The
HILLWALKER'S
GUIDE TO
SCOTLAND

For Ann, my companion along the way

THE HILLWALKER'S GUIDE TO SCOTLAND

Bruce Sandison

CollinsWillow

An Imprint of HarperCollins*Publishers*

First published in 1988 by Unwin Hyman Limited

This edition published in 1993 by Collins Willow
an imprint of HarperCollins*Publishers*, London

Reprinted 1993

**A CIP catalogue record for this book is
available from the British Library**

ISBN 0 00 218416 8

Designed by Julian Holland

Line illustrations by Martin Smillie (Walks 1–50)
and Ann Sandison (Walks 51–68)

Set in Bembo
Printed and bound in Great Britain
by Biddles, Guildford

Contents

Introduction

The first edition of this book marked my half-century and I was relieved to have arrived at that milestone more or less intact – thanks to my wife, Ann, who keeps me fit for the hills in spite of my frequent attempts to undermine her efforts. The present edition contains an additional eighteen walks in north-west and western Scotland, delightfully illustrated by Ann, and I gratefully acknowledge her help and encouragement with the production of this book.

During the last decade much has happened in Highland Scotland that has been highly damaging, not least the monstrosity of taxpayer-funded, factory tree farming, disfiguring many of our moorlands and glens. Even the tree farmers admit that much of this planting was ill-conceived, badly planned and damaging to wildlife – sadly, too late to save the hundreds of thousands of acres now smothered by blanket afforestation.

Worrying also are plans for large-scale commercial peat extraction, particularly in Caithness, where the Highland Regional Council has given planning permission for a charcoal processing plant in the heart of the Flow Country. Moorlands which have lain largely unchanged by the hand of man for seven thousand years are to be sacrificed simply in order that a few already wealthy individuals might profit.

Apart from these threats, fish farming, both in sea and in freshwater lochs, continues, with little regard for damage to aquatic ecology. As always, the promise of 'jobs' opens public coffers and pours forth cash. Super-quarries are another example of insensitivity to Scotland's environment. Plans for quarries at Rodel on the Island of Harris, and at Durness, in north-west Sutherland, will, once again, funnel public funds into a few pockets and irreparably damage the ecology and scenic beauty of the areas concerned.

If you agree, express your views by writing to the Scottish Secretary, New St Andrew's House, Edinburgh, and to the Director of Planning, at the Highland Regional Council, Glenurquhart Road, Inverness, asking them to reconsider their strategy regarding forestry, fish farming, peat extracting and super-quarries in the Highlands. That much at least, I believe, we owe to future generations.

The new walks included in this edition are largely centred around Lochaber, a wild, desolate landscape containing some of Scotland's most dramatic mountains and exciting walks. Exploring them is a never ending source of pleasure, sheer joy, regardless of wind and weather. There is never enough time, that most precious of all assets, and days in the hills seem to speed by faster than regular, lowland hours.

Where to start is always a problem, but a visit to the Tourist Information Centre in Cameron Square, Fort William, is a must for those new to the area. They have a wide range of excellent information regarding Lochaber walks and climbs, and the courteous staff will soon point you in the right direction and give you all the help and advice you need.

Mountain man, hillwalker, or just plain stroller – Lochaber has something for everyone, young and old alike, including absolutely stunning, golden-sand beaches, such as the Singing Sands, where you will find perfect peace and contentment, far from the madding crowd. That is the real treasure of my native land: the opportunity to escape to the lonely places to recharge batteries and emerge refreshed and ready to cope with the outrageous slings and arrows of everyday living.

I have made every effort to ensure that the information given about the walks is accurate, but obviously things change and you should make your own assessment before setting out. Nor do I imply that there are legal rights of way. Always seek advice from the relevant estate, particularly during autumn months when stalking or shooting parties may be active in the hills.

I stress again that this book pretends to be nothing other than a personal account of a number of walks which we have enjoyed. For errors and omissions, I beg your forgiveness, wishing you nothing but joy in the hills and good fortune in all your endeavours. Without our land, we are nothing.

Bruce Sandison
Hysbackie
Tongue
Sutherland
March 1993

Location of Walks

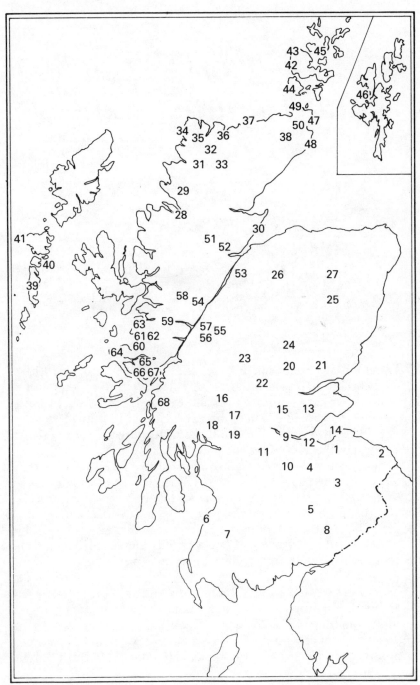

1

Longyester and Lammer Law

FOR THE first year of our married life my wife, Ann, and I lived in a cottage at Fala Dam, a small village sixteen miles south of Edinburgh, close to Lammermuir and Moorfoot hills. We lived the simple life: no running water, no electricity and no inside toilet – just a bucket in an old timber-built shed, disguised by a yew tree at the bottom of the garden.

From October until April, paraffin lamps were lit at 2 p.m. Water was fetched in a bucket from a nearby well. Cooking was by Calor gas. Heating – coal fires and running on the spot, vigorously. Our companions were two kittens, Dolly and Mima, named after mothers-in-law for easier cursing, and a retired sheepdog called Spud, who had spent most of his working life dashing round the Pentland Hills and yet was still game as ever for a long moorland walk.

Changing circumstances, thoughtless ambition and an ever-expanding family moved us from Fala but the fond memory lingers – smoke drifting in cold winter's air, the riot of roses and honeysuckle that was summer, the smell of heather and bog myrtle on moors, the ever-present sound of trout-filled Fala Burn 'loupin ower its linns'.

So it was like visiting an old friend when I passed the village again, on my way to Gifford and Longyester, intent on walking the majestic Lammermuirs. I parked by twitching curtains at Longyester Farm cottages and surveyed the soft shoulder of Lammer Law, rising 1,765 feet before me, grey, blue and green against the horizon. The buzz of busy combine harvesters and barking dogs followed me up the road to Blinkbonny Wood. Rose-hip and raspberry bobbed and danced in mounting wind. My brother, Ian, and I used to make itching powder from rose-hip berries. Drove the girls wild with pretended anger – red hands tussling with long hair and jumper collars.

Squared banks of conifers line the fields, wind-breaks against Lammer storms and welcome shelter for sheep and cattle. To the left of the road are the remains of something intensive – probably a pig-breeding unit. The empty pens are overhung by tall, light-less security lamp-posts, like a Lilliputian greyhound racing track.

Clearing the shelter of the woods, I catch the full force of the wind howling downhill into my face. Butterflies and moths are keeping a low profile this morning. Scabious, tormentil and buttercup toss and bob in the gale. An enigmatic notice warns: 'Danger, Range. Do not pass this point when red flag is flying.'

Should I want shot? I search carefully for evidence of red flags. Higher up the hill, I look back into an old quarry. It must have been used as a Sten-gun range, hence the notice. The sand-backed target and firing point are so close together it could hardly have been anything else. I remember that unless you were actually sticking the muzzle of the gun directly into the middle of the target it was impossible to hit anything with those unruly weapons.

The track up and over Lammer Law is an old drove road, used for centuries to take cattle and sheep to the great southern markets. Whole families would make the long journey – lean husbands, wives, children and dogs, chattering and yapping complaining herds and flocks over the moors.

A magnificent Charolais bull lifts a huge head and stares balefully. Two soft-eyed cows, nuzzled and nudged by new-born calves, chomp contentedly. I call good morning, politely, and hurry by.

My first rest is on a clump of blaze-purple heather by a tiny crystal-clear stream. Westwards, a few lonely sycamores bend against the constant force of the wind. A foolhardy meadow pipit whisks past, followed by an incautious honey-bee. The East Lothian landscape is a patchwork of yellow and green fields, specked white and grey with farmhouses, peeping from dark woods.

Whale-boned Berwick Law broods blackly over fertile fields.

The Bass Rock gauntly guards the Firth of Forth, a grim prison during the seventeenth century. The Romans knew this land and called the inhabitants the Votadini. These ancient Picts peopled the Lothians for a thousand years with hill forts and settlements. I looked towards graceful Tarprain Law, their capital, where, in the early years of this century, a group of workmen discovered an astonishing array of Roman silver and Pictish treasures – a sophisticated, established town enclosing an area of 40 acres.

The wind was even stronger as I struggled on up the hill; it tugged at my coat, whipped tears from my eyes. A brief glimpse of Hopes Reservoir, leaden, sparkling at the foot of Bullhope Law, dotted black by a hopeful fishing boat. At the top of Lammer Law, thankfully, the sun sailed clear from behind thick, dark clouds and the glories of the Lowlands crowded round: Arthur's Seat, a lion crouching over the Auld Grey City of Edinburgh; the blue line of the Pentland Hills; Sir Walter Scott's rounded Eildons and, closer, as though waiting to be stroked, the gentle Moorfoots.

A sudden storm swept in, blanketing the view, and I hurried on towards Tollishill, round Hog Hill and Windy Law to my goal – a single standing stone and the rough outlines of a Pictish fort, ringing the top of a small hill to the west of Tollishill Farm. Vast pylons strode across the hill, like figures from H. G. Wells's *War of the Worlds*. Stark and menacing in the mist. A rabbit scurried over the track, pursued by a bad-eyed stoat. Death in the heather.

Passing under the humming hydro wires I reached Tollishill to be greeted by a laconic collie, securely tied to a barn door. I'm grateful. The outline of the fort is clearly visible: concentric rings, commanding a 360-degree view. These Pictish forts were as much working villages as defensive structures. Gates were barred and spears sharpened only in time of communal danger – generally from the acquisitive aspirations of overbearing neighbours. The single sentinel standing stone is by the side of the road, on the edge of a little wood. Good place for lunch, sheltered and calm.

Wet but refreshed, I retraced my steps back up Crib Law, shadowed by a hungry herring gull and two minister-black crows, wind pushing my back. Before Lammer Law, a deep scar cuts into the hill and I struck right, over the moor, to Bleak Law by Sting Bank Burn. Try falling on your backside to find out why it is so named. On the summit of Bleak Law a tumbled cairn centres a criss-cross of sheep tracks which wind amidst heather and ferns down to a red-rust-roofed shed at the foot of the valley.

Sting Bank Burn bustles into Hopes Reservoir through a wonderland wood of alder, silver birch and hazel. Although Hopes is man-made, it is old enough to have an established, settled look, undiminished by the neo-Gothic water tower and well trimmed lawns surrounding the south end. Beehives nestle in sunny corners and I asked the fishermen how they were getting on. A disgruntled grunt told all.

A dipper, black and white, best-bib-tuckered, kept me company along the outlet burn. The hills around Hopes are scattered with evidence of the Pictish endeavour. Wonder if they had better luck with the fishing? The ghosts of a thousand years keep step with my squelching, sodden boots as I made the last easy miles along tree-lined country lanes back to Longyester.

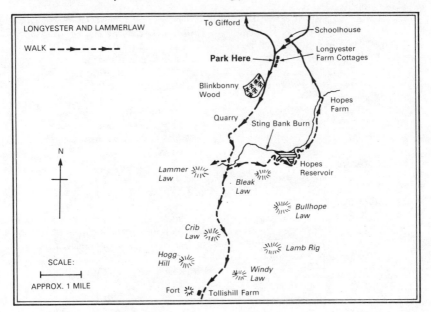

WHAT YOU NEED TO KNOW

Time and effort Allow about five hours for this walk, more if it is a fine day so that you can linger on the way. The climbs are gradual, though fairly steep, and most of the route is along a well marked path. The return journey crosses moorland and you might stumble about a bit; try and stick to sheep tracks and you will come to little harm. In dry weather, the descent from Bleak Law could be sudden if you slip. Carry a tea tray and recapture childhood days if you want to get down very rapidly.

Location Ordnance Survey Sheet 66, Edinburgh, second series, scale 1:50,000.

Grid references Longyester Farm Cottages 545651; Blinkbonny Wood 537642; Quarry 535634; Lammer Law 524618; Crib Law 525598; Tollishill Farm 519581; Bleak Law 538616; Hopes Reservoir 547622; Hopes Farm 559638; old schoolhouse 550655.

Route Park the car on the grass verge by Longyester Farm Cottages and walk south along the minor road towards Blinkbonny Wood. Past the wood, a gate leads onto the hill, following a good track. You will see this track winding up the hill ahead of you.

Strike right from the track, at the highest shoulder, to reach the top of Lammer Law. Walk back to the track and continue south to Tollishill Farm, the standing stone and Pictish fort. Return the same way until you reach the deep scar down which runs Sting Bank Burn. Keep to the right of the burn and work your way round the side of the hill, climbing to the top of Bleak Law.

At the north end of Bleak Law, look down to Hopes Reservoir and you will see a red-roofed shed. Follow a convenient sheep track to the shed. Cross the little burn and you will pick up an ill defined track which leads round the side of Hopes Reservoir, eventually bringing you to the dam at the eastern end.

A minor road exits north from the reservoir, following the outlet burn, past the entrance to Hopes House and East Hopes Farm. Cross the bridge over Hopes Burn and walk on to a road junction, by an old schoolhouse and a telephone kiosk. Turn left here and walk past Longyester Farm, back to the cottages.

14

2

Coldingham Cliff-Tops and St Abb's

COLDINGHAM PRIORY, in Berwickshire, was founded in AD 635. Coldingham Old Church was established on the site of the Priory five hundred years later. Coldingham New Church was built in 1220 and survived intact until the middle of the seventeenth century. Then Oliver Cromwell had a go at it on his way to Edinburgh in 1648.

With the return of Charles II in 1660, and legalised mirth and jollity, the pious people of Coldingham repaired their place of worship, and again in 1854, when a major restoration programme was undertaken. One hundred years later, in 1954, the whole structure was completely renovated and today Coldingham Church is one of the most attractive and best kept churches in Berwickshire.

Understandably, given its turbulent history, the present incumbent, The Revd Daniel G. Lindsay, keeps the little church locked.

When I called recently I had to content myself with wandering round the outside, by trim lawns, through ancient arches, watched by a battalion of suspicious gardeners. Perhaps the same thing happened to Oliver Cromwell and, in order to gain access to his maker, he found it necessary to remove one of the walls permanently.

The village of Coldingham lies amidst fine, fertile, red-soiled Berwickshire farmlands, crowded round a market cross, raised in 1815 by Lord Home to celebrate the defeat of Napoleon – neat red-tiled houses, almost Loire-like in character.

Virginia creeper clings lovingly to the walls of the Anchor Inn but I resisted the temptation for a quick one, striding righteously and soberly past the inviting front door. Never know who might be watching from the shadows of time, bible-breeched and waiting to pounce on poor sinners. Walk first, thirst later.

I walked up the hill, out of the village, and turned right towards Coldingham Loch, two miles distant along a hump-back-bridged country lane, through the old wood that comforts Buskin Burn to Coldingham sands and the North Sea. The sound of running water always reminds me of a senior fishing friend, much given to the love of a dram and always waterless when it came to finding something to dilute his fancy. As the Argo-Cat lurched him lochwards across goat-sided slopes, he would inquire hopefully: 'Is it running water?'

At the top of the first hill, past Bogangreen, a thoughtful bench has been placed in the shelter of the roadside hedge, giving a fine view back to the village, multicoloured roofs across gold fields. Wind whistles through telegraph wires and umbelliferous stalks creak and shake in the breeze.

Hedgerow brambles, missed by birds, prick my fingers and stain my hands. Van-Gogh-black crows hover above stubble and balers work busily up and down the long rows of straw bundles. A fringe of pines guards the road up to Pilmuir Farm and, in the distance, Westloch House and the wood round Coldingham Loch, one of Scotland's oldest and most famous trout fisheries.

Coldingham Estate used to belong to the Scottish brewing family of Usher. It is now owned by Dr and Mrs Wise, who offer a range of well-sited, comfortably furnished self-catering cottages to anglers and other holidaymakers in search of peace and quiet. The loch is regularly stocked with brown trout and has the distinction of being the first loch in Scotland to stock rainbow trout. Both thrive mightily in the lime-rich waters.

The most attractive cottage on the estate is Lochside Cottage, built over a boathouse and the perfect place for an away-from-it-all winter break. Access is either by suspect grass track or by rowing across the loch. The sound of the sea breaking endlessly on mighty cliffs hurried me round the west shore of the loch, past curious head-bobbing white-crested coots and nervous wildfowl.

First sight of the sea, sparkling with a million colours. From the north, a narrow track picks its way along the cliff and I join it close to where a tiny stream blossoms into a silver waterfall, plunging down Heathery Carr, dashing against ebony-black seagull-screaming rocks. On the horizon, the ominous, unmistakable shape of a warship trails a long white furrow northwards, heading for Bass Rock and the Firth of Forth.

The 500-foot hilltop is spread with a continuous array of grass-covered mounds, sudden hollows and heaps of boulders: remains of ancient hill forts and settlements. People lived and worked here for thousands of years and there are outlines of defensive ramparts, ditches and an enclosed fort which measured almost 200 feet across. There are foundations of circular stone-built houses and evidence of a community occupying the site down to post-Roman times. In 1931, relics dated between AD 150 and 400 were discovered during excavation works.

I stopped in the old circles and shared lunch and memories with my ancestors. Must have been a hardy lot to survive here. No danger of a surprise attack from the east, the cliffs would have seen to that, but no way out either. I wondered how many of the villagers had met their pagan gods half-way down the sheer face of the cliff?

After lunch, eastwards along the track to Pettico Wick and my first glimpse of a marine nature reserve. Don't see much of the reserve, not from the shore anyway; but a convenient notice, by the little slipway, tells me that Pettico is jointly sponsored by Britoil and the Nature Conservancy Council. I was reminded that, under-water, spear guns, spears and gaffs were not allowed. Nor was I to disturb marine life or remove any plants. Got to be rules, I suppose, even on the bed of the North Sea.

St Abb's Head, crowned by the white-painted lighthouse with its red-lead fog-horn perched precariously over the cliff, seemed civilization after the wilds of the hill forts. An all-weather road leads to the top and this is much used by visitors to the St Abb's Head Nature Reserve: 200 acres of coastal grasslands and cliffs. More notice-boards. Why does officialdom seem incapable of existing without littering the countryside with notice-boards?

When I first visited St Abb's Head, more years ago than I care to remember, there wasn't a single, solitary notice-board to be seen. Only wild-flower-carpeted cliffs, kittiwakes and puffins and snow-white gannets dashing into blue waves. Now we have high-heeled hair-dressed matrons trailing overweight, grumbling husbands: 'Look at the lovely view, dear, isn't it nice?' So I'm prejudiced? Can't I be fifty and prejudiced?

The path round St Abb's Head is wonderful, and you soon leave most of the single-step-trippers behind. I walked into the tiny fishing village of St Abb's, and back decades in time to a family holiday we spent there in 1947.

The row of brightly painted cottages still crested the hill over-looking the harbour. The bedroom window, where my brother, Ian, and I waited breathless with impatience for the sound of stones rattling on our window – Jake, come to take us to sea.

Jake Nisbet was our hero, full of grand tales of whaling days in the South Atlantic and endless patience with the excited chattering of two small boys. A clinker-built fishing boat edged cautiously out between narrow harbour walls, and I remembered the windy night, sailing home, cold and shaken with rough seas, when mother comforted me with a 'Scotch muffler', a breath-stopping warm hug.

At the white sands of Coldingham Bay I turned my back on the sea and walked slowly back to the present, up the hill to the church. Happily, no one had knocked it down during my thousand-year absence, and the door of the Anchor Inn was still open and just as inviting.

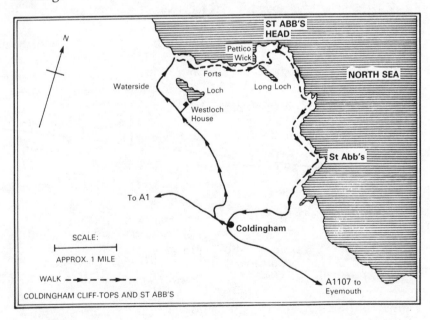

WHAT YOU NEED TO KNOW

Time and effort This is an easy, comfortable walk, with little to make the pulse race; part road, mostly along a cliff track. If you do not have a head for heights, keep well back from the edge. Even if you have, stay clear; the grass can be very slippery and it is a long one-way ticket down. Take extra care to keep well back if it is windy. A sudden gust could catch you unawares. Including a visit to the Priory, allow about four hours for the walk. Longer, if it is a fine day and you fancy a doze on cliffs or beach after lunch.

Location Ordnance Survey Sheet 67, Duns and Dunbar, second series, scale 1:50,000.

Grid references Coldingham 903659; Coldingham Loch 897685; hill forts and settlements 895691; Pettico Wick 908691; St Abb's Head 914693; St Abb's Village 920670; Coldingham Bay 917664.

Route Free parking, last time I was there, opposite Coldingham Priory. Walk past Anchor Inn and up the hill. Turn first right and follow this road out to Coldingham Loch. This is private property and if you wish to view the loch, or walk round the west shore, you must call at Westloch House and seek permission before doing so. Otherwise, continue to the end of the road and at Waterside walk north-east to the cliff path.

Turn right along the cliff path and follow it down to Pettico Wick and the marine nature reserve. A road leads up the hill, through the NCC reserve, past the Long Loch, to St Abb's Head and lighthouse. Climb past the pristine notice-board, round the back of the lighthouse; continue along the cliff, eventually reaching the village of St Abb's.

Walk past the front of the row of multicoloured two-storey cottages on the edge of the hill above the harbour. At the end, you pick up a tarmac path which leads to Coldingham Bay. From Coldingham Bay, walk back to the church. No need to walk on the main road: a good pavement will be found, on the right of the road, behind the hedge. This will almost see you home, safe from oncoming traffic.

3

Eildon, Tweed and Melrose

*H*EATHER-LAZED on Eildon, gazing skyward, lulled by prima donna larks. A soft west wind fingers my hair. White cloud-whisps sail silently by. In the valley, microdot figures inch over golf-green swards. Faint murmers of Melrose, a million miles away, drift up on summer airs. 'God's in his heaven, all's right with the world.'

Abbey pinnacles pierce the trees and, barely discernible amidst the grey cluster of the old Border town, I see the railway station where, centuries past, I parked. Tweed, a silver thread, winds and wends through rich farming lands – squared fields of gold, green and blue – hurrying seawards by deep pools where salmon lie, past the Wallace Monument and ox-bowed Dryburgh Abbey.

The spread of Galashiels edges eastwards and the stark concrete of the County Administrative Buildings in St Boswells intrude harshly onto the gentle landscape. Westwards lies Abbotsford, mighty home of mighty Sir Walter Scott, who made the Eildon Hills his own, his favourite walk, ringed by the magic of Moorfoot,

Lammermuir, Cheviot and Lowther.

The triple hills of Eildon dominate these Border lands. Because the surrounding countryside is flat, they stand proud, like ancient watch-dogs keeping guard over the four abbeys: Melrose, Dryburgh, Jedburgh and Kelso. Melrose Abbey was founded in 1136 by monks from Rievaulx in Yorkshire and for hundreds of years it played an important part in the making of Scotland. King David I granted the abbey the three granges of 'Eildon, Melrose and Darnick together with the royal lands and forest of Selkirk and Traquair with pasturage for sheep and cattle, wood for building and burning and rights of fishing in the Tweed. In addition the monks received Gattonschauch and the lands and woods of Gattonside.'

Like so much of the Borders, Melrose and the other great Scottish abbeys suffered dreadfully during the Scottish Wars of Independence and Edward II sacked the abbey in 1322. Richard II did likewise in 1385 but, in spite of such rough treatment, Melrose Abbey always managed to recover and became the most prosperous religious house in the kingdom.

However, the troubled times of the sixteenth century and constant feuding between Border families brought eventual ruin to the four abbeys. After two successive raids and burnings in 1544–5 the majesty of Melrose Abbey declined. In 1590, 'Jo Watsonn, pensionarius de Melrose, the last member of the convent, passed away' and the great days were over.

The track round Eildon is well marked and earlier that morning I had left the car by the railway station, now a thriving arts and crafts centre, and walked up Dingleton Road, under the bridge, left down the steps and onto the hill. Soon wiping a sweat-wet brow, I rested and looked back, the town turning doll-like below me. Eager midges swarmed in the long grass, anxious for lunch, so I lurched upwards to gain the open heights and welcome breeze.

The track shows well-trodden signs of horses hoofs' in thick red soil and the ground is soft and muddy after overnight rain. An unexpected flag-post marks the way and I begin to think of photographs. Stupid, for, as though reading my thoughts, skies darken and clouds gather. Sat on my lunch-time banana. On the crest, where grass and heather meet, house martins swoop and tumble. Must be on a training exercise, preparing youngsters for their long journey south, fattening them up on Eildon flies.

Before the Romans came, Picts castled the crest of North Eildon with a circular fort. Within the immediate area of the hill, more than three hundred settlements of the Selgovae tribe have been identified. These wild, fearless men must have looked out from their hilltop fastness, over ancient forests, and wondered at the coming of Cnaeus Julius Agricola's legions; the sharp rattle of civilization knocking at old time's door.

The Romans quickly subjugated the Selgovae and routed them from their Eildon fortress. A signal tower was built and a major camp constructed on the Roman road of Dere Street, near Newstead, a mile east of Melrose. The camp was an important staging post for Roman expansion northwards and, at its height, accommodated two legions and a detachment of 500 cavalry.

If you examine Eildon carefully, the outlines of these Pictish settlements are still visible – regular heather-covered ridges, where no ridges should be; strange mounds and hollows on the hillside. The Commendator's House, in the grounds of Melrose Abbey, is a superb museum which includes details and artefacts from the days of Roman occupation.

Another ancient hero, King Arthur, is reputed to have known and loved the Eildon Hills. Romantic legend has Arthur and his knights buried here, awaiting the call for help from a threatened nation; then they will rise from sleep, swords brightly burnished, to vanquish our foes. King Arthur must have been a man of many parts – the same story is told of a dozen other British hills – but I like to imagine the whole Round Table sleeping under tranquil Border skies.

I paid for lunch, a magnificent, well-filled roll, followed by wild bilberries, scattering crumbs amongst the scree for my songstress lark, then stumbled downhill towards the village of Newstead. The track leads to a narrow little wood, famous for the Eildon Tree of Thomas the Rhymer. A stream keeps the track company through the woods and my boots splash droplets over wet socks.

Squirrels dart across the path; stop, bright-eyed and motionless, whisker-twitching, testing the air; then spring, rocket-like, into overhanging branches. A fat pheasant coughs nervously, the sound of its pattering feet quickening as it launches itself into clumsy, frightened flight. Now the main road. The sudden shock of cars.

Newstead is a dream of a village, almost unreal in Scotland – pink-washed cottages, wallpapered with honeysuckle, clematis and roses; trimmed lawns fronting well maintained houses, flanked by two-car garages. Down Clymires Lane, right over the road, then left by the telephone box. The path leads to the River Tweed and my excitement mounts with every step.

For me, the Tweed is the Borders. I grew to love it as a boy, when I first committed the sin of angling amidst its tumbling streams and gentle glides. The Tweed has an unforgettable smell, like no other river I know: warm, friendly, inviting, promising perfect peace, absolute contentment.

By the river, three herons are busy fishing. They flap awkwardly airborne as I arrive. Upstream, a couple of salmon fishers flay the water. Wager the herons have had more sport. A grey wagtail bobs greeting and, in the slow eddies, trout feed hungrily. Mr Dipper watches with tiny-eyed caution.

The riverside track wanders upstream towards the suspension bridge at Melrose. Beech and sycamore shade the water and a salmon turns lazily, silver flanks shining in afternoon sunlight. The urgent buzz of a sawmill startles a flight of mallard from the cover of a reed-covered island. Crows harry a marauding kestrel from their nests and, as I lingeringly watch the river, a stream of ants carry seeds home to their night's rest.

Sitting in the ruined transepts of the great abbey, I wonder where King Robert the Bruce's heart lies. Carried in a silver casket to the Crusades, it was flung by ever-faithful Douglas into the thickest of the fight. After the battle, Douglas was found dead, his body lying over his king's heart. The casket was brought back to Scotland and buried at Melrose Abbey.

Light fades, sending long shadows filtering through the broken windows, washing mellow stones in soft reds and grey. Time stands still, hovering mystically as the sun slowly fades below the gentle peaks of Eildon.

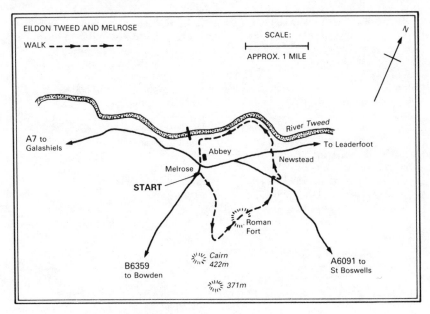

WHAT YOU NEED TO KNOW

Time and effort This is an easy walk which will take about four hours, depending upon how long you spend visiting Melrose Abbey. The climb up to North Eildon may make you puff a bit – it did me – but there is no hurry, so take it at your own pace. The total distance is in the order of seven miles. Wear stout walking shoes – the track gets very muddy.

Location Ordnance Survey Sheet 73, Galashiels and Ettrick Forest, second series, scale 1:50,000.

Grid references Melrose 545343; North Eildon Hill 555328; Newstead 563342; Tweed 563343; Melrose Abbey 549341.

Route In the centre of Melrose, by the Market Cross, follow the B6359. Within fifty yards, before you go under the railway bridge, turn right and within one hundred yards park in front of the old railway station.

Walk back to the road and turn right under the railway bridge. On the left, you will see a notice indicating the start of the Eildon Walk. Go down the steps and follow the track up through the wood onto the hill. After leaving the fields behind the track bears right. Walk round the side of the hill, making for the white-painted flag-pole in the distance.

From the flag-pole, walk directly up to the shoulder between the two hills; thence, an easy walk to the top of North Eildon. From the top, go down the north side, making towards the wood which lies directly below. A track leads through this wood to the main A6091 Melrose–Jedburgh road.

Turn right along the main road and, after about a hundred and fifty yards, left down a muddy track – once again signposted 'Eildon Walk'. Follow this track until you pass under a bridge. Eildon Walk is posted left; you turn right and walk into the village of Newstead.

To the left of the telephone box a track leads past a few houses down to the banks of the River Tweed. At the river, turn left and follow the bankside path back to Melrose. On the way, walk along the top of the well made wall rather than in the field; this leads back to the path.

Just after the sawmill, and before the suspension bridge, turn left, away from the river, and walk into Melrose. There is a motor car museum on your right and the Abbey is signposted on your left.

After visiting the Abbey, walk back past the market cross to the car. There is a café within the old railway station and this will provide you with welcome refreshment – tea or otherwise!

4

The Silver Tyne and Crichton

THE ADMIRABLE village of Crichton is a neat collection of houses thirty minutes' drive south from Edinburgh, but my first journey there took an hour and a half – by bicycle. Couldn't drive at the age of fifteen, although considerate father had given me one or two sneaky shots on quiet country lanes. I had decided to become a world-famous artist and intended to sketch the gaunt ruins by way of a preliminary to fame and fortune.

The Wizard of the North, Sir Walter Scott, had aroused my interest by his description of Crichton in *Marmion*:

> That Castle rises on the steep
> Of the green vale of Tyne;
> And far below, where slow they creep
> From pool to eddy, dark and deep,
> Where alders moist, and willows weep,
> You hear her streams repine.

Or perhaps my imagination had been fired by stories of Mary, Queen of Scots, and her ruthless lover, James, Earl of Bothwell, whose home Crichton was in the seventeenth century. Anyway, I stumbled up and down the jagged stairways and round the well kept courts, sketching busily for most of an afternoon, and the results pleased me mightily: which was all that mattered.

These childish drawings have long since disappeared, which is just as well; but the mystery of the castle, glooming over the silver river from its bracken-covered ledge, remains undiminished, as clear and awesome as ever it was on that first, bright day.

Thirty-four years later, in the warm sunlight of an early-autumn morning, I parked my car by the old parish church at the start of the short track to the castle. Gathering together cameras, notebook, lunch and map, I made for the church, intent upon a few words with my maker prior to setting off for the grim ruins. Best to be prepared.

All the doors of the church were securely locked and bolted. Sad times. I remember, as a boy, when you could walk freely into any Scottish church, Highland or Lowland, without let or hindrance. The Good Lord was always at home in those days.

The parish church was established in 1454 by William Crichton, Lord Chancellor of Scotland, 'as destitute of faith, mercy and conscience as of fear and of folly'. William was one of the most powerful and feared men in Scotland, jealously guarding his privilege of caring for the infant king, James II.

His arch-rivals, and arch-enemies, were the Douglases, and William constantly plotted their downfall. The Lord Chancellor feigned friendship and forgiveness and persuaded the young king to invite the Douglas youths to Edinburgh Castle. The boys stopped at Crichton on the way and, no doubt, were well entertained by William Crichton.

He entertained them better the following evening during the 'dinner of the black bull's head'. At the entry of the platter bearing this ominous sign, Earl Douglas and his brother were dragged from the table and brutally stabbed to death.

As I left the churchyard and walked along the track to Crichton it was as though three decades had vanished. The same clouds seemed to chase the same shadows over the still-golden ferns. Shafts of sunlight danced on red walls and the air was full of the sound of the busy river and sky-high singing larks.

Crichton Castle reached its peak in the ownership of Francis Stewart, Earl Bothwell, when King James VI was entertained there in March 1586. Francis had an unmatched reputation for evildoing and violence, even for those harsh times – 'a terror to the most desperate duellists in Europe and a subduer of the proudest champions'.

Sitting in the courtyard of the castle, gazing up at the superb Italianate Renaissance façade, erected by Francis Stewart, I pondered moodily on my fellow Scots, wondering what manner of men could build such delicate works of art one day and happily murder, rob, pillage and rape the next.

Leaving the castle, I walked past the sandstone ruins of the stable. At first sight, because of the vaulted roof, it could be taken for a chapel but the window above the main door gives the clue: it is shaped like a horseshoe. The stable was a two-storey building – animals below, grooms and retainers above.

To the right of the stables a track leads downhill to the Tyne, crossing a gurgling little tributary on the way. A small meadow, spread with sweet-smelling grasses, carpets the valley and the track then meanders up a muddy slope, through waist-high bracken. Silver-specked spider webs danced between leaves, crystal droplets shaken by my passing, and my trousers clung damply to cold legs when I reached the top.

Here a drunken notice nods the way south to the village of Borthwick. Farmers were busy with harvest as I damply passed. Ahead, the line of the old railway cuts over the hill. Behind, the triple peaks of the Eildon Hills proudly dominate the horizon. On my right, a long line of Pentlands point the way to Scotland's capital city.

From the top of the hill, below me, the tower of Borthwick Castle peeks from surrounding woodlands. The trees are magnificent: oak, ash, beech, sycamore, elm, willow, birch and ancient Scots pine – a proper wood, with space to breathe beneath the leaves.

Woodland birds – blue tit, wren, treecreeper and goldfinch – join me for lunch, as does another sudden rainstorm. I shelter under the umbrella of an old oak. Glossy, aristocratic horses eat also, chestnut and black backs turned carefully against the rain, tails switching as they chomp.

An enigmatic sign offers two ways into Borthwick and I choose to walk left, round the walls of the castle, which is now an exclusive hotel. The road leads down to little Gore Burn, a tributary of the Tyne, made big and proud by heavy rain. Maple trees blush, burnt crimson with the first flush of autumn.

At the end of the road, a wet track invites me down through the woods, leading to a gated wooden bridge and up to Borthwick churchyard. The roof of the church is an intricate pattern of rectangular and diamond-shaped stone tiles, bright and glistening from recent showers. Ranked tombstones tell sad stories of young hopes brought early to earth.

The last time I had walked this way was as a Scout, on a night adventure exercise; two, small, semi-fearful boys, peering at a map by weak torchlight at 3 a.m., hopelessly lost. Then my mind was filled with thoughts of wicked earls and murderous lords lurking behind every bush, razor-sharp blades poised, ready to slit my unsuspecting throat.

Leaving the church, I followed the road through the small village, back over rushing Gore Burn, up to the high bank of the railway, then over the fields to Loquhariot Farm. The view across the valley was dominated by Crichton Castle, softly lit by evening sunlight, with the road leading down to tree-banked Tyne. At the top of the hill, to the left of the village, are the remains of an even earlier fort, dating from the Iron Age, enclosing an area 300 by 190 feet.

I wondered if the inhabitants of these grassy mounds plotted and planned to rule their world as hard and ruthlessly as their latterday neighbours along the road at the castle: Couldn't ask our dour Scots Lord for the answer; when I called at the church again, he was still out.

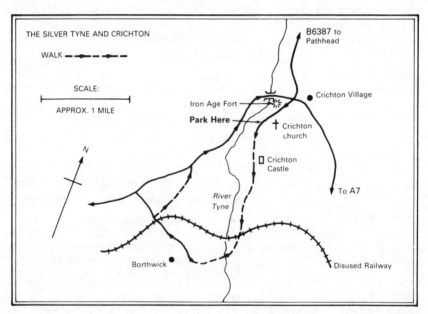

WHAT YOU NEED TO KNOW

Time and effort   This is a pleasant afternoon outing which takes about three or four hours, depending upon how much time you spend exploring Crichton Castle. In wet weather, the track from Crichton to Borthwick can be very muddy, so be prepared. From Borthwick, the route follows a quiet minor road back to Crichton, through farmland and the valley of the River Tyne. There are no harsh hills or heart-bursting climbs and this route offers an easy, gentle, country walk.

Location   Ordnance Survey Sheet 66, Edinburgh, second series, scale 1:50,000.

Grid references   Crichton parish church 381616; Crichton Castle 380612; Borthwick Castle and church 369596; Loquhariot Farm 370608; Crichton Fort 385619.

Route   Park the car at Crichton parish church. Directly ahead lies Crichton Castle, a short walk across the hill. The castle is in the care of the Historic Buildings and Monuments Commission and is open April to September: weekdays 9.30 a.m. to 7 p.m., Sundays 2 to 7 p.m.; October to March: weekdays 9.30 a.m. to 4 p.m., Sundays 2 to 4 p.m. Entrance charge is about £1 per adult.

From the castle walk to the right of the stable building and you will find a narrow track leading down the hill, through a small wood. This track crosses a small tributary of the River Tyne, then over a meadow and up a muddy slope to a stile. Borthwick is signposted here. Follow the sign to the line of the old railway, where there is a farm bridge over the disused track. Take care here and make sure that you cross the track and walk round the side of the hill, to the right, in front of you.

From this hill you will see Borthwick Castle, and the track down through the wood is clearly marked. Once down, cross the stile by the field with horse jumps and walk the few hundred yards to the road. Here turn left, round the side of the walled garden. The road passes over the Gore Burn and wends uphill to a private house. When you see the house, look right and you should find a track down through the woods to a gated bridge over Gore Burn. This path leads up to Borthwick church, through a white-painted gate at the top.

After visiting Borthwick church, follow the little road down through the village to the bridge over Gore Burn. From here, go up the hill and, when you see the railway embankment, turn right and follow the track through the fields to Loquhariot and onto the minor road.

At the next road junction bear right, down into the Tyne valley. On the way up the hill you may if you wish follow the inviting little track on your right, up the hill, through the woods; it leads back to the road. At the top of the hill, at the road junction, turn right. Immediately on your right is the entrance to the site of the Iron Age fort – and a well disguised water storage tank (I think). Walk back to the road, turn right again, and this brings you back to the church and car park.

5

Broad Law, Talla and Tweed

THE BORDER hills of Scotland were born out of millions of years of geological turmoil. Ancient sands and shales, compressed into rock by mighty forces, split by molten lava, crushed beneath ice-sheets and glaciers half a mile thick. The retreating ice left fertile soils which have given comfort and sustenance to man down the ages.

Nearly three thousand years ago our Pictish ancestors tilled these soils and grazed their cattle, protected from attack in fortified villages and hill forts. Double stone walls were laboriously constructed, in-filled with rubble, often up to 15 feet high, surrounded by deep ditches. Huge wooden gates between twin watch-towers guarded the entrance to the village and life was secured only by constant vigilance.

Deep in these green hills, close to the well-springs of Mistress Tweed, I stood by the banks of the gentle river at Hearthstane and looked eastwards, towards the rounded heights of Broad Law, rising 2,723 feet above the stream. I parked the car near to where Hearthstane Burn hurries into Tweed and followed the track, past the farm, along a forest road, up the hill.

This is John Buchan country: writer, soldier, statesman, created Baron Tweedsmuir in 1935 and Governor-General of Canada until his death in 1940. G. M . Trevelyan, the historian, wrote: 'I don't think I remember anyone whose death evoked a more enviable outburst of sorrow, love and admiration.'

Like many boys before me, I had thrilled to the exploits of Richard Hannay in *The Thirty-Nine Steps*; but, to me, the most entrancing piece John Buchan ever wrote was a little memorial poem to a fishing friend, killed during the First World War, called 'Fisher Jamie'. As I climbed the hill, I recited the lines, smiling with pleasure at their simple beauty:

> Puir Jamie's killed. A better lad
> Ye wadna find to busk a flee
> Or burn a pule or wield a gad
> Frae Berwick to the Clints o' Dee
>
> And noo he's in a happier land. –
> It's Gospel truth and Gospel law
> That Heaven's yett maun open stand
> To folk that for their country fa'.
>
> But Jamie will be ill to mate;
> He lo'ed nae music, kenned nae tunes
> Except the sang o' Tweed in spate,
> Or Talla loupin' ower its linns.
>
> I sair misdoot that Jamie's heid
> A croun o' gowd will never please;
> He liked a kep o' dacent tweed
> Whaur he could stick his cast o' flees.
>
> If Heaven is a' that man can dream
> And a' that honest herts can wish,
> It maun provide some muirland stream,
> For Jamie dreamed o' nocht but fish.
>
> And weel I wot he'll up and spier
> In his bit blate and canty way,
> Wi' kind Apostles standin' near
> Whae in their time were fishers tae.
>
> He'll offer back his gowden croun
> And in its place a rod he'll seek,
> And bashfu'-like his herp lay doun
> And spier a leister and a cleek.

For Jim's had aye a poachin' whim;
He'll sune grow tired, wi' lawfu' flee
Made fra the wings o' cherubim,
O' casting ower the Crystal Sea . . .

I picter him at gloamin' tide
Steekin' the backdoor o' his hame
And hastin' to the waterside
To play again the auld auld game;

And syne wi' saumon on his back,
Catch't clean against the Heavenly law,
And Heavenly byliffs on his track,
Gaun linkin' doun some Heavenly shaw.

A sudden flurry of rain sent me chasing for the shelter of a beautifully built circular sheepfold – well-knit grey stones topped with old turf. Crouched inside, sheep-like, it was as though I was on another planet, but the storm soon passed and I trudged on, past numbered posts which zigzag up the slope, each 22 yards apart. Suspicious.

I won't tell you how many posts there are – might be depressing – but when I finally cleared the forest, over a stiled gate, they still marched ahead, incongruous sentinels marking the way. Cattle grazed happily in the wind, cropping fine grass-covered slopes at 1600 feet. A high-altitude pheasant shot past, with startled look and worried shriek. The Lowther Hills crowded the horizon, amazingly folded as though someone had softly smoothed them. God, I suppose.

One of the black cattle had its head up a huge culvert, drinking heavily from the rushing stream which charged down the hill towards Geddes's Well. No sign of Mr Geddes but he must have walked here some time to be so famously remembered on the map. The road is well maintained and, apart from the unremitting marker posts and three-mile slog, going is easy.

As I rounded the final twists and curves, panting, the reason for the well ordered access became clear: a space-age-like structure of dishes and domes, surrounded by a high wire fence, loomed before me. 'Warning, High voltage. Property of the Civil Aviation Authority.' An anxious greenshank flitted by. Hope it has read the warning.

Although the aviation station comes as a bit of a shock, once on top of Broad Law there is a superb panoramic view over half of southern Scotland and the tiresome uphill walk is well rewarded. Unending hills surround me, gentle green-topped slopes full of light and shadow. Hidden corries beckon. White clouds scud over dark ridges. Small patches of bright-yellow fields carpet deep valleys. An empty windswept wonderland. A sweet upland dream.

Leaving the top of Broad Law, I walked in a happy daze along the flat grassy summit to Cairn Law. Talla Reservoir sparkled 2,000 feet below, with the buildings of Talla Linnfoots crouched, tiny black specks, by the edge. Waterfalls on Megget Burn flashed silver as sunlight chased shadows up the sheer sides of Garelet Hill, towering starkly over the west shore of the loch.

I followed a spur to Muckle Side and, after a magnificent two-mile walk, all above 2,000 feet, I rested for lunch. Nestling in a sheltered corner, close to the source of Glenrusco Burn, I attacked a sandwich greedily. By the jagged rocks of the burn, in a warm corner, pale, white flowers nodded sleepily – a sudden, magical garden of grass of Parnassus. A harsh, angry, cackle turned my gaze skywards, and I caught a quick glimpse of a raven slipping away on silent, bible-black wings.

The west shoulder of Muckle Side gives a gradual, safe descent to Talla. Any other way down would be difficult; it is as easy to slip on a grass slope as it is on rock, and from 2,000 feet the result is just the same – not at all nice. Funny how sheep seem to manage. Probably glued to the side of the hill.

The walk north by the side of Talla Reservoir is along a minor road which joins St Mary's Loch with Tweedsmuir, twisting through the Lowther Hills past Megget Stone and Fans Law. During summer months it can be busy, and even in October, when I last walked it, cars passed frequently.

Victoria Lodge, at the end of the loch, sits smothered in conifers like an extravagant lost Highland shooting lodge looking for sport. I walked along the dam wall and down to the keeper's cottage, where fishing permits are issued for those wishing to do battle with Talla trout. Fisher Jamie would have been a regular.

Crossing Talla Water, I found the line of a dismantled railway and followed it round pine-clad Cockiland Hill to Glenrusco, where the old railway bridge still crosses Tweed. There is something special about the scent of Tweed. It has lived with me for nearly forty years, yet it still produces a sense of excitement, of mounting anticipation, and I believe that I could recognize Tweed blindfold from a thousand miles by the magical smell of its tumbling streams.

I paid my respects to Pictish ancestors as I passed their old fort by the stream on the hill across the river. Then, footsore but content, I let lovely Lady Tweed murmur me home.

BROAD LAW, TALLA AND TWEED

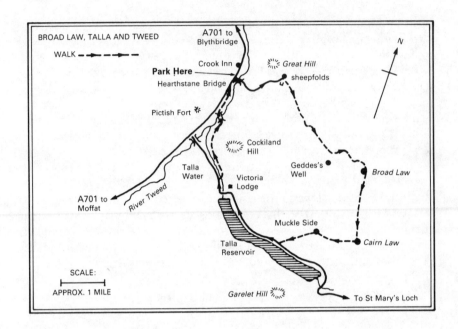

BROAD LAW, TALLA AND TWEED

WALK ▪— ▪— ▪— ▶

A701 to Blythbridge

Park Here

Crook Inn

Great Hill

sheepfolds

Hearthstane Bridge

N

Pictish Fort

Cockiland Hill

Talla Water

Geddes's Well

Broad Law

A701 to Moffat

River Tweed

Victoria Lodge

Muckle Side

Cairn Law

Talla Reservoir

SCALE:

APPROX. 1 MILE

Garelet Hill

To St Mary's Loch

WHAT YOU NEED TO KNOW

Time and effort Quite a lot. Allow about five and a half hours for the round trip – more if it is a fine day, because once up you will not want to come down. The only real slog comes at the beginning, hiking up the rough road to the top of Broad Law. Be like me and stop for plenty of rests. Once up, it is easy all the way. Take great care descending from Muckle Side. Follow the spur and do not attempt a glissade, planned or otherwise, down the steep sides: Talla Reservoir, at the foot, is deep, dark and very cold. The Crook Inn is nearby for welcome after-walk refreshment.

Location Ordnance Survey Sheet 72, Upper Clyde Valley, second series, scale 1:50,000.

Grid references Crook Inn 111265; Hearthstane Bridge 110260; sheepfold 123261; Geddes's Well 137238; Broad Law 147235; Muckle Side 134217: Victoria Lodge 107231; Glenrusco Railway Bridge 105251.

Route Park near the bridge over Tweed at Hearthstane, half a mile south of Crook Inn on the A701 from Blyth Bridge to Moffat. Cross the bridge and at the cottage on your right cut up the hill towards the track you see in front of you. Turn left along this track, round the hill and down to cross Hearthstane Burn.

Then right, and follow the well maintained path, past the sheepfolds, up through the wood. On the top of Broad Law, where you should now be, go past the right-hand side of the civil aviation station and make for the trig. point at the junction of a fence line. The fence pointing quarter-right is your route. Walk due south, over good, springy turf, down and up again to Cairn Law.

Bear right here and go along the shoulder of the hill to the top of Muckle Side. At the west of Muckle Side a spur drops reasonably gently to the road. Walk down this spur, turn right at the road and go on to the head of the loch and dam wall.

Turn left along the dam wall and follow the road down until you reach the cottage where fishing permits are obtained; a notice outside says so. Just past the house, a track on your right leads down to Talla Water. Follow this path, cross the bridge.

Now, angle quarter-left through the woods. Cross a field and you see the line of the dismantled railway. Turn left and follow this back to Glenrusco. Where the old bridges have been removed, you have to leave the track and then climb back up. Don't be tempted to go too fast or you might end up shooting into space where there is no bridge.

Cross the Tweed at Glenrusco, alongside massive water pipes from Talla Reservoir, then a last couple of hundred yards and you are deposited back on the road, where the old railway line used to cross. You should now be able to see your car. If not, head directly for the Crook Inn and drown your sorrows!

6

Culzean Cliffs and Woodlands

MY SECOND son, Charles, recently stayed at the Gas House of Culzean Castle. It was built towards the end of the last century so that Culzean could receive the benefice of carbide lighting. When he told me, I was tempted to remark that he and his colleagues from art school must have felt delightfully at home amidst so much hot air; but common sense and a high regard for personal safety prevailed. Charles Sandison is nineteen years of age, a near-six-footer, fourteen stone square, and notoriously short-fused.

The Gas House, redundant after mains electricity was installed, has been converted into student accommodation used by Glasgow College of Art, and aspiring bands of embryonic Leonardos and Michelangelos rest there between artistic endeavours. Nearby is Culzean Park Centre, where most of Culzean's other 300,000-a-year visitors rest.

Robert Adam designed the beautiful soft-stoned buildings as a home farm in 1777 and the Park Centre, with its dramatic arches and central court, has been carefully developed into a focal point for Culzean Country Park – exhibitions, snack bar, shops and administrative offices.

Which all sounds highly organized, thick with tourists and not really the place for a peaceful afternoon amble. Well, it is and it isn't. Yes, organized and, yes, often busy; but nevertheless a splendid place for stroll and a surprisingly quiet corner of otherwise busy Ayrshire.

The National Trust for Scotland was given Culzean and its 560 acres in 1945, by Charles Kennedy, 5th Marquess of Ailsa, and in 1969 the Trust declared the grounds Scotland's first country park. Herculean effort has restored castle, gardens, woodlands, ponds and pathways to former glory. The result is a wonderful re-creation of a magnificent Scottish estate, complete with swan pond, walled garden, ice house, camellia house, ornamental arches, fountains and delightful tree-shaded walks.

The Castle stands on the edge of 400-million-year-old volcanic cliffs and was originally a square Scottish tower, glowering balefully seawards, defying Atlantic slings and arrows since the Middle Ages. Kennedys have been associated with Ayrshire since the twelfth century; James Kennedy married a daughter of King Robert III in 1407 and he and his five brothers owned half the county between them.

A Kennedy was with Joan of Arc at the relief of Orleans; another fell on Flodden Field with King James IV in 1513. The 2nd Earl was murdered, the 3rd poisoned. The 4th Earl, following the fine traditions of medieval Scottish diplomacy, persuaded the Commendator of Crossraguel Abbey to consign valuable lands to Clan Kennedy – by roasting him alive in the grim dungeons of Dunure Castle.

The present castle is the work of David Kennedy, who succeeded his brother in 1775 and invited architect the Robert Adam to prepare plans for a major restoration and building programme. Of all the splendid rooms Adam designed, in my opinion, there is none finer than the Saloon, a circular, simply-styled, dreamlike room overlooking the Firth of Clyde.

Recitals of Beethoven piano and cello sonatas have been broadcast from the Saloon and a more perfect setting for these glorious masterpieces is hard to imagine. Recently I found myself alone in this sweet room. Soft sunlight streamed through tall windows and I watched, spellbound and silent, as evening stretched out all the Arran hills, and the sun dipped gently into western skies.

Earlier, I walked round the estate on a well marked path, nose-deep in the excellent National Trust booklet which guides you on your way. I started the walk from the main car park, pulling on stiff, cold boots, watched by a herd of haughty red deer, studiously ruminating behind a leap-proof fence, carefully gauging the height to greener grass.

The Gas House was still standing. Given my knowledge of what Charlie does to his room at home, this surprised me. I followed the path down the cliff, onto the foreshore. There are two caves at the foot of the cliffs, reputed home for hibernating moths, and, no doubt, smuggled booty in days gone by.

The shore is an archaeological delight, strewn with pebbles of agate, lava, quartz, flint and calcite. Culzean Park rangers lead parties of visitors on conducted tours and one of the most successful aspects of their work has been the establishment of a young naturalists' club; hundreds of children are introduced to the mysterious world of nature by a team of excellent instructors, adept at capturing youthful imaginations.

Gannets, from their breeding ground on Ailsa Craig, dive spectacularly – spears of white, yellow and black, plunging into the sea from heights of 100 feet. In times past the 'solan goose' was greatly prized for its feathers and soft down. It was also eaten 'by those who can get no better food' and sometimes even domesticated. Sea-swallows, globe-circumnavigating terns, hover and swoop over the waves. Straight-winged fulmars glide by, fingering cliff-side thermals. Red-beaked oystercatchers busily poke.

A total of 155 species of birds have been recorded at Culzean, attracted since the late eighteenth century by the planting of more than five million trees. The Trust has produced an ornithological check-list giving details of residents and visitors, vagrants and rareties. Recent records list goshawk, peregrine, jay, corncrake, grasshopper warbler and barn owl. There have also been single sightings of osprey and little bittern.

There are several buildings along the shore: Dolphin House, a laundry, used until 1900; the Round House, where hardy bathers changed and shivered from the Firth; and the remains of a private oyster pool, to ensure fresh supplies for the great folk at the Castle. Just before the path hikes you back up the cliff, a track goes on to Port Carrick, grander in name than in reality, but a perfect place to stop for a picnic, complete with small sandy beach.

Up Barwhin Hill now, on to the ornate pagoda, fronted by an aviary, built in 1860. I wandered over to Swan Pond, to see what I could see, closely followed by my golden retriever, Breac, the Gaelic word for trout. Still understands English, though, and walked perfectly to heel, eyeing mute swans and wildfowl with feigned indifference.

Morriston Bridge takes the path under a disused railway and the track turns north along the old line. It was opened in 1906 and carried passengers and freight between the village of Maidens, south of Culzean, to Dunure, close to where the old Kennedy stronghold still clings precariously to the cliffs. Left then, leaving the railway at Kennel Mount, and down through the woods, back to the car.

Everything about Culzean charms the senses and delights the eye

– the dramatic arch at the entrance to the castle, creeper-clad, looking like a centuries-old ruin, cleverly designed to do so; Adam and Eve, two Sitka spruce, nodding sleepily in Happy Valley Wood, planted in 1851 and now 140 feet high; and the famous walled garden, with its compass-point corners, ablaze with colour.

I stood in the armoury, surrounded by an astonishing display of weapons ancient and modern, and wondered about the magnificence of Clan Kennedy: great, powerful people; people to be reckoned with, envied and, no doubt, feared. Not so very far distant from the splendour of Culzean, at Alloway, a great man was born – not in palace or mighty castle, but in a simple cottage, shared with his father's cattle.

Whilst David Kennedy and Robert Adam were changing the face of the material world at Culzean, Robert Burns was changing the hearts and minds of people with wild, romantic verses. For all Culzean's grace and glory, perhaps Burns's poetry is the more enduring monument. Souter Johnnie, Tam o' Shanter's drinking partner, lived a mile from Culzean Castle at Kirkoswald. Call at his cottage after your visit, and ponder these matters.

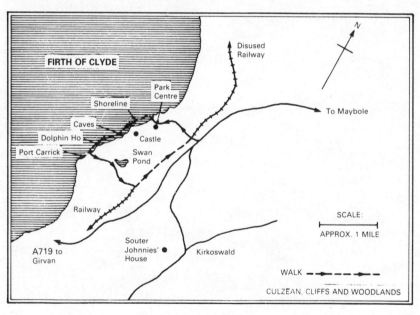

39

WHAT YOU NEED TO KNOW

Time and effort   More of the mind than of the feet. There is so much to see and do at Culzean that you could spend a week there and still not properly explore all that the castle and estate have to offer. Allow at least a whole day. The walk round the boundary takes three hours; more if you are ornithologist, geologist, botanist, or even just plain amateur naturalist. Some of the going is wet and rough so you will probably feel more comfortable in strong walking boots. You can always remove them before you visit the castle. I combined my visit to Culzean with a stop-over at Burns's Cottage in Alloway, near Ayr. You may care to consider doing likewise; the contrast is fascinating.

Location   Ordnance Survey Sheet 70, Ayr and Kilmarnock, second series, scale 1:50,000.

Grid references   Culzean Castle and Country Park 233101; Burns's Cottage 335187; Souter Johnnie's House 241076; Dunure Castle 254158.

Route   You are in good hands. The Park Centre at Culzean will furnish you with an excellent series of descriptive literature, giving details of a number of short and long walks through the estate. The brochure is entitled 'Culzean Country Park Walks'. There are also companion leaflets on other subjects which are invaluable if you wish to get the greatest benefit from your visit. Otherwise, from the Park Centre, follow your nose, and the path, down to the shore and south along the foot of the cliffs.

7

Mary, Merrick and Bruce

*E*LEVEN HECTIC days after her dramatic escape from Loch Leven
Castle, Mary Queen of Scots faced her enemies at the Battle of
Langside on 13 May 1568; but the bleak moorlands between
Dunblane and Comrie saw her father's prophecy fulfilled: 'It cam
with ane lass and it will pass with ane lass.' Mary's forces were
routed and she fled southwards, arriving at Dundrennan on Solway
two days later.

When you come to think about it, Mary never stood a chance
anyway. Her Catholic brother, King Henri of France, and all the
Scots Catholics expected her to re-establish the 'one true church',
preferably by force. Mary resolutely refused. Scottish Protestants,
led by ranting Knox, demanded that she abjure her faith and root
out the evil of Catholicism. This she would never do. With
hindsight, her defeat and downfall were foregone conclusions.

Mary crossed into England, where cousin Elizabeth solved the
problem – by removing Mary's head at Fotheringay on 1 February
1587. She remained steadfast to the end. Dr Fletcher, Dean of
Peterborough, on the scaffold, attempted to persuade Mary to
'repent you of your former wickedness' but Mary replied: 'Mr
Dean, trouble not yourself any more, for I am settled and resolved

in this my religion, and am proposed therein to die.'

Which, a few moments later, she did; and the Earl of Kent stood over her poor body saying: 'Such end of all the Queen's and the Gospel enemies.' Meanwhile, safely on the throne in Edinburgh, her son, King James VI, turned a blind eye, whilst his nobles and clerics no doubt tucked heartily into their sanctimonious Scottish breakfasts. For them, Mary's death in England was a startling break with tradition: normally, they managed to murder their own monarchs.

During her flight from Langside, Mary passed through the wild highlands of Dumfries and Galloway – a desolate wilderness of dangerous cotton-grass-covered silver flows, jagged peaks and windswept moorlands, crowned by mighty Merrick, towering 2,770 feet over tiny lochans with magical names, Neldricken, Valley, Glenhead, Dungeon, Enoch and Aldinna.

There are a dozen hills here, by the ragged Rig of Jarkness and Rhinns of Kells, all over 2,000 feet, including Meikle Millyea, Corserine, Cairngarroch, Cairnsmore, Kirriereoch, Shalloch on Minnoch and Benyellary – ancient granite rocks, laid bare by millions of years of weathering, covered by Caledonian forests, warmed by mild Atlantic winds.

But the forests where Robert the Bruce and Douglas plotted the overthrow of usurping English neighbours were cleared, and now, in their place, we have the new plantations of the Forestry Commission: dense, closely packed, impenetrable conifers, blanketing more than 35 per cent of the south-west. Called 'National Parks', they presuppose some scenic value; in fact, they have created a sterile desert beneath their light-excluding canopy. Colonel Gadaffi of Libya could well declare the Sahara Desert a 'National Garden Centre' and claim for it more beauty and diversity of wildlife than there is in the monotonous, monstrous forests of Dumfriesshire and Galloway.

On a fresh August morning I stopped at the head of Glen Trool and prepared myself for something I had long planned: the ascent of southern Scotland's highest peak, Merrick. Loch Trool – owned by the Liverpool football-pools family, the Moores – winds like a silver ribbon through the glen and I set off, up the side of Buchan Burn, weighted down with cameras, lunch, notebook and pencil.

Heavy rain the previous night had turned Buchan Burn into a spectacular display of waterfalls and deep pools, urging the crystal-clear stream over massive boulders, by banks alive with birdsong and heather so purple it dazzled the eye and dazed the mind. Slender mountain ash arched the torrent, bright red clusters of berries above dancing rainbow spray.

The bad news is that it was also very wet. Can't have it both ways, I suppose – foaming river and dry banks. I climbed hotly over the rocks to the soggy plain above, wading through spongy grass to reach the cottage at Cul Sharg. This is well maintained and provided welcome shelter from a sudden shower. I sprinted the last hundred yards, size eleven boots splashing mud round legs. Took three minutes. Record-breaking for the likes of me.

James Cameron, Toronto, Canada, had beaten me to it – by about a week, according to a name inscribed on the wall of the cottage. Rest and dry, then on again, through the woods, out onto the hill proper. Loch Trool has vanished, hidden in its deep, cleft-like valley. Benyellary looms above, with Merrick lurking north. The sun was very hot so I quickly removed several layers of clothing to ease the steep, relentless climb.

A drystane dyke greeted me on the ridge and I stopped a moment, looking back down the hill, across to Rig of Jarkness – a magnificent crest of jagged peaks enclosing upland valleys, streaked with tumbling streams, caressed by soft shadows of passing clouds.

Some of them weren't passing and, from the west, ominous nimbus gathered. Within minutes a violent storm swept in and I broke more records, struggling back into mountains of pullovers. With wind-driven rain battering my face I battled to the tall cairn of Benyellary and searched through the downpour for Merrick. The top was shrouded in mist, a thick grey bank rolling rapidly to meet me.

Given the broad summit track and small cairns marking the way, I decided to walk on, hoping for a break in the clouds when I reached the top. Hills have a strange, mystical quality in mist. Danger ever-present. Senses sharpened. Caution walking alongside. And something else: an awareness that anything might come charging from the gloom, hobgoblin or foul fiend, and that you are alone in the hands of fate.

The climb had tired me. Mist, rain, wind and cloud depressed my spirits, but I trekked wearily on, determined to reach the top. Nearing the summit, with sudden shock I saw a huge, dark shape ahead, moving towards me through the mist. Was this the black creature of my dreams? I tensed, expectant.

Then clouds cleared, sun broke through and I saw, walking strongly downhill, a hand-in-hand couple, who waved me a cheery good afternoon as they passed. I judged from their appearance that they were at least twenty years my senior, and I won't see fifty again; yet they strode happily across the mountain like a couple of youngsters on a Sunday-school picnic.

The trig. point on top of Merrick is white-painted and surrounded by a circle of heaped rocks. I lunched in solitary splendour in the finest dining room in southern Scotland.

Proud, isolated Ailsa Craig and Arran's 'sleeping warrior' hills shimmered on the white and blue wave-ridged Firth of Clyde. A distant outline of Northern Ireland peaks. Green Lowther Hills and Cheviot, eastwards. South, the flat, blood-stained plain of the 'Debatable Lands' of Border feuds and battles. Beyond, Cumbria's purple-painted lakelands.

The crags north of Merrick, Black Gairy, are daunting and steep, but I followed the eastern ridge and carefully descended, overlooking island-clad Loch Enoch. I made for the little saddle on Craig Neldricken and Helen's Stone; no clear sign of stone, or, for that matter, of Helen either. The ground is rough, wet, tussocked, hollowed and hummocked and I edged my way slowly past Crocket's famous Murder Hole to the side of bleak Buchan Hill at the west end of Loch Valley.

The Gairland Burn, main feeder stream of Loch Trool, chummed me home, singing all the way, a torrent of sound-hurrying water. As the path rose round the hill, glimpses of Loch Trool, cradled between steeply wooded banks, filled the view and I walked past Buchan, uphill to the monolith of Bruce's Stone.

On one side is a description of a battle fought by Robert the Bruce in Glen Trool, when he defeated an English army by rolling mighty stones down onto their unsuspecting heads, thereby causing them great distress and probably quite a few headaches.

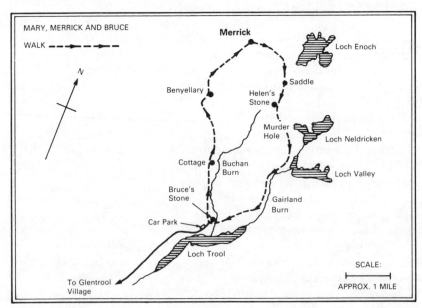

On the other side of the stone is the date when the monument was raised – 1926, if I remember right, but by this time my notebook was a soggy unusable heap and my pencil long lost on top of Merrick. Why, I thought, did it take my fellow Scots more than six hundred years to commemorate our hero king's victory? Luckless Queen Mary would understand.

WHAT YOU NEED TO KNOW

Time and effort Getting to the start, at the head of Loch Trool, is an expedition in itself. The roads through the forest are narrow, twisting and dangerous, with conifers blocking most of the view. The walk I describe takes about six hours so make sure you leave early and plan the day with great care.

Weather conditions change rapidly in this part of the world, so go prepared for the worst, regardless of time of year. I found it a most rewarding, exciting walk – but tiring, probably due to the fact that it was very wet and muddy .

This is particularly so from the bottom of the east slope of Merrick onwards, when you have to plot your own route across the flows. Certainly map and compass country. However, if you want to see one of the finest views in Scotland, then this is a walk you must make; and, once made, it will never be forgotten.

Location Ordnance Survey Sheet 77, New Galloway and Glen Trool, second series, scale 1:50,000.

Grid references Glen Trool car park 417803; Bruce's Stone 419804; Cul Sharg Cottage 416819; Benyellary 415839;Merrick 428854; Descent from Merrick at 420853 towards 437851; Loch Enoch 445850; Helen's Stone 436837; Murder Hole 439830; Loch Valley 445817; Buchan Hill track from 438820 by 428807 to car park.

Route The Merrick Walk is well signposted from the car park at the head of Loch Trool. Follow the signs to Buchan Burn and climb the left-hand side, up a rough, muddy track to the moss above. At the top you will see the little cottage of Cul Sharg ahead, in front of the forest.

Leave the cottage – I did so by the back window – and the track bears slightly right, still signposted, up the hill, through the new plantation. Cross a forest road and continue up, and up and up. As you clear the trees, the summit of Benyellary appears and at the top, a drystane dyke runs northwards. Follow this dyke; it leads to the top of Benyellary and on to Merrick.

The track dips from Benyellary, before the long, gentle ascent to the top of Merrick. From the end of the east spur of Merrick, map in hand, plot your route over the floor of the flow below, marking in your mind the saddle on Craig Neldricken, before you descend. Keep well to the south of Loch Enoch and make for the end of Loch Neldricken.

Skirt the loch – unless it is very hot and you want a cold spash – and trek over the hill towards Loch Valley. From Valley, a wet, broken track leads round Buchan Hill, back to the car park. You empty out at Bruce's Stone, above the track, and a last challenge to tired legs.

8

Riccarton, Hermitage and Roughley Sike

MY WIFE, Ann, doesn't use maps to find out how to get there; she uses maps to find out where she is once she is there, wherever 'there' might be. The woman seems to have an almost supernatural sense of direction. Whilst I ponder at the bottom of a hill, trying to interpret contours, she is half-way up, calling for me to get a move on.

A walk with Ann is an adventure. Others, less considerate, describe her hikes in less kindly terms – such as 'nightmare'. These special days are action-packed, full of incident, never-to-be-forgotten experiences; and when mist rolls down the mountain there is never argument about who should be pathfinder. Breac, my golden retriever, and I fall meekly into step behind Heathcliff, Ann's Yorkshire terrier, and humbly dog them home.

So, when Ann offered to contribute one of her walks to my book, I accepted, courteously but with mixed feelings – anticipation tempered by a strong foreboding of disaster. I had been there before, often. Still, I reasoned, what possible harm could we come to, walking round her childhood, Border hills? During the last war, having been blitzed out of the fair City of York, Ann's mother found employment as schoolteacher at Riccarton Junction, a road-less railway halt deep in the Cheviots fifteen miles south from Hawick.

The construction of a railway line between Hawick and Carlisle was the dream of Richard Hodgson, Chairman of the North British Railway Company in 1858; and, when the decision to start work was announced, Hawick declared a public holiday. But building the line was a Herculean task. The proposed track crossed some of the wildest country in Britain and a tunnel had to be driven 1,260 yards through Limekilnridge. The line between Copshaw and Whitrope Summit was an almost unbroken run of eight miles at 1:75, and the route had sharper curves and steeper gradients than any other track in Britain.

Time and fate eventually caught up with the Waverley Line one hundred and eleven years later. David Steel, Liberal Member of Parliament, rode the last train through Riccarton on the night of 6 January 1969. The following morning a section of track was lifted.

Ann's plan was to retrace one of her favourite walks: round the north side of Arnton Fell and Blackwood Hill, down Roughley Sike, and across the moor to gaunt Hermitage Castle, by Lady's Knowe and Flowsware Rig. In this part of the world, little streams are called 'sikes' and Ann recalled, as a child of seven, swimming in Roughley Sike, summer-warm pools at the foot of a waterfall rushing down the glen.

We knew Riccarton was in ruins, only Ann's schoolhouse being occupied, and that the tree-planters had moved in. However, nothing could have prepared us for the shock of devastation that greeted our arrival: as far as the eye could see, row after row of conifers. Regimented lines of lodgepole pine and Sitka spruce blanketing the horizon, obliterating once open moorlands. Worse, the last traces of the railway village, platforms and signal boxes were being torn up to extract hard core for more forest roads. The route round Arnton Fell had gone for ever.

Sadly Ann abandoned her plan, and we drove back through endless close-packed conifers to the road. But I saw the light of battle glint. 'Just because they have ruined Riccarton doesn't mean that we can't have a walk. Let's go over to Hermitage anyway, and try another route.' Long experience had taught me it was useless to protest. So I turned left on the B6399 and we drove a few miles south, by Whitrope Burn, then up to Hermitage.

My second daughter, Jean, had decided to accompany us. Heaven knows why, given her previous experiences of 'mother's walks'. To get matters off to a proper start, Jean opened the car door and, tangled in the seat belt, tripped into the mud, tearing new trousers and badly grazing her knee. Amidst the ensuing uproar, Heathcliff, having spotted a few sheep and the chance of escape, disappeared over the dyke, a happy brown flash, teeth bared, his face in a hideous grin.

Ann deserted her howling daughter and dashed off in hot pursuit, yelling, uselessly: 'Heathcliff! Come back here at once.' By this time, Breac had found Hermitage Burn and was snorting and snuffling his way quickly downstream. Jean was still hopping around, complaining that she wanted to go home immediately. Good Lord, I thought, and we haven't even started.

An exhausting half-hour later, Clan Sandison reformed. Hot sweet tea was administered and Heathcliff securely tethered to a nearby tree. I managed to get in a surreptitious swipe at the brute whilst 'she' wasn't looking and felt better – not a lot, but better. Breac jumped in to join us, a golden mound of dripping dog. Then Ann announced the fatal words 'I'll just have a quick look at the map.' My heart sank. 'Is there a dungeon in the castle?' I inquired, hopefully.

Hermitage, 'The Strength of Liddesdale', is an overpowering, massive, dark slab of history. Since 1242 it has guarded the south-west gateway to Scotland and throughout turbulent Border feuds and battles Hermitage has occupied a strategically unique position in Scottish history. The castle belonged to the Douglas family and Sir James, 'The Black Douglas', was one of Robert the Bruce's staunchest supporters during the Scottish Wars of Independence.

We explored the castle, marvellously preserved outside but little more than an empty shell inside. The bedroom where Earl Bothwell lay wounded when Queen Mary visited him on 15 October 1566. Mary rode there and back in a day from Jedburgh, over fifty miles of bleak windswept moorlands, to comfort her lover. The great hall, where dubious Francis Stewart of Crichton, 5th Earl Bothwell, entertained – a monstrous, fearful, pitiless prince.

In sombre mood, we left the grim castle and walked down to the road junction. Even Heathcliff was quiet. The cottage on the corner has been converted into a craft centre and shop. Long pause whilst the owner was routed out and forced to sell Jean comforting lemonade and crisps. Turning north, we walked up the road, past Hermitage Cottages.

Ann doesn't like roads. 'Come on now, over the fields and on to Roughley Burn,' she said encouragingly. The roadside dyke scaled, we all landed in a thick, glutinous mire lurking unseen on the other side. Loud howls of protest and outrage from Jean. Heathcliff was instantly transformed into a small, ragged, filthy black ball.

Half-way over the field I spotted the bull. At about the same time it spotted us and lumbered into first gear. Trying to keep calm, I urged the tribe to greater speed and we scrambled over a convenient gate, just ahead of about a ton and a half of steaming, angry Border beef. Roughley Burn lay before us, closely tree-clad, at the foot of a steep slope.

I suggested following the near bank, upstream, until we could find a suitable crossing place; but Ann doesn't like detours. Roman-like, she steers a straight course. Anything in the way has to be surmounted, not rounded or avoided. Just another challenge. Struggling down through the trees, we arrived at the burn, which was full, deep and fast-flowing.

I waded over with Jean first, stumbling amongst slippery stones. Then with Heathcliff: he is afraid of water. Then Ann, although I must admit that she did offer to wade the stream herself. Neat, I thought, standing there, wet to the waist, waiting until then to make her offer. Breac just stayed in the middle of the burn and paralleled our passage up the other side.

Which was not as easy as it sounds. Scrub, bramble, birch and willow crowded the muddy track, bounded by a malignant electrified fence. We crawled, Indian-like, through the tangle. At the first clearing we rested. Within seconds, Ann and Jean had been stung by a resident wasp, sending Jean off into further screams of terror. Me, I thought it was poetic justice.

Roughley Sike reached, we assaulted the hill, searching for the waterfall and pools of Ann's childhood. Sure enough, they were still there, but completely enclosed by mature trees which shaded out all light and gave the glen a forbidding feel. Jean, tired, cold, dismal and disillusioned, grabbed the fence to help her up hill. She shrieked with fright and leapt back. Even here the fence was electrified.

Lunch in the rain at the bottom of the hill. Another ferry session over the river, then the long, wet hike back across the moor to the car. Ahead, the black outline of Hermitage Castle beckoned and Jean and I instictively quickened pace. With any luck, we could get there first and barricade ourselves in. It had held out against invading armies in the past. Perhaps it would protect us today?

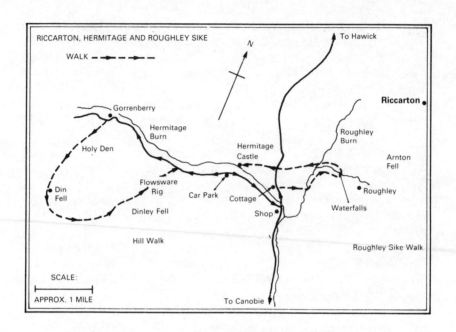

RICCARTON, HERMITAGE AND ROUGHLEY SIKE

WALK

N

To Hawick

Gorrenberry

Hermitage Burn

Holy Den

Hermitage Castle

Riccarton

Roughley Burn

Arnton Fell

Din Fell

Flowsware Rig

Car Park

Cottage

Roughley

Dinley Fell

Shop

Waterfalls

Hill Walk

Roughley Sike Walk

SCALE:

APPROX. 1 MILE

To Canobie

WHAT YOU NEED TO KNOW

Time and effort   A visit to Riccarton Junction will only be of interest to railway buffs or, like us, to people with ancient memories. Forestry has completely destroyed everything else. The walk to Roughley Sike is difficult and tiresome; much of the way is travelled bent double, climbing over and under trees, through tangled undergrowth, across streams. Not long in distance, but long in the mind. If you are foolish enough to attempt it, wear thigh waders and allow about three hours.

I have noted an alternative walk on the map, also starting from Hermitage Castle, but to the south and west: from Gorrenberry to Din Fell, Dinley Fell and Flowsware Rig – a fine moorland and hill walk with excellent views from the top of Din Fell, with summit amble. Be well shod and clad and allow about four hours, plus time to visit Hermitage.

Location   Ordnance Survey Sheet 79, Hawick and Eskdale, second series, scale 1:50,000.

Grid references   Hermitage Castle 497961; craft centre and shop 507952; Roughley Burn 515955; Roughley Sike Waterfalls 522958; Gorrenberry 470970; Din Fell 460960; Dinley Fell 473951; Flowsware Rig 478958.

Route   Leave your car in the car park at Hermitage. For Roughley Sike, walk back down the road to the cottage at the junction with the B6399. Turn left, northwards, and walk up to Hermitage Cottage, on the left of the road. Cross the dyke, into the bog. Stumble over the soggy fields to meet Roughley Burn, a distance of about three-quarters of a mile. Wade the stream and crawl up to where Roughley Sike enters. Climb the hill up Roughley Sike Glen. At the top, by Roughley Cottage, cross the sike and go back downhill. From there rewade the burn and take the most direct route over the moor to the road and Hermitage.

For the hill walk, turn right out of the car park at Hermitage and follow the road west to Gorrenberry. By the telephone kiosk, turn south and climb the shoulder of Din Fell, past Holy Den. This is a steep climb but the ground is relatively dry and going is easy, sort of. From the top, walk south-east, angling down the hill to the promontory of Dinley Fell. From here, an easy walk downhill brings you over Flowsware Rig and back to the minor road. Turn right, alongside Hermitage Burn, back to the car park.

9

Eagle Rock, Romans and Queensferry

ONE OF my best-loved walks near Edinburgh is from the village of Cramond to South Queensferry and back – a distance of ten miles along the shores of the Firth of Forth. As a boy I had often made the walk with my parents so it was with a feeling of returning to an old friend that I once again walked down the winding road to the Firth.

Cramond – Caer Almond, the fort on the River Almond – was an important Roman garrison town, and excavations have revealed much of the signs of early occupation by these methodical early invaders of Scotland. The white-walled Cramond Inn provides a focal point for the village and is well known for the excellence of its food – and drink. Time your walk in accordance with opening hours and work up a thirst for the end of the day.

Robert Louis Stevenson, author of *Treasure Island* and *Kidnapped*, was a frequent visitor to the old inn and, at the other end of the walk at South Queensferry, there is an equally famous watering-hole, the Hawes Inn, built in 1683. Stevenson dreamed up the plot for *Kidnapped* whilst staying at Hawes, in bedroom number 13, 'a small room, with a bed in it, and heated like an oven by a great coal fire'.

It was low tide when I arrived and the Almond lay exposed, mudflatted between tree-lined banks, dotted with small sailing boats. A group of youngsters in kayaks ploughed up and down, yelling with delight when one of their companions capsized. Visitors wandered ice-creamed in warm sun.

A mile off shore, connected to the mainland by a causeway, lies Cramond Island. It is possible to walk over at low tide, but get it wrong and you have a long wait before being able to return. From time to time foolhardy drivers attempt the journey in four-wheel-drive vehicles and, recently, a Range Rover stuck and was soon covered by the incoming tide.

For centuries, passage over the Almond has been provided by a small boat, sculled back and forth on demand by a ferryman who lives in a cottage on the west bank. I stood by the steps leading down to the river, looking hopeful, and in a few minutes the ferryman appeared.

The boat is propelled from the stern, by one oar, manoeuvred in a figure-of-eight rhythm. Not as easy as it sounds. Whilst I was employed by Her Majesty the Queen as a seaman in the Water Transport Regiment, Royal Army Service Corps, I mastered the art of sculling on the River Yar, Isle of Wight. It's like riding a bicycle – once learnt, never forgotten – and it was hard to resist the temptation to ask the ferryman for a go.

I paid my dues of 20 pence and set off westwards along the well remembered path through magnificent woodlands peopled with ancient trees: oak, ash, beech, sycamore, plane, birch, tall Scots pine, larch and nodding old elms, survivors of the dreadful disease that has decimated so many of our native trees in recent years.

A few hundred yards on I turned right, down to the shingle shore to revisit Eagle Rock. As a boy my mind blazed with images every time I surveyed the carving on the face of the huge volcanic boulder. The shape of an eagle has been chiselled in the stone – a Roman eagle, reputed to have been the work of the garrison stationed at Cramond.

Whilst there is no proof that the legionaries actually carved the eagle, I firmly believe they did. Otherwise, all my childhood dreams, wild adventures and fights round the rock would have been pointless. I was always a Pict – and the Romans never won, in spite of what history might say.

On the edge of the tide statuesque herons solemnly stalked lunch;

oystercatchers screamed and squeaked in noisy, black-and-white flights. Long-beaked redshank and curlew poked busily in the sand. Hunch-shouldered mallard stared gloomily at nothing in particular. A pair of mute swans gracefully adorned the flats, haughtily marking my passing.

Walking along the Firth is like a journey in and out of history. The sea is scattered with passing ships: ponderous tankers; a Rosyth-bound Royal Navy frigate, inching menacingly towards port; drilling platforms; and pleasure craft. The Romans would have passed this way, dreaming of distant loved ones and sun-drenched Italian lands.

An RAF fighter plane screams low over Inchcolm, shaking the ruins of the island's ancient abbey, founded in AD 1123, ripping past gaunt pillboxes, relics of Second World War defences. Barnbougle Castle looms near, built in the thirteenth century by the Mowbray family, on the edge of the sea, ideally placed for smuggling; and Hound Point, haunted by the ghost of Sir Roger Mowbray's dog, Baskerville-howling for his dead master, killed during the Crusades.

Glimpses eastwards, of grey-painted Granton Gasworks and Edinburgh and the crouching lion of Arthur's Seat. North over the Forth to the Kingdom of Fife, busy with Burntisland, Methil, Kirkcaldy and Dysart. The view spans the centuries, stretching mind and imagination over Scotland's turbulent past and hopeful future.

Dalmeny golf course interrupts the cool woods, precisely mani-cured in well ordered calm. A notice warns me to take care. Presumably from flying golf balls, but the greens and fairways are empty this morning. Time to visit Dalmeny House, home of the Primrose family, Earls of Rosebery, who have lived there for more than three hundred years.

I never think of Rosebery without reciting to myself the brief lines Robert Burns once gave a previous Lord and Lady Rosebery to say:

> Rosebery to his Lady says,
> My hinnie and my socour,
> Oh, shall we do the thing ye ken,
> Or shall we tak our supper?
> Wi modest face, sae fu of grace,
> Replied the bonnie lady,
> My Noble Lord, do as you please,
> But supper isna ready.

The parents of the present Lord Rosebery divided their time between Mentmore and Dalmeny, 'driving north with two dogs, a cat, a parrot, about twelve staff, three cars and a horse box full of luggage every August in time for the grouse shooting and the Edinburgh Festival'.

Dalmeny House is the work of the 4th Earl, who, one year before the Battle of Waterloo, commissioned the architect William Wilkins to prepare plans for a new house. Barnbougle, the old house, was 'much neglected'. A story is recounted by Lady Rosebery, in her excellent guidebook to Dalmeny, of how the 3rd Earl was once drenched by a wave breaking through the dining-room window of Barnbougle, but the Earl maintained that what had been good enough for his grandfather was good enough for his grandchildren.

Wilkins's building was the first Tudor Gothic Revival house to be built in Scotland and Dalmeny is open to the public. The house contains a wealth of treasures from all over the world: Scottish portraits by Reynolds, Gainsborough, Raeburn and Lawrence; Goya tapestries and the famous Rothschild Collection of eighteenth century furniture, porcelain and other works of art.

From Dalmeny, I walked on to the Forth bridges and Queens-ferry. The railway bridge was designed by Sir John Fowler in 1890 and in its day was one of the wonders of the modern world. Even now, the imposing structure dominates the feather-like span of the new road bridge.

Before the road bridge was built, passage across the Forth was by ferry, established in the twelfth century by Queen Margaret; and the seaside town named for her is now a quiet, traffic-less, peaceful haven. In my young days, the narrow streets were always jam-packed with cars and crossing the Forth could take anything up to three hours, shuttled below the bridge by side-paddle steamers. the *Queen Margaret*, *Robert the Bruce* and *Sir William Wallace*.

Time for a closer look at the Hawes Inn and stirring of old memories before the return to Cramond. Must be back at the Almond before 7 p.m. from April to September or before 4 p.m. during winter months. Otherwise you might end up having to swim for your supper – and who needs that?

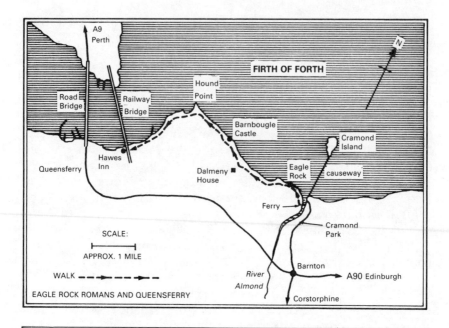

EAGLE ROCK ROMANS AND QUEENSFERRY

WHAT YOU NEED TO KNOW

Time and effort This is an easy walk, along a good track, through woodlands and by shoreline. There and back the walk takes up to four hours, depending upon how long you linger at Dalmeny House. Worth carrying binoculars to get a closer look at wildlife on the shore. The total distance is 10 miles.

Location Ordnance Survey Sheet 65, Falkirk and West Lothian, second series, scale 1:50,000.

Grid references Cramond 190770; Eagle Rock 185775; Dalmeny House 169781; Barnbougle Castle 169785; Hound Point 158796; Hawes Inn 139784.

Route Parking is restricted on the sea-front, so park up the hill in Cramond Village and walk down to the shore. Steps lead down to the ferry. Stand at the top until the ferryman comes over – don't worry, he will see you.

Pass through the turnstile on the other side, by the ferryman's cottage, and the track leads you easily westwards. Within a few hundred yards watch for the little junction on your right, down to Eagle Rock.

Once you reach the golf course, walk inshore of the trees and you will see Dalmeny House set on a promontory to your left. From the house a road continues west, once more through the trees. This soon becomes a track again and leads directly to South Queensferry. Return the same way. Make sure that you check ferry times.

10

Gladhouse, Dundreich Hill and Portmore

TOM WOOD heated milk and poured it over sugar-covered Weetabix. We sat outside our tent by the shores of Gladhouse Reservoir luxuriating in early morning sunlight, the wild, rain-soaked night forgotten. What ever happened to Tom? Thirty-five years have passed since that breakfast, but I still feel its warmth as keenly as though it were yesterday.

We had spent the previous night, on a Boy Scout exercise, walking in the Moorfoot Hills. After gathering up our damp gear, we limped soggily back to Edinburgh and headquarters at Hermit-age of Braid. Although I can't remember the purpose of the hike, I shall never forget that special breakfast. Wherever you are, Tom, thanks again: it was a life-saver.

The little wood we camped in was still there as I lumbered by last summer, heavily booted for the hills. Gladhouse lay calm and peaceful, bedecked with black specks of fishing boats inching eagerly round tree-clad islands, searching shallows for shy brown trout.

Fishing on Gladhouse used to be organized by ballot. In the dark depths of the Water Department of Edinburgh City Council in

Cockburn Street, a mysterious hat was produced and the names of anglers seeking permission to fish on a particular day were chucked in and, presumably, stirred about a bit. First out got the boats. Took me years to realize that in order to be first out you really had to be 'first in' with one of the officials. Father always used to say I was naive.

The road along the south side of the reservoir leads to Moorfoot Farm, a cluster of neat buildings surrounded by well kept, busy fields. Contented cattle and black-faced sheep gazed curiously as I passed, probably wondering if I was for eating. Turning south along a good track, I noted tumbled ruins marking the site of Moorfoot Chapel and Grange.

King David I gave the lands of Moorfoot to the wealthy Abbey of Newbattle in AD 1120. Then, Moorfoot was a considerable community – robe-clad, hooded monks tilling thin soils and tending sheep in upland valleys. Now only bare stones remain by the clear waters of the infant South Esk, as it wends towards captivity in Gladhouse.

The South Esk rises from secret valleys, deep in Moorfoot on Blackhope Scar. It rushes 1,200 feet down Long Cleave to a stem at Gladhouse Cottage, where it is bunched into order for the journey north. The ruins of Hirendean Castle stand on a small knowe overlooking the river – a stark shell guarded by an ancient ash and four windswept sycamores.

I climbed past the sheepfold on the lower slope and sheltered from rising wind in the lee of the single jagged wall. Hirendean was built in the sixteenth century by the Kerr family and little is known of their pastimes and pleasures. Behind me were outlines of a great fireplace, so I was probably crouched in what was once the main hall. Wonder what they got up to, in their balmy days of power and glory? Poor old house; no one seems to care for you now.

'Esk' is the Pictish name for water and the little river glistens and sparkles by an easy track which climbs slowly southwards. Every step of the way is sheer delight. The stream turns and twists, now cascading over tiny waterfalls, now swirling into deep, foam-churned pools. Heather-purple banks and bracken-sided hills colour the scene. Dippers and pied wagtails dart and splash amongst grey and yellow stones. Red-capped grouse wing wildly across the moor and the sound of the stream is never-ending Mozart.

A ford crosses the river at head of Glen Esk, but I balanced, dry-shod, over a twin-poled bridge. As I left the river, I thought how sad it was that the Esk should be so filthy and ill kept downstream by the pits and papermills of Midlothian when it had gone to so much trouble making itself beautiful in childhood hills.

The track reared ahead, climbing round the slope, following a narrow burn bursting with eagerness to reach Lady Esk. A hobgoblin bridge led to a small hut, already winter-fodder-packed for hardy Moorfoot sheep. I turned left, still by the stream, which fell through an ever-darkening, deeply scarred gorge, the sides stripped naked by dashing rivulets. Rowan cling precariously, hopefully berried for autumn birds.

Dundreich Hill, my goal, disappears behind a false summit. Hard going, for me, with plenty of pauses for rest. As I crested the ridge, Dundreich appeared again, a mile distant over an undulating wet moorland plateau. I trudged on, rain now keeping me company. A criss-cross of drainage ditches covers the moor. Deep black and brown peat hags hung dripping with raindrops as I turned and twisted towards the summit.

Dundreich, at 2,040 feet, is second highest of the Moorfoot Hills. A trig. point and cairn of basalt boulders mark the top. Lunch and welcome. The dark ridge of Salisbury and outline of Edinburgh Castle lie enfolded northwards, between Pentland and Lammermuir Hills. Across the Firth of Forth, Ochils and Campsie Fells preamble Highland peaks. Blackhope Scar, Black Knowe and Black Law, a ruffled green carpet, stretch southwards to Tweed.

Below, the dormitory sprawl of Penicuik, 'hill of the cuckoo', edges Edinburgh-wards and the soft Lothian landscape is stabbed with the blades of coal mines, mills, power stations and factories. Godlike on the hill, I ponder man's unending greed and desire to despoil everything around him in the name of commerce and progress. Only the very top of Totto Hill is treeless; Lamb Law, Sherra Law, Dunslair Heights, Cardon Law and Caresman Hill are now smothered by impenetrable conifers.

I walked south from the cairn, along a springy grass summit, to the spur above Portmore Loch. Once spent New Year's Day there, nursing a badly sprained ankle. My fault. Should never have tried to dance a foursome reel, on my own, half-sheets to the wind on Auld Year's Eve. Portmore was always a special place for my wife Ann and me. We used to buy provisions at the Aladdin's cave of Messrs Valvona & Crolla, Elm Row, Edinburgh, and repair to the lochside to eat. Salad summer days, filled with French loaves and cool white wine.

On a small hill south-west of the loch lie Northshield rings – and no finer place to view this Pictish fort than from 2,000 feet above. Three concentric circles of ramparts and ditches enclose an area 240 by 210 feet. The hill is clad with heather and bracken and, from nearby, the outline of the fort is easily missed. Now, from Dundreich, with sun slanting over the shoulder of the hill, I could almost see skin-clad spear-carrying figures, dog-heeled, scurrying homewards.

The reed-fringed south shore of Portmore was clustered with quacking, squabbling mallard. Bad-tempered birds. An expectant angler whisked his fly out over the dimpled rise of a feeding trout. To no avail. I stopped to commiserate and offer advice, conveniently forgetting to mention the fact that during three years of regular piscatory visits I had caught far fewer fish than my wife – who caught only one.

A pleasant lochside track meanders along the east shore to the dam wall and I relaxed for a few moments in a chair outside the fishing hut for coffee. With midges beginning to think I was supper, I started the three-mile walk back to Gladhouse, following the line of an old underground water-pipe. Meant to find out if it was still in use but never did. Ornate iron uprights mark the way, regularly spaced 200 yards apart. They are dated, alternately, 1880 then 1889, and marked as being the property of E & D W T: Edinburgh and District Water something or other?

The wet whirr of snipe, and pheasants, chortling safely from turnips, accompanied me over the fields. By the car I stopped for one last look back up the Esk Valley to Dundreich. Clouds were gathering where I had been. A lone curlew whistled down the hill. I said 'thank you'.

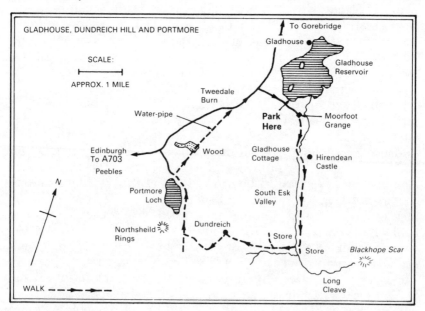

GLADHOUSE, DUNDREICH HILL AND PORTMORE

SCALE:

APPROX. 1 MILE

To Gorebridge

Gladhouse

Gladhouse Reservoir

Tweedale Burn

Water-pipe

Park Here

Moorfoot Grange

Edinburgh To A703

Peebles

Wood

Gladhouse Cottage

Hirendean Castle

N

Portmore Loch

South Esk Valley

Northsheild Rings

Dundreich

Store

Store

Blackhope Scar

WALK

Long Cleave

WHAT YOU NEED TO KNOW

Time and effort About twelve miles and five hours. The only section likely to make you puff – it did me – is the climb up from the head of the Esk Valley to Dundreich Hill. You will require waterproof boots: the plateau before Dundreich is damp and soggy. Nor should you underestimate the rapidity of weather changes in the Moorfoot Hills; modest they may be, but it can be very cold and inhospitable on the tops. Carry spare warm clothing, just in case.

Location Ordnance Survey Sheet 73, Galashiels and Ettrick Forest, second series, scale 1:50,000.

Grid references Gladhouse Reservoir 295535; park at 292527; Moorfoot Grange and Chapel 297524; Hirendean Castle 297513; head of Esk valley 297486; Dundreich Hill 275491; Northshield Rings 257494; Portmore Loch 260500; water line from Portmore at 260508 to Tweeddale Burn at 276526.

Route Park on the minor road leading to Moorfoot Farm, at the south end of Gladhouse Reservoir, in a prepared parking area. Watch out for the inevitable notice-board listing dos and don'ts round the loch. Walk to Moorfoot Farm and turn quarter-right, following the hill track leading to Gladhouse Cottage, on the small hill ahead.

Cross the South Esk by the dam and Hirendean Castle is on your left. The track continues up the valley, eventually leading to a ford across the river and a block-built animal-food store. Turn right, away from the Esk, and follow the track which continues uphill over an attractive little bridge to another winter food store.

Just before this last store turn left by a sheepfold and climb the valley, keeping the stream on your left. This will take you out onto the plateau below Dundreich Hill. From the cairn on the top, walk south-west to the spur overlooking Portmore Loch and carefully descend the hill. When you reach the track at the foot of the hill, turn right, northwards, and follow this path round the east side of Portmore to the fishing hut by the dam wall and car park.

The first gate on your right takes you onto the line of the water-pipe. Look over the field and you will see the route as a straight mound leading towards the conifer plantation in the middle distance. The pipe bisects this wood. At the road at Tweeddale Burn, turn right and walk alongside the massive V-walled outlet stream from Portmore to Gladhouse. Turn first right over this stream, back to your car.

11

Romans, Roundheads and Pentland Picts

I T ALL started in Habbie's Howe, thirty years ago. Mildly protesting, yet anxious to please a new girl-friend, I was chivvied from the comfort of the old inn and marched swiftly to the top of the Pentland Hills. I can't even pretend I enjoyed the experience, walking for walking's sake; but it was immediately clear that, if I wished to retain the regard of this beautiful creature, I would have to start enjoying it – pretty damned quick.

Now, more than half a lifetime and four marvellous children later, I still see that special gleam in her eye when she pores over Ordnance Survey maps during long winter evenings, plotting fresh, lung-bursting expeditions; and, I confess, I have come to enjoy it, very much indeed.

Habbie's Howe was our favourite pub, a few miles from

Edinburgh and made famous by Allan Ramsey in his book *The Gentle Shepherd*, published in 1725:

> Gae faurer doon the burn tae Habbie's Howe,
> Where a' the sweets o' spring an' summer grow,
> An' when ye're tired o' prattling side the rill,
> Return tae Ninemileburn, an' tak a gill.

Which good advice I follow, frequently. As starting point, or perhaps more important, finishing point for Pentland walks, Habbie's Howe is ideal. This small hamlet on the road to Lanark was once a busy staging post for travellers and birthplace of George Mickle Kemp, architect of that famous Princes Street monstrosity the Scott Monument.

Romans also walked this way, spears trailing, wearily to Solway, and Nine Mile Burn lies 1½ miles south-west of Eight Mile Burn, but proper, Scottish miles, neither Roman, nor English. The 'lang Scots miles' which Tam o' Shanter, Kirkton Jean and Souter Johnnie ignored in Burns's poem were 1,976 yards, measured from Edinburgh to the Pentland villages. Not the fancy, foreign, metre things we have to contend with today.

Keeping these old roads in good repair was always a problem – so much so that in 1669 by Royal Statute, it was decreed that every man between the ages of fifteen and seventy should give six days work a year on the roads in his parish. The idea worked as well then as it would now and Scotland's roads had to wait for General Wade, Telford and Macadam and their successors before the 'mosses, waters slaps and stiles' of history were finally smoothed away.

The Pentland Hills were my youthful playground, easily accessible from Edinburgh and a popular weekend retreat for the stolid citizens of Auld Reekie. As a boy, the T Woods near Swanson were a regular haunt, where I wickedly bird-nested amongst whins, searching for pale linnet's eggs.

Robert Louis Balfour Stevenson, the author of *Treasure Island*, lived in Swanson Village as a child and I often hung over the garden wall, gazing at windows, watching for my hero's face. Never saw RLS but I did see my first white blackbird in his garden, an albino oddity which chattered about the trees for years.

Sitting in the car park outside Habbie's Howe last July, ready booted, I stared moodily through the rain, wondering if it would stop long enough for a quick dash up West Kip. Selective mist rolled along the hills, giving the Pentlands an almost feminine outline; they appeared and disappeared, embarrassed by fondling clouds. Still, I reasoned, I can only get wet and the rain might pass.

Through the gate at the end of the car park, and on to the track with Cap Law somewhere ahead, the litany of Monks Burn rumbling nearby. I imagined a holy line of closely hooded figures, wraith-like in the mist, squelching up the path. This is the route Cistercian divines followed from their monastery at Newhall, in the woods south of Habbie's Howe, over the hill to Howlets House, 'the house of the owls', once a lonely chapel, now ruins on the north shore of Loganlee Reservoir.

I stopped by Font Stone, the remains of a cross marking the way. A break in the clouds suddenly exposed the small wood at the head of the glen, like a ghostly army marching downhill. Other, less ghostly armies, stalked Pentland in the past. A few miles north, on the slopes of Turnhouse Hill, at Rullion Green, religious intolerance boiled over into bloody murder.

A Royalist force, commanded by General Thomas Dalyell, fell on a group of 900 Covenanters. Men, women and children were indiscriminately slaughtered. Those who survived were hanged, ten at a time, in Edinburgh, or before their own front doors.

The remainder were shipped to the West Indies as plantation slaves. Dalyell was a devoted Royalist. Since the execution of King Charles I he had never shaved his beard, but even he was appalled by the events of Rullion. He retired from the army, and from public life, immediately after this so-called battle.

Those were hard times to be a Christian. Before the Restoration, the Covenanters had committed equally horrifying acts on Episcopalian fellow Scots. In 1661, blossoming freedom from the Solemn League and Covenant produced these heartfelt hopes, inscribed on an triumphal arch in Linlithgow:

> From Covenanters with uplifted hands,
> From Remonstrators with associate bands,
> From such Committees as govern the nation,
> From Church Commissioners and their Protestation,
> Good Lord deliver us.

In 1687, King James II offered religious tolerance, a final, ill-fated attempt at reconciliation that was to cost him his crown two years later. Gilbert Rule, a noted historian of his time, expressed the church's view of religious freedom: 'To accept this toleration is inconsistent with the principles of the Church of Scotland . . . in which we are all bound to extirpate popery.' The Revd Sheilds, a prominent preacher, put the matter in plainer language: 'To engage in bond of living peaceably is to engage in bonds of iniquity with those who are carrying on Babylon's interest, the mother of harlots and witchcraft.'

Past the wood, I puffed up the shoulder of mist-covered West

Kip, a modest 1,806 feet and second highest of the Pentland Hills. The highest, Scald Law, 1,899 feet, lay somewhere to the north-east, shrouded in cloud and rain.

On a clear day the view from the top of West Kip is spectacular, embracing half Scotland at a glance – Edinburgh, arced and protected by Lammermuir and Moorfoots; distant Cheviots; and, westward, tangled Trossach peaks. Perthshire and the Cairngorms crowd northwards. Largo Law in Fife and Lothian's Berwick Law pillar the Firth of Forth, dotted black by Inchkeith, Bass Rock and the Isle of May.

Not today. I could hardly see my hand in front of my face and stumbled along, searching for the path down to Eastside and Eight Mile Burn. With a sense of relief, I found the track and stamped wetly southwards, eventually arriving on the minor road leading to the A702.

The 200 square miles of Pentland are scattered with Pictish remains – indeed, 'Pentland' means 'the land of the Picts' – and on a promontory at the foot of South Black Hill is the prehistoric fort of Braidwood. There is evidence of two separate periods of occupation and construction. The first fort was probably an all-timber structure guarded by a single wall; the second ring, protected by banks and ditches, is 45 feet from the first, but joined to it by a fence.

As they tramped by, along their neat, well-surfaced road,

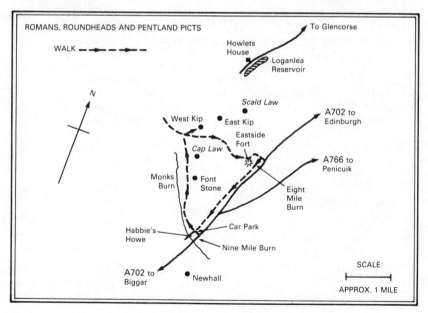

swarthy Roman legionaries must have cursed their luck. What gods had they offended, so badly, to be banished to this last outpost of the Empire, playing watchdog to a bunch of rain-soaked, hair-coated savages? Similar thoughts ran through my mind as I fell in behind a passing cohort and marched back along the Roman road to the car. I left the troop at Nine Mile Burn ad slipped gratefully into Habbie's Howe, to warm my sorrows by the blazing fire.

WHAT YOU NEED TO KNOW

Time and effort All the Pentland Hills are easily accessible from Edinburgh and provide a delightful range of walks, both long and little, strenuous and not so strenuous. The walk described is easy, although sometimes wet, and takes about three hours.

This walk could well be combined with a visit to one of Scotland's most famous places of worship, Roslin Chapel, dating from 1452, and a few miles distant, between Penicuik and Loanhead. The beauty of the Pentland walks is that there is always a quick escape route should the weather turn nasty, and lots of alternative places of interest to visit. Invariably, routes and rights of way are well signposted.

Location Ordnance Survey Sheet 66, Edinburgh, second series, scale 1:50,000.

Grid references Habbie's Howe 178577; Font Stone 175593; Cap Law 175598; West Kip 177605; Eastside 184603; Braidwood Fort 194597; Eight Mile Burn 192593.

Route Drive south-west from Edinburgh along the A702 Biggar road. Park at Habbie's Howe, beside the inn. A gate leaves the end of the car park and the track is signposted, half-left from the gate. Look ahead and you will see the track winding up the hill on the right side of Monks Burn. Half-way up the hill, between Green Law and Broad Law, on your right, is the Font Stone. On the lower slopes of West Kip, go right, round the wood, and on to the summit.

Retrace your steps from the summit and turn south, down the track to Eastside. From here you meet a good, well surfaced road coming up the hill to greet you. Follow this until it takes a 90-degree turn north. Immediately on your right is the site of Braidwood Pictish fort.

Before the little road joins the A702, turn right to Eight Mile Burn. Cross Eight Mile Burn and follow the Roman Road back to the car park and Habbie's Howe.

12

Edinburgh Past
and Present

*I*WAS born and brought up in Edinburgh and wear the 'Auld Grey City' like a garment round my soul. Thirty-two years separate me from Scotland's capital, but a small corner of my heart is for ever Auld Reekie – cautious, reserved, quick to take offence, slow to forgive, essentially parochial and proud of it.

Worse, I was educated in Edinburgh, at Scotland's oldest seat of learning, the Royal High School, founded in 1120 under the Abbot of Holyrood. There I was thoroughly boiled in Bannockburn and stories of Robert the Bruce and William Wallace, imbued with the sad, beautiful poetry of Burns and filled with the stirring novels of our famous former pupil, Sir Walter Scott.

Mathematics and sciences were closed doors, but mention the Battle of Otterburn, Sir Andrew Wood, Montrose or Bonnie Dundee and my interest was guaranteed. Burns's poem 'To a Mountain Daisy' brought tears to my eyes and I laboured for hours memorising 'Tam o'Shanter' rather than Shakespeare. When I finally walked through the memorial doors of the old building, I was about as prepared for the realities of life as King James IV was for battle at Flodden Field in 1513.

My elder brother, Ian, and I used to roam the streets, from Swanson to Leith. Dangerously bird-nesting in private gardens on Calton Hill. Exploring the endless, narrow, dark, secret lanes off High Street. Pushing buttons in Chambers Street museum, watching, fascinated, as stolid models staggered to life. Buying forbidden winkles, paper-poked-and-pinned, from the huge black-clad lady who sat by John Knox's house.

Edinburgh is one of the most beautiful cities in the world, and a walk through 'The Athens of the North' is always an exciting adventure; but, for me, it is not only a walk through Scottish history but also a walk through green childhood years. What was time then? The distance between the top of Arthur's Seat and the hot chiding waiting when we arrived home late for dinner.

The quick way to school was over Calton Hill and this is an excellent starting point for an Edinburgh walk. The hill is an ancient lava flow, steep-cragged to the south and smoothed by ice to the north – ideal for summer sledging on school drawing-boards. Calton is graced by 'the disgrace of Edinburgh', an unfinished monument of classical proportions, the building of which ended when funds ran out – Scottish pragmatism at its best.

I discovered Schubert on Calton, in 1962 when a limousine of a grand piano was placed on the hill, across from the Royal Observatory car park, and two promising young pianists played to an enraptured audience: Vladimir Ashkenazy and Daniel Barenboim.

The path round the west side of the Observatory, above Leith Street, is also an ideal place to watch the last-night sentiment of the Edinburgh International Festival. Castle lights dim, leaving only topmost turrets illuminated. A lone piper laments. Then the blaze and sparkle as fireworks scatter and burst, brightening dark, star-specked skies.

Nelson's Column crowns Calton Hill, a round, ugly monument to Trafalgar's posthumous victor. The firing of the one o'clock gun from Edinburgh Castle is timed at the Column. As one o'clock approaches, a ball slowly ascends a post to the top of the tower. When it falls, half a mile away, the gun fires. Which is why I never mastered the niceties of algebra. At the window of my classroom I could sit, mesmerized, watching this inevitable daily sequence: rise, fall and bang. Much more interesting.

Steps lead down the hill to Waterloo Place, by vast St Andrew's House, pack-full of government bureaucracy, busily administering Scottish affairs. At the east end of Princes Street stand these grand lumps, the Central Post Office and the North British Hotel. Registrar House, a magnificently proportioned Adam building, eyes them warily from across the street, guarded by a bronze statue of the Iron Duke, horse-mounted, arm outflung, pointing towards supposed danger approaching from Portobello.

I always used to return home this way, and wait outside Elliot's bookshop for a number 9 tramcar. Had to be a number 9: that's the one she took. All I needed was the courage to speak to her, but the High School didn't prepare boys for that either.

Across Princes Street, past Waverley Bridge, squats the Scott Monument, like a huge wedding cake waiting to be sliced. Sir Walter sits serenely under his arches, book on lap, studious hands on marble pages, frequently red-nosed – wickedly painted by irreverent pranksters.

Scotland's National Gallery, a few yards further on, is a favourite stopping place of mine. Not the one fronting Princes Street: the one behind, where admission is free. Could never afford the other, and, consequently, always spent my time round the corner. Raeburn's portrait of Mrs Scott Moncrief, the Rembrandt self-portrait, Monet's poplars, Chardin's flowers and McTaggart are my best-loved residents, and I visit them frequently, like old friends.

A road, known as 'The Mound', leads from the galleries up to Castle and High Street. The Nor Loch used to protect these northern walls, and was formed in 1448 when the east end of the valley was dammed. After it had been drained, the mound was built to give access to the 'New Town', built to ease the crush of tenements clustered down Royal Mile from Castle to Holyrood. The foundations of the first of these elegant squares and terraces were laid out on 26 October 1767.

Edinburgh's earliest inhabitants built a fort on Castle Rock, the most easily defensible promontory amongst marshy forests of pre-history. The present castle evolved from these humble timber beginnings and was much needed throughout the ages. Scots were always 'chronically at war', if not with themselves then with the English – a state of affairs only briefly interrupted by Roman domination and lasting until Bonnie Prince Charlie's disastrous visit in 1745.

A Royal Mile of history leads downhill from the Castle Esplanade, past still impressive tenements, called 'lands' in their days of glory. The higher your station, the nearer ground level you lived; but the same entrance was used by mighty lord and humble servant alike and Scottish social distinctions were much formed by these meetings on the stairs. It was hard to be impressed by your neighbour when you were accustomed to seeing him rolling home, pickled and plain, six nights a week. Sundays were soberly kirked.

An amazing array of intellectual ability flourished in the High Street: Allan Ramsey, founder of the Select Society, a literary elite;

his son, also Allan, the portrait painter, and his pupil, Naysmith; philosopher David Hume; Adam Smith, author of *The Wealth of Nations*; William Creech, publisher of the Edinburgh Edition of Burns's poetry; and Scotia's bard himself.

The High street abounded with private clubs of literary, artistic, political and just good old-fashioned Scots drinking men; the Cape Club, favoured by Scotland's unsung poet, Robert Fergusson; the Pious Club, Spendthrift Club, Salt Herring Club, Ten Tumbler Club, and many more.

However, amidst all the bustle of High Street, my most treasured place is round the back of St Giles's Cathedral – an evening sanctuary of peace and solitude, shadowed and softened by lingering sunlight, watched and guarded by the statue of Corollus Secundus, Emperor of Rome, strangely stirrup-less on his mighty horse.

At the foot of the hill stands the palace of Holyroodhouse, residence of Scottish monarchs until the Union of the Crowns in 1603, surrounded by the well kept acres of Holyrood Park, crowned by the proud 'lion' of Arthur's Seat. The Picts built one of their largest forts on top of the hill, enclosing some 20 acres, and Arthur's Seat is easily climbed from St Margaret's Loch. The ruined chapel on the hill overlooking the little loch was built by King Malcolm Canmore's Hungarian-born wife, the saintly Princess Margaret.

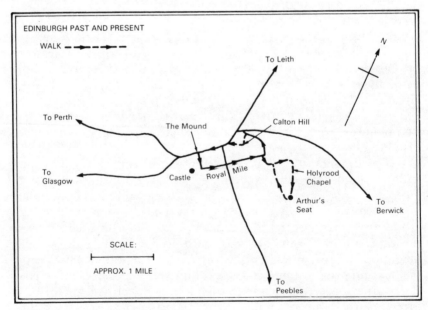

I stood on the lion's rocky head. There was Newhaven Harbour, where Ian and I used to fish; my childhood Edinburgh home; the High School, sad and empty, awaiting the arrival of an ever-absent Scottish Parliament; the hospital, where our first son was born; Jock's Lodge, school playing-fields, where I struggled in winter rugby mud; and, above all, the black-etched castle, rose-hazed and dreamlike, watching carefully over Edinburgh's old grey spires.

WHAT YOU NEED TO KNOW

Time and effort This walk could take a lifetime, there is so much to see on the way. Do your best to allow at least a full day. The walking's easy, but still wear good stout shoes and carry a waterproof: Edinburgh weather, like the city itself, can be fickle. Prepare yourself before setting off by visiting the tourist information centre on Waverley Bridge. Have a street plan to guide you round and mug up basic information about what you hope to visit on the way. For a walk only, allow three hours.

Location Ordnance Survey Sheet 66, Edinburgh, second series, scale 1:50,000.

Grid references Calton Hill 265742; Registrar House 259741; The Mound 255738; Edinburgh Castle 252735; Holyroodhouse 269739; Arthur's Seat 276729.

Route Park your car on Blenheim Place, adjacent to where London Road and Leith Street meet. Walk up the hill to the church on your right. Steps lead to Calton Hill. A track follows a wall up an easy slope to your left. This leads to Edinburgh's Disgrace, the Observatory and Nelson's Column.

Close to the column, an old brass ship's cannon, on wheels, is 'aimed' towards Princes Street. It also points to the steps which lead down to Waterloo Place. On Waterloo, turn right and walk to the east end of Princes Street. Adam's Registrar House is on the right-hand side.

Cross Princes Street and walk through East Princes Street Gardens to the Scott Monument. If feeling particularly energic, stop and climb the stairs that wind up inside, to the top. If not, pass by and visit the Scottish National Gallery at the foot of The Mound.

Walk up The Mound, bearing right round the railing in front of the Assembly Hall, and up the steep stone-flagged slope to High Street and Edinburgh Castle. After visiting the castle, walk down the Royal Mile and call on Holyroodhouse.

Now, into the park, left along the road, past the wishing well to St Margarets Loch. On the far side of the loch a well marked track leads to the chapel on the hill, and then on to the top of Arthur's Seat. Descend by Hunter's Bog, which returns you to the wishing well.

To return to Blenheim Place, walk through the courtyard of Holyrood and turn right on the main road. Twin tunnels under the railway line. Keep left, up Abbeyhill. At the traffic lights, cross, but don't go downhill to Easter Road. Take the road immediately adjacent to it, uphill to Carlton Terrace. This will bring you back to Blenheim Place.

13

Lomond and Loch Leven

*I*LIKED it better the old way. A lonely, broken tower. Moss-covered stones amidst alder, willow and tangled briar. An illkept track. Muddy steps into history. Mary Queen of Scots wandering forlornly by the shore, dreaming of a lost crown. What would I say to her when we met? I was sure, one day, that we would meet, in the woods of Castle Island on Loch Leven.

As soon as the long boat berthed by the wooden landing stage, I felt her presence, and after lunch I haunted the tumbled ruins. Through the stillness of summer noons, humming with insects and secret, deep-thicket birdsong, I walked the little island. She never appeared, but she was always there. Now things have been taken in hand. Daily boat trips from Kinross. Grass neatly trimmed and signposted. Cement and mortar. This way to the Castle. Not the same.

As I stood on West Lomond Hill, overlooking Loch Leven and the fertile Howe of Fife, memories of these youthful fantasies flooded back. My companion, George Reid, pointed skywards, breaking the spell. 'Here they come,' he said. A small aeroplane, climbing through cloudless sky, seemed to splutter and stall, dangerously. Tiny black specks fell from the fuselage. Hope it's not bits of wings and propeller. Then, after a seemingly endless plunge, red, blue and orange mushroom parachutes, figures suspended pendulum-like beneath.

Old and new, the story of Fife. Glenrothes not-so-New Town, an established modern technological centre. Declining coal-mining Cowdenbeath, Leslie and Lochgelly. The industrial pall of Dysart and Kirkcaldy. The Pictish fort on East Lomond. Falkland Palace, favourite home of ancient Scottish kings. From the top of Lomond Hills, a glimpse of things past and things to come.

Earlier that morning we had left a dreach Auld Reekie and made the easy road-bridged journey across the Forth into the Wee Kingdom. Speeding northwards along the A90 towards Kinross, I remembered my first journey to Lomond and Loch Leven, made as a boy of twelve, favoured fishing guest of Mr and Mrs Tom Kelly of Edinburgh – the bustle, steam and shriek of early-morning Waverley; the unforgettable hot smell of the station; rattling, smoke-belching, through the red arches of the Forth Railway Bridge; the wonderful sense of excitement on arriving at Loch Leven pier; the kindness of my hosts and the encouragement of our two gillies.

Today, thirty minutes after leaving Edinburgh, we neatly exited at Junction 5, swept round the south shore, past Vane Farm Nature Reserve and St Serf's Island, through Scotlandwell to Leslie. From here, a convenient, twisting, little moorland road cuts through the Lomond Hills between Leslie and Falkland. We stopped on the highest point, at the thoughtfully provided, well ordered Fife County Council car park and information centre.

A long, well made track leads westwards to the top of the highest Lomond hill, a modest 1,713 feet, but with magnificent views on a clear day. Across Perthshire and Angus, range after range lead to the peak of Ben Macdhui in the Cairngorms. Distant Glen Tilt, crowned by graceful Ben Dearg; Ben Lawers, by Loch Tay; over Ochil and Campsie Fells to Loch Lomond; the stub of Largo Law, on the north shore of Firth of Forth; Edinburgh, Pentlands, Lammermuir and Moorfoots.

Below East Lomond nestles Falkland Palace, built mostly during the fifteenth and sixteenth centuries by successive Scottish monarchs. King James II, by royal charter, proclaimed the tower at

Falkland Palace. Perkin Warbeck, pretender to the English throne, was entertained there by James IV in 1495. Probably Perkin's last good meal – he was hanged by his ungrateful peers at Tyburn in London four years later.

At the age of seventeen, James V was held prisoner at Falkland by the ambitious Earl of Angus and eventually died in the palace in 1542, shortly after being brought news of the birth of his daughter, the future Queen of Scots, at Linlithgow: 'Farewell, it cam with ane lass and it will pass with ane lass.'

Cromwell's men knocked Falkland about a bit and felled the beautiful surrounding woods, where Queen Mary used to hunt, in order to fortify the town of Perth. Most of the present building is the work of Bruce of Falkland, who carefully restored the palace during the early years of the nineteenth century. The ghosts of an earlier age survey the scene. On East Lomond, above the village, lie the remains of an early Iron Age fort. Banked and ditched, this fort was probably occupied for more than a thousand years and during recent excavations hollow glass beads were found among the ruins.

They would not have pleased John Knox, Mary's religious arch-enemy. 'Godless frippery,' I hear him exclaim in disgust. Knox visited Fife in 1559, determined to root out the last vestige of Catholicism. 'We reformed them,' he is reported to have said. Which really meant the ruthless destruction of buildings, books and records, and everything else he and his sanctimonious black-gowned band could lay their hands on. Scotland has no fury like a Presbyterian scorned. On the south-west slope of West Lomond, at the head of Glen Vale, a 'step' at the foot of the cliff is still known as John Knox's Pulpit.

George and I plodged on along the soggy track, occasionally skirting the dampest parts. The way is bounded by a drystane dyke, constructed out of huge round sandstone boulders – a major building feat. A few disconsolate grouse rocketed from the heather, past empty butts, and we noticed the marks of Argo-Cat or Snow-Cat. Visions of tweed-clad men and headscarfed ladies heading comfortably uphill in search of sport.

Craigen Gaw and the Split Nose are on the right – a dangerous climb amidst loose, crumbling rocks. Not for us. As the track edges over the shoulder of West Lomond a well marked frontal route leads straight up the east face. Intent upon a photograph, and worried about fading light, I attacked the slope with gusto – for me, quarter of a mile per hour, interspersed with frequent rests.

The summit is topped by a strange camouflaged rectangular sentry-box, surmounted by an aerial. Strange, because there was no apparent way in. Even here, on top of West Lomond, Fife contrast between ancient and modern persists. Scattered over the hill are the remains of a cairn, built three thousand years ago. When or why the cairn was destroyed is a mystery but it still rises in parts to a height of nearly ten feet and measures almost ninety feet round. What minds and hands planned and laboured these stones to this wild, windswept summit? What hopes and memorials lie buried here?

I stumbled back to the track, dark shadows of departing day chasing me down the steep ridged scree and scrub slope. Sunlight shimmered over a cluster of Fife reservoirs, cupped in the horseshoe of the hills: Ballo, Harperleas, Holl, Drumain and Arnot.

Ahead. the sky behind East Lomond blushed pink and red in the evening. Soft winds sighed over the moor as a last clump of parachutists hurtled earthwards. Wonder what Knox and his dusty band of devil hunters would have made of that lot?

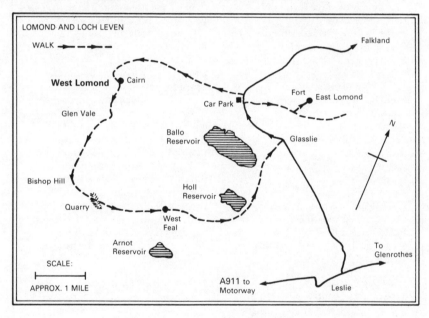

WHAT YOU NEED TO KNOW

Time and effort   It depends upon how much time you have. There and back to the top of West Lomond is an easy couple of hours. Going the other way, the summit of East Lomond is about thirty minutes. If you have a full day, then consider a walk round all the Lomond Hills; from the car park to West Lomond, to Bishop Hill in the south. There is nothing too taxing, providing you follow standard precautions for hillwalking – and choose a good day.

Another good day out may be spent visiting Castle Island on Loch Leven, then Vane Farm Nature Reserve, run by the excellent Scottish Royal Society for the Protection of Birds, followed by a tour round Falkland Palace and a quick dash up to the fort on top of East Lomond. The beauty of the Lomond Hills is that they are so easily accessible and yet wonderfully remote. Back in time for tea.

Location   Two maps needed: Ordnance Survey Sheet 59, St Andrews and Kirkcaldy, and Sheet 58, Perth and Kinross, second series, scale 1:50,000.

Grid references   Leslie 59/ 245015; Falkland Palace 59/255076; East Lomond 59/243063; car park 58/227063; West Lomond 58/ 196066; Glen Vale 58/187059; Bishop Hill 58/185044; Scotlandwell 58/184016; Vane Farm Nature Reserve: 58/160990; Castle Island 58/139018.

Route   In Leslie main street, watch out for a narrow turning on your left, half-way down. There is a notice on the wall, signposting West Lomond, but it is easy to miss. Follow this little road for about four miles, past an interesting-looking restaurant and café on your left, and park in the Fife Regional Council car park. From here, you may strike either right, to East Lomond, or left, to West Lomond. There is an excellent map by the toilet building in the car park and both walks are easy to follow: straight there and straight back.

If you propose a full day's walk, take the track to West Lomond. From the top of the hill, walk due south, keeping as much as possible to the high ground, avoiding the edge of the crags, to Bishop Hill. At the south end of Bishop, look east and you will see an old quarry. A road leads from here, down the hill to West Feal. Walk past the south end of Holl Reservoir towards Ballo and Balgothrie and onto the road at Wester Glasslie, conveniently near the restaurant. Then left along the road, back to the car park.

14
Man Friday in Fife

THE KINGDOM of Fife is a mixture of farming, fishing, mining, heavy industry and some of Scotland's most attractive seaside towns and beaches. I was born in Edinburgh, the wrong side of the Forth as far as Fifers are concerned, but my parents used to take me to Kinghorn for summer holidays. There I learned to love the diversity and dignity of such dissimilar places as Kirkcaldy and gentle Kilconquhar.

I still remember my feeling of excitement upon seeing my first-ever great crested grebe, gracing the calm waters of Kinghorn Loch; and our secret cove, a mile to the east of the town, where my brother Ian and I swam and played with these strange creatures, girls. Days seemed endless then, always sunny, and we quickly befriended the most important people in town: the manager at the local cinema, dispensers of beach-side ice-cream and, our hero, Jake, who ran trips round the bay in a brown clinker-built motorboat.

Fife and golf go together and few areas have so many fine

courses. I have hacked my way round a few, including the 'inner sanctum', the Old Course at St Andrews. Ian, happily ignoring my consistent inability to hit a golf ball with any regularity and frequently not at all, a few years ago invited me to make up a four – all single-figure players. After which I sold my clubs and vowed never again to darken tee or green. My golfing days ended in mortifying ignominy, playing my approach shot to the 18th green from nearly the middle of the main road.

Lower Largo is one of the Kingdom's most attractive towns – well kept cottages lining narrow streets and a tiny harbour backed by a comfortable hotel. The buildings are firmly Scottish domestic architecture in character and appear to have grown, rather than been built. They cluster the shore, leading to a magnificent beach of fine sand that stretches in a golden curve three miles eastwards to Earlsferry and Elie. A relaxing, sea-breeze-refreshing walk; the perfect place to while away a day.

Andrew Selkirk, immortalized by Daniel Defoe as Robinson Crusoe, was born in Lower Largo in 1676. He followed his father to sea and, at the age of twenty-seven years, whilst sailing under Captain William Dampier, was marooned on the island of Juan Fernandez for insubordination. Must have been pretty harsh words to so enrage his captain and merit such cruel punishment.

It takes a lot to keep a Fifer down and Selkirk survived. He was rescued four years later by a passing ship and soon returned to sea, although not under Captain Dampier. Defoe travelled extensively throughout Scotland, as a government agent, or, more accurately, as a spy, reporting the activities and plotting of Jacobites; but it was in London that Defoe met Selkirk and was fascinated by the story of his desert island adventure.

Defoe's masterpiece has captivated readers ever since and a statue of Robinson Crusoe proudly graces Selkirk's birthplace. The figure stands above the door, hand raised, shading eyes, peering endlessly across the street for rescue. Andrew Selkirk died in 1721, in bed, at the tragically early age of forty-five years; but Robinson Crusoe lives on.

I parked my car by the harbour and walked along the quiet main street, past Selkirk's house and up onto the line of the disused railway. Many years had drifted by since I had last passed that way by rail, on gleaming, steam-belching LNER locomotives.

A few minutes' walk left town behind. The long beach, backed by dunes covered in marram grass, was deserted. Square concrete blocks lurched drunkenly from the sand, reminders that Largo Bay was considered a potential landing site for Mr Hitler's happily ill-fated Operation Sea Lion, the invasion of our island fortress during the Second World War. Indeed, the beach was used to rehearse our own soldiers in preparation for the Normandy landings of June 1945.

The dunes play host to a number of rare and beautiful plants, including grass of Parnassus and early purple orchid. They also play host to local sun worshippers, who use the beach for all-over tanning on warm days. The sun was shining brightly, so I joined them, carrying my clothes, bundled under my arm, strolling a couple of carefree miles, naked along the beach.

I stopped to speak to a family, lazing the sun away – two bronzed children, brother and sister, busy with sand castles, watched by relaxed parents. They told me that they used the beach as much as possible during summer months and that many of their friends did likewise. Scotland is blessed with only two official naturist beaches: Lagg at the southern tip of the Island of Arran, and a beach at Saltcoats in Ayrshire. However, there are many unofficial beaches and Lower Largo is one of the most accessible.

At the east end of the beach Cocklemill Burn burbles into Largo Bay and has to be forded – no problem on a hot, clothesless day, but otherwise a long inland detour. There is a large, well ordered caravan site on the other side of the burn at Ford Links, a possible holiday venue, with easy access to the beach.

I followed the track round Shell Bay past Kincraig Point, into Elie, by the golf course – beware of flying balls – and walked through town down to the harbour, a veritable 'Costa', with windsurfing school, instruction in falling in the water, hire of sailboards, sailing dinghies, canoes and pedalos.

In spite of all this activity, Elie is still a working harbour, with local boats fishing for crab, the few remaining lobster and inshore fish. But during summer months Elie is awash with activity and is a popular holiday centre. I sat on the wall by the old granary, used now as sailing club premises, and watched aspiring windsurfers climbing out of and falling into the cold waters of the firth. Cradling a cup of scalding coffee, I pondered man's insanity.

I trudged back through town and headed north, out to Kilconquhar, which has the distinction of being the best kept village in north-east Fife. Looked it, too, and I was almost ashamed to tread the pristine pavements in my muddy boots. No shops as far as I could see, but a fine church and very inviting-looking hotel which offers excellent bar lunches to weary travellers.

The quickest way back to Lower Largo is via the old railway line. This passes close to the A917 Crail–Kirkcaldy highway and from there it is five easy miles home. But, as Daniel Defoe remarked, 'he that will view the county of Fife must go round the coast'. The day was still hot and afternoon sunlight called my soul. Scurrying sandpipers and shrieking oystercatchers dashed and darted in the slow, gravel-tumbling wavelets as I strode the strand, Largo's grey and white houses growing ever larger with every step.

I gave Robinson Crusoe a wink and a nod as I passed – from one lover of quiet places to another. Must find out more about Juan Fernandez; if it was good enough for Andrew Selkirk, it would probably suit me. In the meantime, Largo Bay will do fine – not so far to travel, either!

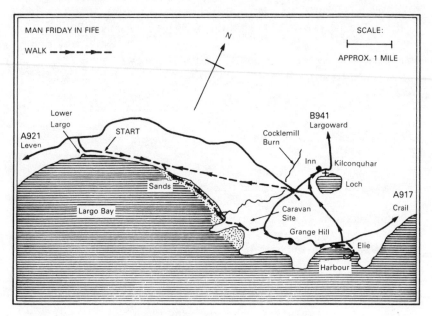

WHAT YOU NEED TO KNOW

Time and effort Allow a full day for this walk and plan your start, if possible, when the tide is full. As you walk eastwards, the tide should be going out. With luck, on your return you should still have flat, clean sands to stamp along, as the tide comes in. For the full effect, choose a warm summer day; you can linger on the beach, dressed or otherwise, as fancy dictates. The old railway line is stony and rough in places so wear strong shoes if you propose to follow it rather than walk both ways along the beach. To save humping food, aim for a pub lunch in Kilconquhar or Elie.

Location Ordnance Survey Sheet 59, St Andrews and Kirkcaldy, second series, scale 1:50,000.

Grid references Lower Largo 415025; start walk 422027; Cocklemill Burn 458008; Grangehill 477002; Elie 492000; Kilconquhar Inn 485020.

Route Park near the harbour and turn right, walking along Main Street, past Andrew Selkirk's house (small museum a few doors on). Look left and you will see the line of the old railway close by above you on the hill. Once on the railway track, walk eastwards. Clear the town and cut down to the beach. From there, follow your nose along the sands.

At the end of the beach, ford Cocklemill Burn and walk through the caravan site. At the entrance, there is a mini-roundabout. Bear half-right and follow a muddy farm track to Grangehill Farm. Do not go up the hill on the 'no exit' road. This track leads, eventually, down to the golf course. Cross the links and make for the shore road that leads along the front to Elie Harbour.

From the harbour retrace your steps and walk, carefully, up the A917 until you see the minor road which leads straight on as the main road turns sharp left. A few hundred yards and one right turn brings you to the village of Kilconquhar – and the excellent inn.

Return from Kilconquhar by the same road as you entered, but do not turn left down to Elie; go straight on. At the A917 you will see the main entrance to the caravan site. From here, you may pick up the line of the railway – immediately on your right – and make a rapid return to Largo; or walk back down to the beach, through the caravan site, and amble along the sands.

15

Glendevon and Tarmangie

*I*KNOCKED on the farm door, wind howling round my bare knees, rain-soaked kilt chapping rudely against frozen legs. A tall, red-faced man answered, and stared, unbelievingly, at the sodden apparition begging permission to camp in his wood. 'I wouldn't put my dog out on a night like this, son. Come in to the fire.'

Warmth and light, mingled with the smell of new-baked bread, flowed invitingly from within, but I had to refuse – I was preparing for my Queen's Scout badge and this journey was the final test. It had to be completed alone, regardless of weather. So I thanked the farmer and strode purposefully into the woods to wrestle with tent and tin-opener.

In spite of the gale, I managed to string main guy-ropes between two pines and quickly weighted down the sides with accommodating stones. Wrapped in a blanket, cold-baked-beaned and pied, I shivered the dark hours away, surrounded by the awful sounds of night. Later, it seemed a small price to pay for that coveted certificate bearing the Queen's arms. Then, it was a nightmare.

That was my introduction to the Ochil and Cleish Hills, of Clackmannan and Kinross, during a rain-filled, stormy two-day expedition thirty-five years ago. But the experience didn't diminish my enthusiasm for their beauty and charm and I have returned ever since to wander amongst these quiet valleys and gentle grass-covered slopes.

The highest of the Ochils is Ben Cleuch, 2,363 feet, flanked to the east by Tarmangie Hill, 2,117 feet, Whitewisp Hill, 2,111 feet, and King's Seat, also 2,111 feet. They crouch over the River Devon and Forth valley in a long unbroken ridge, guarding the towns of Alloa, Alva, Tillicoultry, Clackmannan and Dollar.

Too close for comfort to Caledonia's political heartland, these lands played a constant, often bloody, part in the shaping of Scotland's story. Constantin, son of Kenneth MacAlpine, was defeated and killed at Dollar by the Danes in AD 877; King Alexander II (1214–49) built a fortified tower at Alloa, visited by luckless Mary Queen of Scots, and where King James IV stayed in 1588. Clackmannan had its own tower, home of the great King Robert the Bruce (1306–29), and, in Dollar Glen, between the Burn of Sorrow and the Burn of Care, Castle Gloom – changed in name by Act of Parliament to Castle Campbell by Colin Campbell, 1st Earl of Argyll, in 1465.

The River Devon rises in the Ochil Hills six miles distant as the crow flies from where it joins the Forth at Cambus, west of Alloa. To get there, however, the river winds its way nearly thirty miles through steep-sided Ochil valleys and gorges, past ancient mills and stark, wheel-spindled pit-heads.

I drove north on the A823, by Yetts o' Muchart and Glendevon, with its tiny church, and parked near Glenhead Farm at the start of the water board road leading to Glendevon Reservoirs, aiming for Skythorn Hill and the summit of Tarmangie.

To the left of the road, the waters of the infant river are stemmed, controlled and directed through a large trout farm. More than fifty well ordered tanks lie by the stream, complete with caravan accommodation for supervisors. Good news for Fife and Kinross trout stocks and anglers.

Ragged heaps of stones litter the fields and a small white farmhouse perches uncomfortably on a plateau by the track. I was greeted by barking sheepdogs as I hurried by, trying not to look too much like a stray North Country Cheviot.

Lower Glendevon Reservoir snuggles in the folds of the hills, more like a Highland trout loch in character than a man-made reservoir. A white notice proclaims that all fishing is by fly only. Bad news for Fife fishermen, who, in my experience, would bait a hook with their grandmother if they thought she would attract more trout.

A first hint of winter lingers over the loch and a flight of mallard rise from the reeds, wheeling across the water, turquoise and white flashes against the sombre autumn browns of Common Hill. Wheatears and meadow pipits flit and dance by comfortably supine cattle – must be going to rain. The burn joining the two reservoirs is bursting with the energy of last night's storms, cascading down the valley in an unbridled froth of white-fringed foam. Upper Glendevon is almost waterless, ringed like a badly scoured bath-tub. Bleak stony banks lie exposed, like a woman surprised in the act of undressing. Someone must have left a tap running some-where.

Before the dam wall I turned left and followed the road past the narrow, mud-banked southern finger of the loch, up to Backhills Farm, busy taking sheep to market. Broich Burn tumbles down the hill and the road ends abruptly, changing into a muddy, up-and-downer track.

Shirt off, hot midday sun burning my back, I climbed by the fence, up the ever-increasing slope, into the heart of the valley. Dark shadows from Crodwell and Middle Hills enveloped the stream and I stopped by a waterfall to dress quickly. A dipper bobbed agreement from a stone and a curious wren winked encouragingly from a berry-bedecked rowan overhanging a crystal pool.

Head down, now, on the last heart-throbbing stumble to the ridge. Then, reward. A clear blue sky vista, crowded with snow-fringed mountains to the north and the Firth of Forth, like a silver carpet, shining southwards. Ben Alder, Schiehallion and Angus Hills. Hazy Edinburgh, castle-cragged. Berwick Law and the islands of the Firth, sparkling gems, blinking like young girls before first lovers.

I walked over undulating moorlands, stopping on King's Seat, high above the Forth valley, spread map-like below, studded with Scotland's history; Dunfermline, our ancient capital, last resting place of King Robert. The sudden shock of rock-girt Stirling Castle and Wallace Monument, leaping from the plain. The bright ribbon of the River Forth, edged with the industrial tangle of Grange-mouth and Kincardine power station.

Welcome lunch on Tarmangie, then along the edge of the forest that blocks any simple descent to Glen Sherup, other than through the wide fire-break near the dam of Glensherup Reservoir. One day, I fervently pray, my fellow Scots will waken up to the fact that unrestricted forestry is destroying Scotland, and rise up in arms against these desecrators of our scenery.

Sadly through the regimented rows of lodgepole pine and Sitka spruce, down to the dam wall. A flutter of herons dance long-legged in the topmost branches of a proper wood. Must be difficult, organizing all those legs and wings properly, preparatory to landing. Before the traffic, a perfect 'Tam o' Shanter Brig' crosses the golden Devon and I paused, hiding from evening, thinking not a lot – just content to enjoy the last, warm, lazy moments of a happy day.

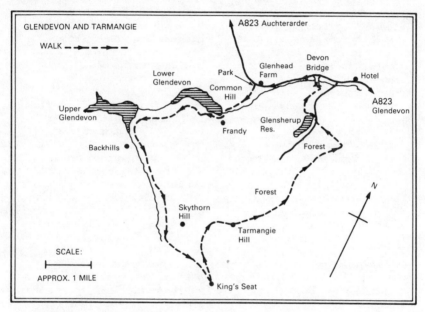

WHAT YOU NEED TO KNOW

Time and effort Took me about five and a half hours, but then I walk very slowly. The first part, on the water board road, is easy. Once you start up Broich Burn the going gets a bit tough. You must wear good walking boots because this path can be very muddy. Once on top, as always, courage and breath return and the rest of the day is just a question of one foot in front of the other over the hill. To have the full benefit of the view from the top, pray for a fine day.

Location Ordnance Survey Sheet 58, Perth and Kinross, second series, scale 1:50,000.

Grid references Glenhead Farm 951053; Lower Glendevon Reservoir 939044; Upper Glendevon Reservoir 914042; Backhills Farm 913036; Skythorn Hill 924013; King's Seat 936997; Tarmangie Hill 942014; fire-break in Glensherup Wood 975037; Glensherup Reservoir 965044; Devon Bridge 966054; Glendevon Castle Hotel 977055.

Route Park just inside the gate at the start of the road up to the reservoirs; there is plenty of room. Follow the road west, past Frandy Farm and Lower Glendevon Reservoir. Just before the dam at Upper Glendevon Reservoir a track leads uphill on your left. Follow this towards Backhills Farm, which is on the other side of the stream feeding the reservoir.

The 'good' track ends here and you now have to try and follow the path south, which climbs up the valley. At times the path is almost too close to the fence by the stream. If this is uncomfortable, there is an alternative path higher up the side of the hill to your left. The sound of water always attracts me so I follow the stream.

Climb out of the valley, onto the shoulder. Still walk south and you see King's Seat ahead. Find your way to the top and then return, north-east, to higher Tarmangie Hill. From Tarmangie, skirt the edge of the filthy forest and, near the end, you will find a wide fire-break. Go down this to the forest road.

As the trees thin out you will see a little track leading down to the dam at the end of Glensherup Reservoir. Cross the dam and follow the road back to the bridge over the River Devon. Turn left here and make your way north along the A823 back to your car. Glendevon Castle Hotel will provide refreshment at the end of your walk.

16

Bad Day on Vorlich

THIS WALK started thirty years ago in Aldershot, where my cousin Bruce Reynolds lived. Big brother Ian and I used to escape there for a few hours each week, a happy release from Her Majesty's cooking and military discipline. Bruce was a small, slightly built boy, much given to television and quick anger if anyone interrupted *Dr Who*, his favourite programme – which, for sheer devilment, Ian and I often did.

In spite of this harsh treatment we remained friends and when Bruce moved to Scotland I was delighted to find that we had a common interest: a love of hill walking. Strictly speaking, Bruce is more a mountain man, infected by the Munro bug, and currently he is attacking Scotland's 3,000-foot peaks with enthusiasm which leaves me speechless. So far he has climbed nearly 200 of the 283 peaks – at great speed and without any sign of the breathlessness which attends my labouring steps up even a modest hill.

Sir Hugh Munro's original list, published in 1891, contained 538 Scottish summits over 3,000 feet, 283 of which were classified mountains in their own right. Sir Hugh climbed all but two: the

Inaccessible Pinnacle on Sgurr Dearg in Skye, which scares the hell out of me, and Carn Clioch in the Cairngorms. Poor Sir Hugh was defeated by bad weather. The first man to surmount the Munros was a minister, the Revd A. E. Robertson, no doubt divinely guided, for he had them all wrapped up by 1901.

Since then, 'Munro bagging' has become a way of life for hundreds of hillwalkers and there is no greater challenge in Scotland. Me, I left it too late. Trout fishing is my excuse. Given a Ross-shire choice between tempting trout in Fionn or life and limb on A'Mhaighdean, the loch always wins. However, pursuit of sport has taken me to some of Scotland's most beautiful mountains, and I honestly admire the determination that drives others up such awe-inspiring heights.

Which is why I found myself, in a blizzard, tramping through Perthshire snow on Ben Vorlich, hopelessly trying to keep pace with my disgustingly fit cousin. Through a mist of pain I longed for the days when it had been possible to 'suppress' him with a single well-aimed swipe. Worse, Bruce was chatting, unconcerned by elements, as though strolling down Sauchiehall Street on a summer evening – and I wished we were.

Earlier that morning, much earlier, Bruce roused me from a warm bed and a particularly comforting dream about a holiday Ann and I once spent on the emerald-green Greek Isle of Paxos, swimming in soft Ionian seas, lazing away blistering days in the shade of olive groves, refreshed by sweet red wine. Snapped to reality, minutes later I found myself shivering out into a grey dawn, muffled and mountainously clothed, Vorlich-bound before I could invent even the glimmer of an excuse.

We drove north from Killearn, through my grandmother's Callander homelands, and followed the long serpentine of Loch Lubnaig to Bonnie Strathyre. The waters of the loch were coloured molten lead and I remembered the last time Ann and I fished Lubnaig. Never caught a thing, other than a shipwrecked bee, floating on a beech-leaf raft. Ann flung him a lifebelt and ferried him safely ashore, where he quickly recovered and buzzed off, presumably seeking swimming lessons.

My cousin and I had ten years of delayed chatter: stories to swop, dreams achieved, grand designs thwarted. Comfortable, relaxing, unimportant bleathers of old friends who had shared baths together as children. Bruce is a member of that famous West of Scotland climbing group The Moray Club – insignia, compass circle, quadrant-filled with ominous words: Hill, Rock, Snow and Ice.

The Moray Club was founded in 1965 by four former pupils of the Moray Outward Bound School and I met some of them during a lecture given by senior Scottish gillie, George Oswald, head keeper on Ben Alder Estate, Inverness-shire. People who walk the hills are nice people – friendly, reliable and patient. Like trout fishermen. I felt instantly at home and welcomed.

When Bruce had a minor accident, falling during a club outing, in an icy car park, not on the hill, he badly sprained his right arm. The offending limb was splinted and strapped in half a ton of white bandage. Nothing daunted – after all, what's a gammy arm to a mountain man – he turned up, slinged and grinning, for the next meet. All the other members emerged from their cars with heavily bandaged right arms, said good morning, and set off up the day's hill.

In 1986, their twenty-first birthday year, Moray Club members travelled the world, exploring distant plains and high peaks. Sheila Fage, three weeks trekking 150 miles in Nepal, climbing 18,000 feet on Annapurna; young Neil Stewart, with the British Schools Expedition to the Yukon; Alasdair Scott, exploring Madagascar highlands; Eric Scott, on Puy de Sancy, the highest point of the Massif Central in France; and a seven-strong team tackling Swiss Alps, Monte Rosa and Matterhorn.

We parked shoreside by Loch Earn at Ardvorlich, where Coire Buidhe burn gurgles past the old house, blushing bride-like under the hump-backed bridge to greet her groom. Bruce and I were greeted less kindly: by bad-tempered wind, glowering clouds and soul-dispiriting, nagging drizzle. Jumpers, jackets, boots, leggings, spare clothing, compass, map, pointless cameras and, most important of all, lunch.

Ben Vorlich, 'the hill of the bay', rises southwards from Loch Earn in a slow shoulder of grassy slopes and jagged outcrops. At the summit, this ridge is joined by three others, crossing to form a welcome plateau, trig.-point-pricked north, grandly cairned south. I had often seen these features from the top of other hills: from West Lomond near Kinross; Tarmangie Hill in the gentle Ochils; and from Pentlands and Arthur's Seat, by Edinburgh.

They looked inviting, from a distance, and I reminded myself of this as I struggled through deepening snow, now falling in thick flakes from mist-grey heavens. Panting like a pensioned cart-horse, I snatched a quick breath from the wind and managed to gasp: 'I suppose you are used to this. One of life's little tribulations.'

Bruce stopped, ear-bending close: 'Are you all right?'

I yelled back, 'Of course I'm all right. I was just asking a question.'

Relief spread across his face. 'I'm so glad. For a moment I thought you were in trouble.'

On a reasonable day, Vorlich is no trouble. Indeed, it is easy to climb and therefore one of Scotland's most popular Munros. Just below the top, for the last few hundred feet, the track does shoot a bit skyward; but with care and caution, and a few rests, the summit is soon reached. So for hillwalkers the ben provides an exciting challenge, magnificent Perthshire views and the pleasure of having conquered a Munro.

However, in bad weather, when icy blasts bustle down the glen, things is different; and, although one travels hopefully, one should always travel prepared. Like the ice axe strapped to Bruce's pack. I wondered where he had secreted the rope. Visions of myself tied to a madman, lost like Mallory and Irvine on their final, doomed assault on Everest.

As far as I am concerned, the actor Vincent Price had it about right when he remarked: 'I once took a climbing expedition as a holiday and found the real reason those mountain climbers rope themselves together. It's to stop the sensible ones going home.' Hiding gloom-laden forebodings, I suggested that perhaps discretion was the better part of valour and our quickest descent was urgently required. 'Thank God,' said my companion, 'I was beginning to think I was climbing with a lunatic!'

As we hurried down the track I cursed the weather, sorry to have missed the summit view and the walk on to Vorlich's neighbour, Stuc a'Chroin. Still, I consoled myself, even the great Sir Hugh Munro had his off days; and there was always another, brighter one, just around the corner.

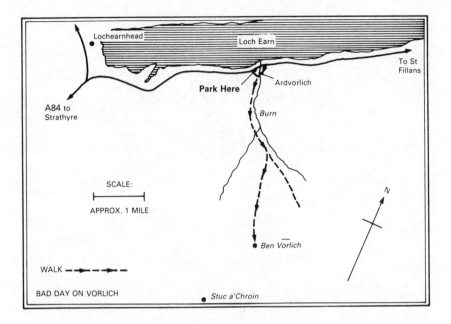

Lochearnhead
Loch Earn
To St Fillans
Park Here
Ardvorlich
A84 to Strathyre
Burn
SCALE:
APPROX. 1 MILE
N
WALK
Ben Vorlich
BAD DAY ON VORLICH
Stuc a'Chroin

WHAT YOU NEED TO KNOW

Time and effort   In reasonable conditions, Ardvorlich to Ben Vorlich and back will take about five hours. If you intend to go on to Stuc a'Chroin, allow another three to four hours. In bad weather, stay in the car and save your breath for a better day.

Location   Two maps are required: Ordnance Survey Sheet 51, Loch Tay, and Sheet 57, Stirling and the Trossachs, second series scale 1:50,000.

Grid references   Ardvorlich 633229; Ben Vorlich 6299189; Stuc a'Chroin 618175.

Route   Park at Ardvorlich House, by the shore of Loch Earn. There are two drives leading up to the house and the estate prefers walkers to enter by the east entrance. The track passes the house and leads uphill, with the burn on your left. Once beyond the trees, you see a good path wending upwards.

There is one 'road junction', just past a well made wooden bridge and marked by a massive boulder. Bear right and look out for stumped posts marking the way ahead. A long and, for me, hard slog. The last section before the top is steep and should be tackled with caution.

If you wish to go on to Stuc a'Chroin, follow the fence posts down to Bealach an Dubh Choirein and then scramble up the crags to the ridge by a twisting path. If you anticipate bad weather, give Stuc a'Chroin a miss and stick to well tracked Vorlich.

17

Venue and the Dancing Stream

I LOOKED towards the summit of Ben Venue, 'the little hill', and smiled at this glorious understatement. At 2,386 feet, little Venue is not. A great, grey slab, thrusting north from Loch Ard in a slow, unrelenting shoulder; rearing north, twin-cragged above Katrine, guarded by the dark cliffs of Beinn Bhreac, streaked silver and shining with streams rushing to Ledard Burn.

Scots are masters of understatement. Ask directions: 'Oh, just a wee bit down the road, you can't miss it.' Meaning at least six miles and out of sight. What time to meet? 'The back of nine' – any time from five past until just before ten. How's the weather? 'Rare!' Guaranteed torrential rain and gale force winds. Getting an exact answer from a Scot is impossible: which is why they make such good politicians.

I suppose, compared with nearby Ben Lomond, at 3,192 feet, and Perthshire's mighty Ben More at 3,843 feet, Venue is modest – but not on a warm morning, hiking burnside to the first ridge. Least of all for my standard of physical fitness. Nevertheless, I made it, and was rewarded by cloud-scattered blue skies and a panoramic view of mind-numbing beauty.

Ben Venue shares the Trossachs with greater neighbours: Ben Ledi, Benvane, Ceann na Baintgherna and Stob a'Choin. They tower proudly over Scotland's 'Lake District', sweet Katrine, Venachar and Lubnaig, where the road wends lochside northwards, through Bonnie Strathyre to Voil and Rob Roy's grave on the Braes of Balquhidder.

Scotland's grand lake, the Lake of Menteith, lies a few miles east of Aberfoyle, capital of the Trossachs. Here, Sir John Menteith earned himself a hated place in Scotland's story when he captured and betrayed Sir William Wallace to the English in 1305. Battles still rage on the lake, but now, they are between anglers and fish, for Lake of Menteith is a carefully managed and popular Lowland fishery.

Inchmaholme Priory graces Menteith's largest island. Here as a child Queen Mary was hidden after the Battle of Pinkie, before being hurried safely to France. A small boat ferries visitors from Port of Menteith to the ruined priory, founded in 1107 by Culdee Monks. For a number of years this little boat was captained by an old friend of mine, Andrew Mair from Dunblane. We gained our seafaring knowledge whilst serving queen and country in the Water Transport Company of the Royal Army Service Corps, overseas on the Isle of Wight.

Andrew introduced me to Stirling and Perthshire. A gentle man, Scots kindly, he showed me Sheriffmuir, where Rob Roy Mac-Gregor lost the Royalists' battle by refusing to charge at the crucial moment, protecting Clan Gregor's future through masterly inde-cisiveness. Andrew and I wandered the old streets of Dunblane, arguing constantly from dawn to dusk, about everything in general and nothing in particular, enjoying every heated moment.

The south route to the top of Ben Venue starts at Ledard Farm, by the shores of fishless Loch Ard – fishless, in my opinion, because of the Forestry Commission's badly planned, insensitive and damaging tree planting. Venue was mist-shrouded when I arrived and parked across the road from the farm. I hopped around, heaving on boots, trying to avoid the worst puddles, in a penetrat-ing Trossachs drizzle. Bound to pass.

As I started up the track the rain stopped, leaving the hills freshly laundered, inviting me in. Then I saw the goat: a tuft beard, long jaw, glazed eyes and ungainly horns sticking through the mesh of a fence. I tried a couple of tentative twists, like an ancient patriarch preparing sacrifice to an old god.

The goat grunted and gripped one of my fingers between blunt, chisel-edged teeth. There's gratitude. It took fifteen minutes man-oeuvring before I eased head and horns back. The bad-tempered beast trotted off bleating to rejoin the herd. Never even said thank you. That's goats. I marched on, nursing bruised ego and finger.

Signpost and stile cross Ledard Burn, pointing the way, stealing amongst magnificent oaks, across a forest floor soft with fallen leaves: a startling gold and brown carpet. Finches flit amidst bare branches, and the white burn leaps in a symphonic chorus over moss-covered boulders, through foam-covered pools, down to Loch Ard.

Out on the hill I stopped by a stile and looked back. Mirror-calm water reflected morning hills. Mist wisps hung like smoke over Eilean Gorm. The Duke of Albany's ruined castle glowered resentfully from its little island below green-clad Bad Dearg Hill – a black speck of black history. For years, by fair means and foul, Albany Dukes were Regents of Scotland, on behalf of disastrously infant and absent monarchs.

Whilst James I was King Henry IV's captive in England, Albany allowed Scotland to fall into a miserable state of anarchy. When James returned, one of his first acts was to collect together the late regent, two of his sons and their father-in-law, the Earl of Lennox. He entertained them at Stirling Castle: on the block.

Lingering sprigs of fading heather purpled the track as I tramped on, hot sun baking my jacket. I lumbered upwards like a mobile sauna, half a gallon of Sandison sweat splashing every step. Red grouse rocketed, cackling with laughter at my startled heart-attack spring from their flight path. Ledard Burn, bursting with energy, criss-crossing the damp path, Highland-jigged beside me.

I stopped by a spectacular waterfall, and from a rowan-crested promontory I watched Ledard hurtle outrageously twenty feet over a heathered ridge into a deep, swirling, back-gorged pool. A dipper bobbed in the stream, keeping me company whilst I stopped for coffee. I left him plenty of crumbs.

Stream-crossing needed watching. Under normal conditions, dry-shod passage; but in heavy water, stepping stones are deeply covered and exposed rocks are ankle-breaking slippy. Wrong footing would mean a soaking, at least. After careful consideration, I jumped, fourteen stone of slow motion, and arrived, knee-deep but safe, by the far bank.

The long ascent gradually tamed the bristling burn and, as I climbed higher, Ledard narrowed, but remained a never-ending pleasure, still challenging the steep cliffs and rocky outcrops, and forcing me to scramble up and down the sides of small tributaries, which armied from Creag Tharsuinn to lend support. Eventually, close to the ridge, Ledard faded into the hill and I sat on a stile by the fence, looking warily ahead towards Ben Venue's twin peaks.

Along the hillside lay a magical track, a narrow, close-cut, dark ribbon overlooking Allt Glasahoile stream in its dash to Loch Katrine. Westwards, by Stronachlachar, I saw the white dot of the *Sir Walter Scott* winking amongst russet trees, drawn ashore for its annual overhaul. Ragged Tinker's Loch sparkled on Druim nan Carn and the way ahead beckoned irresistibly.

I felt a complete sense of belonging. I was the hill. My heart and soul were the rocks around me. As though, giant-like, I encompassed time and space. Married to the wind. Held in the arms of eternity. And other daft thoughts only fools and hillwalkers understand.

Until I began to scramble the west peak. Iron railings stabbed bare rocks. Wind screamed over the crest. Narrow, slow, cautious steps. God, its cold. Stumbling to the shelter of the cairn, crouched, shivering, amazed at the wild landscape – wave after wave of mountain-covered crests guarding a blessing, where all things are possible and all things equal, which I never wanted to leave.

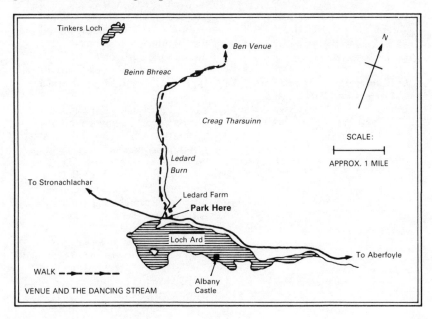

WHAT YOU NEED TO KNOW

Time and effort There and back took me a slow 4½ hours. It's a long haul up to the first ridge and the way is soggy and very wet – even nicer after heavy rain. Be prepared to scramble up and down the sides of a few streams and take great care at the first crossing of Ledard Burn. Otherwise a sprained ankle could ruin your day.

The last hundred feet could be dangerous in bad weather or misty conditions. Even on a good day, some hands-and-knees work is required, but with reasonable caution, and plenty of little rests, you should have no real difficulty reaching the cairn. Always carry extra warm clothing. Be well shod and waterproof.

Location Ordnance Survey Sheet 57, Stirling and the Trossachs, second series, scale 1:50,000.

Grid references Ledard Farm and start point 461023; Beinn Bhreac ridge 462056; Creag Tharsuinn 468049; Venue West Peak 474064.

Route No problem whatsoever, but Ben Venue will be hidden from view until you reach the first ridge. Park across the road from the track up to the farm. There is plenty of room, so make sure you don't block the gate into the field: outraged farmers we do not need. The track passes the left side of the farm buildings and there the way is signposted over an attractive bridge and stile. Say hello to the goats.

Follow the path through an oak wood, with Ledard Burn on your right. Clear the woods and continue up the hill. Look out for the waterfall and make a small detour to the right to view. The first stream crossing requires consideration and caution, particularly after heavy rain. Thereafter, the path crosses the stream several times until you end up walking up the middle of the diminishing burn, on to the ridge.

A fence crosses the path at right angles and from the ridge the track rounds the right-hand slope of Creag Tharsuinn. The twin peaks of Ben Venue can now be seen ahead. Below the summit there is a major 'road junction'. Half-right, downhill, to Loch Katrine. Straight on, slightly right and uphill to the East Peak. You should bear quarter-left, and look for the narrow track that rises steeply to the West Summit.

The last section is very exposed, so in bad weather take great care. The track twists and turns up huge boulders until you come to a small damp plateau. On top of the summit cairn is a strange stone, shaped rather like a hip-bone. You have arrived. Return the same way. You have earned it, and going down is much more sportnik!

18

Bare Bums and Ben Lomond

*M*ANY YEARS ago, my wife Ann and I discovered the joys of naked bathing. Getting dressed to go swimming always seemed the height of lunacy and whenever possible we plunge in birthday-suited. On foreign holidays, we're the luggage-less ones at the airport and since 1978 have been members of the Central Council for British Naturism.

Scotland has its share of sunshine. On hot July days, fishing for wild brown trout amongst lonely hills, I have often waded out, clothesless, to cover rising fish other anglers can't reach; and a summer afternoon snooze on a distant rowan-clad shore is one of life's great pleasures – lulled lazily to sleep by the call of curlew and piping golden plover. However, as in all things, caution is the watchword, and an eye for the weather.

There are a number of official and unofficial naturist sites throughout Scotland and one of the loveliest is on the tree-covered island of Inchmurrin in Loch Lomond. We visited the club. The Scottish Outdoor Club, a few years ago, whilst staying at Rowardennan a few miles north from Balmaha: a perfect holiday which combined marvellous Trossachs walks with lazy, sun-soaked days on Inchmurrin. The name Inchmurrin means 'island of hospitality' and we certainly found kindness in plenty amongst welcoming club members.

Loch Lomond is surrounded by some of Scotland's most dramatic scenery, and some of Scotland's most exciting walks: Arrochar Alps, Cowal and Ardgoil, Crianlarich and Balquhidder. Something for everyone, even sluggards like me. Gentle, lochside strolls along the West Highland Way. The rock-climbing challenge of Cobbler: Gladiator's Grove on South Peak; terrifying Nimlin's and the Chimney Arte on North Peak. Stern stuff. Graceful Ben Lomond towers above all and is favourite with thousands of hillwalkers.

My son Charles and his friend David Martin climbed mighty Lomond from Rowardennan when they were twelve-year-olds, setting the seal on a love of the hills which will stay with them all their lives. My first sight of the Ben was from a less elevated position: afloat on the loch, fishing. Inching over salmon lies round the island-studded south bay: Inchcruin, Inchmoan, Buchin and Tiny Ceardach.

Two friends, Tony Sykes and the late Charles Hodget, had invited me to join them and, happily unsuspecting, I readily accepted. The most productive fishing method is dapping. One angler sits in the middle, wielding a sixteen-foot rod. The cast is made of light floss on the end of which dangles a huge, hairy, artificial fly. This is delicately danced over the waves to attract salmon.

The other two rods fish in the traditional way, with wet flies, from bow and stern. When the man in the middle sees a fish approaching he removes the dap and salmon turn, right or left as the mood takes them, to grab the adjacent wet flies. Which is why I had been invited: all day in the middle, holding a clothes pole whilst they caught the fish.

Loch Lomond is always busy: anglers, sailing boats, canoes, windsurfers, water-skiers – all enjoying the pleasures of this wonderful recreational gem. The *Countess Fiona*, another recreational gem, is owned by Alloa Brewery Company and sails the loch from April until September. An uncle of mine was once the manager of Alloa Brewery, a post I much envied him.

Steaming north, the *Countess* looks as though she had spent all her days plying between Balloch and Inversnaid. In fact, she has had a more chequered career, being tossed about from Loch Awe to Largs during half a century's travel. *Countess Fiona* was built in 1936 for the Caledonian Steam Packet Company and sailed windy Loch Awe under the name *Countess of Breadalbane.*

Dragged overland in 1952, she was set to work in the Clyde, ferrying passengers round Gourock, Holy Loch, Largs and Mill-port. In 1971 she was renamed *Countess of Kempock* and worked for Mr Roy Ritchie; then for Off-Shore Workboats Ltd, battling up and down the broken waters of the Inner Hebrides between Oban, Mull, Fingle-caved Staffa and holy Iona. Her wandering over, the grand old lady serenely sails over her new home.

The *Countess Fiona*, like her famous colleague on Loch Katrine the ss *Sir Walter Scott*, provides an ideal way of combining the beauties of Lomond with a delightful, rewarding, shore-side walk. Best place to start is from Rowardennan, at the end of the road from Balmaha. The *Countess* will collect you at 11.40 a.m. then glide northwards to the busy village of Tarbet on the west shore; from there, over to Inversnaid on the east, arriving close to the long-distance footpath, the West Highland Way. The walk back to Rowardennan is a distance of eight miles and takes approximately three and a half hours. What better way to spend a summer day?

Some famous names have tramped here: Dr Johnson, dogged by the inevitable Boswell; Robert Burns; William and Dorothy Wordsworth, accompanied by Samuel Taylor Coleridge; Robert Southey and the great Scottish engineer, Thomas Telford. Just as well known, although for less respectable reasons, was Rob Roy MacGregor of Inversnaid.

The MacGregor's exploits – cattle stealing and general skulduggery – caused the government to build a fort at Inversnaid, on the land Rob Roy claimed as his own, half-way between Lomond and Loch Arklet. But the garrison had little luck keeping peace. MacGregor attacked, disarmed the soldiers and burnt the fort. Inversnaid was rebuilt. Rob's newphew, Ghulne Dubh, carrying on his uncle's tradition, sacked the garrison again. It was rebuilt a third time and commanded by no less a soldier than Wolfe, soon to meet his fate on the heights of Abraham.

Sir Walter Scott visited Inversnaid in 1792 and found there was still a 'garrison' at the fort: a solitary veteran soldier, contentedly reaping a sparse crop of barley, who told Scott that if he wanted in he would find the key to the fort under the front door. The MacGregors had little use for keys, but Scott did as bid and rested in the old, battle-scarred building.

My most recent visit to Lomond brought near-disaster and a

sharp reminder that in harsh conditions even the easiest of hills can present a daunting challenge. In search of dramatic, panoramic photographs, I parked one wild November morning by the pier at Rowardennan and buckled on boots and camera. A quick dash for the top, superb scenic shots, back in time for lunch.

The fact that Ben Lomond was cloud-shrouded, barely visible through heavy rain, should have deterred me; but I wanted the photographs badly so I set off through the woods, climbing quickly up first gentle tree-clad slopes. The track is well maintained and I blessed the National Trust for their efforts in easing my way.

But as I rose higher, leaving the shelter of trees, the path ahead became a major river and I was soon soaked, both above and below. I passed two other walkers and as I rested by the gate on the hill I saw them tramping back to Rowardennan. As I turned northwards to Sorn Aonaich, the clouds settled ever lower and I found myself plodding upwards through cold, wet, clinging mist.

Rain turned to snow, blown in on the wings of a freezing north-east wind. My right side was covered in a thickening white blanket and I doubted my sanity in continuing. There was no possibility of a break in the clouds that day; and, therefore, no point in continuing. Frozen strands of hair bumped on my forehead. The higher I climbed the more fierce the storm became and I realized that there was not a moment to be lost in getting off the hill.

I turned and, step by careful step, made my way down,

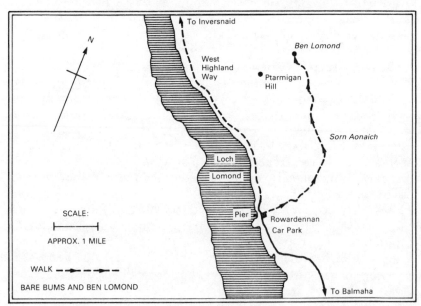

following welcome cairns and my own footsteps, which were fading fast in drifting snow. One slip was all that was required to turn a nightmare into a disaster. What I had done was incredibly stupid, the more so because I certainly should have known better. By luck, rather than by good judgement, I gained the shelter of the woods and safety of the car.

It seemed like an eternity before the effect of the car heater restored some warmth to my limbs and I vowed never to be so daft again. The only comfort I had was my first sight of a rare native Scottish snow bunting, glimpsed fleetingly near the summit. No doubt it was astonished at the stupidity of the human race, walking there by choice rather than of necessity.

WHAT YOU NEED TO KNOW

Time and effort The sail from Rowardennan to Inversnaid and the walk back takes about four and a half hours and is a pleasant, relaxing way to explore Loch Lomond. However, the walk south down the West Highland Way can be busy, particularly during summer months, and the track is often very muddy. So wear strong shoes and always be prepared for Lomond storms.

The ascent of Ben Lomond is another matter. In good weather it is still a long, stiff walk and the round trip from Rowardennan takes five and a half hours. Always remember that what is easy in good summer weather can be dangerous and difficult at other times of the year. If in doubt, don't. No prizes for breaking a leg on the top and a lot of trouble for others if you do.

Location Ordnance Survey Sheet 56, Loch Lomond, second series, scale 1:50,000.

Grid references Inchmurrin 380870; Balmaha 421909; Rowardennan 355986; Tarbet 315045; Inversnaid 338089; Ben Lomond 367029.

Route Information on *Countess Fiona* sailings may be obtained from Alloa Brewery Company Ltd, Anderston House, 389 Argyle Street, Glasgow. Sailing times may also be had by telephone on a recorded message: dial 041–248 2699. In 1987, a single ticket from Rowardennan to Inversnaid cost £2. The boat has snack bar and licensed bar. At Inversnaid, the West Highland Way is well signposted. Make sure that you turn right, otherwise you might end up in Fort William.

The Ben Lomond walk is also well signposted, from near the pier at Rowardennan. There are excellent car park and toilet facilities. Follow the path through the trees, out onto the hill. It just keeps going, up and up, on to the top. Return by the same route. As an alternative, in good weather, cross over from Ben Lomond south-west to Ptarmigan Hill and come down the shoulder to Rowardennan. But he warned: this is a much rougher and more demanding walk. Lomond midges are rough too, in fact 'man-eating', so take along a five-gallon drum of insect-repellent, each.

19

Autumn Trossachs Tales

Trossach rain is the wettest in Scotland. I hunched over the car steering wheel on a cold Stirlingshire morning, parked in Aberfoyle across the street from the newsagent, wondering if they sold boot laces and if I could get there and back without drowning. They did and I didn't, but it was a damned close-run thing.

They don't make boot laces like they used to. My old friends seemed immortal. Now, new pairs come and go with fragile regularity, like snow off a dyke. As if reading my thoughts, the dour Trossach downpour turned to snow, whirling white and wicked through empty streets on the tail of a brash north-east wind. The grey town was soon as devoid of people as Saturday morning kirk.

And I had missed the boat. By about seven days. Moody and miserable, I decided to go on. After all, what's a little rain and snow? My ancestors, Clan MacGregor, would have scoffed at such elements. Indeed, probably welcomed them. Excellent cover from which to mount sharp, cattle-collecting forays on unsuspecting, fire-huddling, soft Lowland neighbours.

The boat I had missed was the ss *Sir Walter Scott*, sailing on Loch Katrine, from Trossachs Pier to Stronachlachar, 4 May to 28

September – £2 a bash or the whole boat on evening charter for £300. Would have been ideal for Rob Roy and his brigands, to hurry them home to Glengyle at the head of the loch, but I very much doubt if he would have parted with any cash for the privilege.

My grandmother, Jean MacGregor, was Trossach-born, in Callander, and I claim rightful kinship with that much persecuted clan, and do so proudly. The lands of Rob Roy lie between Loch Lomond in the west and Loch Katrine in the east – the 'bristling country', of sudden peaks and secret gullies, scanned by mighty Ben Lomond, Ben Venue, Stob a'Chon and Ben Ledi.

Loch Katrine glides through these craggy corries, peaceful and serene, for a distance of eight miles; and the *Sir Walter Scott* rides across summer waters as gracefully as its namesake's creature, the Lady of the Lake, graces the pages of Scott's haunting poem. Dorothy and William Wordsworth visited Katrine on their first tour of Scotland in 1803, when the great English poet was inspired to write that evocative Highland memory 'The Solitary Reaper'.

I turned the engine, and, windscreen wipers working overtime, headed out of Aberfoyle, northwards over Dukes Pass. At the top, by the view-point, snow magically cleared and warm October sun suddenly shone from between rapidly departing clouds. Loch Venachar sparkled west and Ben Ledi, white-fringed and cloud-topped, towered northwards, contrasting brightly with the dark green of stark, tree-covered Ben An.

At the pier, Trossachs Tea Room and Visitors Centre was sullenly shut, the car park deserted, patiently waiting out winter for the bustle and blether of next season's tourists. I unflasked coffee and stood by the car, alone and silent in the fading year, surrounded by the triumphant colours of Trossachs autumn.

Delicate birch dropped silver crystal droplets clinging to precious heart-shaped leaves. Stately pines swayed on rock-girt islands, shimmering fingers of green, mirrored in calm waters. Russet beech scattered last leaves on copper-burnished ferns. Gentle oak sighed, dreaming of long-dead summer days.

Autumn is the best time to visit the Trossachs. By the end of September most tourists have departed and you may enjoy the beauties of the lake in relative peace and quiet. Step on board the *Sir Walter Scott* and book passage to Stronachlachar, five miles' sail up the loch.

From the comfort of the white-painted vessel, enjoy a dramatic journey through some of Scotland's most memorable scenery – and prepare for the walk back. That day, being boatless, I had to content myself with a loch-side walk instead, but you should arrange your visit more carefully, to coincide with the morning sailing which leaves Trossachs Pier at 11 a.m.

The *Sir Walter Scott* is owned by Strathclyde Regional Council and each season the boat is hauled ashore at Stronachlachar, in a small harbour south of the pier, for its regular overhaul: bottom scrape, painting, bilge clean, or whatever else is necessary to satisfy Board of Trade inspectors. So you may board and sail the lovely boat with complete confidence.

Sir Walter arrives in Stronachlachar at 12 noon and as you sail west, two miles before Stronachlachar, on the south shore, watch out for a regal building close to the water's edge, robed in fine woodlands, skirted by neat, well trimmed lawns enclosed by angular, clipped hedges. This striking structure is Royal Cottage, built when Queen Victoria opened Katrine in 1859 as part of the City of Glasgow's water-supply system. Hope she was amused, because in both construction and position Royal Cottage is idyllic.

The road back to Trossachs Pier cuts north, across a tree-covered promontory protecting the mooring, following the shoreline to the narrow head of the loch, where Glengyle Water feeds hungry Katrine. Rob Roy was born in these wild hills and knew every rock and corrie as well as he knew his own name. It was this intimate knowledge of these mountains that saved his life on countless occasions when his arch-enemy, James, Duke of Montrose, pursued him for his life.

In MacGregor's early days, he dealt in cattle – legally, or, at any rate, as legally as one ever could in that notoriously dangerous trade. Rob prospered and became well known for his astuteness and Highland sagacity. However, after a disastrous slump in prices, Rob Roy decided that he had done enough lawful cattle dealing and decamped; he also decamped £1000 of the laird's money.

The infuriated Montrose demanded his capture and, from 18 to 21 June 1712, the *Edinburgh Evening Courant* advertised for his apprehension: 'That Robert Campbell, commonly known by the name Rob Roy MacGregor, being lately instructed by several noblemen and gentlemen with considerable sums for buying cows for them in the Highlands, has treacherously gone off with the money to the value of £1000 sterling.'

Rob always denied having done any such thing, claiming that it was his partner who had vanished with the noble funds. Nevertheless, Montrose visited Glengyle and confiscated Rob Roy's possessions; and made the fatal mistake of turning out MacGregor's wife and children, leaving them defenceless in a harsh, fierce winter. From then onwards, Rob Roy plundered the duke's lands and herds, seeking vengeance for the wrong done to his family and recompense for the wrong done to his sporran.

MacGregor even managed to kidnap the duke's rent collector, Factor Grahame, along with £300 in cash. And, as you walk north up the loch-side, you will see the island where Rob Roy incarcerated the unfortunate man, known to this day as 'Rob Roy's Prison'. MacGregor politely asked the duke to ransom Grahame, but the noble lord refused. So, after keeping Grahame uncomfortably frozen for a week in the middle of the loch, Rob allowed the factor home, unmolested, but rentless.

The MacGregor house still stands at Glengyle, initials 'GM' and date 1704 on a lintel above the door, at the foot of Meall Mor. Urgent, silver streams cascade down savage crags, tumbling into Katrine by the MacGregor graveyard, where Rob Roy's mother lies buried amongst kilted kith and kin. MacGregor himself, against all seeming odds, died in his bed and sleeps life's endless sleep in the old churchyard overlooking Loch Voil, on the Braes of Balquhidder, flanked by wife and family.

The long walk along the north shore of Katrine, back to the car park at Trossachs Pier, is an endless delight, through a constant flutter of red and brown falling leaves and awesome views across the loch to towering Ben Venue. It is easy to imagine how in days past lawlessness reigned amongst these trackless hills, how they were both home and refuge to hunted men whose wayward actions polite society deplored.

But I never pass Brenachoile, near journey's end, without

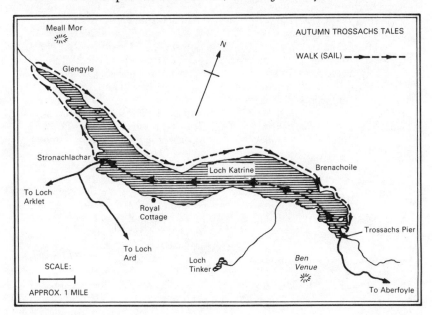

wondering who were more civilized: the untutored men of northern glens or King George's grand ministers in London. For it was at Brenachoile that fate and government soldiers caught up with Doctor Archibald Cameron, brother of Cameron of Lochiel, out with Prince Charlie in the Forty-Five.

Doctor Cameron's only crime was that of tending the wounded after the slaughter of Culloden. For this 'crime' he was branded a rebel and hanged at Tyburn in 1752. No Highlander would ever have been party to a dirty deed like that; and, least of all, Rob Roy MacGregor.

WHAT YOU NEED TO KNOW

Time and effort Great effort required for the first part of this journey: arriving at Trossachs Pier on time for the boat, climbing on board, watching the water slip by, walking round the deck to enjoy the views, remembering to disembark at Stronachlachar. Exhausting stuff.

However, the walk back, round the top of the loch and down the north shore, is about ten miles and could be tiring. Certainly, there is a good road all the way; but still wear strong shoes and take along waterproof clothing.

Because of sailing times, it is best to sail up the loch and walk back. The other way means that you must arrive at Stronachlachar Pier at 12 noon, for there is only one sailing back to Trossachs Pier and if you miss that it's a long walk home.

Sail first, walk later. Then you can amble back at your own pace. Remember, there are no Saturday or Sunday sailings to and from Stronachlachar, so this must be a weekday walk.

Location It is almost impossible to get lost, given that the master of the *Sir Walter Scott* knows what he is doing and where he is going – which he most certainly does. From Stronachlachar, follow the road north, round the loch. It's the only game in town and there are no branch roads. However, maps are comforting and they help identify hills and places of interest. You need two: Ordnance Survey Sheet 66, Ben Lomond, and Sheet 57, Stirling and the Trossachs, second series, scale 1:50,000

Grid references Trossachs Pier 496074; Ben Venue 478061; Royal Cottage 423091; Stronachlachar 403102; Glengyle Water 380136; Gregor MacGregor's Cottage 386135; Brenachoile 478099.

Route Full details of sailing times from Trossachs Pier may be had from Strathclyde Regional Council on 041-336 5333. Ask for Steamer Enquiries. 1987 charges were: adult £1.20 and child £0.60 for the single journey. There is an excellent tea room and visitors centre at the pier. Refresh the body and inform the mind before setting out.

Once at Stronachlachar, simply walk north along the narrow road, round the loch and back to Trossachs Pier. As they say, you can't miss it!

20

Dunkeld Fires and Forests

O NE VICTORY doesn't win a war. Bonny Dundee's Highlanders scored a notable success at Killiecrankie in July 1689, but a few weeks later their kilts were badly singed at the Battle of Dunkeld. Graham of Claverhouse had been killed at Killiecrankie and command of the wild men of the north was now in the hands of the appropriately named Colonel Cannon.

His force of 5,000 Highlanders, with murder in their hearts, marched north intent on a bloody visit to the cathedral city of Dunkeld, ancient Scottish capital, centre of learning and holy bishopric. I suppose the frightened inhabitants of the little town by the banks of the River Tay were used to it, for this was not the first time they had been visited with fire and sword.

King Kenneth McAlpin saved them from an approaching Viking force in AD 845. Sixty years later, Dunkeld was not so lucky when the Norsemen broke through and ravaged the town. They returned in 1027 for another courtesy call, leaving most of the town a smouldering ruin. Very careless with matches, Vikings.

During the religious wars of the sixteenth century, the old

cathedral didn't stand an earthly. Built between 1318 and 1501 and one of Scotland's most beautiful places of worship, it was 'reformed' in 1560: only the nave was left, semi-intact.

In 1689, with the Highlanders advancing, many of the townsfolk must have instantly packed children and belongings and fled. The Cameronians, under command of William Cleland, poet and divine, stayed. It is ironic that, rushing to meet him, broadsword sharpened, was his namesake, Ewen Cameron, wolf-killer of Lochaber – as staunch a Royalist as Cleland was a Covenanter.

Cleland's force of 1,200 Lowlanders, the embryonic Scottish Rifle Regiment, held the centre of town and fought furiously. Cleland soon died, as did his second-in-command, and it was left to Captain Munro, thrust into unexpected authority, to save the day. At the dark hour of midnight, he dispatched a band of desperate men with instructions to lock the unsuspecting Highlanders in their lodgings. Then the Lowlanders passed round the matches.

Few of the attacking force survived the flames; those who did decided that enough was enough, and scampered off, no doubt smouldering, northwards into the night. When dawn broke over sweetly flowing Tay all that remained of Dunkeld were the two dwellings so bravely held by dead Cleland and his powder-stained, weary men. The rest of the town lay utterly ruined.

Dunkeld today is the product of the faith, hope and hard work that rebuilt the town after the battle. The famous 'Little Houses' between Atholl Street and the cathedral all date from this period and are now safe in the caring hands of the National Trust for Scotland.

The Trust has laid out a well planned walk round town, starting at a visitor centre and exhibition near the fountain in High Street. Although the walk is not very long in distance, it is long in content, encompassing all the most notable places of interest: Bakehouse Cottage, Old Smiddy, Stanley Hill, the famous Dunkeld Larches, Cathedral, Dean's House, Ell House, Telford's Bridge and others.

My mother-in-law's family, the Blairs, come from Dunkeld and I first visited the town many years ago, whilst camping as a Boy Scout at Inver Park, just outside town on the banks of the Tay. Sadly, the place where we pitched our tents is now covered by the A9 highway, but I never pass that way without remembering the lumpy nights I slept there, lulled by the sound of the river.

There is something special about this glorious part of Perthshire: the scent of pine trees mingled with wood-smoke; the broad, confident Tay, huge autumn salmon leaping upstream; September browns, reds and russets as leaves turn to winter; the amazing blaze of heather-clad hills; soft-spoken, welcoming people.

From camp at Inver, we marched, Sunday-self-conscious, to the cathedral for morning service. Even the most boisterous were sobered by the sombre magnificence of the grey stones. The first church at Dunkeld was built around AD 570 by Culdee Monks and expanded by Kenneth McAlpin in 848. King David I designated the building a cathedral in 1127. The sanctimonious reformers of 1560, alight with righteous indignation, destroyed one of Scotland's most significant religious monuments 'For the greater glory of God'. He must shake His head in despair.

As boys we ranged wide and wild throughout the magnificent woodlands surrounding Dunkeld, stalking the course of the River Braan to the waterfalls and the deep pools below the Hermitage, where we swam in the clear, tumbling waters.

The Hermitage is easier approached today and the walk starts from a well ordered car park one mile west of town along the A9. The path wends through wonderfully mature, tall trees, alive with birdsong, to an ornate folly, built by the 2nd Duke of Atholl in 1758. Perched high above the Black Linn Fall, there is a balcony overlooking the sparkling, brown-tinged waterfall and even now I still look down expecting to see boys swimming below.

Ossian's Cave is a small, much-reduced building, further up-stream – our headquarters in a day-long game and site of a famous battle between the rival troop patrols of Otter and Beaver. Ossian would have approved, being much given to the Gaelic sport of battle. Legend has it that he was lured away after being defeated in a fight in AD 293 by the Daughter of the Land of Youth, where he spent three hundred years in happy, presumably youthful, exile.

From Hermitage I often walk on through the woods by the Braan to Rumbling Bridge, a little arch where the river is forced spectacularly through a narrow cleft in the rocks. For best effect, make the visit after heavy rain when the Braan is in spate, angry with spume and spray.

Braan meets big brother Tay just upstream from Dunkeld Bridge, where I almost drowned whilst riding a home-made raft downstream in heavy water. We had decided, Viking-like, to give the craft a decent send-off before we returned home to Edinburgh, but when my friend and I found ourselves in the middle of the river, gripped by a fierce current, we threw caution to the winds and dived overboard, striking hopefully shorewards.

I remember the feeling of absolute panic as I struggled in the peat-stained brown waves. More by good fortune than by good sense we both survived, but we had been swept from Inver almost to below Dunkeld Bridge before we reached dry land. Sheepishly, red with embarrassment, we climbed the steps up to the road, swimming-trunk-clad, laughed and pointed at by passing tourists. That was even worse than our dip in the Tay.

The bridge over the Tay at Dunkeld, built by Telford in 1809, was financed by the Duke of Atholl. Not unreasonably, there was a charge for crossing. However, when there was no sign of the toll ever being lifted, in 1868, the good citizens of Dunkeld decided to take matters into their own hands. In the ensuing riots a troop of soldiers had to be rushed from Perth to restore order. Which they did, and the toll stayed until 1879, when the county council finally took over responsibility for the bridge.

Another bridge, much loved by me, is a more modest structure over the Braan at Inver. As a Senior Scout, I was allowed the luxury of an evening stroll by myself once the little ones had been safely tucked up and lashed down for the night.

Watching the moon glinting over Craig a Barns from a blue-black star-specked sky, I recovered from the day's labours: bridge building, knots and lashings, instructing in 'birds and trees', my speciality, which I fondly imagined I knew something about, and the general turmoil of camp cooking.

Neil Gow, that most marvellous and famous of all Scottish violinists, was born at Inver in March 1727; and I know that it sounds ridiculous, but I could almost swear that, sometimes, I heard the haunting strains of his magic fiddle, closely accompanying the soft music of the burn.

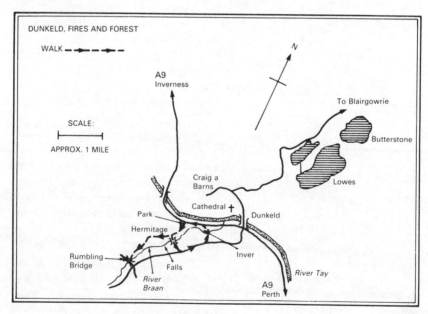

WHAT YOU NEED TO KNOW

Time and effort This walk would make a super break on a journey north or south along the A9. You can follow the Dunkeld Heritage Trail, round town and about an hour and a half; or you can combine that walk with a visit to Black Linn Fall, Hermitage and Rumbling Bridge, which makes a round trip of about four hours. There are no worrying heights to be scaled, just a gentle, peaceful walk along well made paths, amidst glorious woodland and mountain scenery. Stop at the tourist information centre in High Street and obtain copies of their excellent guide.

Location Ordnance Survey Sheet 52, Aberfeldy and Glen Almond, second series, scale 1:50,000.

Grid references Dunkeld 027426; Inver 007423; Hermitage 999418; Rumbling Bridge 997413.

Route Turn off the A9 into Dunkeld and cross the bridge. Half-way down Bridge Street, turn left into High Street. Park here, or, if this is full, there is additional parking at the end of Atholl Road, which is a continuation of Bridge Street. The tourist information centre and exhibition is just opposite the fountain in High Street. Obtain a plan of the Dunkeld Heritage Walk and follow the marked route, round town, a distance of two miles; slightly further if you branch off to visit the Dunkeld Larches.

The Heritage Trail ends at the north of Dunkeld Bridge. Either walk (there is a wide grass verge) or take the car one mile north along the A9 until you see the Hermitage route signposted, from a good car park. The National Trust has an automatic 'booklet dispenser' in the car park and this will furnish you with information for your walk. The track passes under the railway line and leads up the River Braan to Hermitage. From Hermitage, walk upstream to Ossian's Cave and thence on to Rumbling Bridge.

Return to Hermitage and cross the bridge to the south bank of the River Braan. Follow this track to the A822 down the hill to Neil Gow's birthplace, the small forestry village of Inver. Walk through the village to the A9. Turn left and the car park is 100 yards distant.

21

Jam Doughnuts and Brandy

NORMAL people don't have my trouble. They climb straight to the top of a hill. Not half-way up, back to the bottom then up again; followed by three-quarters of the way up, half-way down, then back up again. An assault course, not a walk. However, normal people don't have Jean or Heathcliff. Which is where I went wrong on the Braes of Angus.

There were seven of us, parked by the South Esk at the head of Glen Clova. My wife Ann, and her constant companion – not me, but a rag-haired, black-snubbed Yorkshire terrier called Heathcliff; eldest son Blair and his wife, Barbara; second son Charles and small daughter, Jean.

On either side of the glen mountains tower two thousand feet above the teenage stream and our day's purpose was to explore them. Walking eastwards up Green Hill (2,854 feet), round the horseshoe corrie and down to Loch Brandy, cupped below sheer cliffs, where we planned to have lunch – and, perhaps, a cast or two at some of Brandy's hard-fighting little brown trout.

This is Ogilvie country. In 1432, Sir Wallace Ogilvey, Treasurer of Scotland, was granted permission by King James I to fortify his Tower of Eroly, site of the present Castle of Airlie. James had returned after eighteen years captivity in England, determined to break the power of Lowland nobles and Highland lairds who had ruined Scotland during his absence.

King James paid the customary price for his efforts. On 20 February 1437, as he settled to sleep in the Dominican monastery at Perth, three of his relations – the Earl of Atholl, Sir Robert Stewart and Sir Robert Graham – called to say goodnight, permanently. Catherine Douglas, a lady-in-waiting, barred the door by thrusting her arm through iron clasps, but the murderers snapped it like a twig and defenceless James was dirked to death.

Could never get away with doing that to Heathcliff, although I often feel like trying. What stops me is the sure and certain knowledge that I would meet the same fate as King James's assassins: soundly tortured, pinched wiith hot irons, then hanged. Without mercy.

I looked at the invitingly open door of Ogilvie Arms Hotel whilst the gang got ready. Time for a quick one? 'Boots on, Bruce, I know what you are thinking and the answer's no.' Ann, a true Scot, though Yorkshire born, has a strong streak of Protestantism: labour first, pleasure later, perhaps. 'Have you got my jam doughnuts?' inquired Jean. It was going to be one of those days. My daughter can only be tempted uphill by promise of reward at the top. In this case, half a ton of jam doughnuts – which I was expected to carry.

There are numerous notices at the foot of the hill warning walkers to keep proper control of their animals, presumably dogs and children. One notice explained that keepers had instructions to shoot stray dogs on sight. What about stray kids, I wondered. Bang first, questions later? Traditional Highland welcome.

Sunlight warmed our backs as we fell into line behind Ann, who is the only one who can read a map – at least that's what she says. Making our way past the little school, we followed the narrow track, climbing steeply between Ben Reid and Rough Craig. Grouse-shooting country, dogs too. Early July heather begged to bloom, covering the hill in a dark-green purple-specked carpet. Twin streams chortled busily by. A good-to-be-alive day.

Then I remembered the camera, which I had left on the car roof. In the turmoil of packing and pleading with Jean to behave, I had forgotten the other purpose of the walk: capturing award-winning photographs from the top. By this time, the fit members of Clan Sandison had disappeared over the first ridge. I had been detailed to bring up the rear, which meant helping and encouraging Jean – no mean feat of persuasion, threats and downright violence.

I instructed my complaining daughter to wait and, fingers crossed, set off back down the hill, hoping that the camera would still be there. Thankfully, it was. Grabbing a few lungfuls of air, I hastened hillwards, anxious that my little charge hadn't come to any harm. She hadn't, but was most resentful when I suggested continuing up the track.

We found the others having a leisurely coffee break and I

immediately noticed that Heathcliff had managed to persuade Ann to slip his lead. Would never have happened if I had been there. Just as I opened my mouth to complain, a hare broke cover and bounded over the moor, long antennae ears laid back for greater speed. Heathcliff gave a joyful yelp and set off in pursuit.

I had a vision of a dozen twelve-bore shotguns being raised to twelve tweed-clad shoulders. What would life be like if Ann lost Heathcliff? Could our marriage survive the shock? Throwing down undrunk coffee, I sprinted after the brute, screaming blue murder at him to stop. It was like talking to the wind, or a parliamentarian – complete waste of breath.

The dog had vanished. I stopped on a ridge, panting, heart pounding, covered in sweat. In the distance, a small group of black-faced sheep grazed peacefully. Heathcliff couldn't be anywhere near them. I searched for signs of movement, parting heather, swaying twigs, anything to give me a clue. Failure to find the dog would mean a ruined day and a ruined life. Ann would be broken-hearted.

As I wandered over the moor, calling 'Heathcliff! Heathcliff!' like a hirsute Cathy in search of her Yorkshire lover, my spirits sank lower and lower. Had he gone back to the car? By this time I was half-way down anyway, so I trekked on, fingers once more crossed. No luck. No dog.

Wearily, I started uphill for the third time. All I wanted was a quiet midsummer stroll amongst restful Angus glens. I should be so lucky. The sound of voices raised my eyes heavenwards. The final call? My sinking soul ready to meet my maker? The family lined a ridge, Blair waving. Heathcliff was clutched in his grasp, half-circling overhead.

My worry changed to outraged fury and I increased pace, planning exactly what I would do when I laid hands, feet and anything else lying about on his misbegotten, misshapen body and fog-filled head. Women know these things. When I finally panted up, Heathcliff and Ann were a quarter of a mile ahead. The theory being that by the time I caught them anger and I would be too exhausted to do anything. Which was true.

We laboured up The Snub and stopped to admire our achievement. Glen Cova and Glen Doll lay mistily below. Esk, like a silver ribbon, twisted and turned through small, fertile fields. Driesh, most easterly Scottish Munro, reared west, protected by the jagged scar of Winter Corrie and tumbled rocks of The Scorrie. Sheer hundred-foot cliffs surrounded Loch Brandy and we followed the track, carefully, round Green Hill, down a slow spur to the loch.

With lunch spread and waiting, as if by some devilish command clouds hurtled into the corrie. Rain mixed with sleet drove in horizontally as we rock-huddled, sheltering from the sudden storm. Ann pulled Jean closer. 'Now then, Jean, isn't this fun?' she announced brightly. 'What about my jam doughnuts?' came her angry reply. I had the answer. They were still in the car where I had left them. Nor was I offering to dash back either. Enough was enough for one day.

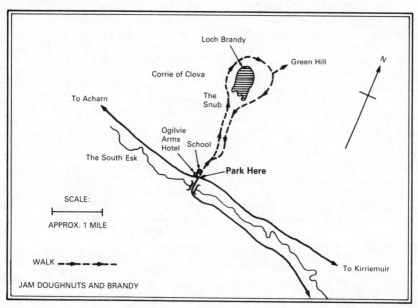

Loch Brandy
Green Hill
Corrie of Clova
To Acharn
The Snub
Ogilvie Arms Hotel
School
The South Esk
Park Here
N
SCALE:
APPROX. 1 MILE
To Kirriemuir
WALK
JAM DOUGHNUTS AND BRANDY

WHAT YOU NEED TO KNOW

Time and effort   Five hours if you are normal; ten if you have Heathcliff or Jean. Either way, this walk should not be undertaken lightly. The way is steep and the crags round the top of Loch Brandy are a dangerous place to be if sudden clouds obscure the route. Regardless of weather, stay well away from the edge and take great care. In winter this route should be attempted only by experienced walkers, in good weather.

If you wish to try your hand fishing for Loch Brandy trout, seek permission first from the Ogilvie Arms Hotel. Don't expect 'one for the glass case'; indeed, don't expect anything at all for Brandy trout are notoriously fickle. Just cross the fingers and keep casting. If you must take a dog, keep it on the lead.

Location   Ordnance Survey Sheet 44, Ballater, second series, scale 1:50,000.

Grid references   Ogilvie Arms Hotel 326732; Corrie of Clova 326755; The Snub 335755; Green Hill 348758; Loch Brandy 340755; Driesh 271736.

Route   The B955 rectangles round Glen Clova and the Ogilvie Arms is at the north end. Park by the hotel and walk past the little school onto the hill. The track is well marked and easy to follow – just very steep. On the first ridge bear left. Ahead, you will see Corrie of Clova and The Snub vee together, with Loch Brandy's horseshoe cliffs east.

The track leads up The Snub and then circles the top of the corrie. As you begin to turn south you come to a path junction. Bear left for a scramble up to the top of Green Hill and then return to the original track. This eases you gently down to the loch, arriving at the south end. A scattering of rocks here provide shelter and a lunch spot.

Follow the path back down the hill to the Ogilvie Arms. If you have your timing right, the doors should be open, and Sid Stephen behind the bar, waiting to help refresh the thirsty inner man and woman. You will have earned it.

22

Panting Round the Knock

THERE WERE nineteen people in the photograph, including Ann's Yorkshire terrier Heathcliff, which she insists is a person. It was taken in woods above Crieff Hydro, Perthshire, outside one of the Hydro's excellent self-catering chalets where Clan Sandison had gathered for a family weekend – Mrs Sandison senior and three daughters-in-law; brother Ian with two of three boys; brother Fergus with two smashing little daughters; my married son, Blair, and his wife; married daughter Lewis-Ann and her husband; Charles, Jean, cousin Bruce Reynolds, Heathcliff and me.

We called the photograph 'the family grope' because, at the critical moment, an unspecified sister-in-law shoved a hand where she shouldn't have, between an unsuspecting husband's legs, causing much merriment to everyone except Mrs Sandison senior, who was very definitely not amused. Still, its a super, happy snap and I treasure it.

Which is more than I can say for some of the memories of that weekend, or rather assault course. The attraction of Crieff Hydro to more youthful Sandisons was splendid recreational facilities: swimming pool and sauna, tennis, table tennis, squash, badminton, golf, riding and billiards. Younger brother Fergus, who is good at things, mapped out a programme of events whereby everyone did everything all the time, and by the end of the first day I felt as though I would never walk again.

I had anticipated a relaxing weekend, striding through old woods on Knock of Crieff, imparting words of wisdom here and there, about birds and trees, to those intelligent enough to listen. Should have known better, much better. My sister-in-law Liz, Fergie's wife, is a keen, fit runner. Come crack of dawn the door of our chalet burst open and we awakened to the sound of a boiling kettle.

Moments later: 'Tea. Outside in five minutes please. We're all waiting. Can't let the side down. Come on, Bruce.' What side? So I'm getting on in years. What do I have to prove to a bunch of fitness freaks? God, its barely light, let alone morning. Never at my best, mornings. 'Come on Uncle Bruce, Auntie Liz is getting cross' from a platoon of nieces and nephews surrounding the bed. Which is how I found myself running, rather than walking, through Creiff woods on a sharp September morning, first frosts of winter ridging the track ahead.

Our bunch set off at the gallop, thankfully downhill towards the stables. Then left. Up a long, slow, wet climb into trees, Liz leading, closely pursued by a brace of teenagers, chattering away as though ambling along Princes Street. Me, I knew I was going to die.

Liz Sandison is an amazingly fit lady. Fell running in the Lake District, several marathons to her credit and seaside runs down the Northumberland coast from Bamburgh Castle. In fact, looking round, they all seemed in good shape and as I found my second breath I hoped I could keep up and not make too much of a fool of myself. Elder brother Ian fell in step beside me and we conversed in convulsed gasps.

'How is it that Ann and Isobel (respective wives) aren't here?' he inquired.

'You're asking me? How should I know? Perhaps they had more sense. Save your breath for running.'

He persisted: 'And what about Fergie? He organized the run and he isn't here either.'

'That's why I'm saving my breath,' I replied. 'I'm going to kill him if I ever get back.'

Jean and Charlie joined us. 'What about a breather?' asked Charles. We crashed together in sudden halt, like a motorway pile-up.

Seconds later, downhill came Liz. 'That's where you all are. On your feet, you lot. Get a move on.' She was running on the spot. 'Think of the good this is doing you. Left, right, left, right, that's it, come on.' Hell hath no fury. We lumbered on.

Knock of Crieff is a gentle wooded hill to the north of the town, criss-crossed by paths, 911 feet in height. Trees vary in type from monotonous conifers topside to magnificent beech, oak and ash on lower slopes. That autumn morning, as the sun sidled up over Mound and Keillour, the world seemed frozen in time and space. Deep wisps of mist valley-lazed below Kate McNieven's Craig and Culcreiff Farm. Dewdrop diamonds sparkled on green larch branches; September golds and browns shaded lingering leaves.

Sounds of awakening Crieff floated upwards, cars busy with early-morning office-bound drivers. The small town lies uneasily between Gaelic-speaking north and anglicized lowlands and was the hub of the Highland cattle trade during the seventeenth century, when southern Scottish and English buyers gathered to argue prices with kilted northern men. As many as 30,000 beasts were bought and sold. More furious arguments raged in 1716 when Jacobite forces set fire to Crieff, destroying every building – no doubt settling a few old cattle-dealing scores in the process.

Like a scene from *Chariots of Fire* we arrived, more or less together, at a heather-clad clearing. I grabbed the concrete pillar at View Point for support and everyone gathered round to squabble over which hill was which. Grampian mountains lay north in faint, distant outline. Eastwards across Strathearn were the Ochil Hills, King's Seat and Tarmangie, resting shadowed in sunlight shafts.

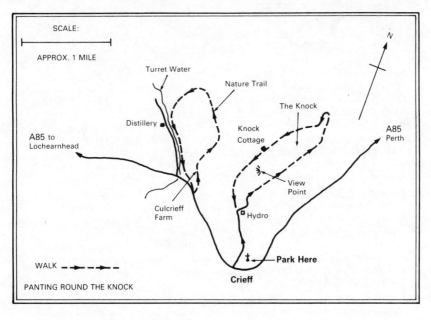

Liz was checking the map. Good grief, I thought, was it that bad? We jogged to the highest point of Knock then turned homewards, down the wide path past Knock Cottage and the Hydro's private gold course. A hopeful golfer, half-way through his swing on the first tee, gave a startled glance as we burst in a baying pack from the trees, and missed completely. Roars of impolite derision and offers of help didn't help. We clattered into the chalets, collected swimming gear and trotted down past tennis courts to the pool. Never had warm water been so welcoming.

Later that afternoon, during a brief lull in hostilities, mother dropped her bombshell. 'You know,' she announced ominously, 'we have enough people to make up two Scottish country dance sets after dinner. Won't that be fun!'

I thought longingly of the high tops of Foinaven and Arkle in darkest Sutherland, and agreed.

WHAT YOU NEED TO KNOW

Time and effort First thing you need to know is that running is not obligatory. Three miles walking takes you round the Knock and it is a delightful journey. The track can be wet at times, awash after heavy rain, but the views from the two high points are worth seeing. In spite of best efforts, giving directions is difficult since there are a number of paths within the woods. Still, you can't go far wrong and they are all pleasing.

As an addition to a walk on the Knock, consider also following the Crieff Nature Trail, one and a half miles in length, well signposted and starting from the car park at Culcrieff Farm. This walk has been prepared by members of the Scottish Wildlife Trust and a useful booklet is available to guide you round. Personally, I haven't seen much of the trail, but I have run round it.

Location Ordnance Survey Sheet 52, Aberfeldy and Glen Almond, second series, scale 1:50,000.

Grid references Crieff Hydro 865224; Knock View Point 867229; summit of the Knock 875235; start of Crieff Nature Trail at Culcrieff Farm 861234.

Route Walk starts from St James Square in the village. Go up Knock Road, through the gates leading to Crieff Hydro. At the stables, bear right and follow the path up into the woods with Crieff Gold Course on your right. This path leads up to the highest point of the Knock. From the top, bear left through the trees and the track brings you back down past Knock Cottage and the Hydro's private nine-hole golf course to the stables.

For the Crieff Nature Trail, leave Crieff by the A85 to Lochearnhead. Just outside the town, turn right along a minor road which leads to Culcrieff Farm. After swatting up local wildlife, trot north to the distillery near Hosh and sop up something else. A guid day deserves a guid end.

23

The Smooth Slope of Rannoch

MORE THAN 1,800 years ago Claudius Ptolemy, Greek geographer and astronomer, author of the *Almagest*, a thirteen-volume work of scientific 'knowledge and explanation', marked the position of Schiehallion on the first map of Britain. Sixteen centuries later another astronomer came to Sidh Chaillean: in 1774 Dr Nevil Maskelyne, Astronomer Royal, conducted his famous experiments there in order to determine the specific gravity and weight of planet Earth.

The only substantial difference in the landscape during the intervening years resulted from the great depredations amongst the forests of pine and oak that once covered Perthshire hills and glens. Ancient trees were felled to make safe the traveller's way: to give security from attack by thieves and robbers and protection from wolves which ranged the woods.

Tree were burnt to make charcol for iron smelting, timber was in constant demand for shipbuilding and sheep cropped regenerating young plants. But there was also great concern for the fast-vanishing forests and in 1579 the death penalty was imposed upon those convicted of destroying trees or broom.

To small effect. All that remains of the Caledonian Forest are woods which line the south shore of Loch Rannoch from Finnart to Bunrannoch – the Black Wood of Rannoch, a magnificent open forest clad in silver birch, alder, rowan, juniper and stately pine, where the Forestry Commission is making valiant efforts to recreate the old forests in the lands of Clan Gregor, the children of the mist.

In 1603 the Privy Council in Edinburgh passed an Act ordering the 'extermination of that wicked, unhappy and infamous race of lawless lymmaris call it the MacGregors'. Men were hunted down like animals, woman branded on the forehead and children transported to camps in the Lowlands and Ireland to serve as cattle boys.

But some escaped to carry on their traditional pastime of relieving softer southern neighbours of anything not nailed down. And two of their descendants climbed Schiehallion's smooth slope in the mid-1970s when my brother Ian accompanied our late father, John MacGregor Sandison, on his last long walk, to the summit.

To reach Schiehallion, follow the winding wooded road westwards from Pitlochry, 'the road to the isles', past Queen's View. No, not unamused Victoria, but a more earthy, Scottish queen. Luckless Mary gave the name, when she visited the rocky promontory in 1564 and was reported to have been very amused with the noble view up Loch Tummel.

In more recent times others less earthy have been just as captivated by that gentle scene. William Wordsworth and his sister Dorothy tramped by during their tour of the Highlands. Alfred Lord Tennyson sought inspiration amongst the tree-lined banks. The great Liberal prime minister, William Gladstone, and Baden-Powell, hero of Mafeking, founder of the Boy Scout movement, both came here to pay silent homage to the beauty of Perthshire.

Ann and I pay homage also and return frequently to Tummel, Rannoch and Laidon to walk the hills and fish clear waters for wild brown trout. Schielhallion, an old favourite, dominates the long glen – a dreamlike, fairy-tale peak, snow-capped, graceful and always welcoming. A friendly mountain.

During recent visits we have stayed in the splendid comfort of lodges at Loch Rannoch Hotel – a far cry from mountain bothy or damp Highland cottage but, after a long day on hill or loch, marvellously relaxing. The lodges are carefully landscaped into mature woodlands and all have magnificent views over Rannoch to Schiehallion. There is an excellent restaurant and, best of all, a swimming pool and sauna complex. Aching joints ease and cold bodies quickly warm in mind-numbing, all-enveloping heat.

Last time, before saying hello to Schiehallion, we took a boat from Moor of Rannoch and sailed up Loch Laidon, across Rannoch Moor, 'the watery place', a desolate plateau a thousand feet above sea level. Laidon lays a silver scar across the moor – horizon crowded west with Black Mount and Glencoe peaks, Black–Corrie north, and bounded south by wild empty moorlands rising to Glen Lyon mountains. We parked the boat three miles down the loch and spent the day hillwalking with only fox and wild cat for companions.

If you have time and relish geographical tricks, sail down Laidon to Tigh na Cruaiche and the north shore bay protected by Eilean Iubhair. Beach the boat and follow up Allt Lochain Ghaineamhaich burn. After a few hundred yards, at streams cross, you may stand in three counties at once, Perthshire, Argyll and Inverness-shire. Presuming, of course, that you have three legs; otherwise, I should imagine you would have to jump about a bit to get the full effect.

A narrow hill road leaves Kinloch Rannoch south to Schiehallion, past shallow, flooded Dunalastair Reservoir. I remember, one cold Easter morning in the early 1960s, going aground in the middle on a barely submerged tree-stump. Whilst Ann gave directions, I stood, waist-deep and freezing, trying to push the boat free.

Our more sensible companions had retired to the pub to roast in front of a blazing fire. Before they had lowered a quarter of their first pint, the door of the bar burst open and a local exclaimed: 'Here! You will never believe what I have just seen. There are a couple of idiots wading in the middle of Dunalastair!' Our friends expressed amused interest but nothing else. We caught nothing.

The tortuous hill road climbs Meall Dubh then falls to Braes of Foss at the edge of a plantation of new trees. The broad shoulder of Schiehallion rises west, still snow-capped in May. Her sister Munros, Carn Gorm, Meall Garbh, Carn Mairg and Creag Mhor, symphony south and the long skirts of the smooth slope cradle tumbling waters of Allt Kynachan stream, pointing the way upwards.

Resting by the summit cairn with Scotland spread before me, I often think of father, labouring up the cairned path to the top, no doubt mightily encouraged by Ian. It was a clear day when he made that last climb. A wonderful memory to sleep with.

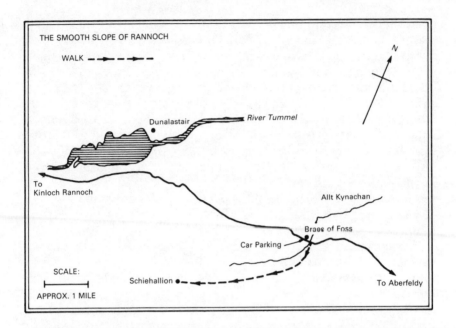

WHAT YOU NEED TO KNOW

Time and effort Be prepared. Although this is an easy walk, in bad weather even Schiehallion can turn nasty. The distance there and back from Braes of Foss is about five miles and you should allow three hours for your journey. The summit is a Munro at 3,547 feet and you will climb nearly 2,500 feet to reach it.

Location Ordnance Survey Sheet 51, Loch Tay, second series, scale 1:50,000.

Grid references Braes of Foss and parking 750559; Schiehallion summit 714548.

Route From the car park at Braes of Foss, to east of the house south of the road, a path leads up a broad valley, on the left-hand side of a small burn. Once you leave the moorland heather habitat and climb higher up the shoulder, a line of cairns marks the way to the summit. On top there is a trig. point and substantial cairn. Return to the car park the same way.

24

Gilbert, Gow and Marble

THE CASTLE at Blair Atholl was built in AD 1269. Oliver Cromwell, that great seventeenth-century demolition contractor, knocked it about a bit in 1653 and the scarred building had to wait until 1872 before being restored. Earls and Dukes of Atholl played a prominent part in Scotland's turbulent story throughout the ages. Much given to royalist tendencies, Atholl dukes and sons were supporters of James Francis Edward Stuart, the Old Pretender, and Charles Edward Louis Philip Casimir, known to his family as Carluccio and to history as Bonnie Prince Charlie.

The dukedom was created when the 2nd Marquess of Atholl fell in with William of Orange in 1688 and was elevated for his pains. Proper pains came later. Like many Scots before and after, the prospect of a Scottish king and expected benefits made the embryonic duke change horses in midstream: from 1703 onwards, Atholl sympathies were pro-Jacobite.

Three of his sons were 'out' in the 1715 rising. The most famous, Lord George Murray, was later pardoned, but failed to profit from such surprising leniency. In 1745 he joined the Young Pretender on his abortive, disastrous bid for the crown of these sceptred isles and was certainly the best of Charlie's rag-bag of generals.

Murray advised against the ill-fated night march to Nairn, before the final battle on Drumossie Moor, and begged the Prince to choose another, more easily defended site. Should have saved his breath. The stubborn Stuarts were incapable of taking advice. Which is how they had got themselves into such a mess in the first place.

Atholl fortunes brightened considerably when the 2nd Duke inherited sovereignty of Isle of Man in 1736. This was sold to the British government in 1765 for £70,000, and in 1828 the 4th Duke parted with his remaining Manx rights for the huge sum of £417,000. A good day's work if ever there was one. The white castle at Blair Atholl is more peaceful now, although more thoroughly besieged by tourists than Cromwell could ever have mustered troops to batter the ancient walls.

Our eldest son is named Blair, his grandmother's maiden name. The family came from Dunkeld and we consider this beautiful part of Perthshire second home – next to Edinburgh, where I was born; the Borders, where my wife was brought up; Caithness, my grandfather's birthplace; and the Trossachs, where Jean Mac-Gregor, my grandmother, lived. Suppose that's more than two, but you know what I mean.

A long track leads north-east from Blair Atholl, knifing thirty-one miles through Glen Tilt by Falls of Tarf and Geldie Burn to White Bridge and Linn of Dee. This is a dramatic, magnificent walk past some of Scotland's grandest scenery, but organizing time and transport is complicated and difficult. The journey takes twelve hours, one way. So you have to rely on public transport at one end or make the walk in conjunction with friends, passing mid-way and picking up cars at the finish. Overnight accommodation for tired feet may also be required.

A good alternative is to do this walk in two parts: from south and north, returning down the glen the same way. Even then it is a long walk, but you can walk as far as you like and the scenery along the path is well worth the effort. Beinn a'Ghlo dominates the eastern slopes of Glen Tilt, hiding from Blair Atholl behind Carn Liath. Munro country. Braigh Coire Chruinnbhalgain, Carn nam Gabhar and Airgoid Bheinn, sparkling white with spring snows, strewn with rough, ankle-twisting boulders.

Deep in the hills (crushed between Coire Cas-eagallach and Meall Reamhar) lies one of Scotland's remotest trout waters, Loch Loch, a narrow ribbon of silver water, shores hour-glassed together. Northwards, Grampian peaks rear skywards: Beinn a'Chait, Braigh nan Creagan Breac, Carn a'Chlamain and Conlach Mhor. In the valley, sweet River Tilt tumbles southwards to its meeting with Garry at Blair Atholl.

Queen Victoria stayed at Blair Castle in September 1844 and fell in love with Glen Tilt:

We drove along Glen Tilt, through a wood overhanging the river; and as we left the wood we came upon such a lovely view – Ben-y-Ghlo straight before us – and under these high hills the river Tilt gushing and winding over stones and slates, and the hills and mountains skirted at the bottom with beautiful trees; the whole lit up by the sun, and the air so pure and fine. But no description can at all do it justice, or give an idea of what this drive was.

Knew a thing or two, did Queen Victoria, amused or otherwise. Each morning a jug of water was placed at her bedside, drawn fresh from a spring high up the glen where she and Prince Albert always stopped to drink and known to this day as a Queen's Well. Little bridges cross the Tilt, each graced by a morsel of history: Gilbert's Bridge, guarded by wonderful beech trees, and named after William Gilbert Robertson, who was 'out' with his laird in the Forty-Five. Near by is Tom na Croich, the hanging hill, last used to dispatch one John Stewart, convicted of murdering a shepherd on Beinn a'Ghlo.

Gow's Bridge, near Marble Lodge, is where marble was quarried and rocks are still chisel-marked where they were struck to split the stones – 'twenty-one shillings a cubic foot, delivered Edinburgh' at

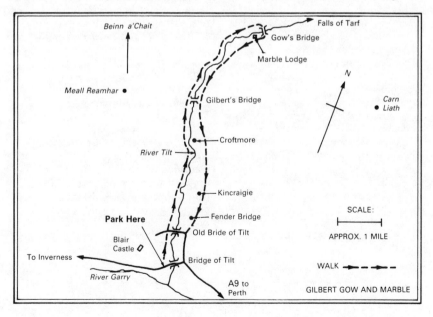

the end of the nineteenth century. Blairuachdar Wood to the north of Old Blair, stands witness to Atholl dukes' pioneering forestry work. James Murray, the 2nd Duke, brought the first larch trees from the Alps to Atholl in 1727 and the 4th Duke became known as 'the planting duke', establishing more than 10,000 acres of forest over a period of sixty years.

Sir Walter Scott, in *The Fair Maid of Perth*, wrote: 'Amid all the provinces of Scotland, if an intelligent stranger were asked to describe the most varied and most beautiful, it is probable he would name the county of Perth.' Spend a day walking in Glen Tilt and you will know why.

WHAT YOU NEED TO KNOW

Time and effort As long and as much as you want. I suggest two alternatives: a walk of about 6½ miles, from Blair Atholl to Gilbert's Bridge and back; or a longer walk of 10½ miles, on from Gilbert's Bridge to Marble Lodge and Gow's Bridge, then back to Blair Atholl. No hardship in either of these walks.

For the hardy, tramp on to Forest Lodge and Falls of Tarf, which is near the half-way mark to Deeside; but allow a good ten hours for the round trip. Shorten this walk by seeking permission from the Atholl Estate office to use their private vehicle access road on payment of a small fee.

Your trip will be greatly enhanced if you buy one of the information leaflets available at the caravan site office. Also seek information concerning stalking in August and October. Who wants shot?

Location Ordnance Survey Sheet 43, Braemar, second series, scale 1:50,000.

Grid references Start point from car park at Blair Castle 866663; Blairuachdar Wood 876684; Gilbert's Bridge 881701; Marble Lodge 898717; Forest Lodge 933741; Falls of Tarf 983797.

Route The start point is at Blair Atholl caravan site and you exit by the first gate to the riverside footpath. Turn left and follow it up through the woods on the left bank of the River Tilt. At Gilbert's Bridge, cross to the east bank of the river and return to the car.

For the longer walk, simply follow the track northwards up Glen Tilt to Gow's Bridge, cross and return south down the east bank to Blair Atholl. The paths are well signposted and you will find it hard to go wrong – unless, of course, you are like me, and congenitally prone to getting lost. In case you are tempted into a little Munro-bashing along the way, don't forget compass and map and be well prepared for the weather.

25

Linn of Dee and Tarf Falls

THE MAN and woman stopped on the banks of the river and took off boots and socks. They were a handsome young couple, bronzed from the hills, laughing in warm September sunlight. Back-packed and barefooted, they stumbled hand in hand across shallow, sharp-rocked Dee. We spotted them an hour since, a splash of white and red amongst heather, inching down from Carn Liath by corries of Dalvorar burn and Carn an Leth-allt.

Obviously, they had tried to shorten their long journey through Glen Tilt by cutting east over Buachaille Breige and Carn Liath to pick up the stalker's path to Inverey. And missed. Not difficult to do in these wild, remote lands. The rough tramp seemed to have dampened only their feet, for as they walked off down the sand-packed road to Linn of Dee happy laughter filled the air.

I was in a Land-Rover, with a Swiss and a Skye man, parked by the side of the river, watching autumn-red salmon surging to upstream spawning grounds beyond Chest of Dee, where silver Dee rises between mighty Ben Macdhui and Cairn Toul in fierce Cairngorms before cascading through Royal Deeside past Balmoral Castle seawards to Aberdeen.

My hosts were from Mar Lodge, a few miles down the glen near Braemar. Mar Lodge was a royal hunting lodge, built in the late nineteenth century by Queen Victoria for the Duke of Fife and Princess Louise, daughter of Edward VII. Nice to be near granny, but not too near.

Great deer drives were held on Mar, hundreds of beasts being driven before the muzzles of expectant royal guns – a tradition going back centuries in the mountains between Blair Atholl and Braemar. Deep in the glen, where chill waters from Loch Loch rush down An Lochain burn to Tilt, the Earl of Atholl built a hunting lodge in 1529 for King James V. More than a thousand men herded deer down from the corries of Beinn a'Ghlo for the king's pleasure. His daughter, Mary Queen of Scots, was similarly entertained in 1564, before she became the hunted one herself.

Today the estate still boasts some of the finest stalking in Europe and Beinn a'Bhuird has a red deer population of 5,000. The ballroom of Mar Lodge is adorned with the heads of 3,000 stags and in days gone by the Mar employed two full-time taxidermists. Grouse on the moor, salmon in the river, stags on the hill. What sportsman could ask for more? Apart from the wherewithal to pay.

Walking is less costly and far less dangerous to fish, fowl and beast. I prefer walking and the only time I interfere with nature is when I attempt to remove a few wild brown trout from their natural habitat, an infrequent occurrence. But I would never begrudge another man his pleasure for it is not my business in life to dictate how others should enjoy themselves. Authoritarian prescription scares the hell out of me. Live and let live – just too bad if you happen to be born grouse, salmon or stag.

Dramatic Linn of Dee is the start of the 31-mile walk to Blair Atholl. The river roars through a narrow defile, cut over centuries by the force of the stream. Dark waters swirl below secret ledges where resting salmon lurk. Cliff-tops are spread thick with pine needles and the smell of resin lingers in mist-fine spray.

A splendid road leads westwards, faced by peaks of Glenfeshie Forest to White Bridge, where the Geldie burn gathers in all the waters from Cnapan Mor and Scarsoch Bheag, sending them chortling to Dee. New trees bunch by the stream as the path climbs slowly past the ruins of Bynack Lodge to the birthplace of the River Tilt.

Loch Tilt lies to the west of the track, hidden from view. In 1769, Thomas Pennant, that caustic Welsh observer of things Scottish, passed that way and described Loch Tilt as 'swarming with trouts'. Pennant had little good to say about Scotland or its people. Further south, he castigated Lowland scenery with his usual brashness and further north he was soon describing the natives of Sutherland as little more than worthless, idle savages.

In the meantime, resting by Loch Tilt, he observed of his journey '. . . the most dangerous and the most horrible I have ever travelled; a narrow path so rugged that our horses often were obliged to cross their legs in order to secure place for their feet.' Welshmen take a lot of pleasing. Unlike Pennant, Queen Victoria enjoyed the trip and wrote in her journal: 'This was the pleasantest and most enjoyable expedition I ever made; and the recollection of it will always be agreeable to me, and increase my wish to make more!' Takes all sorts.

South from Loch Tilt, the infant river is christened Allt Garbh Buidhe, 'the boisterous yellow burn', and the track feints and fades through a long narrow pass, sheer-sloped by Meall na Callich Buidhe. Tarf Water, Tilt's principal companion, slides in a snake-like silver thread from the north, leaping three, final, mighty, waterfalled strides into the waiting arms of Tilt.

A sad bridge was built here nearly forty years after Victoria's merry party trotted by, the Bedford Memorial Bridge. 'This bridge

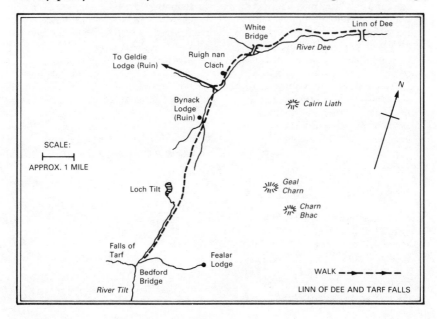

was erected in 1886 with funds contributed by his friends and others and by the Scottish Rights of Way Society Ltd to commemorate the death of Francis John Bedford, aged 18, who was drowned near here on 25th August 1879.' Crossing rivers can seriously damage your health.

Blair Atholl lies ahead, but, unless you have been lucky enough to make arrangements with friends to leave your transport there, turn and retrace steps to Braemar. If you feel very unhappy about turning back, brighten your walk with three of the Munros on the way. A track leads eastwards to Fealar Lodge and you may navigate across the hills to Carn Bhac, Geal Charn and Carn Liath.

Pick up the stalker's path south of Carn Liath summit and follow it down to Inverey. Don't worry too much about getting lost. Head north and wade across the shallow, sharp-rocked Dee. I'll be the guy in the Land-Rover, waiting to greet you on the other side.

WHAT YOU NEED TO KNOW

Time and effort This a long, tiring walk and you should choose the best possible day before getting involved. The total distance is in the order of sixteen miles, there and back so think in terms of an early start and a full day out. High summer with longest days is the best. If you strike east into the hills on your return, make sure you are fully equipped and know how to use a compass and map. Perhaps best to make the high hill walk into a separate outing. Depends upon how fit and experienced you are. Whatever you do, don't take chances.

Location Ordnance Survey Sheet 43, Braemar, second series, scale 1:50,000.

Grid references Linn of Dee 062897; White Bridge 019886; Bynack Lodge 001856; Loch Tilt 993827; Falls of Tarf 983797; Fealar Lodge 009799; Carn Bhac 041828; Geal Charn 032833; Carn Liath 035867; Inverey 086892.

Route From Braemar, follow the minor road west by the side of the river which loops at Linn of Dee. Park here and walk west along the north bank of the Dee. This is an excellent road and takes you smartly to White Bridge, three miles from your start point. Cross the bridge and walk south into the hills.

The main path turns west after Ruigh nan Clach cottage, up the burn to Geldie Lodge. Continue walking south. Tarf Falls are on your right, about five miles from White Bridge. Return the same way, or turn left to Fealar Lodge and get out compass and map.

26

Avoiding Aviemore

I REMEMBER once hearing a lecture by Professor Colin Buchanan on the subject 'Can Man Plan?' Visit the nightmare village of Aviemore on Speyside and make up your own mind. Set amidst some of God's most glorious scenery, this once attractive village has been devastated by mass tourism.

Lord Fraser of Allander, a principal promoter of the development, was much given to referring to scenery and wildlife as 'the merchandise'. With friends like these, Aviemore never stood a chance and the best thing that has happened to Aviemore in recent years is the bypass which excludes its ugliness from view. In my opinion, Aviemore is a fearful monument to man's insensitivity to his environment.

The graceful Cairngorm Mountains have been opened up to allcomers and development is the new god. Conservationists and wildlife bodies are ridiculed when they express concern and nothing must be allowed to stand in the way of commercial exploitation or profit. Those who complain are branded as crackpots, trouble-makers standing in the way of progress.

Wonderful once-remote corries and summits have become easily accessible by ski-lifts and a trip to the high peaks in summer is no less daunting a prospect than an afternoon amble down Oxford Street – and often just as crowded. Ease of access means despoliation: notice-boards, signposts, keep out, private, don't, must and the malignant growth of bureaucracy.

It was not always like that. As a teenager, my wife, Ann, used to visit the Cairngorms during the late 1950s, when Aviemore was just a Highland Blackpool gleam in the developer's eye. She stayed at Carrbridge and each morning a party of young people would set off by bicycle on the fifteen-mile journey to Coylumbridge or Loch Morlich.

From there, they spent their day trout fishing in crystal-clear lochs, scrambling by White Lady Shieling to the summit of Cairngorm, or walking in the Lairig Ghru. But it will never be the same again and something beyond human price has been destroyed for ever.

I first visited Speyside in 1950 as a tenderfoot Boy Scout when the troop camped at Creagdubh near Newtonmoor in the lands of Clan MacPherson. I was homesick, too, but we were kept busy building bridges, hiking into hills, swimming in the little lochans nearby. My interest in trout fishing probably dates from that time. What made those strange, mysterious rings on the calm surface of the loch?

By the time Ann and I met, nine years later, I was a confirmed fisherman and used to boast youthfully about my supposed skill – until one evening, with a quiet smile, she produced from her handbag a photograph of a magnificent two pound trout.

There could be no argument either, because a ruler had been placed above the fish. 'Where did you catch that?' I asked, through gritted teeth. The fish had been caught during one of her days walking in the Cairngorms and was all the more remarkable for having been taken from a tiny mountain stream.

When our children were little we brought them to Speyside and stayed at Nethy Bridge, far from the madding crowd of Aviemore. The old village still retains its ancient charm and we found a perfect cottage close to the banks of gurgling Nethy Burn. The stream rises on Cairngorm's saddle above blue Loch Avon, stumbling down from high peaks between Cnap Coire na Spreidhe and Stac na h-Iolaire to the west and A'Choinneach and Bynack More to the east.

King Edward of England, the 'hammer of the Scots', paused at Nethy Bridge during one of his endless forays north to quell unruly neighbours. Claverhouse and Montrose camped here and General

Hugh MacKay of Scourie, defeated at the Battle of Killicrankie, passed by on his way to disaster.

Communications throughout these wild lands were much improved by that great soldier road-builder General Wade. Between 1725 and 1733 he constructed no less than 250 miles of new ways throughout the Highlands, including the tortuous route over Corrieyairack Pass, employing 500 men in order to do so.

Wade's instructions, as commander-in-chief of government forces in the north, were 'to reduce the Highlands to obedience'; but it takes a 'lang spoon' to sup with a Highlander, as the rebellion of Forty-Five proved. Butcher Cumberland was less delicate in his methods after Culloden and completed the task of subjugation without mercy.

Swiftly flowing Spey meanders past Nethy Bridge in an urgent, silver thread, collecting Nethy Burn and Allt Mor waters into its turbulent arms. One evening after heavy spare, I offered to baby-sit while Ann went to fish where Allt Mor and Spey meet. After an hour or so I began to worry – not so much for Ann's safety, but rather because I suspected that she might be catching lots of fish when I wasn't.

Carrying daughter Lewis-Ann and taking small kilted son Blair by firm grip, we set out through another rainstorm to investigate. We arrived at the river just in time to see Ann landing a lovely trout of about a pound and a half. 'Look, children,' I said, 'isn't Mummy

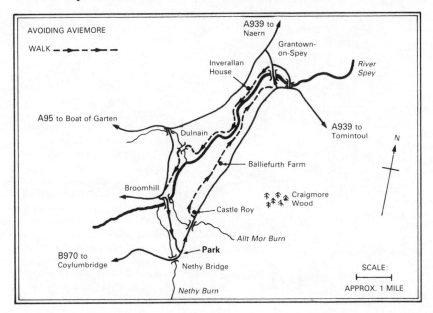

clever. She's caught supper.' Then I looked again and noticed a tear in the corner of her eye. 'What on earth's the matter?' I asked.

'Put it back please. I couldn't kill it. It fought so well.'

I did, but will never understand why.

The Spey is one of Sctoland's finest salmon rivers and a perfect walk leads northwards along the river bank to Grantown and the old arched bridge. One cold night, full of hope, Ann and I fished for sea trout under the bridge. After an hour with nothing to show for our efforts other than freezing faces, we retired under the arches with my hip flask, thoughtfully charged with cherry brandy, and left the fish to get on with it undisturbed.

To complete a memorable Speyside walk, cross the bridge and return to Nethy down the north side of Spey. The banks are busy with salmon fishers and the river busy with fish avoiding them. Above the forests of Craigmore and Abernethy, Cairngorms rise majestically in a mighty shout of mountain triumph.

Before the last ice age, mammoth, musk ox, Arctic fox and lemmings used to haunt these old hills. Ice there still is in plenty, but the only animals haunting hills now are hordes of human lemmings. Wonder if there is any chance of them following the example of their furry, four-legged counterparts?

WHAT YOU NEED TO KNOW

Time and effort Total distance is about nine miles for the round trip and the only obstacles along the way are fences and dykes. Easy walking but can be damp underfoot after rain. Avoid disturbing salmon anglers. They have enough problems as it is and do not take kindly to rocks being hurled into the pools where they are fishing. Have been known to hurl them back. During your day try and fit in a visit to Loch Garten and RSPB-protected osprey nesting site.

Location Ordnance Survey Sheet 36, Grantown and Cairngorm, second series, scale 1:50,000.

Grid references Nethy Bridge 001206; Castle Roy 006219; Speybridge 035268; Old Spey Bridge 040264; Broomhill 995225,

Route Park in Nethy Bridge and walk north out of town along the B970. Past Balliemore and before Castle Roy, turn left and pick up line of dismantled railway. Walk north, and in three miles meet the new bridge across Spey. The old bridge is quarter of a mile further downstream.

Return crossing Spey by the new bridge. Just at the north side, turn sharp left and follow the track along the river towards Inverallan House. Keep to the riverbank and walk beside the Spey, which curves and twists past Dulnain to Broomhill, a distance of about three and a half miles. At Broomhill, cross the river and walk back to Nethy Bridge.

27

Bennachie, the Don and Paradise Wood

I^N 1078 Malcolm Canmore, the one who did for dastardly MacBeth, rested at Monymusk whilst on his way north to quell yet another Morayshire uprising. Using his spear, he marked on the ground an outline of the church he marked on the ground an outline of the church he would build if granted victory over the rebels. He quelled the uprising – a quaint Scottish euphemism for wholesale slaughter – and the church he built still graces the old-world charm of this grey-stoned Aberdeenshire village.

A better-known pattern commemorates the delightful Strathdon hamlet today and is traced on the ground by the feet of Scottish country dancers as they weave and smile their way through the intricate measures of the dance 'Monymusk'. We Scots have always been great ones for dancing. As children, Ann and I were given compulsory lessons in the ancient art. She, more Highland; I, less taxing Lowland shuffles.

One of Scotland's most important relics came from the House of Monymusk, ancestral home of the Grant family since 1712 – the Monymusk Reliquary, a seventh-century casket said to contain a bone of St Columba. Must have been bad news, being an important religious figure. The moment you snuffed, the world beat a path to your corpse, knives poised to cut off bits and pieces for posterity.

The Monymusk Reliquary was at Bannockburn in 1314 inspiring the troops of Robert the Bruce, and can still be seen in Edinburgh at Queen Street, in the Scottish Museum of Antiquities. Another important Scottish antiquity is my mother, Mima Sandison, a wonderful, sparkling octogenarian who still dances three nights a week and is a walking encylopaedia on Scottish country dancing. Eight people together, anywhere, means one thing to my mother: enough for a Scottish country dance set.

Aberdeenshire's two mighty rivers, Dee and Don, ride the county together, from the heights of the Grampian mountains to the cold waters of the North Sea by the honest Granite City. Both are famous for their salmon runs and yet they are entirely different in character. The Dee is essentially a spate river, much given to variations in water level, whilst the gentle Don flows serenely through fine farmlands in unhurried calm. Aberdeenshire farmers, in clipped, sing-song voice, claim: 'A mile o'Don's worth twa o' Dee.'

Bennachie, a smooth range of forested hills, rises quietly over softly flowing Don. Oxen Crag is the highest peak, 1,733 feet, courtiered by Mither Tap, Hermit's Seat, Black Hill and Millstone Hill. The Forestry Commission has laid out a series of pleasant walks through woodlands and across open hills, varying in length from one to eight miles. But, before visiting Bennachie, walk to Paradise, my favourite Strathdon forest, enfolded in a crook of the river by Woodhead and Tilliehashlach.

Paradise Wood is a proper wood, not like today's commercial plantations – dark, impenetrable, sterile deserts. Paradise borders the Don and was beautifully planned and planted by Lord Cullen in 1719. Last year, Ann and I parked the car near the ruined mill on the south bank and walked by the river through a dappled day of sunlight and shadow, amidst friendly old oak and beech, where tall pines swayed sweetly in the breeze and the air was bright with woodland birdsong – Frederick Delius and a 'Walk to the Paradise Garden'.

During that visit I had a close look at the Don. Unexpectedly, dangerously close. I had been fishing Dam Pool, near Forbes Castle. Deep water, clear and slow-moving, alive with summer insects, bordered by high reeds, tree-backed on the north bank – fish-stalking water. Half awake in warm sun, I was taken completely by surprise when a monster fish grabbed my fly. Stepping forward in fright, I performed a neat dive straight into the river.

Fully equipped – waders, fishing jacket and tackle bag – under I went, thinking 'Well, this is it. Wonder what it will be like.' But I managed to struggle upright, head barely above the stream and struggled shaken and dripping ashore. Lost fish, dignity and very nearly life. When I told the family of the near demise of their father I received scant sympathy. 'Not safe to be let out alone.' 'Get your eyes tested.' 'Where did you say the hip flask was? 'How big was this fish supposed to be?'

The climb to the summit of Bennachie is a popular walk and starts from a parking area near Maiden Castle. When we arrived the car park was busy with people preparing for an afternoon stroll. There is an information centre at Don View where a guidebook is available, along with toilets, children's playground and picnic area. The route to Mither Tap is along a well worn track, stamped flat by thousands of feet.

At Pittodrie, on the low east slopes of Bennachie, is a small Pictish fort. The remains of the protecting wall can be clearly seen, enclosing an area 80 feet long by 60 feet wide and there is evidence of further defences, a rampart and ditch. Mither Tap also has hill-fort remains but you may be excused for walking by without noticing for they lie scattered amongst the granite and felspar boulders described in the 'Guide to Prehistoric Scotland' as:

> The outermost wall, about 15ft thick, runs round the bottom of
> the tor for nearly 100ft below the summit; several stretches of its

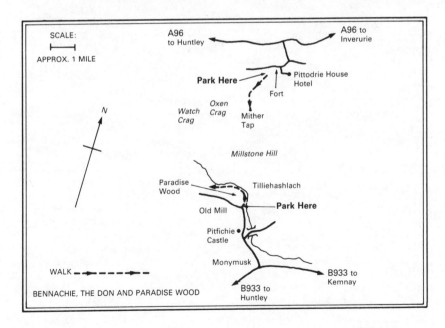

faces can be distinguished, and there are suggestions of a parapet in one place. A second wall encircles the interior of the enclosure thus formed about half way up towards the summit.

A more recent pillar has been erected on Mither Tap, brass-plate-engraved with lines pointing to surrounding peaks. On that fine day, 128 miles north, our Caithness mountains of Morven and the Scarabens were clearly visible whilst the vast bulk of Ben Macdui, Braeriach and Cairn Gorm reared westwards. Patchworked fields, rivers and forests flowed east to Aberdeen.

At the 'back of Bennachie', by the side of a quiet minor road, stands one of Scotland's most beautiful Pictish symbol stones, the Maiden Stone. An ancient slab of red granite, ornately carved front and back with early Christian symbols. On the front, in relief, a man is shown between fish monsters. As I gazed at the elaborate interlace of carvings, a distant bell rang in my mind: I had seen one of these fish somewhere before. Then I remembered. Underwater in Dam Pool on the River Don. Wait until I tell the family.

WHAT YOU NEED TO KNOW

Time and effort Mostly time. The walk up Bennachie, there and back, is only three miles and about a couple of hours' easy stroll; but there is so much else to see nearby that really you should plan a whole day out, driving between various sites.

Apart from Bennachie walk, you should visit Paradise Wood, Pittodrie Fort and the Maiden Stone. Information about other places of interest may be obtained from Gordon District Tourist Board, St Nicholas House, Broad Street, Aberdeen. Tel: (0224) 632727.

Location Ordnance Survey Sheet 38, Aberdeen, second series, scale 1:50,000.

Grid references Monymusk 685154; Paradise Wood 675185; Bennachie car park 691245; Pittodrie Fort 694244; Maiden Stone 703247; Mither Tap 683224.

Route For Paradise Wood, drive north from Monymusk on the west bank of the River Don. Where the minor road turns right to cross the river at Pitfichie, drive straight on past Pitfichie Castle, which is on your left. A mile further, the road bends sharp left. Directly ahead is a track leading down through woods, past ruined mill buildings. Park here and follow the track down to the river and through the woods. Return the same way.

The Bennachie walks are signposted from the car park and you will have no trouble finding your way to Mither Tap. Although often busy, Bennachie is well looked after by a team of men known as the Bennachie Rangers. They are very helpful and will supply whatever information and advice you may require. I suggest you purchase a copy of the excellent guidebook before setting out.

28

Gairloch, Fionn and Fisherfield

URING summer months, Gairloch in Wester Ross is a busy, bustling tourist centre. Thousands of visitors flock to the world-famous Inverewe Gardens, begun in 1865 by Osgood Mackenzie, now containing some 2,500 species of plants from around the world. Children bucket and spade on shining white sands or splash in clear waters warmed by the Gulf Stream. There are excellent restaurants, hotels, museums, craft centres, golf courses, pony trekking, sail-boarding and Highland safaris. Something for everyone.

But the shores of the Short Loch were not always so peaceful; nineteenth-century famines and evictions brought ruin to the north. When Lowland granaries were full, Highlanders starved. People went barefoot, clothed in meal bags, whilst Free Church ministers appealed in vain to London for help. Lord Napier, leading a royal commission in 1882, reported: 'A state of misery, of wrong-doing, and of patient long-suffering, without parallel in the history of our country.'

The open-air pulpit of the Free Presbyterian Church is a reminder of these sad times, when sheep and profit took preference over people; when young and old alike laboured for Destitution Boards or accepted the blandishments of Emigration Societies: bible-blessed with a pound and packed overseas like cattle. Today, a new wind of hope blows throughout the Highlands and the sympathetic development of Gairloch as a major tourist centre is evidence of respect for the past and renewed hope in the future.

North-east from Gairloch is one of Scotland's most beautiful and remote lochs, Fionn, the 'white loch', deep in the heart of turbulent Fisherfield Forest – 180 square miles enfolding thirty-five mountains, eighteen of which tower more than 3,000 feet: a 'thunder' of Munros; a hillwalker's paradise and gamefisher's delight.

In his book *A Hundred Years in the Highlands'*, Osgood Mackenzie describes the most famous basket of brown trout ever taken from Fionn: 'There were four beauties lying side by side on the table of the small drinking room, and they turned the scales at 51 lb. The total weight of the 12 fish caught that 12th day of April by trolling was 87 lb 12 oz.'

Fionn trout are of more modest size today and average half a pound, but there are few more delightful places to fish and the last time Ann and I assaulted Fionn we were rewarded with a dozen brightly marked, sprightly trout. She caught twelve and I managed to catch the rest. Salmon and sea trout also lurk in Fionn's deep waters, making their perilous journey from the sea past anthrax-ridden Gruinard island and up Little Gruinard River to the loch.

There are several fine walks out to Fionn – from the east, from Drumchork near Aultbea, by Loch Mhic 'ille Riabhaich, named after a sixteenth-century outlaw who terrorized the surrounding countryside; from the north, by long climber's path from Corrie Hallie near Dundonnell on Little Loch Broom; and from the west via Poolewe, Loch Maree and Kernsary.

Our favourite approach is from Poolewe, along the banks of the river, where there is always the chance of spotting salmon surging upstream to Loch Maree. Sometimes, surging downhill, come perspiring humans, for this is the line of a fun-run, from Dundonnell, by An Teallach (3,484 feet), Sgurr Fiona (3,473 feet), round Loch na Sealga, down by Ruadh Stac Mor (3,014 feet), past Fionn, then into Poolewe. Twenty-nine miles through Strathnasheallag and Fisherfield forests. Fun?

The road turns north-east at the west end of Loch Maree and climbs the hill to cross Kernsary stream at a high, locked gate. The National Trust for Scotland owns land to the north-west, crested by Meall an Leathaid Dharaich and Carn an Eich Dheirg, and as you hike past new woodlands at the top of the first rise Loch Kernsary sparkles below, spread over the moor in long silver fingers and crooked bays, offering magnificent westwards views to Loch Ewe and the stormy seas of the North Minch. When we passed last summer, a graceful hind, belly-deep in yellow flag and sweet meadow grass, drank from the outlet burn surrounded by clumps of purple heather and backed by the vivid silver-blue loch. An unforgettable moment.

As the broken road twists and turns past Kernsary Lodge, climbing ever higher, majestic mountains bid you welcome. Spidean na Clach, Beinn Airigh Charn and Martha's Peak. Martha was tending cattle on high summer grazings when she dropped a spindle of thread. In attempting to retrieve it she fell to her death and the peak has been known by her name ever since.

A short distance past Kernsary, the track divides and we follow the right hand fork, up the line of Allt na Creige burn, skirting north slopes of mountains, by the forbidding sheer cliffs of Beinn Airigh Charn, past a series of inviting lochs and lochans: na Moine, nan Clach Dubh and finally, Beannach Mor and Beannach Beag. This was the route to the old fishing hut, before things were sited upmarket at north end of Fionn, and it is still known as Old Boathouse Bay. A bustling stream empties into Fionn, a favourite salmon lie.

Climb the headland above Beannach Beag and look east up Fionn. The end of the loch is gripped by seemingly inaccessible, frighteningly steep slopes; Ben Lair leading to Slioch; A'Mhaighdean and Mullach Mhic Fhearchair; Ruadh Stac Mor and Beinn a' Chaisgein Mor. Challenging, difficult climbs and best left alone by unfit, novice, or just plain hillwalkers like me.

A two-mile bankside stumble along the rocky south shore of Fionn leads to New Mooring Bay, protected by scrub-covered Eilean an Eich Bhain. Across the windy loch, in the bay below Beinn a' Chaisgein Beag, is the site of one of Scotland's remotest shops, on the line of a long-dead drove road. As Highland herdsmen cursed lowing black cattle through Fisherfield, the welcome sight must have brought warmth to their hearts and a new spring to their step. For us, a downhill slog to Poolewe before such luck – but wonderful memories to carry on the way.

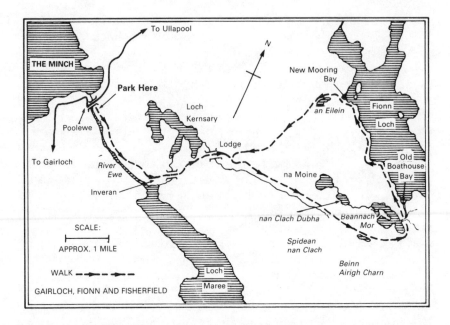

THE MINCH

To Ullapool

Park Here

Poolewe

To Gairloch

River
Ewe

Inveran

Loch
Kernsary

Lodge

New Mooring
Bay

an Eilein

na Moine

nan Clach Dubha

Fionn
Loch

Old
Boathouse
Bay

Beannach
Mor

Spidean
nan Clach

Beinn
Airigh Charn

SCALE:

APPROX. 1 MILE

WALK

Loch
Maree

GAIRLOCH, FIONN AND FISHERFIELD

WHAT YOU NEED TO KNOW

Time and effort Allow a full day for this long, beautiful walk; and choose a good day to do it in. Total distance, there and back, approximately 13 miles. No serious climbs or problems other than the weather and weary legs towards the end. The section along the south shore of Fionn is tiring as there is no real path and the going is rough. Take it easy.

Location Ordnance Survey Sheet 19, Gailoch and Ullapool, second series, scale 1:50,000.

Grid references Poolewe and start 858808; Inveran 874786; Kernsary 894804; fork in track 897803; Old Boathouse Bay 945779; New Mooring Bay 928810.

Route Ample parking space in car park on north side of River Ewe near the school. The road leads south-east from here, along the banks of the river, turning north-east at Inveran. Follow the road uphill to the gate over Kernsary Burn. There is a stile. From there walk on past Loch Kernsary to the lodge.

Past Kernsary Lodge the track forks. Go right. As you climb, the path becomes faint but with common sense and compass and map you will not go far wrong. Keep the large lochs on your left and, immediately past the little loch on your right, bear down to Fionn and Old Boathouse Bay. Follow the south shore, left, to the north end of Fionn, where you will arrive at New Mooring Bay. A good track leads back to the fork in track and Poolewe.

29

The Mountain of the Birds

*B*EINN AN EOIN in Wester Ross is strictly for birds and lovers of wild places. Indeed, the Gaelic name means 'mountain of the birds' and this 2,801-foot peak is home to some of Scotland's most beautiful and elusive species.

Golden eagle nest amongst high corries in nearby Beinn Eighe Nature Reserve, delicately feeding snow-downed chicks on carefully sized morsels of rabbit, hare and anything else stupid enough to move below their fierce gaze. Greenshank flit and pipe over hidden valleys. Dippers dash and splash in shallow, tumbling streams. Snow bunting, dotterel and ptarmigan haunt high tops. Peregrine and raven engage in endless territorial battle. Golden plover dance along the tracks and the hills are loud with the song of curlew, snipe, and sandpiper.

But the grandest prize of all was spotted on 23 June 1970, the first recorded instance of great northern diver nesting in the Highlands of Scotland. Nethersole-Thompson described this historic moment: 'While fishing among wooded islands on a loch in Wester Ross, Eric Hunter saw a large diver with a black head – in sharp contrast to the grey head and hind neck of the black-throated diver. Hunter took no chances. He watched and noted: 'The birds were undoubtedly great northern divers.' This strange diver had two young, which often dived and were hard to see against the background of loch and shore scrub.

Ann and I weren't so lucky when we tramped out into the magnificent wilderness but everything else was perpetual pleasure and for once the weather was spectacularly well behaved – long, cloudless, summer days, warmed by July sun, cooled by soft southerly breezes from the Atlantic. On a calm morning I parked by the hut near Loch Bad an Sgalaig and fell in the troops: Ann, Breac, Heathcliff and me. Our destination, Beinn an Eoinn, Poca Buidhe and Loch na h-Oidhche, 'the loch of the night'.

Civilization lay ten miles distant at Gairloch, where we were staying in one of Harry Davies's cottages at Creag Mhor Hotel. For the time being, however, we were alone amidst a mountain and moorland wonderland, Loch na h-Oidhche is cradled between Beinn an Eoinn to the east and Baosbheinn, 'the wizards' mountain' to the west. From the road, their dark slopes look intimidating. Both are substantial mountains, just below 3,000 feet; but, beside overbearing neighbours, they become mere children.

Slioch spears northwards above the blue waters of island–clad Loch Maree, backed by a mad thrust of Fisherfield peaks. Climbing southwards into the hills, Torridon Mountains line the horizon in splendid array: Beinn Alligin, 'the mountain of beauty'; Beinn Dearag, 'the great rocky peak; Carn na Feola, 'the hill of the flesh'; and, rising above all, the sheer, black, north face of Liathach, 'the grey one'.

Full of hope, we crossed the little wooden bridge over the outlet burn of Am Feur Loch and struck southwards. Well, Ann, Heathcliff and I crossed the bridge. Breac dashed straight into the stream and had to be dragged protesting from his early morning swim. Heathcliff stayed close to heel; he has a long memory and ingrained distrust of water. Can't say I blame him either, given his Scourie experience.

We caught second breath as the stony path climbed between Meall a Ghlas Leothaid and Meall Lochan a'Chleirich to edge round Meall na Meine. Wet, rough going, down the slope to the valley of Abhainn a'Gharb Choire, the outlet stream from Loch na h-Oidhche. We rested, watching the black and white flash of a dipper darting amongst tiny waterfalls. Breac resumed his interrupted swim and charged upstream as we walked on, Beinn an Eionn now tamed in height by our rising approach.

A final valley and slow climb brought us to a flat, boulder-scattered plateau and shining levels of the loch: a narrow, wind-filled channel, one and a half miles long by almost half a mile wide.

Crystal-clear waters lapping a soft, sandy northern bay. Loch na h-Oidhche contains perfectly matched, beautiful wild brown trout which weigh approximately 12 ounces and fight like the devil. High-summer fishing at its finest.

The slopes of Beinn an Eoin rise steeply from the shores of the loch and a path runs down the east shore; but, to fully appreciate this mystical land, climb the north shoulder and walk along the wide ridge to the summit at the south end. Beyond 'the mountain of the birds' lie Gorm Loch Fada and Gor Loch na Beinne: promontories, fishy corners, sandy bays, tempting weed beds – an angler's delight.

But the most startling aspect of the view is the sudden shock of first sight of Ruadh Stac Mor (3,309 feet), Sail Mor (3,217 feet), and the famous Triple Buttress of A'Chonneach: an amazing, uncompromising howl of mountain pleasure, scarred and screed to the shores of lonely Loch Coire Mhic Fheachair, cupped in its bosom. Beinn Eighe, Liathach, Slioch and Fisherfield summits crowd round with golden moorlands brushing their feet, ribboned with silver streams, specked blue with secret lochans – a Bach-like cathedral world of spire and steeple; a glorious hymn of praise to nature.

Descending from Beinn an Eoinn, we spent the night in the bothy at Poca Buidhe, at the south end of Loch na h-Oidhche, by the yellow stone. In days gone by the hollow below this huge boulder used to provide shelter for 'fishers, stalkers and other liars'; now there is a comfortable, well equipped cottage instead.

The following morning we walked south from Poca Buidhe, across wide granite pavements, over rough, trackless moors. For two hours we tramped in solitude, broken only by startled herds of stately red deer, south to a tiny water between Sail Mor and Carn na Feola called Loch nan Cabar, where we caught lunch. Bearing out prize back to Poca Buidhe, we cooked the small fish and ate royally.

In warm afternoon sun, with rising trout stippling the surface of Loch na h-Oidhche, the sense of peace was a tangible, living thing. You feel small and insignificant; yet, more surely than words can ever explain, you know that you also are an important part of this timeless beauty, with as much right to be there as raven, deer or wild cat. If the hills and mountains of my native land mean anything, that is what they mean to me.

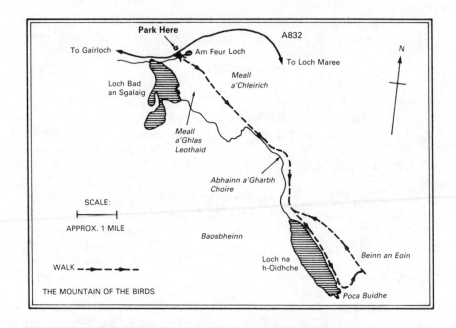

The Mountain of the Birds map. Labels: Park Here; A832; To Gairloch; Am Feur Loch; To Loch Maree; N; Meall a'Chleirich; Loch Bad an Sgalaig; Meall a'Ghlas Leothaid; Abhainn a'Gharbh Choire; SCALE: APPROX. 1 MILE; Baosbheinn; WALK; Loch na h-Oidhche; Beinn an Eoin; Poca Buidhe; THE MOUNTAIN OF THE BIRDS

WHAT YOU NEED TO KNOW

Time and effort   This is a long, rough walk along a stony, often wet track. The total distance from Loch Bad an Sgalaig via Beinn an Eoin to Poca Buidhe and back is approximately thirteen miles and you should allow six hours. Apart from the long slog and the possibility of bad weather, nothing to worry about. If you plan to walk further south from Poca Buidhe, allow another three hours.

Location   Ordnance Survey Sheet 19, Gairloch and Ullapool second series, scale 1:50,000.

Grid references   Loch Bad an Sgalaig 854713; car park and start point 856721; Loch na h-Oidhche 890887; Beinn an Eoin summit 905646; Poca Buidhe 899644.

Route   Follow the A832 from Gairloch to Loch Maree and about quarter of a mile past Loch Bad an Sgalaig there is a hut on your left. Park here. On your right you will see the wooden bridge that crosses the outlet burn of little Am Feur Loch. Cross this bridge and follow the well marked path south. When you reach Loch na h-Oidhche, climb the north shoulder of Beinn an Eoin and walk south to the summit.

Descend carefully from the top, down the west slope, avoiding the crags at the south end, to Poca Buidhe. From here, either walk further south to explore the moorland between Beinn an Eoin and Liathach, or follow the loch-side track northwards, back to the car.

30

Black Isle Fossils and Saints

THE BLACK ISLE is a fertile finger of farmland dividing the Cromarty and Moray firths in north-east Scotland. One explanation of the name is the fact that during harsh northern winters the gentle peninsula is often snow-free when surrounding hills are blanket-white.

A Pictish tribe, known to the Romans as the Decantae, settled and worked the land, blissfully unaware of the turmoil the legions of Rome were causing their southern neighbours. The Roman advance of AD 79 stopped short of Ross-shire, on the south shores of the Moray Firth, and the Picts were left largely to their own devices, to flourish, struggle, and eventually perish at the hands of invading Norsemen. However, these stern Vikings soon succumbed to the persuasive ministrations of the infant thrusting nation of Scots.

One of the Black Isle's most famous sons was Hugh Miller, a stonemason and self-taught geologist of extraordinary ability. He was born in 1802 in the little village of Cromarty, once a busy fishing port, now a cluster of neat houses and holiday homes lining the far north-east shore of the Isle. Hugh Miller's thatched cottage is cared for by the National Trust for Scotland and is now an orderly museum, depicting the life and work of this well-loved humble man of Ross.

Hugh Miller discovered and explored the fossil fish of the Black Isle Syncline, rocks of the Old Red Sandstone period, 350–400 million years old, and described his findings in a book, *The Old Red Sandstone*, published in 1841. I visited the neat cottage to prepare myself for a walk to Hugh Miller's fossil beds, and came away head ringing with strange names but with a clearer picture of our ancient lands and a better understanding of what I hoped to see by the wild shores of the Moray Firth.

On a warm, autumn day, I parked at Eathie Mains Farm and walked back up the road to the end of a mixed plantation of new conifers and old hardwoods. The locked gate is crossed by a wooden stile and a track follows the side of the wood, red-soiled and muddy. Golden barley, heads drooping for harvest, waved and rustled in a soft breeze.

Stately foxgloves lined the woodside bank, watched by lazy bluebells sleeping amidst roots of gnarled oak. The wind whispered through friendly beech, brown with winter's coming. Tiny yellow-headed tormentil peaked at my passing from purple heather and that ultimate botanical survivor, rose-bay willow-herb, grew in profusion along the track.

The sad stones of a ruined croft lie tumbled in a field close to a reed-fringed pond, alive with the hum and buzz of insects, and at the next gate a notice reminds me to 'beware of young trees'. Attacked by bulls and angry farmers, yes, but young trees? I stopped at the gate to munch a good Scots pie, watched closely by a brightly dressed chaffinch, waiting hopefully for crumbs.

The track winds to the top of the cliff where there is a first glimpse of water – the Moray Firth, shimmering, heat-haze-hung to the distant outline of Invernes-shire. Larks twitter and a female corn bunting bustles by, busy with something or other in yellow-flowered whins. On the silver-blue sea an oil tanker heads ocean-wards, small and insignificant against the horizon, and the track plunges down the cliff by heather banks and clumps of orange-yellow ragwort. Butterflies dance in afternoon sunlight amidst gossamer spider webs and the deep throb of the tanker's engine reverberates underfoot.

Black-backed gulls raise noisy protest as I reach the shore by Eathie Fishing Bothy. Southwards, the finger of Chanory Point, crowned by white lighthouse, reaches across the firth to the gaunt symmetry of Fort George, completed in 1769 and used ever since as military barracks. The oil-rig construction yard at Ardersier throws up dark steeples of steel, stark against green and gold Nairnshire fields.

A narrow track runs along the edge of the stony beach, through banks of meadowsweet and tangled rose-hip bushes. Stumbling time, eyes down, watching for pitfalls. After a few hundred yards I am forced onto the boulder-strewn shore. A family of pied wagtails flit and dart welcome on the rocks. Suppose they are being taught the rudiments of feeding; seaweed-covered rocks abound with insects for practice. The parent birds work hard, encouraging their youngsters to ever greater efforts.

Now a different sound of water, and I discover Eathie Gorge, with the old stream chattering down the narrow glen to the sea. More than one hundred years past, Hugh Miller searched for fossils here. I sit on a rock, looking out to sea, surrounded by millennia of history.

Wild, ancient rocks; jagged, red, black, blue, white and grey. Finely weathered into fantastic shapes and patterns, as old as when our world first burst from the darkness of limitless space. Strange marks scar their surface, painting a picture of gasping life struggling from the ocean: 'calcareous shales, containing hard limey nodules with occasional fragments of primitive armour-plated fish'.

The sides of the gorge are a monstrous tangle of birch and bracken, specked yellow with patches of fallen sand, wrenched from the raised beach that runs the length of the south shore. The burn sings softly and I feel a presence: people watching. I turn, expecting to see them, these fantasy figures of my mind, as Hugh Miller saw them – the fairies of Eathie Glen.

I walked eastwards, across the awesome saw-edged rocks, and arrived at a single grass- and daisy-covered stack, linked to the shore by a tide-washed stony causeway. Just the place for lunch, sheltering in the warm lee, lazy lingering. Sleep comes easy here. Too easy. I awoke with a start to find the waves washing the stones and had a wet mad scramble back to the shore.

Round the next headland, where massive rocks have been torn from the cliff and tumbled onto the shore, lies my goal – St Bennet's Well. An inquisitive wheatear guides me through the boulders, white-tailed, bobbing ahead. Then the final bay, watched by a half-hidden ruined shoreside shack, full of dust and old fishing nets.

Alder, birch and willow and waist-high ferns hide the site of the well. I stumble through the tangle until I almost fall into a soft, mossy, emerald-green pool, where the saintly Bennet no doubt stooped to drink. Me, I'm just wet. Retreating to the shore, I sit on a throne-like rock in evening sunlight, tide at my feet, brown-edged waves smoothing wrinkled sand. Fulmers cruise by, stiff-winged. I watch, like some ornithological king presiding over his screaming, squabbling, myriad sea-gull courtiers.

Hard to leave – to start the shore-side stumble, past the fantastic fossil beds, back to Eathie Bothy and up the cliff. On the stiff climb, an anxious lizard scurries across the dusty path. Drops of sweat splash at my feet, I rest. Northwards, the mountain circle of Ben Wyvis colours and changes as clouds throw endless shadows scudding from corrie to summit. A robin, bright-eyed and cheerful, speaks from the stile, keeping me company through the last moments of my sea-walked fairy-spell day.

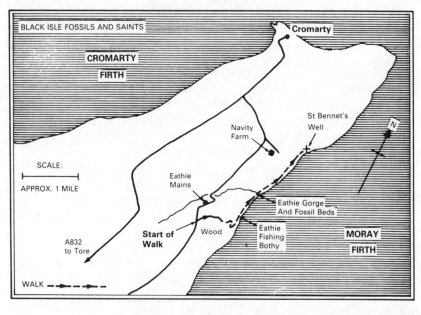

WHAT YOU NEED TO KNOW

Time and effort   Visit Hugh Miller's Cottage in Cromarty first, 17½ miles east of the new roundabout at Tore on the Black Isle. Turn eastwards along the A832. This is a National Trust property, with museum and video display of Hugh Miller's life. Open to the public from Easter to 30 September, Monday–Saturday, 10 a.m. to noon and 1–5 p.m.; Sundays 2–5 p.m., June to September only. Choose a good day for the walk and try to avoid a south wind, blowing onto the shore. The only real effort required is going up and down the cliff. This should be taken gently. Wear stout shoes. The track can be muddy and the shore is rocky. The walk takes four hours, allowing for time to stop and stare.

Location   Ordnance Survey Sheet 27, Nairn, second series, scale 1:50,000.

Grid references   Cromarty 787675; Eathie Mains Farm 771639; Eathie Wood 769636; Eathie Fishing Bothy 777635; Eathie Gorge and fossil beds 784641; St Bennet's Well 792651.

Route   Park the car at Eathie Mains Farm, making sure that you first ask permission to do so. Turn right out of the farm and walk back up the road to the small wood on your left. There is a red–painted gate with a stile over. This is the start of the walk. Follow the track over the field and, eventually, down onto the beach. Turn left and walk on to Eathie Gorge and St Bennet's Well. Return the same way.

31

Stac Polly Saga

ANN AND I arrived late. The drive from Caithness to Assynt had
been difficult – busy, fog-blanketed roads crowded by motorists with little experience of driving on single-track northern
highways. The concept of using passing places to allow overtaking
was beyond them. Darkness had fallen by the time we reached
Ledmore Junction and turned down the thankfully wide A836 to
Elphin.

The old school building at Elphin is used by parties of young
people, accompanied by their teachers, as a base from which to
explore the surrounding area. This time there had been difficulty in
getting a female adult to join the group, in order to keep tabs on the
two girls present. I could understand why this was necessary
because one of the young ladies requiring tabbing was my daughter, Lewis-Ann.

Ann had been roped in to help – much to Lewis-Ann's discomfort. She had been looking forward to a weekend off the lead with
her love of the moment, a large, lanky, speechless boy much given
to nose picking and occasional grunts. I tagged along to provide
moral support, and to introduce a few of the gang to the fine art of
fly fishing.

This was our first visit to Assynt and I rose after a near-sleepless night on a near-springless bed to introduce myself to our new surroundings. Stumbling outside, cursing the weak moment when I had agreed to come, I rubbed sleep from my eyes, and gawped!

Mountains crowded round, startlingly near. I reached out to touch them. Early morning sunlight etched their graceful shapes in a cloudless blue sky. I had never seen anything so magnificent. Which was the start of our love affair with Assynt, Inverpolly and Coighach. We have been returning ever since to walk and fish amidst this awesome mountain and moorland wilderness.

Stac Polly is an old friend: 2,009 feet of crazy peaks and pinnacles. The view from the top is one of the finest in Scotland: island-studded Loch Sionascaig, wandering seventeen twisting miles round hidden bays and dark headlands; a glimpse of tiny Lochan Dearg a'Chuil Mhoir, nestling in the corries of Cul Mor. That great Scottish poet Norman MacCaig, in his poem 'Musical Moment in Assynt', said of Cul Mor: 'And God was Mozart when he wrote Cul Mor.'

Northwards, Suilven, the Vikings 'pillar mountain', thrusts its grey saddled bulk skywards; Suilven's crown, Caisteal Liath, the 'grey castle', towers over desolate, tree-less moors. Quinag and Ben More Assynt line the horizon and the gentle shoulder of Canisp strides by Veyatie and crooked Loch Cama.

Southwards, above the blue and silver of Loch Lurgainn, Ben More Coigach praises the heavens, knifed by the sandstone edge of Sgurr an Fhidhleir, Sgurr Tuath and Sgorr Deas. Across the golden Summer Isles lie the mountains of Harris and Lewis, abed amidst Atlantic haze, Skye Cuillins and majestic An Teallach guarding 'destitution road' at Dundonnell.

One of our favourite walks starts from the old quarry by Linneraineach, on the road between Drumrunie and Achiltibuie. The track follows a fence line, leading gently over the west hip of Cul Beag and down to Loch an Doire Dhuibh, then round little Loch Lon na h-Uamha and up the north face of Stac Polly. A glorious introduction to the delights of Inverpolly, climaxed by a panoramic view from the summit.

However, recently, I made a quicker visit to Stac Polly. In fact three quicker visits, all in pursuit of the photograph which adorns the front of this book. After a meeting in Lairg concerning the damage being done to the north by mass afforestation, I dashed westwards hoping to zip up and snap a gripping sunset. My only companions were Breac, my golden retriever, a self-focusing camera and a tripod.

Littered like a *War of the Worlds* combatant, I approached Polly from the large car park where Lurgainn narrows and struggled up the hill, tripod banging awkardly, Breac bounding ahead, panting to the rocky promontory below the crest on the east flank. Me panting, not the dog. Late afternoon sun was sinking, so, ignoring a growing gale, I set to work with gusto. Position camera, adjust tripod, mark my spot, call Breac to heel, press self-timer, dash to mark.

On the basis that only one out of every hundred photographs I take is usable, I had brought along five million films, and I danced around the rocks, grimacing and leering from all possible angles. Just before shot number 35 of the first reel, whilst I was adopting a particularly dramatic stance, peering eyes shaded into the distance, disaster struck.

The look on my face turned to one of horror as I watched the tripod collapse, blown over by the wind. Tripod and camera hit the deck and the camera back flew open, ruining an hour of jaw-breaking smiles. Worse, the camera was badly damaged, so there was no possibility of starting again. Unsure whether to laugh or cry, I did both and shuffled sadly downhill to face the 130-mile drive home.

My family are very supportive. They can be relied upon to rally round when things go wrong – as they frequently do with me. First, however, I had to keep my hands from their heads as they fell about laughing when I described what had happened. New plans were laid. Ann would accompany me the following morning and take charge of the situation. I was to do nothing other than what I was told, pretty damn quick, no arguing.

Off early at 4 a.m. to catch sunrise. Dawn broke as we reached the car park. So did the weather. Torrential rain, thick mist and not even a finger in front of your nose to be seen, let alone Stac Polly. We sat in the car, sipping coffee. After all, it is well known that west coast weather changes quickly. It did, and got worse. After four hours we abandoned hope and drove home: another wasted 260-mile round trip.

Plan B was then activated. We decided that at the first hint of a good day we would drop everything and dash. Three days later we awoke to a perfect morning, not a cloud in sight and the promise of hours of highly photogenic weather. Within minutes we were in the car, speeding south over the Ord of Caithness, hell-bent for Stac Polly.

Everything went superbly and there were no accidents. I did as I was told and Ann did the camera work. Hard, keeping my mouth shut for such a long time. Hard also keeping warm, whilst we waited for the sun to move along Coigach and Inverpolly crests in order to capture the best shots.

Still, as with most things, Ann had the answer. In between taking photographs, we warmed ourselves by going up and down Stac Polly, like yo-yos. I lost count of the number of times I stumbled up the broken muddy track on the north face. 'Come on, Ann, give it a rest, for goodness sake. I'm knackered.'

Her reply was predictable: 'No arguing I said and no arguing I meant. Stop moaning and get a move on.' By the end of the day I knew every inch of the hill; but I was as warm as toast. When we reached home that evening, for the first time ever Breac was really exhausted – a stone-like golden heap of mud-bespattered dog. I joined him, just as stone-like, and slept the sleep of the just. As we professional photographers say, it was 'in the can'.

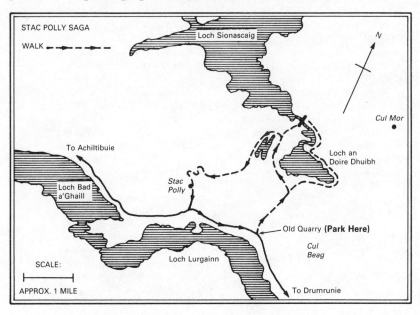

WHAT YOU NEED TO KNOW

Time and effort   The walk from Linneraineach Quarry, round Loch an Doire Dhuibh, then up and over Stac Polly, takes about four hours. You may extend this by turning right at Doire Dhuibh and going round the north shore, crossing the stream by an old bridge just before the river flows into Loch Sionascaig.

This is an easy walk with a good track most of the way, but the hike over the moor to the north face of Stac Polly is rough going, so be well-shod. The hike up Polly is a brief, fierce, stiff climb. Take it easy. No prizes for being there first.

If you do this walk in winter, remember that the north face of Stac Polly is hidden from the sun for most of the day. Consequently, ice will still cling to the rocks, making them very dangerous. The greatest care is advised in all your movements.

Location   Ordnance Survey Sheet 15, Loch Assynt, second series, scale 1:50,000.

Grid references   Drumrunie 166055; Linneraineach Quarry 126090; Loch an Doire Dhuibh 135107; Loch Lon na h-Uamha 128109; Stac Polly 108106; Stac Polly car park 108096.

Route   Park in the old quarry and walk up the hill, following the fence line. The track is well marked. As you come down the flank of Cul Beg, which is on your right, a track branches off left. Go straight on if you want a slightly longer walk. If not, bear left and follow the track between the two lochs. Walk round the north end of the small loch and head straight up the hill towards Stac Polly. As you near the rocky summit, look out for small cairns which line the narrow path up to the top. This path is rough but well defined and it leads you in a gentle series of zigzags to the crest.

Descend from Stac Polly down the steep south face. Descend with maximum caution. The slope is spread with loose rocks. Once off the crest, a wide, soggy track takes you downhill to the car park. At the car park, turn left and walk along the road back to the quarry.

32

Salmon and Suilven

A FEW MILES north from Inverpolly National Nature Reserve near Inverkirkaig, Ross-shire and Sutherland meet. A narrow road crosses Aird of Coigach, twisting and turning towards Sutherland past deep roadside lochans, reaching the sea at Loch an Eisg-brachaidh – a bay of tide-marked rocky islands, alive with Atlantic waves endlessly threatening to tear the little road from the hillside.

Ann and I left early that morning, packing lunch and dogs with urgent speed, bound for Kirkaig river, Fionn Loch and Suilven. But the sudden sparkle of sea at Eisg stopped us and we were happy to watch awhile as curlew and sandpiper went about their business. Oystercatchers poked moodily amongst seaweed-covered stones and a seal popped up to say hello. It was the sort of morning when you knew that all was right with the world.

This was a special day, our silver wedding anniversary, and we planned to celebrate it properly, on Caisteal Liath, Suilven's rounded western peak. Vikings called the mountain Sul-fjall, the pillar mountain, for, as they edged their longships cautiously down Assynt's rocky coast, they saw only the huge bulk of Suilven's west face, rearing above Loch Inver Bay in a mighty sandstone tower.

Suilven is one of Scotland's most dramatic and most inaccessible mountains. You have to work hard to get there. It hearts Glencanisp Forest and no matter how you approach there is a five-mile moorland tramp before reaching the lower slopes. The mountain is only a modest 2,399 feet in height and yet, seen from a distance, towering over a loch-sprinkled landscape, Suilven is a lordly masterpiece of ancient Lewisian gneiss and Torridonian sandstone.

There are four principal lines of attack: from the east from Ledmore Junction and round Cama, the crooked loch; from the north-west, via the estate road and the beautiful Glencanisp Lodge; from the south by following the Kirkaig river; and, perhaps easiest, up the long ribbon of Loch Veyatie by boat. For us, all routes are dangerous because they skirt superb trout lochs, and we find it hard to resist the temptation to stop and fish, getting nowhere fast in the process.

Which is why we planned our visit in April, when only the most foolhardy fish rise and only the most foolhardy anglers brave biting cold to catch them at it. Highland April fanfares spring. Days fight and squabble over whether or not to be reasonable or wild. Sunny mornings change suddenly to nightmare storms. Good weather is a matter of luck and nothing is predictable – other than that you are going to be wet, dry, hot and cold probably several times each day.

Our base was at Achiltibuie in the Summer Isles, where we had rented a comfortable, well equipped cottage for the duration. During summer months this is a busy, popular tourist area but, in early April, delightfully deserted. Days were spent walking in Coigach and Assynt; evenings, relaxing, reading, and watching Turner sunsets from the panorama window overlooking the bay. After a quick dash to the pub.

Before setting off up Kirkaig, Ann and I visited Achins bookshop at the end of a little track leading from the bridge over the river – surely the remotest bookshop in Britain. Alex and Agnes Dickson preside over a stock of 15,000 volumes and have built up the business to include a library service and an excellent range of woollens and tweeds, deerskin, hornware, pottery and paintings.

The path to Suilven follows a good track along the north bank, past deep, silent pools where salmon lie. They run Kirkaig from

March onwards and fishing for them requires strength, skill and feet like a mountain goat's. Near the head of the river are spectacular falls, plunging sixty feet into a dark, sombre, cliff-crowded pool. Instructions for landing salmon from the pool are as follows:

'Slide down to the right-hand side of the fishing stance, and onto a ledge. There is a rope attached to the rock as a handhold. When the fish is gaffed, both gaff and fish are handed up to the angler, who must take care not to let the fish off the gaff and drop on the head of his gillie!'

During the long, slow climb Suilven is hidden from view and it is not until you reach Fionn Loch, the white loch, that Suilven's full majesty is revealed. From the boat mooring bay, across smooth blue waters, the bulk of Caisteal Liath, the grey castle, challenges you to climb him. Skirt loch and at the little sandy bay on the north shore stride across rock-strewn lower slopes to do so.

A wide, steep gully leads upwards to the centre of the mountain, Bealach Mor. No matter what anyone says, a gut-busting scramble. From Bealach Mor a broad ridge points to the summit of Caisteal Liath – sheer round three sides, unexpectedly grassy and sparkled with quartzite boulders on top. More hardy souls than I traverse eastwards along the narrow crest to Meall Mheadhonach, which requires great care and a head for heights.

By the time Ann and I reached Fionn Loch the weather had turned nasty, and decided to stay nasty. We huddled frozen, sheltering by a peat hag, surveying wind-lashed waves screaming down Fionn. Over rims of steaming mugs of coffee, we watched Caisteal Liath disappear in a flurry of snow. Clouds crept down Bealach Mor and soon the whole mountain was hidden from view. To attempt the climb in these conditions would be courting disaster. Discretion and valour time.

But it was hard to leave that wild place and we lingered, thoughtful, silent. Two thirty arrived, the hour when we were hitched near Tron Kirk in the old grey city of Edinburgh.

'What are you thinking, Ann?' I asked.

'You know,' she replied, 'some people would think it madness to spend their wedding anniversary freezing in a snow storm on the shores of a Highland loch.'

I paused, wondering. 'Do you?'

'Of course not, there is no place I would rather be. Happy anniversary, dear.'

Calling dogs to heel, we turned our backs on Suilven and tramped down to Kirkaig. The champagne was on ice, ready waiting at Achiltibuie.

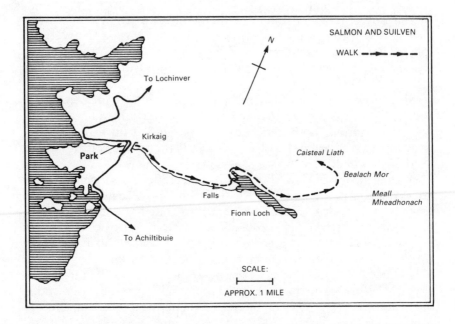

To Lochinver

Kirkaig

Park

Caisteal Liath

Bealach Mor

Meall
Mheadhonach

Falls

Fionn Loch

To Achiltibuie

SCALE:
├───┤
APPROX. 1 MILE

WHAT YOU NEED TO KNOW

Time and effort   A full day's
time and effort. The Kirkaig
approach to Suilven is an easy,
rising walk. Bealach Mor will test
your fitness and stamina, but there
is no need to hurry so take your
time and enjoy the climb. Treat the
summit of Suilven with respect.
Reaching Caisteal Liath is simple
and safe; Meall Mheadhonach
requires caution and is best left
alone if you are inexperienced.

Location   Ordnance Survey
Sheet 15, Loch Assynt, second
series, scale 1:50,000.

Grid references   Loch an Eisg-
brachaidh 073176; car park 086194;
Kirkaig Falls 121179; mooring bay
on Fionn 124177; Bealach Mor
158181; Caisteal Liath 154184;
Meall Mheadhonach 165178.

Route   There is a good car park
near the bridge at Kirkaig river.
The Fionn–Suilven track leads
eastwards from the bridge, through
a gate on the north bank of the
river. Follow your nose. You have
to divert right from the path to
view Kirkaig Falls. Take care in wet
weather.

   By prior arrangement, shorten
your walk by rowing across Fionn
to the north shore. Permission to
do so from Culag Hotel in
Lochinver. Otherwise, tramp
round the west shore and then angle
towards Bealach Mor, which is
easily recognisable. From there on
in it's up. The view from the top is
worth every gasp.

33

Canisp and Inchnadamph Caves

CANISP is a lady. Mature, gentle, serene and welcoming. Her neighbours are more brusque: the sudden, male shock of Suilven 'one sandstone chord that holds up time in space'; masculine Ben More Assynt, long-ridged and pinnacled; the triple sweep of Quinag and corried Cul Mor. Eleven miles of Assynt mountains, none of which falls below 2,000 feet.

Ann and I parked at the roadside by Loch Awe, a tiny shadow of its famous Argyllshire namesake but none the less beautiful – shallow, clear waters, bursting with bright, red-spotted brown trout and an occasional surprise of salmon. Seven scrub- and tree-clad islands scatter Awe, protected by Cnoc an Leathaid Bhuidhe to the west and Beinn an Fhuarain to the east.

Above Loch Awe, Canisp's grey, boulder-strewn shoulder lies like an old dun-coloured skirt; patched purple with heather, silver-threaded by sparkling streams. The walk to the summit (2,779 feet) is an easy three-mile couple of hours' stroll. Indeed, most climbing books describe Canisp as nothing more than a good viewpoint from which to survey surrounding peaks, which is less than true and completely false on the day we chose to mount our assault – mid-April with winter snows covering tops.

Assynt forms the southern boundary between Sutherland and Ross-shire and many years ago the exact boundary line was disputed. In an attempt to end argument, two senior Ross-shire citizens, having first been reminded that their 'feet were on oath', were instructed to walk the marches. They did so, claiming never once to have left Ross-shire soil. Nor had they, for they had filled their shoes with earth from Balnagowan in Easter Ross.

This Highland astuteness is commemorated in the name of the hotel that used to stand at the county boundary on the A837 from Bonar Bridge to Ledmore Junction, Altnacealgach, 'burn of the cheat'. The hotel was once famous throughout Scotland for quality of food, service and sport; but it declined badly and was ravaged by fire in 1985. The last time I passed, even these sad, blackened ruins had been demolished and all sign of the once happy hotel gone.

As we sat in the car by Loch Awe, Canisp looked a daunting prospect. Spring storms raged across the loch, tearing water to shreds, flinging a fine, wet spray over chill moors. The snow line was ominously low. If we wished to reach the top, then we were in for some cold, rough tramping.

Nevertheless, from time to time sun broke through encouragingly and we were prepared for the weather. So, light of heart, we dragged on boots, wrapped up, crossed the outlet stream from Loch Awe and set off uphill, dogs bounding ahead, excited, through the heather.

A faint path pointed the way past lead-grey lochans and, as we climbed, heather receded, giving way to patches of bare, slippery sandstone rock. Weather didn't recede and we were soon walking into the teeth of a howling blizzard. Even the dogs became subdued and we sheltered together, huddled in an untidy human-animal heap. Sunshine again. On up the slow, never-ending slope. Glimpses through the storm of our goal, snow-crowned, shining on the horizon. Then more biting wind-driven sleet.

At about fifteen hundred feet, an amazing tree – someone has planted a little rowan. The infant is protected from Canisp storms by a well built circular wall. Wonder if the tree will survive? Into snow now, hard-packed, thin-crusted over hollows. Every step ever-increasing effort. Summit is cloud-blinded. I feel my body freezing. The animals are miserable. Two thousand five hundred feet. Conference time. We turned back.

Skirting Meall Diamhain we picked up the line of Allt Mhic Mhurchadh Gheir, a long name for such a little stream, the principal feeder burn of Loch Awe. With wicked inconsistency bright sun broke through grey skies and we quickly peeled off heavy layers of clothing, basking in welcome spring warmth. The dogs recovered their spirits and Breac splashed downstream, in and out of crystal-clear limestone pools.

If ever you seek a secret, beautiful place for a family picnic or quiet summer laze, then the upper reaches of this magical burn will provide that location. Even little ones should manage the walk and I know of few more delightful spots in all the Highlands. We arrived back at the car with time to spare and decided to adopt plan B – a visit to Inchnadamph Nature Reserve, a few miles north-east of Loch Awe.

Inchnadamph Hotel is the best centre from which to explore Assynt, a whitewashed fishing and climbing hotel peering west-wards down a wild loch. Willie Morrison presides, greeting guests and visitors alike with old-world Highland charm. Inchnadamph is surrounded by massive limestone outcrops which provide an ideal habitat for rare alpine plants such as sawwort, hawkweed and purple and mountain saxifrage.

Behind the hotel, up Traligill Burn, are the famous Inchnadamph Caves, deep underground passages some five hundred yards long filled with rushing waters. Traligill is the Norse name for Troll's Gill, or Giant's Ravine, and it is believed that mesolithic man inhabited these caves more than six thousand years ago.

We gratefully inhabited one of the caves that afternoon, shelter-ing from another storm that drove huge snowflakes into our numb faces. Then, suddenly, threatening clouds departed, sun shone and

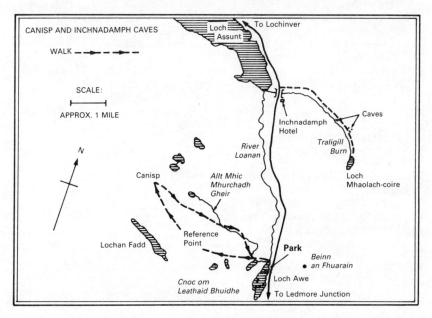

glorious Assynt sparkled before us – the same view hunter-gatherers of old must have blessed and cursed during their endless search for food.

To the north-west the Torridonian bulk of Quinag, snow-capped and glistening, guarding the head of Loch Assynt; graceful, unclimbed Canisp towering to the south-west; whilst above us corries and crags of Conival and Ben More Assynt crowded round. Every step of our day-long snow-swept journey was made worth-while by that single, stunning, humbling vision. We knew we had found something precious: another wonderful memory for the dream bank of the mind.

WHAT YOU NEED TO KNOW

Time and effort In reasonable conditions, this is an easy, delightful walk offering spectacular views from the summit. Seven miles there and back; about four hours. However, take care in bad weather and always go with compass and map. North-east and south-west sides are very steep near the top and, in misty conditions, dangerous.

The walk to the Inchnadamph limestone caves is without problems, other than making sure that you find them all. Ask Willie Morrison in the hotel for additional directions before setting out. Allow about three hours for the round trip.

Location Ordnance Survey Sheet 15, Loch Assynt, second series, scale 1:50,000.

Grid references Park at 249158; Loch Awe 246154; Reference point on hill 229168; summit 204188; stream 232172; Inchnadamph Hotel 251216; limestone caves 272207.

Route There is ample car parking space, off the road, by Loch Awe. Cross the outlet burn at the north end of the loch and find your way up the broad, wide shoulder of the hill. From the top, descend the same way, but angle left to find Allt Mhic Mhurchadh Gheir burn. Follow this back to Loch Awe and the car.

For Inchnadamph limestone caves, park by the hotel and follow the good track that borders the Traligill Burn. There are signposts and you should have no problem finding the caves. One cave is actually in the riverbed. The others are on the south side of Traligill, by the track that leads out to Loch Mhaolach-coire, known locally as the Gillaroo Loch.

34

Seals and Sandwood

THE GREAT fleet sailed south. One hundred warships sparkled with long lines of shields, oars dipping in unison, powered by fierce, merciless men. Men to whom murder came easy. Their leader was old, in a time of youth when survival was chance and old age remarkable. King Haakon of Norway surveyed his force with eagle eyes: eight thousand men, battle-hardened from a hundred fights.

But this was to be Haakon's last battle. Within a few weeks, many of these ships would lie wrecked off the coast at Largs, destroyed by September gales and the cunning of a mere boy – the 22-year-old Scottish monarch, Alexander III. Viking power was broken and Haakon died in Orkney, shepherding the shattered remnants of his fleet home.

When I walk the wild hills and cliffs of the Parph Peninsula I imagine I see this mighty fleet, sailing past Sandwood Bay to meet its doom. Parph means 'turning point' and in August 1263, the year of the Battle of Largs, the Vikings rested weary arms in the long finger of Loch Inchard, close to where the busy fishing port of Kinlochbervie now stands.

Two longships had foundered in heavy seas off A'Chailleach and

Am Bodach – the 'old man' and 'old woman', twin stacks guarding the way south from Cape Wrath. Survivors tried to climb the 300-foot cliffs and the marks of their desperate axe strokes still scar the crags. Six others were killed earlier, when a foraging party was ambushed at Loch Eriboll by clan MacKay, sending Vikings scurrying foodless back to their ships.

The Parph is edged by huge cliffs; 850 foot Cleit Dubh, the 'black cliff', is the highest on mainland Britain. A rutted road wends over desolate moorlands to squat, whitewashed Cape Wrath Lighthouse, completed in 1829. The building stands 370 feet above the sea and its light can be seen from a distance of almost thirty miles. Southwards, Fashven, Creag Riabhach and Farrmheall rise gently from peat-covered moors, and the only way in is by foot.

Sandwood Bay is the most beautiful bay in Scotland. Almost two miles of golden sand, washed clean by long, wind-fringed, blue-green Atlantic breakers born a thousand miles away, sweeping across the ocean to caress desolate Scottish shores. Rocky outcrops, black, sea-sprayed promontories, strut aggressively into the middle of the bay, challenging the elements in an endless battle of surf and thunder.

Northwards, sands mingle with emerald slopes that stride upwards in an amazing array of jagged, dark, stark cliffs, marching to Cape Wrath. South, the slim stack of Am Buachaille, 'the herdsman', breaks the waves in their rush to greet Druim na Buainn. Behind Sahara sand dunes, Sandwood Loch sparkles in summer sunlight, surrounded by green fields specked white with grazing sheep. This is a special, wonderful place. The birthplace of silence. Where time stops and life begins.

This remote corner of north-west Sutherland is one of our secret retreats, frequented by piratical skuas, presided over by golden eagles. When slings and arrows beleaguer flagging spirits Ann and I escape to the Parph, and nothing ever seems so bad when we return. Walking refreshes bits thinking can't reach and there are few finer walks in Scotland than from Oldshoremore to Sandwood.

The road from Laxford Bridge, the A838, turns and twists northwards through a wilderness of heather-clad moorlands, past tiny lochans glimpsed with red-throated divers and hungry grey heron. It climbs, single-tracked, by tumbling, rocky torrents to Rhiconich at the head of Loch Inchard. Turning west to Kinlochbervie is a cultural shock. One moment, wild Highlands; the next, dual carriageway and heavy industry.

Kinlochbervie, packed with piers and boats, is the most important port in Sutherland. Heavy lorries trundle off, loaded with the best of Scottish sea harvest bound for European markets. Those prawns, shrimps and lobsters we gobble greedily whilst on holiday probably passed this way, edging you off the road in the process. Wagons return crowded with Spanish tomatoes and other Continental fruit and vegetables.

Past the port Highland life returns to normal – narrow road bounded by empty hills, sudden clusters of cottages and a heady smell of peat smoke in the air. There are a number of fine, sandy bays along the way; by the crofts at Oldshoremore and Oldshore Beg and just after Blairmore, a notice points north to Sandwood.

Foolhardy or high-wheelbased motorists drive the first two miles of the track leading to Sandwood. Since our last damaged radiator, we park on the road and hoof it. Much more enjoyable, and much less costly. There are tracks and tracks. Some quickly wear you out; others bore you with blank vistas. But this track is the perfect gentleman of all tracks.

A chain of seven shining lochs line the route and the path threads by them. Loch na Gainimh, complete with inviting rowing boat for attacking hard-fighting, red-speckled wild brown trout; delightful a'Mhuilinn, where the track spills onto the sandy east shore, begging you to abandon Sandwood and follow its margins into the hills. My golden retriever, Breac, likes this loch best of all: he swims along, parallel to our progress, and has to be sternly ordered out at the end.

From the highest point of the track the white speck of Cape Wrath Lighthouse blinks above green-brown hills. Reay Forest mountains, bare, scree-scattered, grey peaks, uncompromisingly climb to billowy clouds – the razor-edge of Foinaven and bulky Arkle. Soft winds blow from the dark-gashed gully of Bealach Coir a'Choin, calling you in.

Suddenly, Sandwood Loch, watched by a shepherd's cottage, surrounded by sheepfolds and old stones. Moorland becomes lime-rich pasture, blushing with wild flowers. Then, the glorious, breathtaking, golden sweep of the bay. Footprintless, virgin sands, washed by green seas, surging onto an empty beach.

This is where Sandy Gunn saw his mermaid, sitting on a rocky ledge, gazing wistfully out to sea. At least, that's what Sandy, a local shepherd, reported later; and I believe him. Ann and I were resting on these same rocks last October, watching the endless ballet of dancing, sparkling waves, when a movement in the surf caught our eye. It seemed to be human and, remembering Sandy Gunn's experience, I fumbled for my camera. This would be the photograph of the century and I wanted to be ready.

A young seal was playing in the breakers, surfing to the shore and then swimming out again to repeat the ride. It splashed and

turned, clearly enjoying a moment of most un-seal-like irresponsi-
bility. We watched, transfixed, as the graceful beast turned and
tumbled in the foam.

A large wave washed the seal almost onto the sands and, unaware
of our presence, he flapped ashore in a series of ungainly shuffles.
We could see the whiskered face and bright, black, intelligent eyes
as he settled on the sands to while away a comforting moment in
warm afternoon sun.

After a while, we put the dogs onto their leads and walked
towards the sleeping seal. From about twenty-five yards, he saw us
and decided the sea was a safer place, although we wished him no
harm. We waited as he struggled afloat. The dogs were breathless
with excitement and I slipped Breac. He dashed to the shore,
sniffing furiously, then plunged in. Not a chance, old fellow, I
thought; though I'm sure that they would have been great pals,
given the chance.

A dark head appeared above white foam and we responded with
a cherry wave, thankful for the pleasure he had given us. Then we
turned sadly from the beach to begin the long walk home. The
hardest part was leaving, and we lingered at the top of the hill,
looking longingly back to lovely Sandwood Bay.

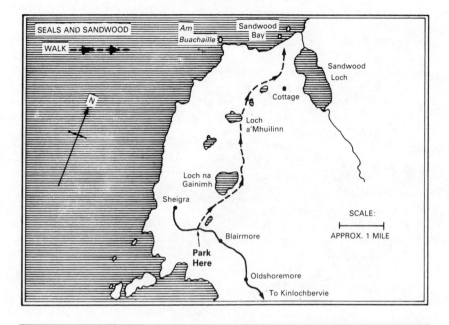

WHAT YOU NEED TO KNOW

Time and effort There and back, this walk is a distance of eight miles along a well defined, easy track. How long it takes depends upon how long you choose to stay at Sandwood Bay. Be warned, once you have seen Sandwood, that could be for ever.

The track is rough so wear stout shoes. Also, be prepared for some muddy splashing after wet weather. Because the walk is relatively simple, it is possible to lug along more than one would perhaps normally carry. Include camera, binoculars and sketch-pad; water colours would be nice too.

Location Ordnance Survey Sheet 9, Cape Wrath, second series scale 1:50,000.

Grid references Laxford Bridge 237468; Rhiconich 255524; Kinlochbervie 220565; Oldshoremore 209585; start of track 195600; Loch na Gainimh 204614; Loch a'Mhuilinn 207630; Sandwood Bay 220650.

Route Drive west from Rhiconich, through Kinlochbervie and Oldshoremore to Blairmore. A few hundred yards past Blairmore you will see a signpost to Sandwood Bay on your right. Park off the road and follow the track. Simple as that. Can't go wrong, but take the map anyway, just in case.

35

Sinking at Scourie

THEY TOOK me for my first real walk when I was six months old. Ten trackless miles across Sutherland moors. I have learned since that puppies should not be exposed to such rigours until at least a year old, but it didn't harm me. Other, that is, than instilling a fear of water – and that was my own fault anyway.

Yorkshire by heritage, I was born and brought up in the old, grey city of Edinburgh. Early days were spent happily under the dining room table, playing with brothers and sisters – a boisterous lot, always ready for a bit of bite-and-tumble. I suppose, being terriers, that's understandable.

Liked the big fellow the moment he appeared in the room, and I rushed round, giving of my best, trying to impress. You see, I heard him say that his wife was a Yorkshire lass and I knew immediately this was the family for me.

My sisters backed off, growling, sensing that silk cushions and fancy ribbons would never be achieved in a home ruled by Him. But who needs ribbons? Should I want to be a canine poof? Great-grandfather Bert, miner's pal all his life, would turn in his grave. So I scuttled to the huge feet and flashed a bright, 9-carat, ear-splitting grin, which secured my future instantly.

That first walk, however, was something else and I confess that there were moments when I wondered if I had done the right thing. Inexperience. After all, coming from Edinburgh, how was I to know the mallard wasn't really injured? She flapped about as though in big trouble. Naturally, I ignored fledglings and chased after her. What would you have done?

Which is how I found myself eyeball-deep in freezing water being blown down the middle of a Scottish loch, whilst the bloody bird made a miraculous recovery, cackling skywards in derision. Cold! Believe me, it was cold. The few scraps of hair I possessed did nothing to protect vital parts and I was certain my last moment had arrived.

It nearly had, and the only reason I'm here telling the tale is because His son, Blair, stripped off and waded after me. Grateful I was, but in retrospect there was no need for Blair to hurl me, like an underdone Yorkshire pudding, twenty yards up the bank. Bruised me something awful. By the time I had recovered and found the scent, the damned birds had flown.

We were staying at Scourie Hotel, which was very comfortable. Every evening, after They went down for dinner, a considerate girl brought me a hot-water bottle. Carefully covering it with blankets, so that I wouldn't be burnt, she gave me a friendly pat, then put the lights out. A real treat, curling up on top of that warm hump. True Highland hospitality.

If I had known then what I know now, they would never have got me out the car. Ben More Assynt, snow and all, I don't mind; even the gut-bursting last hundred feet up the south face of Stac Polly. But Sutherland moorlands are the worst imaginable place for Yorkshire terriers – soggy, bog-filled, heather-humped and tick-ridden.

They walk ten miles. I do forty, at twice their speed. Just to keep up. Do they care? No. It's 'Heathcliff, heel' and 'Heathcliff, come' and Heathcliff do this and Heathcliff do that. First sight of sheep, they have instant apoplexy, particularly Him. Lead-lashed, I find myself being hauled through black, stinking peat hags like some soulless bit of fluff.

We parked that morning by a little lochan, unnamed on the Ordnance Survey map, three miles east along the A894 from Scourie. At least that's what He said. I have come to understand that He couldn't map-read his way out of a paper bag, unless it had hole in the middle and a pint at the end.

Apparently, the proposal was to walk out the Gorm Track (renamed by me 'Gorm-less'), spending the day bird-watching and fishing for something called 'brown trout'. There were six of us: Master and Mistress, Blair and his wife, Barbara, Stanley Tuer, a retired schoolteacher and amazingly fit walker, and me.

The first loch up the hill has one of these funny Gaelic names which I find impossible to pronounce, Loch a'Mhuirt. Apparently it means 'murder loch' and Stan told its story as we tramped by.

Many years ago, a man and his wife lived on one of the islands in the loch. When the Lord of Reay came to stay at Stac Lodge, tenants took him presents. The man sent his wife down to the lodge with a fine hare, but Lord Reay had other ideas about presents and demanded that the woman become his wife. She replied, 'Never, as long as my husband is alive, never.' Reay sent two of his henchmen up the hill to the loch. Seeing them coming, the husband rushed inside and bolted the door.

Flaming arrows set fire to the cottage thatch and when the man ran out they shot him dead. Rowing across, they cut off his head and returned with it to Lord Reay. Bearing the grisly object on a platter, Reay presented it to the woman: 'Madam, your husband is no longer alive and you will be my wife.' Made my skin creep, that story, and I stayed close to Him as we passed the island where the unfortunate man met his doom.

After my escapade with the mallard, I decided to give up swimming and He kept me on the lead all the way to Gorm Loch. Imagine my horror when they piled into a small boat and asked Barbara to lift me aboard. Well, I struggled, of course, but there wasn't much I could do about it. Managed to nip one of His fingers, which made me feel a little better. The next moment we were off, completely surrounded by the cold, dark, awful stuff and escape was impossible.

To this day He claims it was an accident. I know different. He has a nasty streak, usually hidden but sometimes all too obvious. His fishing bag was lying on the stern seat and I had been having a look – you know, just nosing about, chewing the odd glove and reel of nylon, something to do. As He cast, his arm came back and caught me a cracking blow on the side of my head. Next minute I was overboard, fighting for my life again – the second time in two hours.

'Did you hear that fish rise?' He exclaimed. Fish be damned, it was me, going under for the third time. The harder I tried to reach the boat, the further I seemed to drift away. She grabbed the oars and set off after me. 'Hold on, Heathcliff, I'm coming!' She would be too late. My strength was being sapped by freezing water and I knew another ten seconds in the loch and that would be that.

As I sank below the waves my whole life flashed before my eyes: mother's warm tummy, the rag I used to chew, hot milk before the fire. Then, miraculously, I felt myself being lifted to the surface. He had me in his landing net and I was deposited in the bottom of the boat, gasping like a well hooked fish. Fortunately, She is medically qualified and banged and massaged me back to life; but it was a close-run thing.

You would have thought, after such an experience, that the day would have been abandoned, that They would have hurried me home to bed. You would have thought wrong. They asked me if I was all right, tied me to a seat and carried on fishing. I'm dying and they ask me if I'm all right! I will never understand human beings. Sunshine and smiles one moment, drowning you the next.

The rest of the day was spent walking, in pouring rain, and I have never been so cold and miserable in all my life. He must have sensed it because he bent down and, plucking me from the middle of a particularly large clump of sopping heather, stuffed me into the game pocket of his jacket. Thus warmed, I travelled the next three miles, and that rest enabled me to regain sufficient strength to make it back to the car.

In spite of everything, I suppose I really did enjoy the day. The scenery was spectacular: sheep, grouse, deer, ducks and some utterly fascinating smells. The highlight was when I followed one of these scents into a straggle of boulders and came face to face with the most enormous cat I have ever seen.

Cruel yellow eyes blazed from a snarling face and I realized that I would need some help to deal with this fellow. I trotted back and

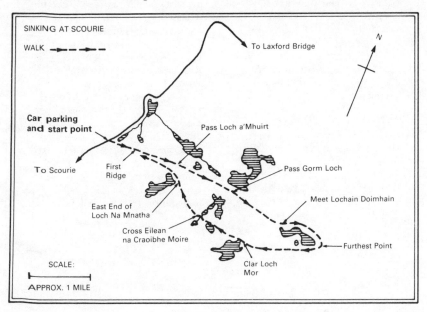

SINKING AT SCOURIE

WALK ▪ ▬ ▪ ▬ ▪ ▬

To Laxford Bridge

N

Car parking and start point

Pass Loch a'Mhuirt

To Scourie

First Ridge

Pass Gorm Loch

Meet Lochain Doimhain

East End of Loch Na Mnatha

Cross Eilean na Craoibhe Moire

Furthest Point

SCALE:

APPROX. 1 MILE

Clar Loch Mor

told Him but he just carried on fishing. I decided that I would have a go anyway, but by the time I got back the cat had escaped. Lucky for him, I thought.

When we arrived at the hotel that evening I was so tired I could hardly eat dinner. My feet were killing me. But She sat beside me, stroking my head, telling that I had been a good boy. I explained about my fear of water and She seemed to understand. That night, when the maid brought my hot-water bottle, I grunted thank you, and was sound asleep before she hit the lights.

WHAT YOU NEED TO KNOW

Time and effort   This is a dramatic walk through magnificent scenery surrounded by mountains, lochs and moorland. Although there are no steep gradients, it is a long, hard walk, particularly in wet weather. The round trip takes about five hours, longer if you wish to have a few casts on the way. If fishing, obtain prior permission from Ian Hay at Scourie Hotel (Tel: 0971-2396).

To follow the route, a compass and map are essential. Even in good weather, it is easy to get lost in this vast landscape. A useful marker in times of trouble is to turn your back on Ben Stack and walk in a straight line. This will, eventually, bring you to the main road. To avoid having to do so, brush up on your map reading.

Location   Ordnance Survey Sheet 9, Cape Wrath, second series, scale 1:50,000.

Grid references   The references given follow the route of the walk from the main road and back again. Start point and car-parking place 185451; first ridge 190449; pass Loch a'Mhuirt at 200445; pass Gorm Loch at 211439; Meet Lochain Doimhain at 222431; furthest point 231427; Clar Loch Mor 214427; cross Loch Eilean na Craoibhe Moire at 205434; east end of Loch na Mnatha 199441.

Route   There are few tracks over the moor so you will have to depend upon accurate map reading to stay on route, which makes this walk a bit of an adventure. Ben Stack is the dominant peak facing you. North-east lie Foinaven and Arkle. So getting your bearings should be easy.

Sometimes, however, it is not; for, apart from the dozens of lochs marked on the OS Sheet, there are others which are not. Nevertheless, with care and caution, you should be able to find your way round. The only steepish part of the walk is when rounding Lochain Doimhain to begin the return journey.

36

The Winds of Hope

Gaunt Dun Dornaigil Broch glowers by the tortuous track through green Strath More in Sutherland. These defensive towers were built by Picts during the final pre-Christian years, sited along fertile, sheltered valleys, close to water and grazing for animals. In wilderness lands, unpenetrated even by the might of Rome, Dicaledonae tended crops, hunted red deer and netted salmon-rich Strathmore River. When danger threatened, families hurried inside and bolted the door.

Brochs were massive structures – drystone built, circular in plan and up to fifty high. Fifteen-foot-thick walls enclosed a space measuring forty feet in diameter and often the marks of timber lean-to dwellings are found inside. They were virtually impregnable, which was just as well, given that the nearest policeman was some two thousand years away.

Strath More is enfolded by graceful Ben Hope, at 3,042 feet Scotland's most northerly Munro and one of the easiest to climb. Westwards, lesser hills rise in tangled ridges to Reay Forest peaks: Cranstackie, Foinaven, Arkle, Creagan Meall Horn and the pinnacle of Ben Stack. Lady Hope towers above all, her craggy cairned head majestically cloud-crowned.

I became interested in Ben Hope, the 'hill of the bay', whilst fishing the loch she guards, one of Scotland's finest sea-trout fisheries. Sea trout and salmon rush short Hope River to the six-mile silver-ribbon loch from May until September; they linger close to shore, scenting gravel spawning beds, freshly washed by winter snows, waiting for egg-heavy, urgent females.

Visitors come from all over the world to battle with the silver inhabitants of Loch Hope, and, to help them find the best places to fish, row the boat and tie on flies, they seek the services of a Highland gillie, the sporting 'gentleman's gentleman'. Even today, many northern gillies speak more Gaelic than English, and prefer to do so; for, in spite of all the efforts of so-called 'improvers' during the eighteenth and nineteenth centuries, the old Celtic tongue survives.

After the taming of the clans, at the terrible carnage of Culloden, in defiance of defeat, Gaelic poetry flourished; and close to the old Pictish tower of Dun Dornaigil is the birthplace of one of the most famous Gaelic bards, Robb Donn, the 'Bard of Sutherland'. Robb Donn, along with others such as Alexander MacDonald, John MacCodrum, Duncan Ban MacIntyre and Dugald Buchanan, created a great lyrical Gaelic history of immense beauty, as alive today as when written two hundred years ago.

Ann and I climbed Ben Hope on a wild October morning. Seeking an early start, we stayed the previous night with Paul Panchaud, at Altnaharra Hotel. Altnaharra is an excellent centre from which to explore the surrounding area and the hotel, at the head of Loch Naver, is one of the oldest in the north – a comfortable, well managed haven, playing host to fishermen and walkers for more than a century.

We parked by the grey broch in torrential rain, wondering at our sanity in even considering an ascent. But the rain passed, tempting us from the warmth of the car. Eager to be off, dogs bounded down to the river, splashing through wet grass, instantly muddied – in Breac's case, being a retriever, up to his middle; Heathcliff, his smaller companion and a brash Yorkshire terrier, just muddy all over.

The keeper's house at Alltnacaillich was busy. Six legs extended from under a sad-looking truck, bits of engine scattered round. Risking rebuke, I checked that a climb on Ben Hope was in order and would not interfere with any stalking parties. Half-Gaelic grunts confirmed we could climb.

Seeing the intense mechanical activity reminded me of the

English visitor whose car had broken down along a wild, lonely stretch of Highland road. After struggling fruitlessly for an hour to restart the engine, the man stopped a passing local riding by on a rusty old bike, chased by a rusty old sheepdog.

The local had a quick look under the bonnet, fiddled a bit and then requested that the stranded motorist turn the ignition key. Magically, the engine fired healthily to life. 'Thank you,' said the visitor. 'You must be a mechanic.' The local paused, considering this statement, then replied: 'Oh, dear me, no. I'm a MacKay from Strathnaver.'

Wind howled as we found and followed the track up behind the house onto the hill. Summer-bleached grass flattened in the gale and Allt na Caillich burn, 'the old woman's burn', rushed white-foamed between steep boulder-strewn banks. The path was soft with autumn rain, marked by deer and sheep, and we struggled upwards, heads bent, shoulders into the storm.

The proud, sheer flanks of Leiter Mhuiseil loomed ahead, thrusting the stream over its ridge in an astonishing sheet of pure silver. Water sprang from rocks, dancing, sparkling droplets, brightening the dark bowl of the corrie. At the foot of the hill the matchbox house seemed an isolated island of calm amidst fierce, timeless elements.

On the exposed ridge, the strength of the wind was an almost animal force and we huddled behind an outcrop of boulders, sipping welcome coffee, assessing our position. The spectacular ridge of Ben Loyal, jagged and knife-like, rose east. The moor shone with lochs and lochans: Meadie, an Dherue, Haluim. West-wards, an azure carpet of Loch Hope; the tiny speck of Loch Bealach na Sgeulachd on Lean Charn; and, beyond, the long finger of sea-Loch Eriboll.

Ahead, the ridge rose gently between Creag Riabhach and the steep cliffs of Leitir Mhuiseil, rearing quickly towards the summit. We walked on for a further quarter of an hour and then decided to abandon the attempt. If the ridge was so exposed and windy, then the summit would be downright dangerous.

Ben Hope is topped by a small, grassy, trig.-pointed plateau, buttressed on three sides by steep cliffs. It would have been impossible to stand there in safety and madness to try. Reluctantly, we turned back down the ridge, promising ourselves that we would return again another, milder day.

As we stumbled, defeated, down the hill, rain fell in solid sheets; the waterfall cascaded endlessly over the cliff. Clouds began to settle on the summit of Ben Hope and we quickened step, anxious to be off the hill before they reached us. Sheep huddled, sodden mournfully, backs against the storm which now raged furiously about our ears.

Back at the broch we leapt, booted, into the car and boosted the heater. The damp smell of wet dogs assaulted our senses. Two tired panting heads thrust between ours, instantly steaming windows. As we drove past Alltnacaillich Cottage I noticed six legs still sticking out from under the truck. Obviously, what they needed was a Mackay from Strathnaver.

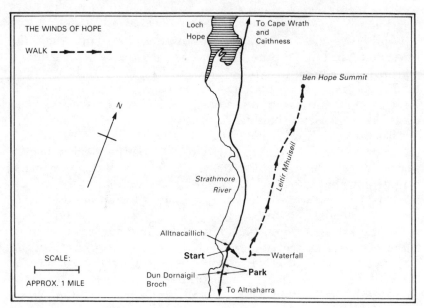

WHAT YOU NEED TO KNOW

Time and effort There and back takes about four hours – a lot more on a hard, windy day. I find the first hike, from the road up to the waterfall, tiring. Maybe its just me, for there is a good track all the way. Anyway, take it easy and take your time.

From the waterfall onwards the route is long but undemanding. Apart from the final assault on the summit, which should be treated with caution, there is nothing much to be concerned about – other, that is, than enjoying yourself.

Location Ordnance Survey Sheet 9, Cape Wrath, second series, scale 1:50,000.

Grid references Dun Dornaigil Broch 458450; Alltnacaillich 459456; waterfall 465455; Ben Hope summit 478502.

Route A word of warning before you start climbing. The little road from Altnaharra to Loch Hope is a very dangerous place, perhaps even more so than the mountain itself. Narrow, single-tracked and nasty; sudden bends, blind summits and then some. Take the greatest possible care if you want to arrive in one piece at the start point for the walk.

There are two parking places, by the broch and a little further north, on the right-hand side of the road, before the keeper's house. Parking near the house is frowned upon, mightily.

Walk from the car towards the house and you will spot the track on your right leading up the hill. It follows the line of the Allt na Caillich Burn to the first ridge, near the spectacular waterfall, where the track crosses the stream.

Walk north along the ridge of Leitir Mhuiseil, which rises suddenly, towards the summit crown, which is guarded on three sides by steep cliffs. In very windy weather, and we get some fierce gales in the north, stay clear of the top, or, if you must, approach on all fours.

37

Invernaver and Torrisdale

FROM THE dawn of history men have lived and worked by the banks of the River Naver in Sutherlandshire. Six thousand years ago mesolithic hunter-gatherers arrived in canoes, hugging the inhospitable storm-torn coastline – long-headed men, clad in furs and animal skins. Others trekked through wolf- and boar-filled forests over windswept mountains to the green and gentle strath.

Two thousand years before the Egyptians built their pyramids, Stone Age men constructed magnificent burial chambers, massive structures which involved placing hundreds of tons of shaped stones. It was a time of constant change: the miracle of fire, flint-tipped weapons, the cultivation of crops, animal husbandry. They built marvellously warm, weatherproof circular homes, and the remains of these ancient dwellings can still be seen today.

These early men were followed by Bronze and Iron Age peoples, aggressive, warlike tribes, constantly seeking better lands. The remains of their fortified towers, the brochs, line the banks of Naver, zigzagging from estuary to source – huge circular stone-built towers. The best preserved, Strathnaver Broch, stands at Grumore, on the north shore of Loch Naver. From its commanding heights, warning of approaching danger could be passed quickly throughout the glen and tribes gathered to defend their lands.

The Romans never subdued these painted northern men, the Picts. Nor did ravaging Vikings, plundering down the gentle strath from their Orkney base. A crueller fate awaited the men of Strathnaver – Clan MacKay. Where Roman legions, Viking raiders and English armies failed, the people of Strathnaver were finally destroyed, not by enemies but by so-called friends, their own lairds. During the infamous Highland clearances of the nineteenth century, the strath was brutally cleared of people to make way for sheep.

Gordons of Morayshire became Dukes of Sutherland in the Middle Ages and as early as 1630 announced that they were determined to 'root out Gaelic barbarity'. The rebellions of 1715 and 1745 changed Lowland attitudes mightily and Highlanders were portrayed as little better than barbarians, a constant danger to civilized life, to be beaten into submission.

In 1770, the Society for the Propagation of Christian Knowledge was set up to administer schools in the Highlands with an express aim: 'To combat the ignorance, atheism, popery and impiety of the Highlands'. Thus the scene was set for the clearances, one of the most inhumane acts ever perpetrated in Scotland. Two thousand men, women and children were evicted, their homes burned and land sold or rented to southern sheep farmers. In vain they prayed:

> O God, shield house and fire and beast
> And all that dwell herein tonight.
> Shield me and my beloved household
> From cruel hands and save us
> From our enemies tonight.

Because of the clearances, Strathnaver has been left almost unchanged, untouched by the hand of man for nearly two hundred years. It is one of the most important archaeological and historical sites in Europe, where the evidence and effect of thousands of years continuous human occupation have been captured in time. The strath is a vast, enduring monument to man's endeavour throughout the ages – a never-ending, constant source of wonder and delight.

After our abortive assault on stormy Ben Hope, Ann and I drove north alongside Loch Hope and then east to the mouth of the dashing little River Borgie. We were determined to save something of the day and decided to walk over the small hills separating Borgie from Naver to look down on the hut circles that crowd the sand dunes on the west bank of the estuary of the river.

We parked just before the Borgie hurries into Torrisdale Bay, where a small bridge crosses the river at Crossburn. The deep pool below the bridge was too much temptation for Breac and he plunged in, regardless of the strong current sweeping round the tree-clad bend. Wide, empty white sands lay ahead, dotted with oystercatchers, and we followed a winding track up past the fishing bothy onto the raised beach above the sea.

This is the site of mainland Britain's most northerly football stadium – a wooden changing hut overlooking a rough rectangle of a pitch with drunken goal-posts at each end. Sheep were the only players that day, so Ann's Yorkshire terror was firmly leaded and restrained from joining their game. We crossed the field and set off up the boulder-strewn slope, climbing the comfortable hills, stopping frequently to admire the wide sweep of the bay, brushed by green, mile-long Atlantic breakers.

Kevin O'Reilly, Department of Geography and Geology, Polytechnic of North London, has written a superb guide to local history and archaeology in Strathnaver, including a description of the Bronze Age settlement at Invernaver – the mouth of the river. We passed the dark blue of Lochan Druim an Duin and stood on the cliffs above Baile Marghait, searching amongst hard-packed sand dunes for outlines of the circular homes of Stone Age men.

The scattered dwellings of Bettyhill, named after the infamous Elizabeth, Countess Duchess of Sutherland, who presided over the clearances, lay eastwards; peat smoke streaming from croft chimneys, whipped skywards in the great gale raging above the river. From the shelter of a massive sandstone boulder we peered wet-eyed through the wind.

'The best preserved circle is situated on top of a mound. You can identify it from a distance by the presence of one slightly upstanding stone. The complete circle is quite impressive; the original wall was clearly several feet high and the stones were laid to give a vertical interior face, particularly evident on the north side. The internal diameter is 40 ft.'

We scrambled downhill and spent an hour exploring the ruins. There are outlines of four hut circles, in one of which is a small cluster of stones which may have been the original fireplace. Within this area there are also the remains of a broch: internal diameter of 28 feet and walls possibly 14 feet thick; two cists, burial chambers:

'bodies were buried individually, each contained in a flagstone coffin, which was covered by a cairn or mound. The bodies were buried in the foetal position – with knees drawn up beneath the chin.'

Tucking our own chins in and calling the dogs to heel, we walked back, north over the sands. Storm particles from the singing sands sprayed our faces; endless waves crested and carolled the deserted shore. Half-way along the beach we found shelter and lunch amongst an outcrop of rocks. We lay on the sands, locked in the timeless, mystical beauty of a wild, unchanging land: and speech seemed pointless.

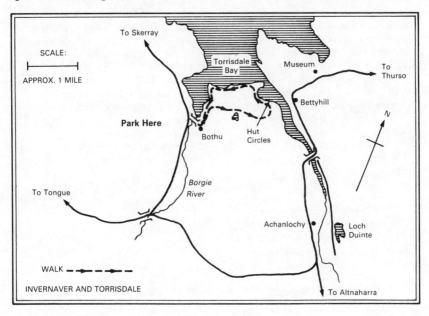

WHAT YOU NEED TO KNOW

Time and effort More mental than physical. For fullest benefit, do your homework first and learn a little about Strathnaver. In order to do so, contact Mrs Elliot Rudie, Strathnaver Museum, Farr, Bettyhill, Sutherland. The museum will be able to supply you with a number of well written and informative brochures describing the history of the strath. Before making the walk, call at the museum and, if you have time, visit the pre-clearance village of Achanlochy, a few miles south of Bettyhill. Allow a full day for your trip. The walk itself takes about two to three hours. Refreshment and bar lunches are available at the Bettyhill Hotel and in the village.

Location Ordnance Survey Sheet 10, Strathnaver, second series, scale 1:50,000.

Grid references Strathnaver Museum 715623; Bettyhill 707617; Achanlochy 717585; start of walk 681621; Lochan Druim an Duin 694621; hut circles 699611.

Route Drive north from the A836, where the main road crosses Borgie River, signposted to Skerray. At the mouth of the river, there is parking space and a track leading down to a wooden bridge. You will see the fishing bothy on the top of the hill at the other side of the river.

Follow this track up and round the bothy and then back down towards the shore. Climb onto the raised beach, by the football pitch and angle quarter-right, aiming for the top of the hill. The track is indistinct and there is a tendency to go too far right. Keep the loch on your right and you eventually arrive on the crags overlooking the hut circles. Scramble carefully down to visit them. Walk back to the car, along the sands, round the coast.

38

Farewell to the Flows

I WAS WITH a Welshman in a small cottage on the north coast of Scotland, talking to the local bard – which was difficult, because, although masterly at stringing together words, he was not so good at the hearing. Our next appointment was with a thatcher, a man versed in the ancient art of covering roof timbers with peat and turf.

Rising, my friend announced: 'Must leave, we have to see a thatcher.'

'You are seeing Mrs Thatcher?' inquired the bard.

'No, a thatcher,' replied the Welshman, struggling.

'And why would you be looking at a tractor?'

'No, Mr MacKay, not tractor, thatcher!' the Welshman yelled.

'Well, be sure and give him my regards for it's a long time indeed since I have seen the factor, and fine man he is too.'

This could only happen in Sutherland, a land full of characters, kindness and patient courtesy and from the window of my work room I look out across Loch Watten in Caithness to where the twin peaks of Ben Grimas rise gently from distant Sutherland moors.

As you drive southwards down Strath Halladle, the grey sentinels of Ben Griam Mor and Ben Griam Beg tower over the narrow road that twists across Badanloch from Kinbrace to Strathnaver. A desolate landscape where human habitation seems improbable. Then, in the distance, like a patch of white moss on a mountain boulder, the Garvault Hotel is glimpsed, lying snug in the folds of gently rounded hills, an island outpost in the wilderness.

Garvault Hotel, owned by Margaret and Tony Henderson, is the remotest hotel on mainland Britain. Its notepaper says so and *Guinness Book of Records* confirms the fact. If you are looking for simple comfort, good cooking and a friendly welcome, then Garvault offers all these and is a perfect centre for exploring the vast moorlands of east Sutherland.

But even this remote and beautiful land is being threatened by the hand of man, for the monotonous green of mass afforestation is creeping over the landscape like some malignant fungus. Northwards, also, in Strath Halladale, tree farmers have moved in, ploughing and devastating moorlands which have remained unchanged and tree-less since the last ice age. These moorland rapists are hell-bent on obliterating every inch from sight in frenzied pursuit of private profit.

For the time being it is still possible to find that special magic of the hills, where:

> Now Turn I to that God of old
> Who mocked not any of my ills,
> But gave my hungry hands to hold
> The large religion of the hills.

Get there if you can and see this amazing landscape before it disappears for ever under regimented rows of tax-avoidance-planted lodgepole pine and Sitka spruce. Fix in your mind the unending beauty of open moors, the cries of curlew, greenshank and golden plover. You will never see the like again.

This is the Flow Country, a far-flung carpet of dark bog pools and ice-blue lochans, blown white with cotton grass, starred with the sudden violet of sundew and milkwort, where bog asphodel yellows warm corners and heather purples autumn days. Hen harrier and golden eagle glide through a vast, endless sky; otters play by tiny lochs; wild cat blaze from behind wisps of shoreside reeds; graceful divers glide over smooth waters where stags stoop daintily to drink.

Climb the Ben Griams to capture the last moments of this precious heritage, and curse with me the thoughtless fools who destroy such beauty.

Ann and I parked behind Garvault Hotel and pulled on hiking boots. Gathering cameras, maps, compass, lunch and dogs, we set off eagerly up the hill. Hardy, thick-coated North Country Cheviot sheep gazed unblinkingly as we struck eastwards towards the shoulder of Ben Griam Beg, anxious to be free.

We crossed the Land-Rover track that leads out to Loch Coire nam Mang and addressed ourselves to the hill. Ben Griam Beg, 1,936 feet, is the higher of the two peaks and the hike to the top is an easy though steep climb. The rounded summit is crested by a cairn and a comfortable seat has been built so that you may rest weary legs after the climb. This seat has been constructed over the years by thoughtful walkers and is made out of grey stone slabs.

Relax here on a warm summer day, gazing southwards over the long splash of Lochs Badanloch, nan Clar and Rimsdale, to the hazed hills of Borrobol Forest: Creag a'Chiore Ghlais, Meall nan Aighean, Creag Mhor and Ben Klibreck. Over the flows, Caithness mountains ridge eastwards to where oil-drilling platforms black-speck sparkling seas. Listen to the constant wind. Feel the silence.

Westwards, range after range of Sutherland mountains shriek to the heavens – the ragged fortification of Ben Loyal; Ben Hope, serenely scaling cloud-wisped skies; Foinaven, Arkle and Assynt peaks. North, over the wild Pentland Firth, lie the hills of Hoy on gentle Orkney, and, abandoned to its fate in the stormy firth, the white star of Pentland Skerry lighthouse.

Ben Griam Beg beckons across a damp valley enfolding two superb trout lochs – Coire nam Mang and Druim a'Chliabhain, boat-housed and bobbed with fishing boats where cross-fingered anglers cast temptingly at the dimples of rising trout. The highest Iron Age hill fort in Scotland crowns the top of Ben Griam Beg, but

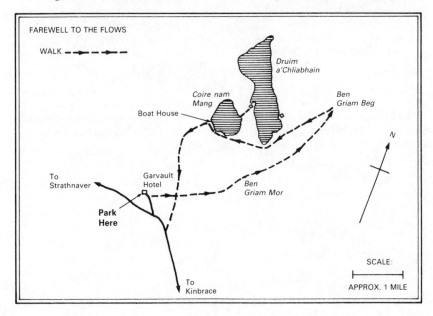

you have to look carefully to mark the ruin – a stone wall 6 feet thick guarding an area 500 feet by 200 feet. Elliot Rudhie, a local archaeologist, has found strange stones here, circular and holed in the middle. Perhaps our ancestors had more direct methods of fishing and used them as weights for nets.

On the long walk back to Garvault, Ann and I rested by the shores of Coire nam Mang. A plaintive, thin, piping voice called from the hill: 'Oh, dear me, oh, dear me!' Bowing on top of a boulder a greenshank warned of approaching rain. The sound of that haunting cry followed us home – another treasured memory of a day in the hills. And it p—— down all the way!

WHAT YOU NEED TO KNOW

Time and effort This is a moorland and hill walk across the Flow Country of east Sutherland. Allow about four hours for the round trip, which covers some ten miles. The ascent of the Ben Griams is not difficult and there are no dangers along the way. The valley floor between the two peaks can be soggy after heavy rain and it is advisable to try and keep to the ridges and higher ground.

Location You will need two maps, Ordnance Survey Sheet 10, Strathnaver and Sheet 17, Strath of Kildonan, second series, scale 1:50,000.

Grid references Garvault Hotel 781388; Ben Griam Mor 805389; Loch Coire nam Mang 800405; Loch Druim a'Chliabhain 810410; Ben Griam Beg 830410.

Route Leave the A897 Helmsdale–Melvich road through Strath Halladale at Kinbrace and turn west along the B871. Park behind the Garvault Hotel. A gate leads from the hotel, half-right across the hill, towards the summit of Ben Griam Mor. Cross the Land-Rover track and climb straight up to the top.

Avoid the crags at the north end of Mor by descending to the left of the top and cross the moor to Ben Griam Beg, with Loch Druim a'Chliabhain on your left. Climb straight up the hill. The return route takes you round the south end of Chliabhain and Coire nam Mang. At the boat-house on the west shore of nam Mang pick up the Land-Rover track which leads back to Garvault.

39

Beinn Mhor Sheep and Eagles

THE BAR at Lochboisdale Hotel on South Uist is the longest I have ever seen. In whaling days, thirsty crews, fresh from South Atlantic storms, disembarked in dry-throated droves, demanding instant service and plenty of space to raise and lower elbows.

When it comes to elbow raising I'm no slouch, but some occupants that night seemed intent upon breaking the world record for the greatest volume of whisky consumed during the course of a single evening. They would have to go some to beat the current holders, though – Creagorry Hotel, just up the road on Benbecula. There, the bar is lined with pre-packed take-aways: a half-bottle of whisky and a couple of cans of export to round off the evening, discreetly wrapped in plain brown paper bags. Keep in trim, Creagorry lads.

Pride of place in Lochboisdale public bar is given over to a huge photograph of the island's patron saint, Saint SS *Politician*, immortalized in Compton Mackenzie's book *Whisky Galore*. Thousands of cases of 'water of life' were 'rescued' when the vessel ran aground in a storm during the Second World War, and I think islanders have been praying for similar heavenly munificence ever since.

A single road runs the length of the west coast. Got to. The rest of South Uist is a desolate, trackless wilderness – moorlands rising to majestic mountains fringed by the most remote, spectacular cliff scenery in the British Isles. There are three main peaks: Hecla, 1,988 feet, to the north; Beinn Mhor, 2,034 feet, to the south and 1,800 foot Ben Corodale, sandwiched between.

Because they rise suddenly from sea level, South Uist mountains look dramatic and daunting; but all three are easy to climb, provided you choose the right route, and right day. The approach to Beinn Mhor, the highest, starts from the coastal road north of Market Stance, past three lochs called Ollay – West, Mid and East. I fished them fruitlessly a few years back and renamed them Dam, Bugger and SFA Ollay. Nevertheless, I am informed that they do contain fish.

This is a compass-and-map country; stout walking boots and full emergency kit. Uist weather is fickle: one moment clear and fine, the next a storm, racing in from the Atlantic. Should mist come down, then you must be prepared; there are steep, dangerous crags on Beinn Mhor and great care must be exercised. In spite of its modest height, treat Beinn Mhor with utmost respect.

A comforting peat track leads eastwards from the A865, egging you on, then deserts you for rough, heather-covered moors. However, the going is not tough and your reference point is the north shoulder of Beinn Mhor, known as Maola Breac. Once there, heather thins and walking becomes easier.

As you climb, the coastal machair plain spreads below – a springtime wild-flower-covered masterpiece fringed by a golden carpet of miraculous empty beaches. A straggle of shallow, blue, lime-rich lochs borders the shore: Fada, Roag, Altabrug – famed salmon and sea-trout fisheries. Grogarry, Stilligarry, Bornish, Kildonan, home of highest-quality wild brown trout in Scotland. Small crofts, smoke-drifting in still air, squat white amidst fertile fields.

A ragged, narrow ridge leads south-east from Maola Breac towards the summit. Pick cautiously upwards. Hardest part is the final scramble, threading carefully over and round jagged boulders. Once crowned, the reward is everything and more you ever wished.

Northwards, across Ben Corodale and Hecla, blush South Harris hills, the 'heather isles'. Over silver seas to Skye, a mighty range of Cuillins: Sgurr Alasdair, Sgurr nan Eag and a'Ghreadaaidh. Beyond, on mainland Scotland, Assynt and Fisherfield peaks: an Teallach, Ben More, Quinag. Small isles lie south: Heaval-topped Barra and, shadowed in distant, shimmering, porpoised seas, Rum, Eigg, Coll and warm-palmed Tiree.

This is the land of golden eagle, rapacious raven and hen harrier. Once, one clear, sunny autumn day, Ann and I gazed from Druidibeg as an eagle circled thermals above the mountain. Even from such distance, the huge, dark shape dominated skies. As we watched, a second bird thrust from Hecla's purple-blue crags to join its mate in soaring, stately flight. If you dream of seeing the 'lord of the skies', then amidst wild Uist mountains that dream will come true.

At the foot of Beinn Mhor, locked in an eastern mountain prison, nestles little Loch Hellisdale. Close by, on cliffs guarding Corodale Bay, is Prince's Cave. The luckless Young Pretender, Bonnie Prince Charlie, hid there after the flight from Drumossie Moor in 1746. Not so bonny either, by all accounts. I suppose that after months running for his life, living wild, that was to be expected, but I have damn-all sympathy for that vagabond prince. He carried with him nothing other than ruin and disaster wherever he went, and he hammered the last nail into Highlanders' coffins.

Similar simple beasts are hunted amongst corries round Beinn Mhor and Corodale. Shepherds comb hills in early summer, searching for sheep, making the long trek to Corodale for 'clippings'. Much easier than flocking herds over tortuous peaks to machair homesteads. They shear during the days and sleep summer-starred nights, well provisioned with good Scotch wine to wet whistles of old stories.

Which seemed a good idea. Ann and I turned from the view and descended to join Gaelic-speaking throngs, elbow-raised by the long bar of Boisdale. We had worked hard for our thirst. At least, that's our excuse.

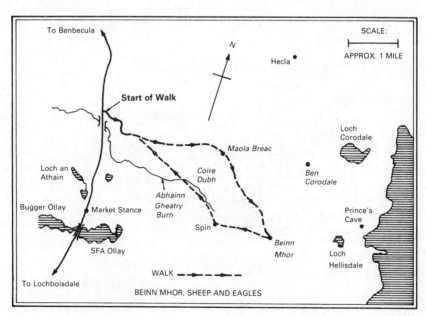

BEINN MHOR, SHEEP AND EAGLES

WHAT YOU NEED TO KNOW

Time and effort   Apart from the final assault on the summit of Beinn Mhor, this is an easy walk, albeit across some pretty rugged country. Compass and map and full service marching order recommended. The total distance is about seven miles and you should allow approximately four hours for the journey, excluding the time you spend in the bar at Lochboisdale. I suggest you leave that part of the walk until last. Don't forget binoculars – for birds on the hill.

Location   Ordnance Survey Sheet 22, Benbecula, second series, scale 1:50,000.

Grid references   The Lochboisdale Hotel is on Sheet 31; find the grid reference yourself or simply follow your nose. Start of walk 768341; Maola Breac 797333; Beinn Mhor 808311; Spin 797314; Coire Dubh 790325.

Route   Drive north from Lochboisdale, past Ollays and Market Stance. Half a mile further a loch borders the left of the road: Loch an Athain. One hundred yards on, two cottages left-right the road. Next right is the parking place and start of the walk.

Follow the peat track onto the moor. Mark the north shoulder of Beinn Mhor and walk directly towards it. This is the easiest way up, and why should we make things difficult for ourselves? On Maola Breac, follow the rising ridge south-east towards the summit. Once on top, you have a choice: either return the same way or be difficult, and edge down the steep west side of Beinn Mhor to the secondary summit of Spin – more climbing than walking but splendid stuff nevertheless. From Spin, angle down Coire Dubh, on the line of the stream, to cross Abhainn Gheatry Burn, thence back to the car.

40

From Market Stance to Scarilode

*B*ENBECULA, Beinn a'faodhia, 'the hill of the fords'; a flat, moorland landscape, dominated by Rueval, the highest hill on the island. Here, in a shallow cave, on the nights of 25 and 26 June 1746, Bonnie Prince Charlie anxiously awaited Flora Macdonald. Flora's stepfather, Captain Hugh Macdonald, was guarding the South Ford, from Benbecula to South Uist, and he supplied travel documents which allowed the prince, disguised as Flora Macdonald's maid, Betty Burke, to escape.

Not a moment too soon. Word was out that the fugitive was hiding on Benbecula and General Campbell arrived on the island commanding a force of more than two thousand men to hunt him down. The following month, Flora Macdonald was arrested by that relentless pursuer of Prince Charles Edward Stuart, Captain Ferguson of *HMS* Furnace and imprisoned in the Tower of London.

Flora was released in 1747, under the Act of Indemnity, and three years later married Alan Macdonald of Kingsburgh. Dr Johnson met her there in 1773, by which time Flora Macdonald was fifty years old, but still a considerable presence.

The good doctor reports: 'We were entertained at Kingsburgh with the usual hospitality by Mr Macdonald and his lady Flora Macdonald, a name that will be mentioned in history; and if courage and fidelity are virtues, mentioned with honour.'

Until recent times, Benbecula was isolated from its near neighbours North and South Uist by the North and South Fords, and passage over the shifting sands was dangerous and difficult. In 1943 a causeway was built over South Ford, still known as O'Regan's Bridge in honour of the priest most active in advocating its construction. Seventeen years passed before Benbecula was linked to North Uist; in 1960 the Queen Mother opened the route over North Ford, completing the link. Island economy was further stimulated by the advent of the rocket-testing range and Ministry of Defence establishment at Balivanich. Of the three islands, Benbecula shows the greatest sign of Hebridean change.

Ann and I first visited Benbecula in 1977. With four children, ranging from two to sixteen years, we stayed in a caravan near Balivanich. One fine, bright morning the family set off to Market Stance, a few miles south of Gramsdale, intent on picnic, fishing and walking. Market Stance was the cattle business centre of the island. In days gone by, mainland dealers would gather there to haggle with islanders and buy their lean black cattle.

Driving past council works and rubbish tip, we parked the car by the shores of Loch Ba Una; where Ann, daughter Lewis-Ann, young Charles and infant Jean disembarked to splash and play in shallow sand-fringed waters. My elder son, Blair, and I set off eastwards, following Clanranald's Kelp Road to the sea. During the Great War kelp was the major industry of Benbecula; potash produced by burning kelp was essential to armaments factories and more than 600 tons was exported each year.

The old track winds round the south side of Rueval through a wilderness of heather-covered moorlands, painted blue-grey with shining lochs and tiny lochans. North-east, behind Rueval, lies one of the most notorious: Loch na Beire.

Two small islands grace the loch, Mheribh Mhor and Mheribh Bheag. On Mhor there is said to be a circular hole, now hidden beneath sad bluebells, carved from ancient rock and once used as a place of execution. Condemned men were bound, thrust into the hole, and left to die. At a convenient time, the corpse was removed and buried on Mheribh Bheag, presumably to make way for further wretched miscreant occupants of that infamous pit.

The track ends on the small sandy beach of a beautiful loch called Scarilode – deep, clear waters surrounded by steep crags, full of responsive, red-spotted wild brown trout. Edge round the west shore, past a bouldered, rowan-decked promontory; on the edge of the rocks, sea-staring the long finger of Oban Haka, are the ruins of a building marked on the map 'Shieling'.

This remote eastern area of Benbecula was once part of a large farm known as Nunton, owned in the 1920s by Lady Gordon Cathcart, resident of Bournemouth. The islanders who survived the carnage of the First World War returned expecting to find, as promised, a 'land fit for heroes to live in'. Instead they found the same old entrenched, enduring divisions they had been told they were fighting to end: landlords protecting imagined hereditary legal rights, and near-destitute tenants, expected to be humbly thankful for the smallest morsel of approbation.

The Crofting Acts of the late nineteenth century ended the monstrous iniquity of summary eviction and gave tenants security to work and improve their lands. However, what it didn't do was to return the land so brutally sequestered by rapacious clearance lairds.

Benbecula ex-servicemen took the law into their own hands and seized their land by force, defying the law and anyone else to remove them. Basking in the glow of Britain's first-ever Labour government, the soldiers succeeded, and the many marks of 'shieling' on Benbecula's map show the results of their desperate efforts to claim and live and work the land they loved and had fought so hard to defend.

Seven years before my first visit, the croft at Scarilode was still occupied, bright with the sound of laughter and smiling faces – in spite of the constant battle against elements to wrest a meagre living from the thin, sparse soils. How much would world-weary, paper-ridden businessmen in City 'trenches', pay for the magnificent, isolated, god-like splendour of Scarilode?

North from Scarilode, in the knuckle of Neavag Bay, sea otters play; Arctic skuas pirate the cliffs; seals nod offshore; green-coated shags spread wet wings to dry in spring-fresh winds. Eternity was born here, amongst the surging foam and singing gulls. Peace beyond price.

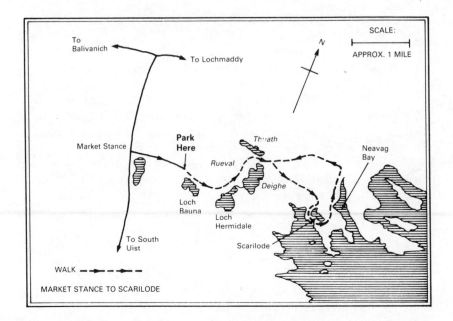

WHAT YOU NEED TO KNOW

Time and effort Apart from the section between Scarilode and the north arm of the Kelp Road, this is an easy walk. Wear stout boots, carry wet-weather gear and you will come to little harm. The round trip covers a distance of eight miles and takes about four hours, depending upon how often and how long you stop to stand and stare on the way. An added attraction would be to climb Rueval on the way home. See how you feel and how much time you have left.

Location Ordnance Survey Sheet 22, Benbecula, second series, scale 1:50,000.

Grid references Market stance 805535; start point 810535; fork on Kelp Road 836535; Scarilode 847523; shieling 846520; north arm of Kelp Road 850535; Rueval 826535.

Route Drive down the A865 and turn left onto the Kelp Road at Market Stance. The 'good' road ends at Loch Ba Una, where there is plenty of room to park. Walk eastwards, following the track north of Loch Hermidale and Deighe, and south of Thuath. One hundred yards past the end of the loch, the Kelp Road divides; take the right fork and walk to Scarilode.

As you approach Scarilode, the track keeps uphill. Leave the track and walk down to the loch and round the west shore. At the south end of Scarilode you will find the ruined shieling. Climb the hill guarding the east end of Scarilode and walk north over the moor, up the side of Neavag Bay. At the end of this sea loch finger you will strike the north arm of the Kelp Road. Follow this back to the start point – with a quick dash up Rueval on the way!

41

Valley and the
Sunken Caves of Hosta

'NAE MAN can tether time or tide.' But you can learn to live with them. As an exciseman, Scotland's national bard, Robert Burns, was well aware of this fact; and so were the smugglers he hunted. Therefore, before enjoying one of North Uist's loveliest walks, carefully check time and tide. Otherwise be prepared for a long wait on Valley Island until seas recede and you can return safely.

At low tide, Valley Island is separated from North Uist by two miles of golden sand. Then it is safe to walk out and explore this secret, summer-primrose-covered paradise. An hour will take you round the coast and on the north shore you will find the finest beaches in Britain, backed by gentle dunes, solitary and remote. It is easy, like Tam o' Shanter, to forget time and tide on Valley and succumb to the 'songs and sweet airs' of this magical isle.

Nor will you be the first visitor to fall under Valley's spell. The old, ruined house that dominates the island was once the home of the Granville family, cousins of the queen, who still own much of Uist. Four thousand years ago, Stone Age man grazed cattle on Valley and even today Uist crofters from the villages of Sollas, Malaclete and Middlequarter take sheep over shining sands to crop summer grass. Bleating flocks herd across wet sands, ankle-snapped by sharp-eyed black collies amidst a chorus of Gaelic shouts from arm-waving shepherds. Memories of times past, when sheep were less welcome, come flooding back.

The 'Children of Colla' were evicted from their homes in 1849, to make way for the 'Great Cheviot'. Godfrey William Wentworth MacDonald, fourth Baron of the Isles, was £200,000 in debt and hard pressed by creditors. Sheep were to be his financial salvation. The only problem was his people. At the first attempt to issue writs of eviction, sheriff officers were sent scuttling from Malaclete in a shower of stones, thrown by angry, fearful tenants.

A force of thirty-three constables, armed with ash truncheons and led by William Colquhoun, sheriff substitute, and Superintendent MacBean, sailed from Oban to beat the men of Sollas into submission. Ever anxious to please his superiors, the Revd Macrae, an island minister, accompanied the force: God's Law as well as man's, would be used to bring the villagers to heel. Alexander Mackenzie, in his 'History of the Highland Clearances' described the scene:

> There was no discussion, no argument, no appeals. The police formed two lines down the street of the township. Sheriff-Officers asked one question only at the doors of the cottages, whether those within were prepared to emigrate on the terms offered. If the answer was no, and it invariably was, then bedding, bed-frames, spinning-wheels, barrels, benches, tables and clothing were all dragged out and left at the door. Divots were torn from the roof, and the house timbers pulled down ready for burning.

The villagers, grouped into a small army, began to hurl rocks and stones at the constables.

> MacBean put his men into two divisions and sent them forward against the crowd with their batons. One took the villagers in the rear, the other in the flank, and drove them over barley rigs and dykes, along the deep-pooled shore.

The end was never in doubt. Three years later, Christmas 1852, the villagers of Sollas, Malaclete and Middlequarter, other than the old, the sick and the lame, left their Uist lands for ever. The frigate *Hercules*, smallpox-ridden, sailed for Australia taking with it the tormented souls of an abandoned people. As you drive past the empty shells of their ruined homes, spare them a kindly thought.

Westwards along the quiet road that circles North Uist is another, less wicked, Victorian folly – the small, ugly, incongruous tower on the south shore of Loch Scolpaig. From behind the croft at the end of the road that divides two 'wings' of the loch, a track leads north along a cliff path, skirting the slopes of Ben Scolpaig, to the Sunken Caves of Hosta.

Sheer cliffs, alive with wild flowers and spring-nesting birds, flank green seas. Natural arches, carved by thousand-year-old waves, throw up endless Atlantic breakers into surging sheets of white spray. Caves probe deep into the rocks and on the cliff-top, near Sloc Roe, land has given up battle, tumbling into a great, gaping hole. On wild days, storm-driven waters howl at the foot of the pit in deafening, defiant roar.

The remains of an ancient Pictish fort lie on the heights above Bagh Blaaskie: Caisteal Odair, 'castle of the dappled hill'. A long wall protects southern approaches to the promontory, pierced by an entrance, 15 feet long and 5 feet wide. The site of the fort must have made it almost impregnable and inside the fortifications are outlines of circular stone foundations, home and hearth to generations of early Gaels.

This is the land where great raptors soar, hen harrier and buzzard, and there is every chance of seeing a golden eagle. Indeed, the varied bird life on North Uist is one of the island's most outstanding attractions. Listen for the rusty-engined coughing of corncrake. The red-necked phalarope also nests nearby in Balranald Nature Reserve.

One year, whilst walking by Loch Eport, in the south of the island, Ann and I saw a rare white stork. The bird was feeding in a roadside loch close to Sidinish and kindly waited until I had assembled zoom lens and taken a decent shot before flapping off over the moor. Round every corner, over every hill, North Uist delights.

The island is two-thirds water, covered with more than a hundred and fifty trout-filled freshwater lochs. Many, like Scadavay, Fada and Obisary, are such a tangled scatter that often the same loch appears to be an endless number of different waters. The shoreline of Loch Scadavay meanders in and out round headlands, bays and corners for a distance of fifty miles, dotted with some two hundred islands, many of which are adorned with their own small lochans.

As the long Hebridean day lingers slowly towards its close over Valley Island, and late sun dips into western seas, there comes a stillness, a moment of timeless beauty, when evening curlew call down the hill and lapwing dip and twist in the gloaming. Then there is no lovelier place in all of Scotland to say goodnight to the world.

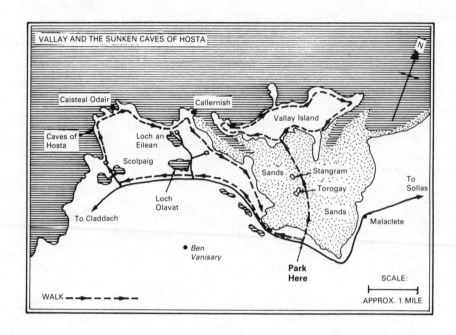

WHAT YOU NEED TO KNOW

Time and effort   This is an easy, though longish walk. It is possible to split it into two separate outings: to Valley Island first and then later, from Scolpaig to the Sunken Caves of Hosta. The full walk covers a distance of twelve miles and is a day's outing. However, if the sun is shining you may be tempted to linger on the fine beaches of Valley Island. Take along a sleeping bag, just in case. Crossing the sands is quite safe but you should seek local advice about the tides before starting. Wellington boots, rather than walking shoes, for this section of the journey.

When walking out to the Sunken Caves of Hosta, it is polite to tell the owner of the croft at the end of the loch, if he is in, of your intention. Keep well back from the edge, particularly from the edge of the cliff-top hole. Remember, the sea is still cutting away below and the perimeter might not be stable. Dogs and children should be kept on a close lead.

Location   Ordnance Survey Sheet 18, Sound of Harris, second series, scale 1:50,000.

Grid references   Parking place 781736; Torogay Island 779746; Stangram Island 778751; Valley Island 775765; Loch Scolpaig 733751; Sunken Caves of Hosta 726765; Caisteal Odair 731769; Loch an Eilean 747760; Callernish 752767; Valley Sound 755756.

Route   Easy parking by roadside. There is a track across the sands marked on the map, but this is not obvious on the ground. You must seek local advice about tide times and route before setting out. The walk over is about 45 minutes and an hour will take you round the island. Return to the car and change into walking shoes for the remainder of the walk.

Follow the road westwards for three miles, past three lochs on your left and then Loch Olavat on your right. A mile past Olavat you will see Loch Scolpaig and the Victorian tower on your right. Walk down the farm road, between the two sections of the loch, to the croft at the end.

A track leads north along the cliff. Follow this out to the Caves of Hosta and then on to Caisteal Odair. From Caisteal Odair, simply follow the coastline round north and east, keeping Loch an Eilean on your right. This leads to Valley Sound and back to the road. At the road, turn left for your car.

42

Skara Brae
and Yesnaby Castle

Y<small>OU NEED</small> good sea-legs for Orkney walking. Not because the
hills are high or hikes taxing, but just to get you safely over the
Pentland Firth. I remember with horror a passage in 1967. The car
was lifted on board by sling and dumped, none too ceremoniously,
in the hold. But that was as nothing compared with the dumping
we humans received when the boat left the comparative calm of
Scrabster harbour.

House-high waves, mad walls of tormented, flying spray, roared
in from all quarters as the vessel corkscrewed and bobbed crazily
northwards. Sea-gulls screamed derision through the storm. My
five-year-old son, Blair, and I, wedged together topside, trying to
pretend that it was really all good fun. Meanwhile, wife Ann and
three-year-old daughter, Lewis-Ann, weathered it out below,
reading, as though a force seven gale was an everyday occurrence.
Strong stuff, females.

Eventually, the boat pitched drunkenly into the lee of Hoy and,
slowly, calmer waters settled pounding hearts. It seemed that we
were not, as I had previously expected, every minute, doomed to a
watery grave. Ashore, surrounded by the solid stones and cobbles
of the old grey town of Stromness, I felt like Mr Fletcher Christian
waving farewell to a mad Captain Bligh. Then, from a great height,
they dropped the car onto the pier – a last defiant gesture of disgust

from seamen to fair-weather sailors.

In spite of that violent journey across Europe's wildest waters the magic of the Orcades has held us enthralled for many years and the journey from mainland Scotland is not always so stormy. We have sailed millpond-calm amidst myriad sea birds, chased and chivvied by porpoise and gannet, lazing sunburnt past sentinel stacks, barely aware of time passing.

One of our favourite Orkney walks starts from the Bay of Skaill in Sandwick, on the west coast of Mainland. The bay is a silver crescent of shining sand, washed by endless green-fringed Atlantic waves. My first golden retriever, Jean, learned to swim there. Jean was a highly-bred bundle of nerves. She required careful persuasion before undertaking any venture faintly dangerous and, as far as she was concerned, water looked mighty dangerous. I waded out into the bay, holding her in my arms, and she swam ashore. Never looked back after that and loved water evermore.

Nestling in the sand dunes at the south end of the bay is the neolithic village of Skara Brae. Five thousand years ago these stone houses must have resounded with the laughter and chatter of farmer-fishermen and their families. The dwellings are wonderfully preserved, lying centuries asleep, undisturbed, under marram-covered sands. A huge storm uncovered the remains of ten houses and they have been carefully excavated to reveal fireplaces, complete with adjacent seat, flagstone box beds, dressers and wall shelves.

On midsummer evenings, amidst cry of sea-gull and twittering late larks, when tourist buses have departed, the ghosts of these small axe-carrying sheepskin-clad men still wander across the dunes, prehistoric dogs yapping busily around calloused, sandalled feet. I know because I have seen them.

Leave Skaill Bay from behind Skara Brae, climbing little Ward Hill, walking over soft, springy, sea-turf specked with wild flowers. The rare Scottish primrose, *Primula scotica*, graces the cliff-tops. Kittiwake, guillemots, razorbill and fulmars squawk and squabble on dramatic crags. The songs of wheatear, meadow pipit and lark sparkle in childhood-crystal air. And, always, the sound of the restless sea.

Eastwards from the hill, Loch Stenness and Loch Harray blue-sweep the moor – two of Orkney's famous trout lochs. Fishermen-filled boats drift the skerry-strewn shallows in endless pursuit of beautifully shaped pink-fleshed wild brown trout. Fish weighing more than 17 lb have been caught and anglers come from all over the world to try their luck – with me it's skill! – in the clear, lime-rich, trout-filled waters.

Close to the deep inlet of Bor Wick, a jagged scar in the cliff, is Broch of Borwick, an Iron Age fort on top of the hill: evidence of changing times, when competition for land and attack by neighbours and newcomers required secure haven for residents – and no visitors were more determined or fiercer than the Vikings.

Skaill is the Norse name for the house of a Viking chief: a good beach and landing place for a longship surrounded by fertile lands. The Norsemen plundered at will throughout Shetland, Orkney, Ireland and mainland Britain until their power was broken at the Battle of Largs in 1261. Even then, the Orkney Islands remained part of Norway and were ceded to Scotland only in 1468 as part of the dowry when King James III married Margaret, daughter of King Christian I.

The Norse influence on the islands is commemorated in names and language as you follow the cliff path south to Neban Point: Edgair, Bor Wick, Qui Ayre, Garthna Geo, Kellyan Hellyan and Lyre Geo. However, when walking along these cliffs it is not the Vikings that you have to fear; a more immediate danger threatens the unwary. Between Yesnaby and Neban Point the moor is owned by a colony of Arctic skuas. During the breeding season they guard their territory furiously, diving fearlessly on intruders, shrieking with anger.

A mighty sea stack, the Castle of Yesnaby has been knifed from the mainland by thousands of years' Atlantic attack. Nearby there is an outcrop of even older rock, start point of the fault known as the Uranium Corridor. Lunch at the view-point on Neban Point, lingering above the waves, watching the changing colours on Ward Hill, highest peak on the Island of Hoy: our next walk.

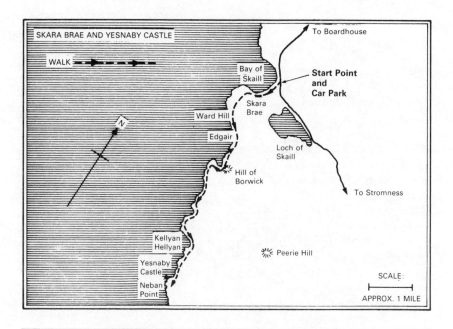

WHAT YOU NEED TO KNOW

Time and effort There and back is a distance of about eight miles. Good walking shoes required and it is advisable to arrive at Skara Brae before 10.30 a.m. After that time, the village gets uncomfortably busy with tourists. This is an easy walk and it will take about four hours, depending upon how long you spend at Skara Brae and how often you stop and stare. As always when on a cliff walk, keep well back from the edge; remember that the cliffs are friable and subject to erosion. Not a good place for dogs. Give the dogs a run on the beach first then leave them in the car for the duration.

Location Ordnance Survey Sheet 6, Orkney–Mainland, second series, scale 1:50,000.

Grid references Start point at Bay of Skaill 236194; Skara Brae 230187; Hill of Borwick 223165; Castle Yesnaby 217134; Neban Point 216132.

Route Park in the car park at Bay of Skaill and follow the signs through the dunes and along the beach to the neolithic village of Skara Brae. Walk south from Skara Brae up Ward Hill and follow the cliff path on to Neban Point. Return to the car park the same way.

43

Orkney, Marwick and Kitchener

HORATIO Herbert Kitchener was the hero of Khartoum and the Battle of Omdurman, Commander-in-Chief of British forces during the Boer War, and Secretary of State for War in 1915, father of the largest volunteer army ever raised – a million and a half scraps of human cannon fodder. I surveyed his memorial on Marwick Head. An ugly tower, like a lost rook searching for a chess-board, perched on Orcadian cliffs 284 feet above the cold waters of the Atlantic where Horatio Herbert met his doom.

On 5 June 1916, three weeks before Kitchener's first hundred thousand went 'over the top' into the hellish Battle of the Somme, the earl sailed from Scapa Flow bound for Russia aboard the cruiser HMS *Hampshire*. That evening, amidst a violent storm, his ship struck a German mine and all but twelve men perished. Kitchener was last seen on deck, 'calm and courageous' as the vessel went down. His body was never found.

I turned from the monument and looked out to sea. Southwards, the jagged stack of the Old Man of Hoy reared, etched starkly against a silver-blue horizon. Purple Hoy hills mingled and merged in midday sunlight. Westwards, limitless white-topped seas waved to Greenland and distant ice-clad polar shores. Perhaps it was as well that Kitchener never survived to see his great army of common men broken and bloody at Picardy. The days of imperialists were gone.

Orkney played host to the Royal Navy during both world wars and the islands are littered with remnants of these horrific conflicts: the Imperial German Fleet, scuttled on 22 June 1919, sparse, rusting hulks and spindle masts, by the grim Churchill Barriers; the delicate filigree wrought-ironwork and paintings of the Italian Chapel, lovingly constructed by prisoners of war, now carefully preserved by their one-time gaolers; broken pillboxes and tank traps; the marks of fighter airfields amongst fertile farmlands.

I first visited Orkney with my family in 1949. We stayed on the shores of Scapa Flow, as guests of the Isbister family, three brothers and three sisters, at Bacakelday Farm. A First World War shell guarded the front door of the cottage and oil slicks from the sunken HMS *Royal Oak*, torpedoed at anchor by a German U-boat during the Second World War, still marked the waters of the bay when high winds blew.

Within the space of two unforgettable weeks I fell in love with Orkney and have returned ever since, trapped by the mystical spell these beautiful islands cast over all but the most insensitive travellers. Orkney is a land of contrasts: of Viking days, when Orkney was ruled by Danes; of turbulent Scottish Middle Ages and the barbaric dominion of Stuart Earls of Birsay; of modern moments of magical music by Peter Maxwell Davies, during the St Magnus Festival; of George Mackay Brown's haunting stories.

The best way to explore Orkney is on foot and a fine walk to start you off is from Birsay to the Kitchener Memorial on Marwick Head. Birsay is a small village in north-east Mainland – a few houses, dominated by the ruins of the Earl's Palace. From Birsay, three hours after high water, it is possible to walk over the concrete causeway to the Brough of Birsay, a tiny island with the remains of a Viking palace and a museum. As small boys, my brother, Ian, and I fought many battles there with fierce, bearded, horn-helmeted Norsemen – and generally came off best. An hour will take you round the island and, providing you have got the tides right, safely back to the mainland.

A bridge in the village leads south to sea links, past the remains of stone-lined pits used to store seaweed during the days of Orkney's booming kelp industry. It was by these shores that I saw my first fulmar, then a comparatively rare bird, now well established along Britain's coastline. This walk is tailor-made for the ornithologist: eider duck, shelduck, dunlin, ringed plover, oystercatcher and curlew call and dance beside you all the way.

Hooded crows shadow your steps, hoping to be guided to eggs

or fledglings disturbed by your passing. Pretend you don't see them and walk smartly on. Common and Atlantic seals, whiskered heads bobbing hello, dot the waves off-shore. In spring and early summer the links are carpeted with wild flowers – *Scilla verna*, thrift, campion and scurvy grass – and at the end of the links, across a low fence, the cliff path climbs gradually upwards to Marwick Head.

Arctic skuas turn and twist overhead. Great skuas, Orkney's bonxies, glide on silent wings, white, under-patches flashing in the sunlight, poised to terrorize their next meal from the gullets of unsuspecting gulls. Marwick Head is an RSPB nature reserve and, during May and July, upwards of 40,000 nesting birds crowd the cliffs in loud, ever-protesting complaint. The path leads down into Marwick Bay by the restored fishermen's cottages and old chapel. Ideal place for lunch.

A narrow track runs eastwards from the bay, crossing a minor road and on to the Loons, a marshland area surrounding the loch of Isbister, home of some of Orkney's spectacular wild brown trout. The RSPB has erected a hide overlooking the wetlands and many a carefully planned and timed walk has come to grief there, watching and waiting for just one more species to brighten the day.

The road back to Birsay ambles along a quiet lane which deposits you onto the links near the cemetery, then over fields to Point of Buckquoy. To the north of Brough of Birsay another cliff path leads to Skipi Geo, where there is a colony of fidgety Arctic terns.

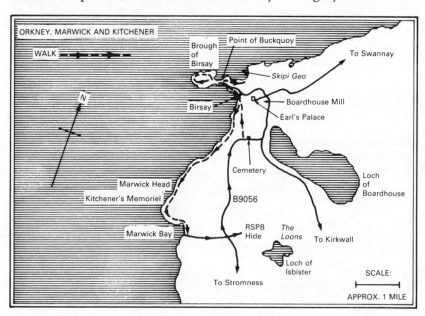

On the shores of an inlet lie reminders of Orkney whaling days – a great whale rib with vertebra attached, set into the ground.

I remember lying on these cliffs as a boy on a windy August day, listening to screaming gulls and the shrieking sea as it battered relentlessly on scarred cliffs. White spray sparkled and flew from mountainous waves, and I saw Kitchener's ship pitching, smoke-belching through the storm, and heard the fearful explosion that carried him into history.

WHAT YOU NEED TO KNOW

Time and effort Distance about nine miles; time is up to you. There is so much to see on the way that you should allow at least five hours – more if you properly explore Earl's Palace and call on the Arctic terns at Skipi Geo. Stout walking shoes are required, and binoculars; however, when using them on the cliffs, lie down first. Orkney cliffs are fragile, dangerous and undercut. Try and plan your trip during May, when the cliffs are sea-bird busy.

Location Ordnance Survey sheet 6, Mainland, second series, scale 1:50,000.

Grid references Start of walk,, Point of Buckquoy 243284; Brough of Birsay 236285; Earl's Palace 248278; Marwick Head 257252; Marwick Bay 259243; The Loons 245242; Skipi Geo 248284; Boardhouse Mill 256275.

Route Park the car at Point of Buckquoy and, after checking the tide times, walk out to Brough of Birsay across the causeway. Visit Viking ruins and early Christian museum. Walk round the island. Return to mainland and walk five hundred yards to inspect Earl's Palace in Birsay.

Cross the bridge in the village and bear right onto the links. Follow the edge of the links where they meet the shore. At the end of the links, cross a low fence and follow the cliff path to Marwick Head and Kitchener's Memorial. In Marwick Bay follow the little road east to the B9056. Cross, and, within two hundred yards, find the RSPB hide.

Return to the B9056 and follow it northwards to a right-angled bend. At this point, by the cemetery, follow a right of way over the fields back to the links and Point of Buckquoy. Skipi Geo is a few hundred yards north from the car park, along the cliffs. End your walk with a visit to Boardhouse Mill, a working mill steeped in history and offering visitors a wide selection of high-quality Orcadian craft products. Well worth a visit.

44

Moness, Ward Hill and Dwarfie

CONSIDERATE parents gave me a small grand piano for my twenty-first birthday and each night, before I go to bed, I play Beethoven. He never wins. After thirty years of combat, he always loses. Night after night I commit murder. Surest way I know of clearing a room of unwanted guests is for me to offer to give them a little tune. People die in the crush for the door.

One night, I discovered Peter Maxwell Davies lurking under a volume of Mozart and thought I would give him a bash. The work in question was *Stevie's Ferry to Hoy*, a simple, haunting, beautiful melody that has stayed with me ever since. Not that I ever mastered the piece with any degree of skill, but I play it recognizably, and that's all that matters to me.

Peter Maxwell Davies, a composer of international repute, has made his home on Orkney and is a mainstay of the Orcadian Annual Festival of Music; arrange your visit in June and hear a hundred glorious voices ringing through the old red sandstone Cathedral of St Magnus in Kirkwall. His music captures the spirit of both people and islands – nowhere more perfectly, in my opinion, than in *Stevie's Ferry*.

The Island of Hoy is an Orcadian enigma, completely unlike the rest of Orkney and more akin in character to the sweeping hills of Sutherland. Most of Orkney is low-lying: rolling, peat-covered moors edged by fine farming lands. Hoy, the Norse word for 'high', is mountainous, almost roadless and absolutely majestic. Ward Hill, the highest peak, is only 1,566 feet, but because it rises so suddenly from sea level it looks daunting, towering and dramatic.

It seems strange to suggest a place to get away from it all on such remote islands as Orkney. Nevertheless, if you really appreciate peace and solitude, head for Hoy. Ferries run regularly from Stromness, through Clestrain Sound, round the little isle of Graemsay to Burra Sound and the pier at Moness. From the pier there are a number of superb walks which vary in length between five and sixteen miles. All have one thing in common: magnificent, unspoilt scenery and rarely another soul along the way.

A circular walk from Moness leads westwards from the ferry, through Cuilags and War Hill, past Sandy Loch and down to the small village of Rackwick, cradled by steep cliffs, fronting the Firth. Wild flowers abound: sundew, butterwort, milkwort, trefoil, woodrush, bog asphodel and dog violet. Where the path meets a narrow single-track road, turn left and walk back across the hill to Moness.

By the corrie of Nowt Bield on your left and the ridge of Dwarfie Hamars on the right, is the Dwarfie Stane. This is a huge sandstone block, a neolithic grave, resting on steep hillsides, measuring 28 feet in length, 14 feet in width and 8 feet in depth. Richard Feacham described it as: 'A passage and two cells have been cut in it, or hollowed out of it. The passage is 7'6" long, 2'4" wide and 2'10" high. A square block of stone lying just outside the entrance was originally used to stop the entrance.'

This burial chamber is unusual because most chambered tombs of the period were built above ground, rather than hollowed out of a convenient rock. Avoid the temptation of trying to crawl in; twentieth-century man is far to large. Walk to the main road – well, the only road on the island – and down onto the beach, which is the quickest way back to the pier.

For a bird's-eye view of Hoy and, on a clear day, half the north of Scotland, climb Ward Hill. After passing Sandy Loch, turn south and follow the line of Water Glen up to the summit. This is an easy climb and an amazing panorama awaits. Sutherland mountains line the horizon – Foinaven, Arkle, Ben More Assynt, graceful Ben Hope and the ragged ridge of Ben Loyal. Over flat Caithness moors, Morven and the Scarabens linger southwards.

North, in a magical multicoloured blue and silver carpet, lie the islands of Shapinsay, Rousay, Eday, Stronsay, Sanday and Westray. Pentland skerries guard the eastern approach to the firth,

Muckle Skerry white-lighthouse-pointed. Across turbulent seas, the deserted island of Stroma, flanked by Duncansby Head, and the massive Caithness cliffs of Dunnet. Descend from Ward Hill to reality, but carefully, down the edge of Howes of Quayawa, a steep, ragged ridge of corries, to White Glen and Moness track.

For the boy or girl who likes a 'proper walk', two miles past Sandy Loch, bear half-right and climb by Berrie Dale onto Grut Fea; westwards across the plateau takes you to the famous Old Man of Hoy – a great stack, rising 450 feet from sea to cliff-top. The moor is home to hen harrier, merlin, buzzard, peregrine, and golden plover. Great skuas preside over the plateau and greet invaders angrily, dive-bombing walkers in mighty swoops of huge flapping dark-brown wings. Walk cautiously and keep a wary eye open for these wardens of the skies.

In the geos that line the sheltered east coast of Hoy another attraction awaits the visitor who is also game fisherman. Sea trout follow the shore and may be caught throughout the year, providing you know where to look. Ask the excellent Orkney Angling Association for advice. They are as friendly and welcoming as their lovely islands and always happy to help visitors find sport and pleasure.

As the ferry pulls away from Moness pier, past the sunken Second World War blockships, rest weary legs and thank the Good Lord for a wonderful day and the physical fitness to enjoy it. Hum a

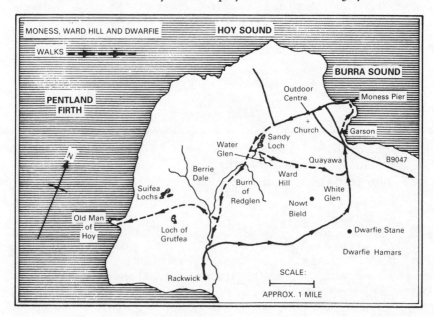

few bars of *Stevie's Ferry* in gratitude. If you don't know the tune, fear not; I will be happy to play it for you at the drop of a quaver – provided you are prepared to take the risk of listening.

WHAT YOU NEED TO KNOW

Time and effort The most important thing is to plan your walks to coincide with ferry times; or take a tent. The longest walk, from Moness out to the Old Man of Hoy, covers sixteen miles and will take up to eight hours. The round trip from Moness to Rackwick and back is eleven miles and about five hours. Moness to Sandy Loch and up Ward Hill is five miles; allow three hours for the journey. Compass and map should be carried and you will need good walking boots.

Location Ordnance Survey Sheet 7, Pentland Firth, second series, scale 1:50,000.

Grid references Stromness 255090; Moness pier 245039; Sandy Loch 219030; Water Glen 220025; Ward Hill 229023; Howes of Quayana 235020; White Glen 242019; The Dwarfie Stane 244006; Rackwick 202992; Berrie Dale 200015; Old Man of Hoy 177008.

Route All the walks start from Moness pier. Walk from the pier to the B9049. Where it turns south, go straight on. This road leads past the little church and outdoor centre. Where the road turns right, go straight on and follow the track out past Sandy Loch, which is on your left.

The route up Ward Hill is on your left, across the feeder stream for Sandy Loch. On top of Ward Hill plot your route down. Bear left along the ridge of Howes of Quayawa and at the end angle downhill into White Glen. At the minor road, turn and leave the road at Garson to stroll along the beach, back to Moness pier.

For round trip from Moness to Rackwick and back, simply follow the track past Sandy Loch westwards. Where it meets the single track road, shortly before the village, turn left and return to Moness via the Dwarfie Stane. The walk out to the Old Man of Hoy departs from the Sandy Loch track where Berrie Dale Water joins Burn of Redglen. Follow Berrie Dale water up the hill for a hundred yards and then bear left. At the top, walk between the little Suifea lochans on your left and Loch of Grutfea right. The Old Man is due west from here. Return to Moness the same way.

45

Rousay Cairns

ORKNEY contains some of the most important archaeological
monuments in Europe: the Stone Age village of Skara Brae;
the dramatic standing stones of Stenness, the Ring of Brogar and
the magnificent Chambered Tomb of Maes Howe. Given the
enormous number of Orcadian neolithic sites, I often wonder how
many people lived on Orkney five thousand years ago. Which is
my trouble – I find it impossible to resist the temptation to
speculate.

Sooner rather than later, and completely unsupported by any
evidence, I build up a mental picture – of busy farmer-fishermen
tending sparse crops; of tousle-haired boys wrestling on ancient
Atlantic sands; of heavy-breasted women grinding corn, warmed
by neolithic sun, chiding scavenging dogs. But there must have
been a thriving community in Orkney, perhaps several hundred
souls; and there must have been great interchange of ideas, tech-
niques and ideals.

There is little evidence of the earliest hunter-gatherer settlers in
northern Scotland, other than sea-shell middens. They lived out
their lives, scrounging and slaying where they could, a bird here, a
beast there, living in caves or rude shelters. On good days, perhaps
the carcass of a washed-up whale; always, the plentiful prehistoric
mussel beds. But their descendants left their mark, particularly by
the manner in which they buried the dead – in great chambered
tombs.

These massive, complicated structures lie scattered throughout Highlands and Islands, memorials of distant, perhaps more civilised days, when, to survive, a community had to work together. Values were more simply expressed, in the everyday necessities of living; and I think that we have more to learn from their lives than dusty archaeological facts. Speculating again.

The Orkney island of Rousay, the 'Holy Isle', has more than its fair share of these monuments, and an easy, delightful coastal walk passes the most impressive. However, the first part of the walk is by sea, providing you don't sit down during the journey – from the pier at Tingwall on Mainland, over Eynhallow Sound, by the island of Wyre to the little harbour at Brinyan.

Rousay is encompassed by craggy shores, scored by rocky bays. Most of the hinterland is gently hilled and there is a fine viewpoint on the highest peak, High Brae of Camps, a modest 800 feet above sea level. High Brae is easily climbed from the road that circles Rousay and the view from the top is spectacular.

Orkney consists of almost ninety islands, some thirty of which are inhabited, and most can be seen from the hill. Northwards lie Westray and its little sister Papa Westray; the wild rocks of North Ronaldsay and the long straggle of Sanday. East are Egilsay, Eaday, Stronsay and Shapinsay, with Auskerry in the distance. South, across Mainland, crowd the ever-present gentle hills of Hoy.

Good news for lighthouse keepers, because nearly all the islands have warning lights – much-needed in these dangerous, turbulent waters, which constantly argue and squabble with deserted black-rock shores, a vast turmoil of tormented seas, empty to Iceland, Greenland and America. Vikings, rather than me, thank you, rowing off into that particular sunset.

The only road round Rounsay is numbered with bureaucratic thoroughness. You would imagine that, being a single road, it would have a single designation. Not so. At the pier it is the B9065; where it joins the loop, right and left, it becomes B9064. A minibus plies the route in an anticlockwise direction, taking forty-five minutes to complete the journey. On the way, the driver will introduce you to the life and times of Rousay, past and present, and this will greatly prepare you for the walk.

Leave the bus at Mid Howe and follow the signposts for the Westness Walk which lead to the brochs and chambered cairn of Mid Howe. At first sight you might be forgiven for thinking that Mid Howe was an old Orcadian cattle byre: drystane walls separated into cubicles. The structure is 106 feet in length by 42 feet wide and the burial chamber takes up 76 feet. There are twelve cells, six on each side, and one side has platforms. Twenty-five skeletons were found here, along with well preserved pottery.

The path leaves Mid Howe and wends its way along the shoreline, by Eynhallow Sound, overlooking Eynhallow and the Church of the Holy Isle. These are fierce waters, where long arms of Atlantic and North Sea race through dangerous narrows with amazing force. Fulmars sweep by, and in spring and summer the path is bright yellow, blue and red with wild flowers. Orkney is devoid of foxes, squirrels, deer and badgers, but if you have your wits about you there is always the chance of seeing an otter.

I decided many years ago that if I were reincarnated I would choose to return as an otter – footloose and fancy free, the outdoor life, as much walking, swimming and fishing as I wanted, and a protected species into the bargain. Who could ask for more?

The path eventually comes back to the 'main' road, but this is a relative statement – expect possibly two or three vehicles an hour. Knowe of Lairo, a long, four-horned chambered cairn, is approached by the track that leads left from the road, past the schoolhouse at Frotoft. It was probably constructed over a considerable period, bits being added at different times. The cairn extends in a long mound for a distance of 180 feet and there is an 18-foot-long entrance passage leading to three burial chambers.

Nearby is another chambered cairn, Knowe of Yarso, a stalled cairn with four compartments, first explored in 1934, when the remains of twenty adults and one child were found. They were well prepared and provided for their last, long journey: '30 individual red-deer, some sheep and a dog. Relics included fragments of food-vessel and beaker pottery, four arrowheads and more than 60 other flint implements, and five bone tools.'

The last of the Rousay monuments is Blackhammar, close to Yarso Cairn, another stalled burial chamber divided into fourteen stalls, measuring 42 feet by 6 feet in width. I wonder if they sang or chanted when they buried their loved ones? How did they mourn? What rites or incantations were performed over the still, sleeping bodies?

Back at Brinyan Pier, as reward for attention, treat yourself whilst waiting for the ferry. The sea-food processing factory at Brinyan offers some of the most splendid lobster, scallop and fresh-cooked crab in Britain. Enjoy a neolithic snack, and spare a crumb for me.

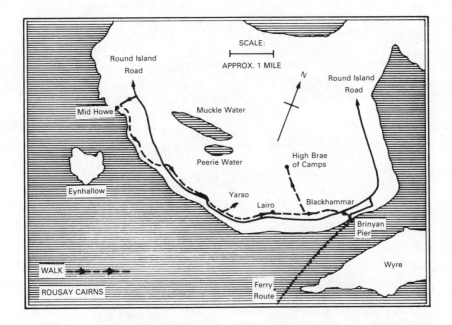

WHAT YOU NEED TO KNOW

Time and effort   Prepare yourself for this visit and read up about the chambered cairns you will be visiting. Best book is a *Guide to Prehistoric Scotland* by Richard Feacham, published by Batsford, London. Make sure to check return ferry times. The walking part is easy and total distance is 6½ miles. Spend the whole day on the island and climb High Brae of Camps after visiting the cairns. Further details from Josh Gourley, Orkney Island Tourist Board, Kirkwall. Telephone: Kirkwall (0856) 2856.

Location   Ordnance Survey Sheet 6, Orkney – Mainland, second series, scale 1:50,000.

Grid references   Ferry at Tingwall on Mainland 403228; Brinyan Pier 436275; start of walk at Mid Howe 375310; Mid Howe Cairn 371308; Yarso Cairn 404281; Lairo Cairn 414277; Blackhammar Cairn 425275; High Brae of Camps 419290.

Route   Sail from Tingwall to Brinyan and take the minibus round the island. Get off at Mid Howe and follow the signposts marking the Westness Walk, eastwards along the coast. The cairns are on the left of the road and High Brae of Camps is easily accessible to the north.

46

From Skelberry to Birka

THE SHETLAND ISLANDS have provided home and haven for the world's travellers for more than four thousand years. At Jarlshof, near Sumburgh Airport, there is evidence of continuous occupation since Stone Age, Bronze Age and Iron Age times, right down to the days of Viking domination. The 'Temple' at Stanydale, a communal building near Bridge of Walls, is a remarkable structure, standing amidst the ruins of a settlement of nine houses, surrounded by the outline of ancient fields, clearly worked by a small neolithic community.

Early writers referred to Shetland and Iceland as ultima Thule and in the 4th century B.C. Pytheas of Marseilles, astronomer and geographer, sailed 'six days from north Britain' to reach them. These remote northern lands are a wild scatter of more than a hundred islands resting in the storm-tossed bosom of the mighty Atlantic Ocean, covering an area of more than 550 square miles.

The largest island is Mainland and other principal islands are Yell, Unst, Fetlar, Bressay and Whalsey. They are an endless delight of sunlight and serenity, guarded by huge, sea bird-clad crags, fringed with deserted white sandy beaches. Moorlands are specked silver with more than three hundred freshwater lochs peopled by Arctic skua, red-throated diver and golden plover. Springtime is a riot of wild flowers and in high summer the endless days of the 'simmer dim' banish night.

Most people have only a vague idea of where Shetland really is – other than being in that little box, top right of the map on evening weather charts. In fact, the islands lie on the same latitude as Bergen in Norway and the southern tip of Greenland, as close to Norway as they are to Aberdeen and vastly proud of Viking traditions.

The Gulf Stream warms and washes Shetland's shores and the islands are never too hot or too cold, though at any one time weather conditions vary greatly throughout the island: the east coast may be basking in sunshine at the same time as the west coast is cringing under lead-heavy rain. Only one thing is constant: the ever-present wind; and what the Shetlander calls a gentle breeze BBC weathermen in London generally report as a force eight gale.

I first visited Shetland in 1983, delighted to be amongst so many fellow Sandisons, for mine is a Shetland name. The old capital was Scalloway, on the west coast, but this distinction now belongs to Lerwick in the east. Lerwick is a busy, bustling town and its harbour plays host to Europe's fishing fleet. Boats from Russia, Poland, Denmark, Norway, Germany and France crowd the anchorage off Commercial Street and a dozen different dialects may be heard in shop and bar.

Visitors admire and buy the famous handmade knitwear, which uses the natural colours of hardy Shetland sheep, fleece taken in handfuls from their stout sides. There is delicately spun lace from the island of Unst, soft sheepskin rugs and traditionally designed fine silverware.

The islands provide a wealth of interest for archaeologist, ornithologist, botanist, geologist, historian, game fisherman or just plain 'escapist' – enough to keep every member of the tribe fully occupied and interested, and the only danger is the all-pervading, overwhelming temptation – never to leave.

During my visit, I spent most of my time walking and fishing the lochs of Mainland in company with Rae Phillips and Bobby Tulloch, expert anglers and well accustomed to finding their way over trackless moors to wonderful places. Their boats were wonderful too: sleek, narrow-bowed, finely crafted works of art, owing as much to Viking traditions as to the skills of modern day boat-builder. There is a saying in Shetland: 'You may do as you please with another man's wife, but you must never touch his boat.'

A walk of outstanding beauty and interest is from Skelberry, in North Mainland, out over the moors to Lang Clodie Loch. It is a long, tough way and very definitely compass-and-map country.

When you climb onto the moor an amazing vista opens. Scattered granite boulders glisten in the sun; golden plover flit and pipe over rough peat hags. Scootie Allan, the Shetland name for the Arctic skua, tumble and twist in stunning aeriel mock-combat; the constant wind tugs at your clothes.

We threaded our way across the moor, edging round peat banks, past a string of dark blue trout-filled lochs and lochans with magical names: Roer Water, Maadle Swankie, Tonga and Muckle Lunga, Many Crooks, Moshella and the Loch of the Grey Ewe. But the most dramatic of all is lovely Birka Water, 700 yards long by 300 yards wide – easier to measure its extent than to describe its beauty.

Birka is crystal-clear and at the east end there is a sandy beach which makes a perfect picnic spot. Opposite the beach is a magnificent waterfall, dropping from high crags along the south shore. I first saw it after heavy rain, on a warm, sunny afternoon: full, silver, thunderous, tumbling sparkling into the waters of the loch, sending urgent wavelets rippling over the calm surface.

We walked round the loch to the foot of the falls and then climbed slowly to the tiny, narrow lochan at the top. As I reached the crest, head level with the outlet falls, I found myself eyeball to eyeball with a red-throated diver. The bird was half a dozen yards away – the 'rain goose' of the Shetlands. As more of my bulk appeared, the graceful creature gave a wink of welcome and splashed noisily skywards, seeking a less busy feeding place.

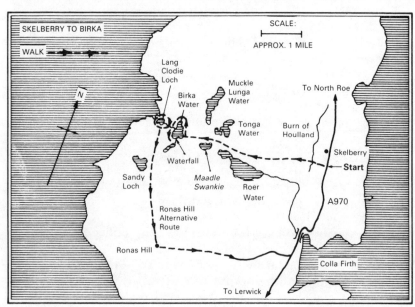

Birka collects together all the waters from the lochs on the north slope of Ronas Hill, the highest point on Shetland, and hurries them seawards down a splendid outlet burn on the west shore, a narrow, boulder-strewn, living stream, chattering and singing in still summer air. Far below, on a green plateau, tiny Lang Clodie Loch gathers the streams into her arms then shoots them out over vast, red-ragged cliffs into the Atlantic wilderness.

Bobby Tulloch and I walked homewards that evening, over the marvellous wonder of the moors, stopping once or twice for a few casts in little lochans along the way, talking about this and that, and mostly not at all. Before descending to the road, I paused and looked back, trying to fix the memory and scent and sounds of the moorlands in my mind. As I write, they are still as fresh and startlingly clear as on that first, memorable, sunny Shetland day.

WHAT YOU NEED TO KNOW

Time and effort As the crow flies, seven miles there and back. For humans, twisting and turning over the moor, probably about another mile. This is a hard walk and there are no tracks or paths to ease the way. Essential equipment are strong walking boots, compass and map. If mist comes down, even with compass and map it will be hard to find your way, so do make sure you are well prepared for all eventualities.

Location Ordnance Survey Sheet 1, Shetland – Yell and Unst, second series, scale 1:50,000.

Grid references Start of walk 362862; access onto hill 360863; Roer Water 335864; route between Tonga Water and Maadle Swankie 322872; Birka Water 316875; Birka waterfall 315872; Birka outlet burn 316875; Lang Clodie Loch 312878.

Route Park the car just before the houses at Skelberry. There is a gate on your left, leading down through a grass park to the foot of the hill. Cross the burn and climb the gully leading up to the plateau.

Walk westwards, keeping Roer Water on your left. Take frequent bearings to check direction or you may find yourself going too far north. Pass between Tonga and Swankie, then walk in a straight line, as far as possible, on to Birka. If you get it right, you should arrive at the sandy beach.

Walk round the north shore of Birka to reach the waterfall, crossing the outlet burn on the way – step nimbly to avoid wet feet. Climb the waterfall and say hello to my red-throated diver, then return to the outlet burn.

Follow the outlet burn down the narrow defile to the cliff-top plateau and Lang Clodie Loch. Stay well back from the edge of the cliffs. I suggest you return home the same way but, if you feel really adventurous, angle south past Sandy Water and Swabie Water to climb Ronas Hill. The way down follows the east shoulder of Ronas and this leads to a hill track which will take you back to the A970, then north to your car. Be warned, this will add five more miles.

47

Caithness Castles, Cliffs and Shores

THE SHORE and cliff path from Keiss to Staxigoe in Caithness is a walk for all seasons. I have tramped that way battered by winter gales, grateful for every sheltering dip, watching white showers of snow buntings peck stubble fields and huge, heavy-billed great northern divers haughtily riding the endless waves of Sinclair Bay; and enjoying the sudden pleasurable company of sombre-eyed, whiskered and curious Atlantic seals.

Arctic winds chase mountainous seas eastwards, dashing them in white-sprayed fury against Old Red Sandstone rocks weathered by millions of years into stark, jagged stacks, knifed by black, sea-booming fiords and secret caves. Sinclair Bay is a scimitar of gold, enclosing green-crested breakers, sweeping southwards by gaunt Ackergill Tower, past grim Girnigoe Castle to lighthouse-topped Noss Head.

Springtime flowers peep from rocky corners: *Primula scotica*, light-green leaves cupping vivid purple flowers. Sea rocket and sandwort, scruvy-grass and sand sedge adorn the beach. High dunes host chickweed and hawkweed, backed by field gentian, campion, wild pansy and knapweed. Cliff-tops riot with thrift, sea-pink, rose-root and vetch.

Fulmar, kittiwake, guillemot, razorbills and puffin tenement crags in never-ending squabble. Turnstone, purple sandpiper and sanderling flight the shore. Solan geese, Sule Skerry gannets from Orkney, turn and dive, stiff-winged flashes of brilliant white. Emerald-green and black shags cluster the rocks, wings out-stretched, like old men waiting for tea time.

I have wandered, summer lazy, splashing through River Wester where it marries the sea, sunbathing on warm sands, lulled to dreamless sleep by oystercatcher and curlew. Walked south into a theatre backdrop clad with graceful mountains; conical Morven, Madiens Pap, Ben Alisky, Clas Choire and bare-breasted Scarabens.

Keiss, the 'rounded ridge' of the Vikings, is a tiny village clinging to Caithness cliffs. A small harbour plays host to a few colourful craft fishing for crab and lobster, and there is a busy salmon-netting station. From a rocky promontory, the dark ruins of Keiss Castle guard the neat cluster of grey houses, as they have done for more than four hundred years.

Keiss produced one of Scotland's most famous engineers, James Bremner, born on 25 September 1784. The only schooling he had consisted of the customary three Rs of the eighteenth century: reading, writing and religion. His father apprenticed him as a carpenter in Greenock and, after six and a half years and two voyages to America, Bremner returned to Wick, where he set up as shipbuilder and fish curer.

James Bremner invented a suspension crane, with a jib capable of extending from 80 to 120 feet; a pile driver which drove three piles simultaneously; the world's first 'Mulberry' harbour, constructed as a series of watertight compartments, which could be floated into position prior to being sunk; and a system of buoyancy bags, used for floating heavy foundation stones into position for building harbours.

His most notable triumph was refloating ss *Great Britain*, then the world's largest ship. The *Great Britain* ran aground on the rocks of Dundrum Bay in Ireland on Friday 27 August 1847. For a year, the best engineering brains in the country tried to rescue her. Eventually, Bremner was asked to help. Not only did he refloat the mighty vessel, but within a few weeks he sailed her back to Liverpool under her own steam, inventing a super-capacity water pump in order to do so.

As a mark of esteem, Bremner was awarded the Telford Medal of the Institute of Civil Engineers and when he died in August 1856 Caithness mourned the loss of a much-loved son. Flags were flown at half-mast and shops along the funeral route pulled down shutters. James Bremner was laid to rest in the grounds of the old parish church of Wick.

The Wester river is a barrier along the way. Wading time. Cold legs in high water, damp feet in midsummer. Sea trout and salmon run the short river to Loch of Wester, the 'loch of the ford', now greatly disfigured by the clutter of huts and workyards of under-sea pipe fabricators, Kestrel Marine. The mouth of the Wester is a favourite fishing spot, where local anglers gather to tempt sea-liced, silver fish as they splash through salty waters to upstream spawning grounds.

Behind marram covered dunes lies one of Scotland's oldest golf courses, Reiss, founded more than one hundred years ago and a traditional Scottish 'links' course, flat and sand-blown, covered with wild flowers and cursing golfers. Whenever I forget that my greatest golfing handicap is a complete inability to hit the ball in a straight line, a few holes at Reiss remind me. I see a lot of wild flowers and do a lot of cursing, searching for lost balls.

At low tide, wide sands between Wester and Ackergill make easy walking. Our two dogs love the beach and tear about like mad things, up the dunes, dashing in and out of the sea. Well, Breac does the sea bit; Heathcliff is more circumspect about water, having almost drowned as a puppy in a cold Sutherlandshire loch.

This is our Boxing Day family walk, regardless of weather – though sometimes Caithness weather is so mild that dafter members of the tribe paddle, blue-toed and screaming with delight. At the age of twenty-five? Everyone comes home wet.

Ackergill Tower, one of the oldest inhabited houses in Scotland, dominates Sinclair Bay. Five-storeyed and nearly seventy feet high, Ackergill was once protected by a moat and high wall. Cromwell's troops used the Tower as headquarters during their visit to Caithness in the seventeenth century and in 1699 it was bought by the Dunbars of Hempriggs.

Ackergill is in new hands – completely refurbished as a 'think tank' for business executives seeking privacy and seclusion whilst they make world-shaping decisions about toothpaste sales and paper-clips. Tiptoe by. Great men should not be disturbed by simple strand strollers.

Past the little community of Ackergill, with its high-legged lifeboat-launching station, the track edges a rocky shore, climbing up sheer hundred-foot cliffs. Not a place for dogs or people without a head for heights. Like me. I keep well back, inching cautiously along the windswept tops.

Sinclair and Girnigoe Castles beckon, perched on a sharp, almost inaccessible promontory: dark ruins of dark days. Clamber down into the dungeon where George Sinclair, 4th Earl of Caithness, left his son James to die in 1576 – 'keiped in miserable captivity for the space of seven years'. James had incurred his father's wrath for failing to murder hostages taken during the siege of Dornoch. The hapless young man was starved for two weeks then given well salted meat. When he asked for water to slake his raging thirst none was given and James died in agony, chocked by his own tongue.

Ann and I often visit the grim castle, which provides a sheltered, skua-eyed view of the bird-busy bay. Eider duck, male birds with neatly parted black-and-white backs, dive in the clear waters. Summer terns flit and dance over the waves. And, sometimes, carried on the wind, a starker, more distant, blood-chilling call seems to echo through the cold ruins.

Close to Sinclair and Girnigoe Castles is another summer favourite of ours, Sandigoe Bay – a scrap of yellow sand, backed by scarred cliffs, rarely busy, ideal place for warm after-church Sundays. Nearby, at Noss Head, in a deep gorge, is a natural rock 'seat', one hundred feet above the sea. Approach carefully and not at all in high winds.

Puffin-watching time. A few yards over the void, in the cliff face, a small colony of puffins have burrowed nests. They sit, firework-beaked and serious, doing what puffins do – whirring off in endless food-hunting forays for hungry offspring. Funny birds, puffins: when the parent birds reckon that youngsters are big enough, they abandon their squawking brood. Chicks stumble light-wards, topple down the cliff, and learn – very quickly – to fly.

Across the fields from Noss is the fishing village of Staxigoe, where my grandfather was born. Time was when this small harbour was more important than neighbouring Wick. Timber from Sweden arrived at Staxigoe and the rocky harbour might be packed with up to eighty ships. Today things are a lot quieter; a few, small inshore boats moored fore and aft across the bay.

I feel at home in Caithness, and nowhere more so than by Staxigoe. Elsay Farm, once owned by an uncle of my father, George Reay; the war memorial, standing on land given to the community by a long-departed relative. Sounds stupid, but I'm sure some of them join me on my walks from Keiss to Staxigoe, and I'm always glad of their company.

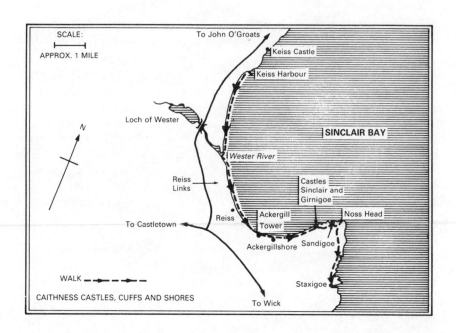

SCALE:
APPROX. 1 MILE

To John O'Groats

Keiss Castle

Keiss Harbour

Loch of Wester

N

SINCLAIR BAY

Wester River

Reiss
Links

Castles
Sinclair and
Girnigoe

To Castletown

Reiss

Ackergill
Tower

Noss Head

Ackergillshore

Sandigoe

WALK ━ ▸ ━ ━ ▸ ━

Staxigoe

CAITHNESS CASTLES, CUFFS AND SHORES

To Wick

WHAT YOU NEED TO KNOW

Time and effort   Allow about five hours for this walk. Even better, when the sun is shining, make a day of it. There is a lot to see along the way, including Sinclair and Girnigoe Castles, which are an outing in themselves. Take along a towel for drying feet after crossing Wester river.

The cliffs towards the south end of the bay are very high and great care must be taken walking along the tops. Also when visiting the castles. There are sharp drops and in the summer the grass is smooth and slippery.

It is possible to climb down to the shore through a dark stairwell at the end of the promontory upon which the castles stand. Only do so when the sea is mirror calm. At other times waves could wash you off to Norway – and who needs that? Keep children under strictest supervision. Dogs should be left tied up outside.

Location   Ordnance Survey Sheet 12, Thurso and Wick, second series, scale 1:50,000.

Grid references   Keiss 346713; Keiss Castle 357616; Wester river 339577; Ackergill Tower 354547; Ackergill 359545; Castle Girnigoe 379549; Sandigoe Bay 385550; Noss Head 388551; Staxigoe 385525.

Route   Leave your car at Staxigoe, by the harbour, and travel by taxi, bus or a good friend out to Keiss. If you propose to visit the old castle of Keiss, first ask permission to do so at the farm on the way down to the shore. From the harbour at Keiss walk south along a track which edges the fields, leading to a car park overlooking the shore.

If the tide is out, cut down onto the beach. Otherwise, follow the track along the top of the dunes until you find space on the sands. Place to come down is at a ragged, barbed-wired fence. Cross the river Wester as best you can and simply follow the beach south.

As you near Ackergill Tower, you will be forced off the beach by rocks. Walk along the foreshore past the tower and then, keeping up, make for Ackergill village. A well marked path exits from the village and this leads up and along the cliffs to Castle Sinclair and Girnigoe.

After visiting the castles, walk towards Noss Head. A fence line cuts your path and a signpost will direct you down a steep gully to Sandigoe Bay. Climb back up the hill and make for the little lochan by the side of the lighthouse. On the cliff, close to the west of the lighthouse, you will find the puffin colony – open from April until June – and the rock seat.

Walk back down the road which leads to the lighthouse and at the car park turn left and walk over the fields to Staxigoe. This will bring you to the harbour.

48

Herring and Hill Forts

WICK IS a ragged little town clustered round a shallow wave-swept bay. Even today, in good weather, gaining access to the harbour is hazardous; in days of sailing boats it could be downright dangerous. During the great herring fishings in the nineteenth century boats stayed at sea overnight, returning the following morning, and often had to anchor in the bay to await favourable tide conditions for entry. It was then that Wick Bay could be most wicked for if a sudden storm caught the fleet at anchor they were forced to run for safety before an onshore wind chased by huge, merciless breakers.

The worst disasters happened in the 1840s. In 1845 ten men drowned when a fierce onshore wind whipped shallow waters into a frenzy of foam and surf. Three years later, 37 men perished in a single night of terrible gales. Thousands of people gathered on harbour walls, helpless, as boat after boat came to grief in tormented, boiling waters. Those days have long since gone, although Wick is still a busy fishing port; but the 'silver darlings' are remembered in an imaginative exhibition in the Wick Heritage Centre, housed in an old grey building close to the harbour.

There are superb photographs from the famous Johnson Collection: furnished interiors of fishermen's homes; complete boats in a mock harbour, rigged and crewed; and a full-scale model of a herring curing house. A host of personal effects and documents are displayed, including the sad little school bag of a child who died, the books of his brief life spilling from the open flap.

Although unkempt and untidy, Wick has its own special charm and character. Wickers are self-reliant, friendly, hard-working people, used to making their own entertainment. The town's only cinema closed a few years ago and until then was one of the few places of entertainment. However, not so very long since, when silent films were shown, a visit to Wick cinema could be a less than entertaining experience.

One of the Caithness clans was blessed with large numbers who could neither read nor write, and when they filled the front rows the rest of the audience had to contend with a commentary as their spokesman translated, in a loud voice, the subtitles at the bottom of the screen.

Caithness coastlines are dressed with harbours which flourished in the glory days of the herring fishings: Scrabster, Thurso, Castletown, Ham, Scarfskerry, Huna, Groats, Skiraz, Keiss, Staxigoe, Wick, Sarclet, Whaligoe, Lybster, Latheron and Dunbeath. All had their complement of sturdy boats which each summer sailed the stormy waters of the North Sea to reap sparkling harvest.

Whaligoe is one of the most dramatic of these little harbours and lies south from Wick, near Ulbster. The sea has cut a narrow cove into the cliffs and more than three hundred steps lead down to a tiny, now deserted harbour. Wives used to carry heavy crans of dripping herring up the steep steps and everything required to service the small boats had to be laboriously transported down the flagstone stairwell.

Although fisherfolk have gone, the old steps are still carefully cared for by a local lady. Her belief is that since Jesus was a fisherman, and will come again, He might well arrive at the foot of Whaligoe Steps. She is determined that the good Lord should have easy access to the top.

West of Whaligoe is Hill of Yarrows, a rounded summit 696 feet in height. There are more than eighty prehistoric sites in the vicinity, dating from almost five thousand years ago. Chambered tombs, standing stones, stone rows, hill forts and settlements and brochs – perhaps one of the most extensive and least explored archaeological sites in Britain.

Garrywhin Fort crests a ridge overlooking the tiny, reed-covered Loch Watenan and is 590 feet in length by 300 feet wide. A stone wall runs for a distance of 450 feet, pierced by entries lined with stone slabs. At the foot of the ridge, close to the shore of the loch, is a short horned chambered cairn where neolithic pottery was found amidst skeletal remains. At Mid Clyth, nearby, are magnificent stone rows: twenty-two rows of eight stones locked fast in the soil, their purpose and function as yet unknown.

Loch Watenan is home for wading and diving birds, which flock there in hundreds to quack and croak amongst thick weeds. It is also home for some beautiful wild brown trout – deep-bodied, golden and wild fighters. Earlier this year I caught a fish of two pounds on a Slazenger 4 golf ball. No, not a 'fisherman's story' but quite true. Well, nearly.

I was half concentrating, casting, gazing round at the endless delight of wildlife, when a glint of white under the water drew my attention. A golf ball. Never one to look a gift horse in the mouth, I bent forward, scrabbling about under the surface trying to pick it up without getting my sleeve wet – but to no avail.

I tried kicking it shorewards, forgetting all about my flies, which were somewhere out in the middle of the loch. When the fish grabbed and shot off, rocket-like, I overbalanced and fell on hands and knees. Soaking wet now, I grabbed the ball and stumbled ashore. Which is how I managed to catch a trout on a Slazenger 4.

A track leads from the south end of the loch up into the hills, wending past Cairn of Get towards Loch of Warehouse. South-west of Warehouse are more chambered cairns and a standing stone, and the hill is scattered with the boulders and stones of other ancient monuments.

Warehouse is one of my favourite places and the view from the top is perfect. The tower of Old Parish Church in Wick, where my daughter Jean was christened; Keiss and the wide sweep of Sinclair Bay, rising over moorlands to John o' Groats and the hills of Hoy on Orkney. Morven and Scarabens look close enough to reach out and touch whilst westwards, over the flow country, Sletill Hill and Ben Griams nod sleepily in Sutherland.

Walk north down the hill to Loch of Yarrows and back in time once more to the hut circles, brochs and cairns of neolithic man. Must have been a busy place then, bright with children's laughter and busy families in the fresh dawn of time. I never pass this way without wondering what they would all make of our fretful, complicated lives now.

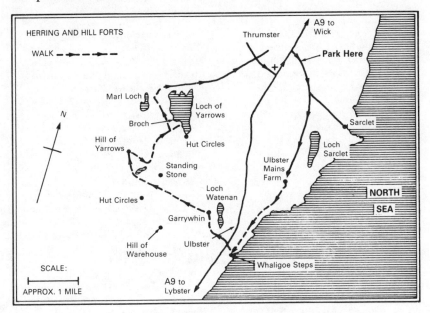

WHAT YOU NEED TO KNOW

Time and effort   Visit Wick Heritage Centre first and then set off on this delightful ten-mile hill and coastal walk. Good walking boots should be worn for the way is often rough and wet – but few problems. Keep back from the edge of the cliffs, however, and be warned: going down the steps at Whaligoe is a lot easier than climbing back up them. Before visiting the Watenan neolothic sites, arm yourself with a copy of either the *Caithness Book*, editor Donald Omand and published by Highland Printers, Inverness, or Richard Feacham's excellent *Guide to Prehistoric Scotland*, published by B. T. Batsford Ltd, London.

Location   Ordnance Survey Sheet 12, Thurso and Wick, second series, scale 1:50,000.

Grid references Wick Heritage Centre is at Bank Row 365506; Car parking at Thrumster 338452; Mains of Ulbster 335421; Whaligoe Steps 321406; Loch Watenan 319410; Garrywhin 318414; Loch of Warehouse 300424; Loch of Yarrows 310440; Yarrows Broch 308435.

Route   After visiting Wick Heritage Centre, drive south down the A9 to the village of Thrumster. Turn left, and you will find parking space by the small playing field on your left, a hundred yards from the road junction. Follow the minor road south past Loch Sarclet to Mains of Ulbster and on to the cliffs. A mile further brings you to Ulbster and Whaligoe.

The first large house on the cliff is a converted mill. The top of the steps is further on, to the left of the row of cottages. Up and down the steps. They are very steep and if you have any doubts about climbing back up only go half-way down, to the first 'twist', and view the harbour from above. No prizes for having a heart attack in Caithness.

From Ulbster, cross the A9 and take the little road directly in front of you. It leads up to Loch Watenan. The hill fort and archaeological remains are all close together. Climb north from the loch, using compass and map, which you have not forgotten, and admire the view from Loch of Warehouse and Hill of Yarrows.

Descend from the north end of the loch down a narrow gully and on to Loch of Yarrows and Yarrows Broch and the hut circles, which are all at the south end of the loch. Follow the rutted farm road up the west bank, passing Marl Loch on your left, not shown on Ordnance Survey sheet.

Turn right along the north shore of Yarrows and follow this little road to its first major crossing. Turn right here, back to the A9. North up the A9 to Thrumster. Take great care on this last section. Cars travel very fast up this long, straight part of the A9.

49

Forss and Scrabster

A FEW MILES west from Thurso in Caithness, along the last road on mainland Britain, lies Forss House, an old grey building nodding sleepily over the Forss river in a small wood, carpeted in spring with celandine, snowdrop and bluebell. Treecreepers study the bark of insect-rich pines. Woodcock whirr stiff-winged through dark forests.

A pair of buzzards rule the valley from a new plantation throne and below Forss Falls, where brown and white waters dash over shining black rocks, Atlantic salmon hurl themselves in silver bars at cascading torrents, urgent for upstream spawning grounds.

Forss House has been converted into a comfortable hotel, home for passers-by and fishermen who come to do battle with salmon in the narrow little river. To the left of the house, by the side of the lawn, a path leads to a promontory overlooking the falls. A thoughtful seat comforts you as you wait and watch for the sudden splendour of the king of fish, rising majestically to challenge the stream.

Early one morning I watched an otter sidle cautiously into the pool. His eyes sparkled and whiskers twitched as he scented the air for the smell of danger, but the wind was right for me and I watched him pursue, capture and land a salmon of about nine pounds in weight, rushing the doomed fish into the undergrowth, anxious for breakfast. Wish I could catch them so easily.

A track leads from the back of the house, through an iron gate, along the side of pine-wooded hills above the river. Forss slides gently seawards through green meadow lands, decked with purple and spotted orchid, tormentil, bugle, milkwort and primrose. Grey and pied wagtail dip and bob by the stream as it hurries under a footbridge to greet the cold Atlantic in Crosskirk Bay.

On the cliffs above the west shore cluster the ruins of one of Scotland's oldest places of worship, the twelfth-century St Mary's Chapel. Close by, bristling with fiercesome antennae, is a US Air Force base, endlessly searching the ether above ragged seas for warning of who knws what. Opposing cultures. One born out of a love for God; the other out of fear of man.

Long wave-washed rocky ledges wed the Forss river to the sea in an everchanging pattern of crests and tiny storms. Oystercatchers pipe by the shore and seals black-bob the bay. Brisk eider drakes, escorted by dowdy-grey females, roller-coast the tide. A small boat snuffles round the rocks, seeking lobster pots and anything else that happens to be passing.

Fertile fields rise in low sea-girt cliffs and a faint path runs eastwards along the jagged tops towards Brims Ness, fanned by dangerous, skerry-fingered shoals and shallows. Seas tumble and turn in contrary currents and wide waves sweep the shore. Surfers from all over Europe gather here for international events. Crowds of men and women, in skin-tight colour-striped wet-suits.

Off shore, other Europeans seeking international fame speck the sea with fishing boats, dredging the depths for record-breaking fish. Recently, whilst millions watched on television, three well-heeled pleasure-chasing Londoners roared and laughed drunkenly as one of their party took pot-shots at passing sea gulls. Our local sheriff took his own pot-shots at this stupid man in court a few months later.

Past the scratchy harbour at Brims, flat fields covered in wild flowers margin the sea. Marwick Head on Orkney rears northwards, pricked by the dark shape of Kitchener's Memorial. Ward Hill on the Island of Hoy shimmers blue in hot afternoon haze and on the forward slope of the cliffs, in warm corners, *Primula scotica*, that rarest of Scottish plants, blushes purple-pink in summer sunlight. Tiny streams chortle down rocks by bright clumps of yellow primrose whilst curlews engineer busily under stones on the shore below.

A mile from Brims, on a tall promontory, separated from the
mainland by a narrow ridge, lie the remains of a Pictish hill fort.
Little can be seen of the fortifications but the air is full of the sound
of these hardy painted men going about their business, keeping
careful watch seawards for marauding Norsemen. There is a private
swimming pool near here. A shallow, clear pool, left by receding
tides, backed by high cliffs. A secret, silent place to laze away tired
hours.

On Brims Hill old quarries echo empty, relics of the great days of
the Caithness flagstone industry at the turn of the century, when
each year 16,000 tons of Caithness flagstone was exported throughout the world. London's Strand and docks were paved with
Caithness flag, as were Leith Walk and Parliament Square in
Edinburgh. The ever-increasing railway stations used Caithness
flag and there was a constant demand for this fine-quality stone.
Until some unkind person invented concrete.

The cliffs now cry to Spear Head and Holborn Head, towering
almost a hundred feet above Thurso Bay. On wild days I have seen
waves crashing at their feet, shattering spray in wind-driven sheets
to the top. During the terrible times of the Highland Clearances,
America-bound emigrant ships would gather in Thurso Bay to
await the arrival of their cargo of human misery, torn from
Sutherland glens to make way for Lowlanders and their sheep.

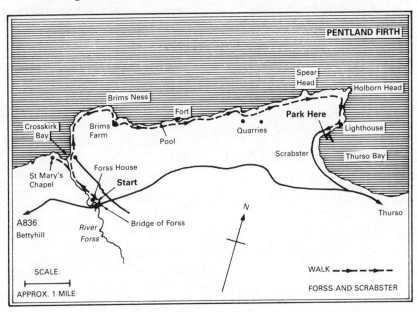

The tall stub of Holborn Head lighthouse points the way to Scrabster harbour. The Orkney ferry, *St Ola*, lies snug against her pier. Fishing boats and sailing craft throw colourful reflections over smooth, oil-calm waters. Like a crow's nest above the scene, the Upper Deck restaurant beckons. They serve the best steak in the whole of Britain. Treat yourself after the long walk. You deserve it.

WHAT YOU NEED TO KNOW

Time and effort Eight miles from Bridge of Forss to Scrabster harbour and about four hours' walking, more if you stop and look a lot. I suggest that you leave your car at Scrabster harbour by the Orkney ferry terminal and take a taxi out to Bridge of Forss. Make sure that you tell the driver that it is Forss/Thurso you want. There is another Forse, to the south of Wick, and they are often confused. If it is a fine day pack a picnic and take longer, stopping for lunch in the cove by my 'private swimming pool'. The only danger is the cliffs. Keep well back from the edge, particularly in windy weather and on Holborn Head.

Location Ordnance Survey Sheet 12, Thurso and Wick, second series, scale 1:50,000.

Grid references Bridge of Forss 037687; Crosskirk Bay 029700; St Mary's Chapel 025701; Brims Ness 040714; swimming pool 058709; fort 063710; quarries 079707; Holborn Head 109716; Scrabster harbour 100700.

Route The entrance to Forss House Hotel is well signposted before Bridge of Forss. Have a stirrup cup. Turn left out of the hotel, past the two chalets, and follow the track through the trees to the iron gate. Right from here, along the bank above the river. After a few hundred yards you are forced downhill. Scramble over the bluff and walk down the flat fields to Crosskirk Bay.

St Mary's Chapel is on the west side of the river and is reached by crossing the bridge near the ruined stone buildings on the shore and walking uphill on a well marked track. Return to the east bank and follow the cliff round past Brims Ness to Brims Farm. Walk up the farm road for a little way and then cut back left to the cliff-top.

As the cliffs grow in height, look out for the swimming pool and hill fort promontory. The track now runs close to the edge of the cliff, protected by a fence. Keep on the landward side and walk out to Holborn Head. From Holborn Head angle down towards the lighthouse and walk back to Scrabster harbour. And the Upper Deck.

50

'Sheer Greed
of Materialism'

BLAR NAM FAOILEAG in Caithness is a beautiful, living, growing
peat bog which has survived six thousand years since the last
ice age and is still busy today, laying down layer after layer of peat
over flagstone and sandstone of the Middle Old Red Sandstone
series. During glacial times Caithness was invaded by ice from two
directions, the principal body moving in from the North Sea and
covering the county east to west.

When the ice retreated it left behind a large, shallow inland lake,
fed and drained by river systems, and a barren landscape of bare
rock mixed with fragments dredged from the sea bottom. This
formed a stiff boulder clay, almost impermeable to air and water,
and the only plants able to establish themselves were shallow-
rooted creeping species such as mosses, lichens, marsh flowers and
small windswept trees. Perfect conditions for the growth of peat.

A section through the peat shows, at lowest levels, remains of
dwarf willow and alder which survived in the subarctic tempera-
tures. Then remains of birch and hazel, with many of the hazel nuts
showing that they had been gnawed at one end by small rodents.
Uppermost layers contain buried roots and branches of stunted
woods.

Blar nam Faoileag is an SSSI, a site of special scientific interest,
alive with history, a precious part of our national heritage. But we

live in strange times, when man constantly disregards his environment and seems to care for it only in so much as it might yield him financial return.

The previous owner of Blar nam Faoileag was the local 'laird', Lord Thurso, and he proposed a plan to extract peat from the bog on a commercial basis. A very considerable sum of public money was paid to compensate him for not doing so. More recently, the same 'laird' sold substantial tracts of the Flow Country to private tree-farming contractors, thereby allowing them to devastate ancient Altnabreac moorlands by planting millions of foreign species of conifer.

In a speech to the House of Lords on 12 April 1976, Lord Thurso is reported in the *John o'Groat Journal* as saying: 'The sheer greed of materialism threatens these rural communities'. In my opinion, Lord Thurso's actions clearly demonstrate the truth of his own statement, and his complete disregard for the Caithness landscape.

The land south of Blar nam Faoileag, round Loch Ruard, is safe in more enlightened hands and there is little danger of man's 'sheer greed' destroying these wonderful open moorlands. To walk amongst them is an unforgettable experience – a vast, silent, unchanging landscape, heather-purpled under God's great heaven.

Golden plover and greenshank pipe crossly from red-specked sphagnum tussocks. Winter brings flocks of graceful whooper swans and greylag geese. Great skua and Arctic skua make long sweeps over the moors. Hen harrier and peregrine ply the wilderness in search of prey and black-throated divers feed in trout-filled lochs.

Tiny streams, banked bright with wild flowers, flow endlessly over lichen-covered boulders, past water-gardens of yellow flag. Sundew, butterwort, crowberry, bog asphodel, blue and pink milkwort, tormentil, spotted orchid and marsh violet blush shyly from warm corners.

One hot summer's day, Ann and I were fishing in Loch Ruard. A light breeze gently ruffled the surface and fish were rising to our carefully presented flies. By mid-morning we had caught our fair share. Which was just as well. Because, for no immediate apparent reason, everything went quiet. Where, but a moment before, trout had been rising, now complete silence reigned.

'Don't turn round too quickly,' said Ann. She was sitting in the stern, looking over her left shoulder, smiling. I eased round and saw the reason for the smile and the sudden absence of fish. Lying on its back, 'arms' folded across downy chest, was a magnificent dog otter. Long, white-tipped whiskers twitched. Intelligent, sparkling eyes gazed at us curiously, following our every move.

The otter turned over and swam slowly round the boat, then dived soundlessly, a stream of bubbles disappearing amongst small waves. That was the last we saw of him but the memory of that glorious moment will remain with me until my dying day.

The walk out to Ruard and Blar nam Faoileag starts from the A895 Latheron–Thurso road a mile from Achavanich and another delightful Caithness water named Loch Stemster. At the south end of Stemster is a dramatic circle of Bronze Age standing stones, the grey sentinels of Stemster: 'It may originally have comprised about 60 stones, but one third have weathered or have been removed. The stones are thick slabs of flagstone, protruding on average about 5 ft above the ground'.

Little Loch Rangag lies south, close to the main road, and on the east bank is a rock-covered promontory, the home of Grey Steel, a Caithness robber-baron. His stock in trade was to greet travellers on the steep-sided Ord of Caithness, inviting them to contribute to the Grey Steel Preservation Fund. Those unwilling or unable to do so were hurled to their deaths over the cliffs.

The story goes that eventually Grey Steel pushed his luck too far. He kidnapped a young lady from my village of Watten and carried her off to Rangag to work his evil pleasure. The lover of the lass on Grey Steel's castle, catching the inmates drunk from an even- was not amused and gathered together an angry gang of friends. On a dark night they crossed the moors to Rangag and descended

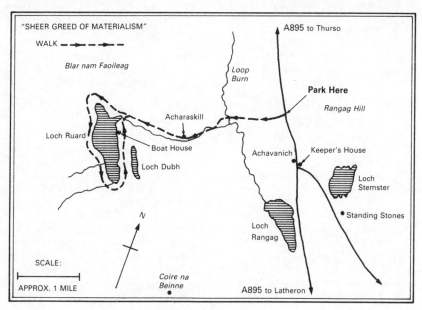

ing's jollity. Which they rounded off by the removal of heads and complete destruction of the tower.

Harsh times, when often the only way of redressing wrongs was to take the law into your own hands. When I look at the mindless destruction of irreplaceable Caithness moorlands by mass afforestation, I'm not so sure that our ancestors were all that wrong. So, if you will excuse me, I'm off to organize the troops – and there will always be room for you, or any other man or woman who loves Scotland's wild and wonderful places.

WHAT YOU NEED TO KNOW

Time and effort The first part of this walk is along a good track which leads almost half-way to Loch Ruard. From there on the going can be rough and wet, particularly after heavy rain. So go prepared and make sure you are well shod. Also, pack compass and map. If a Caithness mist comes down you will need them out on the moors. The total distance covered is approximately eight miles and this will take about four and a half hours – as always, depending upon what distracts you along the way.

Call first at the house of the keeper, Mr Munro, to check that you will not be disturbing any stalking parties. His is the large detached white house on the east side of the road at Achavanich, opposite the farm and on the way to the Stemster Standing Stones.

Location Ordnance Survey Sheet 11, Thurso and Dunbeath, second series, scale 1:50,000.

Grid references Keeper's house 180427; Loch Stemseter 190424; Stemster Standing Stones 189417; car parking and start of walk 178436; Acharaskill Steading 158432; Loch Ruard 140435; Blar nam Faoileag 135445.

Route Visit the standing stones first and then drive north. There are two empty cottages by the east side of the A895 about half a mile north of Achavanich. Park here. Across the road, is a track leading down into the valley. Walk this way.

Cross the gate at the bottom and follow a well made Land-Rover track up the hill. The track criss-crosses the Loop Burn, eventually abandoning it to lead to the farm steading at Acharaskill. This is set amidst a patch of green field which is easily seen from the start point.

A faint path runs west from the steading, up the north side of the outlet stream from Ruard. It is bad news to walk on the south side of this stream. The ground there is very rough indeed and hard going. This track will bring you to Loch Ruard.

Strike right at the loch, round the shore to the north bay. This is the southern edge of Blar nam Faoileag. Return from the bog by walking down the west bank of Ruard, round the south bay, where there is a good sheltered picnic spot under high peat banks. Complete the circle round the loch to the boat house and follow the track back down the burn and on to the car.

51

Strathpeffer and the Hill of Terror

A S TITLES go, one could be forgiven for thinking that *A Treatise on the Sulphureous Mineral Waters of Castle Leod and Fair Burn in Ross-shire and the Salt Purging Waters of Pitacithly in Perthshire*, by Doctor Munro, is hardly likely to win any prizes for bringing in the crowds. In fact, Dr Munro's book, written in 1772, did just that. Within a generation, thousands of people from all over Britain and Europe were flocking north to Easter Ross to sample Dr Munro's waters in the burgeoning spa town of Strathpeffer.

In its Victorian heyday, Strathpeffer was as popular as any of the spas then in vogue, and was known as the 'Harrogate of the North'. Originally, the town was popularized by Anne Hay Mackenzie, Countess of Cromartie, and the Duchess of Sutherland, aided by the convenient arrival of the railway. Strathpeffer flourished, attracting such luminaries as Princess Mary of Texk, daughter of the Duke of Cambridge and cousin of the unamused Queen of the British Empire. Grand hotels were opened, fine shops built and all the bustle of Victorian England seemed to be epitomized in this strange, most un-Highland-like little town, nestling below the majestic heights of Ben Wyvis. Even George Bernard Shaw came to ease tired muscles here.

Today, the town is just as busy, not with those seeking ease of body, but with tourists and visitors seeking peace of mind.

Throughout the year, Strathpeffer bustles. The Victorian character of the town has been carefully retained, shops renovated in the nineteenth-century style, and a Victorian Week is staged each September, when villagers dress in appropriate costume.

The station, a single-platform terminal opened in 1885, is magnificent: a long, single-storey wooden structure with a ten-bay glazed awning supported upon cast-iron columns. This has been marvellously restored to its original pristine splendour, and although the trains no longer run, the station is now home to a series of delightful small shops, a craft centre, and the nostalgic Highlands Museum of Childhood exhibition.

On a blisteringly hot July morning, Ann and I sampled the sulphureous waters before exploring the town, guided by Douglas Murray's booklet *Victorian Strathpeffer*: solid buildings, protected from prying eyes by well-kept flower, tree and shrub gardens.

After an hour or so of stately Victoriana, we followed the A834 out of town to Contin and the A832 road towards Wester Ross and Ullapool, heading for Garbat, our objective for the day being the summit of shapely Ben Wyvis, 3,433 feet, 'the hill of terror' and highest mountain on the east coast of Scotland, north of Inverness.

But not before paying our respects to the Falls of Rogie, a dramatic waterfall on the River Black Water, a tributary of that famous salmon stream, the River Connon. There is a large car park by the road and the walk down to the falls takes only a few moments; and, given good water levels, there is always the chance of seeing salmon leaping the falls.

In Celtic Scotland, for hundreds of years, the salmon was thought to have supernatural powers, being regarded as a symbol of knowledge and of freedom. Even the Picts, who left few relics other than their ornately carved stones, venerated fish; many stones carry the symbol of the fish, surely *Salmo salar*, the leaper.

There is not much leaping about Ben Wyvis, rather a long, unrelenting slog up to the summit; but the views from the top are more than ample reward for the effort involved, and so we parked at Garbat eager to be off.

In recent years Ben Wyvis has suffered dreadfully from the ungentle administrations of commercial forestry, with much of the lower slopes and surrounding levels being smoothed by Sitka spruce and lodgepole pine. Worse, entrepreneurs and developers are currently examining the possibility of constructing a railway to the top, and of developing the Ben as a centre for ski-ing.

A gate in the wall of trees leads to a muddy track and we hurried along, anxious to be free of their cloying darkness. The 'burn of the pass', Allt a'Bealach Mhoir, kept our spirits high as we broke clear and climbed to the saddle between Tom na Caillich and glowering An Cabar. A buzzard circled overhead, busy looking for an early lunch. A grouse rocketed away over the heather.

Ben Wyvis looks deceptively simple, from a distance – a gentle old lady, dominating the view. On my return from business sorties in the south she always bids me welcome from the A9 above Inverness. But for me, there is something special about her greeting as I speed over the Black Isle to the Dornoch Bridge. Glancing westwards to her shapely form, I know that I am home.

The haul from the road, up to An Cabar, 3,116 feet, involves a stiff climb of some 2,500 feet. So we deserved a coffee break once there and rested thankfully amidst the sphagnum moss and heather, catching our breath, both from exertion and from the stunning view that, foot by foot, opened before us. It was one of those rare, blue-sky, glorious days in the high hills, when it is possible to discard the usual protective layers, which we did, happily, before marching along the magnificent summit plateau of Glas Leathad Mor towards the wall surrounding the Ordnance Survey marker.

The angry eastern face of the grand dame lay exposed: tumbled crags and corries of Coire na Feola and An Sochach, and Loch a'Choire Mhoir glinting far below, with the thin, silver ribbon of Allt nan Caorach hurrying east to Glen Glass. Northwards, I saw the mountains of my Caithness ancestors, peaked by Morven; south, a glimpse of Cairngorm; west, the wilderness of Torridon

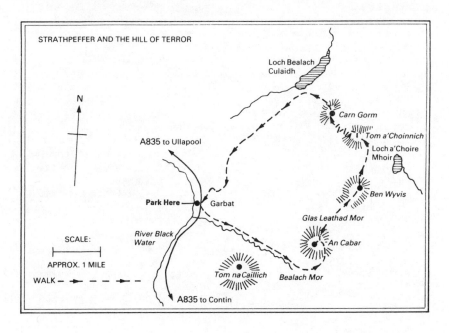

STRATHPEFFER AND THE HILL OF TERROR

Loch Bealach Culaidh

N

A835 to Ullapool

Carn Gorm

Tom a'Choinnich

Loch a'Choire Mhoir

Park Here — Garbat

Ben Wyvis

Glas Leathad Mor

SCALE:

River Black Water

An Cabar

APPROX. 1 MILE

WALK — ▸ – – ▸ –

Tom na Caillich

Bealach Mor

A835 to Contin

and Coigach; east, intimidating waters, over the sea to Norway.

Offer me the finest, best-renowned restaurant in the world for lunch; ply me with promises of haute cuisine, truffles and caviar; tempt me with Château Mouton Rothschild, or even cask-strength Tain Glenmorangie: I would forego them all, unhesitatingly, for a coffee and sandwich on the summit of Ben Wyvis.

Ann had to drag me protesting from the top but eventually we set off down the twisting track to Tom a'Choinnich, by Carn Gorm, and then made our way back through the forest to the car.

WHAT YOU NEED TO KNOW

Time and effort Not much, wandering around Strathpeffer, but watch out for the traffic, particularly in high summer, for the town can often be very busy. The walk down to the Falls of Rogie takes about ten minutes and the drive from there to the start point of the Ben Wyvis walk is about six miles. Allow a whole day for the full expedition, making an early start in Strathpeffer.

The first part of this ten-mile walk is unrelentingly upwards, for some 2,500 feet, as you climb to the summit plateau; but thereafter the going is easy, apart from during or after heavy rain, when the tops are wet underfoot. The principal danger on Ben Wyvis lies in loss of direction, should you be enveloped in mist. It is very easy to wander off-course. You must always carry compass and map – and know how to use them.

Location Two maps needed: Ordnance Survey Sheet 26, Inverness, and Sheet 20, Beinn Dearg, second series, scale 1:50,000.

Grid references Strathpeffer 483583; Falls of Rogie 445584; Garbat car park 418678; Bealach Mor 448654; Tom na Caillich 439654; Ån Cabar 450667; Glas Leathad Mor 460680; Ben Wyvis summit 463684; Tom a'Choinnich 463700; Carn Gorm 456710.

Route The best way to explore Strathpeffer is by using Douglas Murray's booklet *Victorian Strathpeffer* obtainable at the Tourist Information Centre in the centre of town. Thereafter, follow the A834 to Contin and join the A832. Two miles north along the A832 brings you to the Falls of Rogie car park, on the right of the road. The walk to the falls is clearly signposted.

At Gorstan, one mile north from Garve, follow the A835 Ullapool road to the car park at Garbat, on the left by the River Black Water. On your right you will find the gate leading through the forest to the Ben Wyvis track. Follow the track through Bealach Mor, then bear left up the hill to the top of An Cabar.

Walk north-east along the plateau to the OS Post at the summit. Edge round the crags above Loch a'Choire Mhoir, which is on your right, and descend to Tom a'Choinnich. A steep, zig-zag path hurries you down to Carn Gorm. Descend from Carn Gorm, keeping Loch Bealach Culaidh to your right, and pick up the path back to the car park at Garbat.

52

Knock Farril and the Friendship Stone

ALTHOUGH THE town of Strathpeffer is of recent origin, the surrounding area has been home to man for thousands of years, since Mesolithic times. Consequently, the day after Ann and I had enjoyed the dubious delights of the spa's Victorian architecture, as mentioned in the previous walk, we set off in search of a somewhat older dwelling, probably built more than two thousand years ago.

The Iron Age hill fort on Knock Farril, resting on the highest point of the long ridge which shelters Strathpeffer from south-east winds, is one of the most dramatic and enigmatic in the north of Scotland. At the Ben Wyvis Hotel, we turned right and followed the signpost to Knock Farril. The dogs did likewise, panting in the heat, pink tongues lolling, ready for anything, particularly rabbits.

Walking quickly up the tarmac road from town, our first stop was involuntary, when a proprietorial sheepdog took a lunge at Ann's little treasure. Heathcliff was rapidly scooped up out of harm's way, barking furiously – from the safety of his mistress's arms – and the sheepdog retreated, thwarted. Away from the road, the track leads up the side of a neat field, edged with several iron seats, conveniently sited to calm the heaving lungs of passers-by.

As always, I was astonished at just how quickly, as we gained height, the town shrank to model-like proportions, church-spired and gardened in Victorian calm. A large, commercial conifer plantation, euphemistically named Blackmuir Wood, wrapped itself around the western end of the hill and we entered through a traditional, binder-twined, Highland gate. Where would the farmer be, I thought, without binder twine, the mainstay of every agricultural repair.

The way through the wood winds up the hill along a forest track, marked by colour-tipped posts. The margin of the track is clustered with wild flowers, but beneath the dark, closely packed conifers little grows. As we neared the top, the trees thinned, letting in life-giving light, but it was with a sense of relief that, after a fifteen-minute hike, we cleared the trees and reached the top.

The Firth Lands of Ross and Cromartie lay before us: a bright patchwork of woodlands and tidy, fertile fields, golden barley, splashed with the yellow of oilseed rape. Smoke drifted lazily from the chimneys of the small cottages fringing the shores of Loch Ussie, blue and silver in the morning haze. The hill ahead was covered southwards in green bracken and the dogs dashed off into the undergrowth whilst we stopped for coffee.

Castle Leod, ancient home of the Mackenzies of Kintail, thrust aggressively from the grasslands of Blairinich to the north, backed by forest-clad Ben Wyvis. The Mackenzies, astute operators in the politics of Scotland's Middle Ages, assisted King James VI to quell disturbances in the Outer Isles, and as their strength and importance grew, so also grew the strength and importance of their magnificent, five-storeyed tower.

A more modest, yet none the less dramatic monument rests on the crest, a few hundred yards east of the forest: the Friendship Stone, a head-and-shoulder, bronze sculpture of a woman holding two children. After the dreadful Yerevan earthquake in Armenia, pupils of Dingwall Academy raised money for children who had suffered in the tragedy, and subsequently, a party from Dingwall visited Ycharents School in Yerevan.

When the visit was returned, the Armenian children brought with them the Friendship Stone, which they had made, and at a moving ceremony on Knock Farril on Saturday 15 September 1990, attended by more than 150 pupils and parents, the sculpture was unveiled. The present bronze monument is a replica of the original, which is now housed in Dingwall Academy. Mr Alexander Glass, Rector of Dingwall Academy, is planning another school visit to Yerevan, with a Scottish Friendship Stone, as soon as political conditions permit.

Relics of more ancient politics may be found at the end of the crest overlooking Dingwall and the Dornoch Firth: the vitrified hill fort of Knock Farril, a massive array of remains of walls and ditches on the grassy summit. The principal part of the fort measures 425 by 125 feet, but it is the extent of the subsidiary structures which makes Knock Farril notable, and the clear evidence of the process of vitrification.

These structures were invariably built in exposed, windy places, providing maximum, all-round visibility and maximum defensive capabilities. Walls were constructed of closely knit, interwoven timbers, bonded together in order to support considerable weight. If the structure were set on fire, either deliberately or by accident, the heat generated by the conflagration could melt the lower stones – as is evidenced at Knock Farril by the remnants of a vitrified wall.

Ann and I lunched in the fort, and I swear that I could feel the presence of its long-departed, skin-clad inhabitants. A feeling of contentment, not oppressive; of happy children and barking dogs; of parents, busy with the small tasks of living, bringing up their families, hunting, fishing and tending their sparse crops. The people may have gone, but at Knock Farril their spirit lingers.

Barking from Breac and Heathcliff roused us, and we called the dogs to heel. They arrived, rabbitless and absolutely shattered by their exertions amidst the bracken. We gathered our bits and pieces together and left the ridge, both animals limping tiredly behind, and continued down the long crest of the hill towards the line of the old railway at Fodderty Lodge.

Half-way down the ridge we stopped for a swing, from a red and white rope strung from the gnarled branches of one of a beautiful stand of old Scots pines. A well-dressed chaffinch eyed us curiously. A lazy heron flapped by overhead. The dogs flopped, grateful for a moment's respite, and then dashed off again, unable to resist the temptation of the chest-high bracken almost smothering the path, as we continued down the hill.

At the bottom we turned left and walked to the end of the field, before climbing a broken stile to the arrow-straight railway track, pointing back to Strathpeffer. Indentations of sleepers ridged the sad route, once proud with hissing, puffing steam locomotives, packed with excited, spa-bound passengers. Sheep languished in the shade of fine chestnut trees growing in the middle of the track.

The sun dipped behind a low bank of clouds, highlighting the almost sheer, dark south face of Knock Farril. Knew a thing or two, did Iron Age Man, about defensive situations. I would not have relished the prospect of charging up that cliff in order to attack.

Insects hummed in the stifling, fly-happy heat. I waved a silver birch branch around my head to discourage them. A number of broken bridges forced us to leave the track and take to the muddy field to the north of the railway. Breac benefited immediately, finding a tiny stream in which to quench his thirst. He fell, legs spread-eagled, in the middle, lapping furiously. Heathcliff next. Hope the stream keeps running until the dogs are satisfied.

Back, at last, on the railway track, Breac and I steamed on, Ann trailing behind. Heathcliff, already exhausted, dashed back and forth between, checking that we were still there. A pheasant, golden-brown, scuttled across the path. Breac was too tired even to blink an eye. Can't say he hadn't been told. I warned him about the dangers of over-exertion in pursuit of rabbits.

Suddenly, the end of the line, and a neat cottage, obviously a converted railway workers' building, and then, the station itself: the same view the driver must have had as he applied the brakes. Quite magnificent. And welcome shade after the heat of the sun. I mounted the platform, Breac dragging himself after me, and we

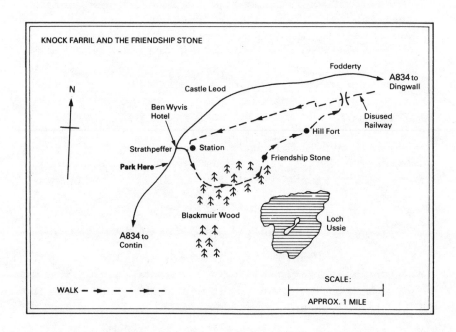

KNOCK FARRIL AND THE FRIENDSHIP STONE

wandered along to an outside table by a little tea-room.

Stripping off my dripping shirt, I sat, gratefully. 'A bowl of water, two cups of coffee, and scones, please.' Whilst I sipped my coffee, Breac, legs spread-eagled once more, lapped at the water, sending spray splashing over the stone platform. A tiny, dark-eyed robin bobbed onto the back of a chair, looking for crumbs. He would have to be patient. Ann arrived with Heathcliff and we ordered more water. More lapping.

When Ann finished her coffee, we paid the bill, tethered the dogs, and, wearily, hauled them back to the square where the car was parked. Heathcliff managed to jump aboard. Breac had to have a lift. They settled silently and, almost instantly, were fast asleep. Homeward-bound, I looked southwards to Knock Farril, the Friendship Stone and the old fort on the hill, and smiled my thanks.

WHAT YOU NEED TO KNOW

Time and effort Strangely enough, although this modest walk involves hardly any extraordinary effort, being only six to seven miles in extent, like the dogs I found it very tiring indeed. Perhaps it was due to the heat of the day, the muggy atmosphere, or perhaps it was simply due to the previous day's long hike. Whatever, it is an easy, very enjoyable stroll and highly recommended. In winter, however, or in wet weather, be prepared for a muddy tramp in the field to the north of the old railway track.

Location Ordnance Survey Sheet 26, Inverness, second series, scale 1:50,000.

Grid references Strathpeffer 483583; gate into Blackmuir Wood 490577; exit from Blackmuir Wood 496577; the Friendship Stone 499580; Knock Farril hill fort 506585; Fodderty Lodge railway bridge 514591; Strathpeffer Station 486585.

Route Park the car in the main square, by the post office and fountain, and then walk left, down the main road. After a hundred yards or so, you will see the Ben Wyvis Hotel across the road. Immediately adjacent to the left of the hotel is the minor road leading up to Blackmuir Wood and the start of the Knock Farril walk.

On entering the wood, bear left and follow the track up the hill to the bare ridge. Walk eastwards along the ridge, past the Friendship Stone, down to a farm, then back up the final slope to the hill fort. Walk through the fort and you will pick up the track which continues gently down the hill to Fodderty Lodge railway bridge.

At the end of the field, join the railway track and follow it back to Strathpeffer Station. Along the way, you will be forced by thick undergrowth to leave the railway and walk in the field to the north. This can be soggy going, so make sure that you are well shod and prepared. At the railway station, simply follow the road back to the main square.

53

Battles, Young and Old

IT WAS all over in about half an hour. By midday on Wednesday 16 April 1746, 1,500 men of Prince Charles Edward Stuart's army lay dead or dying on Drumossie Moor. The rest, including their 'Bonnie' commander, were flying in disarray, or lying helpless, waiting for Cumberland's eager bayonets to end their misery.

As the Duke rode through the field of battle, he complained that a wounded Highlander had looked at him insolently. Turning to one of his companions, Wolfe, he ordered him to shoot the man. Wolfe refused, replying that the Duke could have his commission before he would carry out such an order. A few years later, Wolfe gained his place in history by leading his army to victory, and by dying, on the Heights of Abraham in Canada.

The brutality with which government forces acted on that cold spring day after the Battle of Culloden, encouraged by their commander, the King's son, and his officers, slaughtering prisoners and the wounded, burning many alive, is a dark, indelible stain on British history. Long after the Young Pretender had escaped to France, Butcher Cumberland's brigades continued to ravage northern straths and glens, burning castles and crofts, raping defenceless women, murdering young and old, often simply for their own barbaric amusement. Cattle, sheep, oxen and horses were stolen in their thousands and sold to rapacious English and Lowland Scots dealers who flocked north like scavenging vultures. Houses were stripped of their valuables, which were then auctioned, the spoils being divided amongst officers and soldiers who were thus encouraged in their barbarity.

Rebel or not, to be a Highlander was enough. The innocent and the guilty, without discrimination, were to feel the full wrath of a badly frightened Parliament: 'People must perish by sword and famine.' The strength of the clan system and the dignity of the Highland way of life.was to be destroyed for ever.

I never walk in gentle Strathnairn or Stratherrick, south from Inverness, without thinking of these desperate, terrified, fleeing men – men without hope, home or comfort, deserted by their chiefs, whose outrageous vanity had forced them, unwillingly, onto the field of slaughter – or of Butcher Cumberland, who returned to London a hero and had a flower, sweet William, named in his honour. To this day, in Scotland, the plant is still known as 'stinking Billy'.

We discovered the area many years ago, one sharp spring, when we stayed in a house overlooking Loch Ruthven. Most travellers hurry up and down the busy A9 and few bother to turn west along the little road that marries General Wade's old way through the Great Glen to Fort William. It still fingers the wild shores of Loch Ness, winding through tree-clad slopes to Foyers, then climbing by Glenlia into Stratherrick, and on to one of the most stunning views in the north at the head of Gleann nan Eun, overlooking island-scattered Loch Tarff.

Thomas Pennant, that dour Welsh observer of things Highland, passed this way in 1769 and reported: 'In many parts we were immersed in woods; in others, they opened and gave views of the sides and tops of vast mountains soaring above. The wild animals that possessed this picturesque scene were stags and roes, black game and grouse; and on the summits, white hares and ptarmigans. Foxes are so numerous and voracious that the farmers are sometimes forced to house their sheep, as is done in France, for fear of wolves.'

Our home for the week was Tullich House, a rather grand farmhouse on the north shore of Loch Ruthven, well furnished and very comfortable. Since our visit, a number of other properties have been renovated and are available for rental, and this area is ideal for introducing little ones to the delights of hillwalking. At least, that is what we told Charles and Jean, our two younger children.

Charles has always been suspicious of my expeditions, ever since, at the age of three, I took him up a steep hill near Yetholm in the Borders. Under duress. In retrospect, it was a big walk for a little fellow, and it was January, cold and snowing. But he made it.

Three quarters of the way up, with me pulling and heaving, coaxing and cajoling, he suddenly stopped and refused to go a step further. Until then he had been concentrating on the ground immediately under his feet. Now, as the sun broke through, he turned round to see exactly where he was, expecting, I imagine, to see the land behind him.

I will treasure for ever the look on his face as he was confronted with nothing other than blue sky. Startled, Charles looked down, amazed at just how high he was; then, gritting his teeth, he strode past me and almost ran the rest of the way to the summit. In such a fashion are hillwalkers born. I laboured after him, mightily relieved, but the experience engendered in him a dark suspicion of my stories about the wonders of Scotland's remote, high places.

The first walk we took Charles and Jean on from Tullich, some years later, was an easy stroll up the hill behind the house, to the top of Stac na Cathaig, 1,463 feet. There is a forestry track and, at the end, a good scramble up and down over heathery tussocks to the top. Both enjoyed the experience, particularly Charles, who collected a fine antler along the way, which he used to great effect every time his small sister complained that she was tired. He still has the antler. And Jean claims that she still has its marks.

The following morning dawned spring-bright and sparkling, so we decided that it was a good time to walk Stac Gorm, 1,410 feet, on the south side of Loch Ruthven. Stac Gorm is far more demanding for children, because there is no recognizable track and the undergrowth is deep and clinging, at least on the lower slopes.

Jean set to with a will and managed well, apart from a few places where she insisted upon being carried. Which was good for me, I think. In spite of the sun it was cold, but as we climbed, our bodies warmed considerably. Once on the summit plateau, we marched west to the trig. point where photographs were duly taken to record Jean's achievement, and then west again to the far end of the ridge at Craig Ruthven.

Charles and Jean have long since flown the nest, Charles developing a career as an artist, Jean developing into a wonderful mother.

On long winter evenings, when I drag out the inevitable box of photographs, there they both are, standing freezing on Stac Gorm with mountain peaks all round, Ann in the middle with a supporting arm about each of them. And I am pleased for them, and pleased that we encouraged them to appreciate 'the large religion of the hills'.

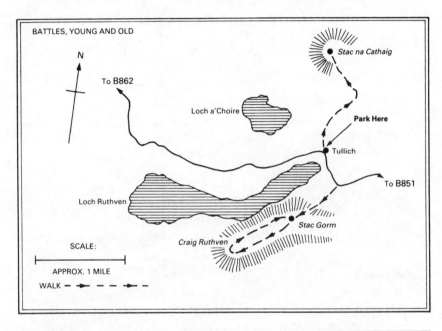

BATTLES, YOUNG AND OLD

N

To B862

Loch a'Choire

Stac na Cathaig

Park Here

Tullich

To B851

Loch Ruthven

Stac Gorm

Craig Ruthven

SCALE:

APPROX. 1 MILE

WALK

WHAT YOU NEED TO KNOW

Time and effort Not much for adults, but, depending upon their age, a good challenge for children. The walk to the top of Stac na Cathaig is a good morning or afternoon expedition and should present no problems. Obviously, the better the weather, the better the walk. Stac Gorm is a much rougher six-mile tramp, mostly trackless. Make sure that you take with you energy-inducing barley sugar or other treat of your choice.

Location Ordnance Survey Sheet 26, Inverness, second series, scale 1:50,000.

Grid references Tullich 638286; Loch Ruthven 620276; Stac na Cathaig 640301; Stac Gorm 631274; Craig Ruthven 621270.

Route The hill behind Tullich has been planted, but a track leads through the forest out onto the slopes of Stac na Cathaig. Simply follow the track up the hill, returning by the same route. For Stac Gorm, walk down to the east end of Loch Ruthven and climb the hill from the road. Once up, pick your way west along the top to Craig Ruthven. Return the same way you came.

54

Glengarry and Ben Tee

'ON REACHING Glengarry the first place we came to was Greenfield, possessed by Mr McDonald. The house was really a curiosity. It was built of earth, and the walls were all covered with a fine verdure, but on calling, we were conducted into a cleanly and neat-looking room. . . . The ladies, Mrs McDonald and her sister, were handsome and genteelly dressed, although unappraised of our arrival, unless by the second sight. They were very easy and agreeable in their manners, and very unlike the outside of their habitation.'

James Hogg, the Ettrick Shepherd, thus described his arrival in Glengarry during his tour of the Highlands in 1803. His friend, Sir Walter Scott, had persuaded Hogg to send him a series of letters along the way, recounting his adventures, and Scott arranged to have them published in *The Scot's Magazine*, probably the oldest magazine in the world.

An equally hospitable welcome awaits travellers in Glengarry today, at the Tomdoun Hotel, across Loch Inchlaggan from Greenfield, although in Hogg's day the River Garry still ran free through the glen. Loch Inchlaggan was formed in the mid-1950s, the hydro-electric boom time in the Highlands, when Loch Quoich, further up Glengarry, was also formed, drowning the river.

A line of tree stumps, still pokes above the surface of Loch Inchlaggan towards the south-west shore, marking the site of 'The Island of the Children'. Highland folklore tells of a group of children harvesting corn on the island many years ago. A water horse, white and magnificent, came up out of the river and the youths eagerly clambered onto its back, trapped by the animal's magic spell. The only survivor was one boy, who, finding his thumb stuck to the side of the horse, severed it with a stroke of his sickle.

There has been a coaching inn at Tomdoun for more than a hundred years. *Murray's Handbook*, by Sarah Murray, in 1894 notes that 'carriages may be hired there' for the journey through Glen Shiel, past the Five Sisters to Kyle of Lochalsh and Skye. The road beyond Tomdoun is the longest dead-end route in Britain, following the gloomy shores of Loch Quoich and reaching the sea at the head of Loch Hourn, 'the loch of hell', in Knoydart.

The dark ruins of Invergarry Castle are all that remains of the ancient home of the Macdonnells of Glengarry. Charles Edward Stuart rested here, briefly, during his flight west after the Battle of Culloden. Two years later, Butcher Cumberland's troops arrived at Craig an Fhithich, 'the rock of the raven', ravaging the people and their lands, and burning Glengarry's ancestral home in the process.

The River Garry now links four lochs, Quoich, Poulary, Inchlaggan and Garry, and these waters are famous throughout Scotland for the size of their ferox trout – huge cannibal fish, feeding on their smaller brethren and particularly on the shoals of Arctic char that thrive in the deep, cold waters of Loch Garry.

South from Loch Garry the view is dominated by the graceful shape of Ben Tee, 'the hill of the fairies', 2,957 feet in height, from the summit of which walkers are rewarded by one of the grandest views in all of Scotland. The lower slopes are thickly forested with the commercial plantations which so disfigure much of this lovely Scottish glen, but once clear of the dark trees, a moorland wonderland opens up, making for a splendid day out in the hills.

Ben Tee is also known as Glengarry's Bowling Green, and stones from the mountain were used to build the old castle by the shores of Loch Oich. Getting the stones down from Ben Tee was achieved by forming what is probably the longest human chain in history – a line of men passing the stones, hand to hand, from the slopes of Ben Tee to Loch Oich, a distance of more than five miles.

In times past Glengarry was a wildlife paradise and, indeed, it still is, but not to the same extent. Victorian sporting gentlemen wreaked havoc on much of Scotland's wildlife, conscientiously recording their deeds. One such note gives gamebook details for shooting in Glengarry between 1837 and 1840: 198 wild cats, 246 pine martens, 67 badgers, 48 otters, 27 sea eagles, 15 golden eagles, 18 osprey, 275 kites, 63 goshawks, 656 buzzards, 462 kestrels, 63 hen harriers, 6 gyr falcon and 106 assorted owls.

Ben Tee can be climbed from two directions – from the shores of Loch Lochy, in the Great Glen, and from Glengarry. The Lochy access is from Laggan Locks and Kilfinnan, and involves a very sharp ascent by the north bank of the Kilfinnan Burn, via dramatic falls, along a narrow, often muddy track. The Glengarry access, from Greenfield, although somewhat longer, offers a less daunting approach. Both routes, however, are demanding, arduous tramps.

A drove road used to run south from the edge of the forestry plantations, but walkers now keep to the hill, beyond the forestry, along the delightful track that borders the little Allt Ladaidh. The real fun begins a mile further on, where the track branches left, heading up the Allt Bealach Easain, 'the pass of the little falls'. From there, it is teeth-gritting time, and a hard haul to the summit.

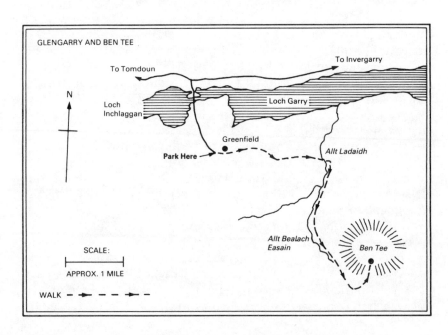

Few Scottish views can match the splendour of the vista from the top of Ben Tee. Half of Scotland seems to be displayed for your pleasure. Northwards, the mountains of Glen Affric, Kintail and Clunie; east, the blues and greys of the Monadhliath, Corrieyairack and Creag Meagaidh; to the south, the mighty bulk of Ben Nevis, the Grey Corries and Glencoe; westwards, the wild, tumble of crags and peaks of Knoydart and Morar: Sgurr na Ciche, Luinne Bheinn, Sgurr Thuilm, Sgurr nan Coireachan. A majestic, unforgettable, wilderness panorama.

James Hogg never climbed Ben Tee — at least, if he did, he left no record of having done so — but I thought of the Ettrick Shepherd as I surveyed the stunning view. There is a memorial to Hogg, near his border home, at the south end of St Mary's Loch. The stone statue is inscribed with the line: 'He taught the wandering winds to sing'. An appropriate sentiment on the summit of lovely Ben Tee and my heart sang also, with joy at the marvellous beauty of my native land.

WHAT YOU NEED TO KNOW

Time and effort From Greenfield, the walk is about twelve miles, there and back, and can take up to eight hours, depending upon weather conditions and how long you linger along the way. The early stages are over easy forestry roads, but once out onto the hill, the going is rough and the way steep.

Select a good day in order to enjoy the splendid summit view, but always be prepared for bad weather. Compass and map-reading skills are essential, and you should make sure that you are thoroughly prepared for every eventuality. This walk should not be underestimated, but provided that you take care, and are reasonably fit, you should come to little harm.

Location Ordnance Survey Sheet 34, Fort Augustus, second series, scale 1:50,000.

Grid references Tomdoun 157011; Greenfield 202005; Allt Ladaidh 230003; Allt Bealach Easain 226984; Ben Tee 241972.

Route Cross the bridge over the narrows between Loch Garry and Loch Inchlaggan and start the walk one mile further south, at Greenfield. A gate takes you into the forestry plantation, and a good track leads east through the trees, meeting the Allt Ladaidh Burn after some two miles, by a derelict hut at the side of the stream.

Turn south here, following the track on the east side of the Allt Ladaidh, and climb out of the forest and onto the hill. The track crosses the Allt Bealach Easain, with Ben Tee glowering above you on the left, and at this point you should bear left and follow the track up the bealach. At the end of the track, take a deep breath and angle left up the final slopes to the summit. Return the way you came.

55

Ptarmigan Tops

LOCHABER WAS good to Prince Charles Edward Stuart. After the rout at Culloden in April 1746, the Young Pretender spent six months fleeing government wrath, wandering through the area, aided by Cameron of Lochiel's tenants and, in particular, by Donald Cameron of Glen Pean. Ordnance Survey maps are littered with references to his hiding places: Prince Charlie's Cave, Charlie's Cave, the Princes's Stone, the gully above Loch Quoich, the cave in Coire Dho, and Cluny's Cave above Loch Ericht on Ben Alder. The fugitive passed twice through the head of Glen Roy, over the steep shoulder of Creag Meagaidh: on 28 August, fleeing south, and again on 14 September, hurrying north to Loch nam Uamh where a French ship was waiting to take him to safety.

Our purpose was a long, invigorating ridge walk, taking in three Munros and seven tops, starting from Aberarder by Loch Laggan. The car park was busy: climbers and walkers, tumbling out of cars and vans, dragging on jackets and well-worn boots. Much of the walk is through a National Nature Reserve and it seemed as though it was going to be a busy day in the hills.

Ann examined the map, getting her bearings. Bad news. Ominous glint in her eyes. Determining the route. Knowing her, it would be pretty uncomplicated – simply straight up. The vast bulk of Carn Liath, 3,298 feet, glowered above us, head in the mist. As we followed the trail onto the hill the sun blazed down.

The path winds up, heading for Lochan a'Choire, nestling below the dark crags of Stob Poite Coire Ardair, and, happily, our companions marched on towards the loch. Our intention was to traverse the ridge from east to west and, consequently, at a clump of wizened silver birch, we turned right and headed for the clouds.

With Ann already a hundred yards ahead, I puffed behind, marvelling at the contrary nature of Lochaber weather. One moment, the sun shone brightly, casting long shadows into Stob Poite Coire Ardair; next, a sudden storm swept in, blotting everything from sight. Rain now, then more sunshine, now more mist. We skirted the rocky outcrops guarding the south face of Carn Liath, edging higher.

The hill was alive with wild flowers: meadow cranesbill, heath bedstraw, lady's bedstraw, tormentil, bog asphodel, bell heather, bilberry, cloudberry, cow-wheat, with its pale, milky coloured pods, and wonderful patches of wild thyme. A line of old iron fence posts marked our way. Four ptarmigan appeared, coyly picking amongst the boulders. We stopped for a chat. The birds were well turned out in black and white summer plumage.

A broad, thyme-strewn plateau leads to the tumbled summit cairn of Carn Liath, and we huddled there, grateful for shelter. My hands were numb and I quickly dragged out heavy trousers and struggled into them, pulling on a second jumper and a pair of fingerless gloves. Hot coffee warmed us and the sun broke through once more, opening up a marvellous view back down to Loch Laggan, silver and blue, far below.

Our way lay along the top of the ridge, but our next objectives, Meall an-t-Snaim and Sorn Garbh Choire, were enshrouded in white clouds. Stay and shiver, or march on? We rose and headed west, down the broad top. More sun and a superb prospect of the sheer, ragged crags encircling Lochan a'Choire. Easy walking.

We passed Meall an-t-Snaim and its small cairn, staying on the track, well back from the lip of the corrie, as the path ran perilously close to the edge. Above us the sun was working hard to break through, and as we strolled up the grassy slope to Stob Poite Coire Ardair it succeeded, at least ahead. Behind us, however, Carn Liath disappeared completely.

Below us, on a plateau above Loch Roy, a cluster of tiny blue lochans guarded the northern approach to the famous Window. As Ann and I stood on the north side of it, 3,000 feet above Loch Laggan, where Charles Edward Stuart had passed, it was clear that someone had left it 'open', for a fearsome gale howled through the dark cleft in the ridge below Creag Meagaidh. I saw a trout splash in the shallows of the loch as we laboured up the 500-foot west side and headed on to our third Munro, mighty Creag Meagaidh, 3,700 feet.

At the summit cairn we lunched on top of the world, bright

sunlight and clear skies now firmly established. I saw Ann scanning the upland plateau that lay below us – the incredibly beautiful ridge that leads round to Meall Coire Choille-rais and An Cearcallach. 'What about walking on, Ann?' I enquired. Seconds later she was on her feet, galloping down the slope.

It was a magical walk, peering into the secret, un-named lochan below Meall Coire Choille-rais, feeling utterly elated, striding back along the ridge to An Cearcallach. A time for running. Glen Spean lay before us, backed by the ridges and peaks of Ben Nevis and the Grey Corries, with the whale-shoulder of Beinn a'Charainn so close in the evening sunlight that it seemed as though we could reach out a hand and stroke its grey rocks.

Neither of us wanted that day to end. Sadly, we moved off westwards along a narrow path to the steep edge of the mountain. We picked our way down carefully, following ill-marked tracks, clutching at heather and boulders, along rocky ledges, across rushing streams. A tortuous, difficult descent that seemed to take ages.

Off the mountain the terrain became even rougher and by the time we picked up a good path, even though it pointed too much to the west for us we gratefully followed it, by Moy Burn, to the road – arriving five miles from Aberarder. Line astern, we set off in the gathering dusk. I tried a few army and Boy Scout marching songs to keep our spirits up as we went past grim Moy Lodge and the

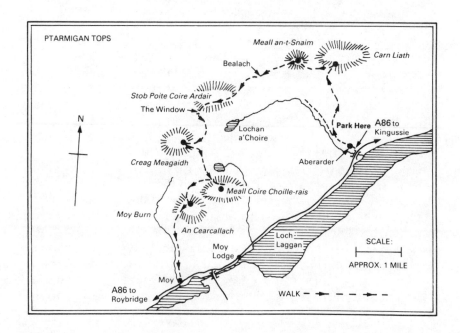

little camp site at Rubh na Megach, finally reaching Aberarder an hour and a half later.

As we sat in the car, looking up at the wonderful ridge towards Carn Liath, Meall an-t-Snaim and Stob Poite Coire Ardair, I knew that we had experienced something very special; that I would be unable to describe it fully to anyone else; that we would never forget that day as long as we lived – and that it was time for a well-earned pint.

WHAT YOU NEED TO KNOW

Time and effort Allow about ten hours for this strenuous walk of some seventeen miles. There are few hazards along the way, provided that you observe the normal mountain safety precautions. Some of the gradients will make you pant a bit, but there is nothing to worry anyone who is reasonably well preserved and reasonably fit.

Problems will arise, however, in bad weather. Great caution is then required as the ridge, although wide, has a sheer drop to the south for much of the route, particularly when ascending from the Window to Creag Meagaidh. The tendency is to stray too far to the left, onto the edge of the precipice overhanging Lochan a'Choire.

I found the most difficult part of the walk to be the descent from An Cearcallach, which is very steep and should be avoided in bad weather or winter conditions. Plan the timing of your assault carefully and make sure that you are not caught out on the tops, unprepared, in the dark.

Location Ordnance Survey Sheet 34, Fort Augustus, second series, scale 1:50,000.

Grid references Car park at Aberarder 482874; Carn Liath 472904; Meall an-t-Snaim 459905; Stob Poite Coire Ardair 429889; the Window 425886; Creag Meagaidh 417877; Meall Coire Choille-rais 435863; An Cearcallach 425854; Moy 422827.

Route The first part of the route from the car park at Aberarder is a clearly marked path, with railway sleepers laid over the bogs. Watch out for the clump of silver birch on your right as you ascend so that you locate the faint track up the south side of Carn Liath.

Keep to the left of the intermediate crest, Na Cnapanan, and you will soon pick up the line of iron posts that lead to the plateau and, eastwards, to the summit cairn. Walk back, westwards, and the way ahead is obvious, along the ridge towards Stob Poite Coire Ardair and the Window.

A track wends up from the north side of the Window, leading to a broad, grassy plateau, past Madman's Cairn to the summit of Creag Meagaidh. From the cairn the rest of the walk is laid out, map-like, below you to the south. Descend from the final top, An Cearcallach, via Moy Burn, to the road at Moy, and thence back along the A86 to the car park at Aberarder. Better still, have someone meet you at Moy.

56

A Splendid Day Out

ANN HAS been talking about going on a proper walk. I know exactly what she really means – straight up the side of some ruddy great mountain. She is engrossed in Ordnance Survey Sheet 41, Ben Nevis, thickly contour-packed, including Carn Dearg, Carn Mor Dearg and the Grey Corries. My only hope is to remain absolutely silent, fingers crossed.

I have always loved walking, through sylvan glades, by babbling brooks, over heather-covered moorlands. But it was not until I fell in with Ann that I discovered the delights of more elevated, elongated hikes. When we first met, more than three decades since, we used to explore the Pentland Hills which guard the auld grey city of Edinburgh, within easy striking distance of Habbie's Howe, a convenient, famous Lowland hostelry.

Shortly afterwards, I was introduced to the Yorkshire Dales, where Ann had walked in her youth. An aunt lived at Redmire, a wonderful little stone-housed village in Wensleydale. We had marvellous walks in Bishopdale, Apedale, Coverdale, Swaledale and Wharfedale. The dales are gentle, easy-going lands, full of magic and mystery, and in those days they were relatively quiet.

My first long walk, a distance of some twelve miles, was from the market town of Hawes. We climbed south by Wether Fell to the summit of Drumaldrace Hill and followed the Roman Road eastwards, then down to Semer Water. Skirting the south shoulder of Addlebrough, across Thornton Rust Moor, we arrived at Aysgarth and the Red Lion, two pints before the bus back to Hawes. Unforgettable.

The map grunted decisively and I knew the die was cast. 'What about a couple of Munros this morning?' she enquired, casually. 'After all, it's a super day and you might even get a few decent photographs from the top.' The inducement. 'Exactly which Munros do you have in mind?' I asked. 'Stob a'Choire Mheadhoin and Stob Coire Easain, by Loch Treig. You can look for trout as we go. Won't it be fun?' Resigned, I started packing.

These two peaks are part of a continuous, long shoulder, running south from the A86 near Tulloch Station. Loch Treig, impounded by a dam to provide water for the British Aluminium plant at Fort William, lies to the east, the magnificent Grey Corries to the west. Stob a'Choire Mheadhoin is 3,610 feet and its neighbour, Stob Coire Easain, 3,658 feet. A splendid day out, according to her.

An hour later found us winding up the narrow road to Fersit by the Allt Laire Burn, An Dubh Lochan and the River Treig. It had been a good year for foxgloves. Everywhere we travelled in Lochaber these graceful flowers greeted us, even by the side of the busy road between Spean Bridge and Fort William. The verges near Torlundy were a wild flower garden, bright with buttercup, clover, meadowsweet, wild thyme and foxglove.

We parked the car at Fersit and set off along the track towards Loch Treig, Breac splashing happily in the clear waters of the river. Heathcliff, soundly leaded, scuttled along by his mistress's heels, tongue lolling, straining to be off. A locked pole-gate bars vehicle access below the dam, and the dam itself looked hideous. The lower water level had exposed acres of sand and silt, and as far as the eye could see, the sad loch was ringed by a jagged, water-level tide mark.

The track along the west side of Loch Treig is the route of a disused company railway and at the end is an untidy cluster of steel and iron, black-painted buildings. Across the loch, the railway line to Corrour and Rannoch Moor dives into a dark tunnel and we watched as a near-empty train trundled by, hooting. Ahead reared the twin peaks of our mountains and we happily left the shore and began angling up the side of the hill, heading for our first objective, the plateau below Stob a'Choire Mheadhoin.

Patches of silver birch clung precariously to the side of the hill. Rocky outcrops, lichen-clad, blocked our way. Cautiously, we skirted round them, climbing ever higher through clumps of amazingly bright bell heather. Burgeoning ling was bursting to take its place, anxious to purple the hill properly.

It was a stiff haul, at least for me, from the lochside up to the plateau and then on to the summit of Stob a'Choire Mheadhoin, and I called for an immediate halt when we reached semi-level ground by the cairn at the south end. Clutching hot coffee, and my breath, I gazed in wonderment at the surrounding vista, happy and grateful, as always, that Ann had dragged me out to enjoy the miracle of beauty that is my native land.

Westwards lay Stob Choire Clàurigh, dominating the Grey Corries, then Aonach Beag and Aonach Mor and mighty Ben Nevis; south, the sharp glen carrying the railway, through Corrour to Rannoch Station and desolate Rannoch Moor; eastwards, the green heights of Stob Coire Sgriodain, Beinn na Lap, overlooking Loch Ossian, and a distant prospect of Ben Alder; to the north, our recently discovered friend, Creag Meagaidh.

Heartened, we carefully picked our way down to the bealach between the two peaks and then set our shoulders to the final, steep assault on the summit of Stob Coire Easain, enjoying every moment of the ascent. I always dread the prospect of getting there, being an essentially lazy sort of person, but oh, my goodness, once there, however distant there might be, how thankful I am that I made the effort.

We lunched on Stob Coire Easain, Loch Treig sparkling far below, and immediately afterwards had an elongated photo-session, which, given my ability with a camera, is always very much a question of luck, in spite of alleged idiot-proof, point-and-shoot modern machines. We then retraced our steps to Stob a'Choire Mheadhoin and north across the ridge, reluctant to leave the high tops with their stunning views.

The way let us down gently and we followed the shoulder over Meall Cian Dearg, avoiding the steep descent to the lochside and the black buildings, on to Creag Fhiaclach and the car at Fersit. As we approached civilization, Heathcliff, complaining bitterly all the time, was tethered. Breac? Back in the river, soothing his aching feet. Ann, as usual, had been right: a splendid day out.

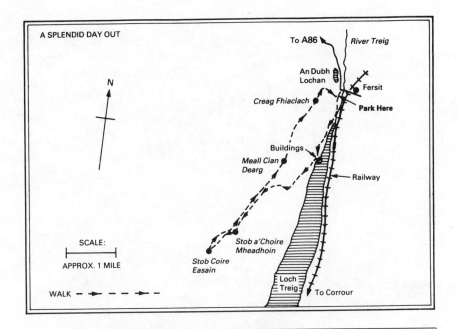

A SPLENDID DAY OUT

To **A86**
River Treig

An Dubh
Lochan

Fersit

Creag Fhiaclach

Park Here

Buildings

Meall Cian
Dearg

Railway

Stob a'Choire
Mheadhoin

Stob Coire
Easain

Loch
Treig
To Corrour

N

SCALE:
APPROX. 1 MILE

WALK ‑ ‑ ‑ ‑ ‑

WHAT YOU NEED TO KNOW

Time and effort Allow a good six hours, longer if the weather is fine, for this nine-mile walk. The most strenuous part, which engendered serious huffing and puffing from me, is the climb from the lochside up to Stob a'Choire Mheadhoin. Once there, it is relatively easy going, although the way ahead is broken and stony.

The south side of Stob a'Choire Mheadhoin is very steep, dropping to Loch Treig, as is either side of the bealach between the peaks, and the crags of Irlick Chaoile on Stob Coire Easain. Take the greatest possible care in bad weather conditions. It is a long way down.

Location Ordnance Survey Sheet 41, Ben Nevis, second series, scale 1:50,000.

Grid references An Dubh Lochan 349788; car park at Fersit 350782; Loch Treig dam 349772; black buildings 343760; Stob a'Choire Mheadhoin 316736; Stob Coire Easain 308731; Meall Cian Dearg 333760; Creag Fhiaclach 345780.

Route From the car park, follow the track south to the dam at Loch Treig, then on to the end of the path at the buildings by the shore. From this vantage point, plan your route up the side of the hill, skirting the obvious crags. Return by keeping to the high ridge all the way. On Creag Fhiaclach, turn east, back to the car.

57

Glen Roy and the White Falls

THE ROYAL High School of Edinburgh is a bad place to learn spelling. At least, during the late 1940s and early 1950s, it was for me. Then, the principal inducement to effort was the strap: a thick, tongued strip of leather which I dreaded as much as I dreaded the finer points of i before e except after c. Thrice weekly lashings had little effect, other than producing red palms and sullen resentment. Yet in spite of this rough introduction to the delights of language, I survived, and even began to make up whole sentences; and, eventually, I realized that writing was the only thing I really wanted to do.

However, my learning curve was excruciatingly slow. In order to avoid academic enterprise, I eagerly embraced outdoor interests – ornithology, wildlife, hillwalking, hiking, camping – indeed, anything that would separate me from flying chalk, smudged jotters and conjugated verbs. Which is, I suppose, how I became a hillwalker and fly-fisherman. On mountain or moor, river or loch, I was in control, confident and competent.

Forty years on, hillwalking and fly-fishing remain my first loves. There are few pleasures in life that can compare with a day out amidst Scotland's glorious hills and mountains, regardless of wind and weather, walking and fishing, exploring this lovely land.

Lochaber epitomizes everything I mean: it is a wild, distant country, crowded with fine peaks, fast-flowing rivers and silent lochs; where you may discover an eternity of joy on the high tops, with snow bunting and ptarmigan for companions; where scented bog myrtle lulls the senses and wild thyme blooms amongst boulder-strewn screes; where salmon lurk in deep, heather-banked pools and brown trout stipple calm, distant lochans.

Ann and I recently spent two weeks walking and fishing in Lochaber, based at Roybridge and covering some hundred and fifty miles. Within a radius of twenty miles from Roybridge there is a great variety of excellent game fishing to suit all levels of expertise and expenditure; and there are more than enough hills and mountains to keep even the most dedicated walker happy for years.

Glen Roy and the River Roy are amongst our favourite locations. The hills surrounding the glen make marvellous walking country and are less frequently visited that their higher neighbours, ensuring perfect peace and seclusion. The little river is divided into three fishing beats, Club, Top and Forest Beat, and, provided that there are good water levels, there is always the chance of a salmon.

The most famous landmark in the glen is the Parallel Roads – regular, 30-foot to 90-foot wide terraces, running along the side of the hills. Their regular pattern gave rise to the theory that they had been constructed by man, and tradition supposes that they were once the hunting paths of ancient Celtic heroes. They are in fact a geological feature, formed during the ice ages, each line marking the gradually decreasing level of water impounded behind the ice dam blocking Glen Roy: as the dam melted, so the level lowered.

Ann and I spent a day walking in the hills above Forest Beat, upstream from Brae Roy Lodge, leaving the track by the river at Glen Turret, climbing the long shoulder of Carn Dearg, 2,520 feet, and crossing the Parallel Roads along the way. From the summit we walked eastwards across Carn Dearg Beag to Glas Bheinn, where we paused for well-earned coffee. In the distance, the Corrieyairack Pass zig-zagged over the Monadhliath Mountains to Fort Augustus; Loch Spey, the source of Scotland's fastest-flowing river, sparkled in the flat lands below Creag Meagaidh; and, at the foot of the hill, the White Falls, our first destination, by lonely Luib Chonnal bothy.

Ann and I lunched at the falls, serenaded by the sound of the shining stream thundering into a deep, peat-stained pool. A solitary, damp rowan overhung the flow; green ferns and purple foxgloves nodded in the gentle breeze; yellow saxifrage, stonecrop and northern bedstraw blushed from sunny corners. Heathcliff settled by his mistress, begging for scraps. Breac dived straight into the pool to ease his aching feet. I did likewise.

After lunch we tramped south, following the course of the River Roy upstream from the falls, bearing right at the Allt nan Luibhean Burn, into the bealach between Carn Dearg South, 2,913 feet, and Meall a'Mheanbh chruidh, 2,680 feet. A sharp haul took us to the summit of Carn Dearg South, giving dramatic views down into the corrie of Loch Roy, then we went back to the bealach to climb the long shoulder to the top of Meall a'Mheanbh chruidh.

A most convenient stalker's path greets you to the south of the top, and we walked down the glen with the gurgling burn of Uisge nam Fichead keeping us company, past the charming cascades known as the Dog Falls. Annat Cottage and the levels of the river valley gave us welcome relief. From here on the going was easy.

At Brae Roy Lodge, a hundred sheep greeted us, much to Heathcliff's delight, his face instantly twisted into a hideous grin as he strained at the lead. The only way through was to skirt the farm

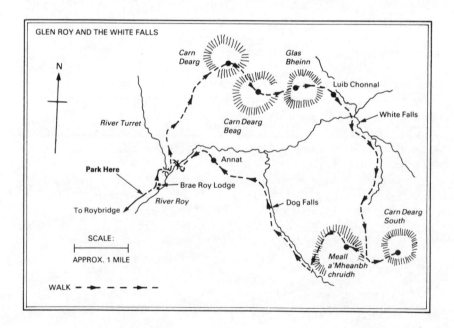

GLEN ROY AND THE WHITE FALLS

N

Carn Dearg

Glas Bheinn

Luib Chonnal

River Turret

Carn Dearg Beag

White Falls

Annat

Park Here

Brae Roy Lodge

River Roy

To Roybridge

Dog Falls

Carn Dearg South

Meall a'Mheanbh chruidh

SCALE:

APPROX. 1 MILE

WALK

buildings, so we edged round, clambering over several well-made fences in the process. My final test of stamina was helping Breac over the last fence, otherwise impassable because of its height. A tired, eight-year-old golden retriever is no lightweight, believe me, especially after an eight-hour walk.

Back at the car park, I dragged out the notebook I always carry on our expeditions, to note the names of the wild flowers we had seen. 'How do you spell saxifrage, Ann?' I enquired. 'Is bedstraw all one word?' My better half, grunted in disbelief: 'Didn't they manage to teach you anything at the Royal High?' 'Not a lot, dear. But I still manage to catch the odd trout and climb the odd hill.'

WHAT YOU NEED TO KNOW

Time and effort This is a long, but easy hill walk, covering approximately fifteen miles, and you should allow a full day for the journey. The ascent of Carn Dearg, above the River Turret, is steep and sudden, but once up the remainder of that section of the walk, the route on and down to the White Falls is delightful.

On the other side of the glen, the trek up to Meall a' Mheanbh chruidh and Carn Dearg South is over rough, trackless ground, but the way down is much easier, following the stalker's path. In poor weather conditions, exact map reading is essential, for it would be very easy to wander off-course in the mist.

Location Ordnance Survey Sheet 34, Fort Augustus, second series, scale 1:50,000.

Grid references Roybridge 273810; car park 335912; Brae Roy Lodge 336914; Glen Turret 340920; Carn Dearg 358948; Carn Dearg Beag 365942; Glas Bheinn 378941; Luib Chonnal bothy 395936; White Falls 398933; Carn Dearg South 410894; Meall a'Mheanbh chruidh 395894; Dog Falls 374896; Annat 363921.

Route From Roybridge on the A86, follow the minor road up the glen. This is tortuous and twisting, with dangerous blind summits, and requires great care. At the end of the road, park on the left, before the entrance to Brae Roy Lodge. Walk north past the lodge and follow the sand/gravel track by the River Roy to its meeting with the River Turret. Climb to the summit of Carn Dearg and from there, walk on to Carn Dearg Beag and Glas Bheinn, then down to the White Falls.

From the White Falls, follow the course of the Upper River Roy to its junction with the Allt nan Luibhean Burn and then bear right for the bealach between Carn Dearg South and Meall a'Mheanbh chruidh. After visiting these two summits, pick up the stalker's path to the south, which leads back down the hill to Annat. Cross the river by the new bridge and walk back to the car.

58

Lunch in the Clouds

Aᴺᴺ ᴡᴬˢ straining at the leash, eager to be off. The dogs, more sensibly, had decided to have a day in bed. Their normal response to the appearance of walking boots and jackets is a frenzied yapping from Heathcliff and a great trampling of feet from Breac. That morning, however, lazy eyes blinked sleepily, so we left them, resting luxuriously.

I looked at my better half, suspiciously, then glanced at what lay ahead: Carn Ghluasaid, 3,140 feet, glowering in the mist, towering over the north shore of Loch Cluanie in the Ceannacroc Forest. 'If the weather improves,' she announced brightly, 'we can walk on to Sgurr nan Conbhairean and Sail Chaorainn.' I muttered a silent prayer, these peaks being 3,639 feet and 3,287 feet respectively, and continued fighting with my recalcitrant laces.

Four cars were parked by the lochside at Lundie – early birds, already on the hill – and we made out two matchstick figures disappearing into the clouds above us. The Lundie Burn gurgled happily, flinging its cold waters over a fine little waterfall. A spruce wheatear bobbed us good morning, snow-white rump a bright speck in the gloom. Wind-driven rain stung my face. We crossed the iron and concrete bridge onto the old military road and tramped soggily up the hill to the start of an old stalker's path.

West Highland weather is, however, notoriously fickle. Half an hour later the sun broke through, filling the glen with light and warmth, easing tense muscles, and encouraging us upwards. Already the cars parked by Loch Cluanie were small specks, as we gained height. To the south, across the loch, ridge after jagged ridge reared skywards: Creag a'Mhaim, Aonach air Chrith, Spidean Mialach and Gleouraich. A busy stream hurried down the hill, criss-crossing the track. A good-to-be-alive day.

We make our first stop. She is consulting the map – always a bad sign, particularly since the weather has improved. A family of meadow pipits are having a singing lesson. A lone grouse rockets from the heather. Three sad-eyed, dripping, black-faced sheep appear over a crest, followed by several more. As we watched, we heard a shepherd whistling, and then saw him, far below, working his dogs over the hill with military precision.

A marvellous, tiny, wild flower garden lay at our feet: spotted and purple orchid, bog asphodel, eyebright, wild thyme, cotton grass and bell heather. Four dogs now quartered the hill, collecting together small bands of sheep, dashing hither and thither, one moment squatting, statue-like, the next, at a call from their master, flying over the hill, tongues lolling, black and white streaks of lightning.

Climbing on, we crossed a large, bare, rock pavement where single stones have been placed to mark the direction to the track at the other side. Very convenient. The shepherd's whistling grew ever fainter, lost in the sound of the rising wind as we wended our way, tacking, up the mountainside. A sudden, unexpected gust could topple the unwary from the narrow path, which became unrelentingly steep. A storm swept in and, instantly, we were enshrouded once more in mist.

Some years ago John Ridgeway kindly autographed a copy of his super book *Flood Tide* for me. 'Into the mist' was his inscription, and now, looking ahead, I finally realized what John had meant. I experienced a sharp pang of excitement, pleasure and anticipation, rather than dismay at the deteriorating state of the weather. Suddenly, we were on the summit plateau, searching for the cairn, and we carefully followed the track to the edge of the sheer cliffs overlooking Allt Coire Sgreumh.

Retreating to the second cairn, a little way south and east from the crags, we huddled in the shelter of the old stones, shivering over hot mugs of coffee, wondering whether to go on or to abandon the day and retreat to the car. Visibility was virtually zero. In these situations, out in the hills, discretion is always the better part of valour and, reluctantly, we decided to descend. But as we rose to go, the clouds miraculously lifted, stunning us with an amazing view north-westwards to Sgurr nan Conbhairean. Irresistible.

A long, sharp ridge swings out from Carn Ghluasaid, wild with near-vertical rocks and corries, rising to the conical peak of Sgurr nan Conbhairean. Smooth, almost manicured grass, scattered with small boulders, leads along the shoulder and we determined, regardless of what the heavens might do, that we just had to walk on and attain the summit. Nothing else seemed to matter. We set off, the light of adventure glinting in our eyes.

Keeping well back from the edge, we inched along the misty top to the cairn by Creag a'Chaorainn, 3,276 feet, then across Glas Bhealach to the beginning of the final haul up to Sgurr nan Conbhairean. Again, the clouds lifted, giving us a quick glimpse of the summit; then just as quickly, the white, clinging mist swirled back to envelop us in a strange, silent, visionless land.

We were on him almost before we realized he was there: a snow bunting, head tilted, watching curiously. He hopped closer, pecking occasionally amidst the thyme. For me, it was one of the most glorious moments of my life, finding at last one of Scotland's most elusive and greatest characters. How I wished that I could thank him for his presence, for the great gift that he had given me. Ann and I stood motionless, hardly daring to breathe, speechless, until the tiny bird flitted off into the mist.

Moments later, still unable to see a hand before our faces, we reached the summit and, mindful of the fearsome drop to the north, moved carefully to the small, stone-tumbled cairn. I worked my way round and, delight of delights, found the small, drystane-built stall that offered us, as it has offered many like us in the past, welcome respite from the wind – shelter and comfort. Gratefully, we tumbled in to wait out the worst of the storm.

Utterly secure, with the wind howling around us, we lunched, deep in the clouds; and, as though rewarding us for effort, Lochaber relented and the afternoon remained as bright and sunny as anyone could wish. From our lofty perch, the finest self-catering restaurant in Scotland, we surveyed Glen Affric to the north; the Five Sisters of Kintail, the Rough Bounds of Knoydart, Morar, Moidart and Loch Eil to the west and south – half of Scotland, laid out map-like for our pleasure.

After lunch, we left Sgurr nan Conbhairean and descended to walk north along the fine ridge to Sail Chaorainn, searching on the

way for Prince Charlie's Cave, a few, tilted boulder slabs on the
north face of the encircling corrie where the fugitive is reputed to
have hidden for several days after his return from South Uist in the
Outer Hebrides. Little enough good have I to say of BPC. He was a
disaster for Scotland. But even I have to admit that he must have
been quite a walker.

Happily, we made our way back along the ridge and up the lower
screes of Sgurr nan Conbhairean again, swinging right to the
narrow ridge above Gorm Lochan, a tiny, dark-blue circle, surrounded by bright green slopes. Below, Loch Cluanie sparkled in
evening sunlight, and the long descent by Meall Breac to Allt Coire
Larr was a constant joy. The little burn greeted us with deep pools
and crystal-clear waters, swirling over dramatic, bouldered falls.

We crossed the stream and stopped in a small wood of oak, birch
and rowan, where foxgloves, ferns, buttercups and butterflies kept
us company. Reluctantly, back at the military road, stiff-upper-
lipped, we joined a party of ghostly government troops, slogging
back to barracks. They complained bitterly about being posted to
such a desolate, uncompromising wilderness. Their officer rode up,
belligerently. 'Any rebels in the hills?' he demanded. 'None,' I
replied, confidently, in spite of everything, crossing my fingers
behind my back.

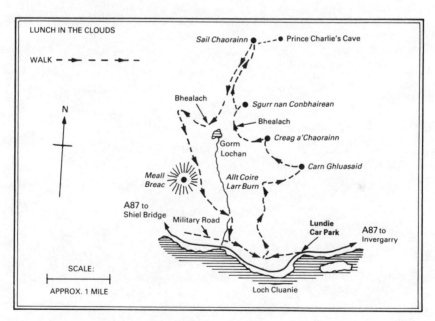

WHAT YOU NEED TO KNOW

Time and effort The ascent of Carn Ghluasaid from the shores of Loch Cluanie involves a fairly unrelenting, 2,500-foot climb. The good news is that there is an excellent, well-marked track all the way. Once on the plateau and ridge, the going is easy. The only other ascent is the steepish slog up to the summit of Sgurr nan Conbhairean – and, having gone down the other side to reach Sail Chaorainn, you have to go some way back up again on the return journey. You really get to know that slope.

When the tops are cloud-covered it is easy, and dangerous, to go astray. Double-check your map reading and hasten slowly; there are sheer drops along the way. In windy weather, watch out for that sudden gust that might catch you unawares. Keep back from the edges and ledges. Apart from these obvious dangers, this is a straightforward walk of about ten miles. Take as long as you like. There are no prizes for speed.

Location Ordnance Survey Sheet 34, Fort Augustus, second series, scale 1:50,000.

Grid references Car park at Lundie 145105; start of stalker's path to Carn Ghluasaid 137103; Carn Ghluasaid 146125; Creag a'Chaorainn 149132; Sgurr nan Conbhairean 130139; Prince Charlie's Cave 139155; Sail Chaorainn 136155; Gorm Lochan 124133; Meall Breac 124117; military road on return journey 127106.

Route The Lundie car park is part of the old road, now bypassed by the A87 route to Shiel Bridge, on the north shore of Loch Cluanie. A gate leads onto the hill and the military road. Watch out for the stalker's path, on your right, which takes you up to Carn Ghluasaid. From the summit cairn there is a magnificent vista of the way ahead to Sgurr nan Conbhairean, along a broad ridge, sheer to the north, steeply sloping to the south.

From Sgurr nan Conbhairean the route to Sail Chaorainn and Prince Charlie's Cave is obvious. On the return, walk back up to Sgurr nan Conbhairean, bearing right before the top, heading towards the knife-like bhealach above Gorm Lochan. Walk past the lochan to the next top, then begin your descent to Meall Breac. From Meall Breac, come down to the Allt Coire Larr Burn, aiming for the trees a few hundred yards from the road. Cross the burn and pick up the track on the opposite bank. This leads back to the military road. Turn left on the military road and walk back to Lundie.

59

Glen Dessarry and
Carn Mor

WE LABOURED up the steep slope in white mist, a knife-like
wind urging us on. To our right the cliffs plunged, almost
sheer, into Gleann an Lochain Eanaiche. The thin, spongy topsoil
overlaid bare rock, carpeted with yellow-gold bog asphodel and
delicate purple thyme. Ahead lay our goal, the cloud-covered
summit of Carn Mor, 2,700 feet, guarding the head of Glen
Dessarry and Glen Pean in Lochaber.

At the top we paused for coffee and, as though in reward for
uncomplaining effort, the clouds lifted, opening up one of the most
magnificent views in all of Scotland. Northwards, the River
Dessarry turned and twisted down the glen to blue Loch Arkaig.
Upper Glendessarry Cottage and Glendessarry Lodge sparkled
2,000 feet below – tiny, bright specks by the silver stream. The
Rough Bounds of Knoydart and the mountains of Morar crowded

round – Sgurr nan Coireachan, Sgurr na Ciche and Meall Buidhe. To the south lay the thin ribbon of the River Pean and a wonderful prospect of the sharp cliffs and corries of Sgurr Thuilm, 'the peak of the rounded hillock', Streap, 'the climbing hill', and Gulvain, which is also known as Gaor Bheinn.

However, even in this remote wilderness, intensive afforestation was in progress, busily establishing taxpayer-subsidized rows of lodgepole pine and Sitka spruce. Just how these trees, if they ever grow and if they are ever economical to harvest, will be transported to a sawmill is beyond me. The road along the north shore of Loch Arkaig is a nightmare to drive, even for cars. To upgrade it so that it could carry heavy, timber-laden lorries would cost a fortune, no doubt requiring even more public funds.

Perhaps the intention is to float the timber down the loch itself? If so, I have no objection to any damage that might be caused to the hideous fish farm at the east end, but I would be horrified to see this remote area becoming yet another example of the superiority of private profit for a few over the legitimate recreational aspirations of the many.

We turned our backs on the ghastly plantations, our intention being to follow the four-mile-long ridge eastwards, by Meall nan Spardan and Monadh Gorm, to photograph Loch Arkaig prior to descending to Strathan, fishing rods ready, in search of something for supper – a brace of Loch Arkaig's lovely wild brown trout.

Loch Arkaig lies fifteen miles north from Fort William along the B8004. This narrow, twisting track, via the Dark Mile, was the route used by Prince Charles Edward Stuart, fleeing westwards after his defeat at the Battle of Culloden in April 1746, past the home of Cameron of Lochiel, the first of the Highland chiefs to support the disastrous uprising. Lochiel paid for his folly, materially at least, when 320 soldiers, under the command of Lieutenant Edward Cornwallis, arrived at Achnacarry and burned his fine house and gardens as he lay watching, helpless, in the hills. His clansmen paid more dearly for their reluctant support of their chief and the Young Pretender, many being murdered by government troops whilst their laird slipped off to safety in France.

After he escaped from Benbecula in the Outer Hebrides, with the assistance of Flora Macdonald, Prince Charles arrived at Loch Nevis, hoping to find a boat to take him back to France. But news of his arrival spread quickly and, once more, the hunt was up.

General Campbell, with 400 men, marched east; Captain Scott, with 500 men, blocked the western routes; a chain of interlocking camps was established: escape seemed impossible. However, Donald Cameron of Glen Pean came to the rescue, guiding the

Prince through the hills, at times so close to their pursuers that they could clearly hear them talking by their camp fires.

The little road along the north shore of Loch Arkaig, past the dramatic Eas Chia-aig waterfall, is more peaceful today, and a number of small sites amidst the birch and rowans host neat holiday caravans. Fishing boats bob by the shore and children play in the shallows. On a calm summer evening it is difficult to imagine the hardship and suffering that stalked the glen nearly two hundred and fifty years ago.

High above Loch Arkaig, in glorious evening sunlight, we rested again. The dogs, having covered three miles for every one that we had marched, collapsed, exhausted, at our feet. A tiny lochan sparkled nearby, bright with white cotton grass, bobbing in the breeze.

The farm cottages and buildings of Strathan lay far below as we contemplated our descent from Monadh Gorm. The way down the hill was steep, dangerous even in summer, requiring step-by-step judgement, avoidance of rocky outcrops, and careful progress through knee-high bracken and heather. The scent of bog myrtle filled the air as we edged lower, until we finally reached the forest track, hot, foot-sore, but happy.

On the wooden bridge over the River Dessarry we stopped, and I clambered down to the fast-flowing stream to collect a cup of sweet, peat-stained water. The dogs rushed for the river, too,

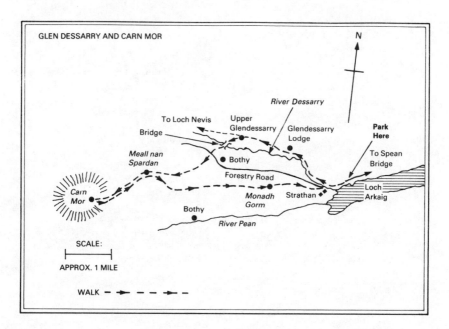

eagerly quenching their thirst in the flow. An early owl flitted by as a late-hunting heron flapped homewards. Half an hour later we followed, complete with a fine brace of trout for dinner. Ann caught two; I caught the rest. Such is life, but they were magnificent.

WHAT YOU NEED TO KNOW

Time and effort This eleven-mile walk takes about six hours, depending upon how long you stop along the way. The first part is on a good track from the head of Loch Arkaig. We followed the old route, along the north side of Glen Dessarry, rather than the new forestry road. A matter of principle. At Upper Glendessarry Cottage the route continues on to Loch Nevis, a further, rough, three-hours' tramp, passing the start point for climbing Sgurr na Ciche.

For those wishing to stay out longer, there is a bothy, A'Chuil, on the south side of the River Dessarry and, over the ridge, in Glen Pean, another bothy by the River Pean. Take care crossing the Dessarry: there is an old bridge, but it is not entirely complete and it is probably better, water levels permitting, to wade the river, downstream of the bridge.

The long haul up the summit of Meall nan Spardan is taxing, but once there the worst is over and you enjoy the delights of ridge walking in a glorious setting. On the way east along the ridge to Loch Arkaig, beware of the forestry fence. There are no gates that I could see, and you have to climb it as best you can, close to one of the heavy posts.

Descending from Monadh Gorm requires care and takes some time. As can catching supper in Loch Arkaig. Fishing is very much a matter of being in the right place at the right time, as I know, all too well, to my cost. Best of luck in your efforts.

Location Two maps needed: Ordnance Survey Sheet 34, Fort Augustus, and Sheet 33, Loch Alsh and Glen Shiel, second series, scale 1:50,000.

Grid references Car park 988916; Glendessarry Lodge 968927; Upper Glendessarry Cottage 951931; bridge 944929; A'Chuil bothy 945924; Meall nan Spardan 920920; Carn Mor 903911; Monadh Gorm 962915; Strathan 980915.

Route Park the car at the end of the little road along the north shore of Loch Arkaig. Follow the track westwards round the hill, past Strathan, and on past Glendessarry Lodge to Upper Glendessarry. A track leads down the hill to the river and an old, broken bridge.

Cross the river, and the new forestry road. Climb the shoulder of Meall nan Spardan. This takes you onto the ridge. Follow the ridge west to Carn Mor. Return via Meall nan Spardan and walk east to Monadh Gorm. Descend to Strathan, the car park and Loch Arkaig.

60

The Singing Sands

*I*HAVE absolutely no problem lying doing nothing on a sun-drenched beach. Provided that it is a naturist beach, for it has always seemed to me to be the height of lunacy to get dressed up to go either swimming or sunbathing. Happily, my view is shared by ever increasing numbers of people, influenced by their experiences whilst on holiday abroad.

When Ann and I manage to escape to the sun, which is an all-too-infrequent occurrence, we are the ones at the airport with minimal baggage and bright, anticipatory smiles. Our destination is invariably a remote corner of the Mediterranean, or south-west France, where we can obtain an all-over-tan, soak up the local atmosphere and wine, and explore the countryside.

However, my better half believes in pain before pleasure and, after much map-scouring, invariably selects a beach involving a brisk two-hour walk or a vigorous burst of biking to reach. We have had wonderful holidays – on the delightful island of Formentera, amidst the forests and sand dunes of the Landes in south-west France, and, a few years ago, in south-west Crete, where we spent marvellous days in the White Mountains.

Such pleasures are also easily found in Scotland, on dozens of hidden beaches along the north and west coasts, such as Torrisdale, Strathan, Faraid, Keisgaig, Sandwood, Droman, Lag na Saille, Camus na Ruthaig, Slaggan, Uags, Ardintoul, Inverguseran, Pean-meanach, Gortenfern, and many more; as well as the hundreds of soft, sandy shores fringing distant hill lochs and lochans. Ideal post-lunch resting places during a day out in the hills.

Most recently, we discovered Gortenfern, the Singing Sands of Ardnamurchan, a series of small, golden coves with stunning views across green and blue waves to the purple islands of Eigg and Rhum. Ardnamurchan means 'the promontory of the great seas' and the peninsula is the most westerly point of mainland Britain, dominated by the slender, 118-foot column of a lighthouse designed by Alan Stevenson and built in 1846 for the Northern Lighthouse Board.

Ardnamurchan light is now automated, but I knew one of the last keepers, Jim Hardie, and his wife Nan, with whom I used to work in Caithness in the 1970s. Jim was every inch the lighthouse keeper, a resilient, self-possessed man of great character, and I was thrilled to read one day in *The Scotsman* that the Queen had visited them at Ardnamurchan for tea and chat. Nan would have enjoyed that, enormously.

As much as we enormously enjoyed our gentle day at Gortenfern, self-awarded after three days of strenuous effort on the high tops of Lochaber. And, joy of joys, the sun was shining brightly as we set off from Roybridge, picnic-packed and ready for adventure, accompanied by two excited dogs, Ann's paints and sketching pad, assorted bird and wild flower books, and binoculars.

At Kinlochmoidart we stopped to say hello to the Seven Men of Moidart, represented by five beech trees near the shore. The trees were planted in the early years of the nineteenth century through the authority of the Kinlochmoidart Estate, whose ancestors were Jacobites and supported Prince Charles Edward Stuart during the 1745 rebellion. Two of the original trees fell foul of the elements and have been replaced by saplings.

The Seven Men arrived with BPC in 1745: William Murray, Marquess of Tullibardine; Sir Thomas Sheridan; Sir John Macdonald; Aeneas Macdonald, younger brother of the Laird of Kinlochmoidart; John William O'Sullivan; the Revd George Kelly; and Francis Strickland. After the defeat at Culloden, Tullibardine died in prison, Sheridan, O'Sullivan and Kelly escaped to France, Aeneas Macdonald was banished, and Francis Strickland died at Carlisle.

Far better that they had all stayed at home, along with their leader. Better by far that they had never set foot on Scottish soil, for in doing so, and in their encouragement of a highly impressionable youth, they sealed the fate of the old Highland way of life for ever, and caused untold misery to many thousands of decent, simple people, whose only crime was to be Highland.

The narrow A861 road twists over Cruach an t-Aon Bhlair, past Captain Robertson's Cairn, down to the little village of Acharacle at the south end of Loch Shiel. Just before the village, we turned right along the B8044 and thence left towards Arivegaig and Torran Iamhair.

A beautifully converted, white-walled croft house called 'Spin-drift' lies adjacent to the parking area and the owners were busy licking their garden into shape as we parked. The sand flats of Kentra Bay lay exposed, shining in morning sunlight, and we stopped on a fine wooden bridge to peer into the dark waters of Allt Eas an Taileir Burn in search of sea trout or salmon.

The bridge across the stream was built in June 1985 by the Second Troop of the 11th Field Squadron of the Royal Engineers. And a very good job they made of it, including a neat bypass to the left of the main gate which allows you to cross without having to heave the main gate open. Most civilized and much appreciated by both dogs and humans. However, watch out for the handrails on the structure because they are flimsy: an over-serious lean could give you a much closer look at the fish than you had anticipated.

We followed the excellent track that margins the bay, alive with early birdsong, silver birch and rowans bursting with berries. Tiny streams, big from recent rain, cascaded down from Bruach na Maorach, cutting neat channels through the grey mud flats to an astonishingly blue sea. Freshly laundered sheep grazed by the shore, staring at us with dark, uncomplaining eyes as we strode by.

The ford at Gorteneorn is guarded by a sad grey house sur-rounded by woodlands: elm, beech, pine and oak. The oak trees are magnificent and some are obviously very old, their gnarled bran-ches being supported by moss-covered dykes. Nor have they squandered their years, for the forest floor is scattered with their offspring: delicate shoots, thrusting upwards, bright green leaves luxuriating in the mild, west-coast weather.

Beyond the oaks, a few yards up the hill, lies the harsh reality of so-called modern forestry: serried ranks of Sitka spruce and lodge-pole pine, packed tightly together, blanketing out all light and life from beneath their branches. If I had my way, I would sentence the perpetrators of the factory tree farming that is destroying my native land to a lifetime in the middle of their hideous plantations – they deserve nothing less.

The track down to the Singing Sands is marked by a signpost

and, when we passed, a line of stones formed as an arrow. Shades of Boy Scouts days. Rough rocks gave way to gentle sand and the trees reverted to those of a proper, Scottish wood, reminiscent of the forests of the Landes in south-west France which we so admired. Wren, finch and tit chattered from the branches and then, suddenly, Gortenfern beach, splendid and magnificent, lay before us – golden sands, washed by crystal-clear seas.

A few families lazed in the sun. A group of boys played football. Oystercatchers busied themselves in the margins, hunting for lunch. Herring gulls and black-backed gulls wheeled overhead. As we walked over the sands, our feet breaking the thin crust formed by the prevailing winds, Gortenfern sang to us – a mystical, shimmering melody, promising peace and serenity.

The beach extends eastwards, separated into five coves, each one seemingly more delightful than its neighbour, and we clambered over rocky headlands, exploring each beach, before finally arriving at the most easterly cove ready for sustenance and sunning. This last beach is backed by superb sand dunes and we circled inland, behind the dunes, to the shade of a clump of small oak trees. Bog myrtle scented the air as the temperature by the trees soared into the 80s.

After lunch Ann dragged out the sketch pad whilst the dogs hid under the oaks. I wandered to the crest of the dunes, looking out over the sands and the Sound of Arisaig to the Point of Sleat and

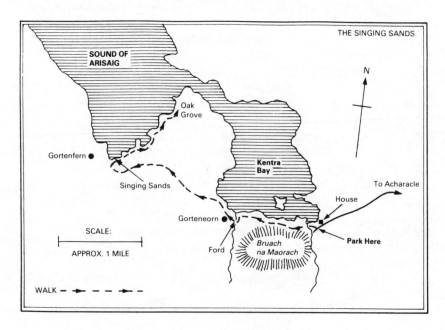

Skye. Otter country. The Cuillin Hills lined the horizon: Sgurr Dearg and Sgurr Alasdair, towering over the cold waters of distant Loch Coruisk.

Back in the oak grove Ann was busy sketching an unsuspecting bird's-foot trefoil. I watched for a few moments as she worked, admiring her skill and dexterity. A male Common Blue butterfly flitted by. The sun grew even hotter. . . . I lay back, content. I have absolutely no problem lying doing nothing on a sun-drenched beach.

WHAT YOU NEED TO KNOW

Time and effort   Very little of the latter and quite a lot of the former, depending upon the weather. Obviously, you should choose a good day for the expedition. This easy, delightful walk is ideal for a family outing, and even little ones, with some encouragement, should find it well within their capabilities.

The main beach is three miles from the car park and the last beach is a further one mile east: a total of some eight or nine miles there and back, depending upon how much you wander once there. Remember to take along all the essential items for a lazy day: bread, tomatoes, salad, cheese, wine and water. The more active might care to pack a good book.

Location   Ordnance Survey Sheet 40, Loch Shiel, second series, scale 1:50,000.

Grid references   The Seven Men of Moidart 704726; Acharacle 665679; car parking 650677; Gorteneorn 635678; the Singing Sands 614688; oak grove 625697.

Route   Park near the house called 'Spindrift' and cross the wooden bridge over the river. The track leads westwards along the margin of Kentra Bay, past Gorteneorn, up the hill, through the commercial forest, and down to the signpost indicating the beach.

A word of warning is perhaps appropriate regarding the return journey. Ann and I thought that we would return via the coast, avoiding the forestry, but found that we were unable to do so, due to the nature of the terrain. Away from the beach, the coastal rocks are deeply fissured and smothered with dwarf trees, heather and ferns. This makes finding a route not only difficult but also very dangerous, because it is all too easy to slip into one of the hidden crevices, risking severe injury. After stumbling around for an hour, searching for a way through, we eventually retraced our steps and returned to the car park by the outward route. There may be a path, but if there is we failed to find it.

61

The Silver Path and Castle Tioram

AFTERNOON SUNLIGHT sparkled. So did the dogs, sensing a
walk. With Heathcliff on the lead, sheep-proof, and Breac
bounding ahead to the first muddy stream, we left the car and
walked north along the shore by Castle Tioram and Loch Moidart.
The tide was out, leaving golden sands specked dark green with
seaweed, hosting busily probing, red-billed, black and white
oystercatchers.

Walk first, castle later. Skirting a happy group of campers,
holiday-makers, windsurfers and cyclists, close to a large sign
declaring 'NO CAMPING', we followed a well-made trail into a
woodland wonderland. Oak, wych-elm, silver birch and ash
shaded our way; sunbeams dappled the forest floor. Wild flowers
blinked from rocky crevices and the gentle path led us upwards,
through a rust-covered, wrought-iron fence and gate.

The track hugs the steep shoreline, washed by the crystal-clear waters of Loch Moidart. Across the bay lie the islands of Eilean Shona and Shona Beag, joined together by a narrow isthmus. Eilean Shona has a number of beautifully situated, self-catering cottages, tucked amidst ancient trees, overlooking the sea: the ideal location for an away-from-it-all, family holiday.

Castle Tioram dominates the westward view, backed by a distant prospect of the crags and peaks of Rhum and Eigg: An Sgurr, with its Pictish hill fort, on Eigg, and the dark heights of Trallval, Ainshval and Sgurr nan Gillean on Rhum. Tiny, low-lying Muck nestles a few miles south, across the blue Sound of Eigg.

The shore track we followed is known as the 'Silver Path' and in places it is very rocky, with plenty of scrambling up and down over lichen-covered rocks. Perfectly safe, but, as always, caution is required at all times. Who needs a sprained ankle? The dogs seemed impervious to danger, dashing around, sniffing and snuffling under every boulder and fallen log.

Entirely content, we ambled along by the sea, stopping frequently to enjoy the sheer beauty of our surroundings, and dipping down to a small, rocky bay where a little stream tumbles from the shoulder of Beinn Bhreac (790 feet). The path continues eastwards but a small cairn marks our route south, up the line of the stream, onto the hill. Calling the dogs to heel, we began the climb.

Tall, green ferns brushed our sides as we tramped up the muddy track, awash with recent showers. A wren chattered noisily from the undergrowth. Shining droplets of water clung to silver spider webs and sparkled on delicate birch leaves. A heron flapped lazily by, shorewards to fish. Insects buzzed and hummed; brilliant butterflies fluttered in the light breeze. There was no place that we would rather have been. Peace was a tangible, living reality.

Clearing the trees, the path led us onto a verdant plateau, clustered with the ruins of a small crofting settlement – perhaps half a dozen buildings, grey stones tumbled over thick turf. Foxgloves nodded from derelict hearths; smokeless chimney stacks and broken walls filled the scene with a sense of sadness. A startled deer, head high, gazed at us inquisitively, before breaking through the bracken and bounding off.

It must have been a good place to live. A hard life, but complete and self-contained; where children could grow up and grow old in safety. A few cattle, hens, a patch of barley, and a firm belief in the awesome power and majesty of the Almighty. What did they feel, those long-departed Highlanders, when they were forced to leave their homes so many years ago? Whatever, they have left behind a kind legacy in their glen, a lingering song of happiness.

Beyond the crofts the track climbs easily round the west shoulder of Beinn Bhreac, through a narrow pass, where we turned east to scramble up to the ragged summit. At the top a magnificent vista greeted us – of wild mountains, rearing north, east and south: shapely Rois Bheinn in Moidart, Beinn Odhar Mhor by Loch Shiel, Sgurr Dhomhnuill in Ardgour, and Beinn Resipol in Sunart. Westwards lay the endless charm of Ardnamurchan and the graceful Atlantic.

With typical west-coast wickedness, the weather suddenly turned nasty. A knife-like rain storm rushed in, sweeping us off the summit, sending us scurrying downhill in search of shelter. We shivered our way past a weed-fringed lochan, Breac plunging happily into the muddy margins and emerging, with difficulty, black to the waist. Heathcliff, distinctly pipe-cleaner-looking in the rain, tripped delicately and disconsolately behind Ann.

Over a brow we found cover in an open wood by the side of Loch Blain and huddled beneath the dripping trees, gratefully sipping hot coffee. A pair of red-throated divers eyed us suspiciously from the middle of the loch. At the far side, a sudden movement: a fisherman, or rather, woman. Seemingly oblivious to the storm, she cast away, hopefully. Further along, her husband and son were similarly engaged. Not a sign of the snout of a single trout disturbed the calm.

We left them, still busily casting, and retraced our steps past the first lochan, to pick up the track. It climbed from the glen to a crest and then ambled delightfully downhill past a fine-looking, deep lochan, full of rising fish. Breac immediately plunged in and swam parallel to our path, high above the shore, down to the far end, where the waters had been impounded by a large, concrete dam.

Our party, now completely wet but happy, wandered through the dripping trees back to the little road by Eilean Uaine and, turning north, returned to the car park and Castle Tioram. As we arrived at the narrow causeway leading to the castle, the sun broke through from behind dark clouds, bathing the majestic ruin in brilliant light. A place to be reckoned with. The home of powerful men.

Castle Tioram was built in the fourteenth century and for generations was the principal mainland residence of Clanranald. It is wonderfully preserved, without the disciplined neatness that spoils so many of our ancient monuments. We explored the old rooms and staircases, peering through broken windows, expecting at any moment to be confronted by a claymore-wielding custodian, demanding to know what right we had to be there.

Throughout its history, Castle Tioram was never taken by force. The end came, in 1715, when the last occupant, Allan Clanranald, ordered it to be burnt, lest it should fall into the hands of government forces during the Jacobite Rebellion, disastrously led by that arch-schemer, the Earl of Mar, better known as 'Bobbing Johnny'.

Clanranald was said to have had a vision of death before he left to join the fray, and his 'second sight' proved all too accurate: he was killed a few weeks later at the Battle of Sherrifmuir, near Dunblane, fighting for his 'king across the water'. As he died on the moor, a second fire broke out at his newly built Hebridean home, Ormiclate Castle on South Uist, completely destroying the building.

We paused and pondered on the sad fate of war-like Clanranald, and on the even sadder fate that was to befall his people in the aftermath of the war. But, leaving the castle and walking back across the shining sands, dogs scampering ahead, it was hard to remain sombre on such a glorious evening. Let Clanranald lie in peace – the sun shines on.

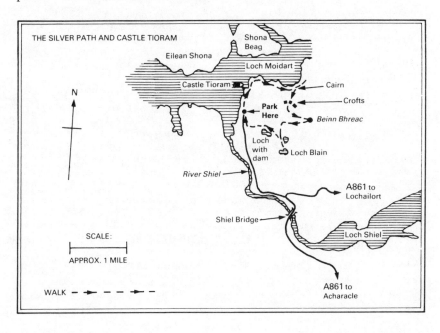

WHAT YOU NEED TO KNOW

Time and effort This is a comfortable walk of about five miles, including the climb to the top of Beinn Bhreac and a wander round Loch Blain. Stout walking shoes are required, as well as the usual wet-weather gear. Be prepared for all conditions. Take care on the coastal path: there are a few narrow ledges, as well as a 'balance' along a section of wire-encased rocks, directly above the sea.

Once you leave the shore the track can be very wet, as can be the plodge up to the top of Beinn Bhreac; but it is easy going and you should allow plenty of time simply to stand and stare and to enjoy the wonderful view. If you are an angler, packing a portable fishing rod will be even nicer, offering the opportunity of a few casts in Loch Blain and the other small lochan on the way back down to the road.

The walk can take three to four hours, or all day, depending upon what you wish. However, do remember to leave enough time to explore Castle Tioram properly. Mind the tide. In certain conditions you might find yourself wading back to the mainland or, at worst, stranded in the castle until the next low tide. There are worse places to

be stuck – provided that you have a good supply of midge repellent.

Location Ordnance Survey Sheet 40, Loch Shiel, second series, scale 1:50,000.

Grid references Car park 685721; Castle Tioram 663725; small cairn 679724; ruined crofts 677720; Beinn Bhreac 684715; Loch Blain 674707; loch with dam 672711; Eilean Uaine 664714.

Route If approaching from the Lochailort road, just before Shiel Bridge, where the River Shiel leaves Loch Shiel, turn right along a narrow road signposted to Tioram Castle. Park in the car park and walk along the track by the shore, past the castle and round the bay. The 'Silver Path' starts here and is very easily located.

The only possibility of going off-route is at the small bay where the cairn stands. If you do miss it, you will soon know, because the path ends a few hundred yards further on. Once on the track, the rest is simple: past the crofts, to the summit of Beinn Bhreac, down to Loch Blain and back to the road. The route over to Castle Tioram is across the sands.

62

Dreams of
Peanmeanach

*I*F SCOURING maps is the sign of a dreamer, then dreamer I am. When winter winds batter our windows I invariably curl up with Sheet 15, Loch Assynt, Sheet 9, Cape Wrath, or indeed, any of the eighty-five Ordnance Survey sheets which cover the land I love.

Happily, I have been fortunate enough to find a partner with similar interests, and for the past thirty years we have walked, climbed and hiked over most of Scotland; fishing, exploring, probing and prying into the remotest corners of our wonderful country, never tiring of its endless diversity and charm.

Ann specializes in wild flowers and I have an interest in birds, so we get along just fine – in spite of frequent collisions caused by her stumbling about peering earthwards, while I sky-gaze the moors and corries in search of feathered friends. But, by and large, we cope and, in the process, learn from each other.

I first noticed the track on the map when I was plotting an assault on some of the peaks surrounding Loch Shiel. Because there appeared to be a fine beach at the end of the trail, and because it passed close to an interesting-looking loch, it seemed the natural place to go, promising to be 'far from the madding crowd'.

As we sped past Loch Eilt along the road from Fort William, sunlight sparkled and an urgent train busily chugged the West Highland Line. We paused near Polnish to visit the little 'Church in the Hills', the place of worship of the local lairds, the Cameron-Heads, who for many years owned fishing rights on Loch Eilt. The track from the road to the church starts by a broken notice-board, bereft of messages. At the railway crossing – stop, look and listen – we were advised that long, slow or heavy vehicles should contact 0977 02335 prior to crossing.

God was out when we reached the church and the tiny building was securely locked. Paint flaked from the walls. Patterned windows glinted. Rois-bheinn cast gloomy shadows over the sad church with its memories of a bygone age.

The railway separating the church from the road was built in 1901 to service the fishing port of Mallaig and the ferries which still ply the islands of the Inner Hebrides. It extends for forty-two miles through some of the most dramatic scenery in Lochaber, crossing the famous viaduct at Glenfinnan, the first structure in the world to be built entirely of concrete.

The Mallaig Extension Line is a Mecca for thousands of steam-railway enthusiasts. LMS (London, Midland & Scottish) and LNER (London & North Eastern Railways) locomotives attract more than 20,000 passengers each year, the trains huffing and puffing their way up the steep gradients, past trout-dimpled lochs and grand peaks, by Loch Morar and the Silver Sands to the Sound of Sleat and Mallaig.

We began our huffing and puffing a mile or so from the 'Church in the Hills', near Arnipol. There is a large, safe, car parking area to the right of the road and with both dogs on the lead we crossed and walked west for a couple of hundred yards to pick up the well-marked track which leads onto the Ardnish Peninsula.

The ground was soggy after recent rain. In Lochaber it has either just stopped raining or is just about to start raining again. The area has the highest rainfall levels in the British Isles. But it was a glorious morning. Tiny crystal rain-drops shone from delicate silver birch; spider webs clung precariously from green ferns. Breac was in his element, black mud to the waist in seconds. August heather purpled dark, wet crags and the air was full of the scent of bog myrtle. Wonderful old oak trees bid us welcome, their young off-shoots scattering the open forest floor, regenerating their species.

A billy-goat-gruff bridge spans the railway – guarded by dire warnings about weight limits – which curves round the south shore of Loch Dubh. We spotted a fishing boat tucked safely amongst the trees as we made our way carefully over the wooden planks crossing the outlet stream of the loch, and continued onto the hill.

The track, although wet, is excellent, which makes this walk easily accessible to explorers of all ages, ideal for little legs and families. The sun shone brightly as we splashed up a tree- and heather-filled gully to the first crest. Loch nan Uamh lay below us, where Prince Charles Edward Stuart first set foot on mainland Scotland in August 1745, and from which point he finally escaped to France.

By the shore, at Mullochbuie, are the outlines of an old crofting village: tumbled grey stones surrounded by green patches of cultivated grass. A serious stream cascades down the hill, entering Loch nan Uamh close to the settlement.

Climbing steeply out of the gully, the track takes on an altogether more organized look. More major road than simple walkers' path, clearly the result of great effort, with neat steps cut into the side of the hill and paved with convenient rocks. St John's wort, milkwort and bog asphodel blush in the sphagnum moss as the track wends upwards over false top after false top.

At the highest point on the track, by Cruach an Fhearainn Duibh, we were rewarded by an amazing vista of the Small Isles – Rhum, Eigg and Muck – with a distant prospect of Sgurr Alasdair and the Cuillin on Skye. On our left lay Loch Doir a'Ghearrain, with its wild scattering of coves, promontories and headlands, divided into two large bays by jagged narrows.

We wandered on happily, the most convenient track leading us down into a gentle glen, past more remains of earlier settlements. Bright green, moss-covered boulders lined the path as we pushed our way through tangled birch and bracken. A solitary raven soared over the waterfall at the outlet of the loch, and ahead, across a wide, fertile plain, lay a golden beach, washed by emerald waves.

The ruins of Peanmeanach village are impressive, and one of the old cottages has been made into a comfortable bothy where walkers may spend the night, or which they can use as a base for further expeditions. West of Peanmeanach are the ruins of another village, Glasnacardoch, and it is possible that more than eighty people once lived and worked by this distant shore. Hence the well-cared-for track, back to 'civilization'.

We walked past the bothy, with its green door, red-painted windows and white, stone-lined path, and continued down to the beach, our footsteps cushioned by springy turf. Sitting, sheltered from the wind in a rocky corner, we lunched gratefully. Oystercatchers dashed about importantly, probing for food in the shallows.

Sun-warmed, we dozed, and, in dreaming, I heard the sound of children's laughter and saw men tending cattle by the shore – and, coming down the hill to the village, a party of sheriff's officers, with the factor, bearing notices of eviction.

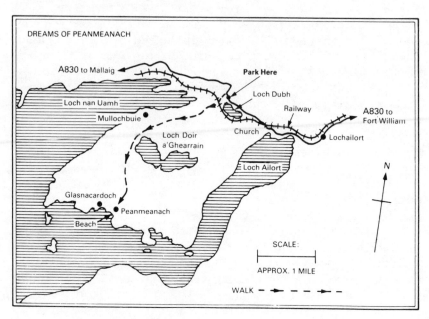

DREAMS OF PEANMEANACH

A830 to Mallaig

Park Here

Loch Dubh

Loch nan Uamh

Railway

A830 to Fort William

Mullochbuie

Church

Lochailort

Loch Doir a'Ghearrain

Loch Ailort

N

Glasnacardoch

Peanmeanach

Beach

SCALE:

APPROX. 1 MILE

WALK

WHAT YOU NEED TO KNOW

Time and effort Eight easy miles there and back, although the track can be very wet and soggy. This is an ideal walk for a family outing to the beach at Peanmeanach. The bothy is a good base if you wish to stay out for a few days, or as a place to shelter in adverse weather conditions. Those who fish for brown trout will be delighted with Loch Doir a'Ghearrain, which is full of fine, hard-fighting little fish, and the odd much larger specimen, to keep you alert at all times.

Location Ordnance Survey Sheet 40, Loch Shiel, second series, scale 1:50,000.

Grid references The 'Church in the Hills' 751828; car parking 743834; start of track 740835; Loch Dubh 744832; Mullochbuie 721830; Loch Doir a'Ghearrain 725817; Peanmeanach 712805; Glasnacardoch 707806.

Route Follow the A830 road from Fort William, past Glenfinnan and Lochailort. Just before Arnipol and where the road widens at Loch na Uamh, park on the right of the road in a wide, hard-surfaced area. Cross the road – take care of fast traffic – and you will find the start of the track, just before the private road down to Polnish House. Follow the track out to Peanmeanach. You can't go wrong.

63

Morar and Morag

THE WHITE Sands of Morar are one of the most photographed views in all Scotland, and one of the most popular stopping-off places for visitors to the area. Consequently, during the tourist season, Morar loses much of its charm. But it is easy to escape the crowds, and all you need in order to do so is Ordnance Survey Sheet 40, compass and map, stout walking boots and a willing heart. The hinterland of this wilderness wonderland is a hillwalker's joy – wild and desolate, where you may walk all day without meeting another soul.

Two long, narrow sea lochs enclose the Rough Bounds of Knoydart, beyond Morar, lying betwixt heaven and hell: Loch Hourn, 'the loch of hell', to the north, and Loch Nevis, 'the loch of heaven', to the south. A small ferry plies Loch Nevis, the only easy means of access to Knoydart. Another ferry calls at the remote hamlet of Tarbet on the Morar shore of Loch Nevis, and by diligent use of these ferries, marvellous walking and climbing opportunities in Morar and Knoydart await the adventurous traveller.

One of the best ways to appreciate all that region has to offer is to make a circular walk of North Morar, along the north shore of Loch Morar, the deepest freshwater loch in Europe, to Swordland, and north to Tarbet, returning via the south shore of Loch Nevis by Stoul and Lochan Stole. The depth of Loch Morar is recorded at just over 1,000 feet. However, recent soundings show that the loch is in fact closer to 1,100 feet in depth; and, like Loch Ness, its more famous neighbour to the south, Loch Morar is also reputed to be the home of a 'monster', affectionately named Morag.

I would be the last to deny the existence of some prehistoric creature inhabiting the grim confines of either water. Certainly, as far as Loch Ness is concerned, there is now too much circumstantial and factual evidence to write the probability off as fantasy. I am sure, therefore, that Loch Morar also holds deep, unfathomed secrets beneath the turbulent security of its shining surface. Prove me wrong.

What is beyond doubt is the fact that Simon Fraser, 12th Lord Lovat, one of Prince Charles Edward Stuart's most controversial supporters, was apprehended, hiding in a tree trunk, on one of the islands at the west end of the loch. Lovat, who had fought on the Hanoverian side during the 1715 uprising, capturing Inverness on behalf of the government, felt that he had not been sufficiently rewarded for his trouble, and joined Bonnie Prince Charlie during the '45. Lovat has the unenviable distinction of being the last person to be publicly beheaded in Britain, cheerfully mounting the scaffold on 9 April 1747, in his eightieth year.

In my fiftieth year, I parked the car by Bracorina and set off eastwards along the shores of Loch Morar, accompanied by my faithful (most of the time) hound, Breac. Loch Morar was formed some 60 million years ago, during the Tertiary period, when massive land movements and upheavals gave birth to many of our most dramatic mountains and the Hebridean islands. To the east, towards the head of the loch, rocky, moorland hummocks mount unrelentingly to the high tops: Sgurr na h-Aide, Carn Mor and the shapely pinnacle of An Stac.

Loch Morar is about twelve miles long and is estimated to contain some 81,000 million cubic feet of water, impounded behind a rock shelf just below the surface at the shallow, western end of the loch. The River Morar, exiting from the loch, is the shortest river in Scotland, being only 300 yards or so in length. Loch Morar is deeper than the neighbouring Atlantic, until that ocean plunges over the continental shelf, 130 miles west of the White Sands. Salmon and sea trout run the little river, to join the native wild brown trout for which Loch Morar is famous.

Past Brinacroy, the rough track wends tortuously along the crags overlooking the loch, eventually bringing me to the Victorian splendour of Swordland Lodge, close to where Loch Morar attains its greatest depth. I scanned the waters hopefully, in search of Morag. The margins of the loch shelve very steeply, but even so, in some of the bays that most charming of aquatic plants, water lobelia, grows profusely, its pink stems carrying slender, lilac flowers, and often close by, the green, non-flowering quillwort.

So much of Scotland is now owned by non-Scots and absentee landlords that it is very hard not to be somewhat resentful of the grand, private shooting lodges that scatter our glens; hard to forget that not so long ago these lands were busy with people who inhabited them by right of ancestry, and who were removed from them by laws designed for the benefit of their alleged superiors.

The crofting Acts, passed at the end of the nineteenth century, certainly helped redress the balance, giving tenants a degree of security of tenure; but they did nothing to assist the tens of thousands of people who had already been evicted. Today, one of the most cheering events taking place in the history of land ownership in Scotland is the plan of the Assynt crofters to purchase their lands, on the open market, rather than allow them to fall into the hands of yet another clutch of would-be Highland gentlemen.

I left Swordland and swung north, tramping through the dark, narrow pass between the sides of Cnoc a'Bhac Fhalaichte to the east and Eun-tuim to the west, down to the shore of Loch Nevis and the pier at Tarbet. Knoydart beckoned, bathed in bright sunlight, its mountains shining jewels against a blue-white, cloud-scattered sky: Meall Buidhe, Beinn Bhuidhe and Sgurr Coire Gobhar.

My way west from Tarbet followed the rough, south shore of gentle Loch Nevis: trackless, wild, stumbling country, by the ruin of Ardintigh, hugging the contours of the steep hills, down to the tiny wood by the shore at Torr nan Gamhainn and the scattered buildings at Stoul.

Wearily, I heaved myself south over Bealach nan Sac, Breac plodding dolefully at my heels, to the stepping stones across Lochan Stole. I carefully noted, for future reference and a further, fishing expedition, brown trout rising, feeding eagerly. Breac did likewise, whilst busy slaking his thirst by trying to drain the loch.

As I wandered down the moor to Bracorina, graceful Loch Morar glistened in early evening sunlight. In the west, Rhum, Eigg and Canna settled to sleep on their Atlantic pillow. Beyond the Sound of Sleat, the misty-blue Cuillin Hills were fringed with the fire of the setting sun. A proud, noble land, where 'the blood is strong'. A land to love and to cherish.

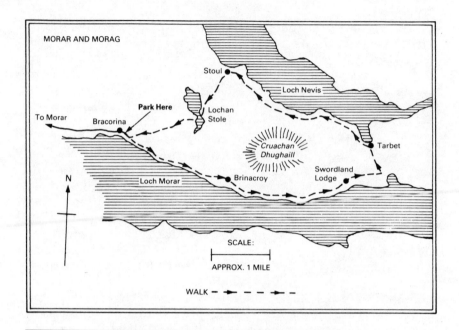

MORAR AND MORAG

Stoul

Loch Nevis

Park Here

To Morar
Bracorina

Lochan
Stole

Tarbet

*Cruachan
Dhughaill*

Swordland
Lodge

N

Loch Morar

Brinacroy

SCALE:

APPROX. 1 MILE

WALK ━ ➤ ━ ━ ➤ ━

WHAT YOU NEED TO KNOW

Time and effort This is an
arduous tramp of about ten miles,
over some pretty rough country,
particularly along the south
shoreline of Loch Nevis. Allow
about five hours for the round trip
and try to select a good day. Make
sure that you are well shod and
carry a compass and map. If the
weather deteriorates, you will need
them.

Location Ordnance Survey
Sheet 40, Loch Shiel, second series,
scale 1:50,000.

Grid references Morar 678930;
Bracorina 725928; Brinacroy
754914; Swordland Lodge 789914;
Tarbet 793924; Ardintigh 778931;
Stoul 757943; Lochan Stole 745935.

Route Follow the minor road
east from the village of Morar along
the north shore of the loch, past the
boat mooring bay. Bracorina marks
the end of the road. Park here and
walk east, along the rough but
well-marked track by the loch,
noting as you do so the track on
your left, by which you will later
return to the car.
   A few hundred yards past
Swordland Lodge, bear left/north
through the narrow glen that leads
to Tarbet. From Tarbet,
westwards, you are very much on
your own. Simply keep to the
higher ground above Loch Nevis
until you reach Stoul. Pick up the
track again at Stoul and follow it
steeply uphill over Bealach nan Sac
and on to Lochan Stole. Cross the
loch at the south end and walk back
to the car at Bracorina.

64

Ardnamurchan Volcanoes

SOUTH FROM Loch Shiel, the A861 touches Loch Sunart at Salen before swinging east towards the village of Strontian at the head of the loch. Strontian is famous as the place where, in 1791, Charles Hope discovered the element strontian, isolated in 1806 by Sir Humphrey Davis. The Strontian mines, closed since 1871, were opened again in 1983 to supply the North Sea oil industry with barytes.

Less well known is the story of the only floating church in Scotland, built in Glasgow and paid for with money raised in Sunart. After the Disruption of 1841 and the formation of the Free Church of Scotland, the local laird refused to allow the new church to be built on his land. Hence the floating church, which served the community faithfully for many years.

At Salen a minor road, the B8007, wends westwards along the north shore of the loch, past Glenborrodale Castle and St Columba's Well to Ardslignish. Ardslignish Point dominates the immediate view, and below the headland, where the clear waters of Allt Tor na Moine flow into Camas nan Geall Bay, is the slender column of Cladh Chiarain, dedicated by St Columba and marking the grave of St Ciaran, who died in AD 548. The stone is inscribed with a cross and a dog.

The west of Ardnamurchan is a hillwalker's delight. There are miles of empty moorlands, scattered with tiny blue, trout-filled lochs and lochans, surrounded by craggy peaks and dark cliffs. Much of the coastline, particularly in the north, may only be visited by means of man's oldest method of locomotion – his feet. The landscape is dominated by a series of modest hills, the highest of which is Ben Hiant, 'the holy mountain', 1,732 feet in height. Few roads intersect this wilderness and those that do are tortuous, narrow, and single-tracked.

The unique geological feature of Ardnamurchan is the great Tertiary Ring at the western end of the peninsula, formed 58 million years ago by a vast volcano, one of the many which gave birth to much of north-west Scotland and the Inner and Outer Hebrides. Massive explosions showered the surrounding area with molten rocks, the most notable example of which is known as Maclean's Nose, the jagged cliffs below Ben Hiant and Stallachan Dubh overlooking the Sound of Mull.

The best way to appreciate the character of these superb crags is from the sea. The circular core of the Ardnamurchan volcano covers an area of some six by nine miles, the centre being midway between Achnaha and Glendrian, to the north of the small village of Kilchoan, which is the principal, indeed the only, source of supplies and comforts in the west of Ardnamurchan.

A more ancient and more uncertain source of comfort was Mingary Castle, a cliff-top eyrie between Maclean's Nose and Rubha Aird an Iasgaich. After the Battle of Bannockburn in 1314, King Robert the Bruce consolidated his power and control over his barons by grants of land to those who had supported him during the war with England. The Coymns, implacable enemies, were banished and their lands given to Angus Og of Islay, including a charter to Morvern and Ardnamurchan.

Future Scottish kings also experienced difficulty in controlling their wild, western subjects, who often acted as though the Lordship of the Isles was a kingdom in its own right, quite separate from the rest of Scotland. The young King James IV settled the problem by taking the lands back into his personal ownership, much to the dismay of MacIan of Ardnamurchan. The King and his court arrived in force at Mingary Castle in May 1495 and there received the submission of the unruly isles where, it was claimed, 'the pepill ar almaist gane wilde'.

Portuairk is a small hamlet at the end of the B8007, and a good starting place for an easy, long walk northwards to Lochan an

Dobhrain and a traverse of the rim of the extinct volcano. Sanna Bay is a popular picnic spot because of its delightful little sandy beaches, and in summer the warm, shallow waters make it perfect for a family outing.

The old crofting community at Sanna suffered the same fate as so many of the other settlements in the area when, during the middle years of the nineteenth century, the people were evicted to make way for more profitable sheep. Alisdair Maclean graphically describes these sad events in his book *Night Falls on Ardnamurchan*. Allt Sanna Burn flows gently by the ruins of their lives, the broken remains of a once bustling, happy village.

More happily, because of the rugged, inhospitable nature of the landscape, the west of Ardnamurchan has been spared the attentions of commercial tree farmers; but, sadly, the waters of Loch Sunart have been severely affected by another man-made disaster – fish farming. This beautiful sea loch is disfigured by cages and ancillary buildings, producing, in my opinion, a suspect product.

Loch Sunart is a long, narrow, shallow loch, famous for its marine life: sponges, corals, common sea-fingers, red sea-fingers, cushion starfish, white trumpet anemone, sea-fan, football sea-squirt, and much more, warmed by the waters of the North Atlantic Drift. Waste from the fish farm cages sinks to the bottom of the loch and nobody seems to have investigated the effect this has upon other creatures.

It is time for the Crown Estate Commissioners – the body which issues licences to fish farmers operating in the sea – to insist, prior to giving them permission to proceed, that developers produce scientific evidence to demonstrate that their activities will not be environmentally damaging. Either that, or the responsibility for giving consent to fish farming schemes should be placed in the hands of regional planning authorities.

I attended to more personal planning matters after crossing the Allt Sanna Burn, walking east over the floor of the extinct volcano to the far ridge of Meall an Fhir-eoin. From the top, the edge of the volcano circled south and west, enclosing a broken landscape ringed by hard, dark hills. Once on the summit of Meall nan Con, 1,434 feet, I was rewarded with a magnificent view encompassing Ardnamurchan, Mull, Sunart, Moidart and Ardgour.

The beautiful islands of Tiree and Coll shimmered in a blue haze and, on the horizon, I glimpsed a distant prospect of the Outer Hebrides, the magical 'heather isles'. My day was filled with a deep awareness of my small presence in these silent places, where eagles soar and otters play; where the only enemy was my own restless spirit, and my greatest friend, the calm hills.

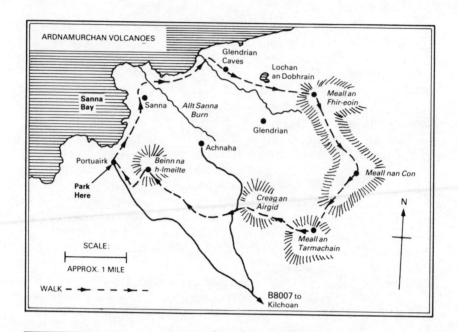

WHAT YOU NEED TO KNOW

Time and effort   This is an easy, ten-mile walk which takes about five hours. It can take much longer, particularly if you spend some time in the lovely little coves by Sanna Bay, or walk out to Glendrian Caves. The going is fairly rough, across broken ground, and, as always, it is very easy to get lost if the weather deteriorates. Don't forget your compass and map.

Location   Ordnance Survey Sheet 47, Tobermory, second series, scale 1:50,000.

Grid references   Portuairk 440680; Sanna 446696; Glendrian Caves 464708; Lochan an Dobhrain 479701; Meall an Fhir-eoin 490698; Meall nan Con 505681; Meall an Tarmachain 493664; Creag an Airgid 477669; Beinn na h-Imeilte 459671.

Route   Park at the end of the B8007 at Portuairk. Walk north from Portuairk, crossing a burn and over a slight ridge to the beach at Sanna Bay. Explore the coves and then head north-east to Sanna. From there, follow the coastline round the next large, rocky bay to Glendrian Caves. Now walk south, following the line of the Allt Mhic Cailein Burn, and bear left to scramble up Meall an Fhir-eoin, a long, jagged spur and the start of the circuit of the volcano edge.

There is a fair bit of up and down along the way, but simply circle the ridge south and then west, heading for Meall nan Con, Meall an Tarmachain and Creag an Airgid, eventually crossing a minor road before climbing again to the last ridge, Beinn na h-Imeilte. From there, descend to the B8007 and follow it back to the car park at Portuairk.

65

Black and White in Morvern

W<small>HEN THE</small> government vessel H<small>MS</small> *Harebell* arrived at Lochaline on the evening of Friday 29 August 1930, on board were
the people of St Kilda, evacuated from their distant island home on
'the edge of the world'. The Scottish Office had arranged for
twenty-seven of the islanders to be resettled at Larachbeg, Ardtornish, in Morvern.

As Ann and I wandered by Larachbeg, where the River Aline
flows to the sea, we paused and remembered the St Kildans. From
1925 until 1930 the islanders had cost the government £2,388.
Evacuation was the obvious solution. Twenty-five years later,
more than £500,000 was spent to establish a missile tracking station
on Hirta, the main island. If only the St Kildans had been able to
hold on until then.

The arrival of the St Kildans in Morvern reversed the trend of
depopulation that had been in progress since 1813, when more than
2,000 people lived on the peninsula. Until then, no Lowlander
owned a single Morvern acre; but between 1813 and 1838, every
property changed hands, due largely to the profligate life-style of
the 6th Duke of Argyll, the owner of Morvern, who reduced his
family's fortune by about £2 million. Clearances and evictions soon
followed.

In 1838 Patrick Sellar acquired 6,816 acres of land around Loch
Arienas and brought sheep down from his Sutherland estates.

Forty-four families, amounting to 230 people, were immediately evicted. Sellar, an agent of the Duke of Sutherland, was well practised in the art of eviction and few of the dispossessed protested.

John Macdonald was one such casualty of these ruthless clearances and he was appointed spokesman when, in 1883, the Napier Commission came north to hear evidence of these events. At a meeting in the Free Church hall the old man, when asked by the Commission what he wanted, replied: 'I would like to be the way I was before, if it were possible, that is. I should like to have a croft and my cows back again, as before.' Lord Napier heard this same, sad plea everywhere he travelled in the Highlands.

There is nothing at Larachbeg to mark the passing of the St Kildans, nor any other monument in Morvern in remembrance of the suffering the clearances brought to these gentle glens.

A mile beyond Larachbeg, at Claggan school, where the River Aline tumbles through a ragged gorge, we crossed the A884 and walked north to Acharn. Here the Black Water, flowing south down Gleann Dubh, the Black Glen, from Loch Clachaig, meets the White Water, which rises from the moorlands at the head of Gleann Geal, the White Glen. When either or both of these streams flood, such is the force of the flow that, rather than sweeping into the River Aline, they swing westwards into Loch Arienas.

At the bridge over the Black Water we turned north along the path by the stream, enfolded between the firm slopes of Braigh Uladail to the east and Meall Achadh a'Chuirn to the west, on the edge of the John Raven Wildlife Reserve. John Raven, the previous owner of the Ardtornish Estate, was an eminent botanist and an expert on the mountain flowers in the area. Would that more Highland lairds were like him.

The reserve covers an area of 4,200 acres, spreading west from Gleann Dubh, encompassing Beinn Iadain, Beinn na h-Uamha and the long arm of Loch Teacuis. There are four designated sites of special scientific interest, and the reserve was established by the Royal Society for Nature Conservation in 1975. Since then, through the support of the Ardtornish Estate, the area protected has been considerably extended and is particularly noted for species such as purple saxifrage, yellow rose-root, red campion, white campion, and alpine lady's mantle.

Red deer also abound and may often be viewed at the end of the little road that twists out past Loch Arienas and Loch Doire nam Mart to Kinlochteacuis – grand bucket-and-spade country for little ones. More than 136 different species of birds have been recorded in the reserve, and as we tramped up the Black Glen, a solitary golden eagle soared westwards and a white-rumped wheatear flitted ahead, bobbing from stone to stone by the stream.

A dam has been built across the pool below the falls in the Black Glen gorge, to encourage salmon upstream. It is surrounded by a magnificent oak wood, full of the song and chatter of finch, wren and warbler. The ancient trees are coated with lichens and mosses and are also home to a wide variety of insects, the most spectacular of which is the golden-ringed dragonfly.

Our most convenient track crossed the silver river beyond the gorge and gently led us round the slopes of Monadh Meadhoin to Crosben. From there, we contoured the hill to Loch Clachaig and paused for coffee in the morning sun – and for a few casts at the bright little brown trout dimpling the calm surface of the loch – the perfect place to introduce beginners to the gentle art of fly-fishing.

A brief struggle with the slopes of Beinn Chlaonleud gave us the grassy plateau of a gentle ridge and we strolled happily south to the third summit, a mile distant, and 1,526 feet above Gleann Geal and the White River. We lazed at the top, watching the world go by.

After lunch we began our descent to the road and a small bridge across the river at Alltachonaich, following the busy, winding stream down to the waterfall at Eas na Mucaireachd, then on to our last top, the rounded summit of Meall Damh, 1,122 feet. Loch Tearnait and Leacraithnaich bothy lay to the south, with the cluster of lochans by Meall nan Clach glinting in the distance.

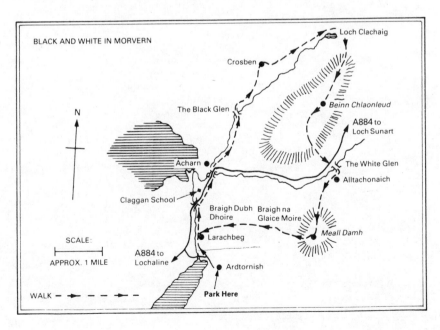

BLACK AND WHITE IN MORVERN

The wild peaks and ridges of Beinn Mheadhoin, at 2,425 feet the highest mountain in Morvern, reared west. A raven eyed us curiously, then flew off purposefully in the direction of craggy Meall a'Chaorunn – a dark, diminishing speck in the clear blue sky.

A long, moorland plodge past the pool on Braigh na Glaice Moire and the woods of Braigh Dubh Dhoire brought us back to Larachbeg and the River Aline. Evening caught us as we walked by the river, admiring the well-maintained banks and classic pools. We paused on the old bridge, peering into the white waters. A huge, silver shape lifted itself clear of the flow, plunging through the foam. We held our breaths, enchanted. All was well with *Salar*.

WHAT YOU NEED TO KNOW

Time and effort   Choose a good day for this delightful, fourteen-mile walk through the Black Glen and the White Glen in Morvern, and allow about eight hours for it. Even if the weather is variable, it is well worth doing.

In summer months you may also join a conducted party, hosted by one of the Scottish Wildlife Trust's wardens, to appreciate properly the delights of Glen Dubh and the John Raven Wildlife Reserve. Details of these conducted walks may be obtained at the Ardtornish Estate Office and you should remember that, otherwise, access to the reserve is strictly limited and is by application only. Given the very special quality of the flora and fauna of the reserve, this policy should be welcomed by all who love and appreciate the countryside. The walk described here is not covered by these restrictions but, as a matter of courtesy, you should still check with the Estate Office before setting out.

Location   Ordnance Survey Sheet 49, Oban & East Mull, second series, scale 1:50,000.

Grid references   Ardtornish 704475; Larachbeg 696485; Claggan school 700498; Acharn 703504; Crosben 720542; Loch Clachaig 744563; bridge at Alltachonaich 747508; Meall Damh 740485; Braigh na Glaice Moire 725486; Braigh Dubh Dhoire 715485.

Route   Park at the Ardtornish Estate Office and walk back towards the bridge over the River Aline. Turn right through the woods, up a good track by the river which leads past Larachbeg and Claggan school. Cross the main road here and walk on north to Acharn. Pick up the path on the east side of the Black Water and walk north up the glen, crossing the stream after a mile and a half, to Crosben.

The way from here on is trackless, but the going is relatively easy, provided that you maintain height along the slopes of the hill. At Loch Clachaig, walk round the north shore of the loch and then climb the long ridge of Beinn Chlaonleud. From the top you will see the bridge over the A884 at Alltachonaich, and your route to Meall Damh. From Meall Damh, walk west back to Larachbeg and Ardtornish.

66

Ardtornish Great and Mighty

*E*IRICH AGUS tiugainn, O! Which, being translated means: Get up and come along! Such was the Gaelic invitation to visit Morvern, issued by Dr Norman Macleod, the minister of St Columba Church in 1810. One hundred and eighty years later, Ann and I did and we found a gentle paradise of snow-covered mountains, curlew-calling hills, sparkling lochans, wild moorlands and tumbling rivers; an area alive with ancient woodlands, spring-busy with nest-building birds; where primroses nodded from sunny corners and best-bib-and-tuckered dippers darted in crystal-clear streams.

Morvern is one of Scotland's least visited areas and still retains a sense of peace and quiet all too often lacking in many of Caledonia's more famous, popular resorts, remote or otherwise; and although the hills and glens of this gentle land hardly match, in either grandeur or height, the splendour of other areas, Morvern is the ideal place to introduce newcomers, old and young alike, to the delights of hillwalking.

Even today, there is no easy way in to the magnificent wilderness that is Morvern. The best route is by the short ferry crossing over Loch Linnhe at Corran Narrows, eight miles south of Fort William. But even then, for most of the way you find yourself in the grip of a tortuous, single-track road, climbing through Glen Tarbert, down to the sea at the head of Loch Sunart; then, the A884 south, winding up the long hill from the shore between Beinn nam Beathrach and Taobh Dubh, into Gleann Geal, the White Glen of Morvern.

I became interested in the area after reading Philip Gaskell's excellent book, *Morvern Transformed*, a wonderfully detailed and well-researched social history; and because of the exploits of Patrick Sellar, still one of the most hated men in the north of Scotland and better known in my home county of Sutherland as the principal agent of the infamous Strathnaver clearances in the early years of the nineteenth century.

After the clearances, two men owned most of the land: Octavious Smith, who bought Achranich Estate in 1845, building what is now known as Ardtornish House; and Patrick Sellar, using the fortune he had amassed from his acquisition of the lands he had so brutally cleared, who bought Ardtornish and built himself a grand house near Ardtornish Castle, overlooking the Sound of Mull.

Smith, who was born in 1796, made his fortune out of a gin distillery at Pimlico Lane in London. Sellar's holdings, to the east and west of Achranich, were divided by Smith's property. With two such determined, strong-willed personalities, dispute was inevitable and it eventually centred upon salmon fishing rights in the River Aline, the 'short river', a delightful, classic, Highland spate stream, full of deep pools and urgent glides – and, frequently, even today, full of silver salmon, heading for upstream spawning grounds in the principal tributaries, the Black and the White Rivers.

Smith owned one bank, but discovered to his horror that Sellar owned the whole of the fishing rights. As relations deteriorated, he refused Sellar permission to fish. Smith immediately retaliated by denying Sellar right of way across Achranich, to tend to his business at Loch Arienas in the west. The matter was placed in the hands of their respective lawyers and the young families of the stubborn men were ordered to ignore each other, on pain of severe retribution.

Happily, before the matter came to court, the disagreement was settled. In 1850 they signed a binding document giving Sellar legal right of way across Achranich, in return for which Sellar sold half of his fishing rights on the River Aline to Smith, for the sum of £400. Victorian propriety and honour were satisfied.

Thereafter, the two families lived happily and Eleanor Sellar later recalled: 'I remember Gertrude, Mr Smith's youngest daughter, telling me how the new peace was inaugurated by her mother and herself, then a child of eight, lunching at Ardtornish. Mr Sellar set her beside himself and called her his little lady. The goings to and fro between the two places were as perpetual as they had been strictly forbidden the year before.'

In time, the families were united in marriage and the estates merged into what is the present Ardtornish Estate; and, as was the custom in Victorian Scotland, many great and famous people travelled north to enjoy Ardtornish hospitality. Alfred, Lord Tennyson, poet laureate, accompanied by Francis Turner Palgrave of *Golden Treasury* fame, visited William Sellar, Patrick's heir.

William was Professor of Humanities at Edinburgh University and the two poets stayed with him in 1853, whilst on their way to visit Loch Coruisk in Skye. Utterly captivated by Ardtornish, they never reached Skye, and Tennyson wrote:

> For though he missed a day in Sky,
> He spent a day in heaven.

John Buchan, statesman, soldier, author, poet and angler, met Gerard Craig Sellar, Patrick's grandson, in South Africa in 1902, and he and his wife stayed regularly at Ardtornish. Indeed, Buchan probably conceived the idea for his book *John Macnab* from the earlier dispute between Smith and Sellar, and used Ardtornish as the setting for his wonderful tale, dedicated to Rosalind Maitland, Craig Sellar's sister.

I am fascinated by the character of a man such as Patrick Sellar, obviously highly educated, a caring husband and father, and yet so utterly ruthless in his dealings with hundreds, even thousands, of defenceless, simple people, whose only crime was to be in the way of his self-interest. It is not for me to judge his actions. He has left his own legacy to history, and a black legacy it is.

Ann and I set off one morning to complete our journey through the times of Smith and Sellar, crossing the little River Rannoch by Ardtornish House and making our way southwards along the track by the shore of Loch Aline. It was a happy morning, sun-bright and gull-wheeling, with both dogs dashing about, busy with whatever dogs are busy with amidst thick fern and bracken.

The careful, caring hand of John Raven, the late owner of Ardtornish Estate, is evidenced everywhere in the woodlands bordering the track – oak, ash, birch, pine and larch – a natural wood of great charm and beauty. Unlike the monstrosity that has been created across the bay – the Fiunary Forest, a vast mass of commercial conifers, planted by the Forestry Commission. Below the forest are the Lochaline sand mines, vital to Britain's war effort during the Second World War, producing high-quality material used in the production of optical glass, and still busy today.

A thin ribbon of woodland edges the track as it leaves the shore and winds up the slow hill towards Ardtornish Point and a grey cluster of semi-derelict farm buildings with old flagged courts and moss-covered roofs. A low wall borders Sellar's grand mansion, surrounded by tangled undergrowth, bramble thickets and tumbled trees. Little remains of its former serenity, so much enjoyed by Tennyson, Palgrave and Buchan. As we poked and pried amongst the ruins, I noticed that few birds sang.

Under the high, wooded cliffs overlooking Ardtornish Bay, a neat cottage nestles by the shore at Inninbeg, with a small boat ready for expeditions buoy-bobbing a few yards from the shingle. Sheep and cattle had marked a muddy track to the headland and Ann and I walked out to the dramatic ruins of Ardtornish Castle, glowering towards Mull from its lofty perch above the waves. Had Tennyson stood amidst these grey stones, searching for inspiration?

A chill wind slid down the Sound of Mull, slipping through the empty castle, quietly engulfing us. Time for home. Calling the dogs to heel, we walked up the hill, past the tangled gardens, and back along the track to Ardtornish. The smell of wood-smoke greeted us, drifting lazily from the chimneys of warm cottages amidst the trees. Dinner – and the glass that cheers.

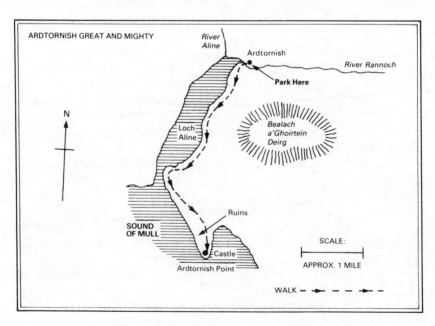

WHAT YOU NEED TO KNOW

Time and effort The walk is about seven miles, there and back, along an excellent, although at times muddy track. This makes it ideal for a morning or afternoon stroll. Avoid doing the walk in the evenings during summer and autumn, unless you are well prepared with midge repellent.

Most of the effort should be expended before setting out, by reading about the area, its history, and the history of the Highland clearances. In this way you will fully appreciate and enjoy all that the walk, and, indeed, Morvern, has to offer.

Location Ordnance Survey Sheet 49, Oban & East Mull, second series, scale 1:50,000.

Grid references Ardtornish House 703475; site of Patrick Sellar's house 693433; Ardtornish Castle 692426.

Route Cross the bridge over the River Rannoch and simply follow your nose. The track leads right out to Ardtornish Point and a cluster of farm buildings. A track to your right takes you down to the ruins of Ardtornish Castle. In wet or windy weather, take care along the way.

67

Tearnait and the Table of Lorn

Dogs can be difficult on holiday, even proper dogs like mine, my golden retriever Breac, the Gaelic word for trout. Yorkshire terriers are even nicer, like Heathcliff, Ann's pride and joy.

Which is why Ann and I were particularly impressed with the Ardtornish Estate in Morvern, where we stayed for a week at Easter a few years ago. There are excellent, virtually dog-proof fences in all the important places. Nevertheless, as we have found from bitter experience, Ann's little treasure is always safest on the lead, except in the remotest, sheepless tracts.

Ardtornish is a welcoming place where the emphasis is on providing everything for a relaxing holiday for every member of the family, including dogs. Bicycles, with baby seats on the back, are available for hire; there are good laundry facilities; and there is even a lending library for fireside evenings. John Hodgson rents out canoes, sailing dinghies, rowing boats and outboard motor-powered boats. And if you fancy catching your own supper, John will even provide the necessary tackle, prawn-creels and bait.

During our visit we stayed in Kinlochaline Cottage, a comfortable house near the black tower of Lochaline Castle. In spite of variable west-coast weather conditions, we managed to spend most of our time out-of-doors, exploring the wilds of Morvern, walking and fishing along the way, and including a visit to the famous Ardtornish Gardens – 28 acres of superb parkland, shrubs and trees.

The woodlands are magnificent: native birch, larch, firs and pines, dark green against the pink sandstone of Ardtornish House, bought by Owen and Emmeline Hugh Smith in 1930. Each year they received presents of named and un-named hybrid rhododendrons from Sir John Stirling Maxwell, of Pollock House, Glasgow. Consequently, the Ardtornish plants are famous throughout Scotland for their colour and variety.

Most of the ancient Morvern woodlands were destroyed in 1745, during the Jacobite Rebellion, when General Campbell ordered the 'wasting of Morvern' for supporting the Young Pretender, Prince Charles Edward Stuart. The work was carried out on 10 March by Captain Robert Duff, RN, with marines and sailors from the sloops *Terror* and *Princess Anne*. Forests were set alight from Drimnin in the west to Ardtornish, a distance of eleven miles.

To the east of the gardens an estate road leads past Achranich, by the banks of the River Rannoch, out onto the hill. It climbs steeply through old woodlands as the river charges down a long, spectacular series of falls and white-churned pools. At the top of the hill, trees give way to a wide, moorland strath, enclosed southwards by Glais Bheinn and the Table of Lorn, a dramatic long ridge guarding Coire Slabhaig.

The going is easy, along a well-defined track which cuts through the mountains of Morvern and Kingairloch, reaching the sea by the ruined castle of Glensanda on the shores of Loch Linnhe. A number of fine streams flood into the River Rannoch from the Table of Lorn – Allt na Socaich, Allt Strath Shuardall and Allt na Feinne – flowing over a fertile, grass-covered plain, scattered with derelict cottages.

Spring in Morvern is a contrary affair, one moment sunlight, the next moment storm. As we reached the confluence of Allt Dubh Doire Thearnait Burn with the River Rannoch, a storm whistled down from Meall a'Chaorunn, bringing with it huge flakes of driven snow. Seconds later we were white-fronted and gasping, anxious for shelter.

We found relief at a mountain bothy, conveniently sited overlooking Loch Tearnait. Stumbling in thankfully, we lit a fire.

Warmed by hot soup, sandwiches and coffee, we relaxed, closely guarded by two steaming, dripping dogs, alert for anything that might come their way. We had brought our fishing rods, in the hope of an early trout, and we eyed them wishfully, given the snowstorm raging outside.

The bothy was spotlessly clean and tidy, wind- and watertight, and had a logbook wherein previous users had recorded their exploits, both on the hills and in the loch. Reading the stories, I was reminded of a text I had once seen, many years ago: 'This hut is for the comfort and convenience of walkers, shooters, fishers – and other liars.' Time changes little.

Then, miraculously, the storm passed, the sun shone, and we noted a few dimples on the calm surface of Loch Tearnait. Quickly putting up our rods, we marched purposefully lochwards, the light of battle shining in our eyes. Now or never time. The dogs appeared from the bothy. Breac, well insulated by thick fur and seemingly impervious to cold, splashed in, immediately scaring every trout for miles. Heathcliff, still suffering from the effects of the storm, found a sunny spot and luxuriated on a flat rock.

After half an hour's fruitless effort we abandoned all hope of supper and decided to walk on, our objective being Meall a'Chaorunn and the traverse of the long ridge westwards, over An Sleaghach, Mam a'Chullaich to Glais Bheinn, including the summit of An Dunan – the Table of Lorn – a modest 1,572 feet in height.

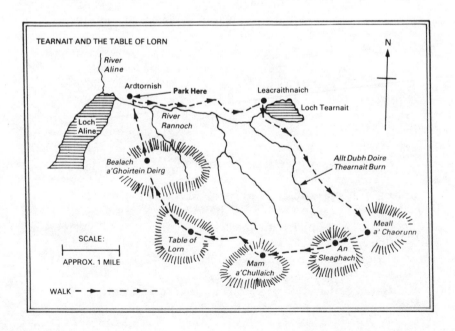

But height is of little relevance, at least to Ann and me; more important is the simple pleasure of being there, part and parcel of the joy that is Scotland.

We walked happily along the tops, dipping down into secret glens, climbing grassy slopes, to our evening table. The blue mountains of Mull beckoned from across the narrow waters of the sound: Sgurr Dearg, Beinn Talaidh, and the island's solitary Munro, Ben More, 3,169 feet. Carefully noted for another day.

Lengthening shadows, fingering the sides of Coire Slabhaig, hurried us down the smooth slope to Bealach a'Ghoirtein Deirg and the banks of the River Rannoch. Loch Aline shone like well-used pewter in the April evening as we nodded to the stately pines by the Tam o'Shanter bridge across the River Aline. 'What's for supper, Ann?' I mused. 'Not trout, dear, that's for certain,' replied my better half, unkindly.

WHAT YOU NEED TO KNOW

Time and effort This is a long, invigorating walk, covering a distance of some thirteen miles, giving absolutely splendid views over Lismore Island in Loch Linnhe towards Glencoe and Ben Cruachan to the east, and towards the hills of Mull in the west. There are no problems along the way and the going is easy.

You don't have to be an angler to enjoy this walk, but if you are, stop for a few casts in Loch Tearnait. Obtain permission first from the Ardtornish Estate Office. How long the walk takes depends entirely upon how long you wish to linger, either by the loch or in the hills. Ideally, make it a full day out. You will not be disappointed.

Location Ordnance Survey Sheet 49, Oban & East Mull, second series, scale 1:50,000.

Grid references Ardtornish House 703475; start of track 708474; Leacraithnaich bothy

742471; Loch Tearnait 750470; Meall a'Chaorunn 769445; Mam a'Chullaich 741432; the Table of Lorn 722438; Bealach a'Ghoirtein Deirg 710457.

Route If you are not staying at Ardtornish, call at the Estate Office prior to walking, to receive directions. The path passes the office, before crossing a bridge over the River Rannoch. Follow this well-made path all the way to Loch Tearnait and Leacraithnaich bothy. From the loch, cross the outlet burn and skirt Guala an Tur, keeping to the higher ground, with Allt Dubh Doire Thearnait on your right.

From the summit of Meall a'Chaorunn, the way westward to the Table of Lorn is obvious. Leave the Table by walking north-west along the ridge of Coire Slabhaig, down over Bealach a'Ghoirtein Deirg to Fountainhead and the River Rannoch. Walk back to the Estate Office and your car.

68

Gunpowder, Treason and Plodge

EVERYONE NEEDS pampering from time to time. I was re-minded of this recently by my nearest and dearest when we were caught on Ben More Assynt in Sutherland in a sudden snow-storm: 'Why do you do this to me?' she complained, bitterly. Grunting apologetically, I guided Ann down to the shelter of one of the famous Inchnadamph limestone caves, where we huddled together like Mesolithic hunter-gatherers, waiting for the storm to pass.

I decided there and then that it was pampering time, and when Charles Stott of the Melfort Club at Kilmelford near Oban suggested a visit, I agreed with alacrity. We would have a few days walking, fishing and being pampered. Melfort cottages are won-derfully comfortable, superbly fitted with every conceivable con-venience, and have the added advantage of being close to a sports complex complete with swimming pool, sauna, solarium, gym, billiard room, library and first-class restaurant.

The buildings housing these facilities were originally used for the manufacture of gunpowder, until the invention of dynamite ended that dangerous occupation. Charles Stott has renovated them to form a self-catering village of considerable charm and character.

The restaurant is called The Shower of Herring, named after the following occurrence: 'On a small eminence above Melfort House, a shower of herring fell in 1821, in every respect so large and good that the tenants by whom they were found were reduced to send some to their landlord, then residing in Edinburgh.' (From the *Edinburgh New Philosophical Journal*, October 1826.)

Mesolithic man also left reminders of his passing at Melfort, near a cave on An Sithean, 'the hill of the fairies'. Before Hydro Board blasting operations covered the site in 1956, hundreds of flint and quartz artefacts were discovered, including scraps of teeth and charcoal fragments dating back more than seven thousand years.

Melfort is Clan Campbell country, the ownership of which was hotly disputed by neighbouring Clan Macdonald. In one incident Alexander Macdonald descended on Melfort intent upon wreaking havoc while the laird, John Campbell, was absent. The laird's wife, with great perspicacity, in order to minimize damage to her husband's property, laid out a magnificent banquet for the invaders and then retreated with her family to hide in the woods nearby.

Delighted with this reception, Macdonald gave orders that Melfort should be spared; but as he stopped to rest on the pass north of Kilninver and looked back, he was horrified to see the Campbell home going up in flames. Three Irishmen were found guilty of starting the blaze and they were hanged on the spot – known to this day as Tom a'Chrochaidh, 'the mound of the hanging'.

Campbell lairds owned the Melfort lands in unbroken line of succession from the fourteenth century until the middle of the nineteenth century – by which time the family had supplied the Crown with two admirals, one naval captain, one commander RN, four generals, four colonels, two majors, six army captains, and six lieutenants. A war-like bunch.

In keeping with family tradition, in 1838 Colonel John Campbell, the last laird, sold the property to Messrs Harrison & Ainsley, an English gunpowder manufacturing company – thereby inadvertently being responsible for causing the 'big bang' on 9 March 1867 when a massive explosion destroyed the whole place.

I first travelled that way more than forty years ago on a family holiday, when we spent a night on the lovely Island of Eriska, overlooking the Lynn of Lorn. Whilst mother, father, and my younger brother, Fergus, stayed in style in the Eriska House Hotel, my brother Ian and I were given permission to camp out on the west shore of the island.

That was my introduction to the Highlands of Scotland, and when we awoke Ian and I washed ourselves in the sea, surrounded by seals and the cry of gulls. Across Loch Linnhe, the mountains of Kingairloch shimmered in morning mist, a magic wall of myriad colours, and I realized that I had found something very special.

Later that day we continued south, our destination being the slate island of Easdale, where father wanted to look at a cottage. I was far more interested in looking at the hills and mountains – and the narrow stream which exits from Loch Seil to join the sea just south from Clachan Bridge, the famous 'bridge over the Atlantic'. It was raining, as it frequently does in these 'airts', and I noticed a man in an old army-style officer's mackintosh, straddling the stream, fishing. To me, then, he seemed to be wasting his time, but, in later years, I discovered that the stream was a notable sea-trout fishery.

Fearnach Bay, close to Melfort House, was crowded with sailing boats when Ann and I arrived. The Melfort Club also offers guests a wide range of water sports, including boat hire, windsurfing, canoes, water ski-ing and scuba diving. These activities are directed from the old pier which used to service gunpowder-packed vessels as they edged their way carefully out of the rock-strewn confines of Loch Melfort. Dangerous, nail-biting work.

A perfect little track twists west from Melfort, hugging the shoreline, then winds uphill through delightfully wooded crags, past the small hamlet of Kilchoan to the end of the road at Degnish. Just before Degnish, on the right, a track leads north into the lands of Kilbrandon and Kilchattan, heading steeply up the southern slopes of Dun Crutagain. Ignoring the track, Ann and I, and the inevitable dogs, tramped straight up the shoulder of the hill to the modest summit 896 feet above sea level.

From the top a magnificent panorama of scattered islands greeted us: Seil, Easdale, Torsa, Luing, Shuna, Lunga, Scarba, and the Garvellachs. There are the remains of a fort on Dun Chonnuill, the most northerly Garvellach isle, and the ruins of a monastery on Eileach an Naoimh to the south. Until recently, a cottage could be hired on Garbh Eileach, the largest of the Garvellachs, making it one of the most remote holiday locations in the world.

Swinging north-east, we angled down Dun Crutagain towards the track, joining it where an old drystane wall divides moorland from cultivated pastures to the north. We crossed the top of Bealach Gaoithe, 'the pass of the wind', and walked down to the gnarled hawthorn tree, known as the Lucky Tree, by the side of the track. The lower trunk of the tree is covered with coins, hammered into the bark: the custom is reputed to bring good luck. I produced a coin, to leave our mark – after all, who needs bad luck?

Then, blessed with the prospect of good luck, we returned to the top of the pass and struck off eastwards over the hill towards the Kilchoan Lochs, in search of supper. There are two lovely little lochans, nestling between high crags, and we spent a happy hour exploring their delights, Breac more intimately than us, swimming and paddling around, scaring every fish for miles.

As the sun sank beyond the misty islands, we walked back to the track and down the hill to the car. In the distance, over Luing, the crags of Scarba sparkled, and beyond, the Garvellachs settled to sleep under the dark-blue blanket of night.

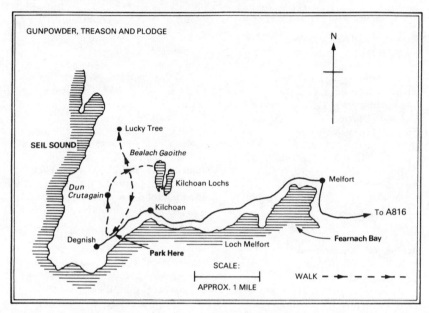

GUNPOWDER, TREASON AND PLODGE

N

• Lucky Tree

SEIL SOUND

Bealach Gaoithe

Kilchoan Lochs

Dun Crutagain

• Melfort

Kilchoan

To A816

Degnish

Loch Melfort

Fearnach Bay

Park Here

SCALE:

WALK ‑ ‑►‑ ‑ ‑►‑ ‑

APPROX. 1 MILE

WHAT YOU NEED TO KNOW

Time and effort This is an easy walk of about eight miles, there and back from Degnish. You may extend the walk by beginning at Melfort and walking along the coastal road to the start of the track. This adds six miles to the total distance. On the hill, no problems or difficulties, but, as always, be cautious should the weather deteriorate.

Location Ordnance Survey Sheet 55, Lochgilphead, second series, scale 1:50,000.

Grid references Melfort 834142; Kilchoan 795135; Degnish 782126; start of the track 786126; Dun Crutagain 785137; Bealach Gaoithe 789151; Lucky Tree 788152; Kilchoan Lochs 798143.

Route Leave Melfort and turn right along the narrow road towards Kilchoan and Degnish. Just before Degnish, on your right, you will find the track up the hill. Ignore the track and climb through the thin strip of woodland, to the top of Dun Crutagain.

From the top, angle north-east to pick up the track again and follow it northwards to Bealach Gaoithe and the Lucky Tree. The Kilchoan Lochs are to the east of the track and are easily found by walking due east from GD 790148.

Return from the Kilchoan Lochs to the track or, as an alternative, follow the outlet stream of the east loch back down to the road at Kilchoan Bay. At the road, turn right and walk back to the car.

Select Bibliography

Bennet, Donald, *The Munros* (Edinburgh, Scottish Mountaineering Trust).

Bennet, Donald, *The Southern Highlands* (Edinburgh, Scottish Mountaineering Trust).

Bingham, Caroline, *Land of the Scots* (London, Fontana).

Burnett, Ray, *Benbecula* (Benbecula, Outer Hebrides, Mingulay Press).

Butterfield, Irvine, *The High Mountains of Britain and Ireland* (London, Diadem Books).

Culzean (Edinburgh, National Trust for Scotland).

Dunkeld and Birnam (Perth, Dunkeld and Birnam Tourist Association).

Feacham, Richard, *Guide to Prehistoric Scotland* (London, Batsford).

Gordon, Seaton, *Highways and Byways in the West Highlands* (London, Macmillan).

Grimble, Ian, *The Trial of Patrick Sellar* (London, Routledge & Kegan Paul).

Lamont-Brown, Raymond, *Walks for Motorists* (London, Warne).

Lindsay, Maurice, *The Lowlands of Scotland* (London, Robert Hale).

MacKenzie, Agnes Mure, *Scottish Pageant* (Edinburgh, Oliver & Boyd).

MacKenzie, Alexander, *History of the Highland Clearances* (Inverness, Melven Press).

Melrose Abbey (Edinburgh, HMSO).

Moir, D. G., *Scottish Hill Tracks* (Edinburgh, John Bartholomew).

Murray, W. H., *The Companion Guide to the West Highlands of Scotland* (London, Collins).

Nethersole-Thompson, D., *Highland Birds* (Inverness, Highlands and Islands Development Board).

Omand, Donald, *The Caithness Book* (Inverness, Highland Printers).

Pennycook, Andrew, *Literary and Artistic Landmarks of Edinburgh* (Edinburgh, Albyn Press).

Poucher, W. A., *The Scottish Peaks* (London, Constable).

Prebble, John, *Highland Clearances* (Harmondsworth, Mx, Penguin).

Randall, Eric, *The Merry Muses* (London, Luxor Press).

Rintoul, and Skinner, *Poets Quair* (Edinburgh, Oliver & Boyd).

Rosebery, Countess of, *Dalmeny House* (Queensferry).

Simpson, Douglas, *Hermitage Castle* (Edinburgh, HMSO).

Smith, Sydney, *South West of Scotland Rambles* (Glasgow, Richard Drew).

Steven, Campbell, *Glens and Straths of Scotland* (London, Robert Hale).

Stevenson, Robert Louis, *Songs of Travel*.

Thompson, Francis, *Portrait of the Spey* (London, Robert Hale).

Thorne, and Collocott, (eds), *Chambers Biographical Dictionary* (Edinburgh, Chambers).

Tranter, Nigel, *Portrait of the Lothians* (London, Robert Hale).

Walkers' Britain (London, Pan/Ordnance Survey).

Walk Perthshire (Edinburgh, Bartholomew).

Wilson, Ken, and Gilbert, Richard, *The Big Walks* (London, Diadem Books).

TOURISM AND VIOLENCE

New Directions in Tourism Analysis

Series Editor: Dimitri Ioannides, E-TOUR, Mid Sweden University, Sweden

Although tourism is becoming increasingly popular as both a taught subject and an area for empirical investigation, the theoretical underpinnings of many approaches have tended to be eclectic and somewhat underdeveloped. However, recent developments indicate that the field of tourism studies is beginning to develop in a more theoretically informed manner, but this has not yet been matched by current publications.

The aim of this series is to fill this gap with high quality monographs or edited collections that seek to develop tourism analysis at both theoretical and substantive levels using approaches which are broadly derived from allied social science disciplines such as Sociology, Social Anthropology, Human and Social Geography, and Cultural Studies. As tourism studies covers a wide range of activities and sub fields, certain areas such as Hospitality Management and Business, which are already well provided for, would be excluded. The series will therefore fill a gap in the current overall pattern of publication.

Suggested themes to be covered by the series, either singly or in combination, include – consumption; cultural change; development; gender; globalisation; political economy; social theory; sustainability.

Also in the series

Tourism and Violence

Edited by

HAZEL ANDREWS
Liverpool John Moores University, UK

ASHGATE

Published by
Ashgate Publishing Limited
Wey Court East
Union Road
Farnham
Surrey, GU9 7PT
England

Ashgate Publishing Company
110 Cherry Street
Suite 3-1
Burlington, VT 05401-3818
USA

www.ashgate.com

British Library Cataloguing in Publication Data
A catalogue record for this book is available from the British Library

The Library of Congress has cataloged the printed edition as follows:
Andrews, Hazel.
  Tourism and violence / by Hazel Andrews.
    pages cm. -- (New directions in tourism analysis)
  Includes bibliographical references and index.
  ISBN 978-1-4094-3640-9 (hardback) -- ISBN 978-1-4094-3641-6 (ebook) --
ISBN 978-1-4724-0253-0 (epub) 1. Tourism. 2. Tourism--Social aspects. 3. Emotions.
I. Title.

  G155.A1A5644 2014
  338.4'791--dc23

                                                                    2014016684

ISBN 9781409436409 (hbk)
ISBN 9781409436416 (ebk – PDF)
ISBN 9781472402530 (ebk – ePUB)

Printed in the United Kingdom by Henry Ling Limited, at the Dorset Press, Dorchester, DT1 1HD

Contents

List of Figures

List of Tables

Notes on Contributors

Hazel Andrews is a social anthropologist and Reader in Tourism, Culture and Society at Liverpool John Moores University. With a particular focus on practices of embodiment, consumption, habitus and place, Hazel's research and publications have examined social and symbolic constructions of national, regional and gendered identities in the context of British tourists to Mallorca. Her current research involves the application of theories of existential anthropology to understandings of tourists' experiences and an examination of discourses of nationalism in tourism imagery. Hazel is the author of numerous texts on her work in Mallorca including *The British on Holiday. Charter Tourism, Identity and Consumption* (2011) and *Liminal Landscapes: Travel, Experience and Spaces In-between* (2012). She is also a co-founder and an editor of the *Journal of Tourism Consumption and Practice.*

Wolfgang Aschauer completed his academic training in sociology, psychology and communication science at the University of Salzburg in 2007 with a dissertation entitled 'Tourismus im Schatten des Terrors. Eine vergleichende Analyse der Auswirkungen von Terroranschlägen (Bali, Sinai, Spanien)'. It was published as a monograph in 2008 (Profil Munich-Vienna). Since 2007 he has been a Postdoc at the Department of Sociology and Cultural Science at the University of Salzburg. In 2009 he received the award for innovative teaching for an applied research practical course on migration and integration (together with Dr Manfred Oberlechner). His main research areas are migration and racism, cross cultural research, tourism sociology and tourism psychology, empirical methods and statistics. Currently he is working on a third-party project in cooperation with the PMU Salzburg (together with AO. University Professor Dr Martin Weichbold). He recently applied for a FWF-Stand Alone Project on Ethnic Prejudice and Islamophobia in Western European States (habilitation project).

David Botterill is a freelance academic and higher education consultant and Senior Research Fellow in the Oxford School of Hospitality Management at Oxford Brookes University, Visiting Research Fellow at the Centre for Tourism at the University of Westminster, Professor Emeritus in the Welsh Centre for Tourism Research, Cardiff Metropolitan University and Fellow of the Association for Tourism in Higher Education. He holds a Visiting Professorship at the Breda University of Applied Sciences, the Netherlands, and in 2011 was a visiting scholar at James Cook University, Australia. In 2012 he was a FAPESP sponsored Visiting Scientist at the State University of Campinas (UNICAMP), Brazil. Recent books include: *Tourism and Crime: Key Issues* (2010) with Trevor Jones, *Key Concepts in Tourism Research* (2012) with Vincent Platenkamp and *Medical Tourism and Transnational Healthcare* (2013) with Guido Pennings and Tomas Mainil.

Alan Clough is recognised in Australia for his significant contribution to research and practice in the challenging field of substance use problems in Indigenous communities. He brings to his work the unique perspective of having lived and worked in and for remote communities in the Northern Territory's 'Top End' for 20 years. Over the past two years he has developed similar relationships with Aboriginal and Torres Strait Island communities in far north Queensland. In the past five years, he has published 24 publications in refereed journals and two are currently under review. From 2005–2008 he held a NHMRC Postdoctoral Fellowship. He is developing a collaborating centre for prevention studies to address substance abuse and other public health problems in northern Australia and the Asia-Pacific.

Charmaine Hayes-Jonkers is Program Support Officer and Evaluator at Cairns Safer Street Task Force, James Cook University. Ms Hayes-Jonkers has predominantly worked in the alcohol-related assault field, but is also involved in research and training with private security officers in licensed premises and CCTV camera operators and street-based security. Her research interests include: youth violence and crime; fear of crime studies; community peoples' transitions from prison and hospitals back to country; crime and antisocial behaviour, culturally appropriate housing and effective service provision.

Anne Hertzog is a geographer. After the Aggregation of geography (1997), she studied at ENS Ulm and EHESS in Paris (1997/1998). She began to develop her research about geography of heritage, museums and tourism during her PhD doctorate (thesis supported in 2004 – University Denis Diderot, Paris). She teaches at Cergy Pontoise University France as a 'Maitre de conférences' (university lecturer) where she pursues her research about geographical approaches of heritage, museums and tourism. The question of war heritage is one of her main current subject of research.

João Luiz de Moraes Hoeffel completed a PhD in Social Sciences at Campinas State University (IFCH/UNICAMP), São Paulo, Brazil, with a focus on environmental issues and undertook Post-Doctoral research at the Center for Environmental Education and Public Policies at São Paulo University (ESALQ/USP). He teaches at Atibaia College (FAAT), Atibaia, São Paulo, where he also coordinates the Center for Sustainability Studies (NES/FAAT) developing research projects on Natural Resources Conservation, Environmental Education and Environmental Planning, and at University São Francisco, Bragança Paulista, São Paulo, Brazil. He contributes to the NEPAM/UNICAMP research programme on Global Environmental Changes and Quality of Life as a Collaborating Researcher.

Born in Palestine, **Rami Isaac** did his undergraduate studies in the Netherlands, graduate studies in the UK and has earned his PhD from the University of Groningen, the Netherlands, in Spatial Sciences. He is currently a senior lecturer in tourism teaching at the undergraduate as well as postgraduate levels at the Academy for Tourism at the NHTV Breda University of Applied Sciences in the Netherlands. He was the external assessor of Bethlehem TEMPUS (2004–2006) curriculum development project in Palestine in the field of pilgrimage, tourism and cultural industries. His research interests are in the areas of tourism development and management, critical theory, and political aspects of tourism. He has published numerous articles and book chapters on tourism and political (in)stability, occupation, tourism and war, violence and transformational tourism.

Trevor Jones is Professor of Criminology at the School of Social Sciences in Cardiff University where he has worked since 1998. Prior to this he lectured in the Law School at the University of Edinburgh, and worked as a Senior Research Fellow at the Policy Studies Institute (PSI) in London. He has researched and published extensively in a range of fields including policing and crime prevention, private security, comparative criminal justice policy-making, and workplace bullying and harassment. He is author/co-author of six research monographs, co-editor of two major edited collections, and author of a large number of journal papers, research reports and book chapters. His research interest in the relationship between crime and tourism resulted in the co-edited volume (with David Botterill) *Tourism and Crime: Key Themes* (Goodfellow Publishing 2010), in which he authored a chapter on the policing of tourist spaces.

Kristin Lozanski (PhD University Alberta, 2008) is an Associate Professor of Sociology at King's University College at the Western University, Canada and an affiliate of the Graduate Program in Migration and Ethnic Relations at the Western University. Her research interests bring together globalisation, neo-liberalism, mobilities, gender and racialisation through theoretical and empirical analyses of travel and tourism. She has published several articles in the area of critical tourism studies, which have appeared in *Annals of Tourism Research*, *Tourist Studies*, *Social Identities*, and *Critical Sociology*. More recently, her work has led her into the realm of medical tourism, with a specific focus on transnational surrogacy.

Catherine Palmer is a social anthropologist at the University of Brighton, UK, where she is a principal lecturer in tourism anthropology. Her research interests encompass identity and belonging; embodiment; the heritage; culture of the coast/seaside; materiality, space and place. She is a member of an interdisciplinary research cluster *Understanding Conflict: Forms and Legacies of Violence* where she focuses on the role of tourism in the cultural construction and experience of post-conflict memorial landscapes. She is published in journals such as *Annals of Tourism Research*, *Tourist Studies* and the *Journal of Material Culture* and has edited books on research methods (CABI) and visual culture (CABI).

Louise C. Platt completed her PhD at Liverpool John Moores University in 2010 and teaches on the BA (Hons.) Tourism and Leisure Management and BA (Hons.) Events Management programmes at LJMU. Her PhD is an ethnographic study of the performance of local identities in relation to the European Capital of Culture in Liverpool 2008. The theoretical underpinnings derive from social anthropology and performance studies. It considered the balance between creative improvisation and the constraints of social and cultural norms in forming identities. The study asked how far the celebrations were a chance to redefine local identities and whether there were opportunities for experimentations with those identities in order to present a new version of Liverpool. The work provides a nuanced approach to understanding a large-scale cultural event by focusing on lived-identities. Her research interests include: identity performance, mundane leisure and urban 'happenings'. Prior to commencing her PhD, Louise completed an MA in Arts and Museum Management at Salford University and then worked in the performing arts sector in Greater Manchester.

Shane Pointing is a Senior Research Officer with The Cairns Institute at James Cook University. He is a Realist researcher into a range of complex social problems, including the role of CCTV in reducing alcohol-related assault in the night time economy, co-ordinated quantitative data linkage across health, crime and service delivery agencies, and different aspects of homelessness. He has extensive experience in designing, implementing and evaluating partnered community projects. Prior to his research career he was a policy advisor to Queensland Government ministers, and a civilian in the police service. He continues to make outcome-based connections across networks, and discovering and facilitating the flow of evidenced-based knowledge and locally contextualised information.

Michelle Renk is a PhD student in the Center for Environmental Research (NEPAM / UNICAMP) on a FAPESP fellowship. Michelle is currently working on the NEPAM research teams investigating the 'Quality of life and energy in coastal locations: socioeconomic and environmental implications of the oil and natural gas' and 'Global environmental changes, vulnerability, risk and subjectivity: a study on the North Coast of São Paulo State'.

Les Roberts is a Lecturer in Digital Cultures in the Department of Communication and Media at the University of Liverpool. His research interests are in the cultural production of space, place and mobility, with a particular focus on film and popular music cultures. He is author of *Film, Mobility and Urban Space: a Cinematic Geography of Liverpool* (2012), editor of *Mapping Cultures: Place, Practice and Performance* (2012) and co-editor of *Locating the Moving Image: New Approaches to Film and Place* (2014), *Liminal Landscapes: Travel, Experience and Spaces In-between* (2012), and *The City and the Moving Image: Urban Projections* (2010). For information on recent research activities and publications see www.liminoids.com.

Cristina Rodriguez holds a Master degree in Human Geography from the University of Campinas, Brazil and was awarded a PhD in Tourism from James Cook University, Australia. She has several years' experience as a lecturer in tourism in two private universities in Brazil and has worked as a casual lecturer for the School of Business, James Cook University in Australia, where she taught classes on destination management. She has published on the topics of backpacker tourism, community based tourism and nature based tourism in the Brazilian Amazon region.

Nancy Scheper-Hughes is Professor of Anthropology and Director of the programme in Medical Anthropology at the University of California Berkeley. Her research, writings and teaching focus on violence, suffering, and premature death as these are experienced on the margins and peripheries of the late modern world. For the last decade she has been involved in a multi-sited, ethnographic, and medical human rights oriented study of the global traffic in humans (living and dead) for their organs to serve the needs and desires of international transplant patients. Nancy continues to conduct research on transitional violence, justice and reconciliation in the slums, shantytowns, and squatter camps of Brazil and South Africa.

Sônia Regina da Cal Seixas has a PhD in Social Sciences from Campinas State University (IFCH/UNICAMP), São Paulo, Brazil, with a focus on Global Environmental Changes, Quality of Life and Subjectivity. Sônia is a leading member of the Center for Environmental Studies, NEPAM, Campinas State University, UNICAMP, full Professor at the PhD Environment & Society Program (NEPAM-IFCH-UNICAMP), and Professor at the Energy Systems Planning Program (FEM-UNICAM). Sônia is also a Fellow-2 of the CNPq – Brazil's National Council for Scientific and Technological Development – and Group Leader of the Quality of life, environment and subjectivity programme.

Tom Selwyn is Professor of the Anthropology of Tourism in the Anthropology Department of the School of Oriental and African Studies University of London. Professor Selwyn gained his training in anthropology from LSE and has many years teaching experience both in Anthropology and the Anthropology of Tourism at the LSE, the University of Tel-Aviv, London Metropolitan University and the University of Surrey Roehampton where he was responsible for establishing the first MA in the Anthropology of Tourism. Tom is also a co-founder of *Tourism Concern*. He has published widely in the fields of tourism, landscapes, and issues relating to Israel-Palestine. Tom has attended numerous international conferences and headed several EU funded programmes.

Paula V. Carnevale Vianna is a physician and teaches and researches Public Health in the Regional and Urban Planning programme at the University of Vale do Paraiba (Univap), Brazil. She has published in the area of urban health and public policy. Her major area of interest is the history of health policies and their relationships with the urbanisation process.

Chapter 1

Introduction

Hazel Andrews

In a BBC Radio 4 programme entitled 'Itchy Feet' (1997) the broadcaster and travel writer Rory MacLean was considering the place of postcards in our travels. Drawing on a range of voices MacLean invited listeners to hear spoken the words that people write on their postcards. Most of these were drawn from the post Second World War tourism boom and contained the sort of information we might expect to find on a communication about a holiday – the weather, the accommodation, activities etc. – on the back of a picturesque image of the vacation location. However, towards the end of the programme a very different kind of image is presented with the following details of a postcard sent to Le Havre, France in 1906 read out:

> 'Canton – Torturing Prisoners' – several Chinese males at full stretch with legs dangling just above the ground. This was a slow method of strangulation. The message is very simple, it says 'A thousand best wishes'.

This is both a disturbing image and message that has haunted and puzzled me since I first heard it. Some years later I read Leon F. Litwack's (2004) *From 'Hellhounds'* which describes and explores the brutality of racist murders in the southern United States between 1882 and 1968. During this period approximately 4,742 black people died at the hands of lynch mobs. The victims were frequently put to a long, slow agonising death – by hanging or burning – on the basis of false allegations of crime and often by lynch mobs. The abuse did not end with death as this was often followed by 'the dismemberment and distribution of severed bodily parts as favors and souvenirs to participants and the crowd' (2004: 125). As if the use of the word 'souvenirs' is not enough to set in motion the idea of a touristic edge to the appalling events Litwack discusses he further notes that these atrocities were often associated with a 'carnival-like atmosphere' (2004: 124) in which on-lookers frequently recorded the activities by way of photography. In addition these photos found their way to becoming postcards and trade cards used to 'commemorate the event' (ibid.). This circulation and mobility of human suffering was also not restricted to the image but, as Litwack (2004: 125) notes, people travelled to witness the executions, responding to their prior advertisement in newspapers and taking advantage of the

> special 'excursion' trains [which] transported spectators to the scene, [and] employers sometimes released their workers to attend, parents sent notes to

school asking teachers to excuse their children for the event, and entire families attended, the children hoisted on their parents' shoulders to miss none of the action and accompanying festivities.

The horror of these two examples – from Canton and the United States – demonstrate how closely tourism and violence are intertwined and for how long the activity so often associated with pleasure and leisure has been enmeshed with the violently macabre.

Of course we can go much further back in history to find examples of the connection between travel and violence. For instance the Colosseum in Rome was a focal point to which people journeyed to witness the violent and bloody conflicts of gladiatorial combats; but yet the coupling of violence and tourism is rarely starkly stated. By which I mean the violent underpinnings and violence of tourism are infrequently expressed with the use of the words *violent* or *violence*. There are of course exceptions, for example the works of Kristin Lozanski (2007); Darlene McNaughton (2006) and Erika Robb (2009). All three prove instructive in understanding how violence and tourism are interwoven. For example, by examining the relations between independent western female travellers and local Indian men as they emerge in the sexual harassment of the former by the latter and the often violent retaliation – both physical and verbal – Lozanski argues that this particular type of touristic encounter allows for the deconstruction of the gendered and racialised interaction which demonstrates 'the racist, misogynist and colonial discourses within which independent travel is embedded' (2007: 296). McNaughton's work considers a different type of interaction hewn under the development of tourism. Writing again in the context of India she points to the violence that many of the migrant workers responsible for the facilitation of tourism services in the area are subject to from the local indigenous and wealthier population who consider the seasonal workers as outsiders: 'they are often heavily marginalized ... while they act as hosts to international tourists, many local residents see them not as guests or as hosts but as uninvited interlopers' (2006: 659). Robb's work in Brazil considers 'dark tourism', its basis in historical violence and how it is manifest also in 'violence that is current and live' (2009: 57). She notes (ibid.)

> Even as I write this, a group of tourists are riding motorcycles up through the narrow alleys and paths beneath my window, thrilled at the sight of Uzi submachine guns cradled in the arms of the teenage drug traffickers. Although organized tour companies in the favela maintain that the tours are about social justice and claim to be raising tourists' awareness of poverty, racism, and class discrimination, it is hard to determine whether tourists truly engage with these goals or whether they are attracted by the titillating potential for danger, personal injury, or even death.

These three examples show the rich seam the context of tourism is to mine for understanding violence in contemporary times; as McNaughton attests 'there is violence in tourism as a modern expression of capitalism, with its associated flows of people and capital' (2006: 660). However, mostly the connection is not made explicit finding a home in the euphemism of dark tourism or in the guise of crime and of course acts of terrorism. As such the discussions of violence in connection with tourism have mainly centred around the following themes: 1. Political stability and the often associated terrorism (e.g.: Sonmez 1998, Bhattarai et al. 2005); 2. Ideas of safety and security (e.g.: George 2003); and 3. Links with crime (e.g.: Brunt et al. 2000). There has been considerable focus on 'dark tourism' relating to those sites premised on acts of violence in connection with war, death and suffering (e.g. Lennon and Foley 2000, Stone and Sharpley 2008, Strange and Kempa 2003). It is not the intention to dismiss these important areas of enquiry. Indeed they make their presence known in this collection (see, for example, Chapter 6 and Chapter 10) but rather to make more explicit the place of violence within tourism and in so doing not to confine it to areas of certain touristic products, practices and occurrences but to bring to the fore the problem of the violence of the everyday which seeps into all areas of life – including that of the pleasure seeker – and often goes unnoticed. The not noticing serves to enforce and make violent, usually with impunity, social relations that go far beyond the reach of that which is normally described as taking place within the context of tourism.

I have already referred to the work of Lozanski, Robb, and McNaughton to illustrate the place of violence in tourism but would like to further the point by considering a few more examples. An obvious area of consideration is that of the connection between tourism and war, and Adam Weaver (2011) reminds us that some of the foundations that allow modern tourism practices are rooted in the modus operandi of war. Indeed 'technologies that have had a profound impact upon the conduct of war have, equally importantly, contributed to the speed and accessibility of civilian air transport' (2011: 677). By way of example Weaver cites the Boeing 747, once a military transporter, now a commercial airliner, and further contends that some pleasure-based activities are made safe as a result of military technologies. Vicuña Gonzalez (2013) argues that the national security interests of the United States have been well served by tourism and militarisation in the Philippines and Hawai'i. They have worked together to inform for example tourist itineraries which help to further the American strategic and economic interests in the Pacific. As noted earlier where violence has been discussed in the study of tourism it is often connected with human conflict and political instability. We might also note that this often comes to the fore in discussions of terrorism. An insightful paper by Raoul Bianchi draws attention to the structural power relations that cause violence to be done to those at tourism destinations in the aftermath of terrorist attacks. It is worth quoting an example at length (2006: 71):

> Following the attack on an Israeli-owned hotel in Mombasa killing 17 Kenyans and three Israelis, and the simultaneous attempt to shoot down an Israeli airliner

on 28th November, 2002, the British government warned against all non-essential travel to Kenya. Subsequently, on 15th May, 2003, British Airways was urged to suspend all flights to the country. These were only re-instated on 4th September, 2003, over two months after the UK Foreign Office had lifted the advice against all non-essential travel (Tourism Concern, 2003). According to Kenya's Tourism Minister, the Kenyan tourism industry lost Sh.1bn within days of the travel warnings being issued and BA's suspension of flights, not to mention the loss of wages incurred by the local workforce due to the inability of hotels to pay their staffs' wages (*Daily Nation*, 21st May, 2003). The US and UK governments made the lifting of terror related travel warnings subject to the Kenyan government implementing numerous anti-terror and security measures, further increasing the financial burden on a country already suffering considerable financial losses as a result of the travel bans (*eTurboNews*, 20th June, 2003). Not only did ordinary Kenyan citizens suffer as a result of the collapse of their tourism industry, but it is they, rather than foreigners or tourists, who have borne the brunt of the terrorist bombings, not to mention politically motivated violence in recent years.

The effect that 'large-scale' acts of violence have on the lives of 'ordinary' people and their interpersonal relations is also evident in Bowman's (1989) discussion of sexual relations between Palestinian men and foreign women tourists in Jerusalem. Writing before the 1987 intifada Bowman contends that encountering feelings of subordination in dealings with more economically and socially 'superior' tourists some market vendors had developed 'an aggressive sexuality focussed on the women of the tourist population … [and their] use of sexuality [was] a means of expressing and challenging economic and political inequities' (1989: 77). According to Bowman through the 'conquering' of the western female tourists the merchants can express their power in the face of the 'structural inequalities built into the relation of tourist and tourist merchant by economic inequality and the hostility of the Israeli-run tourist industry' (1989: 87).

The last example I want to draw attention to is Nancy Scheper-Hughes's work on the global trafficking of human organs. Scheper-Hughes has written extensively on this subject. Cross-border medical based tourism is now a well-established 'niche' in the practice of tourism where people move across national boundaries to undertake plastic surgery, fertility treatment (for examples see Connell 2006, De Arellano 2007, Jones and Keith 2006) and in some cases routine operations (news. bbc.co.uk/2/hi/health/1770348.st). Scheper-Hughes (2011) draws our attention to the illegally organised transplant tourism in which the people and body parts are trafficked from the poorer echelons of global society to and for those with greater economic capital. The outcome of such activities often result in poor outcomes for both the donor and the recipient, the former encouraged to sell a body part on the promise of great financial reward and the latter travelling in the hope of achieving a prolonged and better quality of life. Such suffering that Scheper-Hughes describes is all neatly wrapped in the language of tourism by those who benefit the most from such exploitation: the traffickers or brokers and surgeons. Indeed the '"transplant tour" packages [include]: travel to an undisclosed foreign and exotic setting; five-star hotel accommodation' (2011: 56). By examining this aspect of tourism the violence that is uncovered can be used to make comment on the social world we inhabit, as Scheper-Hughes contends: 'transplant tourism casts light on the dark underbelly of neoliberal globalization, on the rapacious demands it creates and the predatory claims it makes on the bodies of the "bio-disposable"' (2011: 85).

The foregoing discussion has highlighted the commingling of violence with tourism showing the deep and long standing connections between the two. Violence is manifest in many aspects of touristic practices and encounters which includes: violence between individuals, violence as an attraction, the interconnections of violence and tourism with structural inequalities which can impact not only on the political economy of whole destinations but also personal relations and health or the practicalities of touristic activity in the form of technological developments. Having established the intimacy of violence and tourism I now wish to explore briefly how we can understand more closely what violence in fact is.

It is not my intention to explore the category of violence in great detail as this has been well rehearsed elsewhere (see for example Scheper-Hughes and Bourgois 2004, Das et al. 2000, Arendt 1970) and each chapter in this book in its own way defines what violence is. What is important to emphasise is that violence is manifest in many different forms and that these are not necessarily physical. Das et al. (2000) have highlighted the various levels at which violence is produced and 'consumed', relating it to how the inner world experience of the individual is connected to sets of social power relations often involving global flows of images, capital and people. There is also a recognition that there is a need to examine violence 'as a cultural expression or as a performance' (Whitehead 2004:1). As such violence as an object of study cannot be understood as occurring in only large scale events and at times of conflict but also forms part of the 'ordinary' or 'everyday' social world (Bourdieu 1991, Bourdieu and Wacquant 1992). Rather than a physical demonstration of violence the 'ordinary' or 'everyday' aspects of violence often appear in a symbolic form. Such expressions of violence occur at all levels of the social world. As Bourdieu (1991) outlined in his discussion of various forms of symbolic domination in which fields of power relations between social actors are established, the acts and practices of everyday life are underwritten by 'silent and insidious' (1991: 51) acts of violence.

As already noted the field of tourism provides a fertile ground for furthering understandings of violence both in its physical and symbolic senses because due to its very nature it involves the global flows that Das et al. (2000) refer to, and it is also a major item in western consumer consumption practices. Further, to reiterate the violence of tourism as 'violence' (that is stated as violence) has not been prominent in the study of tourism, rather being 'hidden' with different labels in discussions of 'dark tourism', 'terrorism' and 'crime'. Dark tourism is the lens which presents itself as one of the most obvious through which to view tourism and violence as the very products on which this category of touristic practice relies are often derived from violence manifest on a large scale in the form of state, and inter-state conflicts. It is different from crime and terrorism because it is unlikely that anyone seeks to become a victim of crime or terrorism during their holiday (albeit some tourists do deliberately seek out danger – see Lozanski Chapter 3 this volume), but dark tourism sites are chosen, are travelled to and form part of the leisure and pleasure mobilities regardless of whether they are for 'remembrance' or 'educational' purposes. The study of tourism has a duty to think through violence to examine not only tourism but also the nature and place of violence in society at large. This book draws on a range of international contexts to deepen the understanding of the role of violence in shaping touristic practices. Of central importance to the work presented in this volume is the way in which the violence that moulds tourism products, as well as the violence within them, inform the social world and the power relations and moral order that 'orient norms and normality' (Das et al., 2000: 5).

In Chapter 2 Les Roberts examines the intersection of violence and travel in the in-between spaces of transit: spaces that encompass what from Augé we have come to understand as 'non places'. Noting that such intersections may take the form of literal and metaphorical forms of violence, for example the scuffles of drunken stag tourists or football fans and the carnage of the tube train suicide bomber; it can also assume less tangible forms, for example: the surrender of identity and somatic rights at airport security; or the 'extraordinary renditions' of itineraries designed to circumvent international human rights legislation. He argues that whilst these examples are topographically embedded in the material and symbolic landscapes of global travel more generally they are, nevertheless, no less illustrative of experiences and geographies specific to touristic practices. Drawing on a selection of cinematic, textual and ethnographic spaces of transit, Roberts sets out to explore the violence of non-places and to cast closer critical reflection on the spatial anthropology of these landscapes as spaces of violence. As such the chapter sets out to explore their imaginary and affective potency as spaces where violence (and the violent) remains a latent but frequently active energy that haunts and commingles with the everyday rhythms of travel and tourism.

Using India as an example, Kristin Lozanski in Chapter 3 looks at violence as it is manifest in tourists' search for otherness. This otherness, she argues, is informed by a desire to see the otherness of a post-colonial imaginary which operates through Orientalist discourses that cast the 'Third-World' and its citizens as irrational, chaotic, hedonistic, and violent against a West that is dialectically constructed as logical, orderly, self-restrained, and safe. These discourses of the Other coalesce in the desire of many travellers to obtain experiences outside of enclavic tourist spaces. Such spontaneous encounters enable claims to risk, a key principle used by travellers to distinguish themselves from tourists. In this context, violence is a particular form of risk that reinforces narratives of the volatility of the Orient, which in turn provides the markers of difference through which they, as individuals, are able to make themselves and, ultimately, participate in nation-building projects that reify Western countries as 'safe'. Lozanski notes that while recent scholarship has argued that adventure travel has become merely a performance of adventure in which travellers are insulated from virtually all forms of risk, individuals, and as members of a supranational bloc, travellers expect to be able to encounter risk, while simultaneously remaining exempted from it. By theorising the relationship between risk and violence, Lozanski explores the ways that travellers' narratives are predicated on risk while exposure to violence is actively mitigated at both individual and structural levels. She also explores the obverse which is the violence done by travellers to the places and people to which they travel. Incorporating violent events such as the bombing in Delhi's Paharganj market (2005); the terrorist attacks at Mumbai's Taj Mahal Hotel (2008); and the rapes of German travellers in Rajasthan in 2005 and 2006; as well as incidents of violence committed by travellers against Indians, this chapter examines the tangled contradictions between travellers' fantasies of and aversions to violence, as well as the ways in which they themselves are complicit in violence.

In Chapter 4 Hazel Andrews explores the role of symbolic violence in examples of touristic practices and products drawn from the popular charter tourism destinations of the Mediterranean Islands of Mallorca and Menorca. Based on ethnographic field work she argues that the non-explicit forms of violence found in both places reflect and inform power relations within society, often serving to legitimise those relations. Basing her ideas on Bourdieu's discussions of the misrecognition of violence, Andrews further contends that the fact that the violence is not in overt physical form means that it is un-remarked upon, which serves to instil the events she describes with a sense of insidiousness and everydayness. The first example is taken from Menorca and considers the way in which a particular representation of gendered relations serves to inform constructions of those relations, trivialise acts of violence towards women and endorses the role of women as belonging to the domestic sphere. The second example is based on Magaluf, Mallorca and provides instances of the way in which elements of touristic practice are underwritten by violence and serve to legitimate the continuation of violence in the home world of the tourists.

Louise Platt takes us to the city of Liverpool in the Northwest of the UK in Chapter 5. Liverpool held the title of European Capital of Culture (ECoC) in 2008. Platt argues that the city used the award to try and reinvent and re-imagine its image, in particular on a national level. She explores the way in which prior to 2008 a myth of Liverpool as an undesirable destination had developed based on economic and urban decay, crime, riots, poverty and radical politics all of which became key features which blighted the way the city was viewed. The ECoC year and the corresponding rebranding activities were used to construct a transformed place image and thus with the hope of increasing tourism to the city. Platt's analysis is based on an ethnographic study of the city during 2008 and 2009. She draws on the work of Judith Butler and the notion of injurious speech or linguistic violence. The chapter asks if the negative interpellation of place constitutes the way that it performs its identity and therefore impacts on how the place is presented and seen as a tourist destination. Platt argues that to understand the image of a place is to interrogate how it is constructed through branding activity but also through embodied processes of engagement with place. This includes a consideration of power relations and notions of dominance and resistance. By considering the linguistic and symbolic violence that Liverpool has endured, and how these became myths and stereotypes, the chapter assesses the impact that this has on embodied performances of Liverpudlian identity. This in turn, allows for the possible transformation of the city's identity, through the creative potential of the relationship between symbolic violence and everyday sociality.

In Chapter 6 Anne Hertzog looks at the recent French historiography of the First World War which, she argues, tends to break with unemotional approaches of the war and questions the 'incredible' and 'unprecedented' violence of the Great War (Audoin-Rouzeau, Becker, 2000). She asks that we may wonder what the place and the status of violence in the process of making battlefields touristic places is, arguing that it is a process that implies a great multiplicity of actors (local, national and foreign in the case of the Somme, for example). Hertzog contends that choices of the representation of war violence are complex: the role of national traditions (historiography, for example) but also the image of the way of fighting (the battling parties) that each nation intends to show to the world through the eyes of tourists. She argues that the treatment of violence in the process of tourism development – which suggests communication to others – deals with politics, culture and identity. When sightseeing is seen as a means for territorial development and planning, as an agent of spatial and social change, a specific use of war violence can be observed in the process of attraction in order to make the places 'appealing'. The result is that peace or 'shared memory' are frequently put forward in the process of making battlefields touristic places. The rise of such discourses, that in no-way dismiss war violence, but grant it a specific role, can be linked to the pacifying function, at times, assigned to tourism. Hertzog attests that in this way, such a vision is closely linked to Knafou's (2009) analysis which defines tourism as the biggest mass movement of populations coming peacefully to other places. This positive vision of the touristic phenomenon as a way to connect nations and people, the ultimate war aftermath in other words, nevertheless clashes with a mistrust from other battlefield tourism stakeholders which those of the positive view associate with merchandising or entertainment, leading to a kind of symbolic violence against what should be considered as sites of sacrifice and mourning.

In Chapter 7 Tom Selwyn reflects on the connections between tourism and violence within the context of Bourdieu's and Passeron's (1977) concept of symbolic violence as it relates to education. Selwyn builds upon these ideas to demonstrate their effectiveness as a means to think about contemporary political issues. He examines some of the central ideas and practices of some types of tourism and the cultural industries in Israel/Palestine and BiH to explore the role both have in producing and reproducing views of the world based on nationalist sentiments. The chapter considers the idea of 'cultural shutdown' in relation to

Sarajevo where the main museums and galleries have been allowed to run out of money ultimately forcing their closure arguing that it is an extension of ethnic cleansing begun during the war and that this feeds into separatist notions of the future. The language of separation is also found in Israel quite literally and symbolically in the presence of the wall that divides it from Palestine. Selwyn notes the close relationship between separatist agendas and economic success. He also argues that a culture of resistance exists in both BiH and Israel/Palestine which build on ideas of cosmopolitanism and cultural pluralism.

Remaining in Palestine, in Chapter 8 Rami Isaac notes that tourism destinations reinvent themselves for various reasons ranging from intrinsic characteristics of tourism demand, economic behaviour and attitudes towards the local culture and environments. In this chapter he uses the case of Palestine and the violence, tension and political instability that has existed there since 1948 to examine the processes and instruments in shifting from tourism based on pilgrimage to 'other types' of tourism, in particular 'atrocities' tourism. Isaac explores answers to some basic questions of shifting tourists' motivations; the processes and thus consequences of such changes; the main conditions for successful transition, and he sheds light on how tourism and touristic practices in Palestine endorse to legitimise the Palestinian 'right of return', and eventually the acknowledgement of '*Al Nakba*' in 1948 and 1967 (the uprooting of villages and the creation of refugees).

In Chapter 9 Sônia Regina da Cal Seixas, Luiz de Moraes Hoeffel, David Botterill Paula V. Carnevale Vianna and Michelle Renk explore issues of tourism and violence in the context of the 'litoral norte' (north coast) of Brazil. Exploring the city of Caraguatatuba and the surrounding area they note that from the early 1980s this stretch of coastline has been subject to a rapid process of modernisation, industrialisation, and demographic growth driven by speculation and unplanned tourism that have caused great impacts on the quality of residents' lives. The extensive urban expansion, particularly the construction of holiday and second home condominiums, has attracted a significant migrant labour force – who themselves have created a demand for new housing in often unplanned developments. Seixas et al. argue that these rapid changes in demography and economy have produced a myriad of new social problems, for example, in 2008 Caraguatatuba was the most violent city in the State of Sao Paulo and the 91st most violent in Brazil. The chapter opens up some new research lines concerning the interrelationships between social and environmental change in the region and violence, tourism and crime.

Chapter 10 takes us to an examination of the relationship between tourism and terrorism by Wolfgang Aschauer. He argues that the loss of tourism demand after terrorist attacks is documented quite extensively in several publications (Aly and Strazicich 2001, Pizam and Smith 2000, Pizam and Fleischer 2002, Frey, et al. 2005, Aschauer 2008). Aschauer, contends however, that quantitative data relating to the flow of tourists allows only speculative assumptions about the causes of spatiotemporal fluctuations in tourism whilst other potentially influential considerations, for example, psychological factors (tourist mentality), economic-societal factors (crisis management, media) and political-cultural factors (travel alerts, cultural distance to locals) have remained less examined areas of tourism research. Aschauer draws our attention therefore to the importance of not limiting the discussion to tourism statistics but rather including understandings by travellers of the destination image (both on location and in the generating market). The chapter considers the results of a 2007 survey of 132 inhabitants of the Austrian city of Salzburg about the destination image of Bali and the Sinai region. The results are compared to an earlier survey conducted in 2005 with tourists on location (Aschauer, 2010). The study integrates new approaches to the research of tourism demand which can be ascribed to tourism mentality. It is assumed that a higher risk propensity, a higher travel experience and higher information needs lead to lower fears of terrorism and to a better image of terrorism-affected destinations. Aschauer's work furthers our understanding of crisis management as it measures the differences in the destination image between travellers on location and those potential travellers in source markets, highlighting which psychological requirements lead to a persistent motivation to travel despite terrorism threats.

David Botterill, Shane Pointing, Charmaine Hayes-Jonkers, Trevor Jones, Cristina Rodriguez, and Alan Clough provide a critical realist perspective in Chapter 11. They explore the juncture between tourism and violence in the city of Cairns, in the far north of Queensland, Australia. Botterill et al. use the chapter to explore the connections between enduring backpacker motivations and practices, the hidden sensitivities of tourism stakeholders to the projection of negative destination images, and the turn to crime prevention initiatives as a central plank of government policy. The chapter provides evidence from an extensive research project into alcohol-related violence and illustrates how these mechanisms interact. The empirical evidence suggests that there are un-reconciled tensions between these mechanisms, and that further 'deep' mechanisms sit below them, namely: collusion of denial, the demarcation of civility, and its contrasting figurations. The authors summarise their critical realist explanations and consider the implications in other backpacker contexts.

In an extended Chapter 12 Nancy Scheper-Hughes explores in some depth her work which explores the transplant tourism phenomenon as a part of medical tourism which includes a whole range of medical interventions which are now motivational factors for global travel. The afterword (Chapter 13) contributed by Cathy Palmer draws out some of the main themes presented in this volume and argues that violence within tourism is akin to matter-out-of-place, 'polluting' the social order which asks tourists to question how they live with others. Palmer goes on to suggest questions and issues that may inform future research directions for examining the relationship between tourism and violence.

References

Aly, H.Y. and Strazicich, M.C. 2001. Terrorism and Tourism. Is the Impact Permanent or Transitory? [Online]. Available at: http://fama2.us.es:8080/turismo/turismonet1/economia%20del%20turismo/economia%20del%20turismo/terrorism%20and%20tourism.pdf [accessed: 1 February 2012].

Arendt, H. 1969 *On Violence.* New York: Harcourt, Brace and Company.

Aschauer, W. 2008. *Tourismus im Schatten des Terrors. Eine vergleichende Analyse der Auswirkungen von Terroranschlägen (Bali, Sinai, Spanien).* München: Profil.

Aschauer, W. 2010. Perceptions of Tourists at Risky Destinations. A Model of Psychological Influence Factors. *Tourism Review*, 65 (2), 4–20.

Audoin-Rouzeau, S. and A. Becker. 2000. *14/18, retrouver la guerre,* Paris: Gallimard.

Bhattarai, K., Conway, D., and N. Shrestha. 2005. Tourism, Terrorism and Turmoil in Nepal. *Annals of Tourism Research*, 32 (3), 669–688.

Bianchi, R. 2007. Tourism and Globalisation of Fear: Analysing the Politics of Risk and (In) Security in Global Travel. *Tourism and Hospitality Research*, 7 (1), 64–74.

Bourdieu, P. 1991. *Language and Symbolic Power.* Cambridge: Polity Press.

Bourdieu, P, and L. Wacquant. 1992. *An Invitation to Reflexive Sociology.* Cambridge: Polity Press.

Bowman, G. 1989. Fucking Tourists: Sexual Relations and Tourism in Jerusalem's Old City. *Critique of Anthropology*, 9 (2), 77–93.

Brunt, P., Mawby, R. and Z. Hambly. 2000. Tourist Victimisation and the Fear of Crime on Holiday. *Tourism Management*, 21 (4), 417–424.

Connell, J. 2006. Medical Tourism: Sea, Sun, Sand and … Surgery. *Tourism Management*, 27 (6), 1093–1100.

Das, V., Kleinman, A., Ramphelle, M. and P. Reynolds (eds). 2000. *Violence and Subjectivity.* London: University of California Press, 1–18.

de Arellano, A.B.R. 2007. Patients Without Borders: The Emergence of Medical Tourism. *International Journal of Health Services*, 37 (1) 193–198.

Frey, B.S., Luechinger, S. and Stutzer, A. 2005. Calculating Tragedy: Assessing the Costs of Terrorism. *CESifo Working Paper*, 1341, 131.

George, R. 2003. Tourist's Perceptions of Safety and Security While Visiting Cape Town. *Tourism Management*, 24 (5), 575–585.

Gonzalez Vicuña, V. 2013. *Securing Paradise. Tourism and Militarism in Hawai'i and the Philippines.* London: Duke University Press.

Jones, C.A. and L.G. Keith. 2006. Medical Tourism and Reproductive Outsourcing: The Dawning of a New Paradigm for Healthcare. *International Journal of Fertility and Women's Medicine*, 51 (6) 251–255.

Knafou, R. 2009. Heritage & Tourism Cities in Europe. Proceedings of Urban Tourism, Heritage and Urban Quality in Europe. March 2009.

Lennon, J.J. and M. Foley. 2000. *Dark Tourism: The Attraction of Death and Disaster.* London: Thompson Learning.

Litwick, Leon F. 2004. From 'Hellhounds', in *Violence in War and Peace: An Anthology*, edited by N. Scheper-Hughes and P. Bourgois. Oxford: Blackwell, 121–128.

Lozanski, K. 2007. Violence in Independent Travel to India. *Tourist Studies*, 7 (3), 295–315.

McNaughton, D. 2006. The 'Host' as Uninvited 'Guest' Hospitality, Violence and Tourism. *Annals of Tourism Research*, 33 (3), 645–665.

Pizam, A. and Smith, G. 2000. Tourism and Terrorism. A Quantitative Analysis of Major Terrorist Acts and their Impact on Tourism Destination. *Tourism Economics*, 6 (2), 123–138.

Pizam, A. and Fleischer, A. 2002. Severity vs. Frequency of Acts of Terrorism: Which has a Larger Impact on Tourism Demand? *Journal of Travel Research*, 40, 337–339.

Robb, Erika M. 2009. Violence and Recreation: Vacationing in the Realm of Dark Tourism. *Anthropology and Humanism*, 34 (1), 51–60.

Scheper-Hughes, N. 2011. Mr Tati's Holiday and João's Safari – Seeing the World through Transplant Tourism. *Body and Society*, 17 (2&3), 55–92.

Scheper-Hughes, N. and P. Bourgois. 2004. Introduction: Making Sense of Violence, in *Violence in War and Peace: An Anthology*, edited by N. Scheper-Hughes and P. Bourgois. Oxford: Blackwell, 1–31.

Sönmez, S.F. 1998. Tourism, Terrorism, and Political Instability. *Annals of Tourism Research*, 25 (2), 416–456.

Stone, P. and R. Sharpley. 2008. Consuming Dark Tourism: A Thanatological Perspective. *Annals of Tourism Research*, 35 (2), 574–595.

Strange, C. and M. Kempa. 2003. Shades of Dark Tourism: Alcatraz and Robben Island. *Annals of Tourism Research*, 30 (2), 386–405.

Weaver, A. 2011. Tourism and the Miltiary Pleasure and the War Economy. *Annals of Tourism Research*, 38 (2), 672–689.

Whitehead, Neil, L. 2004. Rethinking Anthropology of Violence. *Anthropology Today*, 20 (5) 1–2.

Chapter 2

The Violence of Non Places

Les Roberts

Kurtz on the tube

Sometime in the mid-1990s I was walking along Earl's Court Road in London when I noticed something of a commotion kicking off by the entrance to the Underground Station. As I drew nearer I saw a number of what were clearly very frightened passengers running out of the station into the mid-morning throng. Behind them, crashing through the ticket barriers and bulldozing everything and everyone who got in his way, charged a hulking powerhouse of a man whose ferociously intimidating presence radiated pure aggression. The indiscriminate rampage, seemingly fuelled in part by drugs, alcohol or quite possibly both, was over almost as quickly as it had begun. But the incident left behind an intensity of feeling that was as palpable as the panic and pandemonium it had induced: an ambient sense of unease and mild terror that hung in the air for several minutes and which epitomized, for me at least, what might best be described as a *spatio-temporal moment of violence*.

Stripped of any wider socio-political or historical context the phenomenological significance of this moment lies in the particularities of a chance commingling of place and affect. Irrespective of the form it had taken, whether in terms of the physicality of the act or the emotional convulsions it precipitated amongst those caught in its destructive path, the violence that this example serves to illustrate finds resonance with the wider themes explored throughout this chapter. That the memory of this episode has continued to impress itself upon me is doubtless attributable to the visceral intensity of the violence I had encountered, but it is no less on account of the constitutive *transitoriness* of that particular spatio-temporal moment; transitory in terms of the fleeting and contingent eruption of the violent event, but also insofar as the drama unfolded in a quintessential space of transit: the non-place setting of an Underground Station.

The recollection of the moment as an affective residue of violence, an embodied and spatial as much as temporal 'moment', outstrips that of the individual himself, whose bald head and monstrous frame conjures the memory of a vaguely Kurtz-like image that probably owes more to Marlon Brando's character in the film *Apocalypse Now!* than that originally created by Joseph Conrad in his novella *Heart of Darkness*. Reflecting on this Kurtzian association, the contextual framing of this narrative as a travel story, albeit one played out in rather different 'contact zones' than those Pratt (1992) adumbrates in relation to European colonial encounters with the 'other', nevertheless brings with it the sense of a legacy of violence that is deeply rooted in an imperial imaginary of Western conquest and colonization. As a place or space through which travellers pass en route to *other* places and spaces, whether these be far-flung sites of exotic adventure or the everyday landscapes of mundane urban habiting (Lefebvre 2003: 81), the train station, or rather this particular train station, is part of a wider geo-historical constellation through which the threat of violence (symbolic or otherwise) runs like a thread.

Indeed – and to continue this anecdotal prolegomenon for a moment – Earl's Court was the tube station I had passed through several years earlier when visiting a travel agency that specialized in backpacking and adventure tourism. I was planning a round-the-world trip that took in, amongst other destinations, former British colonies: developing nations my Lonely Planet guidebooks reliably informed me were a mecca for those with a taste for 'alternative', 'budget' and 'exotic' travel. Moreover, not un-coincidentally, Earl's Court is a part of London where many backpackers – most notably Australians, New Zealanders and South Africans – themselves form a sizable transient population. I recall the transparent plastic wallet that my travelling companion and I obtained as part of our travel pack accessories. On it was printed the Lao-Tzu aphorism (and well-worn travel cliché) 'A journey of a thousand miles begins with a single step'; a truism that speaks well to the fact that the step out of a London tube station is but a short step away from that which imprints (and implicates) itself in the altogether more politically and ethically fraught landscapes of the 'other'. The non-place, by this reckoning, represents a heterotopic space of violence inasmuch as the potential of such is rarely far from reach. When, from deep in the shadow of London's luminescent gloom, Marlow, Conrad's narrator, utters the immortal line 'And this also has been one of the dark places of the earth', the estuarine landscape of the Thames becomes as redolent of the horror of colonial violence as the Congo River, the symbolic and geographic 'heart' of *Heart of Darkness* (Scheper-Hughes and Bourgois 2004: 7). Similarly, geographies of transit and mobility in everyday 'home' environments exact, or at least, in latent form, harbour forms of symbolic violence in ways that are analogous to that visited symbolically and/or physically in travel and tourism destinations across the globe. Violence, like those who perpetrate it, is shaped by the spaces in and through which it is transacted and produced and from which, lurching forward, it strikes its blow.

In setting out to explore the violence of non places the aim of this chapter is not to contribute towards a spatial taxonomy of violence insofar as, symbolic or otherwise, it might be held to constitute one of the defining attributes of non places (as if it were somehow imprinted into the architectural DNA of spaces such as underground stations, airports, service stations, or modes and types of transport). Nor is it to sketch or identify a 'canon' of narratives and symbolic events in which the themes of violence and non places come together in some ill-defined or arbitrary way. Its altogether less concrete objective is to contribute towards a space of reflection given over to a spatial anthropology of these landscapes as spaces and places of violence. As such it sets out to tap their imaginary and affective potency as spaces where violence (and the violent) remains a latent but frequently active energy that haunts and affects the everyday rhythms of travel and tourism. Drawing on a selection of textual, cinematic and ethnographic spaces, the chapter offers a tentative and impressionistic investigation into the violence of non places; one in which the baleful ghost of Kurtz is never far from the surface.

The Moment of Violence

Measured against the scale of atrocities routinely unleashed in the name of violence, not least those more prominently linked with London Transport such as the 7/7 bombings in July 2005, the Earl's Court 'moment' described above barely registers. However, by the same token it is the very everydayness and mundanity that characterizes it as a moment of violence that is the focus of concern here. The implications of this more prosaic or banal form of violence, which are examined in more detail below, are two-fold. Firstly, inasmuch as it is defined in terms of its unexceptional or even routinized status within everyday socio-spatial practice, what we might understand by violence in this context differentially encompasses its more 'symbolic' (Bourdieu and Wacquant 1992) and 'everyday' (Scheper-Hughes 1993) forms. Paying heed to the everyday, lived, and symbolic dimensions to violence demands, in turn, closer critical awareness of the constitutive spatialities of violence and the temporal geographies by which these are framed. Secondly, relating these discussions to travel and tourism practices, the spatial question brings with it consideration of the geographies of travel, tourism and transit and the different ways these inform and reflect the anthropological dimensions to violence: how it is lived, imagined and experienced in the social world.

In geographical terms, then, the intersection of violence and travel is one that is at its most fraught and uncertain when enacted in the in-between spaces of travel and transit: spaces that encompass what from Augé (1995) we have come to understand as 'non places'. Such an intersection can take various forms: the airport scuffles of drunken stag tourists or football fans; the carnage of the tube train suicide bomber; the penetrative assault of the roadside rapist; the strike of a mugger in a multi-storey car park. It can also assume less tangible forms: the surrender of identity and somatic rights at airport security; the liminal suspension or denial of selfhood at borderzones or transit camps; or the 'extraordinary renditions' of itineraries designed to circumvent international human rights legislation (Gregory 2006: 225–7). To the extent that these examples are topographically embedded in the material and symbolic landscapes of global travel more generally they are, of course, no less illustrative of experiences and geographies specific to tourism and tourists.

Given that the concept of violence is more than a little 'slippery' (Scheper-Hughes and Bourgois 2004: 1) its permutations and forms are manifold and quite often discreet. The idea of violence, as Springer notes, 'is open to significant spatio-temporal variation that depends on the individuals and groups concerned'

(2012: 137). Consequently, as an object of analysis violence demands critical interventions that are attuned to the specificities of the violent act and the discursive and experiential landscapes that nurture the potentiality of its fomentation and growth. For Benjamin, 'the critique of violence is the philosophy of its history' (2004: 251). In its possessive form, the 'history of violence', as David Cronenberg's 2005 film of the same name tantalizingly suggests, highlights an ambiguity of meaning that takes us from the grand sweep of historical time to that enacted in the singularity of place and body: the spatio-temporal moment when that history reveals itself. If we say 'he or she has a history of violence', or 'this place has a history of violence' it is an embodied history we are referring to: a *habitus* of violence that denotes a teleology or trajectory made manifest in the biographical and bio*geo*graphical disposition of the subject. Accordingly, tweaking Benjamin's formula slightly, we could just as well argue that the critique of violence is the philosophy of its *spatiality*, or, given the affective dynamics that imbue spaces with an intoxicating and at times seductive volatility, the philosophy of its spatio-temporal *moment*.

Approaching violence through the conceptual prism of the 'moment' is, as Springer suggests, to draw an analogous parallel with what he describes as the exemplary violence of neoliberalism. 'Within the current moment of neoliberalism', he writes, 'violence is all too often a reflection of the turbulent landscapes of globalised capitalism' (2012: 139). For Springer, the implications of this are that exceptional violence – that is, violence that falls outside of the norm and which thus retains its capacity to shock and horrify us – 'risks becoming exemplary, or so routinized and quotidian that we no longer feel an affective response to its appearance' (2012: 139, 140). In his study of Cronenberg's adaptation of J.G. Ballard's 1973 novel *Crash*, Iain Sinclair remarks that it as a film that captures 'the death of excitement. A riposte to Hollywood's mega-budget prostitution of the senses … an elegy to boredom, loss, futility: to Ballard's "death of affect"' (1999: 57). The idea that the erotic potential of the violent car crash might stir a latent post-humanist sensibility inured to (or bored by) a culture predicated on hyper-sensorial excess is one that finds resonance with Springer's dialectic of exceptional and exemplary violence. Indeed, the ascription of the term 'Ballardian' to those landscapes that the novel, and Cronenberg's film, pay inglorious tribute is a testament to a millennial vision in which violence seeps inexorably from the mundane spaces and 'dead zones' of everyday urban entropy. The exceptional becomes the exemplary insofar as it opens up a space, critically and aesthetically, within which to surf the tension between the two. The geographical correlate to these imaginary and textual spaces of violence are the material landscapes from which they draw their inspiration: motorways, flyovers and expressways, slip roads, verges and embankments, the seemingly endless perimeter zones of major airport hubs, retail complexes and business parks, or the pockets of in-between or negative space that provide the setting for Ballard's subsequent novel *Concrete Island* (1974), in which an architect finds himself marooned, like a latter day Robinson Crusoe, on a patch of wasteland in the middle of a motorway intersection in west London.

The affinities between the chronotopic spaces of Ballard's dystopian fiction and the 'supermodern' non places that Augé describes have been well documented (Luckhurst 1996; Roberts 2002; Sellars 2011). Although not couched in such terms by the anthropologist, symbolic violence underpins much of the conceptual edifice and ethics of non places insofar as they function to direct our critical gaze to a rapidly deterritorializing world 'where transit points and temporary abodes are proliferating under luxurious or inhuman conditions (hotel chains and squats, holiday clubs and refugee camps, shanty towns threatened with demolition or doomed to festering longevity); where a dense network of means of transport which are also inhabited spaces is developing' (Augé 1995: 78). Manifest in the non places of, for example, Fortress Europe, the exceptional violence of global economic disparity is rendered exemplary by a discursive mediation that reduces the subjectivity of migrants and refugees to that of 'illegals' or 'clandestines': identities which reinforce their status as transient and aberrant and which thus legitimize their necessary removal by state authorities. The demolition in 2009 of the so-called 'Jungle', a transit camp near Calais on the north coast of France, which provided the temporary home for nearly 800 migrants, was gleefully reported in the right-wing British newspaper the Daily Mail, which lent its moral legitimacy to the eventual mobilization of bulldozers, and up to 500 French riot police armed with flamethrowers, stun guns and tear gas (Howarth and Ibrahim 2012: 200). In 2003 the then opposition Conservative party in Britain advocated that asylum seekers be housed on what they euphemistically termed 'offshore havens' – essentially floating, or actual islands on which claimants are detained pending the decision of the authorities as to their fate (Travis 2009). The wringing out of policy ideas such as this reveals a spatial logic that paints a particularly vivid picture of the ways that violence, through official mechanisms of displacement, suspension and incarceration, is visited upon the very notion of citizenship and *place* (in the sense of that which Augé's concept is relationally defined against). The transitory, liminal and deterritorial are rendered permanent and *concrete*, in both the architectural and figurative meanings of the word. These are non places whose affective in-between-ness is that of *zones of stasis*, marked by 'the temporal unfolding of spatial restriction' (Roberts 2002: 82), rather than, in terms of the agency of mobility that might characterize the spaces of dwellings such as the Jungle, *zones of transition*: the unfolding potential of as yet unrealized (or contingently realized) goals, hopes or desires (ibid: 85; Andrews and Roberts 2012: 12).

The journey from Ballard's marooned motorist adrift in the non places of London's motorway network to the virtual strip-search of air passengers as they pass through the 'totalitarian space' of the airport body scanner,[1] or to the plight of the asylum seeker caught in the interstices of place and identity, is one that, while otherwise uneven and elliptical, finds common ground insofar as it is open to the rhythms, affects and cadences of violence that reverberate throughout

---

1   The Disorder of Things, 'American Vignettes (I): Totalitarian Undercurrents' (January 2013): http://thedisorderofthings.com/2013/01/09/american-vignettes-i-totalitarian-undercurrents/ [accessed: 11 January 2013].

these non places. Violence that flares and burns, like a comet trail, in the spatio-temporal moment.

In 'The Theory of Moments' published in the second volume of his *Critique of Everyday Life*, Lefebvre writes: 'The moment is born of the everyday and within the everyday. From here it draws its nourishment and its substance' (2002: 351). Attention to the everyday is a crucial element of any critique of violence. It is within the realm of the everyday that the exceptional and exemplary square off in a dialectic that brings with it recognition that what in any given circumstance we might regard as 'the violent', whether in terms of the act or its perpetrator, is situated and brought into being in lived time and affective space. Accordingly, Lefebvre remarks that, 'Like time, the moment reorganizes surrounding space: affective space – a space that is inhabited by symbols which have been retained and changed into adopted themes (by love, by play, by knowledge, [and by violence])' (2002: 353).

The concept of 'everyday violence' as set out by Scheper-Hughes refers to 'the little routines and enactments of violence practiced normatively on vulnerable bodies in families, schools, hospitals, medical clinics' and other institutional and bureaucratic settings (2004: 253). Although Scheper-Hughes's idea of everyday violence allows for a more fine-grained analysis attuned to the 'daily practices and expressions of violence on a micro-interactional level' (Bourgois 2004: 426), critical emphasis on the disciplinary and discursive mechanisms by which violence is enacted need not preclude consideration of the wider social and spatial practices of everyday life; i.e. those enacted outside clearly defined institutional settings, in spaces of everyday encounter, consumption and mobility, including – but not limited to – those non places of transit and exchange that are the focus of the current discussion. The recognition that space, in the Lefebvrian sense, is socially produced brings with it a countervailing emphasis on the ways violence is lived, practiced and experienced as part of everyday forms of socio-spatial engagement. In other words, violence as a diffuse, affective and embodied element of spaces and temporalities that are dynamic and processual.

Reinforcing this contention, Springer argues that 'violence acquires meaning through its affective and emotional content, where it becomes literally *felt* as meaningful' (2012: 137, emphasis in original). As he notes, coming at the question of violence from a theory of the moment, 'we suddenly become much more aware of its spatio-temporality as we are forced to acknowledge the complexity of process, or the *momentum* that goes into any single 'act' of violence. A moment is not a still picture but a moving one' (2012: 138).

The Horror of Non Places

Moments of violence, however fleeting or evanescent, invariably leave a trace, whether physical or emotional. They can also imprint themselves on memory in ways that both bookmark the event in time and re-situate the self in specific places and landscapes. I recall as a young child seeing the film *The Long Ships* (1964) one morning on the television. The film includes a scene where Viking prisoners are executed by being pushed from a platform atop a wooden construction on which a giant curved blade had been mounted, down which the condemned are forced to slide. At the tender age of four or five this scene left something of an impression and in the days and weeks that followed I would obsessively switch on the television in the hope that I might witness a similar spectacle of violence, something I had hitherto had no real comprehension of, and certainly no previous visual memory. Like many reared on a 1970s and 1980s feast of horror and gore the capacity for films to shock and leave an affective trace in this way has inevitably diminished over the years, to be resurrected only briefly with the all-too-real horror of internet snuff videos I found myself viewing in the early 2000s in the form of jihadist beheadings of Western hostages.

One film, however, that I do recall leaving something of a distinctly unsettling sensation for several days after watching it owes as much of its horror to the geography and locatedness of the violence around which the film narrative is centred as to the specific form and content of the horror itself. The latter, the only actual evidence of any violence having taking place in the narrative at all, comes at the end of the film. Rex, a man in his early twenties who has been obsessively trying to get to the truth of his girlfriend's disappearance while holidaying together in France, wakes up in darkness underground. He has been buried alive. Unquestionably, much of the horror of *Spoorloos* (*The Vanishing*) (George Sluizer, 1988) is on account of its flirtation, by way of grisly conclusion, with vivisepulture, an archetypal horror theme most notably associated with the gothic fiction of Edgar Allen Poe. Indeed, perhaps one of the reasons the film continues to haunt the viewer long after the video has been put back on the shelf is the extent to which it taps into a culturally deep-seated psychopathology of fear, or *taphophobia* to give it its technical name: the irrational fear of being buried alive.

However much the film's ending has bearing on the impact of *Spoorloos* (the literal translation of this Dutch word is 'without a trace'), what is more significant here is the location of the disappearance and abduction ('the vanishing') of Saskia, Rex's girlfriend, the event that precipitates the fatalistic narrative that unfolds. The effectiveness of *Spoorloos* as a horror film lies in its near-forensic examination of a moment of violence that is critically bound up with the sense of irresolution and absence that engulfs Rex and which drives his dark quest for knowledge. This moment – sustained, convulsive, inert, destructive – has its spatial counterpart in the motorway service station where Saskia disappears. The endless to and fro of people across the station forecourt – holidaymakers, commercial travellers, local motorists stopping off for groceries or petrol; the flow and stutter of cars, trucks, and vans; the tireless murmur of motorway traffic streaming by, seemingly indifferent to the fleeting flurry of roadside activity – the '*metaphorai* of the pause', as Morris seductively puts it (1988: 41); this restless geography of transit and circulation also denies resolution. As a non place, its emptied and contingent sociality negates the slow accretion of memory and identity. Time is measured in other peoples' comings and goings. For Rex time stands still, he is unable to go forward or back. Only absence and the crushing oblivion of an arrested narrative define his being-in-the-world, as if a film inside Rex's head has stuck on pause: an alternative narrative that will never be played.

The existential limbo that the film illustrates, while in this case a protracted moment of horror, can, for some, have its attractions inasmuch as the non place offers the possibility of embracing the very negation of 'anthropological place'[2] that liminal spaces of transit and mobility can incite in the imagination. Approached in this way, the non place provides a means of divesting oneself of established social responsibilities and memories, and the identities that bind these together. If, as I will go on to argue in the following section, this can also be approached from the perspective of symbolic and everyday violence, then it is the *habitus* of place and identity that becomes the object of that violence, the familiarity and grounded-ness of which, by virtue of its absence, is precisely that which prevents Rex from moving on (geographically and psychologically). The service station, which he returns to time and time again, becomes a spatial metaphor for his overriding sense of loss and absence. It becomes an affective zone of stasis on the terms elaborated above.

The horror of *Spoorloos* I have thus far been circling around has led us along a deliberately oblique path towards violence by accentuating the affects of the spatio-temporal moment. In the first instance this is felt empathetically in terms of my own response to the film as a dramatic representation of violence and its horrific aftermath. Secondly, and by extension, the film's diegetic spaces of horror and violence are durational, that is they mobilize an affective and embodied semiotics that is attributable to their ontological status as 'time images' (Deleuze 1989). Indeed, from a Deleuzean perspective they more explicitly resemble what Deleuze dubbed *espace quelconque*, translated (rather awkwardly) as 'any-spaces-whatever'. Describing the transition from the aesthetics of the 'movement-image' – cinematic images predicated on action, linearity, and spatial contiguity – to those of the 'time-image', Deleuze argues that, in the post-war period

> a crisis of the action image [developed]: the characters were found less and less in sensory-motor 'motivating' situations, but rather in a state of strolling, of sauntering or of rambling ... The action-image then tended to shatter, whilst the determinate locations were blurred, letting any-space-whatever rise up where the modern affects of fear, detachment, but also freshness, extreme speed and interminable waiting were developing. (1986: 120–21)

Fear, detachment, speed, waiting: these are all affects that describe Rex's existential world. The any-space-whatever of the motorway service station reflects the suspended animation of time that has become unbuckled from the social world

---

2   Defined in Durkheimian terms, for Augé, anthropological places are 'relational, historical and concerned with identity' (1995: 77).

speeding to and fro around him. In the same way that *Spoorloos* doesn't neatly fit the genre conventions of the horror film, neither is it in any obvious sense a road movie. If it is it is a road that goes nowhere. The violence inflicted on Rex's sense of being-in-the-world is what we are privy to for the duration of the film. As its totem and centre of axis the service station becomes an architectural embodiment of that violence and its affects.

The violent act itself, and the motivations of its perpetrator, are, by comparison, little more than a back story. A young Dutch couple on holiday together stop at a service station in France. A middle-aged man – bourgeois, respectable, a loving father and husband – abducts the woman traveller. He is, we will discover, driven by a desire to explore his capacity for evil, for inflicting suffering, torture and death on an innocent victim, chosen at random, by burying them alive. Like Kurtz's odyssey before him, this too is a Nietzschean journey into the heart of extreme darkness. In the years that follow, the boyfriend remains haunted by the vanishing. When, towards the end of the film, the killer makes himself known to the boyfriend, he offers him a chance to finally learn the truth. However, this resolution is only attainable on the condition that the boyfriend allows himself to be drugged; a journey of transition which takes him from the site of the abduction – the service station – to the claustrophobic interiors of a coffin; a journey of elliptical blackness broken only, as for the viewer, by the faint glow from a cigarette lighter.

The horror, as we have seen, relates to the violence and psychological upheaval that 'the vanishing' exacts on those left behind. As an any-space-whatever the transitory geography of the service station, with its relentless throughput of arrival and departure, connects with an indeterminate cosmology. The sheer infinitude and unknowableness of this potentiality of moments – of communication and reconnection beyond the existential present – lends an almost transcendent quality to non places of transit such as motorway service stations or airports. In his book *Angels: A Modern Myth*, a series of philosophical reflections on the global networks and intercommunications of message-bearing systems ('the metaphysics of the service industries', as he puts it), Michel Serres recounts the imaginary exchange between two service personnel attached to Charles de Gaulle Airport in France. One, an airline worker, is constantly on the move; the other, based permanently at the airport, stays put while everything moves around her:

> I spend my life here, in this never-ending flow of passengers, communications, conveyors, messengers, announcers and agents, because my work is at this intersecting point of a multitude of networks all connected to the universe … I hear the sounds of these clouds of angels. (Serres 1995: 9)

Serres's poetic allusion to an infinitude of connections radiating out from the otherwise still axis of the non place takes on another, more poignant meaning when considered in the context of those who have vanished without trace whilst travelling, leaving their loved ones stuck in limbo, yearning for some form of closure or resolution. In 2008 the British parents of the missing four year old Madeleine

McCann, who vanished from a holiday apartment in Portugal in 2007, released a family photograph of their daughter, dressed as an angel, taken in Christmas 2006. A newspaper headline that featured the image read: 'Our angel! Please let this be our last Xmas without Madeleine'.[3] Clouds of angels – messengers from utopic and virtual dimensions: the inverse cosmology that Serres invokes – haunt the transitory spaces and non places of travel, whether as immaterial traces of memory, or, as with the missing posters displayed at airports by the McCann family, visible markers of an absence made present. When in 2007 the McCanns attempted to put up posters at Lisbon airport it was reported that the Portuguese authorities tried to prevent them from doing so, fearing it might damage the country's tourism industry.[4] In 2012, five years after her disappearance, age progression images showing what the missing girl might look like at the age of nine were displayed in airports and other locations around the world. In April 2012 a German tourist claimed to have spotted the girl boarding a transit bus at Ibiza airport in Spain, one of many reported sightings worldwide.[5] No one, apart from the person(s) who took Madeleine can claim to know what has happened to her, yet the violence of the act in terms of the processes and impacts of the abduction, the trauma of the police investigation (which at one point implicated the parents), and the intrusive and relentless media scrutiny of the McCanns[6] are no less a part of the constellation of affects and narratives that had their origins in a spatio-temporal moment sprung from a holiday apartment in the Algarve one evening in May 2007.

There are, of course, countless numbers of missing persons who disappear each year from any number of locations and places. Not all of these will involve death, violent or otherwise. And not all of these missing persons will remain missing. There are as many possible scenarios and contingent possibilities as

---

3   http://www.mirror.co.uk/news/uk-news/our-angel-please-let-this-be-our-last-xmas-without-367005 [accessed: 18 January 2013]. A religious tribute to the missing girl posted on YouTube features photographs of Madeleine McCann and her family interspersed with drawings and images of angels, constellations and stars. The song 'Missing Angel' by the country and western singer Jim Reeves provides the soundtrack to the video: see http://www.youtube.com/watch?v=l6XqkCgcJSk [accessed: 18 January 2013].

4   http://web.archive.org/web/20070621061029/http://www.express.co.uk/posts/view/9320/Maddy:+Now+Portuguese+police+object+to+'missing'+posters [accessed: 18 January 2013].

5   http://www.thesun.co.uk/sol/homepage/features/4516642/Why-every-Madeleine-McCann-sighting-is-crucial-and-cant-be-ignored.html [accessed: 18 January 2013].

6   Gerry and Kate McCann were amongst the witnesses who gave evidence at the judicial public enquiry led by Lord Justice Leveson in 2012, which was called following the News International phone hacking scandal. Extracts from Kate McCann's personal diary, which had been leaked by the Portuguese police, were published in the British newspaper News of the World without her consent or knowledge. Her husband said that she had felt 'mentally raped' by the publication of the diary, in which she had recorded her private thoughts and feelings about her missing daughter. See http://www.independent.co.uk/news/media/press/kate-mccann-felt-violated-by-newspaper-6266466.html [accessed: 18 January 2013].

there are trajectories, encounters and (mis)connections that form the complex and infinite patterns of everyday mobility. The point is not that violent events and their ramifications have a locatedness and that that has somehow eluded critical attention. It is that acts and events that have violent affect are bound up with spaces and non places of transit in ways that are homologous to those processes that imbue these spaces with properties that are constitutive *of* non places. Non places, by definition (or at least by that advanced by Augé) exert forms of symbolic violence by virtue of their capacity to haemorrhage those structures and symbols that function to nurture the 'organically social' (1995: 94); forms which otherwise inhibit the 'emptying' of place and memory and the advance of 'solitary contractuality' that follows in its wake. The intersection of violence and non places is thus a process that sharpens critical awareness of the spatio-temporal moment of violence; an observation, moreover, that highlights the limitations of an anthropology of non places in the form expounded by Augé in his short, but hugely influential work. Many of these limitations relate to what the anthropologist does not say about the emotional and experiential dynamics of non places, an area that, as I discuss further below, has drawn more engaging and illuminating responses from artists, filmmakers and psychogeographers.

In terms of an anthropological critique of violence that seeks to take up the same slack as that which pertains more specifically to Augé's theory of non places, Whitehead suggests that 'To come to terms with violence properly we must go beyond the anthropology of identity, and embark on an anthropology of experience, to which individual meanings, emotive forces and bodily practices are central' (2004: 2). One way we can begin to approach this is to consider the attraction of non places for those seeking either to exploit their violent potential or to embrace the affects of violence that appear to attach themselves so readily to these spaces.

The Seduction of Non Places

> [Non Places] are radically *new ontological types of place*, constituted *qua* places through their relations to *another* spatiality. (Osborne 2001: 189, emphasis in original)

In the introduction to the second edition of *Non Places*, Augé writes: 'Perhaps, today's artists and writers are doomed to seek beauty in "non places" ... They are further fragments of utopia, in the image of our time divided between passivity, anxiety and, despite everything, hope or, at the very least, expectation' (2008: xxii). Striking a more ambivalent tone with regard to their emotional geographies, this shift in emphasis towards recognition of the aesthetics of non places is partly reflected in the cover images that adorn the respective editions of Augé's book. In the first (1995), a handful of weary-looking passengers sit hunched over reading material at an otherwise deserted airport departure gate. Peeking in through the window behind them is the nose of an airliner framed against the night sky. By contrast, the cover of the 2008 edition features an impressionistic (and colour) image of the interior of an airport terminal, with light reflecting off the vast expanse of empty floor space in what looks like a concourse building or the connecting passageway between terminals. The faint silhouettes of passengers moving along a travelator can just be made out in the distance.

If the realism of the former conveys a sense of longueur, immobility, passivity and social anomie, the painterly quality of the latter, whose human subjects, unlike those stuck at the gate, appear to be actually in motion, could quite readily be matched with J.G. Ballard's altogether more sanguine view that '[airport] concourses are the ramblas and agoras of the future city, time-freeze zones where all the clocks of the world are displayed, an atlas of arrival and destinations forever updating itself, where briefly we become true world citizens' (1997: 11). At first glance, Ballard's observation that '[airports] constitute the reality of our lives, rather than some mythical domain of village greens' (ibid.) would appear to concur with Augé's distinction between anthropological place and non place. Yet in dismissing the organic sociality of the former ('a mythical domain'), Ballard, unlike Augé, embraces the airport not as a symptom of supermodernity that warrants sociological concern, but as a positive and 'benevolent social and architectural influence' (ibid.). Welcoming its 'transience, alienation and discontinuities' (ibid.), the writer champions the airport precisely because it has succeeded in evacuating history (Pascoe 2001: 32).

In terms of tourist and leisure travel, negotiating the necessary disenchantments of the motorway or airport in order to arrive, as quickly and efficiently as possible, at the holiday destination would, in most instances, be to discount the possibility that these spaces of transit might be considered as viable tourist 'places' in their own right. The backseat mantra of 'Are we there yet? Are we there yet?', known all too well by families enduring the tedium of long car journeys, hints at the desire of spatial and temporal ellipsis and the 'editing out' of this part of the holiday narrative. Indeed, the fact that motorways, service stations, airports and similar spaces of transit are less likely to feature in holiday photographs or videos, and thus may be considered to be, at best, at the very margins of the mainstream tourist gaze (Urry 1990), suggests that these are landscapes that few would consider 'authentic' in the terms outlined by MacCannell in his seminal work *The Tourist* (1976).[7]

That said, despite a burgeoning academic literature on what some, but certainly by no means all, would readily confer the term 'non places' of transit, there remain few if any sustained and detailed ethnographic studies of these spaces by which we might gain deeper understandings of how tourists and other travellers make

---

7   This is not to suggest that motorways and their service areas have never been a focus of spectacle, touristic or otherwise. When the M1 and other of Britain's motorways first opened in the 1960s, as Merriman notes, for some they represented 'places of spectacle, dwelling, socialization and excitement' (Merriman 2004: 159). Similar observations have been made in respect of airports in the UK, see Adey 2006.

sense of, ascribe meaning to, and *experience* these spaces. In this respect, Augé's call to 'imagine a Durkheimian analysis of a transit lounge at Roissy' (1995: 94) remains unchallenged if the yardstick by which such things are measured is the degree to which non places negate or are deficient of the qualitative attributes of 'anthropological places'. However, if pushed further into the sphere of the imagination, the same cannot be said in respect of filmmakers, writers and artists who have long been drawn to these spaces, not least on account of their capacity to exact forms of symbolic violence and of disrupting everyday structures of habitus (Andrews 2009).

The use of airport locations in films exploring themes of displacement, alienation or emotional stasis can be traced back to the modernist cinema of the French Nouvelle Vague, perhaps most notably Chris Marker's *La Jetée* (1962), but also François Truffaut's *La Peau douce* (1964), or Jean-Luc Godard's *Une femme mariée* (*A Married Woman*, 1964), both set in Orly airport in Paris. Commenting on Jacques Tati's *Play Time* (1967), again set at Orly (or at least a replica of the airport which Tati had constructed), Pascoe notes that in the choreographed movement of Hulot (Tati's eponymous alter-ego) through the airport Tati 'presents us with a void – a *duty-free* zone' (2001: 261, emphasis added; 258–273). A more recent elaboration of these themes is provided in Roch Stephanik's *Stand-By* (2000), a film which revisits the same vast, inert spaces of Orly that the new-wave directors had set out to explore back in the 1960s. Hollywood's contribution to the genre of 'non place airport films' includes Steven Spielberg's 2004 *The Terminal* (the tag-line of which is 'life is waiting'), or *Up in the Air* (Jason Reitman, 2009).[8] In all of these films the airport terminal represents as much a space of habiting and dwelling as transit. Their characters appear permanently adrift in placelessness, either intentionally (embracing the 'duty-free zone' of the airport) or as victims of circumstances over which they have no control or agency.

If we extend this list to encompass automotive spaces of transit, the sheer number and breadth of films that could be cited here is, of course, almost limitless. However, this is only really the case if applied to the more general chronotope of 'the road'. When narrowed down to those that conform to a spatio-temporal moment constitutive of the non place – i.e. those disproportionately specific to high-speed roads (motorways, highways, expressways, and so on) and their supporting infrastructures – there are a surprisingly few examples that present themselves for analysis (perhaps representing a cinematic analogue to the 'unmarking' of the motorway in visual cultures of tourism). Moreover, despite being as emblematic of modernity as the rapidly evolving cityscapes and 'centripetal' urban environments that have remained such a prominent feature of the post-1930s cinematic imaginary, the 'centrifugal' spaces of the motorway, as Dimendberg has noted (1998: 56), have remained far less studied that filmic representations of the city. Alongside

---

8   It can be noted in passing that the photograph used for the publicity poster for *Up in the Air* bears close resemblance to that on the cover of the first edition of Augé's *Non-Places* (1995).

the aforementioned *Crash* and *The Vanishing*, films such as *Time Out* (*L'Emploi du Temps*, dir. Laurent Cantet, 2001), *Butterfly Kiss* (dir. Michael Winterbottom, 1994), *London Orbital* (dir. Chris Petit and Iain Sinclair, 2002), or *Content* (dir. Chris Petit, 2009) are amongst those handful of cinematic attempts to venture deep into the experiential and affective landscapes of motorways, service stations and related topographies of the road. As I have argued elsewhere, these are films that sit less comfortably within the generic category of 'road movie' than that of the 'off-road movie' (Roberts 2005; cf. Ward 2012). Their constitutive geographies are fashioned not by neo-Kantian *a priori* conception of road space and the neat linearity of time. It is the embodied topographies of spaces that inhibit processes of (straight-*forward*) navigation and delineation that are of significance here. Space is contingent; attuned to the corporeal sensibilities and affective modulations and variegations of time. For those seeking 'off-road adventures', like the travellers in the films cited above, non places are therefore seductive in that they are potentially transformative and transitional spaces: they may not necessarily 'go' anywhere in the geographical sense, but facilitate the passage to (or through) other states of being, consciousness or selfhood (see also Giles 2006).

In *Time Out*, Vincent, a middle-class executive conceals from his family and friends the fact that he has been sacked from his consultancy job. Maintaining the illusion that he has secured a prestigious new position in Geneva working for the United Nations, he spends most of the week in his car driving through the French and Swiss countryside, telephoning his wife from car parks or motorway service stations, and pretending that he has just come out of business meetings. The abstract spaces of the motorway become a welcome refuge from the responsibility and complexity of his situation. Indeed, as Vincent later confides, it was an increasing reluctance to leave his car that precipitated his eventual dismissal from his consultancy position. Driving hundreds of kilometres to attend pointless meetings was, he confesses, the only thing about the job he enjoyed. Like an errant tourist increasingly unable or unwilling to return to the home world, Vincent's flirtation with danger – the inversion or deferral of a social identity he has become increasingly alienated from – brings with it the risk of spilling over from symbolic to physical violence the more his liminal world starts to collapse around him.[9] Motorway space plays host to a different manifestation of violence in *Butterfly Kiss*. Shot on and around the motorways of Lancashire in the north west of England, the film follows the actions of a sado-masochistic lesbian serial killer and

---

9   The film draws much of its inspiration from the real-life case of the Frenchman, Jean-Claude Romand, who, like Vincent, was a Mr Ripley character living a life of deception, pretending to his family and friends that he worked as a doctor and researcher at the World Health Organisation, while in reality spending his days driving aimlessly around the Alps. Incredibly, Romand somehow managed to sustain this for 18 years, his otherwise normal middle-class lifestyle financed by money embezzled from friends and relatives. When, in 1993, Romand's double life was finally exposed, he responded by murdering his wife, children and parents, and by attempting to take his own life.

her impressible lover. Tramping maniacally across a landscape of hard shoulders and petrol station forecourts, the killers cut a violent and psychopathic swathe through these non places, tapping and channelling their latent energies along the way. Picken describes *Butterfly Kiss* as 'A tentative experiment in fusing narrative with psychogeographical enquiry' (1999: 229; see also Roberts 2012: 60).

The idea that violence of non places (symbolic and/or physical) might be a quality – an *energy* – that conveys not so much horror, as discussed in the previous section, but excitement and possible transcedence, finds resonance with those that increasingly inform the development of alternative or 'radically different' (Picken 1999: 229) geographies – or *psychogeographies* – of travel and tourism. There is not the space here to explore in any great detail the relationship between 'psychogeography' and tourism, this is an area to be taken up more fully and more critically elsewhere. But it should be noted that, against the backdrop of global consumer cultures that are evermore in thrall to the spectacle, what is or might be meant by the term 'psychogeography' has become increasingly detached from its moorings in the revolutionary praxis of the Situationists and the writings of Guy Debord (2010, 2004). Indeed, for a Marxist thinker such as Debord, or, indeed Lefebvre, whose theories have strong affinities with Situationist ideas on urbanism and space, the very coupling of 'psychogeography' and 'tourism' would be anathema. Culturally, the deeply compromised nature of the concept has been noted by figures such as Patrick Keiller and Iain Sinclair, who are often held up as exponents of a British psychogeographic tradition. Commenting on its banalization, Keiller suggests that, by the 1990s psychogeography had become an end in itself, reduced to little more than the 'Time Out Book of London Walks' (2003: 377).[10] Sinclair, in turn, is wary of the dangers or making what 'it' is too concrete and formalized or over-fetishized as a style or genre. Commenting on the idea of a 'psychogeographic tour', something the London-based writer is often asked to do, Sinclair explains: 'It's one of the reasons I hate "doing a walk" ... it would be awful, it would be the exact opposite of what the experience is supposed to be which is like a forgetting and an absorbing and an emptying-out and a letting-things-happen' (in Cooper and Roberts 2012: 91). Sinclair's epic trudge around London's M25 orbital motorway (which formed the basis of *London Orbital*, the book (2002), and the film of the same name made with Chris Petit) for obvious reasons, not least practical, but also asthetic and political, is an

---

10 Amongst other things, psychogeography has become a label for niche, slightly 'off-beat' forms of urban tourism. By way of illustration, *The Lonely Planet Guide to Experimental Travel* (Antony and Henry 2005) is a guide book marketed at people 'who like their travel a little less formulaic ... Experimental Travel', it declares, 'has its roots in the varied practices and philosophies of modern alternative thinkers from the Surrealists to the Psychogeographers. Experiments such as travelling to a particular grid reference on a map, or simply wearing a horse's head around town, are all classic examples'. www.lonelyplanet.com/experimentaltravel/about (accessed 14 October 2010). See also Crab Man's *Counter-Tourism: the Handbook* (2012).

example of 'psychogeographic' cultural mobility that very much goes against the grain of formalized (hence reproduceable and standardized) tourist practice and the mainstream tourist gaze. 'Violence', in the more diffuse sense of a radically disrupted spatial habitus, is precisely the point.

For these reasons it is counterproductive and reductive to attempt to define what might be meant by a 'psychogeography of violence' in respect of non places of travel. Nor is it necessarily a worthwhile exercise to set this up against what might count as tourism 'proper' (whatever, exactly, that is) in terms of the motivating factors and attractions that draw travellers to seek out and explore landscapes such as those discussed in this chapter. What it is or is not is adumbrated by the arguments and illustrations that I have presented here, the point being to draw attention to the ways in which violence, in all its forms and slipperiness, is lived, felt, imagined and *experienced* in material and affective landscapes of travel. In relation to alternative forms of tourist activity, psychogeography, if we insisted on forcing the term, could be quite readily applied to Laura Ruggeri's experimentation with 'abstract tours', designed to prompt anti-touristic engagements with urban spaces, and to foster embodied knowledge and experience of space over purely visual consumption (Ruggeri 2007). It could equally well be attached to strategies of place-hacking and 'Urban Exploration', an umbrella term for practices in which participants try to gain access, often illegally, to locations that offer experiences beyond the everyday, particulary sites of decay or abandoned industrial buildings and other forbidden locations (Fraser 2012: 139). As Fraser argues, 'The pursuit of real or authentic experiences, as opposed to the contrived spectacle of traditional tourism, is [one of the] common element[s] between the UE [Urban Exploration] traveller and the adventure/disaster tourist' (2012: 141; see also Ninjalicious 2005).

Whether or not specific types of travel and their related spatial practices might be categorized in terms of 'touristic', 'anti-touristic', 'counter-touristic', 'psychogeographic', 'alternative', 'experimental', and so on, arguably has little bearing on questions pertaining to *how* these practices are experienced, and the intensities and temporalities of the affective spaces embodied by the tourist, psychogeographer, urban explorer, or whoever. The theme of violence provides an instructive means by which to explore the experiential spaces of travel and tourism. It sharpens critical awareness of the emotional geographies of non places and highlights the different ways these both shape and are shaped by the movements, trajectories, desires, fears, anxieties, and hopes of those who pass through or inhabit them.

Tourism as a Moment of Violence

As I have argued, violence can be shown to have spatial and temporal affects that are homologous to those that constitutively negate structures of anthropological place. Symbolically and materially the ceding of these social, cultural and historical structures of identity represents violence not so much in terms of *event* or the consummation of an *act*, but in the processual undoing of a sense of social or corporeal being that weakens the links that securely anchor the self in place and time. The violence of non places is the disruption of the habitus of place. These violent affects can be experienced as horrific and destructive, but they may also allow for the cultivation of more positive feelings of dislocation, 'letting go', and a renewed sense of agency and creativity. If, as Andrews (2009) has suggested, tourism can be experienced as a moment of being, then, by the same reckoning, tourism may also be considered a spatio-temporal moment of violence.

References

Adey, P. 2006. Airports and Air-mindedness: Spacing, Timing and Using the Liverpool Airport, 1929–1939. *Social and Cultural Geography*, 7 (3), 343–63.

Andrews, H. 2009. Tourism as a 'Moment of Being'. *Suomen Antropologi: Journal of the Finnish Anthropological Society*, 34 (2), 5–21.

Andrews, H. and L. Roberts. 2012. Introduction: Re-mapping Liminality, in *Liminal Landscapes: Travel, Experience and Spaces In-between*, edited by H. Andrews and L. Roberts. London: Routledge, 1–17.

Antony, R and J. Henry. 1995. *The Lonely Planet Guide to Experimental Travel*. Melbourne: Lonely Planet.

Augé, M. 1995. *Non-Places: Introduction to an Anthropology of Supermodernity*. London: Verso.

Augé, M. 2008. *Non-Places: An Introduction to Supermodernity*. London: Verso.

Ballard, J.G. 1997. Airports. *The Observer*, 14 September, p. 11.

Benjamin, W. 2004. Critique of Violence, in *Walter Benjamin Selected Writings, vol. 1: 1913–1926*, edited by M. Bullock and M.W. Jennings. Cambridge, MA: Belknap, 236–252.

Bourdieu, P, and L. Wacquant. 1992. *An Invitation to Reflexive Sociology*. Cambridge: Polity Press.

Bourgois, P. 2004. The Continuum of Violence in War and Peace: Post-Cold War Lessons from El Salvador, in *Violence in War and Peace: An Anthology*, edited by N. Scheper-Hughes and P. Bourgois. Oxford: Blackwell, 425–34.

Cooper, D. and L. Roberts. 2012. Walking, Witnessing, Mapping: An Interview with Iain Sinclair, in *Mapping Cultures: Place, Practice, Performance*, edited by L. Roberts. Basingstoke: Palgrave, 85–100.

Crab Man. 2012. *Counter-Tourism: The Handbook*. Axminster: Triarchy Press.

Debord, G. 2004 [1967]. *The Society of the Spectacle*. London: Rebel Press.

Debord, G. 2010 [1955]. Introduction to a Critique of Urban Geography, in *The Situationists and the City*, edited by T. McDonough. London: Verso, 59–63.

Deleuze, G. 1986. *Cinema 1: The Movement-Image*. London: The Athlone Press.

Deleuze, G. 1989. *Cinema 2: The Time-Image*. London: The Athlone Press.

Dimendberg, E. 1998. The Will to Motorisation – Cinema and the Autobahn, in *Speed – Visions of an Accelerated Age*, edited by J. Miller and M. Schwarz. London: Photographers Gallery, 56–69.

Fraser, E. 2012. Urban Exploration as Adventure Tourism: Journeying Beyond the Everyday, in *Liminal Landscapes: Travel, Experience and Spaces In-between*, edited by H. Andrews and L. Roberts. London: Routledge, 136–51.

Giles, J.R. 2006. *The Spaces of Violence*. Tuscaloosa: University of Alabama Press.

Gregory, D. 2006. Vanishing Points: Law, Violence, and Exception in the Global War Prison, in *Violent Geographies: Fear, Terror, and Political Violence*, edited by D. Gregory and A. Pred. Abingdon: Routledge, 205–36.

Howarth, A. and Y. Ibrahim. 2012. Threat and Suffering: The Liminal Space of 'The Jungle', in *Liminal Landscapes: Travel, Experience and Spaces In-between*, edited by H. Andrews and L. Roberts. London: Routledge, 217–33.

Keiller, P. 2003. City of the Future. *City*, 7 (3), 376–386.

Lefebvre, H. 2002. *Critique of Everyday Life, Volume II*. London: Verso.

Lefebvre, H. 2003. *The Urban Revolution*. Minneapolis: University of Minnesota Press.

Luckhurst, R. 1996. *'The Angle Between Two Walls': the Fiction of JG Ballard*. Liverpool: Liverpool University Press.

MacCannell, D. 1976. *The Tourist: A New Theory of the Leisure Class*. London: Macmillan.

Merriman, P. 2004. Driving Places: Marc Augé, Non-places, and the Geographies of England's M1 Motorway. *Theory, Culture and Society*, 21(4/5), 145–167.

Morris, M. 1988. At Henry Parkes Motel. *Cultural Studies*, 2 (1), 1–47.

Ninjalicious. 2005. *Access All Areas: A Users Guide to the Art of Urban Exploration*. Canada: Infiltration.

Osborne, P. 2001. Non-places and the Spaces of Art. *The Journal of Architecture*, 6 (2), 183–94.

Pascoe, D. 2001. *Airspaces*. London: Reaktion Books.

Pratt, ML. 1992. *Imperial Eyes: Travel Writing and Transculturation*. London: Routledge.

Roberts, L. 2002. 'Welcome to Dreamland': From Place to Non-place and Back Again in Pawel Pawlikowski's *Last Resort*. *New Cinemas: Journal of Contemporary Film*, 1 (2), 78–90.

Roberts, L. 2005. *Utopic Horizons: Cinematic Geographies of Travel and Migration*. PhD thesis, Middlesex University. Available online at: http://www.liminoids.com/LesRoberts_PhD_2005.pdf. [accessed: 18 January 2013].

Roberts, L. 2012. *Film, Mobility and Urban Space: a Cinematic Geography of Liverpool*. Liverpool: Liverpool University Press.

Ruggeri, L. 2007. The Poetics of Urban Inscription: From Metaphorical Cognition to Counter-Representation, in *Critical Architecture*, edited by Jane Rendell, Jonathan Hill, Murray Fraser and Mark Dorrian. London: Routledge, 103–11.

Scheper-Hughes, N. 1993. *Death Without Weeping: the Violence of Everyday Life in Brazil*. Berkeley: University of California Press.

Scheper-Hughes, N. 2004. Who's the Killer? Popular Justice and Human Rights in a South African Squatter Camp, in *Violence in War and Peace: An Anthology*, edited by N. Scheper-Hughes and P. Bourgois. Oxford: Blackwell, 253–66.

Scheper-Hughes, N. and P. Bourgois. 2004. Introduction: Making Sense of Violence, in *Violence in War and Peace: An Anthology*, edited by N. Scheper-Hughes and P. Bourgois. Oxford: Blackwell, 1–31.

Sellars, S. 2012. 'Zones of Transition': Micronationalism in the work of J.G. Ballard, in *J.G. Ballard: Visions and Revisions*, edited by J. Baxter and R. Wymer. Basingstoke: Palgrave Macmillan, 230–48.

Serres, M. 1995. *Angels: A Modern Myth*. Paris and New York: Flammarion.

Sinclair, I. 1999. *Crash: David Cronenberg's Post-mortem on JG Ballard's 'Trajectory of Fate'*. London: BFI Publishing.

Sinclair, I. 2002. *London Orbital: A Walk Around the M25*. London: Granta.

Springer, S. 2012. Neoliberalising Violence: Of the Exceptional and the Exemplary in Coalescing Moments. *Area*, 44 (2), 136–43.

Travis, A. 2003. Tories Plan Island Refugee Centres. *The Guardian*, 9 September, p. 10.

Urry, J. 1990. *The Tourist Gaze: Leisure and Travel in Contemporary Societies*. London: Sage.

Ward, S. 2012. 'Danger Zones': The British 'Road Movie' and the Liminal Landscape, in *Liminal Landscapes: Travel, Experience and Spaces In-between*, edited by H. Andrews and L. Roberts. London: Routledge, 185–99.

Chapter 3

Desire for Danger, Aversion to Harm: Violence in Travel to 'Other' Places

Kristin Lozanski

Introduction

In his grapplings with the definitions of violence, Raymond Williams (1983) highlights the complexity of the many senses in which it can be understood. The five senses he identifies – physical assault, physical force, media coverage of violence, the threat of violence, and unruly behaviour – overlap with one another, making it difficult to maintain these distinctions. For the purposes of this chapter, I am interested in elaborating Williams' observations regarding the manifestation of violence displayed in 'physical assault' and 'physical force' as these forms operate in parallel or tension with abstracted or potential forms of violence present in 'violence as threat' or 'violence as unruly behaviour' (Williams 1983: 330) These categories are difficult to maintain as they are necessarily entangled and, as Williams notes, they may be mutually constitutive.

For my purposes, the distinctions highlighted by Williams are productive points of entry into a necessarily messy analysis of violence in the context of ethnological travel to Other places. Such forms of travel emphasize encounters with Otherness in order to obtain social capital: 'The exaggeration and promotion of difference is especially ostentatious in what is referred to here as ethnological tourism – or the commodification of so-called "primitive peoples" and their semiotic sister, the natural landscape – where tourists have shown to be highly concerned with procuring a distinguishing experience' (Conran 2006: 275–6). This difference is constructed through Orientalist narratives (Said 1979) in which unruly – as 'not amenable to rule or discipline; ungovernable; disorderly, turbulent' (OED 2013) – contrasts the discipline, governability, and order that is presumed, by Westerners, of Western subjects and societies (Rose 1999).

While I am aware of the symbolic violence imposed upon Others through Orientalist discourses that emphasize savagery, unruliness, and threat – mythological qualities imposed upon Others through colonial scripts (Memmi 1991) – I am more interested in the ways in which travellers' desires for such symbolic forms of violence stand in sharp contradistinction to physically manifest violence. That is, travellers desire danger while they refuse harm. I begin from William's (albeit collapsed) distinction between violence that is physical (assault and force) and that which is potential (threat and unruliness) and use this framework to consider the tensions vis-à-vis violence that exists within travel that is culturally-focused. Specifically, ethnological travel is contingent upon unruliness, as *potential* violence; meanwhile, within any form of tourism, including ethnological travel, there is little (if any) tolerance for *physical manifestation* of violence enacted upon the bodies of travellers and tourists. While travellers to Other places desire Otherness, which is typified through unpredictability, chaos, and disorder, they simultaneously assume a subject position outside of any actualized violence associated Otherness. Thus, in this chapter I explore the contradictory relationships between the desire for violence and the assumed exemption from violence.

The Other of Ethnological Travel

In Other places, the reasoned, rational Self of Western modernity (Goldberg 1993) encounters a dialectically constructed Other, a racialized Other that is characterized through what the western Self is not: primitiveness. Others and their associated culture are understood to occupy anachronistic spaces (McClintock 1995), in which their presence in a contemporary geography indicates a temporal disruption: 'Colonized people … do not inhabit history proper but exist in a permanently anterior time within the geographic space of the modern empire as anachronistic humans, atavistic, irrational, bereft of human agency – the living embodiment of the archaic "primitive"' (McClintock 1995: 30). Mbembe elaborates this temporal distinction in his critique of theoretical assumptions which assert 'compared to the West, other societies are primitive, simple or traditional in that, in them, the weight of the past predetermines individual behavior and limits the areas of choice – as it were, a priori' (2001: 10). As a marginalizing discourse, primitiveness is characterized through binary distinctions from civilized societies.

> nomadic rather than settled; sexually promiscuous, polygamous and communal in family and property relations rather than monogamous, nuclear and committed to private property; illogical in mentality and practicing magic rather than rational and scientific. In popular terms, non white primitives have come to be conceived as childlike, intuitive, and spontaneous; they require the iron fist of 'European' governance and paternalistic guidance to control *inherent physical violence* and sexual drives. (Goldberg 1993: 156, emphasis added)

There are further binaries through which Others are represented. Dominant travel narratives construct Others as impoverished but happy (Lozanski 2010), spiritually immune to hardship (O'Reilly 2006), and outside of the capitalist practices of commodification and exchange (Kontogeorgopoulos 2003). These narratives stand against a dominant representation of Western lives as unhappy, spiritually devoid, and fragmented by capitalist consumption and, in so doing, represent nostalgia for the alleged social cohesion and satisfaction of pre-modernity (MacCannell 1976).

While contented Others are necessary as 'picturesque' (Bhattacharyya 1997) contributions to both culture and landscape (Conran 2006), a more rigorous experience is required to narrate the transformative experience critical to Western Self-making, itself a process deeply embedded in travel as an alternate to tourism (Lozanski 2011, Munt 1994): 'The extended trip ... although constructed as strenuous and at times risky (*and perhaps precisely because of this construction*), is unanimously viewed as a highly positive experience, generating sought-after and valuable personal changes' (Noy 2004: 84, emphasis added). As a means of self-construction, Elsrud points to the distinction between risk as a 'material, physical fact' and 'a device used to construct a story' (2001: 598). Thus, while invisible Others provide travellers with material services such as housekeeping, food preparation, and transportation (Azarya 2004) and picturesque Others provide travellers with narratives of authentic and non-commodified engagement (Lozanski 2010, Conran 2006, Kontogeorgopoulos 2003), unruly or threatening Others provide a rhetorical background of difference upon which narratives of conquering both Self and Other are presented.

Violence as Elsewhere

Other places – those defined through racialized, religious, and cultural differences from Western-centric norms – map onto tenuous categorizations of so-called 'developing' or Third World geographies. Yet despite the discursive troubling of such representations of Otherness and categories of relative affluence and poverty, there is a materiality to the violence that exists in ostensibly-Other places. A 2002 report by the World Health Organization indicates that in 2000, the estimated proportion of violence-related death (homicide, suicide, and conflict-related) that took place in high-income countries was 8.9 per cent, in contrast to the 91.1 per cent of violence-related death that occurred in low-to middle-income countries (World Health Organization 2002: 7). Even considering per capita rates, there were 32.1 violence-related deaths per 100,000 in low-and middle-income countries in contrast to 14.4 per 100,000 in high-income countries (World Health Organization 2002: 7). These data suggest that there are indeed higher risks – more physical assault, more physical force – for violence-related death in Other places.

While violence may be more prevalent in the global south, violence is pervasive throughout the world. Many travellers, as citizens of the West, assume a lack of violence within their communities: 'we often don't associate violence as a mundane feature of our existence' (Tyner 2012: 2). Instead violence is something that disrupts, that is extraordinary: 'Indeed, it is something that happens to someone else, someplace else; not us, and certainly not here' (Tyner 2012: 2). The (incomplete) erasure of violence as a defining characteristic of the West is enabled by the *removal* of violence rather than the *elimination* of violence. In the West, violence takes places within enclosed spaces, away from public view (Ray 2011): prisons serve as sites of both capital punishment and the symbolic and physical

violence experienced by inmates, while abattoirs enable consumers to purchase
and eat meat with wilful blindness to the process of its production. Similarly, the
private space of 'home' serves the narrative purpose of safety and belonging while
providing the setting for much of the physical and sexual assault that occurs in
Western countries (Tyner 2012).

In contrast, violence in Other places is more visible. This violence is more
visible for several reasons. First, violence in Other spaces often takes the form of
armed conflict.[1] This violence takes place in public spaces (although it may also
penetrate private spaces) and, often though not always, receives media attention.
Through such media coverage of violence – the third of Williams' (1983) senses
of violence – colonizing tropes reiterate an ahistorical and decontextualized
portrait of violent Others. This homogenizing effect introduces the second reason
violence is more visible in Other places. While violence in the West is attributed
to dysfunctional individuals, violence within marginalized (racialized, colonized)
communities is understood to reflect the community as a whole (Bannerji 2000).
Through media coverage, unusually violent stories such as death by stoning in
Muslim countries or the vicious gang rape of an Indian woman in December 2012
receive disproportionate attention. Such extreme cases, despite being rare (at
least in their extremity), come to represent norms of legal proceedings or gender
relations, respectively. Moreover, attention on the rate of sexual assault in, for
instance, India (India's National Crime Records Bureau indicates that one woman
is raped every 20 minutes in India, Bohmwick 2012) occludes the presence of
sexualized violence in other locales. Based on Department of Justice data from
2006 to 2010, the Rape, Abuse, and Incest National Network reports a woman is
sexually assaulted every two minutes in the United States (n.d.). Drawing on data
from the Office of National Statistics in the United Kingdom, 536,000 individuals
experienced sexual assault in 2011/12, a number that translates to roughly one
sexual assault every minute (Office of National Statistics 2013), a rate that is
similar to that reported in Canada: 512,000 sexual assaults were reported on the
General Social Survey (approximately 1/10 of which are reported to police) in
2004 (Brennan and Taylor-Butts 2008).

It is not possible to draw direct comparisons between these rates of sexual
assault because of discrepancies between rates that are self-reported on anonymous
surveys and those rates that are calculated based on police statistics. Additionally,
rape is a far more specific act of violence than the broader category of sexual
assault, a precision that necessarily curtails the number of rapes reported. Yet,
even if it is not possible to directly compare India to the UK, the USA, and
Canada the data describing the rates of sexual assault in the latter three countries
indicate that that sexualized violence is a significant, if not epidemic, problem
in those countries themselves. Thus, even if one made the highly arguable claim

---

1   Notably, the West is often involved in such armed conflict, either directly through
military presence or political interference, or (arguably) indirectly through the arms trade
or historical practices of colonization and/or exclusion.

that sexualized violence is more frequent in 'Other' places, sexualized violence is clearly problematic in much of the so-called developed world.

'Elsewhere', violence is understood through the culture of violence theory, in which violence is assumed to inhere in cultural norms and practices. In this way, violence is 'entirely context specific, related exclusively to particular places and having no relationship to the global political economy' (Springer 2009: 306). Either interest or disinterest on behalf of individuals in the West with regard to violence in Other places/upon Other bodies can be legitimated because while interest represents a charitable (rather than self-interested) action, disinterest is justified on the grounds of irrelevance to one's own sphere of responsibility. In either case, Other violence is understood as elsewhere, entirely dissociated from quotidian Western lives.

Violence and Tourism

Several countries have tourist police. For instance, a Google search will quickly yield results reflecting the establishment of tourist police in many countries which have strong or developing tourist industries, including India, Nepal, Kenya, and Sri Lanka. Stated explicitly, or embedded implicitly, as the mission of these police forces is the personal security of the tourist and their property. Subsequent responsibilities include keeping hawkers away from tourists to prevent their experience from being disrupted (Nepal Police 2011) and protecting tourists from harassment (Kenya Ministry of Tourism 2013).[2] In this way, tourists are accorded special status within tourism-dependent countries and this status works to provide them with a material separation from the unruliness of locals, unruliness that ranges from harassment by beggars or touts to physical violence.

Given the relatively minor experiences against which tourist police are intended to insulate tourists, it can be argued that the tourist police are, in fact, present not because there are great risks to tourists and travellers, but rather because there are not significant risks. Tourist police can assist with the provision of an ideal experience free from Others who inconvenience tourists and travellers through their unruliness. The presence of tourist police, then, emphasizes the possibility of violence that provides meaning to ethnological travel at the same time that this presence indicates a lack of manifest physical violence.

In those cases in which tourists do experience physical violence, juridical processes favour speedy prosecutions and harsh sentences for those who inflict violence upon tourists. In the case of sexual assault of travellers and tourists, for instance, such violence is quickly and severely sanctioned:

---

2 Only the Sri Lankan Tourist Police indicate that their responsibilities include 'safeguard[ing] Sri Lankans from negative practice such as use of children for commercial sex, drugs, and other undesirable activities' (Sri Lanka Tourism Development Authority 2011).

- Two Thai men were sentenced to death within weeks of having raped and murdered an English tourist in Ko Samui, Thailand (Guardian Staff and Agencies 2006).
- In two separate incidents, when German travellers in Rajasthan, India were raped, the men who assaulted them were sentenced within one month of the assault (Chatterjee 2006, Indo-Asian News Service 2005).
- Three Bihari (India) men sentenced to life imprisonment after raping a Japanese tourist in May 2010, less than a month after charges were filed (Gaya 2010).
- Five Indian men were arrested the day after a Swiss tourist was gang-raped (Associated Press 2013).

The expedited indictments and tough sentences in these cases stand in considerable contrast to the bureaucratic sluggishness that characterizes the investigation and prosecution of sexual assaults of local women or of tourists when in their own countries.[3] These efforts to make quick convictions and administer harsh punishments reflect a deliberate decision by the governments to set an international precedent against violent sexualized crime against tourists, women in particular (Lozanski 2007: 312 n2). These decisions, in turn, reflect the negligible tolerance for violence that is manifest upon the bodies of travellers and tourists.

Indeed, the volatility of the tourism industry vis-à-vis violence has been demonstrated in high profile incidents of violence. For example, several scholars (Smyth, Nielson, and Mishra 2009, Putra and Hitchcock 2006, Henderson 2004) have identified the significant, if temporary, consequences of the bombings of two Bali nightclubs in a tourist district on 12 October 2002 for tourist arrivals to the island and to the country. In the aftermath of the bombings, those working within the tourism sector had to negotiate the material loss of tourism revenues and symbolic shift in Bali's reputation as a safe destination, an experience that flagged the inherent precariousness of tourism (Baker and Coulter 2007). Yet these bombings were not read as an attack on Bali, but rather an attack on tourists.

Given the proximity of the Indonesian island to Australia, Bali's reputation as a tourist destination for many Australians, and also the number of Australians who died as a result of the attack (88 of 202 people), the bombings were also read through lenses which cast Australia and Australians in particular as victims not just in the sense of the immediate attack, but in terms of a broader attack on culture and ideology (West 2008, Lewis 2006): 'the Bali bombing, despite its own international dimensions, became understood as an Australian disaster, primarily narrated through national mythologies and concerns, and conceived as a threat to the Australian way of life' (West 2008: 342). While West speaks to the attacks as a 'threat' towards Australian culture, I would suggest that the threat, if one existed, was not in and of itself adequate as a means to signify victimhood. Rather, it was

---

3   Indeed, India's National Crime Records Bureau indicates that one woman is raped every 20 minutes in India.

the transformation of this threat into a suicide bomb and a car bomb, subsequently detonated upon the bodies of (Australian) citizens that was significant. Following the bombings, Australian, American, British, Canadian, Scandinavian, and Japanese governments issued travel advisories for not just Indonesia, but Southeast Asia more broadly (Henderson 2004), thereby institutionalising a specific threat directed towards travellers and tourists and dissuading their citizens from taking on the role of travellers and tourists in these locations.

In addition to these governmental efforts to protect tourists, there are also preventative measures in place at the industry level to remove tourist vulnerability, at least vis-à-vis locals. For instance, many venues do not permit locals on the premises[4] as locals are understood, within tourist discourse, as a source of threat to person or property (Hutnyk 1996). Additionally, desirable spaces are designated as tourist spaces and mobility of locals into those spaces may be barred. Such barriers exist through direct prohibitions, such as those practiced at Varkala, Kerala in India in which the responsibilities of the lifeguards are not only to provide relative safety for the swimmers, but also to prevent Indian men from entering the space (Lozanski 2007). More indirectly, mobility is impeded through capital, or lack thereof. Highly desirable beach spaces are often held privately by the accommodations which front onto them. As a result, only guests within the hotel or resort are able to access the beach (Nowicka 2007). These practices highlight travellers' minimal tolerance for actual violence. While violence is understood to inhere in the locals, the tourism industry itself produces the idea of potential violence (Lozanski 2007) that creates ethnological desire and at the same time that the industry mitigates against the possibility of physical violence.

Travel as Edgework

Parallel to the violence that is understood to be outside of and distinct from the West, Others are also understood to be distinct, both physically and culturally. Tourists are understood to experience this difference via 'hermetically sealed' encounters (Lozanski 2013: 53). However, it is precisely through proximity to Others and to violence that travellers highlight their difference from tourists. Responding to a caricature of tourists as oblivious, camera-toting, resort-isolated individuals, many individuals who seek travel or tourism that is less damaging and more ethical (Butcher 2003) from their travel do so through the active construction of contrast vis-à-vis tourists. One means through which this construction takes place is through the purposeful avoidance of enclavic tourist spaces (Edensor 1998). Enclavic spaces, such as museums and memorials, are constructed with the tourist gaze – both domestic and international – in mind. The consumption of these

---

4   Notably, local Balinese were not permitted into the Sari Club – one of the bars bombed in Bali – thus limiting the number of locals who were killed in the October 2002 attacks (West 2008).

spaces is defined a semiotic architecture that gives physical direction and often also substantive insight through which tourists are guided through the space and content. Thus, the audience is directed both in their understanding or knowledge and their movement or participation in the site.

By contrast, travellers seek heterogeneous spaces – those characterized by spontaneity, the mundane activities of everyday life, and performances directed towards or intended for other locals. Such spaces include public squares, marketplaces, or other spaces in which cultural rituals or festivals are performed outside of formal venues (Markula 1997). These are 'unruly' spaces which are, through their production (Lefebvre 1991), 'not amenable to rule or discipline; ungovernable; disorderly, turbulent' (OED 2013): heterogeneous spaces are unruly spaces. They are spaces in which it is difficult to defend against violence either at the level of organized violence (Coaffee 2009) or in terms of interpersonal violence. The desire for heterogeneous spaces, for spontaneity, and for volatility points to travellers' expectations of non-violence, while that very physicality of violence enacted upon the bodies of locals, serves to define local people and geographies as appropriate sites of alternative tourism.

Additionally, travellers seek unmediated engagement with locals and local culture. Rather than conceptualizing their encounters with the individuals who work in the tourism industry to facilitate their experience, travellers are inclined to see such individuals (including guides, touts, and taxi drivers) as tainted. Bhattacharyya's (1997) analysis of guidebooks – a significant, though relatively informal way, through which alternative forms of travel culture are institutionalized and reproduced (Sorenson 2003) – indicates that those do not provide 'service with a smile' are undesirable (Bhattacharyya 1997), in contrast to the 'picturesque Others'. The former are designated by travellers to be 'unruly' and are questioned as to whether they are 'real' representatives of their culture (Lozanski 2010). More desirable Others have no direct financial interest with the traveller (Kontogeorgopoulos 2003) and are submissive either as they facilitate the travellers' experiences or as they provide foci for the tourist gaze (Urry 1990). They also do not disrupt narratives of Otherness and instead can be easily incorporated into travel narratives.

This story is constructed through a traditional narrative architecture in which the traveller-cum-Hero encounters a Villain – as troublesome local, dangerous situation or strenuous experience – and ultimately the Hero conquers the Villain. In this metaphoric analysis, Whitehead's (2005) theorizing of masculinity through the Hero-Villain interaction is productive: masculinity must be produced through Heroic acts (i.e. conflict with a Villain), however these acts are always finite and subject to being undone. As such the production of masculinity is a necessarily reiterative process. Transposing Whitehead's Hero-Villain from masculinity model onto travel, travellers construct themselves through ongoing encounters that are crudely dichomotized into hostile confrontations with 'unruly' Others or meaningful encounters with 'real' Others (Lozanski 2010). In the former, it is the Other him/herself who is overcome in order to achieve traveller status; in the latter, it is instead the cultural difference presumed to inhere in the Other that must be overcome in order to successfully construct the identity of a traveller. Notably, Whitehead's Hero requires not just a Villain, but also a 'non-man' against which to construct himself. While the Villain is granted agonic status, the 'non-man' represents the failure of masculinity through his failure to engage in the confrontation crucial to the production of manhood. In travel discourses, 'tourist' replaces 'non-man' as one who does not engage in ongoing practices of challenge in order to establish status as an active, rather than passive, subject.

Despite efforts by many travellers to distinguish themselves from tourists, travel still operates with reference to tourism and the security it provides. As literary scholar Paul Fussell suggests:

> If the explorer moves towards the risks of the formless and the unknown, the tourist moves towards the security of pure cliché. It is between these two poles that the traveller mediates, retaining all he can of the excitement or the unpredictable attaching to exploration and fusing that with the pleasure of 'knowing where one is' belonging to tourism. (1980: 39)

As a practice situated between the unknown and cliché, travellers participate in contradictory desire for both safety (exemption from physical violence) and risk (potential violence). In this way travellers engage in '"edgework", an attempt to negotiate the razor's edge between life and death, order and chaos, control and uncertainty, and so forth' (Fletcher 2010: 8). Fletcher (2010) explores constructions of edgework through the concept of a 'public secret'. In his ethnographic analysis of adventure tourists, Fletcher finds that these tourists wish to be in danger – a means to highlight extent of their adventurous Self – while simultaneously remaining safe – due to the extensive protocols and expertise of the organizations facilitating their adventures. Those engaged in ethnological travel, I argue, similarly desire to be open to the risks of Otherness while simultaneously assured that they are in no imminent danger. In Wendy Shaw's reflections on ethnographic fieldworkers-cum-travellers/tourists, Papua New Guinea provides the backdrop against which researchers and travellers have the 'potential for encountering a consumable moment of danger' (Shaw 2011: 470). Emerging from the distance/difference collapse of Othering, the structure of travel narratives reflects the edgework between unruliness and the threat of physical violence and manifest physical violence: 'travellers tell tales of amazing landscapes and local peoples, but often set the scene to enhance the impact of the frightening punch line. Our narrations become polished recitations of narrow escapes and thwarted horrors' (Shaw 2011: 474).

Managing these situations – or at least subsequently narrating these situations as if they were coolly and successfully managed – is key to maintaining 'road status', the cultural capital associated with independent forms of travel (Sorenson 2003). Road status emanates from 'hardship, experience, competence, cheap travel, along with the ability to communicate it properly' (Sorenson 2003: 856). This desire for hardship and experience, in order to demonstrate competent navigation, necessarily involves moving beyond the metaspaces (Hottola 2005) – typically the backpacker slums or other spaces constituting on-the-'off-the-beaten-trail'-trail – of physical and cultural comfort. Yet even outside of these spaces, travellers expect(and often receive) safety in the face of unruliness or of threat – either individual (as in mugging) or contextual (as in civil unrest).

As travellers do not understand themselves as unruly or uncivilized Others, there is an expectation not only of difference, but of occupying a space outside of that difference. While travellers seek heterogeneous spaces that reflect more off-the-beaten-path experiences and operate outside of the safety and cultural controls of enclavic spaces, there is also a mostly implicit (though sometimes explicit) sense of entitlement to control and safety within those spaces. Although travellers desire spontaneity, as well as the chaos and risk that is associated with Otherness, they also desire to be exempted from it.

Reflecting on the interruption of her anthropological fieldwork by a massacre of tourists and locals by Rwandan rebels in the immediate area in which she was staying, Elizabeth Garland (1999) suggests this expectation of exemption is not without basis. Following the massacre, she was evacuated to the relative safety of the United States while residents of the community in which she was studying were left behind to negotiate the devastation to their community. Yet, Garland recognizes, this expectation is also entirely illegitimate in the sense that the narrative of difference – a difference through which Otherness is constituted and the Self achieves the cultural and social capital of encounters with that Otherness – is, in part, constructed through both narratives and material realities of volatility in the daily lives of those Others. Thus, expectations of exemption from violence exist not as personal ignorance or arrogance, but part of the same cultural discourse that recognizes and values travel:

> By traveling to them [dangerous places] anyway, we unconsciously assert ourselves as the sort of people who are intrinsically invulnerable to the dangers those places represents. One might even say that it is the prospect of encountering and surviving danger – or at least a bit of 'excitement' – that motivates us to leave home in the first place. (Garland 1999: B5)

Although danger may be knit into Western travellers' rationale for travel as a marker of difference from much of the Western context (Spilerman and Stecklov 2009), the transformation of danger – insomuch as danger reflects threat or possibility of harm – into material harm is inconsistent with travel discourse. I invoke 'discourse' here not to refer to narratives of travel, but instead in a Foucauldian sense in which discourse outlines the parameters of what it is possible to think. That is, while danger underpins the discourse of travel, actual harm cannot be understood within the discourse of travel, but rather undoes the possibility of travel as both an individual experience and a cultural practice for which individuals are recognized.

At a cultural level, manifest violence – in contrast to threatened violence – flags travellers' position both outside of and inside of difference: while travellers can never fully overcome the difference through which cultural travel is framed as a result of their very subject position as travellers, they can never fully be outside of that difference either. If violence is manifest upon the bodies of locals, it may similarly be manifest upon the bodies of travellers. Thus, manifest violence rejects the erroneous expectation of universal security for citizens of the West and highlights the possible hostility of those who cannot travel but are themselves subjected to travel (Kincaid 1988). Manifest violence also reflects the classed inequalities and individual negotiations of gendered/racialized power that inflect ethnological travel (Lozanski 2007) and thus rejects the hyper-individuated Western self of travel. Thus, culturally, manifest violence emphasizes shared physical vulnerability, a similarity that disrupts the Self-Other dichotomy upon which much travel is predicated, and the broader socio-political and economic contexts within which travel operates.

At an individual level, the actualized experience of violence challenges travellers' claims to cultural savvy, as travellers' experiences of manifest violence may be interpreted as their inability to read a situation as overly perilous or to successfully negotiate the edge between risk and safety. These possible misjudgements undermine claims of competence which are critical means to establish travellers' identities as such (Sorenson 2003). Moreover, the experience of manifest violence recalls the oblivion or naivety associated, in the discourse of travel, with tourists.

The Intrinsic Violence of Travel

If travel is indeed a means to cultural engagement, that engagement necessarily takes place in a context of violence. Much like the violence that, noted above, takes place privately within travellers' home communities, violence of a more public nature exists in many spaces of difference, spaces that are deemed worthy of travel because of that very difference. Certainly, violence inheres in the at-home lives of many travellers and thus it is specious to expect that violence is not woven through spaces away from home. Moreover, it is the case that travellers are themselves implicated in the commission of manifest violence, violence against locals (Lozanski 2007) and, undoubtedly, violence against each other.

If there is to be an actual effort to overcome cultural difference, violence has to be recognized first of all as embedded in the lives of people who are more vulnerable. Participating in any kind of way in these lives means, therefore, exposing oneself to the corresponding threats of and manifestations of violence. Secondly, travellers must understand themselves as coming from a context of violence: that is, violence is not just 'over there' it is within their communities, and sometimes themselves, as well. In fact, Goldberg argues:

The generic image of the savage [that emerged historically] represented violence, sexual license, a lack of civility and civilization, an absence of morality or any sense of it ... . [w]ith the psychological interiorizing of the moral space in late medieval thinking, the savage man came to represent the wild man within ... that confronts each human being. (1993: 23)

It is essential, then, to shift the focus of travel away from the technical details of difference which obscure the significant overlap in our lives, in our experiences of violence, in our complicity with violence, and – more generally – in our complex personhoods (Gordon 1996). It is only through recognition of shared qualities, characteristics, vulnerabilities, and shortcomings that meaningful exchange is possible.

References

Associated Press. 2013. Men arrested in India after Swiss tourist gang-raped: Woman reported attack near Orchcha, in central state of Madhya Pradesh. *CBC News Online,* 17 March. Retrieved 11 April 2013 from http://www.cbc.ca/news/world/story/2013/03/17/swiss-tourist-gang-raped-india-arrests.html.

Azarya, V. 2004. Globalization and international tourism in developing countries: Marginality as a commercial commodity. *Current Sociology*, 52(6), 949–967.

Baker, K. and Coulter, A. 2007. Terrorism and tourism: the vulnerability of beach vendors' livelihoods in Bali. *Journal of Sustainable Tourism*, 15(3), 249–266.

Bannerji, H. 2000. *The dark side of the nation: Essays on multiculturalism, nationalism and gender*. Toronto: Canadian Scholars Press.

Bhattacharyya, D.P. 1997. Mediating India: An analysis of a guidebook. *Annals of Tourism Research,* 24(2), 371–389.

Bohmwick, N. 2012. Brutal New Delhi Gang Rape Outrages Indians, Spurs Calls for Action. *Time World Online Edition,* 19 December. Retrieved 2 May 2013 from http://world.time.com/2012/12/19/brutal-delhi-gangrape-outrages-indians-spurs-calls-for-action/.

Brennan, S. and Taylor-Butts, A. 2008. *Sexual assault in Canada: 2004 and 2007*. Ottawa: Statistics Canada. Retrieved 2 May 2013 from http://www.statcan.gc.ca/pub/85f0033m/85f0033m2008019-eng.pdf.

Butcher, J. 2003.*The moralisation of tourism: Sun, sand ... and saving the world?* New York: Routledge.

Chatterjee, R. 2006. Delay and denial. *The Tribune (India) Online Edition*, 26 April. Retrieved 17 September 2006 from http://www.tribuneindia.com/2006/20060426/index.htm.

Coaffee, J. 2009. Protecting the urban: The dangers of planning for terrorism. *Theory, Culture & Society,* 26(7–8), 343–355.

Conran, M. 2006. Commentary: Beyond authenticity: Exploring intimacy in the touristic encounter in Thailand. *Tourism Geographies*, 8(3), 274–285.

Edensor, T. 1998. *Tourists at the Taj: Performance and meaning at a symbolic site.* New York: Routledge.

Elsrud, T. 2001. Risk creation in traveling: Backpacker adventure narration. *Annals of Tourism Research,* 28(3), 597–617.

Fletcher, R. 2010. The emperor's new adventure: Public secrecy and the paradox of adventure tourism. *Journal of Contemporary Ethnography,* 39(1), 6–33.

Fussell, P. 1980. *Abroad: British literary travel between the Wars (electronic version).* Oxford: Oxford University Press.

Garland, E. 1999. An anthropologist learns the value of fear. *The Chronicle of Higher Education,* 7, B4-B5.

Gaya. 2010. Trial begins in Japanese tourist rape case. *The Indian Express,* 22 April. Retrieved 11 April 2013 from http://www.indianexpress.com/news/trial-begins-in-japanese-tourist-rape-case/609980.

Goldberg, D.T. 1993. *Racist culture: Philosophy and the politics of meaning.* Malden, MA: Blackwell Oxford.

Gordon, A. 1996.*Ghostly hauntings: Haunting and the sociological imagination.* Minneapolis: University of Minnesota Press.

Guardian Staff and Agencies. 2006. Pair face death penalty over student's murder, 18 January. Retrieved 17 September 2006 from http://www.guardian.co.uk/uk/2006/jan/18/ukcrime.travelnews.

Henderson, J. 2004. Managing the aftermath of terrorism: The Bali bombings, travel advisories and Singapore. *International Journal of Hospitality &Tourism Administration*, 4(2), 17–31.

Hottola, P. 2005. The metaspatialities of control management in tourism: Backpacking in India. *Tourism Geographies*, 7(1), 1–22.

Hutnyk, J. 1996. *The Rumour of Calcutta: Tourism, charity and the poverty of representation.* New Jersey: Zed books.

Indo-Asian News Service (IANS). 2005. Rapists given life term. *The Tribune (India) Online Edition,* 2 June. Retrieved 17 September 2006 from http://www.tribuneindia.com/2005/20050602/nation.htm#10.

Kenya Ministry of Tourism. 2013. Security. Retrieved 21 April 2013 from http://www.tourism.go.ke/ministry.nsf/pages/security.

Kincaid, J. 1988. *A small place.* New York: Farrar Straus & Giroux.

Kontogeorgopoulos, N. 2003. Keeping up with the Joneses: Tourists, travellers, and the quest for cultural authenticity in Southern Thailand. *Tourist Studies*, 3(2), 171–203.

Lefebvre, H. 1991. *The Production of Space*, trans. Donald Nicholson-Smith. Malden, MA: Blackwell.

Lewis, J. 2006. Paradise defiled the Bali bombings and the terror of national identity. *European Journal of Cultural Studies*, 9(2), 223–242.

Lozanski, K. 2007. Violence in independent travel to India: Unpacking patriarchy and neo-colonialism. *Tourist Studies*, 7(3), 295–315.

Lozanski, K. 2010. Defining 'real India': Representations of authenticity in independent travel. *Social Identities*, 16(6), 741–762.

Lozanski, K. 2011. Independent travel: Colonialism, liberalism and the Self. *Critical Sociology*, 37(4), 465–482.

Lozanski, K. 2013. Encountering beggars: Disorienting travellers? *Annals of Tourism Research*, 42, 46–64.

MacCannell, D. 1976. *The tourist: A new theory of the leisure class.* Berkley, CA: University of California Press.

Markula, P. 1997. As a tourist in Tahiti: An analysis of personal experience. *Journal of Contemporary Ethnography*, 26(2), 202–224.

Mbembe, J.A. 2001. *On the postcolony.* Berkley, CA: University of California Press.

McClintock, A. 1995. *Imperial leather: race, gender and sexuality in the imperial context.* New York: Routledge.

Memmi, A. 1991[1965]. *The colonizer and the colonized.* Boston, MA: Beacon Press.

Munt, I. 1994. The 'other' postmodern tourism: Culture, travel and the new middle classes. *Theory, Culture & Society*, 11(3), 101–123.

Nepal Police. 2011. Tourist police: Tourist police for tourists' safety. Retrieved 21 April 2013 from http://www.nepalpolice.gov.np/tourist-police.html.

Nowicka, P. 2007. *The no-nonsense guide to tourism.* Toronto: New Internationalist.

Noy, C. 2004. This trip really changed me: Backpackers' narratives of self-change. *Annals of Tourism Research*, 31(1), 78–102.

Office of National Statistics. 2013. *Violent crime and sexual offences, 2011/12.* London: Office of National Statistics. Retrieved 2 May 2013 from http://www.ons.gov.uk/ons/rel/crime-stats/crime-statistics/focus-on-violent-crime/index.html.

O'Reilly, C.C. 2006. From drifter to gap year tourist: Mainstreaming backpacker travel. *Annals of Tourism Research*, 33(4), 998–1017.

Oxford English Dictionary Online. 2013. "un'ruly, adj. (and n.)" *Oxford University*, 13 March. Retrieved 18 April 2013 from http://www.oed.com/view/Entry/217421?redirectedFrom=unruly.

Putra, I.N.D. and Hitchcock, M. 2006. The Bali bombs and the tourism development cycle. *Progress in Development Studies*, 6(2), 157–166.

Rape, Assault, and Incest National Network. N.d. *How often does sexual assault occur?* Retrieved 2 May 2013 from http://www.rainn.org/get-information/statistics/frequency-of-sexual-assault.

Ray, L. 2011. *Violence and society.* Washington DC: Sage.

Rose, N. 1999. *Powers of freedom: Reframing political thought.* Cambridge: Cambridge University Press.

Said, E. 1979. *Orientalism.* New York: Vintage.

Shaw, W. 2011. Research journeying and the adventure/danger impulse. *Area*, 43(4), 470–476.

Smyth, R. Nielsen, I. and Mishra, V. 2009. 'I've been to Bali too' (and I will be going back): Are terrorist shocks to Bali's tourist arrivals permanent or transitory? *Applied Economics*, 41(11), 1367–1378.

Sorensen, A. 2003. Backpacker ethnography. *Annals of Tourism Research*, 30(4), 847–867.

Spilerman, S. and Stecklov, G. 2009. Societal responses to terrorist attacks. *Annual Review of Sociology*, 35, 167–189.

Springer, S. 2009. Culture of violence or violent Orientalism? Neoliberalisation and imagining the 'savage other' in post-transitional Cambodia. *Transactions of the Institute of British Geographers*, 34(3), 305–319.

Sri Lanka Tourism Development Authority. 2011. Tourist police. Retrieved 21 April 2013 from http://www.sltda.lk/tourist_police.

Tyner, J.A. 2012. *Space, place, and violence: Violence and the embodied geographies of race, sex and gender*. New York: Routledge.

Urry, J. 1990. *The tourist gaze: Leisure and travel in contemporary societies*. Thousand Oaks, CA: Sage Publications.

West, B. 2008. Collective memory and crisis: The 2002 Bali bombing, national heroic archetypes and the counter-narrative of cosmopolitan nationalism. *Journal of Sociology*, 44(4), 337–353.

Whitehead, A. 2005. Man to man violence: How masculinity may work as a dynamic risk factor. *The Howard Journal of Criminal Justice*, 44(4), 411–422.

Williams, R. 1983. *Keywords: A vocabulary of culture and society*. Rev. ed. New York: Oxford University Press.

World Health Organization. 2002. *World report on violence and health: Summary*. Geneva: World Health Organization.

Chapter 4

The Enchantment of Violence: Tales from the Balearics

Hazel Andrews

Introduction

In 2008 a disturbing case of false imprisonment and rape came to the World's media attention. It was the by now infamous case of the Austrian Josef Fritzl who in March 2009 was found guilty of rape, incest, murder and enslavement. Fritzl had imprisoned one of his daughters beneath the ground in a specially built cellar where she was held for 24 years during which time she gave birth to seven children as a result of the rapes suffered at her father's hands. The horrific story was greeted with shock and outrage not only that such horrendous crimes had been committed but that they had gone undetected for so long under the noses of other people. Fritzl was sentenced to life imprisonment in a secure institution for mentally ill offenders.[1] Sadly, Fritzl's case is not entirely unique; Natascha Kampusch was kidnapped and held in a cellar (also in Austria) for over eight years. During her time of incarceration she was allowed periods of respite from the prison, albeit under the watchful eye of her captor. In Belgium the serial killer and sex offender Marc Dutroux also had an underground dungeon in which he held many of his victims. In another case based in California USA, Jaycee Dugard was kidnapped and held for 18 years during which time she was repeatedly raped.

How do we feel when confronted with these stories? Certainly many feel disgust, horror, shock, outrage, distaste and discomfort. We may ask questions about how anyone can inflict such abuse and violence on other human beings. We experience feelings and ponder questions while the global media thrusts the incidents into our faces with sensationalist headlines, see for example the British tabloid newspaper *The Sun*'s 'Monster Fritzl's "animal children"'.[2] But what should our responses be when the incarceration and abuse of women are based on fun, are used to tell a story to entertain us? Do we feel or exclaim the same reactions to Gaston Leroux's eponymous phantom who kidnaps Christine to imprison her in the secret underground chambers of the Paris Opera house when we read the book, watch the film, go to the musical or listen to the CD as when

---

1   http://news.bbc.co.uk/1/hi/7371959.stm. Accessed October 2012.

2   http://www.thesun.co.uk/sol/homepage/news/1111698/Monster-Josef-Fritzl-Animal-children-Dungeon.html. Accessed October 2012.

we learn of Josef Fritzl? *Is* the *Phantom of the Opera* different because it is, after all, just a story?

Doubtless different interpretations can be applied to Leroux's work and its subsequent popular manifestations. It is not my intention to interrogate them here, but rather, by drawing attention to the work, to demonstrate that acts of violence (and particularly those against women) are often interwoven in what appears to be quite harmless entertainment, suitable for all ages, and are rendered innocuous in the guise of fun. It is the apparent ordinariness or everydayness of story-telling, of which the *Phantom of the Opera* is an example, that makes the plot seemingly benign. As Das contends 'violence, far from being an interruption of the ordinary, is folded into the ordinary' (Das 2008: 283). However, both the *fiction* of the Phantom and the *facts* of Fritzl have in common a desire to secret a woman away and have total domination over her.

This chapter is a discussion of the ways in which violence towards women appears to be sanctioned in aspects of the everyday practices of tourism. By examining two examples, one from Menorca and the other Mallorca (both islands in the Balearic chain located in the western Mediterranean), I will demonstrate that aspects of storytelling as part of tourists' entertainment and leisure activities and related touristic practices take the form of symbolic violence (Bourdieu 1991) which serves to reinforce structural relations of male power and dominance over women.

I will begin with the example from Menorca followed by the example from Mallorca outlining the field of action and associated practices and performances in both settings. Each example involve a form of story-telling based on the activities of pirates, they both form part of tourists' and leisure seekers' entertainment on the different islands. The discussion that follows will focus on ways in which both stories allow for a misrecognition of violence by serving to reinforce and naturalise unequal gendered relations casting women as the property of men and belonging to the domestic sphere all in the guise of fun.

Into Xoroi's Cave

Menorca is the second largest of the Balearic islands and a popular holiday destination. It offers typical sun, sea and sand holidays as well as an array of other facilities and attractions that fall into the pantheon of tourism products – historical monuments, gastronomy, sport, festivals and so on. The island is well renowned as a family destination catering for children of all ages (Obrador-Pons 2012). The official on-line tourism portal of the Balearic Islands[3] lists the many attractions and activities that Menorca has to offer, including the itemisation of a number of 'don't miss it' and 'get to know' attractions. On this inventory is Cova d'en Xoroi (translated as Xoroi's Cave).

---

3   http://www.illesbalears.es/ing/minorca/home.jsp. Accessed October 2012.

Cova d'en Xoroi is in the municipality of Alaior on the Island's south coast. It is a natural formation in that the cave system on the cliff edge is the result of geology and processes of erosion and weathering. The caves are put to good use as a tourist attraction and leisure facility offering night-time entertainment in the form of clubbing and during the day fulfilling the role of a café-bar. The site consists of a number of connecting caves where it is possible to wander through, buy refreshments, and either sit inside or outside on one of the terraces and admire the view over the sea. The latter is a particularly popular activity around sunset when the terraces afford views over the sea towards the setting sun (Figures 4.1 and 4.2 below).

Marketing material attached to the caves describe them as 'spectacular', 'impressive', 'steeped in mythology' and 'touched by history and washed by the sea'. The history and mythology referred to relates to a story about a man called Xoroi after whom the caves are named. Xoroi is described as both a man with an unknown past[4] and a legendary Turkish pirate.[5]

The story goes as follows: Xoroi arrives on Menorca by sea, although there is a mystery as to exactly how he came ashore being thought to be the only survivor of a shipwreck. He sets up 'home' in the caves. Coincidentally nearby dwellings are subject to break-ins and thefts which become attributed to Xoroi. During one of these incidents Xoroi is said to abduct a young woman – described as a 'damsel' and 'beautiful young girl' – who is about to be married. Neither Xoroi nor the young woman are seen for many years. Then one winter Menorca experiences an unusually heavy amount of snowfall and footprints leading to the caves appear in the snow. Local men arm themselves and follow the prints to the caves. Upon arrival at the caves Xoroi is discovered with a woman (the victim of the kidnap) and three children, described as 'the fruit of their love' in the cave's publicity material. Realising that he is cornered Xoroi throws himself into the sea, followed by his eldest son. Neither is ever seen again. The woman and the surviving two children are taken to the settlement of Alaior where they live out the remainder of their lives.

I visited Cova d'en Xoroi in 2008 with my family. The entrance fee cost ten Euros per adult and a 'free' drink was included as part of the cost. Once inside the cave complex one is free to wander between the various caverns which are generally dark and smell damp and musty, music is played. In places steep steps link the different levels of the cave system and terraces together. Tables and seating are both inside the caves and outside on the terraces. During the late afternoon of our visit the caves are already quite crowded and there is no seating available on the outside terraces. We wander around the site alternating between inside and outside, and claim our 'free' drink. As the sun begins to lower in the sky more and more people on the terraces are taking photographs of their partners, friends, and families against the backdrop of the setting sun.

---

4 Cova d'en Xoroi information booklet, 2008.

5 http://www.illesbalears.es/ing/minorca/home2.jsp?SEC=HOM&lang=0004&id= 00001051. Accessed October 2012.

Figure 4.1 Caves and Terrace Cova d'en Xoroi
Source: © Les Roberts 2008.

As part of the overall 'product' there is a souvenir shop. The shop sells postcards of the caves, CDs of music made by in the in-house production company Sa Cova Productions. Among the souvenirs are t-shirts, tea-towels, ashtrays and

Figure 4.2 A terrace, Cova d'en Xoroi
Source: © Les Roberts 2008.

information about the caves. Included in all this material are products aimed specifically at children which include an eight page paperback story booklet entitled '*Xoroi el pirata de los mares del sur*' (Xoroi the Pirate of the South Seas). The cover of the booklet depicts a colourful scene of a man floating in the sea clinging to a log and staring up with his un-patched eye at a cliff face pocked with the mouths of caves. Behind him is a ship's mast flying a flag with a crescent moon. All of this is in cartoon form. The story continues inside in black and white, simple cartoon drawings depicting the different elements of the story: Xoroi stealing chickens; Xoroi abducting the young woman; Xoroi, the woman and a dog in a happy domestic scene inside the caves; a group of angry local men; following the footprints in the snow; discovering Xoroi and his family in the caves; Xoroi and son jumping from the cliff-face to their deaths in the sea. Each drawing is accompanied by a short explanatory text. The image on page three of the booklet is the abduction scene: a smiling Xoroi is shown bounding off carrying the nameless young woman who has a clear look of distress and is tied with rope from upper waist to mid-calf, her arms flailing. Two hapless looking adults – presumably her parents – peer from around the front door of a house.

Part of the official tourism discourse of Menorca the story is presented as a tale of love, romance and passion. One of its main functions is to make the caves an

Figure 4.3 Pirates Adventure building
Source: © Hazel Andrews 2009.

attractive tourism offer. As my discussion will demonstrate the marketing material and merchandise associated with the caves makes no acknowledgement of the violent reality of piratical practices and in effect trivialises the abuse of women.

The second example, to which I now turn, is based on a particular piece of entertainment – again involving pirates – aimed specifically at the tourist market visiting Mallorca. It is taken from a much larger ethnographic study involving periods of participant observation in the resorts of Palmanova and Magaluf located to the south west of the capital Palma in the municipality of Calvià.

Aha Me Hearties!

Mallorca is the largest of the Balearic islands and a very popular tourist destination receiving in excess of eight million tourists in 2011.[6] The island attracts visitors from a number of European countries of which Britain is one of the lead suppliers. The dominance of some nationalities in certain areas has given many resorts a distinctive 'national' character based on the origin of the visitors. Magaluf and Palmanova,

---

6   http://www.caib.es/sacmicrofront/contenido.do?mkey=M10072911244127834137& lang=EN&cont=27994. Accessed October 2012.

Figure 4.4 Entrance to Pirates Adventure
Source: © Hazel Andrews 2009.

but especially Magaluf, can be understood as having a particular 'British'[7] feel. This quality is not just based on the derivation of the holidaymakers but also in the

---

7   A word I use advisedly but as a means of 'short hand' to encompass all those originating from England, Wales, Scotland and Northern Ireland. It is also the case that the descriptors of British and English are often used interchangeably.

facilities that can be found in the resorts. The shops, bars, restaurants and hotels cater for the demands of their clients. This is a two-way process in that what is offered helps to shape demand. Thus the flavour of the resorts is shaped by the presence of British imported food and drink: bacon, sausages, breakfast cereals, milk, bread, beer and so on. Many of the establishments carry 'British' names: The White Horse, The Tartan Arms, The Geordie Pride and The Willows to name but a few. In addition the Union Jack is used as a way of signalling a sense of identity (and common language) appearing in shop signs, on menus or flown from balconies by tourists, along with flags – St George, St Andrew and the Red Dragon flag of Wales – that specify more explicitly the origin of the tourist. The Britishness of the resorts is also heightened by the main language of communication being English, added to by the broadcasting of English language television in the form of satellite programmes from soap operas to talent shows and endless repeats of British sitcoms.[8] I will now discuss my second example *Pirates Adventure*, which although located in Magaluf attracts British tourists from all over the island during the main tourist season.

Pirates Adventure

Pirates Adventure is part of late evening and night-time entertainment on offer to tourists visiting Mallorca during the high summer season. The performance is aimed at, and predominately patronised, by British tourists and is one of the main attractions in the area (if not the island) for the charter tourism market, with coach loads of tourists brought from other parts of Mallorca. Tickets to the performance are sold by all the major British tour operators as well as the independent travel agents in the resorts. The performance takes place in a purpose built building (Figures 4.3 and 4.4). *Pirates Adventure* can be interpreted in many different ways for example what it tells us about constructions of national identity and gendered spaces (Andrews 2009, 2011). However, my purpose here is to examine the show more explicitly in relation to the misrecognition of violence because it exemplifies so well the 'innocence' of violence in everyday practices which in turn serve to underscore and legitimise the violence of structural relations. I will begin by describing the show.

There are two types of performance on offer: Family Pirates and Adult Pirates. The differences between the two are that the former starts and finishes earlier in the evening than the latter, a couple of the games played differ and the family show is toned down in terms of the type of language used. For example, one of the main characters in the show, the French Pirate – Jacques Lafitte – is in Adult Pirates referred to as 'that French Bastard', in the family show this is moderated to 'that French poof' or 'that French pillock'. However, the format and story line of the performance is more-or-less the same for both versions.

---

8 For a more detailed discussion of the nationality of Palmanova and Magaluf see Andrews 2005, 2010, 2011.

Queues begin to form outside the venue for both versions of the performance well before it is due to begin. For Adult Pirates the show starts at 11.30pm, but by 10.15pm people are queuing to get in. At 10.45pm, by which time the queue is considerably longer, people are admitted to the building. As the line moves towards the entrance each individual is given a strip of black material depicting a skull and crossbones and the wording pirates. These pieces of material can be worn as a bandanna around the head or tied around the neck or wrist. Everyone has their (group) photo taken along with a Pirate and these are presented for purchase later on in the evening.

Once inside as people are being seated and waiting for the show to begin other merchandise is offered for sale including plastic silver swords and black pirates scarves decorated with a skull and cross bones. During this waiting period each table is visited by a member of the cast drawn from the lead British Pirates. In doing this the audience is divided into four teams with the idea that they will support 'their' pirate and be, at various points in the show, in competition with each other. Advice is also given as to how to get more drinks. For sangria it is a case of holding an empty jug in the air and for beer raising a copy of the menu. The four teams are based on the British pirates Blackbeard, Captain Scarlet (the only lead woman pirate), Barbarossa, and Sir Francis Drake.[9] The story line of the show is as follows: The British pirates have been recruited by Sir Henry Morgan to help him to maintain his position over Jacques Lafitte in the ownership of some Moroccan treasure. The main narrative of the show is based on this conflict with each side demonstrating its abilities through acrobatics, dancing and gymnastics. In the first act the French are vanquished and the British reassert their authority.

The performance begins with Captain Darling (on other occasions Sir Henry Morgan opens the show) advising the audience 'if you are easily offended, if you don't like blue things or swearing piss off, you know where the door is'. The next step is to explain the background story. The attention of the audience is drawn to a treasure chest, which is full of Moroccan gold, jewellery and crown, which is held in the air by Darling. He points to the back wall of the theatre upon which is a cartoon-like painting of a beach scene depicting a treasure chest and a number of human skulls. The character of Jacques Lafitte is introduced as 'that evil French Bastard', which the audience are encouraged to shout at him every time he appears on stage. Among the hostile comments aimed at the French is 'we don't want the French here do we?' In one show the audience are told that Lafitte could be a German. Every time the French are mentioned members of the audience boo.

The next step is the playing of the 'Yes/No'. There is an audience representative of each Pirate's team. The object of the game is to answer all of the questions put by Captain Darling without using the words 'yes' or 'no'. This ranges over several questions with the prize for succeeding in answering all questions without using

---

9   For a fuller discussion of the names and histories of these characters and the conflating of history and geographical distance see Andrews 2011.

the prohibited words being a bottle of champagne. There are occasions when no-one wins. The men are often insulted by the compère and the physical appearance of the women commented upon. In the Family Pirates version of the game the contestants are also adults, but when they are tripped up their treatment is less brutal than that in the adult version of the show, and rather than insults from the compère the audience are told to shout 'adios', after a count of three. There is a sense of fun but there are also feelings of discomfort as the participants are laughed at and humiliated through insults from the master of ceremonies. The playing of this game at the very beginning of the show serves to instil a sense of competition between members of the audience whilst also subjecting them to a form of control by the performers. The sharing of enjoyment in the put-down of the contestants makes the audience complicit with the aim of the show's narrative, which is not just about defeating the 'French Bastard' but also belittling him.

The entertainment proceeds with the British pirates celebrating their victory over the French, the wrecking of their ship La Hispaniola and the capture of the treasure. At this point the performance involves acrobatics, juggling and twirling fire torches. During this part of the show Captain Scarlet is the object of attention from the other male 'British' captains as they attempt to kiss her, but never succeed as she ducks out of the way and the two men almost embracing are left poking their tongues out at each other. The whole time the audience are shouting, cheering and clapping for their captain. There is an air of excitement and people are laughing and joking. This part of the performance is followed by an interval for dinner. During this time people engage in mock fights with recently purchased plastic swords and can become even more like pirates by having their faces painted and buying more pirate souvenirs.

The second half of the production is mainly given over to the 'French' pirates. Jacques Lafitte appears and shouts of 'you French bastard' come from the audience. Some people stand-up and gesticulate angrily as they yell at the pirate. Even at the end of the show when the audience applauds the performers 'Jacques Lafitte' is greeted with boos and insults. As the French and British fight the audience cheers on their designated captains. Finally, the British are overcome and it is the French turn to party. This section of the play consists of very skilled gymnastics, acrobatics, and some dancing.

The story continues and the British re-emerge for a final battle in which they defeat the French. During this scene a 'French' woman pirate is about to be killed, but orders are given 'put her below deck there's washing-up to be done. It's women's work'. The captured Jacques Lafitte is made to walk the plank, as he goes down behind the ship two inflatable sharks are thrown in the air and there is a burping noise. In Family Pirates the audience are asked 'shall we kill him?' to which the response is 'yes', then he walks the plank, the sharks burp, 'he is dead' is announced and everyone cheers. The crown from the treasure chest is lifted into the air accompanied by more cheers from the audience. At this point members of the audience are encouraged by the tour operator representatives to stand up and sing along to the songs that are being played and to wave their arms in time with the music.

Following the main part of the show there is another audience participation game in which eight contestants play a version of the game musical chairs. That is they to go to the audience to collect items and in the meantime the chairs on stage are reduced in number. The participants return to the stage after each object is collected and are then told what to get next. There is an emphasis on speed as the contestants are in competition for a seat on stage. Objects for collection might include a pair of boxer shorts, a white bra, condoms, or a 20 pound note. In Family Pirates different items are asked for, such as a pair of sunglasses, laces and a postage stamp.

Whatever the combination of goods, in Adults Pirates there is one 'article' that is always put up for collection: a topless woman, or a woman who is prepared to bare her breasts on stage. At this point in the game the audience and contestants are egged on by the presenter with the constantly cited quip of 'get your tits out for the boys'. During one show the women come on stage topless and sit on the laps of the contestants, one participant bounces the breasts of his partner up and down as she sits on his knees. One young woman is pulled on to the stage but she does not want to go topless. Another more willing young lady comes on to the stage and sits on the lap of the first woman. Once each player has a woman on the stage topless or otherwise the women are then asked to stand up one at a time and exhibit their breasts to which the audience cheers. The compère tries to cajole the more reticent woman by repeating what has by now become the mantra-like 'come on get your tits out for the boys', when she still refuses to do so he states 'don't worry lads it wouldn't be worth it'. One woman has not been sunbathing topless so her breasts are white and the host says 'I tell you what love don't you ever think of getting them out on the beach?' In one show the women all enter the stage clothed and are lined up in a row. Each one is asked to expose her breasts, with constant references to 'getting your tits out for the boys'. One young woman with a large bust is requested to show her breasts three times and to come to the front of the stage to do so. Another of the women does the splits, and is asked 'can you do it with your tits out?' She is asked to repeat the feat twice. Following the exhibition of bare breasts the entertainer advises 'you notice we didn't take any chairs away then, that's because we're sexist'.

During a performance of *Family Pirates* another audience participation game is played. This involves a woman contestant. On stage is a large wooden board against which 'Sir Francis Drake' demonstrates axe throwing. The woman is asked to stand against the board with her arms stretched out and she is blindfolded. She is told that on the count of three an axe will be thrown. At three Drake walks up to the board and bangs an axe into it and close to the contestant. Each time this happens the blindfold is lifted so the woman can see where the axe 'fell'. Captain Darling, who is compèring, comments, 'I bet you wish you'd shaved your armpits'. The woman is then asked to stand with her legs apart, as she complies Darling shouts 'open wider this is Magaluf' and the audience cheer. He then says, 'your legs are crying', implying that she has wet herself. When the game is over the woman has won a bottle of champagne. As she goes to collect the drink from the bar Darling calls out: 'by the way the toilets are over there'.

The Enchantment of Violence

Pirates Adventure can be deconstructed and read at a number of different levels and for different meanings in terms of how it can be understood as entertainment, promoting a sense of national identity based on foregrounding historical Anglo-French conflicts, as well as those with other European neighbours in reference to the Germans and through the historical pastiche by which some of the characters in the story represent the Spanish (Andrews 2011). However, it is what it tells us about the role of symbolic violence and in particular the contribution that makes to how women are viewed which is my main concern in the present discussion and it is to the analysis of both the pirate story from Menorca and the Pirates Adventure performances in Mallorca that I now wish to turn.

I completed the fieldwork on Mallorca for my PhD quite some time (nine years) before I holidayed in Menorca and visited the Caves D'en Xoroi. On Mallorca I was engaged in 'scholarly activity' and was by-and-large on my own; on Menorca I was on a family holiday and for a much shorter period of time compared to my fieldwork. Does this then bring to the fore of the discussion possible different epistemological foundations for understanding my interpretations or is that having conducted participant observation my ethnographer's eye accompanies me everywhere? I do not have a ready answer but what I can say is that there are two stories both of which involve pirates, both of which are premised on ideas of fun, indeed highlight fun, can be easily understood as entertainment and as such are stories based on the misrecognition of violence (Bourdieu 1991) because within all the fun and frivolity are stories of abuse, power and domination which appear so ordinary that the violence within them is legitimated.

In the *Logic of Practice* Bourdieu (1990) makes the point that in the context of the Kabyle House – the name given to the homes of the Kabyle Berbers of Algeria – there are few institutions that dominate the social world, instead domination is achieved through inter-personal relations in the form of gift giving, obligation and hospitality which disguise and/or emolliate the power relations symbolically expressed in object and actions. As Thompson comments 'it enables relations of domination to be established and maintained through strategies ... which conceal domination beneath the veil of an enchanted relation' (1991: 24). Of tourism, Selwyn (2007) has made the case that tourism sets out to enchant. In his work on the political economy of enchantment, he argues that the processes involved in, and the elements designed to attract tourists to destinations, are premised on a symbolic exchange, and that part of this enchantment derives from 'an industry fuelled, inter alia, by ideas, values, and symbolic structures the purposes of which are to enchant, that is to shape imaginations, interpretations, and memories, and to otherwise enhance cognitive and emotional transformations' (2007: 49). I wish to extend this analysis and argue that the stories and mythologies woven within the two examples discussed in the preceding sections not only shape social relations and the imagination but feed off the imagination and reinforce pre-existing notions and fantasies. In general tourism businesses use myths to appeal to the imaginations and prior knowledge of potential tourists. Indeed, Urbain (1989) has observed that representations used in tourism narrate the consciousness and memory of the traveller. In the cases under consideration in this chapter through the stories and enactments of piratical activities a direct appeal is made to fanciful ideas of pirates and pirating in the minds of the tourists.

The Figure of the Pirate

It is worth reflecting on the figure of the pirate given that, as Cordingly (1995) notes, ideas about pirates are deep rooted in western imaginations. Indeed, Skoronek claims: 'at the dawn of the twenty-first century hardly a week passes without a discussion in the media about the topic of "pirates" and "piracy"' (2006: 286). What is being referred to by Skoronek encompasses a wide range of activity including illegal download of digital information: films, music, and software as well as the theft of ships and kidnapping of sailors and holiday makers.[10]

The figure of the pirate has been the subject of various discourses for over two centuries. One of the earliest accounts is Charles FL. Johnson's book of the 1700s *A General History of the Robberies and Murders of the Most Notorious Pirates* which claims to detail the lives and actions of notorious pirates and includes illustrations of some of the, by-now, best known characters, such as Edward Teach (alias Blackbeard). More recently we can identify children's classics – *Peter Pan* and *Treasure Island* – and more recently still Disney's *Pirates of the Caribbean* film series and Aardman Animations' *Pirates! In an Adventure with Scientists!* which are part of a long lineage of Pirate-based films to emerge from the popular film industry. The pirates that we encounter in these representations are often presented within a discourse of romance, adventure, fun and heroism, as 'lovable rogues' as well as being liminal-like figures tinged with danger who stand between authority and the 'common' person with the latter's interests at heart. However, as more recent piratical incidents demonstrate,[11] and as Cordingly reminds us, 'the real world of pirates was harsh, tough and cruel … Pirate captains were often vicious and sadistic villains' (1995: 282). I contend that the representation of pirates in both Menorca and Mallorca in the ways described in the preceding discussion fit the more romanticised version of who pirates were without reference to acts of torture and murder perpetrated by actual pirates. In

---

10 see for example *Somalia's Face of Modern Piracy* http://www.time.com/time/photogallery/0,29307,1858572,00.html.

11 BBC News – UK couple kidnapped by Somali pirates fear for lives www.bbc.co.uk/1/hi/england/kent/8371446.stm.

order to make clear the violent reality of pirates the following example describes one approach developed by a Pirate called Montbars of Languedoc: 'he would cut open the stomach of his victims, extract one end of his guts, nail to a post and then force the wretched man to dance to his death by beating his backside with a burning log' (Cordingly 1995: 157). Women would also be subjected to torture and this often took the form of disrobing and sexually abusing the victims. Acts perpetrated against women included that they were 'burned in parts that for decency' could not be named which suggests the genitals, stripped naked and burnt, and, in one case, stripped naked, stood in a wine barrel full of gunpowder and threatened with a lighted fuse (Cordingly 1995: 156). In addition in reporting on the antics of a Captain Gow, Cordingly draws on the work of Defoe (1725) explaining that in a raid on the island of Cava, Orkney 'they abducted three women [who were] "kept on board some time, and used so inhumanly, that when they set them on shore again, they were not able to go or to stand"' (1995: 150–51).

What interests me here is that whilst the entertainment of *Pirates Adventure* does not engage in acts of physical harm it nevertheless focuses on the body as a site for symbolic violence primarily through the sexualisation and disrobing of women almost mirroring the very sadistic and sexualised violence inflicted on the real life victims. Women in *Pirates Adventure* are presented as objects for titillation and partially stripped, the only lead woman pirate is made benign in not being named after a real life pirate – for example Anne Bonny and Mary Read – and therefore ideas of violence enacted by women are somewhat muted. Captain Scarlet, as she is called, is the focus of attention from male pirates who in their attempts to kiss her make her an object of desire and help to foreground ideas of romance and/or lust which along with the naming of part of the Pirates Adventure set as 'the pussy hole' clearly positions women, if not defines them, as sexual beings. I now wish to focus my analysis on what both sets of pirates (Xoroi from Menorca and Pirates adventure in Mallorca) and tourist attractions tell us about the role and treatment of women.

The Figure of the Female

As noted the character of Captain Scarlet is a lead pirate, as such she plays a role in commanding members of the audience in terms of audience participation. As one of the 'British' pirates she is on the winning side and this also affords her a certain degree of power but in comparison to her male counterparts her overall role in the show is less. However, she also serves a purpose – a possible romantic interest at best, and, as previously opined, the subject of unwanted male attention. In her studies of the militarisation of everyday life Cynthia Enloe (1988 and 2000) examines the way in which seemingly harmless practices serve to militarise and underscore actions with unrecognised violence. Thus militarisation is not just about being a member of the armed forces *per se*, but is 'a far more subtle process' (2000: 2). Enloe uses the example of Star Wars shaped pasta pieces in children's food, or condoms that have a camouflage pattern. 'Militarization does not occur simply in the obvious places but can transform the meanings and uses of people, things, and ideas located far from bombs or camouflaged fatigues' (2000: 289). With specific regard to women Enloe notes that in earlier days of western-based warfare women formed part of the army camps in their roles as domestics looking after the all-male soldiers. These 'camp followers' were ideologically marginalised from the main purpose of the military and their value understood as being able to 'service' the men. Both of these aspects can be applied to Scarlet who, I contend, is ideologically marginalised by the lack of a proper pirate's name but is seen as having a use value as a possible sexual partner. Enloe notes: '[i]f the husband was killed, his comrades vied to gain her services for themselves' (1988: 4). The playful competition between two of the lead male pirates for Scarlet's attention occupies the position of 'vying for her services'.

The usefulness of women is also recognised in the treatment of the captured female French pirate. Rather than kill her (which is the violent fate awaiting Lafitte) instructions are given to 'put her below deck there's washing-up to be done. It's women's work'. Not only does this seemingly flippant quip raise a laugh with the audience it serves to reinforce the role of women as belonging to the domestic world, and to perpetuate, through an act of symbolic violence, existing gendered power relations. The role of women in the domestic sphere and servicing men is further exemplified in the 'tits out for the boys' aspect of the musical chairs game. The exhortation of the women to bare their breasts and their admonishment if they do not places women not only as objects of sexual arousal and gratification for men but in the reduction of the women to a pair of breasts serves to de-humanise them. Elsewhere in Magaluf and Palmanova it is possible to purchase postcards of naked women exhibiting their breasts and genitals. More-often-than-not these poses are faceless. It is immaterial who the woman is, her personhood and identity is lost as she is reduced to her naked, natural – 'animal' – state in which her biological functions of reproduction and suckling are highlighted. Perniola (1989: 237) makes the following observation:

> Clothing prevails as an absolute whenever or wherever the human figure is assumed to be essentially dressed, when there is the belief that human beings are human, that is, distinct from animals, by virtue of the fact that they wear clothes. Clothing gives human beings their anthropological, social and religious identity, in a word – their being. From this perspective, nudity is a negative state, a privation, loss, dispossession.

The focus on reproduction and suckling primarily support the idea of the mother as nation. That is the connection between women and ideas of motherhood, family and associated thoughts about comfort and nurturing often lead to nations being represented in female form (Andrews 2011). As White (2003) observes, based on research undertaken in Russia, women reproduce the nation biologically, culturally and symbolically. To be able to dominate a woman is a way to also exercise power over her ability to reproduce and over the outcome of that reproduction. The assignation of the French woman pirate to below deck as a domestic removes her from the possibility of the reproduction of France due to the absence of French men to the possibilities of the reproduction of a form of Britishness as her new role is likely to include (forced) sexual activity with the British.

That women are sexual objects is further reinforced during the axe-throwing stunt when the female contestant is cajoled to open her legs wider. Again, Enloe's (1988, 2000) work is insightful, as she argues women did have value in army camps in terms of providing services for men – sexual, sanitation, food provision, care of the wounded – but could easily be dispensed with or subjected to violent punishment if it were thought that they were in the way. 'Women camp followers were barely tolerated by military commanders. So long as they provided supplies and services ... But as soon as a commander decided that they were slowing down the march ... camp followers were summarily purged' (1988: 2). Therefore, the domestic sphere to which women are assigned in Pirates Adventure, the normative gender relations presented elsewhere in the resorts and the violence exhibited towards women speak not even of a domesticity of a happy, warm, cosy home let alone equal standing between genders. Rather it is a world in which women must always be sexually available, as the 'tits out for the boys' mantra suggests; working within a framework of a stereotypical gendered division of labour; and always marginal to the main action of the male counterpart (Andrews 2009). There are two other features that the tales from Menorca and Mallorca link to with regard to the violent treatment of women and that is the figure of the 'abducted woman' (Das 2006) and as I will demonstrate 'the figure of the woman in the damp below'.

The Figure of the Abducted woman

The young woman in the story of Xoroi in Menorca is kidnapped and in the story of the defeat of the French in Pirates Adventure reference is made to the capture and imprisonment of women in the form of the woman pirate 'put below'. The disturbing events with which I opened this chapter all involve the removal of women from their homes and lives. In short all the women are abducted.

Writing in relation to Partition in India in 1947, itself a bloody and violent event in which hundreds of thousands died, Veena Das (2006) notes that on both 'sides' of the divide women were abducted and raped. What followed were attempts to 'recover' the women, restore them to their 'correct' place on either side of the divide, and re-establish the sexual contract in which a woman bears legitimate children fathered by her husband. Das links these events to the control and legitimisation of the sexual and reproductive functions of women as resolutely placed in the realm of a family in which men are the heads and that this, in turn, upholds the State: 'the *mise-en-scène* of abduction and recovery places the state as the medium for re-establishing the authority of the husband/father. It is only under conditions of ordered family life and legitimate reproduction that the sovereign can draw life from the family' (Das 2006: 36).

In the story of Xoroi there is a figure of an abducted woman, removed from her family and therefore taken out of circulation for marriage and reproduction within the legitimate social order. She is kidnapped by 'the other' and in her recovery the pirate and the couple's eldest son (the future head of a household) die. The state cannot be upheld by the position of an outsider as the head of family and nor by his son as he is a product of an unsanctioned union. In the story the maiden upon her 'rescue' (and as was often the case of the abducted women in Partition it is not necessarily obvious that she wishes to be restored to the social order from which she came) goes to live with her two children in the village and is thus repositioned in her rightful place. As the preceding discussion has shown real pirates engage in the abduction of women but the outcomes have been and are far from romantic.

Pirates Adventure removes a woman from her potential to reproduce the nation. The female French pirate put below deck is taken out of circulation for a French coupling and placed in a situation which opens her, as already observed, to the possibility of the reproduction of a form of Britishness, with the unspoken idea that she is likely to be the object of sexual attention in her new role. In addition, as noted, the statement that accompanies her incarceration 'there's washing up to be done, it's women's work' places her firmly within the domestic sphere, which is also her correct place in the social order. Both Pirates Adventure and the story of Xoroi draw attention to the role of women as procreators. In Pirates Adventure the audience is reminded of the sexual and reproductive role of women in the demands to get their tits out for the boys, often under much coercion, and refusal to participate in this is met with admonishment 'don't worry boys it wouldn't be worth it'. In other words for a woman to refuse to reveal her breasts on demand is to challenge her role in the sexual contract. The way to deal with her noncompliance is to punish her. What Pirates Adventure also does is link the idea of nation to woman and the role of the male in upholding that. The effervescence of Britishness that is evident in the show (and elsewhere in the resorts) is based on ideas of conflict. As Das comments 'women's allegiance to the state is proved by their role as mothers who bear legitimate children … and men learn to be good citizens by being prepared to die to give life to the sovereign' (2006: 35–6). Pirates Adventure works to show men as fighting heroes defending the honour of their country and ensuring that women know their correct place in the kitchen and bedroom.

In the preceding discussion I argue that we need to think carefully about such activities as Pirates Adventure and the story of Xoroi because they cloak violence towards women in the guise of fun. We can see from the news items presented at the beginning of this chapter and the reference to Das's work on Partition that such stories are also reality. Another element that the stories from Magaluf and Menorca have in common with the kidnappings and imprisonment of the women in the news stories from Europe and the United States is the secreting away of the abductees in places associated with below and dampness.

The Figure of the Woman in the Damp Below

In his classic text on the Berber House Bourdieu's (1973) discussion of the Kabyle dwelling provides an interpretation of the nature of its space. The lower part of the house is dark and damp and connected with sexual intercourse and giving birth; it is a place associated with women and animals. The upper part of the house is light and dry and seen as the sphere of men and fire. The positioning of people within the house is argued to be an expression of the organisation and wider structure of Berber society. 'The low and dark part of the house is also opposed to the high part as the feminine is to the masculine ... the opposition between the upper part and the lower part reproduces within the space of the house the opposition set up between the inside and outside' (1973: 100).

Female sexuality and the creation of desire can hold much power over men in their need for their bodily urges to be satisfied. For women, power can lie in the ability to refuse or accept intercourse and with this feelings of pleasure and intimacy. In Magluf the over valorising of the female breast serves to show women as sexual beings. At the same time, as Valerius observes, '[t]here is a close correspondence between the nation and women's bodies, whether they are material bodies biologically reproducing the nation ... or targets of ethnic rage and humiliation' (2003: 43). The role of women as reproducing the nation is argued by Das to be distinct from that of men. Men, she argues, are assigned a role in which they 'should be ready to bear arms for the nation and be ready to die for it' (2008: 285), whereas 'women's reproduction is seen to be rightly belonging to the state ... so as citizens they are obligated to bear "legitimate" children who will be, in turn, ready to die for the nation' (ibid.).

In the stories and events recounted above we see women placed in underneath, moist places – cellars, caves, lower deck. That which is associated with the 'natural' role of women is concerned with the lower, sexually productive parts of the female body. Part of the sexual allure of women is in the attraction of the vagina as dark, hidden and damp. Women incorporate and consume men during intercourse, they can hide and use the most potent part of the male body inside this damp, dark 'hole'. Problems arise when women refuse access, when they are seen to be too powerful and as a challenge to the dominant role of men and by corollary their place as the head of family and state and the natural protector of women in the wider social order. It seems that both the blatant (Fritzl and his ilk) and latent misogyny (in the form of symbolic violence) that accompanies many of these ideas is to subjugate women. The desire to maintain or reassert the social order as that dominated by men finds expression in both literally and metaphorically putting women below and reminding them of their need to be dark and damp.

Conclusion

Both women and men get kidnapped and undergo all sorts of violent treatment and abuse as part of this process. Not all women who are taken are held in 'places below'. However, as the start of this chapter demonstrates many women are incarcerated in such sites. These stories are troublesome, upsetting and are met with anger and the need for justice. After a time these events probably, for many, fade from memory and are largely forgotten, until the next time a similar scenario arises. The men who have perpetrated the acts in the news items cannot and should not be excused for what they have done. However, when reflecting on such heinous crimes it might also be worth thinking on how the micro-social order that they have sought to create is present in the wider social order in the symbolic language of touristic practices and how through the misrecognition of violence the various audiences are enchanted into the 'natural' order of things.

References

Andrews, H. 2009. '"Tits Out for the Boys and No Back Chat": Gendered Space on Holiday'. *Space and Culture* Vol. 12 (2): 166–182.

Andrews, H. 2011. *The British on Holiday. Charter Tourism, Identity and Consumption*. Bristol: Channel View.

Bourdieu, P. 1973. 'The Berber House', in Douglas, M (ed.) *Rules and Meanings: An Anthropology of Everyday Knowledge*, Harmondsworth: Penguin.

Bourdieu, P. 1990. *The Logic of Practice*, Cambridge: Polity Press.

Bourdieu, P. 1991. *Language and Symbolic Power*, Cambridge: Polity Press.

Cordingly, D. 1995. *Life Among the Pirates. The Romance and the Reality.* London, Abacus.

Das. V. 2006. *Life and Words. Violence and the Descent into the Ordinary*, Oxford: Oxford University Press.

Das, V. 2008. 'Violence, Gender, and Subjectivity'. *Annual Review of Anthropology* 37: 283–99.

Defoe, D. 1725. *An Account of the Conduct and Proceedings of the Late John Gow, alias Smith, Captain of the late Pirates, executed for Murther and Piracy committed on board the George Galley* London: John Applebee.

Enloe, C. 1988. *Does Khaki Become You? The Militarization of Women's lives*, London: Pandora.

Enloe, C. 2000. *Maneuvers. The International Politics of Militarizing Women's Lives*, London: University of California Press.

Johnson, C. 1962. *Lives of the Most Notorious Pirates*, London: Folio Society.

Leroux, G. 1995. *The Phantom of the Opera*. London: Penguin.

Obrador-Pons, P. 2012. 'The Place of the Family in Tourism Research: Domesticity and Thick Sociality by the Pool'. *Annals of Tourism Research* Vol. 39 (1): 401–420.

Perniola, M. 1989. 'Between Clothing and Nudity', in Feher, M (ed.) *Fragments for a History of the Human Body Part Two*, New York: Urzone Inc.

Selwyn, T. 2007. 'The Political Economy of Enchantment. Formations in the Anthropology of Tourism'. *Suomen Antropologi* 32 (2): 48–70.

Skowronek. Russell K. 2006. 'X Marks the Spot–Or Does It?: Anthropological Insights into the Origins and Continuity of Fiction and Fact in the Study of Piracy', in Skowronek and Ewen, Charles, R. *X Marks the Spot. The Archaeology of Piracy.* Gainesville: Florida University of Florida Press.

Urbain, J.D. 1989. 'The Tourist Adventure and His Images', *Annals of Tourism Research* Vol. 16 (1): 106–118.

Valerius, J. 2003. '(Dis-)Embodying the Nation: Female Figures, Desire and Nation Building in Early Twentieth-century Finland', in Cusack, T. and Bhreathnach-Lynch, S. (eds) *Art, Nation and Gender Ethnic Landscapes, Myths and Mother-Figures*, Oxford: Blackwell.

White, A. 2003. 'Mother Russia: Changing Attitudes to Ethnicity and National Identity in Russia's Regions', in Andall, J. (ed.) *Gender and Ethnicity in Contemporary Europe*, Oxford: Berg.

Chapter 5

Dealing with the Myths: Injurious Speech and Negative Interpellation in the Construction of Tourism Places

Louise C. Platt

Introduction

Whilst it must be acknowledged that the notion of injurious speech as a form of linguistic violence in relation to place image is not as serious as physical, and even, we can argue symbolic violence, the analytical scope that it offers us allows a nuanced consideration of how tourist places are created over time. Building on the very rationale of this collection, the chapter is responding to the call from Whitehead to explore violence, 'as a cultural expression or as a performance' (2004: 1). The representational forms of violence through the myths that have contributed to the construction of the identity of the city of Liverpool in the North West of England will be interrogated here framed by the work of Butler (1997a) on injurious speech and negative interpellation. The theories of Butler will be utilised as an analytical lens through which to examine the example of Liverpool and provide an interpretation of how place is (re)imagined.

Within tourism studies, it has been identified that myths contribute to the constitution of places, in both the consumption and in the constructions of the destination (in particular see the work in Selwyn 1996b). This chapter will consider how the myths of the city of Liverpool can be linked to popular culture, in particular on a national level. It will also briefly explain how the rebranding of Liverpool in 2008 for the European Capital of Culture (hereafter ECoC) depended on the mythologisation of the greatness of Liverpool's past. Myths are perpetuated through the rebranding process and the ECoC in Liverpool was a large scale event which looked to utilise these myths of greatness to 'shake off' (Boland 2008: 366) negative perceptions of the city. As Hall ponders,

> Yet it has to be questioned how far residents themselves use this discourse, or whether it is one provided by those in power both to justify their actions in regeneration and also to justify their inability to transform the landscape. (2003: 195)

There is a balance between reimagining the identity of a much-maligned city and responding to the lived identities of local people. The complex processes of power and subjection to power are key in the framework presented here in this chapter.

Whilst much of Butler's work (in particular 1993, and [1990] 2006) focuses on gender being performatively produced, Borgersonis adamant that Butler is primarily a phenomenologist in that she, 'has sought to understand the paradoxes and complexities of meaning and being' (2005: 65) and her theories are about processes of becoming beyond solely gender identity. Butler developed her notions of performativity as a method to critique and challenge the ways in which gender is constituted. She rejects the notion that gender is innate, but rather, 'a kind of becoming or activity'([1990] 2006: 152). This suggests that it is not a fixed idea but is a process. In Butler's work, the subject is formed through a process of citationality. She draws on Derrida who argues that, '[c]ould a performative utterance succeed if its formulation did not repeat a "coded" or iterable utterance[...]?'(1988: 18). Indeed, what he is pointing out is that through processes of citation, performatives hold their power. Butler argues that it is precisely through iteration that we present a performance of normative identity, '[s]uch norms are continually haunted by their own inefficacy; hence, the anxiously repeated effort to install and augment their jurisdiction' (1993: 237). She is asserting that speech acts only provisionally succeed due to processes of reiterative convention (1997a). Therefore, in the interpellation we are subjected but the instability of this allows for creativity, and in this case, the resignification of place.

The example offered in this chapter is based on an ethnographic study conducted during 2008 and 2009 of Liverpudlian identity using the ECoC award through which to study the place and people's identities. The chapter will begin with an outline of the field of action and how Liverpool came to hold the ECoC award. The chapter will proceed by providing depth to the theoretical underpinning introduced above and explore how by using the notions of injurious speech and negative interpellation an understanding can be achieved of the creation of place image and, in turn, how it also leaves space for creative resignification.

Liverpool and the European Capital of Culture Award: A Brief Background

Liverpool is a port city in the North West of England. It resides within the borough of Merseyside and has a population of around 450,000. The city is made up of 30 wards and statistics from the 2011 census state that 14 per cent of the population are of a black or minority ethnicity (University of Liverpool 2012). The city is ranked as the most deprived local authority in England (Department for Communities and Local Government 2010). Due to its maritime and musical heritage Liverpool has many tourist attractions which continued to be a draw for visitors throughout the ECoC year in 2008. The tourism industry in Liverpool prior to the ECoC year was healthy (with a reported 57 million visitors in 2004[1]) but the award contributed to a rise in visitor numbers. The Mersey Partnership[2] stated that visitor numbers to the city increased through 2008 from 63 million to 75 million, with an increase of 6 per cent in hotel occupancy.[3]

In 2004 Liverpool was awarded the ECoC title for 2008. The European Commission states that the ECoC's purpose is, 'to highlight the richness and diversity of European cultures and the features they share, promote greater mutual acquaintance between European citizens, foster a feeling of European citizenship' (2010 online).[4] Research carried out between 1995–2004 found that the title was beneficial to the host cities (Palmer et al. 2004a and 2004b). This report concludes that,

> The European Capital of Culture (ECOC) action of the European Union is a powerful tool for cultural development that operates on a scale that offers unprecedented opportunities for acting as a catalyst for city change. (Palmer et al. 2004a: 188)

The ECoC title, since Glasgow held the award in 1990, has become strongly associated with regeneration (Garcia 2004). Due to this there was some expectation on the part of communities in Liverpool for the award to be a solution to problems of social deprivation. Jones and Wilks-Heeg discuss how, 'the notion of Liverpool ECoC 2008 as an inclusive, community-based process emerged' (2004: 342) which led to a myth of the title being a panacea for the city's problems.

Historically, Liverpool had been in a period of decline as, whilst the docks had previously provided work for the men of Liverpool, by the 1960s the changing patterns of transportation and the dawn of the 'container revolution' (Murden 2006: 430) led to the decline of the city, aided by de-industrialisation and global economic recession. Events such as the Toxteth riots in 1981 left community/council relations broken and unemployment rates continued to rise. Murden explains that the media focused attention on Liverpool at this time although the same issues were being experienced nationwide. The result of economic decline in the city and a weak local leadership in the shape of a Conservative-Liberal coalition in the early 1980s was a turn to an alternative leadership, the Labour party. Popular within the party were Militant activists and those from trade unions who had worked alongside the activists in the factories. De Noyer explains,

---

1   Data taken from http://most.merseyside.org.uk/site/research [accessed 21/09/10].

2   This was the tourism and investment agency for the region – the organisation no longer exists under this name but is now part of the Liverpool City Region Local Enterprise Partnership.

3   Data take from The Mersey Partnership www.merseyside.org.uk [accessed 21/09/10].

4   http://ec.europa.eu/culture/our-programmes-and-actions/doc433_en.htm

Religious divisions scrambled party loyalties. Strikes were often wildcat, beyond the unions' control. The corruption of Liverpool's politics was, like the waterfront architecture, normally compared to Chicago's. And when the Catholic mafia passed into history, the moribund rump of Liverpool Labour was Militant's for the taking. (2007: 175)

This further alienated Liverpool from the rest of the country as the Labour Party was not keen to be associated with the Militant Tendency and by 1985 those that had risen to power in Liverpool such as Derek Hatton found themselves removed from the party. The legacy left to the city of this period was one of mistrust.

Therefore, attempts to deal with 'the Liverpool problem' began before the ECoC title was fought for. For example, in 1981, in the wake of rioting and unrest in the inner city, the Conservative Government, headed by Michael Heseltine MP put together a task force of civil servants and private companies to look at the regeneration of the city. The Merseyside Development Corporation was established in 1981 to regenerate the city and they looked to tourism and leisure to change the fortunes of the city. An International Garden Festival was organised to take place on undeveloped land in 1984. The event cost £30 million and despite attracting over three million visitors over the six months that it took place it only recuperated 20 per cent of the cost (Parkinson 1988) and the site remained unused until development began in February 2010 to restore many of the garden features and build new apartments. However, the Corporation saw that culture-led regeneration was a key economic driver and the development of Albert Dock in the 1980s was seen as a great success in bringing employment and investment into the city. In particular, the opening of the Tate Liverpool in 1988 was seen as a positive move forward for the city.

In 1993 the city acquired 'Objective One status' from the European Union. Liverpool qualified for this by having a Gross Domestic Product lower that 75 per cent of the average for the EU. By gaining this status the city became eligible for regeneration funding from the EU.[5] The election of New Labour in 1997 and the party's focus on social inclusion led to the creation of the economic and physical regeneration organisation, Liverpool Vision in 1999. The creation of the tourism and investment agency, The Mersey Partnership[6] in 1993 also saw a push in promoting Liverpool as a tourist destination and a desirable location for investment driven by campaigns such as 'Making Merseyside', which had the aim of changing perceptions of the city (see: Kokosalakis et al. 2006 and Selby 2005).

From this brief overview it is clear that the ECoC award could be potentially contentious. The city had been through intense periods of decline with many organisations intervening to solve the social and economic problems. There was a

5   By 2006 this status was removed due to the economic growth of the city making Liverpool no longer eligible.

6   As mentioned previously, The Mersey Partnership ceased to exist in 2012 and is now part of Liverpool City Region Enterprise Partnership.

strong legacy of political instability which had the potential to hinder the process of developing a successful year (O'Brien and Miles 2010). Indeed, the discourse of rebranding activities of organisations such as The Mersey Partnership and The Liverpool Culture Company, the organisation set up to oversee the ECoC year, do not explore the complexity of lived identities, the daily realities for the inhabitants of the city. To illustrate this point, Griffiths, in analysing the bid documents of all the UK cities which competed for the title that year, comments that there lacks an approach of, 'culture being viewed as a medium for a collective emancipation; of culture as a field of struggle and resistance; of culture as a source of oppositional identities [...]' (Griffiths 2006: 430). It is true that place-identities are not singular, as Boland explores in his work (2010: 2). As a result the images and stereotype of a city often do not reflect the actual identities of those that reside there, but, on the other hand, they are not created out of a vacuum as the proceeding section will address.

Injurious Speech and the Myths of the City

In order to examine the image of Liverpool, this chapter will draw on Judith Butler's notion of injurious speech or negative interpellation (Butler 1997a) which derives from Althusser's theories of interpellation (Althusser 1971). In his work on ideology, Althusser describes a scenario in which, through interpellation or a 'hail', the subject is constituted. The process of turning towards that which interpellates confirms the subject as a concrete subject. In Althusser's theoretical scene a man [*sic*] is hailed in the street by, for example, the police, 'Hey, You there!' to which the 'hailed individual will turn round [...] he becomes a *subject*. Why? Because he has recognised that the hail was "really" addressed to him' (1971: 48 original emphasis). He is suggesting that ideology acts, 'as that very precise operation which [he calls] interpellation' (1971: 48). According to Althusser 'ideology is eternal' (1971: 49), we are '*always-already subjects*' (1971: 50 original emphasis) and therefore predisposed to turn towards the 'hail'.

Althusser's thesis is examined and rejected by Butler on the basis that he sets up, 'an impossible scene' (Davies 2012: 887). She states that the success of the interpellation is based on a Foucauldian account of power/ideology (Foucault, [1975] 1991) and it is processes of citation and historicity, 'repeated action of discourse' (Butler 1997a: 27), of the interpellation rather than the 'voice' (i.e. in Althusser's scene, the police) from which it is derived. She questions why we readily turn towards the 'law' – presuming our guilt. She states that the reason that one turns towards the hail is because, 'it promises identity' rather than creates identity (Althusser 1997b: 108). Indeed, we turn towards the hail, as we are dependent on 'the law' (or the Panoptican power in a Foucauldian analysis) in the constitution of our identity. According to Butler, drawing on Foucault, that which is the source of subjection is also, 'what we depend on for our existence' (Butler 1997b: 2). Therefore this suggests that the process of interpellation, even negative interpellation, plays a part in constituting identity and we are complicit in this. This idea of being complicit in the interpellation through turning towards the 'hail' will be developed further in relation to Liverpool's identity and it will be argued that the city is complicit in the image constituted.

To now embed this theoretical underpinning within the context of the creation of touristic places we need to address the implications of the perspective. If we consider the notion that the interpellation is an iterative process we can see that Liverpool has been negatively interpellated throughout popular culture and by the UK media. Cultural products of the city have played a role in the development of stereotypes that people associate with Liverpool and have contributed to the iterative process of negative interpellation. Boland states that, 'such is the extent of 'cultural knowledge' about Liverpool that almost anyone in the UK and significant numbers across the world, would be able to posit a view of the city and its people' (2008: 356). Liverpool born Alan Bleasedale's BBC TV social realist drama *Boys From the Blackstuff* brought to the screens the struggles that working men were experiencing in the late 1970s. Whilst problems of unemployment were not just characteristic of Liverpool, the programme created the image of the unemployed Liverpudlian man and the slogan, 'gissa job', a colloquial phrase for asking for employment became an iconic slogan for the years under Margaret Thatcher's Conservative Government. From 1986 to 1991 the success of Carla Lane's (also Liverpool born) TV comedy *Bread* also brought the myth of Liverpool to the small screen. The programme revolved around the survival of a family living in the Dingle area of the city and included their many fraudulent and 'dodgy' deals. The image of Liverpool prevalent in the media and popular culture contributed to a negative stereotype of the city and its inhabitants on a national scale. Within popular culture comedians have created caricatures of Liverpudlians which have both been embraced and rejected by locals. Most famously Harry Enfield's *The Scousers* sketch led to an image of the city as being full of curly haired, moustached, argumentative football fans.

The tragic events in the city's footballing history of Hillsborough in 1989[7] and, earlier at Heysel in 1988[8] did nothing to help the city's external image. The British tabloid newspaper *The Sun*[9] accused Liverpool fans of stealing from victims of the Hillsborough disaster and urinating on victims of the crush. As Murden comments, 'the very fact that they felt it acceptable to make such comments in the wake of such a tragedy gives some indication of the depths to which Liverpool's stock had

---

7   96 Liverpool fans died as the result of a human crush in the stadium during an FA Cup match between Liverpool FC and Nottingham Forest. This event led to the conversion of many football stadia into seated only arenas.

8   Juventus and Liverpool fans clashed leaving 30 people dead.

9   *The Sun* newspaper is boycotted by many Liverpool Football Club fans with some outlets refusing to stock it.

sank' (2006: 470).[10] Once again the city was negatively interpellated through the reporting of this event. Even in the aftermath, several inquiries and investigations later the image of Liverpool was harmed and even led to accusations of the city being too sentimental and emotional. In particular, anger was felt deeply within the city when one of Liverpool's home-grown talents made scathing remarks about his hometown. Alexei Sayle caused controversy when he commented that, 'Liverpool people are so sentimental anyway and even more so with this – oh, we are the greatest people and you'll never walk alone ... and all this sh-te [...]' (Sayle quoted in: Baxter and Hookham 2003 online, original omission of letters). Sayle was criticised for leaving the city and forgetting where his roots were and what he owed to the city for his success (Baxter and Hookham 2003).

Boris Johnson, the current Conservative Mayor of London was implicated in the further iteration of this injurious discourse of 'sentimentality'. In 2004 the *Spectator*, a weekly Conservative magazine then edited by Johnson, published an unsigned editorial accusing the people of Liverpool of wallowing in victim-status.[11] This example of the iteration of 'sentimentality' from differing sources from within and beyond the city highlights Butler's thesis around the power of the performative. The very furore surrounding the *Spectator*'s article and the subsequent visit of penitence to the city by Boris Johnson, suggests that the injurious speech act is, 'mobilised by that long string of injurious interpellations' (Butler 1997a: 49). The violating nature of the speech act is only successful through processes of citation and derivation. Butler continues to clarify that, 'precisely the iterability by which a performative enacts its injury establishes a permanent difficulty in locating final accountability for that injury in a singular subject and its act' (Butler 1997a: 50). Indeed, what this suggests is that the 'myth' of Liverpool is being constituted, and as Selwyn (1996a: 3) states, myths can be created to either 'forget' or 'over-communicate' information and stories. This 'over-communication' can be considered as iterated injurious speech due to the repetition of the discourse of 'sentimentality' in the public domain by high-profile figures. The uproar from within Liverpool further 'over-communicates' the notion facilitated by the national media.

To develop this latter point of uproar within the city, we need to not forget the aspect of Butler's thesis, which is concerned with complicity, that the interpellation, 'promises identity' (Butler 1997b: 108). Therefore, it can be argued that the identity that the injurious speech promises may not be what Liverpool is hoping for but it has become ingrained in the city that it depends on it for success and, I argue for its sense of community and thus the reason why the ECoC title

---

10   The Hillsborough Independent Panel produced a report in September 2012 forcing *The Sun* to apologise and led to the resignation of the Chief Constable of West Yorkshire Police over allegations of police cover-ups.

11   Original link to article no longer exists, however the immediate aftermath is covered by the BBC News here http://news.bbc.co.uk/1/hi/uk_politics/3756418.stm [accessed 27/11/12].

was awarded to the city in the first place (BBC News 2003). The injurious speech became a unifying force for the city. Murden explains that by the 1980s the image of the city had never been worse,

> Britain had fallen out of love with Liverpool, and the violent, argumentative, thieving, badly dressed scouser caricatured by Harry Enfield was how the world now viewed the city's inhabitants. Economic decay, unemployment, poverty, riots, strikes and radical politics all made Liverpool bad news, representative of the dark side of Thatcher's Britain. (Murden 2006: 469)

Yet, in relation to this idea of the city's negative image, when interviewed for this research, Roger Hill from BBC Radio Merseyside and also a performance artist, commented that he feels Liverpool would rather be seen as on the outside and not as accepted as part of the Nation. Hill comments that Liverpool, 'does not want of a part of a club that would accept [Liverpool] as a member' suggesting that it revels in its negative image. If we refer to Bourdieu's notion of symbolic violence, because the violence can, 'only be exerted on a person predisposed (in his habitus) to feel it ...' (Bourdieu 1991: 51). In a sense, the city had turned towards the 'hail' and the interpellation was successful.

Therefore the efficiency of the stereotyping of the city is not only based in the iterative processes of the injurious speech but also in the active complicity of the subject, in this case in the identity construction of Liverpool. Items and events from the past take on symbolic form to create an understanding of identity for the present and the future. Strategic decisions around the promotion of a place results from, as Pritchard and Morgan (1998) tell us, are ideological and borne from political processes and therefore have a specific 'message' to convey about a place. As we have seen above, more informally, the organic image of place is also constituted through channels which may be ideologically driven, for example the print media. Alternatively, organic images are created through popular cultural products, which may not be overtly political but may arise from the political and social climate of the time. Bauman reiterates this by stating that, '[m]yths do not tell stories to amuse. They are meant to teach, by endlessly reiterating their message: a kind of message that listeners may forget or neglect only at their peril' (2001: 8). Through the rebranding processes prior and during the ECoC celebrations there were attempts to re-mythologise the city using the slogans which drew on the previous glories on the once thriving and prosperous city, 'A World in One City' being particularly utilised, albeit critiqued (Jones and Wilks-Heeg 2007) and eventually side-lined. Stories, or myths of the community are shared and it may be that these are nostalgic or romanticised versions of the past, as Cohen states, a community uses myths to deal with change and create a 'collective response' (1985: 99). Kearns and Philo comment that the centrality of local history is key to processes of self-identification which is then manipulated to whatever ends. They conclude that, 'manipulation of culture involved in the selling of places will tend also to be a manipulation of history' (Kearns and Philo 1993: 5). This can also, by extension, include the manipulation of the negative interpellation that the city is complicit in. It becomes part of the self-identification of the city, and thus, part of the reimaging. To borrow a phrase from Butler, the reimaging can be seen as, 'misappropriating the force' (Butler 1997a: 40) of injurious speech and it is this that I will turn to next.

Resisting Injurious Speech and Negative Interpellation

We have already seen that Butler considers the instability of the performative offering up the potential for resignification. The very need to iterate the citation to ensure its success suggests that there is a space for ambivalence. Medina on referring to the discursive potential of agency suggests that, '[t]he performative reiteration of symbolic violence can be disrupted and even subverted' (Medina 2006: 116) further suggesting the ability to restate or 'restage' the identity performance. I have introduced the idea of 'misappropriating the force' of the negative interpellations (Butler 1997a: 40) and I feel that it is worth quoting Butler at length to clarify this point,

> The political possibility of reworking the force of the speech act against the force of injury consists in misappropriating the force of the speech from those prior contexts. The language that counters the injuries of speech, however, must repeat those injuries without precisely re-enacting them. (Butler 1997a: 40–41)

Related to this, and returning to the core theme of violence, is Rapport's (2000) thesis of violence and creative potential. Both Butler and Rapport are suggesting that the space of ambivalence in violence acts/injurious speech allows for creativity, a resignification to emerge.

This resignification of the image of the city through reference to the injurious speech, can be seen in one event which formed part of the build-up to the 2008 ECoC celebrations. *The Liverpool Nativity* employed the literal narrative of the story of the birth of Jesus but in turn became a narrative of the city on that particular evening. The event was a precursor to the launch of the city becoming ECoC and was part of the official cultural programming. It was developed by the team behind *The Manchester Passion* and *Flashmob the Opera*[12] and was a modern reworking of the traditional Christmas story played out on the streets of Liverpool set to the music of some of the city's most famous artists and bands.

---

12   'The Manchester Passion', broadcast live on Good Friday in 2006 on BBC TV and 'Flashmob the Opera', staged live in London in 2004. Like The *Liverpool Nativity*, The Manchester Passion updated a biblical tale and set it to the music of the city and was performed by local actors and musicians. They were both street performances produced by BBC Classical Music Television. The *Liverpool Nativity* was written by Liverpudlian Mark Davies Markham and directed by Mancunian actress, Noreen Kershaw.

In brief, the story is narrated by Gabriel, a security guard standing in front of CCTV screens which broadcast the action of the story to the gathered audience. The action concerns Mary, a white waitress and her black boyfriend Joseph, an asylum seeker who must report to the passport office in the city centre at the demand of Herodia, a power-hungry minister looking to make her mark on politics in the city and then advance her career. Mary is informed by Gabriel over a TV in the café that she is to have a child. Joseph storms off, as he believes Mary to be a virgin. Mary receives a call on her mobile from Gabriel telling her it will be the Son of God so Mary and Joseph must quickly make their way to the city. Their journey begins aboard the Mersey Ferries which have become an icon of the city, in particular through the 1960's popular music song by Gerry and Pacemakers, *Ferry Across the Mersey*.[13] This song is given further import in the nativity through the presence of Gerry Marsden, the singer from the band, welcoming the couple on board the ferry. The couple reconcile whilst making the journey. On arrival they face both well-wishers (in the form of a gaggle of drunken girls) and derision by a group of thugs who shout abuse at Joseph, telling him to get back to where he came from (along to the tune of *Get Back* by The Beatles). The theme of racial (dis)harmony is prevalent during the performance and the slogan of *The World in One City* was still at this point being utilised. Mary and Joseph are rescued from this incident by a Salvation Army marching band playing *All You Need is Love* to which the gathered crowd sing along to enthusiastically.

In the meantime, an Angel visits a group of shepherds in the guise of homeless people, and tells them of the news and leads them to the place where the baby will be. The Magi are also on their way but make a stop to see Herodia who demands they tell her where the child is. When Herodia realises that the Magi will not reveal the child's location she orders the murder of all newborn babies in the city. By now Mary (who is heavily pregnant) and Joseph have successfully made it to the city and are offered a 'lean-to' round the back of a pub in which to rest. The action now moves to the stage outside St George's Hall and a curtain opens to reveal Mary and Joseph and the newborn child, who is placed in a shopping trolley as a crib. The Angels lead a procession of the shepherds and the Magi through the crowds who come onto the stage to greet the child. Herodia has been unsuccessful this time and Gabriel requests that the crowd welcome the family into their arms as Mary and Joseph carry the baby down from the stage and into the audience.

The citation of images of poverty in the context of the performance are examples of this misappropriating that Butler talks of as they 'restage' the negative images of the city in a creative manner. The live performance, in particular the 'stable' scene where baby Jesus is laid in a shopping trolley as a crib, challenges the perceptions of poverty by re-signifying the image in a humorous way. The negative interpellation is repeated without 'precisely re-enacting it' (Butler 1997a: 41).

---

13   'Ferry Across the Mersey' was a huge hit for Gerry and the Pacemakers released in 1964 and it is still played on the boat which travels between the Wirral and Liverpool city centre.

The audience, both at home and in the live crowd, recognise this image as a representation of Liverpool and therefore are able to understand the humour of its misappropriation.

In another scene in the performance, one 'shepherd' berates another for sounding, 'like a Scouse stereotype' when, on being told an Angel will guide them to a 'special place', responds by saying excitedly, 'free all you can eat buffet, sound'.[14] The 'shepherds' then proceed to squabble and antagonise each other much like British comedian's Harry Enfield's 'The Scousers' sketches which often ended in a cartoonish fight. This links back to the 'cultural knowledge' that Boland speaks of (2008). The 'Scouse stereotypes' are acknowledged directly in the performance ranging from the example of the shepherds offered above to the Angel being a blonde 'WAG'[15] style character in a silver catsuit. The label of 'Scouse' in fact was found to be contentious during my research with some older participants finding it offensive and associated with be 'rough' and 'loud' (these were the words of a lady who was part of a reading group in an over 55s housing complex that I spent many weeks attending) meaning uncouth and unrefined. The origins of the label is said to lie in the dish 'lobscouse' which was a stew eaten by the sailors and workers on the docks in the 19th Century. The word is used to describe the local accent and the label 'Scouser' to describe a person from Liverpool.[16] As Boland (2008 and 2010) comments, the 'Scouse' identity is so easily recognisable that the negative connotations are part and parcel of the success of the Liverpool Nativity's performance of 'Scouse' identity.

Similarly, to return to the iteration of the notion of 'sentimentality' the city also resignified this through creative misappropriation. In a promotional film for ECoC[17] we are presented with a clip of Boris Johnson. In the film he is seen at an event in Liverpool and turns to the camera saying, 'well done Liverpool … Can I go home now?'. The city is repeating the injurious speech, but turning it on its head in order to re-imagine the identity of the place to a city that is capable of laughing at its own stereotypes.

In the discourse of the organisers of the cultural programme, this misappropriation of injurious speech was also evident. The antagonistic stereotype of Liverpudlians as portrayed by Harry Enfield and the shepherds in the nativity (as discussed above) was further iterated by Phil Redmond, Creative Director of the Liverpool Culture Company who was brought in four months before the start of the ECoC to oversee the year's celebrations after resignations and in-fighting amongst the board of the company. Redmond, a Liverpudlian television producer of famous UK shows such as Grange Hill, Brookside and Hollyoaks, was a popular

---

14　'Sound' is a colloquial term of 'good' or 'great'.

15　The label given to the wives and girlfriends of footballers by the UK's tabloid media.

16　Further discussion on this can be found in (Belchem 2006).

17　This film was aired on the Sky channel Information TV in January 2008. The channel provided much coverage of events and activities throughout the year.

addition to the creative team. He most famously commented, 'I felt as if I'd been put in charge of organizing a typical Scouse wedding, with everyone telling me, "I'm not going if she's going" or, "You can't have those two on the same table together". But in the end everyone turns up, makes up and has a great party' (quoted in: Hickling 2009), suggesting that the chaos was part of the identity of the place, further negative interpellation being misappropriated. This complicity with the stereotype works in part due to Phil Redmond being from the city and he has been rather scathingly called a 'professional Scouser' by one blogger.[18] In a similar way that the comedy of the Liverpool Nativity worked the 'insider' is *allowed* to resignify or restage the interpellation in the creative act.

Conclusion: The creative potential of negative interpellation

The title of this chapter is concerned with how people deal with place myths. It has already been established that in the making of tourist places, myths play a significant role (Selwyn 1996b) and this is particularly true of the case study presented here. Liverpool has been negatively interpellated so that the image of poverty and urban decay has become part of the UK's national consciousness. The award of the ECoC title in 2008 was the opportunity for the city to present the city on an international stage and in particular change the national perception about Liverpool and its cultural identity. There was always going to be those who were sceptical that this could be achieved and in fact, whether it can be maintained in the long-term remains to be seen. By using the notion of negative interpellation, as put forth by Butler (1997a), as a framework to consider the constitution of place image, we can see that the place is accepting of the negative perceptions and creatively misappropriates them.

It is possible to consider how negative interpellation leaves space for creative potential in the reimagining of place identity. We have seen how Butler considered that the subjects are complicit in their own negative interpellation by turning towards the 'hail' in the first place. The promise of identity is too tempting. In the case study of Liverpool the promise of some sort of recognition and attention led to the 'absorption' of the negative interpellation and a perpetuation of the stereotypes through restaging and resignification.

In 2008 Liverpool was looking to reposition itself and the ethnographic data suggests that people will revel in those stereotypes out of familiarity and comfort but there is always the potential for, as Dewsberry stated, 'emergent structure' (2000: 494). The Foucauldian account of power which Butler draws on, that being depending on the structures and norms for our existence, opens up the possibility for agency and potential creative transformation. The application of this theoretical lens to the construction of tourist place, in reference to Liverpool, has allowed for a view of place which does not put negative interpellation as something which

---

18   www.liverpoolpreservationtrust.blogspot.com.

is 'bad' per se but something which enables or facilitates a creative reimagining. This chapter is not necessarily looking to measure the success of this reimaging by the people of Liverpool and the structures and organisations involved in the official ECoC programming and branding, but it offers an alternative analysis on place image.

Linguistic violence, in the framework presented here, offers the chance for resignification of place due to the contingent, social and collective nature of how a place is constituted. This chapter is not looking to trivialise the serious nature of hate speech or negative interpellation but rather utilises the theoretical notions outlined as a method to explore how Liverpool attempted to change and challenge perceptions that were prevalent at a national level in particular. Turning attention to the creativity of violence, although not on an individual level as per Rapport's analysis (2000), in dealing with the myths is what this chapter has set out to explore.

This chapter has shown that linguistic violence can be enabling when applied to the case of place image and myths of place. The 'pre-disposition' of Liverpool to 'feel' the symbolic violence (to paraphrase Bourdieu 1991: 51) can be seen on the one hand as being open to the injurious speech and therefore having no right to complain about it, but on the other, it allows a new image of place to emerge in a performative sense which is perhaps more reflective of the lived identities and encompassing of a view of 'culture as a field of struggle and resistance', that Griffiths (2006: 430) called for in his analysis of Capital of Culture bid documents. The collective response to myths, to the negative interpellation, is very much dependent on being complicit in it and this is what we can see in the case study of Liverpool in and prior to 2008 ECoC.

References

Althusser, L. (1971). *Essays on Ideology.* London & New York: Verso.

Bauman, Z. (2001). *Community: Seeking Safety in an Insecure World.* Cambridge: Polity Press.

Baxter, L., and Hookham, M. (14 August 2003). It's Alexei Sneer. *icLiverpool. co.uk* Available from: http://icliverpool.icnetwork.co.uk/0100news/0100 regionalnews/tm_method=full%26objectid=13290629%26siteid=50061-name_page.html [accessed: 27 June 2008].

BBC News. (4 June 2003). *Why Liverpool Won.* Available from: http://news.bbc. co.uk/1/hi/uk/2962008.stm [accessed: 10 January 2009].

Belchem, J. (2006). *Mersey Pride: Essays in Liverpool Exceptionalism.* (Second ed.). Liverpool: Liverpool University Press.

Boland, P. (2008). The Construction of Images of People and Place: Labelling Liverpool and Stereotyping Scousers. *Cities*, 25 (6), 355–369.

Boland, P. (2010). Sonic Geography, Place and Race in the Formation of Local Identity: Liverpool and Scousers. *Geografiska Annaler: Series B, Human Geography*, 92 (1), 1–22.

Borgerson, J. (2005). Judith Butler: On Organizing Subjectivities. *The Sociological Review*, 53 (s1), 63–79.

Bourdieu, P. (1991). *Language and Symbolic Power.* Raymond, G., and Adamson, M., Trans. Cambridge: Polity Press.

Butler, J. (1993). *Bodies That Matter: On the Discursive Limits of 'Sex'.* London: Routledge.

Butler, J. (1997a). *Excitable Speech: A Politics of the Performative.* New York & London: Routledge.

Butler, J. (1997b). *The Psychic Life of Power: Theories in Subjection.* California: Stanford University Press.

Butler, J. ([1990] 2006). *Gender Trouble.* New York: Routledge Classics.

Cohen, A.P. (1985). *The Symbolic Construction of Community.* London: Routledge.

Davies, N. (2012). Subjected Subjects? On Judith Butler's Paradox of Interpellation. *Hypatia*, 27 (4), 881–897.

Department for Communities and Local Government. (2010). *The English Indices of Deprivation 2010.* London: Department for Communities and Local Government.

Derrida, J. (1988). *Limited Inc.* Evanston: Northwestern University Press.

Dewsberry, J.D. (2000). Performativity and the Event: Enacting a Philosophy of Difference. *Environment and Planning D: Society and Space*, 18, 473–496.

Du Noyer, P. (2007). *Liverpool: Wonderous Place – From the Cavern to the Capital of Culture.* London: Virgin Books.

European Commission. (3 February 2010). *About the European Capitals of Culture.* Available from: http://ec.europa.eu/culture/our-programmes-and-actions/doc433_en.htm [accessed: 15 February 2010].

Foucault, M. ([1975] 1991). *Discipline and Punish: The Birth of the Prison.* Trans. Sheriden, A. London: Penguin Books.

Garcia, B. (2004). Cultural Policy and Urban Regeneration in Western European Cities: Lessons from Experience, Prospects for the Future. *Local Economy*, 19 (4), 312–326.

Griffiths, R. (2006). City/Culture Discourses: Evidence from the Competition to Select the European Capital of Culture 2008. *European Planning Studies*, 14 (4), 415–430.

Hall, D. (2003). Images of the City. In: Munck, R. (ed). *Reinventing the City: Liverpool in Comparative Perspective.* Liverpool: Liverpool University Press, 191–210.

Hickling, A. (5 January 2009). Follow that Spider. *The Guardian.* Available from: http://www.guardian.co.uk/culture/2009/jan/05/liverpool-year-culture-verdict [accessed: 10 April 2009].

Jones, P., and Wilks-Heeg, S. (2004). Capitalising Culture: Liverpool 2008. *Local Economy*, 19 (4), 341–360.

Jones, P., and Wilks-Heeg, S. (2007). Packaging Culture, Rethinking Cultures: The Re-branded City. In: Grunenberg, C., and Knifton, R. (eds). *Centre of the Creative Universe: Liverpool and the Avant-Garde*, 204–219.

Kearns, G., and Philo, C. (eds). (1993). *Selling Places: The City as Cultural Capital, Past and Present*. Oxford: Pergamon Press.

Kokosalakis, C., Bagnall, G., Selby, M., and Burns, S. (2006). Place Image and Urban Regeneration in Liverpool. *International Journal of Consumer Studies*, 30, 389–397.

Medina, J. (2006). *Speaking from Elsewhere: A New Contextualised Perpective on Meaning, Identity, and Discursive Agency*. Albany: State University Press of New York.

Murden, J. (2006). 'City of Change and Challenge': Liverpool Since 1945. In: Belchem, J. (ed.). *Liverpool 800*. Liverpool: Liverpool University Press, 393–485.

O'Brien, D., and Miles, S. (2010). Cultural Policy as Rhetoric and Reality: A Comparative Analysis of Policy Making in the Peripheral North of England. *Cultural Trends*, 19 (1–2), 3–13.

Palmer, R., Richards, G., and Dodd, D. (2004a). *European Cities and Capital of Culture: Part 1*. Brussels: Palmer/Rae Associates.

Palmer, R., Richards, G., and Dodd, D. (2004b). *European Cities and Capital of Culture: Part 2*. Brussels: Palmer/Rae Associates.

Parkinson, M. (1988). Urban Regeneration and Development Corporations: Liverpool Style. *Local Economy*, 3 (2), 109–118.

Pritchard, A., and Morgan, N. J. (1998). *Tourism Promotion and Power: Creating Images, Creating Identities*. Chichester: John Wiley & Sons.

Rapport, N. (2000). 'Criminals by Instinct': On the 'Tragedy' of Social Structure and the 'violence' of Individual Creativity. In: Aijmer, G., and Abbink, J. (eds). *Meanings of Violence: A Cross Cultural Perspective*. Oxford and New York: Berg, 39–54.

Selby, M., (2005). *Understanding Urban Tourism: Image, Culture and Experience*. London: I.B. Tauris & Co Ltd.

Selwyn, T. (1996a). Introduction. In: Selwyn, T. (ed.). *The Tourist Image: Myths and Myth Making in Tourism*. Chichester: John Wiley & Sons Ltd, 1–32.

Selwyn, T. (1996b). *The Tourist Image: Myths and Myth Making in Tourism*. Chichester: John Wiley & Sons Ltd.

University of Liverpool. (18 December 2012). *Study of 2011 census reveals greater diversity and integration*. Available from: https://news.liv.ac.uk/2012/12/18/study-of-2011-census-reveals-greater-diversity-and-integration/ [accessed: 17 February 2013].

Whitehead, N.L. (2004). Rethinking the Anthropology of Violence. *Anthropology Matters*, 20 (5), 1–2.

Chapter 6

Re-inventing Battlefield Tourism 'In Times of Peace': Connecting Tourism and the Remembrance of Violence

Anne Hertzog

Introduction

Battlefield tourism is an interesting case study by which to explore the connections between tourism and violence. This is because this type of tourism illustrates how the violence of war alongside the macabre and dangerous generates tourism (Lloyd 1998; Ryan 2007) and constitutes one of the oldest motivations for tourism (Sharpley and Stone 2009). In addition tourism has often been seen as an inappropriate activity on battlefields because it is deemed to generate practices and values seen as incompatible with the memory of suffering and the violence of war. In France, since the 1980s, battlefield tourism has been reactivated in particular through the emergence of tourism policies based on war heritage valorisation. This renewed interest in battlefield tourism is characterised by an increase in the exhumation of the traces of the war and as such serves to highlight the deep impact on the societies and territories of France's north. It also leads to a differentiation between various forms of war violence that have been sometimes concealed or erased by veterans, inhabitants, or even historians (Audoin-Rouzeau and Becker 2000: 24). It raises the questions of the incomprehensibility and incommunicability of war violence for today's visitors 'because nothing of what contemporaries of the conflict has experienced can be understood and even approached so far' (Audoin-Rouzeau and Becker 2000: 18).

As the question of violence has now become increasingly significant in the recent French historiography of the Great War, we may question the place and status of war violence in the process of making battlefields tourist places. In this chapter I will demonstrate how the treatment of violence in the process of tourism development deals with politics, culture, and identity. I will analyse how actors try to conciliate development of tourism, a place's attractiveness and remembrance of war violence, in the French case. I will also show how the invention of 'remembrance tourism' as a form of cultural tourism during the 1990s serves to legitimate tourism, often seen as a type of symbolic violence when it comes to war sites.

The Reactivation of Battlefield Tourism since the 1990s in Response to Globalised Paradigms and Local Interests

For two decades, we have been witnessing an unprecedented recollection of the remains of the war after a long period of rejection or denial. Trenches are being rebuilt, ruins of destroyed villages are being restored and forests are being cleared to reveal the chaotic aspect of the former battlefields. Never before had the number and variety of informative posters and signs been so important to mark the landscape and give interpretations of 'what happened'. From Flanders to Alsace,[1] historical routes, works of art, museums or visitors' centres depict the war and its violence in a renewed way.

The 'marking' (Veschambre 2008) of landscapes and places which used to be scenes of fighting, began during the war itself. In the 1920s, both the 'commemorative fever' (Baioni 2004: 1139) across Europe and the fast obliteration of the traces of war due to rebuilding in the devastated countries, led to the preservation of many battlefields by the nations involved in the conflict. Because some of the bloodiest war zones were regarded as symbolic places of the birth of a national awareness and pride (Audoin-Rouzeau 1998: 123), they became the main sites of mourning, and pilgrimage. They also became tourism attractions. This political process of transforming battlefields into symbolic national places of remembrance created a hierarchy among the various battlefields leading to the eclipse of certain sites in favour of those 'imposed' by the state and veterans (Verdun for the French, Ypres or the Somme for the British, Beaumont-Hamel for the Newfoundlanders, Vimy for the Canadians).[2] For veterans, the fearful of the traces of war disappearing and the associated violence being forgotten, led to the will to preserve battlefield landscapes and to the invention of new symbolic landscapes: in Vimy for example, the planting of thousands of trees represented missing soldiers; everywhere, the inscription of thousands of names on memorials showed the massive scale of the massacre. But of course, nowhere was violence tangible anymore and only the emptiness of the former battlefields remained. As Paul Gough writes:

> while the native populations in France and Belgium toiled to reconstruct their homes and land, pilgrims and veterans roamed the former battlegrounds to locate places that might contain the memory of significant events. Outwardly there was nothing to see; the landscape that drew them was an imaginary one. It was a place of projection and association, a space full of history, yet void of obvious topography, where physical markers had been obliterated but the land overwritten with an invisible emotional geography. (Gough 2010: 13)

---

1   The Western Front stretched out from Flanders to Alsace in the north and east of France from 1914 to 1918.

2   For example the French historian Antoine Prost shows how Verdun became the 'main' battle in the collective French memory of the Great War, due to the dominant position of the Veterans in French society during the after war period (Prost 1986).

Ruins or mine holes were however sometimes carefully preserved like memorials to 'prove the barbary of the enemy' (Danchin 2008: 240). Many tourism guides, for example *Michelin Battlefields Guides* (1917) which proposed routes through the devastated countries, also narrated enemy actions and violence with a patriotic rhetoric, even after the war ended. Providing detailed historical and geographical accounts, they were illustrated by many pictures of ruined landscapes, and in order to foreground violence repeating the numerous postcards and paintings that were produced in France at that time (Danchin 2008: 240).

After the Second World War the increasing number of visitors from the former Commonwealth countries in contrast to a decline of French visitors shows different relations to the history of war and sites of memory, depending on the political, cultural and national backgrounds of the visitors (Nivet 2008: 9). More generally, there was a real lack of interest for the First World War in French society – apart from, for example, First World War veterans – from 1950s to the 1980s as it was overshadowed by the nearer memory of the Second World War. Since then many signs of a 'return' of the Great War have been visible, along with a renewed interest in academic research, an increasing presence in culture, media and art (cinema, literature, song, art photography) and also in political spheres (Offenstadt 2010). This revitalised attention took place in a new global context, characterised by important social (disappearance of the last veterans), cultural (the 80–90 year anniversaries of the war) and political (end of Cold War) changes. Thus, since the 1980s, French tourism policies in the regions on the former front are based on the recognition of a patrimonial value of war heritage (Hertzog 2010, 2012). In these tourism policies, remembrance remains an important output, since the aim is to remember the sacrifice of the fallen soldiers and to restore the place of 'forgotten' battles in national memory.

The involvement of local actors in the valorisation of this heritage also reveals the new French political context of decentralization of decision making. Since the 1980s, the increased power of local authorities has allowed them to promote regional planning and large-scale renovation works based on the Parisian model (for example building new war museums). Promoting equal access to culture and art is part of these tourist and cultural local policies. War heritage promotion is also seen, by most of the public stakeholders, as a new tool in economic and regional development, as well as a means to erase the negative image associated with certain places by creating new cultural and economic resources. Against a background of de-industrialisation or urban decline, heritage in the form of war memories, provides a possible response. This renewed manner of dealing with memories of the Great War is now a common approach in all areas of the former front; but it has emerged at different times in different areas: early in the 'British' area of the Somme but much more recently in other territories as in the Nord/Pas-de-Calais, Champagne or the Vosges – still considered in 2008 as 'virgin land' in the process of tourism development of 'unknown' and 'forgotten' battlefields (Prouillet 2008: 325).

At the same time, this renewed interest in the Great War and its material traces takes place in the growing interest for places symbolising extreme suffering and violence all over the world. A report published in 2009 in order to promote tourism of memory in the Meuse connecting different historic sites, shows how the remembrance of war, massacre or sufferings is now a globalised phenomenon, and produces a new category of tourist destinations, which we could call 'sites of globalised memory':

> The tragic history that the Meuse underwent is today an opportunity, the opportunity to make the Meuse become the great "department" of remembrance needed by the world, on a par with Auschwitz, the beaches of Normandy and Hiroshima, who welcome more than one million visitors. It is towards this tourist model that the Meuse must turn to, today.[3]

The transformation of former war zones (including more recent sites for example: Vietnam, The Balkans, Rwanda) into tourist destinations is now a globalised phenomenon, due to both the rise of world tourism (MIT 2005) and the global spread of remembrance (Assayag 2007: 6–25; Rousso 2007: 3–10). For many historians and philosophers, occidental societies have developed a common attitude towards the past, determined by the 'Holocaust as a negative founding event' (Ricoeur 1991: 39, in Garcia 2008: 374). According to Assayag (2007: 5–7), '"the slaughtering" history of modernity has not disappeared from our horizons', as if 'our peaceful lives need the vision of the past human disasters'. Thus, according to this author, we need to focus more on 'the catastrophic complex of modernity', a modernity based on the enigmatic connection between 'democratic safety' and 'extreme violence'.

This new context is also characterised by the emerging notion of the 'duty of remembrance', first linked to the Holocaust. This concept, that appeared in France during the 1990s, can be defined as the social 'injunction to remember' (Lavabre 2000: 48), a moral duty to maintain the memory of sufferings and injustices endured by a certain part of the population in the past. It has become a central concept in UNESCO cultural and tourist policies (for example the Slavery Routes project in Africa). According to French historian Sébastien Ledoux (2009: 2) this 'duty of remembrance' refers to a specific relationship to the past based on the collective 'conscience of crisis', a new glance at oblivion – seen as a moral fault – and the primacy given to the victim status. The increasing use of the 'duty of remembrance' as a new value in social and political spheres can be seen as a sign of a 'weakening of the Nation-State which must face the internationalization of the laws and the globalisation of the ways of thinking', and at the same time the

---

3   Barcellini, S. 2009. *La Meuse face au défi du centenaire de la Grande Guerre. 2014–2018. Propositions pour une refondation de la politique mémorielle*, Rapport pour le Conseil Général de la Meuse, p. 3. Available from: http://www.verdun-meuse.fr/images/ files/LA_MEUSE_FACE_AU_DEFI_DU_CENTENAIRE.pdf.

seeking of a redefinition of a 'national account, in the name of the human rights, in a multicultural dimension' (Ledoux 2009: 8). This duty of remembrance can take various forms and social practices: official declarations, law texts, international treaties, education or research programmes, commemoration days, publications, and memorials, as well as tourism.

Representing War Violence in Tourist Places

New scientific ways of exploring the Great War has come out of the renewed interest in this event since the 1980s. The will to break with a 'smooth' history of the war has led some historians to re-highlight war violence, studying it not only on large scales through political history – conflict between states – but also as a cultural phenomenon and individual practices through new anthropological approaches (Audoin-Rouzeau, Becker, Ingrao and Rousso 2002). For example, French historian Stéphane Audoin-Rouzeau, following the British John Keegan,[4] defends an 'anthropology of fighting' paying particular attention to the use of arms as 'instruments of violence', individual behaviour during battles and fight experiences. For him, the only way to seize violent practices – '*what exactly happened on the battlefield*' – is on the ground (Audoin-Rouzeau and Becker 2000: 28–9). When it comes to 'war violence' archives, writings and even testimonies, do not seem to be sufficient because they are silent and act to exclude some voices. Other types of occulted violence, like brutality against prisoners or atrocities inflicted on civilians have also become important points. According to Annette Becker the history and memory of civilian sufferings have been long overshadowed by 'a remembrance of the war identifying the conflict almost exclusively with violence endured by combatants' (Audoin-Rouzeau and Becker 2000: 59). These renewed academic approaches have influenced French museography and tourist narratives. Since 2000, many tourism projects have contributed to illuminating these specific types of war violence. For example, the 'Remembrance Route' in North Pas de Calais created by the Conseil Regionalin 2007 focuses on the question of German atrocities against inhabitants and, more generally, refers to both combatant and civilian collective memory of the Great War. Yet, the growing interest in war heritage by tourists still focuses on battlefield violence with most of the tourist projects leading to an 'immersion in the universe of the trenches'.[5]

The question of how war violence is, or should be, represented has become an academic research subject in several fields, such as History, Sociology of

---

4   Author of *The Face of Battle: A Study of Agincourt, Waterloo, and the Somme*, Penguin, 1983.

5   For example in the *Programme de valorisation du patrimoine et de la mémoire de la Grande Guerre. Site national du Hartmannswillerkopf Vieil Armand*, Dossier de Presse, octobre 2008.

Media and Philosophy.[6] Through this chapter, we may wonder how professionals involved in tourist and cultural projects deal with the subject.[7] It appears that even though war violence has been highlighted in French historiography for several decades, the fact is it is yet still often 'unthought-of' in tourism and cultural projects, or even the construction of war museums and exhibits. Firstly, violence 'obviously' accompanies *any* narratives about war or interpretation of war sites. A historian working with a cultural agency on the museography of Suippes war museum remarks: 'Never had war violence been considered as a specific question or problem, either by the scientific committee or by the [planning] agency. No specific reflection was made on this point: it went without saying that violence was an integral part of the exhibition' [PO]. Secondly, the question of war violence is associated with disciplinary fields not necessarily represented in the processes of the cultural or tourist projects. The director of the *Chemin des Dames* museum notes, 'The question of war violence is not tackled directly, maybe because we would have needed a philosopher or an anthropologist to help us to think about violence' [AB]. Lastly, this question supposes 'scientific' and 'historiographic' steps which turn out to be sometimes secondary in tourism planning projects as an expert involved in the Vosges tourist development explains 'The questions of improvements of the sites and economic development overrun the scientific approaches and the historical debates' [YP].

The very possibility of explaining and showing war violence to visitors, for whom it is an 'imagined' but finally intangible experience, is often put forward by actors involved in a museum or site's interpretation. 'The question of war violence in a museum is essential for me at the time when the Western societies have expelled death from their concerns and rejected war in a remote and exotic world' [YLM]. The visual representation of scenes of fighting, corpses or mass graves is sometimes put forward to cause a 'necessary and salutary shock' in order to 'reintroduce reality in a whole of virtual representations (video games ...)' [YLM]. However, war violence as an unknown experience for the majority of the visitors raises the question of their perception of the violent images and narratives: 'How can one comprehend the violence felt by the combatants in today's society, as we live in a world of peace, with relative comfort, with very different experiences and landmarks?' [AB]. This remark – which questions the tourist experience on battlefields – is closely akin to what historians stress about how contemporary

---

6 See for example Assayag, op. cit. 2007; Olivera 2011; Trouche 2010; Wahnich 2001, 2010.

7 Several professionals have been interviewed about this issue: YLM, historian, is the former director of a museum devoted to the two world wars in the department of Pas-de-Calais. He is now on the head of a public structure devoted to the remembrance, cultural and tourism policy in the same area [YLM]; PO took part in the scientific programme of a museum devoted to the Great War in the Marne built in 2005 [PO]; AB is the director of a WW1 museum, in Aisne, she is an art historian [AB]; YP is an expert historian and coordinates the actions of valorisation of the battlefields in the Vosges [YP].

European societies can handle this event. The 'return' of the Great War, interpreted as a 'return of the repressed', even an 'interminable mourning' supposes at the same time a major 'cognitive rupture' (Audoin-Rouzeau and Becker 2000: 19). According to Audoin-Rouzeau and Becker, this rupture is defined by the impossibility for today's societies to adopt and admit 'the same system of values and perception developed about the Great War than the contemporaries did' (2000: 18). Moreover, war is now a remote phenomenon in French society: 'the war, which marked the successive generations of the 20th century with its recurring presence until the end of the Algerian conflict, is from now on in position of complete externality' (Audoin-Rouzeau and Becker 2001: 18). And more generally, violence has been excluded from the social norms as Muchembled shows it (2008: 22), and has even become a 'taboo' in Western Europe.

So in this specific social and cultural context, how is war violence represented? In many museums, realistic representations are presented. In the museum of Albert in the Somme (opened 1992), the curator (non-professional) claims to have been originally inspired by the Imperial War Museum in London, UK, building realistic war scenes of fighting and using sound effects. In the Meaux Great War museum (2011), the large scale reconstruction of trenches aims at making the public understand 'the soldiers' experience'. These sort of realistic settings, now very common in many French war museums (public and private ones), try to induce the visitors to 'experience' the violence in the trenches in a pedagogical as well as spectacular way.

However, other museums like the 'Historial de Péronne' in the Somme (1992) clearly refuse to have visitors 'enjoy' war as a show and wish to spare them the emotional effects created by the staging of distressing scenes. In this museum, the very idea of representing the fighting is debated. The battle is simply not portrayed in the exhibition, and an informative note even underlines that '*battles are unimaginable experiences for those who didn't fight them*'. Jay Winter, a British historian who participated in the creation of the museum draws attention to 'the radical *otherness* of the battle experience' (2008: 34). Therefore, according to him, any attempt at the 'reconstitution of the horror' is in vain: '*it is impossible to reproduce the odour,the light, the emotions of the war in the trenches without being kitsch*' (2008: 35).

The Historial of Péronne distances itself with the pseudo-realism of the war museums which propose to tell visitors what the war *really* was. Moreover, the museography offers a representation of war violence which shows above all the suffering, and seeks to avoid triumphalism or heroism. Historian Sophie Wahnich analyses how the soldiers' uniforms and belongings instead of standing, are laid out in white pits: this specific scenography denies war action but emphasises death and mourning. According to her, this museum overlooks a part of war violence and 'produces an effect of war denial' (2001: 23). However, Winter argues 'a vertical representation is that of hope, while a horizontal one suggests mourning. The purpose of this museum is to convey the notion of a shared disaster' (2004: 156). Opened in 1992, the museum was the first in France to introduce an explicitly

European dimension in its exhibition by the use of three languages and showing the war as an experience held in common across Europe, a 'shared disaster'. Sophie Wahnich clearly identifies apolitical dimension in the representation, 'holding back the memory of war conflict' (2001: 30) in order to promote a vision of the Great War as a joint experience for Europeans, linked with political contemporary ideas – the construction of the European Union during the 1980s–1990s.

These cultural choices are also rooted in theoretical issues, developed by the group of historians having worked on museum narratives ('l'École de Péronne'). Winter is one of them, and he states, 'to *feel* the war, it is necessary to be able to imagine the *pain* of others' (2008: 34). This method puts emphasis on a cultural, anthropological and comparative approach to the violence of war, while rejecting traditional factual takes on 'military history'. The treatment of war violence in cultural and tourism policies is now often linked to specific historiographic traditions or methods, as the importance of an 'available corpus' of historical sources is often pointed out by professionals: 'Finally [we had] only few images of atrocities (and few serious testimonies)' [PO], 'In the representation of war violence, we have to face the impossibility – or its limits, because the available material is missing' [AB]. The question of what is fit to be seen depends on material conditions – access to archives, acquisition of new objects and so on – and influences narratives about war violence. Yet, historians rarely work on their own constructing accounts for museum exhibitions or tourist routes. One notes '*the historian should not yield to the concerns of the public stakeholders or the visitors demands*' [YLM].

Representations of war violence depend on the actors involved in the projects. Since the 1980s, the development of tourism and cultural policies has caused a shift in the make-up of the actors involved in the conservation and valorisation of battlefield heritage. Besides the traditional '14/18 community' (Offenstadt 2010: 9) composed of veteran or heritage associations, new categories of professional stakeholders have arisen, including academics, curators, tourism promoters or artists without forgetting politicians, who order and support the projects (Hertzog 2012). Moreover, the majority of the projects financed by public stakeholders involve scientific committees, increasing give greater weight to the role of academic historians in the formation of narratives.

These actors do not always share the same concerns, interpretation of the past, or vision for the organisation of the sites. Thus, the question of representing war violence can crystallise the tensions between them. For example, historians often plead for the exclusive use of authentic documents whereas museographers impose 'more spectacular' reconstitutions in order to make the museum or the place more attractive (Olivera 2011). Whereas historians can defend portrayals of the harshness of warfare in name of the 'historical truth', politicians can be reluctant to accept the same for fear of shocking 'families and the youngest visitors'.[8] It is

---

8   This example has been given by the director of one war museum in the department of Pas-de-Calais opened in the late 1990s. As a famous historian, he finally succeeded in imposing the pictures, but visitors are warned of the violence shown in the scenes.

sometimes difficult for curators or tourism professionals to make choices based on different theoretical approaches to historical events:

> As far as I'm concerned, I don't know what to do with the interpersonal violence by the "cleaners of trenches". I am aware of the debate between various historiographic theories: on one side, this example is used to demonstrate a form of brutalization in the fighting; on the other side, we are reminded these practices were marginal. How can we deal with that consequently in a museum? The question is not simple, all the more so because the visitor can remember the object (for example a trench knife) and not read the text which would bring a nuance in the use of this type of weapon. (AB, war museum curator in Aisne)

The motives influencing the treatment of war violence hint at historiographic traditions, collective or individual representations of the war and the ways in which war is historically and culturally referred to. But they also reveal how people today appropriate battlefields according to political, cultural or economic issues. The choices made in the war museum of Péronne (the Historial) illustrate tendencies during the 1990s, to revive past warfare with an emphasis on tragedy rather than heroism. Most of the public art pieces commissioned by public actors in the cultural and tourist development of battlefields since the 1990s depict suffering rather than military heroism. For example, Haim Kern's sculpture – 'They did not choose their grave' – commissioned by the French Ministry of Culture in 1998 to commemorate the battle of the Chemin des Dames[9] delivers a universal message of shared pain. This is also the case of 'Constellation of pain', a work chosen by the local authorities of Aisne in 2005 in order to celebrate the role of colonial troops. Contemporary art is used in a way to modernise the commemoration of the Great War but it is also used to make battlefields 'attractive' places for visitors. Clearly, the finality of such artistic choices is to diversify the tourist 'offer'; to make this kind of tourism become 'cultural tourism', able to fulfil contemporary needs and demands, rather than only 'battlefield tourism' associated with war violence and thus of limited attraction.

Local interests in tourism policies might be for reasons of economic development or regional planning. Therefore tourism is perceived as a vector of change and an opportunity. This can lead to a particular use of the register of violence in the construction of 'appealing' places in order to make them 'desirable'. For example, the theme of nature is often mobilised in the narratives about areas previously affected by war violence, as a positive value of the place:

> Walk through the battlefields [...] Feel the emotion in these places today full of calm and serenity. The Somme Valley is green again, flowers have invaded

---

9   It used to be one of the bloodiest battlefields, often seen like a disaster because of the lack of organisation and the incapacity of the military chiefs during the 1917 offensive. See Loez (2010).

the fields, big trees watch over the Chemin des Dames again, landscapes are amazingly beautiful. Nature is back, quiet Picardy pays tribute to men who have fallen for its liberty.[10]

The need to communicate a seductive image of the place, while integrating the war as part of its identity also leads to the development of positive interpretations of this heritage. For example, in order to give a positive image of the country, the document for the Tourism Planning of Lorraine proposes a re-interpretation of war heritage and even war history: the battlefields are depicted as sites where '*the battles made Europe and brought people together*. [...] The stake is to communicate an image turned towards the future, the meeting of the people more than the war.'[11]

The issues related to the representation of war violence are complex. Whether they favour the beauty of sacrifice or heroism, the realism of fighting or the refusal to see war as a show, these representations serve various purposes.

'Remembrance Tourism': A Tool for Legitimating Tourism Development on Battlefields?

In 2008 Dominique Camus, the Head of Tourism Development in the Somme Department, stressed the 'difficulty' of developing tourism based on war heritage and such 'painful memories'.

> According to both public and private actors of our department, the development of tourism on such a sensitive theme needs to be handled with precaution. Obviously, war tourism cannot be treated as seaside tourism, golf or hiking. Local actors have already made sure that the tourist development of sites of memory should conform to the spirit and values of respect and contemplation.[12]

This quotation reveals the tension between tourism for pleasure purposes and more serious modes of travel in remembrance of conflict. After the war, former battlefields were transformed into sacred spaces of remembrance and sites of mourning. They were however also 'profane' places 'haunted by tourists' (*The War Illustrated* 1914, in Danchin 2008: 240), journalists or bystanders coming 'to see the war' and 'to contemplate the destruction' of the 'martyr cities' (Nivet

---

10   Regional Comity for Tourism, Picardy, website: http://picardietourisme.com/fr/index.aspx, consulted in 2007.

11   *Schéma Régional de l'économie touristique et des loisirs 2007–2012*, Stratégies et plan d'action, Conseil régional de Lorraine, p. 28. Available at: http://www.tourisme-lorraine.fr/pages/fr/schemaregional_strategielorraine.pdf.

12   Speech given during a conference about 'Remembrance Tourism' in Picardy, in 2008: ONAC, *Le tourisme des mémoires au service du développement économique et culturel de la Picardie*, Colloque d'Amiens.

2008). From the war itself, these practices have triggered a negative representation of tourism, associated with voyeurism, plundering and disrespect, and perceived in many ways as 'symbolic violence'. During the interwar period, many criticisms were levelled at tourism in the European press, especially among veterans' organisations. For example, in 1919, the *Newspaper of the Devastated Areas for the Defense of the Disaster Victims from the North and the East* stated 'the crowd of people that has nothing to do, or the snobs who go there as if they went to the races. Their cheeky and turbulent nature takes the top and their attitude becomes a profanation for us' (Danchin 2008: 255). The tourist is the one who does not belong to this 'us', expressing a 'community of suffering' to which the veteran or the 'pilgrim' does belong. Compared to the 'profiteer who neither took part in the war, nor in the sacrifice' (Danchin 2008: 255), the tourist represents a negative figure opposed to the veteran-pilgrim. The presence of tourists on the battlefield is thus seen as an intrusion in this sacred place. This social and cultural construction of tourists which appeared during the war actually reveals the dominant position of veterans in European societies during the interwar period (Prost 1986). The stigmatisation of the figure of the tourist partly draws its origin from the ways in which veterans remember battlefields as places of sacrifice.

Immediately following the war, the stigmatisation of tourism was not founded exclusively on the opposition between tourism and pilgrimage. It also revealed the existence of competition between organisers and financial beneficiaries of the trips. In 1919, a deputy of the Meuse attested 'the question is, if the spectacle of our destroyed houses, our demolished hamlets, our sorry and barren campaigns, is, yes or no, going to be exploited and to benefit travel agencies or merchants of tourism, or rather will it benefit the ruins themselves'. Thus, if tourism is often seen as a possibility of enrichment which can contribute to the rebuilding of devastated areas (Danchin 2008: 256), there is a strong criticism of the marketing of the battlefields and the exploitation of suffering for commercial reasons.

These negative representations of tourism, emerging from the time of the war, have had long effects on perceptions of battlefield tourism. Because of the extent of the phenomenon (visitors coming from all over Europe, and other parts of the world), the expanse of the territories and the debates provoked by its development, the interwar period might constitute a key moment in the history of tourism associated with war zones. The 'war' between tourism and pilgrimage, the criticism of a '*spectacularization*' of the suffering, through the transformation of the places of death into visitor attractions, the trivialisation of war and violence, these representations have known re-actualisation today. The speech given in 2006 by the then Australian Minister for Veterans, Bruce Billson, about the development of the Australian battlefields shows that such sensibilities still have resonance in the present. 'We have to remember that our ultimate goal is to commemorate the services rendered and the sacrifices made, and not to create a tourist attraction. The criticism of the "marketing of the battlefields" (Saunders 2008) is still evident and even develops in the context of an emerging "market of the memory"' (Barcellini 2008).

On another level, the denunciation of the damages of tourism through the 'plundering' of the sites by visitors scouring the battlefields in search of objects also intensifies. The reasons are mainly the increasing trade in 'militaria'[13] as we approach the centennial of the war. It also reveals the rise of new categories of professional actors, namely, Great War archaeologists, instituting new representations of battlefields as 'archaeological heritage' or 'heritage in danger', and thus, new 'professional' norms and good practices emerge. More than ever, the 'battlefield explorer' or 'amateur' is now the prototype of the figure of the contemptible 'violent' tourism, incarnating venal, destructive and disrespectful practices. More generally the institutionalisation and professionalisation of battlefield tourism in France since the 1980s has led to the disqualification of former practices or actors. Conflicts and tensions have become very frequent between 'amateurs' belonging to local veteran or heritage associations handling 'their' battlefield and professionals of culture or tourism taking control of the management of the sites. For the traditional actors of the '14/18 community', this new symbolic domination by professionals is often seen as a violent loss of control of the sites but also of the memory of war (Hertzog 2012).

Not without paradox, a decline in or absence of tourism is also greatly deplored, as developing tourism in the battlefields is now an important issue for many stakeholders, especially the public sector. The growing lack of interest by the French for battlefields heritage between the 1960s and 1970s, and the neglected state of many memorials or sites have often been denounced by veteran organisations or local heritage associations, who saw evidence of neglected memories and signs of a collective amnesia (see Offenstadt 2010). Thus, there always seems to be either too many or too few tourists on battlefields!

Because the battlefield symbolises for many a place of suffering, tourism has often been judged as out of place, associated with a form of 'symbolic violence' or 'indecency' towards sacred landscapes and memory of the dead. Nevertheless it has found a renewed legitimacy over the past few decades, through the invention of 'remembrance tourism' ('tourisme de mémoire'[14] a new category of cultural tourism, supported by the State. Institutional actors, experts and professionals of tourism now use this category in France, rather than 'battlefield tourism', 'history tourism' or even 'pilgrimage'. Remembrance tourism implicitly refers to the rhetoric of the 'sites of memory' ('lieux de mémoire': Nora 1986). The concept of remembrance tourism has become a sort of 'verbal convention' sufficiently shared and developed in France to become a 'legitimizing obviousness' just as the notion of 'duty of remembrance' (Ledoux 2009: 1). In 2006, one could read on the French Ministry website that 'the phrase remembrance tourism may be surprising. We may see a contradiction between the term "tourism" that recalls holidays and

---

13   Military objects sold on the world wide web.

14   The English translation of 'tourisme de mémoire' can be 'remembrance tourism' or 'memorial tourism' (both can be found in UNESCO texts or declarations for example).

"remembrance" which is marked by gravity and contemplation. But critics have been rare until today; this denomination is now accepted and used by everyone'.[15]

Remembrance tourism was officially given license by a convention signed between the Ministry of Defense and the Tourism State Secretary in 2004. Since then, it has been reinforced by several texts, declarations and, lastly, a second convention between the two institutions in 2011. Several objectives are expressed: to highlight the importance of French military heritage, to affirm 'its economic role in the development of the territories' (Convention 2004) and to contribute to 'the formation of a civic consciousness',[16] as well as to further the knowledge of history. The same kinds of objectives appear in several UNESCO declarations and projects since the 1990s in which remembrance tourism is presented as a way to protect heritage, link people and contribute to cultural, social and economic development (for example the Slavery Routes project in 2004). For the French Ministry of Defense it is also a way to legitimise some of its strategy in a context of professionalisation of the French army.

More generally, this tourism policy offers a way to authorise tourism, often perceived as 'taboo' or 'negative', in response to the need for making 'tourism development'. Locally, this kind of tourism is perceived as a means of rejuvenating broken territories and local communities traumatised by war violence. In this sense, it is from now on seen as a component of the identity of the territories enabling them to overcome the damage wrought by war. Dominique Camus, in charge of the tourism development, Council of the Somme District, (op. cit. 2008) claims:

> Remembrance Tourism enables the rebuilding of a new identity for these territories (East of the Somme). This new identity is founded on welcoming others, being open to them, in order to encourage trade and mutual enrichment. Battlefield Tourism is beneficial to the inhabitants of these areas, both traumatized by tragedies and the weight of history as they need to evolve. The invaded territories thus become welcoming lands.

Camus also offers the following definition for such tourism 'a form of tourism where the ethical and moral value will be even more present, where the visit of these places of memory will be a means of giving a direction to our future'. Thus, remembrance tourism is defined as 'ethical' and 'sustainable' tourism. It is perceived as a way of reconciling the protection of heritage, economic development and ethical and social values. It offers a prospect which could sound paradoxical: a project of reinvestment in the past, supposed to propel society towards the future.

---

15   Les Chemins de Mémoire, Ministère de la Défense, website: http://www.chemins dememoire.gouv.fr/page/affichepage.php?idLang=fr&idPage=2784.

16   'Tourisme de mémoire', brochure, April 2011, Ministry of Defense, website: http://www.defense.gouv.fr/site-memoire-et-patrimoine/memoire/tourisme-de-memoire-et-memoire-partagee/tourisme-de-memoire, consulted 2012.

Remembrance tourism is thus closely defined as a form of tourism charged with values and 'more sense'. More than any other kinds of tourism it should lead to the 'meeting' between people and is seen as an instrument of peace. This 'peace-making' function of tourism is particularly expressed in the Convention of 2004: 'during a period disturbed by great international events, remembrance tourism seems to be a vector of peace, a means of exchange and an instrument of mutual respect between the peoples'. This rhetoric of peace is generalised and largely drawn upon by all the actors: remembrance tourism is presented as a means 'of celebrating peace between the nations' by the Department of Somme. On another scale, the cross-border network programme between France-Wallonie and Flanders created in 2007 to develop tourism and cross border cooperation is also presented as a 'call for common peace'. This positive representation of tourism, seen as the greatest mass movement of people travelling peacefully to other countries, is sometimes upheld by some academics, but is considered as 'optimistic' or 'naive' by many others (see for example Doquet and Evrard 2008: 12). Nevertheless, the topic of peace is now very common. Since the 1990s, this value has been attached to tourism in order to reach political goals, namely promote European identity. Linked to the notion of 'shared memories'[17] often highlighted in remembrance tourism, the promotion of peace also serves political and diplomatic interests – reconciliation between former enemies, peaceful diplomatic relations, and affirmation of the French position in a globalised world. Locally, plenty of actors use the topics of peace, shared memory, and remembrance tourism to develop didactic tourist tours or international youth camps. Museums and cultural centres also promote peace and shared memory, for example the World Centre for Peace founded in Verdun in the 1980s. Although some voiced doubts about the project, local politicians insisted on creating a cultural place dedicated to peace, close to the most symbolic and highly visited French battlefield. This national site of memory should become an international peace symbol, in an environment full of sites, monuments and numerous war museums, but confronted with the loss of interest in commemorative places a modern museum dedicated to cultural activities was seen as an opportunity to develop a renewed tourist attraction.

Remembrance tourism as an ideal tourism, or rather this ideal of tourism, has emerged as a variation, on a national and local scale, of what Saskia Cousin (2007) calls the globalised 'doctrine' of cultural tourism. Remembrance tourism is endowed with qualities recognised as 'cultural tourism', which have been imposed under the aegis of UNESCO (Cousin 2007). Just like cultural tourism, remembrance tourism is 'sustainable' and makes it possible for 'cultural diversity' to be expressed. For example, this concept was precisely mobilised to promote the tourism development of a Chinese cemetery in the Somme in 2008. As a form of cultural tourism, remembrance tourism policy is 'a way of combining economic

---

17   This notion has been discussed during the 1st International Conference on Shared Memory in Paris in 2006, organised by the French Ministry of Defense and UNESCO, with 24 delegations from countries involved in French military history.

development and visits of heritage sites, practices and cultural exchanges, market of goods and services' (Cousin 2007: 55). At the same time, it incarnates a 'duty of remembrance' in practice. As a type of cultural tourism, tourism of memory is built as an 'ideal mobility, a method of cultural exchange and a development tool' (Cousin 2007: 44). It makes it possible to combine economic exchanges and moral values, and thus realises an inversion of the representations of tourism traditionally associated with symbolic violence.

Conclusion

Battlefield tourism constitutes an interesting case to study the connections between tourism and violence. The reactivation of battlefield tourism over three decades in France make local societies renew associations with a painful and violent past that has long been ignored. Battlefield tourism reveals the complexity of the relationships between French society and the Great War, but also representations of violence as social and cultural constructions and representations of tourism. Thus, peace or 'shared memory' are frequently put forward in the process of making battlefields tourist places. By corollary there has been a rise of registers that do not dismiss war violence, but elevate its status. In a context of important socio-spatial changes, on local and global scales, remembrance tourism is promoted as cultural and ethical tourism and a pacifying function is assigned to this kind of tourism. This positive (thus problematic) vision put forward by certain actors nevertheless clashes with a scepticism about battlefield tourism by some others, which they associate with merchandising or entertainment, and construe a kind of symbolic violence against what should be considered as sites of sacrifice and mourning.

References

Assayag, J. 2007. 'Le spectre des génocides. Traumatisme, muséographie et violences.extrêmes', *Gradhiva*, 5: 6–25, online 12 July 2010. Available at: http://gradhiva.revues.org/658.

Audoin-Rouzeau, S. 1998. 'Le front en Picardie en 1914–1918: creuset et frontière idéologique', in Duménil, A. and Nivet, Ph. *Picardie, terre de frontière*, Amiens, Encrage: 123–32.

Audoin-Rouzeau, S. and Becker, A. 2000. *14/18, retrouver la guerre*, Paris, Gallimard.

Audoin-Rouzeau, S., Becker, A., Ingrao, Ch. and Rousso, H. 2002. *La violence de guerre (1914–1945)*, Paris, Complexe.

Baioni, M. 2004. 'Commémoration et musées', in Becker, J-J. *Encyclopédie de la Grande Guerre*, Paris, Bayard: 1139.

Barcellini, S. 2008. 'Souvenir, mémoire et marché' ('Remembrance, memory and market'), *Le Monde*, 11 November.

Cousin, S. 2008. 'L'Unesco et la doctrine du tourism e culturel', *Civilisations* 57, online 30 Dec 2011. Available at: http://civilisations.revues.org/index1541. html.

Dagen, Ph. 1996. *Le silence des peintres. Les artistes face à la grande Guerre*, Paris, Fayard.

Danchin, E. 2008. 'Héroisation des ruines et des combattants: la mise en place d'un tourisme de champ de bataille (1914–1921)', in Auzas, V. and Jewsiewicki, B. (dir.) *Traumatisme collectif pour patrimoine: regards croiséssur un mouvement transnational,* Presses de l'Université de Laval, Laval, Canada: 237–60.

Doquet, A. and Evrard, O. 2008. 'Introduction: Tourisme, mobilités et altérités contemporaines', *Civilisation*, 57: 9–22, online 30 Dec 2011. Available at: http://civilisations.revues.org/index1541.html.

Garcia, P. 2008. 'Quelques réflexions sur la place du traumatisme collectif dans l'avènement d'unemémoire-Monde', in Auzas, V. and Jewsiewicki, B. (dir.) *Traumatisme collectif pour patrimoine: regards croisés sur un mouvement transnational,* Presses de l'Université de Laval, Laval, Canada: 373–80.

Gough, P. 2010. 'The living, the dead and the imagery of emptiness and reappearance on the battlefields of the western front', in Maddrell, A. and Sidaway, J. (eds) *Deathscapes: New Spaces for Death, Dying and Bereavement*, Ashgate, Farnham: 263–81.

Hertzog, A. 2010. 'La valorisation du patrimoine de la Première guerre mondiale en Picardie. La fabrique d'une ressource culturel le territoriale', in Fournier, L-S., Bernié-Boissard, C., Crozat, D. and Chastagner, Cl. *Développementculturel et territoires*, Paris, L'Harmattan: 189–208.

Hertzog, A. 2012a. 'War battlefield, tourism and imagination', *Via@ International interdisciplinary review of tourism*, 1. Available at: http://www. viatourismreview.net/Article6_EN.php.

Hertzog, A. 2012b. 'Cultural policy and the promotion of world war in heritage sites in France: Emerging professions and hybrid practices', in Paquette, J. *Cultural Policy, Work and Identity*, Ashgate: 56–78.

Lavabre, M.-C. 2000. 'Usages et mésusages de la notion de mémoire', *Critique Internationale*, 7: 48–57.

Ledoux, S. 2009. 'Pour une généalogie du devoir de mémoire en France', Centre Alberto Benveniste. Available at: http://centrealbertobenveniste.org/formail-cab/uploads/Pour-une-genealogie-du%20devoir-de-memoire-Ledoux.pdf.

Lloyd, D.W. 1998. *Battlefield Tourism: Pilgrimage and the Commemoration of the Great War in Britain, Australia and Canada, 1919–1939*, Berg Publisher.

Loez, A. 2010. *La Grande Guerre*, Paris, La Découverte.

MIT, 2005. *Tourismes 2. Moments de lieux*, Paris, Mappemonde, Belin.

Muchenbled, R. 2008. *Une histoire de la violence*, Paris, Seuil.

Nivet, PH. 2008. 'Les origines du tourisme de mémoire: Le tourisme des champs de bataille pendant et après la première guerre mondiale', in ONAC *Le tourisme des mémoires au service du développementéconomique et culturel de la Picardie*, Colloque d'Amiens.

Nora, P. 1986. 'Introduction', *Les lieux de mémoire*, Vol. 1, Paris, Gallimard.

Offenstadt, N. 2010. *La Grande Guerre aujourd'hui*, Paris, Odile Jacob.

Olivera, Ph. 2011. 'Marne 14–18 à Suippes: La réalisation d'un musée local du front', *Le Cartable de Clio*, 11: 91–100.

Prost, A. 1986. 'Verdun', in Nora, P. (dir.) *Les lieux de mémoire*, 1986, 1997, Paris, édition Quarto.

Prouillet, Y. (dir.) 2008. *La grande Guerre dans les Vosges*, Conseil Général des Vosges.

Rousso, H. 2007. 'Versunemondialisation de la mémoire', in Rousso, H. *Mémoires Europe-Asie, Vingtième siècle*, 2/94: 3–10.

Ryan, C. 2007. *Battlefield Tourism: History, Place and Interpretation*, Elsevier.

Sharpley, R. and Stone, P.R. 2009. *The Darker Side of Travel: The Theory and Practice of Dark Tourism*, Bristol, Channel View.

Trouche, D. 2010. *Les mises en scène de l'histoire. Approchecommunicationnelle des sites historiques des guerresmondiales*, Paris, L'Harmattan.

Veschambre, V. 2008. *Traces et mémoires urbaines. Enjeux sociaux de la patrimonialisation et de la destruction*, Rennes, PUR.

Wahnich, S. 2010. 'Transmettrel'effroi, penser la terreur', *Gradhiva*, 5, 2007, online 12 July 2010. Available at: http://gradhiva.revues.org/692.

Wahnich, S. and Gueissaz, M. 2001. *Les Musées des guerres du xxe siècle: des lieux du politique?* Paris, Kimé ('Tumultes').

Winter, J. 2008. 'Présentation de la muséographie de l'Historial', in Becker, J-J. *Les collections de l'Historial de P*éronne, Paris, Ed. Somogy.

Winter, J. and Prost, A. 2004. *Penser la Grande Guerre. Un essai d'historiographie*, Paris, Seuil, Point Histoire.

Chapter 7

Tourism, Sight Prevention, and Cultural Shutdown: Symbolic Violence in Fragmented Landscapes

Tom Selwyn

Let us go in together, and still your fingers on your lips, I pray. The time is out of joint – O cursèd spite, That ever I was born to set it right! Nay, come, let's go together.

Hamlet, I, v

Preface

There are few territories in or around Europe whose political, geographical, and symbolic landscapes are as fragmented as those within the State of Bosnia-Herzegovina (hereafter BiH) and those between the Mediterranean sea and the River Jordan.

In the former case we find a single state divided into two so-called 'entities'. On the one hand there is the Federation of Bosnia-Herzegovina, with a population made up (mainly) of Muslims, Catholics, Jews, and agnostics and, on the other, Republika Srpska (hereafter the RS) with a population (mainly) of Orthodox Christians. The capital cities of these 'entities' are Sarajevo and Banja Luka whilst the capital of the State of BiH is Sarajevo. West Mostar is effectively the cultural centre of the Bosnian Croat population of BiH who are thought of as a third ethnic group in the country. These political and supposedly ethnic divisions resulted from the extensive 'ethnic cleansing' of the 1992/1995 Bosnian War and the Dayton Peace agreement signed in December 1995 that brought it to a close by legitimating the consequences on the ground of the violent mass civilian displacement that took place. Moreover, amazingly (and amazingly confusingly) Bosnian Serbs may obtain passports issued by the State of Serbia in addition to passports issued by BiH, whilst, in a comparable way, Bosnian Croats may obtain Croatian passports.

In the case of the area between the Mediterranean and the Jordan there is one state (Israel), increasing numbers of whose citizens now live in the neighbouring non-state of Palestine, within which there is another territory (even more of a non-state, one might say), namely Gaza. The map of that part of Palestine known as the

'West Bank' (the land to the west of the Jordan) has a lace or lattice like quality: areas of land punctured by over 200 island-like Israeli so-called 'settlements' and 'outposts' along with military bases, and nature parks controlled by Israel, all of which are attached to the Israeli mainland by an integrated system of mainly straight and wide roads whilst the Palestinian towns and villages are connected within the territory to each other by roads that are older, narrower, more sinewy and difficult to negotiate, routinely blocked by hundreds of check points. And then of course there is the enormous wall that careers its way through Palestine, from north to south, spawning many other walls along the way (like those that cut into Bethlehem, for example, around the area of Rachel's Tomb) one effect which is literally to prevent citizens in Israel actually seeing Palestinians in Palestine, and vice-versa.

In short, both territories are examples of landscapes that are deeply 'out of joint'. States, non-states, 'entities', 'settlements', divided cities, parks, military bases, refugee camps, checkpoints, walls, barriers, good roads for drivers of one ethnic affiliation, bad roads for drivers of another, flyovers, tunnels: all jostle and overlap. Furthermore, existing refugee camps in one territory (Palestine) will necessarily bring to mind memories of wartime camps and 'safe havens' in another (BiH), one of the most infamous examples of the latter being the town of Srebrenica in which military forces of the 'international community' allowed many Bosniaks (Muslim citizens) to be killed. Such memories will be propelled further back to a time in Palestine of war, violent dispersals of population, the sacking and destruction of villages, of cultural erasure. These memories will, in turn, give rise to memories more distant still of ghettoes, camps and mass murder in places far away from the Mediterranean.

Presently, tourists, visitors, and citizens who now traverse these fragmented spaces are subject to wide varieties of interpretations. Like landscapes everywhere, the fractured contours of BiH and Israel/Palestine are nothing less than canvasses upon which are inscribed multi textual, if deeply contested, narratives about how the world has worked in the past and how it works now. Moreover, landscapes of the external world are, of course, experienced, felt, and expressed internally both cognitively and emotionally. External landscapes and internal landscapes mirror each other in many senses.

Introduction

This chapter considers the relationship between tourism and violence by using the idea of *symbolic* violence – first explored by Bourdieu and Passeron (1977) with regard to education in general – to look at the politics and political implications of certain types of tourism and the 'cultural industries' (including painting and the visual arts, design, sculpture, work in museums, galleries, libraries, forms of intellectual work, and forms of tourism itself) in BiH and Israel/Palestine. The use to which the idea of symbolic violence is put here is to illuminate a discussion about the role of tourism and the cultural industries in the production and reproduction of nationalist views of the world, on the one hand, culturally pluralist and interculturalist views (cf. Khan 2006, for a powerful definition and exploration of this term in the British diaspora context) on the other.

The chapter's title picks out two particularly potent symbolic features of the contemporary cultural landscapes of BiH and Israel/Palestine both of which have to do with questions of identity, identity formation, and identity boundaries. These are, firstly, what has come to be known at the 'cultural shutdown' in Sarajevo and, secondly, particular (and particularly characteristic) types of tours in Israel – and by Israelis abroad – both of which are linked metaphorically in the chapter, in ways that will become clear, to 'the Wall'[1] that physically separates Israel from Palestine.

In addition to looking at the deployment of symbolic violence in the construction of nationalist/exclusivist versions of human and political relationships the chapter also reflects on ways in which these versions of how the world works are being challenged and resisted by alternative modes of tourism in the Israeli/Palestinian case and a bold initiative in the field of visual art and sculpture in the BiH case. The chapter further argues that academic work in tourism and the cultural industries carried out in the early years of the 2000s under the auspices of the European Commission's TEMPUS (Trans European Mobility for University Studies) Programme by staff and postgraduate students in networks of universities centred upon the Bosnian cities of Sarajevo and Banja Luka and the Palestinian city of Bethlehem were, and remain, committed quite precisely to undermining nationalist and culturally separatist ideas and practices in both BiH and Israel/Palestine. Our TEMPUS work aimed, and aims now, to contribute to the work of a growing number of movements and initiatives in the tourism and cultural industries field aiming to replace such dispositions with sets of ideas and practices founded upon and embracing cosmopolitanism and cultural pluralism.

What follows thus opens with a brief recollection of the notion of symbolic violence as expressed by our two authors. There follows an ethnographic section in which their ideas are applied, first of all, to certain types of tours in Israel/ Palestine (with a short reference to tours by Israelis to Poland) and, secondly, to the 'cultural shutdown' (to be described below) in Sarajevo.

One preliminary point needs making. Bourdieu and Passeron use the notion of symbolic violence to reveal how education works ideologically and politically. The assumption here (hardly controversial) is that tourism and the arts are both educative practices: both are firmly in the business of education. The proposition seems extremely clear with regard to the particular cases discussed in this chapter.

---

1 'The Wall' has different names ('Security Wall', 'Apartheid Wall', and so on) which reflect ways that different people perceive it. In this chapter we will simply refer to it as 'the Wall'.

Symbolic Violence

Bourdieu and Passeron introduce their 'theory of symbolic violence' by stating 'Every power which manages to impose meanings and to impose them as legitimate by concealing the power relations that are the basis of its force, adds its own specifically symbolic force to those power relations' (op. cit.: 4). They add 'All pedagogic action (PA) is, objectively, symbolic violence insofar as it is the imposition of a cultural arbitrary by an arbitrary power'[2] and that 'PA necessarily implies, as a social condition of its exercise, *pedagogic authority*' (op. cit.: 5, authors' italics). The authors thus identify the terms *symbolic violence* and *pedagogic authority* as being indispensable to any analysis of the way that educational structures and processes work. The present chapter builds on the applicability of these propositions to ideas and practices beyond the formal education system to other sites and fields such as the tours and forms of cultural work discussed here.

Pedagogic work (PW), they add, amounts to 'a process through which a cultural arbitrary is historically reproduced through the medium of the production of the *habitus* productive of practices conforming with that cultural arbitrary ... and is the equivalent, in the cultural order, of the transmission of genetic capital in the biological order' (1977: 32). In short, it is through pedagogic work that *cultural capital* is produced and reproduced. In this chapter we are concerned with the cultural capital produced and reproduced in BiH and Israel/Palestine by aspects of tourism and the cultural industries widely defined. We may pause to record Bottomore's (1977: vi) foreword to the English edition of Bourdieu's and Passeron's *La Reproduction* in which he observes that the theory of symbolic violence traced by the authors has a direct link to the well-known proposition by Marx that the ruling ideas in every age are the ideas of the ruling class.

Here is the central point for us. We are concerned here with two sets of phenomena in two different Mediterranean territories. We will look at both with a view to interpreting the stories/narratives in and around them as pedagogic work and action with the same political and cultural purposes held by the ruling political authorities. The first of these is to assert the absolute primacy of ethno-religious identity in human affairs, the second is to close down the possibilities – precisely in territories so transparently demographically defined by people and groups of differing cultural dispositions – for serious thinking about cultural pluralism, interculturalism and cosmopolitanism.

---

2   The adjective *arbitrary* may refer not only to decisions and/or understandings that are capricious and/or unrestrained by reason but also to a government that wields power unrestricted by law. One may speak, for example, of 'arbitrary government'.

Sight Prevention and Cultural Shutdown

The Tours of the Society for the Protection of Nature in Israel (SPNI)

I have written elsewhere (Selwyn 1995, 1996) in some detail about the tours organised and run by the SPNI. Founded in 1953 the SPNI was born from a collection of ideas and practices that included East European walking and hiking traditions, workers' education movements, scouting and other activities associated with the emerging military formations in pre-state Palestine (including the *Palmach*, the élite commando unit of the new army) all of which came together to create a disposition towards land and landscape that came to be known as *Yediat Ha'Aretz*, 'knowing the country'.

The SPNI is a membership organisation as well as a very successful tour operator, addressing itself primarily to Israeli residents as well as to visitors to the country from the Jewish Diaspora. A small number of non-Jewish visitors find their ways on to SPNI tours. Prominent SPNI members routinely take part in media debates having to do with nature protection and conservation in Israel.

The society has a very substantial budget made up of membership subscriptions, payments for trips, and (above all perhaps) grants from the Israeli Ministry of Education with which it has a very close relationship. A large proportion of the tours devised and managed by the SPNI take tourists into the Israeli countryside where they are taught about the flora and fauna in what they term a 'holistic' way, or a way that ties the natural world inexorably into specifically Jewish and Israeli history, society, and culture.

There are a large number of SPNI field schools to be found all over Israel. These are normally stocked with guidebooks and maps about the areas around the schools as well as basic cooking facilities and (in some cases) accommodation. Members of staff of the field schools are mostly young post-army personnel who fulfil various functions including tour guiding.

I have described SPNI tours as 'myth collecting tours' (Selwyn 1996), an expression echoed by Whitman (2011) who speaks of the participants of *Birthright* tours (discussed below) as 'absorbing Jewish-Israeli myths'. Thus I have described how the SPNI tours combine at least four registers in managing to be (mainly through the skill of the guides) at the same time scientific, emotionally demanding, physically testing, and rhetorically extremely inviting. Thus, to start with, they will all include detailed analyses of the flora and fauna encountered, together with detailed references to significant examples of the built heritage (Roman remains of one kind or another, Crusader's castles, sites of biblical significance, and so on). Secondly, partly because the SPNI tours (like the others described here) are *group* events, partly because of the key role of the guide in assuming the role of *mora/madrich* (teacher/leader) and thus being the focus of admiration and identification, the tours tend to engage their participants in noticeably strong emotional attachments and feelings of kinship with each other and with the land and landscape through which they are taken. Thirdly, part of the intellectual and emotional power of the SPNI tours derives from the physical experiences they involve. These range from difficult and sometimes dangerous climbs up or down gorges or ravines to much more gentle but nevertheless physically significant visits to streams and waterfalls which involve participants being in turn wet and cold (from the water) and dry and hot (from the sun) and so on. Such physical experiences, allied as they inevitably are with powerful oratorical accompaniment (through the voice of the tour guide), are the foundations of the processes of ideological embodiment with which a considerable amount of the present volume is concerned. These kinds of experiences provide the contexts in which SPNI tourists are exposed not just to sight but to all sorts of other sensations (such as smell, taste, feeling generally) as well, all of which, fourthly, tend, to emphasise the point the *rhetorical* claims of the guide more convincing and seductive. One is, so to speak, *drawn in* to a mythical/ideological landscape in which one can come close to being in touch with very ancient roots indeed. As one SPNI advertisement puts it about one stretch of landscape its tours cover, it is 'the only biblical landscape in the world' (cf. op. cit.: 123).

This is much too brief a summary indication of the SPNI and its tours, but at least it enables us to begin to recognise the direction to which the sociological/ anthropological signposts are pointing. We are, to use favourite expressions used by both Durkheim and Mauss, in distinctively 'effervescent' cognitive and emotional territory.

And Palestinians are absolutely nowhere to be seen.

Taglit-Birthright Tours

We are fortunate in having an extremely thoughtful and detailed description and analysis of the *Taglit-Birthright* (*Taglit* meaning discovery) programme in Kelner's (2010) *Tours that Bind: Diaspora, Pilgrimage, and Israeli Birthright Tourism.*

Kelner describes how at the core of *Birthright* are 10-day-long tours of Israel for young Jewish Americans. Between 30–40 young people are given an all-expenses-paid tour to many of the more famous sites in Israel led by young Israeli (post-army) guides. The tours involve powerful physical experiences (hiking, climbing, swimming, eating, drinking, generally having communal fun) and intense meetings and discussions with representatives of important Israeli institutions such as local community leaders, army personnel, university staff, and comparable others. There may very well also be meetings and discussions with Palestinian spokespersons.

Whitman (2011) estimates the cost of the *Birthright* programme (up to 2011) at $500 million collected and donated by a combination of Jewish philanthropic associations, community organisations, the Jewish Agency – in addition to the Israeli government itself (Glassenberg 2011).

Birthright tours are powerful experiences that mirror those of SPNI tours. Both originate from a common ideological source and work cognitively, emotionally, and psychologically in similar ways. Glassenberg (loc. cit.) captures it well. Speaking of *Birthright* he writes that we have

… a picture of dynamic interplaying factors: a highly structured manipulating of variables and circumstances on the part of *Taglit-Birthright* and the various trip organizers, the conscious and semi-conscious framing of sites by tour guides, the teasing out and highlighting of strictly Jewish meanings and identities by American teachers. [The tours are underpinned by] the natural tendency of tourists to seek meaning everywhere, on the 10-day high of unique physical experiences and pleasures, on the intimate group dynamic, and on the agency of the free-thinking independent tourist trying to make sense of it all.

Kelner demonstrates the ways that the tours are designed to foster close attachments of participants to each other as well as to the land and landscape of Israel. The microcosmic experiences of the tours are intended, at a more macro level, to engender a comparable sense of closeness amongst the American Diaspora community and to ground such feelings of solidarity upon recognition that they are produced and reproduced by a relationship with Israel that is, so to say, umbilical. The tours achieve this partly or mainly by weaving this attachment into a strong sense that it is also an integral part of a *personal* transformative experience. It is common, he reports, to hear an individual participant reporting that the trip 'changed my life'.

Kelner argues that *Birthright* is as much concerned with the continuing existence of the American Jewish Diaspora as it is with the task of persuading young Jewish people to emigrate to Israel. Building on this insight, Saxe et al. (2010) have linked *Birthright* to the growing anxiety in the American Jewish Diaspora that it is threatened by inter-marriage.

SPNI, Birthright, Cultural Capital and Pedagogic Authority

The SPNI and *Birthright* tours share a narrative with an extensive number of other tours organised for Israeli residents, Jewish and non-Jewish visitors to Israel, potential immigrants to Israel, Israeli schoolchildren to Poland and the camps (Feldman 2008), and others. This powerful and very familiar narrative speaks about what it means to be Jewish in the post-Holocaust world and (which is our particular focus here) how Jews and non-Jews alike should relate to and think about the Israeli State. Golden (1996) puts it succinctly in her description and analysis of the 'story' told in the Museum of the Jewish Diaspora at Tel-Aviv University. The museum tells of the ways that Jews, Muslims, and Christians used to live more or less harmoniously in Spain before its re-conquest by Ferdinand and Isabella and the consequent expulsion of both Jews and Muslims from the country. In 1492, the museum tells us, the hundreds of years of co-existence came to an end, never to re-appear. The museum further tells its visitors that Jews living in pre-Second World War Europe did not heed the lessons of 1492, many paying the price in Hitler's death camps. In short, the museum's narrative underpins those of our tours. They tell us that it is fundamentally unsafe for Jews to live in a cosmopolitan world; that great emphasis needs placing on community solidarity and, for example, the concomitant avoidance of intermarriage; that the need is paramount to bind the strongest possible relationship between Jews and the land of Israel as the only safe home for Jewish people. Furthermore, as Wesley (2006) shows in such detail in relation to planning decisions in Nazareth, it is not only those sources reputed (particularly by rightist Israeli and American political rhetoric) to be flamboyantly 'obvious' dangers – Iran, Hizbollah, and 'Hamastan' – that are thought potentially threatening but ordinary Arab/Palestinian residents and citizens of Israel living in Israeli towns and villages.

In short, the cognitive and emotional bases of the cultural capital and pedagogic authority of our tours (backed up and complimented as these are by institutions and politico-cultural processes of various kinds) is to be found not just in the real historical violence experienced by Jews at various historical moments but also in the pedagogic work and political production and reproduction of cultural capital that ensures a framework of *symbolic violence* that comes in the present to be *frozen* in time. Before returning to some of the corollaries of this for contemporary Israel/Palestine, we will turn our attention back to BiH.

'Cultural Shutdown' in Sarajevo

In June 2012 there was a meeting of young professionals in the field of arts and the cultural industries in the Historical Museum of Sarajevo to discuss the closure/semi-closure/partial operation of seven institutions in Sarajevo. These are The National and University Library which was the first building in the city to be bombed at the beginning of the siege, destroying two million items of priceless books, documents, and archives from various parts of the world in a variety of languages; The National Museum of Bosnia and Herzegovina: closed on 4 October 2012 but now active again; The Art Gallery of Bosnia and Herzegovina: still closed; The Museum of Literature and Theatre Arts of Bosnia and Herzegovina, closed for a while as a political protest; the National Film Archive of Bosnia and Herzegovina which is unable to appoint a management board without sponsorship/support from government; The National Library for the Blind and Partially Sighted Persons, which is open but which has had considerable difficulties appointing a board; and the Historical Museum itself which Susan Pearce (2013) has described as a (still) battle-scarred crumbling façade next door to a gleaming shopping centre. There is no permanent funding for these institutions and no ministry formally in charge of them.

This gloomy catalogue of failing cultural institutions does not mean, of course, that there are *no* spaces in the city where cultural work takes place. Of course there are: bookshops, faith based spaces within or beside mosques/churches/synagogues, a cinema complex, cafés, the vibrant streets themselves, music venues of various kinds, even universities: not only centres of intellectual activity and the cultural work which accompanies it but sometimes also centres of *familial* cultural life: Burch University (one of the three Turkish-funded universities in Elija, a suburb of the city, which are all doing well) holds regular festivities for children and families.

Nevertheless the closure/semi-closure of the seven named centres of artistic and cultural life in Sarajevo does have enormous practical and symbolic significance for the life of the city and its visitors. In order to think through what the significance might be we need to lay some basic foundations by sketching some of the politico-economic contours of the historical governance of arts centres compared with how they are run today.

Historical and Contemporary Politico-economic Contexts of the 'Cultural Shutdown' in BiH

This is assuredly not the place to make any more than a fleeting and programmatic note about the contexts of the 'cultural shutdown' in Sarajevo (even if the present writer had any competence to do so which he does not) except to make the obvious point that any half decent account of the historical emergence of each of the seven would constitute fascinating and important research topics. Here we can only glimpse at some of the possibilities. For example, what became the National and University Library under Tito after the Second World War was located in a building designed by Austrian architects and opened in 1896 as Sarajevo's town hall. The stories about the library I have heard contain reference to the Austrian authorities encouraging one of the building's architects to visit Cairo to learn about buildings in Egypt on the grounds that a 'pseudo Moorish' building, as people refer to it, would be congenial to the city's Muslim population and fit into the Ottoman old town which the Austrians preserved. As a library in post-war Yugoslavia it became famous for its collection of books, documents, manuscripts, and archives from all parts of the Muslim, Jewish, and Christian world in languages from Farsi to Turkish, Hebrew to Arabic, German to Bosnian as well as others. This priceless heritage was inherited by independent BiH in April 1992 and incendiary bombed (with inflammable bullets) shortly afterwards by the military forces that later besieged the city for three years. It was as if for one brief moment BiH held a prize – some would say *the* prize – that has clearly eluded the world ever since. It was as if for those few days in 1992 a building and all its books in Sarajevo became a sign that there *was* a time in Europe when a cosmopolitan world had existed and flourished based on a largely productive co-existence – notably in such fields as the arts, medicine, and science – between Jews, Muslims, and Christians. Shortly after their expulsion from Spain in 1492 a Jewish community took root in Sarajevo, a thought that reminds us that during the siege of Sarajevo this community was entrusted with keeping some of the most valuable Islamic treasures safe during the siege. Whilst glad that the latest *Visitor's Guide to Sarajevo* (2013) assures us that the building will open in 2014, thanks partly to EU funding, it is still hard to find words adequately to describe the failure of the local and international authorities in allowing the building *still* to be more or less empty in 2013.

As we have noted above, the Dayton Agreement signed in 1995 effectively legitimated the physical results of the war and divided the country in the way described in the Preface above. The effect of the war and its endorsement by Dayton for our present purposes is that the responsibility/governance for 'culture' and cultural work has been – precisely – split up, fragmented, and has no coherence. Or, to put it more exactly, the coherent policy towards 'culture' in BiH is resolutely to have none and to ensure that any sign of an emergence of any was and is simply blocked. One example of this was the prevention of Ars Aevi to bring an exhibition of works by Bosnian artists to represent the country for the second time in history at the Venice Biennale in 2009, on the grounds that the collection contained no work by Serb artists. When it was pointed out that in fact the selection did have work by several 'Serb' artists, including one of the most famous of all contemporary Bosnian artists, Braco Dimitrijevic – who at one time was resident of Sarajevo and who now lives in Paris – and who could be recognised as a Serb by origin and name, whilst being a known cosmopolitan – the Ars Aevi organisers were met by a response from counterparts appointed by the state Ministry of Civil Affairs, which at the time was headed by a minister from the RS, that would have warmed the heart of any British Rail user who has been faced with the explanation that trains were late because of the 'wrong kind of snow'. Dimitrijevic was effectively the 'wrong kind of Serb' in the sense that he neither lived in the RS nor subscribed to its state building tendencies. Dimitrijevic's monumental exhibition did take part in the Biennale, but as an Ars Aevi project, selected by the artistic of the Biennale, and not by the state ministry.

Given this kind of blockade and obfuscation it comes as no surprise that our seven institutions are drifting in a sea of near bankruptcy blown around by capricious and malicious political forces drawing them towards the rocks of permanent closure and dissolution.

Shutting Down, Preventing Sight, Cementing Fragments: The Triumph of 'Entities'

We may now return to the consideration of the political and cultural corollaries both of our tours in Israel/Palestine and the cultural shutdown in Sarajevo.

Earlier comments about the former BiH National and University Library being at the very epicentre of European and global cosmopolitan memory could be extended in different ways to others of our closed institutions. The 'cultural shutdown' in Sarajevo is, in several senses, a reflection of the fact that military force-of-arms and an international peace agreement have gone some way to undermining multi-cultural BiH itself: the same can be said of cosmopolitan Palestine.

It is worth a sentence or two to think about what is at stake. Programmatically (as that is all we can do here) we might think of juxtaposing nationalist projects with cosmopolitan projects by taking a leaf out of Karl Popper's (1945) work and thinking about two possibilities, the Open Society and the Closed Society. In the context of BiH, Popper's spirit is evident in the pages of Landry's (2002) Council of Europe Report *Togetherness in Difference: Culture at the Crossroads in Bosnia Herzegovina*. For this author, an Open Society in BiH would be one in which senses of personal, social, and cultural security are approached through mutual recognition, in which intercultural ideas and values are expressed in many ways including in artistic work, in which the writing of history gets done professionally and with a maximum of negotiation between parties. By contrast a Closed Society is one in which the primacy of ethno-religious identity is said to be primary, cultural mixing seen as a source of danger, and the seeming inevitable need is ideologically established for a 'security' enforced by force of arms alone. The only way in which people in this latter kind of territory can physically and metaphorically get around is through, along, under, over, and around corridors, 'by-pass roads' (Selwyn 2001) tunnels, flyovers, and walls. In a 'Corridor Society' (R. Selwyn 2013) – effectively what the territory between the Mediterranean and the River Jordan has become – one does not actually *see* the other: he/she remains invisible, unknowable, unrecognisable.

As far as the disjointed spaces of BiH and Israel/Palestine are concerned we may note a recent report by the International Crisis Group (ICG) speaks of a 40 per cent unemployment rate and multiple blockades of state wide economic and cultural policies in BiH. The former High Representative, Paddy Ashdown, routinely writes and speaks about the country sliding backwards into conditions comparable to those of pre-war days. Many of the personnel and departments in the institutions of the EU, UN, World Bank, and other bodies have moved on, leaving the door open for a type of frontier capitalism that pays scant attention to the demands of the Bosnian environment, society, or culture. As for Palestine, its natural and cultural assets and heritage are being stripped and degraded by the day. The winner of the 2008 Orwell Prize for Literature, Raja Shehadeh (2007) describes how 'The hills (on which I started walking as a child) were like one large nature reserve with all the unspoiled beauty and freedom unique to such areas'. Now, however, the region is promoted to would-be Israeli settlers in terms of the desirability of its biblical landscape. But, as the Israeli architects Rafi Segal and Eyal Weizman (2003) have observed:

> that which renders the landscape "biblical" – its traditional inhabitants, cultivation in terraces, olive orchards, stone building, and the presence of livestock – is produced by Palestinians whom the Jewish settlers came to replace. The very people who cultivate the "green olive orchards" (of the brochures) and render the landscape biblical are themselves excluded from the panorama. The Palestinians are there to produce the scenery and then disappear.

Indeed, the suffocation of Palestinian towns, cities, and villages, continues apace.

In both territories there are, of course, obvious politico-economic consequences of the increasingly closed and divided societies. In BiH along with ubiquitous signs of dysfunctional government, there are, as we have noted, sites of real poverty. Palestine is witness to deepening occupation, ghettoisation, and ethnic cleansing in all but name. The International Community[3] arrives periodically with

---

3   The term International Community (with its upper case initial letters) is used here loosely to point towards international organisations such as the Office of the High

spectacular and trumpeted gifts ('$4Billion to double the Palestinian economy in three years' as John Kerry puts it) but then retreats into the background as if it, too, was terminally subject to local/regional political forces.

At a recent public lecture in London, Daniel Seidemann (2013) the founder and organiser of the organisation Ir-Amim (http://eng.ir-amim.org.il/) asked rhetorically whether Israel/Palestine had 'become so Balkanised' as to be beyond repair. The solution of his organisation to the fragmentation of the territory lies in the rapid agreement to enable two states to co-exist in the region. This is also the rhetorical solution of spokespersons of the International Community. If there is not such an agreement soon (within two years, he says) Seidemann predicts that the area will inevitably experience what he describes as 'the slow train wreck' that is well on the way to happening as the 'two state solution' would be completely impossible to reach.[4] There is an increasing number of observers who would regard his remedy, even if it were desirable, as utopian. Looking at Israel/Palestine from BiH, as we have done here, and observing the actual reality of its physical landscape it is clear that the 'spatial shaping' of the territory undertaken by the Israeli state since 1967 has long since rendered any two state solution impossible realistically to conceive let alone achieve. The physical and political reality is that the territory between the Mediterranean and the River Jordan is a single, if deeply fragmented, territorial unit in which, as we have observed earlier, a state rules a non-state by military force. Furthermore, looking at this geographical space using a Bosnian lens, then it is not so much 'just' a state, but an '*entity* state' ruling a non-state in the Israel/Palestine region.

Tourism and the Arts as Resistance to Fragmentation: Responses in BiH and Israel/Palestine

We started by considering the uses to which the idea of symbolic violence might be put in two cases within the tourism and cultural industries. These cases consisted of mainstream tour operations (SPNI, *Taglit-Birthright*, tours to Poland organised by the Israeli Ministry of Education, for example) and the 'cultural shutdown' in BiH. Bourdieu and Passeron defined the purposes of symbolic violence in education in terms of the extent to which the pedagogic work and consequent cultural capital help legitimate ruling ideas and values in any society. The pedagogic work in the case of the Israeli tours and the Sarajevo 'cultural shutdown' clearly share a similar aim, namely to promote the idea that ethnic and religious identity is the primary principle upon which social and political organisation is (and must always be) based.

Representative (OHR) in BiH and other affiliated organisations of the UN and comparable institutions as well as the bilateral and multilateral initiatives undertaken by allied states.

    4   Cf. the texts and maps on Seidemann's *Terrestial Jerusalem* (http://www.t-j.org.il/) for example.

However, we may now consider the fact that in both our territories we also find radically alternative ideas and values within the spheres of tourism and the cultural industries. These are to be found in the structures and processes of a number of organisations, initiatives, and projects. We can only give the briefest of insights of what these consist of here, so will confine our considerations to three sets of activities: the Ars Aevi collection in BiH, a variety of 'alternative' tour operations in Israel/Palestine, and work carried out within the EC's TEMPUS Programme in BiH and Palestine.

BiH: Ars Aevi, Sarajevo

The Ars Aevi project is arguably one of the most remarkable art collections/ collaborations in the world. One of its catalogues (Ars Aevi 2006) outlines and describes not only the art objects in the collection but also the history and genesis of the project itself. Originally conceived in the early 1990s and realised in the years during and after the Bosnian War, it consists of a network of artists and cultural institutions and museums, in Milan, Prato, Ljubljana, Venice, Vienna – and shortly (the present chapter is written in 2013) Belgrade. Each of these co-operating cities has constructed collections of art works that are exhibited specifically as part of the wider Ars Aevi project: each city thus has an artistic nucleus connected with Sarajevo. For example in the year 2000 the Modern Art Museum in Vienna held an exhibition entitled 'Sarajevo 2000'. Writing in the catalogue to this exhibition (quoted in Ars Aevi, op. cit.: 374), Alexander Zigo traces the historical and cultural background of the Bosnian War and, in turn, to Ars Aevi. Looking back to the fall of the Berlin Wall in 1989 and the start of the disintegration of Yugoslavia which had arguably begun in 1980 with the death of Tito and gathered steam with the independence of Slovenia in 1991, Zigo wrote of the 'new nationalism' that emerged in central and eastern Europe. One of the features of this, he wrote, was the spreading pattern in the region of political rhetoric that presented certain national minorities as scapegoats. The example of Sarajevo, a 'small capital in a small republic in the Balkans with a historically grown multicultural centre which has experienced the mutually beneficial coexistence of different cultures for several centuries' was seized on by many artists and intellectuals because 'they perceived the experience of the city as a real alternative' (to the growing nationalism elsewhere in the region). This was the context in which the Ars Aevi project was developed.

The list of globally distinguished visual artists who have worked, and continue to work with Ars Aevi, is a very long one and includes Anish Kapoor, Braco Dimitrijevic, Michelangelo Pistoletto, and at least 100 others, all amongst the most distinguished workers in the arts of our time. It is, of course, totally impossible to write in any detail here, but there are three examples of work displayed in the collection held in 1996 in Ljubljana that give the briefest of tastes of what a more extended account might cover. Yves Klein's *l'État*, part of the *oeuvre* of the Ljubljana-based artistic network IRWIN, shows a thin, arguably slightly vulnerable, and undoubtedly beautiful young woman, naked and surrounded by five men in blue suits holding paint brushes. This picture is placed within a box-like structure on top of what appears to be parts of an engine. The text within the work reads '*Certificate d'Authentication, Cette oeuvre est un original Yves Klein – IRWIN*'. Viewers may wonder, though, whether the 'authentication' at issue refers to the painter or to the title of the work, *l'État*. Perhaps the painting is about the authentication of the state by official looking men, whose people are represented by the vulnerable naked woman. Such an interpretation would, after all, touch a very familiar vein of nationalist symbolism in Europe upon which trope the work casts a sardonic gaze. Then there is Marjetica Potrc's *A House with a Room for Possessions* that consists of an expansive wooden balcony with a door leading into a wall. It is as if the viewer was led towards a room to view objects of value which (as precious objects do) bear upon the subject's identity, only to find his or her sight blocked (and, indeed, mocked) by the fact that the door opens on a wall where of course there is nothing to be seen. Finally, there is the ironic box with a slit in the top (as it were a box for placing voting slips) produced by Evgeny Asse, Vadim Fishkin, Dimitri Gutoff, and Viktor Misiano, that turns out to be a receptacle for donating money. The text superimposed on the box is '*Donate for Artificial Reason*'.

These works point us towards a collection which, indicative of the Ars Aevi project in general, is concerned with providing artistic spaces in which viewers, as active participants, are encouraged to think through a number of fundamentally interconnected issues. The three examples above suggest that these include: the interplays between identity/identities, nationalism, legitimation processes and the symbolic role in these of men and women, objects, their meanings and the relations between them, spatial symbolism, reason and unreason, vulnerability, malleability, propaganda and ideological mobilisation, and (profoundly shown within each case quoted here) democracy – or more particularly (since democracy suffers from rhetorical overuse) – the capacities of individuals and collectivities to think together, flexibly and freely, about how relationships between them may be framed and re-framed.

Israel/Palestine: ATG (Beit Sahour), Zochrot (Tel-Aviv), Kairos Palestine (Jerusalem), ICAHD (Jerusalem), Open Bethlehem (Bethlehem)

There is a growing number of civil society organisations in Palestine/Israel who are working to counter the mainstream discourse of officially supported tour operations in the region of which the following are a sample.

The Alternative Tourism Group (ATG) (info@atg.ps) is a tour operation directed by Rami Kassis based in Beit Sahour, neighbouring Bethlehem. It organises tours for all types of tourists from university students to diplomats and pilgrimages for those looking for alternatives to more traditional mass pilgrimage in the Holy Land. Its itineraries include visits to and discussions with Palestinian and Israeli activists in Palestine, olive picking tours, and has produced the most comprehensive guidebook to Palestine and Palestinians presently in publication (Sabri et al. 2005). It has also developed a Code of Conduct for tourists in Palestine that has been adopted by the Palestinian Ministry of Tourism, and works with a number of Israeli/Palestinian human rights organisations, including Zochrot, Breaking the Silence (whose membership is made up of Israeli soldiers dedicated to documenting their experiences in occupied Palestine), the Alternative Information Centre, Rabbis for Human Rights, B'tsalem, the Israeli Information Centre for Human Rights.

Zochrot is an organisation founded by Eitan Bronstein and managed from its office in Tel-Aviv. Its home website (zochrot.org) informs readers that Zochrot 'will act to challenge the Israeli Jewish public's preconceptions and promote awareness, political and cultural change within it to create the conditions for the Return of Palestinian Refugees and a shared life in this country'. To this end Zochrot runs tours for Israelis and visitors to Israel/Palestine to Palestinian villages destroyed in 1948, working with former residents to recall and describe the buildings, and the social and cultural life of the villages. The group presents the 1948 *Al Nakba* as 'the destruction, expulsion, looting, massacres and incidents of rape of the Palestinian inhabitants of this country [...] keeping refugees out by force at the end of the war, in order to establish the Jewish state'. It does so by exhibiting 'photographs, testimonies, maps, prose, and more'. As they (rightly) state the aim of the group is to 'seek recognition for injustice and new paths toward change and repair'.

Kairos Palestine (kairospalestine.ps) is a predominantly Christian ecumenical group that has an extensive inter-faith network of members in Christian, Jewish, and Muslim communities in and around Jerusalem. One of its leaders, Yusef Daher, has an extensive knowledge of tourism, pilgrimage, and hospitality in Palestine, having worked in the industry for many years. Like Rami Kassis of ATG, Daher is a TEMPUS graduate (see below). The group has a high standing in many Christian churches throughout Europe and beyond and takes on extensive advocacy obligations abroad. Its discourse is more distinctively religious than, for example, ATG and Zochrot, using biblical quotations (for example, from Psalm 24:1 – 'The earth is the Lord's and all that is in it, the world, and those who live in it') to argue against injustice and war. As they say 'God has put us here as two peoples, and God gives us the capacity, if we have the will, to live together and establish in it justice and peace, making it in reality God's land'.

The Israeli Committee Against House Demolitions (ICAHD) (www.icahd.org) was founded by Jeff Halper (a former member of the Anthropology Department at Ben Gurion University, Beer Sheva) and colleagues in 1997 and is an Israeli/Palestinian organisation based in West Jerusalem. Specifically committed to opposing Israeli demolition of Palestinian houses and ending the occupation, ICAHD's website presents the group as 'a critical, "radical" organization which can envision a single democratic state in Palestine/Israel'. A central part of the work of ICAHD involves running 'alternative' tours that seek to inform visitors to the region about the 'political realities that affect Palestinians and Israelis'. Those taking the tours organised by ICAHD meet both Palestinian and Israeli witnesses to the politics of the area.

Open Bethlehem (openbethlehem.org) was founded by the film maker Leila Sansour in 2005 and is an organisation committed to recovering an open city from its present position of being surrounded by the Wall (Selwyn 2009, 2011). In the group's own words 'Ultimately, it is the forging of a lasting peace agreement between Israel and Palestine that will eventually lead to the dismantling of the wall around Bethlehem, and the rest of Palestinian cities, and the preservation of Bethlehem's heritage – both its living communities and their land. It would be impossible to save Bethlehem without granting Palestinians the right to self-determination. It is equally impossible to envisage a pluralist Middle East, a major factor for the future of democracy and open society in the entire region, without saving model cities like Bethlehem. These beliefs lie at the heart of the Open Bethlehem campaign. Open Bethlehem has been championed by political and religious leaders throughout the world, including Desmond Tutu, who has written about 'Open Bethlehem's nonviolent attempt to save a city that belongs to many in the world. It is unconscionable that Bethlehem should be allowed to die slowly from strangulation' (cf. openbethlehem.org).

BiH, Palestine, Europe: The TEMPUS Programme

I have written in more detail (Selwyn and Karkut 2006; Selwyn 2010a, 2010b) about the TEMPUS projects that I and colleagues conducted in BiH and Palestine from 2000 to 2006 (and continuing).

The TEMPUS Programme (see above) was initiated by the EC in 1990 as a response to the fall of the Berlin Wall in 1989 and the prospect of Eastern European countries joining the EU. In 2002 it expanded to include the Mediterranean region with an overall aim to encourage inter-university co-operation structured around projects that focus on academic subjects identified as being priorities by the partner countries concerned. The two projects with which we were involved in BiH (Selwyn and Karkut, op. cit.) and Palestine were concerned with pilgrimage, tourism, and cultural heritage and consisted of working with networks of universities in and next to the EU (Sarajevo, Banja Luka, Bologna, and London in the BiH case; Bethlehem, Joensuu (Finland), and London in the Palestinian case) to compose and deliver Master's courses in Tourism, Pilgrimage, and the Cultural Industries. Additionally, the two projects produced a national tourism strategy for BiH and contributed to policy and planning strategies for tourism and pilgrimage in Palestine.

Amongst the more original outcomes of the BiH and Palestinian TEMPUS projects was a number of suggestions about projects for the future. They were all presented in some detail to representatives of the International Community in Sarajevo and Bethlehem.

In the case of the BiH TEMPUS we put forward a plan for the restoration of the library system throughout BiH. The original (Yugoslav) national library system was set up under Tito by the novelist and Nobel Prize winner Ivo Andric (with his Nobel Prize winnings). We proposed the setting up of a single and unified tour guiding school in two BiH cities of Sarajevo and Banja Luka. This would work on the development and teaching of a cosmopolitan history of BiH and the region. Thirdly we suggested that the Muslim pilgrimage site at Ajvatovica (presently the largest Muslim pilgrimage site in Europe) be further incorporated into the municipal and national framework of the BiH economy. Finally, we proposed the setting up of a national design centre in which professional designers from all quarters of BiH and beyond could explore designs from the varied cultural traditions of the country.

The Palestinian team produced other projects of which the following four are examples. Firstly, we proposed a strategy for re-integrating local municipalities, such as Bethlehem's neighbour Beit Jala (traditionally an attractive holiday spot in the summer because of its relatively high, and thus cool, position in the area) into the overall Palestinian tourism economy. Then we devised a plan for small-scale tourism in the village of Battir, near Bethlehem which would engage the village municipality, the women's association, and a nascent craft industry. Thirdly we proposed the setting up of a Palestinian tourism board, on the grounds that tourism development cannot be led either by the public or private sectors alone. Fourthly, we demonstrated the need to develop the Visit Palestine website (visitpalestine.ps) subsequently brilliantly realised by one of the TEMPUS graduates, Sami Khoury.

In both BiH and Palestine we suggested the setting up of a research centre for the study of tourism, pilgrimage, and the cultural industries. The purpose of such centres was, and remains, very precise, namely to provide an intellectual and practical space for research into and development of regional tourism/pilgrimage/ cultural work founded upon the principles of interculturalism and cultural pluralism. In so doing we were guided mainly by ongoing work in the two regions some of which we have just described.

Before concluding there is a final observation to be made that bears upon the role of the International Community in the two territories. The aim of the TEMPUS Programme at its conception was to provide support for co-operative and collaborative work between an international organisation (the European Commission), international networks of universities, and regional civil society organisation as outlined here. As the International Community seems (yet again) to be generating discourse about peace and normalisation it might consider enhancing this approach. After all, conventional states, 'entities' and 'entity states' have a poor record in this sphere.

Conclusions: Looking Ahead

In this chapter we have used the cases of the 'cultural shutdown' in Sarajevo and a mainstream of officially sponsored tours in Israel and beyond to discuss the role of tourism and the cultural industries in the pedagogic work engaged in the production, reproduction, and counter production of cultural capital. In the BiH case artistic and cultural spaces (the seven main museums, galleries, and museums in the country's capital city) have been allowed to run out of money and staff and thus to close. These institutions are *precisely* those that (like the National Library) hold powerful memories of cosmopolitanism and pluralism and *precisely* those in which such ideas and values may be explored and constructed for the future. That is why they have been targeted in and after the war leaving the ideological field open for the spinning of nationalist and separatist narratives. In the Israeli case we have seen how mainstream tours are shaped, just as the actual landscape between the Mediterranean and the Jordan has been shaped (Israeli government spokespersons term the process 'spatial shaping'[5]), by an ideological regime governed by belief in the necessity of walls and corridors with nationalism, and separate development at its core. However, we have also seen that in both BiH and Israel/Palestine there is active resistance to those bleak political visions. Thus Ars Aevi in BiH (within its network of co-operative European cities) and a collection of institutions operating tours and associated educational projects in the Israel/Palestine region are at the forefront of pedagogic work shaped by ideas of the Open Society and a commitment to building cultural capital made up from narratives of cosmopolitanism and cultural pluralism.

In short, we have arguably not only shown the relevance of Bourdieu and Passeron to the field of tourism and the arts but have, in the process, built upon and contributed to the development of their ideas by showing their usefulness in contemporary political and ethnographic settings. During the course of this we have touched on several overlapping and interweaving topics: symbolic violence, cultural capital, political fragmentation (and fragmentation more generally), tourism studies themselves, and the role of tourism and the arts in international relations. We may conclude with one or two sentences about each.

Contextualising our studies of symbolic violence in the history and politics of BiH and Israel/Palestine, we have pointed towards the kinship between symbolic violence, the formation of cultural capital, and real physical violence in both cases. In the former, closure of the cultural institutions is closely related to, if not a virtual continuation of, the ethnic cleansing that took place at the time of the war, the legitimation of this by Dayton, and the dreams of separatist futures by the leaders of at least one of the two 'entities' in BiH. The separatist rhetoric in Israel, symbolised and actualised by the Wall, is framed by the actual and remembered violence of wars, ethnic cleansing, and dispersals of refugees from (at least) 1492 to 1967 and thereafter. Moreover, ideas about the primacy of nationalism and ethno-religious separatism, are, so to say, good for business. Thus, for example, *The Guardian* newspaper (17/7/13) reported that Israel recently purchased £7 billion's worth of cryptographic equipment from Britain. The report promotes the reflection that cultural capital is characteristically grounded in the possession of real financial capital. Wall-building, military security and the arms industry in

---

5   Cf. Ir Amin website.

general are all highly lucrative to some economies, especially those struggling out of recession.

We need to emphasise, however, that *cultural* capital involves reference to *internal* as well as external landscapes, states of mind and emotional disposition as well as political states. This is a topic for another day but we could offer a shorthand comment here that given that external and internal landscapes tend to mirror and reflect each other, the Freudian notion of compulsive repetition seems highly relevant in both cases.

Before coming to a close we need to anchor our thoughts within a tradition of academic, historical, and literary writing about the Mediterranean and Balkan regions. Thus, for example, Amin Ma'alouf (2000) has written of the multiple collective and individual identities in the region whilst Amitav Ghosh's (1992) reading of one of the greatest sets of documents about medieval Jewish life in the Muslim world, the *Cairo Geniza*, recalls a world defined by interculturalism and cultural pluralism. Ammiel Alcalay (1993), from a distinguished Bosniak Jewish family, has looked backwards and forwards to times 'beyond Jews and Arabs', whilst Claudio Magris (1999) writes of the cosmopolitanism of Trieste and the geographical regions to its north, south, and south-east. Such writers all follow Fernand Braudel (1972) himself in defining the political and demographic shape of a region composed of many fragments (of identity, tradition, faiths, languages, and so on) that is, at the same time, structurally coherent. This line of thought underpins the work of our TEMPUS graduates, and colleagues from Ars Aevi, the Alternative Tourism Group, Zochrot, Kairos Palestine, Open Bethlehem, as well as other regional and international networks of libraries, galleries, museums, and universities, and others working in the field of tourism, pilgrimage, and the cultural industries. All invite us to look towards a future for the cultural heritage of the Mediterranean, including BiH and Israel/Palestine that is rooted in the realities of the region's history, geography, and demography.

References

Alcalay, A. 1993. *After Jews and Arabs*, Minneapolis: University of Minnesota Press.

Ars Aevi Collection, Sarajevo, 2006.

Bottomore, T. 1977. Introduction to Bourdieu, P. and Passaron, J-C. Op. Cit.

Bourdieu, P. and Passaron, J-C. 1977. *Reproduction in Education, Society, and Education*, London: Sage.

Braudel, F. 1992. *The Mediterranean and the Mediterranean World in the Age of Philip I*, London: Collins.

Feldman, J. 2008. *Above the Death Camps, Below the Flag*, Oxford: Berghahn.

Ghosh, A. 1992. *In an Antique Land*, Delhi: Ravi Dayal.

Glassenberg, E. 2011. 'Review of Kelner 2010', *Journal of Jewish Education*, 77, 272–6.

Golden, D. 1996. 'The museum of the Diaspora tells a story', in Selwyn, T. (ed.) *The Tourist Image: Myths and Myth making in Tourism*, Chichester: Wiley, 223–50.

The Guardian (newspaper), 17 July 2013.

Ir-Amim website (ir-amim.org.il), accessed 27 July 2013.

Kelner, S. 2010. *Tours that Bind: Diaspora, Pilgrimage, and Israeli Birthright Tourism*, New York: University Press.

Khan, N. 2006. *The Road to Interculturalism: Tracking the Arts in a Changing World*, Crewkerne: Comedia.

Landry, C. 2002. *Cultural Policy in Bosnia Herzegovina: Togetherness in Difference, Culture at the Crossroads in Bosnia Herzegovina*, Strasbourg: Council of Europe, (MOSAIC project).

Maalouf, A. 2000. *On Identity*, London: Harvill.

Magris, C. 1999. *Microcosms*, London: Harvill.

Pearce, S. 2013. 'Culture shutdown? A plea for museums, galleries, and libraries in Bosnia and Herzegovina', *Deliberately Considered Website* (deliberatelyconsidered.com/2013/01), accessed 27 July 2013.

Piquard, B. 2007. 'The politics of the West Bank Wall: Symbolic violence and spaciocide', in Swenarton, M., Troiani, I. and Webster, H. (eds) *The Politics of Making*, London: Routledge.

Popper, K. 1945. *The Open Society and Its Enemies*, London: Routledge.

Sabri, G., Scheller-Doyle, C. and Shomali, W. 2005. *Palestine and Palestinians*, Beit Sahour: ATG.

Saxe, L., Phillips, B. and Sasson, T. 2010. Intermarriage: The impact and lessons of Taglit-Birthright Israel, *Contemporary Jewry*, 31(2), 151–72.

Segal, R. and Weizman, E. 2003. *A Civilian Occupation: The Politics of Israeli Architecture*, Tel-Aviv: Babel.

Seidemann, D. 2013. Public lecture, Belsize Park Synagogue, London, June 2013.

Selwyn, R. 2013. Personal communication.

Selwyn, T. 1995. 'Landscapes of liberation and imprisonment: Towards an anthropology of the Israeli landscape', in Hirsch, E. and O-Hanlon, M. (eds) *The Anthropology of Landscape*, Oxford: Oxford University Press, 114–35.

Selwyn, T. 1996. 'Atmospheric notes from the fields', in Selwyn, T. (ed.) *The Tourist Image: Myths and Myth Making*, Chichester: Wiley 147–62.

Selwyn, T. 2001. 'Landscapes of separation: Towards an anthropology of by-pass roads in Israel/Palestine', in Bender, B. and Weiner, M. (eds) *Contested Landscapes*, Oxford: Berg, 225–41.

Selwyn, T. (with Karkut, J.) 2006. 'The politics of European co-operation: An account of an EC TEMPUS project in Bosnia-Herzegovina', in Burns, P. and Novelli, M. (eds) *Tourism and Politics*, London: Elsevier, 123–45.

Selwyn, T. 2009. 'Ghettoising a matriarch and a city: An everyday story from the Palestinian/Israeli borderlands', *Journal of Borderland Studies*, 24(3).

Selwyn, T. 2010a. 'The EU in the Balkans: The case of a TEMPUS project in Bosnia-Herzegovina', *Anthropological Notebooks*, University of Ljubliana, May 2010.

Selwyn, T. 2010b. 'Pilgrimage and tourism in Bosnia-Herzegovina and Palestine: Reporting from two of the European Commission's TEMPUS projects', in McLeod, D. (ed.) *Sustainable Tourism in Rural Europe*, London: Routledge, 137–50.

Selwyn, T. 2011. 'Tears on the border: The case of Rachel's Tomb, Bethlehem, Palestine', in Kousis, M., Selwyn, T. and Clark, D. (eds) *Contested Mediterranan Spaces*, Oxford: Berghahn, 276–96.

Shehadeh, R. 2008. *Palestinian Walks: Notes on a Vanishing Landscape*, London: Profile.

Terrestial Jerusalem website (t-j.org.il), accessed 27 July 2013.

Visitor's Guide to Sarajevo 2013. Sarajevo.

Visit Palestine website (visitpalestine.ps), accessed 27 July 2013.

Wesley, D. 2006. *State Practices and Zionist Images*, Oxford: Berghahn.

Whitman, S. 2011. 'Review of Kelner 2010', *Contemporary Sociology*, 40(3), 317–18.

Zochrot website (zochrot.org/en), accessed 27 July 2013.

Websites

Alternative Tourism Group (ATG) (info@atg.ps)

Cultureshutdown (cultureshutdown.net)

Deliberately Considered (deliberatelyconsidered.com)

Israeli Committee Against House Demolitions (ICAHD) (icahd.org)

Ir Amim (ir-amim.org.il)

Kairos Palestine (kairospalestine.ps)

Open Bethlehem (openbethlehem.org)

Terrestrial Jerusalem (t-j.org.il)

Visit Palestine (visitpalestine.ps)

Zochrot (zochrot.org/en)

Chapter 8

A Wail of Horror: Empathic 'Atrocity' Tourism in Palestine

Rami Isaac

Introduction

Perceptions of violence, political instability and safety are a prerequisite for tourist visitation. Violent protests, social unrest, civil war and violence, terrorist actions, the perceived violations of human rights or even the mere threat of these activities can all serve to cause tourists to alter their travel behaviour (Hall and O'Sullivan 1996: 117).

Tourists are regarded as longing for relaxing and unconcerned holiday-making and therefore are sensitive towards violent events in tourism destinations. Paradoxically, for most of human history, travelling has been associated with risk and fear for the physical integrity and the belonging of the traveller (Neumayer 2004). As Hall (1994: 92) points out, 'the origin of the word "travel", to travail, to overcome adversity and hardship, gives evidence of the difficulties which the many travellers faced'. Yet, tourists are only willing to travel to foreign destinations if their journey and stay are safe.

Any violence where people are dying certainly results in a negative impact on local tourism businesses and influences the flow of tourists to the countries directly involved in the violence; although it depends who is dying. Tourists easily visit poor countries where people may be regularly dying either from hunger (although this in itself is a form of violence) or violence, as long as they do not perceive a threat to themselves (Isaac and Ashworth 2012). The perception of personal threat to the visitor is crucial. However, many studies have shown that violence and conflict may have severe impacts on tourism (Sönmez 1998, Roehl 1995, Hall 1994, Richter and Waugh 1986). In addition, evidence from around the world reveals that conditions of safety and security (Pizam et al. 1997, Sönmez 1998) and security anxiety, either from war, violence or civil unrest may have highly destructive impacts on tourism.

Within the field of tourism studies, 'dark' tourism is the lens which presents itself as the most obvious through which to view tourism and violence. This is because the very product on which it relies is derived from violence manifest on a large scale, in the form of state, and inter-state conflicts.

The empirical context of this chapter – Palestine – is crucial. This chapter examines the motives, processes and results of one particular type of repositioning of tourism destinations, which is the potential shift from pilgrimage based to 'atrocity' based tourism. This may include a fundamental change from the so-called 'Holy Land' as a pilgrimage destination to a tourism product range redefined to rest on the 'political instability', in general, and the 'violence' of the Israeli occupation in particular.

This chapter also explores the answers to the basic question of why the shift from pilgrimage to 'dark' tourism?; the process and thus consequences of such change. In addition, it sheds light on how atrocity tourism and touristic practices in Palestine can serve to legitimise the Palestinian 'right of return', the recognition of the Palestinian '*Al Nakba*' (The Catastrophe) in 1948 and 1967 (the uprooting of Palestinian villages and the creation of refugees) and ultimately to send a strong political message about the Palestinian people as human beings.

Success in Tourism: Recent Progress and Visions

Several models have been developed since the early 1960s that describe the evolution of tourism destinations through a life-cycle process (Butler 1980, Christaller 1963, Gormsen 1981, Miossec 1977), but Butler's model has attracted most attention. This is because it is credited with providing 'an analytical framework to examine the evolution of tourist destinations within their complex economic, social and cultural environments' (Cooper and Jackson 1989: 382).

A tourism destination has two main roles and a number of important supporting roles. First, and foremost, it must seek to enhance the social and economic well-being of the local inhabitants who live and work in tourist destinations. Secondly, in order to be labelled a tourist destination it must not only enhance resident well-being but also offer a range of products, activities, services and experiences to satisfy tourists' expectations (Ritchie and Crouch 2003: 191). The supply of these products and activities, when enjoyed by the visitor, at a price they are willing to pay, and which allows the destination to operate in a sustainable and prosperous manner (economic, environmental, and socio-cultural) for the benefit of residents, might generally be regarded as successful (Bornhorst et al. 2010). Other measures of success have been identified by Ritchie and Crouch (2000, 2003) Otto and Ritchie (1996), Pearce (1997) and Kozak (2002). In addition there is a bulk of studies conducted on a single aspect of destination performances and success, such as marketing (Buhalis 2000), pricing (Dwyer, Forsyth, and Prasada 2000, Keane 1997, Mangion, Durbarry and Sinclair 2005), product offerings (Faulkner, Oppermann and Fredline 1999, Judd 1995, Murphy, Pritchard and Smith 2000), membership (Donnelly and Vaske 1997), and quality (Go and Govers 2000).

Research conducted by Bornhorst et al. (2010) reveals that the determinants of destination success can be grouped into five distinct key themes:

1. Economic success,
2. Product and service offerings,

3. Effective marketing,
4. Quality of visitor experiences,
5. Internal stakeholder interaction.

As Bornhorst et al. conclude, these broad variables can be categorised as input, process and performance.

The interaction of stakeholders involved in tourism are confirmation of the density and complexity of the system and indeed, validates the need to examine the phenomenon from several different angles, in order to accurately assess destination success. Consequently, destinations are no longer only reactive in their undertakings but also take a proactive approach to ensure they remain relevant in the industry.

Palestine: The Dark Periods

For a comprehensive overview of the geopolitical history of Palestine, see Isaac and Platenkamp (2010) and Isaac and Ashworth (2012). Nevertheless, a brief outline of the events that have shaped the current socio-political conditions will be explained below.

After the dissolution of the Ottoman Empire in the 1920s Palestine came under the British mandate and lasted until 1948. The British promised Palestine sovereignty but also agreed with European and American Zionists, in the Balfour declaration of 1917, to build a Jewish national home in Palestine.

The UN General Assembly resolution 181(II) of 29 November 1947 incorporated a plan for the partition of Palestine into two States (one Arab and one Jewish), for economic union between them, and for the internationalisation of Jerusalem. This vision was firmly rejected by David Ben-Gurion, then the undisputed leader of Israel. He actively encouraged the dispersal of Jewish immigrants across confiscated land, not seeking a peaceful solution to the issues the area was confronted with (Avnery 2011).

The war of 1948 is known by the Palestinians as '*Al Nakba*' – The Catastrophe. The forced expulsion of 800,000 Palestinians from 1948–49, was part of a long-standing Zionist plan to manufacture an ethnically pure Jewish state (Pappé 2006), directed by Prime Minister David Ben-Gurion, whom Pappé labels the 'architect of ethnic cleansing' (2006: 21). The second catastrophe was during the 1967 war, when 350,000 Palestinians were forced out of the West Bank and Gaza Strip. The slow transfer policy of the State of Israel added another 500,000 Palestinians to the list of homeless Palestinians (Andoni 1993).

In general, after 1948 and as a result of war, displacement and forced migration, the West Bank and Gaza Strip entered into what Taraki and Giacaman (2006: 1) call a 'dark' period of closure and insularity. The areas were cut off from the dynamic social and cultural currents of the region and the world.

Since the June 1967 war Israel has been in occupation of all Palestinian areas beyond the Green Line 1967 borders (international delineation of Palestine), where Israel occupied the West Bank including East Jerusalem and the Gaza Strip (UN Resolution 242 calls on Israel to withdraw to the Green Line). Since the occupation began in 1967, there has been two big *intifadas* (uprisings, in Arabic, *Al-Aqsa*) with the intention to end the occupation. The First *Intifada* started in 1987, and lasted for six years and included demonstrations, strikes, boycotts and refusal to pay Israeli taxes. The Second *Intifada* erupted in September 2000.

Notwithstanding, Palestine is now in crisis. The current situation sees Palestinians subjected to daily human rights abuses, living in devastating poverty in refugee camps, and under Israeli occupation. In addition Palestinians face restrictions on their movements both within and to Palestine. Illegal practices by the Israelis in the occupied West Bank and the Gaza Strip are well known and documented by both Palestinian and Israeli non-governmental organisations. For example, B'Tselem, the Israeli Information for Human Rights in the Occupied Territories, states that as of December 2007, there are 99 permanent Israeli checkpoints throughout the West Bank (B'Tselem 2007). The United Nations Office for the Coordination of Humanitarian Affairs (UNOCHA) also lists the number of flying – the so-called 'surprise' – checkpoints, which vary from an average of 69 a week in October 2007 to 141 a week in May 2007 (OCHA 2007). More recently, the total number of closures and obstacles of mobility and movements of the Palestinians documented by OCHA (2010a) at the end of the reporting period stood at 505, down from 626 in March 2009.

Practically, all Palestinians living in and outside the West Bank and the Gaza Strip face serious obstacles to their mobility when deciding to travel through the West Bank, and a range of related problems when moving outside the West Bank, for example travelling to Europe or to neighbouring countries such as Jordan (Barghouti 2000, Halper 2008, Harker 2009, Isaac 2009, 2010, 2010a). The Gaza Strip has become totally out of bounds for Palestinians from the West Bank. As Shehadeh (2008) observes a merchant from Ramallah finds it easier to travel to China to import cane garden chairs than to reach Gaza, a mere 45 minutes' drive away.

In July 2011, Europe's airlines enforced an Israeli travel ban on activists hoping to repair Palestinian schools. More than 100 activists, planning to visit Palestine, travelling from various European countries, reached Tel Aviv airport, but upon arrival they were detained by Israeli forces, and subsequently deported (Nieuwhof 2011). The activities of these activists included renovating a kindergarten, planting trees and repairing water wells, and were coordinated with 25 local Palestinian organisations. As a result, in April 2012, Bethlehem hosted the international event 'Welcome Palestine', a gathering arranged in order to bring to public attention the issue of freedom of movement and difficulties faced on trying to visit Palestine within the framework of the restrictions imposed by the occupation (author's experience).

In June 2002, the state of Israel approved the erection of the Wall separating Israel from Palestine. Israel uses concrete and metal walls to segregate, displace and apply control over Palestinians living in the occupied Palestine. The Israeli apartheid Wall is actually a series of walls, razor wire, electrified fences, trenches and watchtowers flanked by a 27.5 metres 'buffer zone' which the Israeli military patrols (Isaac 2009). The Wall's total length is 707 km – the distance between London and Zürich, and more than four times as long as the Berlin Wall (154.5 km). The Wall is more than twice the length of the Armistice line (Green Line), the international delineation of Palestine (OCHA 2010b).

The route of the Wall has been designed so that it encircles 80 illegal (by international law) Israeli settlements indicating that its primary function is to incorporate these communities into any future Israeli state. Israeli planners place these Jewish settlements on the hilltops of the West Bank and plan them strategically to dominate and control the valleys in which most Palestinian villages are located. It is also usual to find that the names of Palestinian villages on road signs have been deleted with black paint by Israeli settlers (Shehadeh 2008).

Approximately 30,000 Palestinians are trapped between Israel and the Wall, cut off from friends and relatives and isolated from the economic and urban hubs of the West Bank. Around 28,000 more Palestinians are completely imprisoned by the Wall, connected to the rest of the West Bank only by a tunnel or a gate controlled by the Israeli military. An additional 126,000 Palestinians are surrounded by the Wall on three sides, their freedom of movement severely curtailed (OCHA 2010b).

The construction of the Wall affects Palestinian life in general and education in particular by presenting more obstacles restricting the movement of teachers and students. A total of 22 local communities have been separated from their schools as a result of the Wall, so nearly 3,000 students and their teachers need to pass through the Wall's 'gates' every day (Affouneh 2010, see also Harker 2009).

Tourism Potential to Palestine

The tourism sector has always been a primary sector in the Palestinian economy and a key income-generating industry accounting for 15.2 per cent of GDP in 2004, and a generator of jobs accounting for 19.9 per cent in 2004 (UNCTAD 2005, as cited in Zoughbi-Janineh 2009: 153).

Since the establishment of the Palestinian National Authority (PNA) as a result of the Oslo Peace Process in 1993 between Israel and Palestine, the Palestinian Ministry of Tourism and Antiquities was established (MOTA). The MOTA took responsibility for the tourism industry in the Palestinian cities and towns and made several steps to enhance the tourism developments in their territories.

The year 2010 proved to be another record-breaking year for tourism in Palestine. The number of foreign visitors to Palestine reached a record high with over two million foreign tourists. Overnight stays in Palestine hotels increased by 40 per cent in 2010 reaching a record high of 1,400,000 (including both foreign and domestic overnight stays and staying in East Jerusalem). Overnight stays by foreign visitors to the West Bank increased by 51 per cent. These growth figures and the increase in demand are met by a significant growth and renewal of the tourism infrastructure. New hotels, restaurants, cultural centres and resorts are opening across the West Bank and East Jerusalem. Both public and private sectors are investing millions of dollars in developing, restoring and upgrading the tourism industry (MOTA 2010).

Currently a pilgrim-tourist spends nine to 10 days in the Holy Land. An average itinerary includes four to five days in Jerusalem (including visits to Bethlehem, Jericho and the Dead Sea) and three or four days in northern Israel, where the focus is on Nazareth, the Sea of Galilee and other Israeli sites. Nearly 90 per cent of inbound visitors to the Holy Land visit Palestinian towns such as Bethlehem, Jericho, East Jerusalem, and Nablus, while many of these tourists are day-visitors spending only a few hours before returning to Israel (MOTA 2010).

Despite the optimistic numbers of tourist arrivals to Palestine, there are a few well-researched underlying tendencies that have an influence upon this form of tourism. There is one major trend that is perceived as a potential threat to the phenomenon of pilgrimage in Palestine. First, many Palestinians feel that their contemporary culture and the political realities of their lives are not adequately expressed or articulated in conventional pilgrim-based tourism. The development of new forms of tourism (such as 'atrocity' tourism), could be a response to Israel's policy of cultural domination. Israel succeeded in labelling Palestine as an unsafe tourist destination, subverting of its identity, and causing restrictions, and complications for tourists entering Palestinian cities and towns (see Isaac 2010a, 2010a). As Palestinians face increased restrictions on their movements, Israel has recently (2011, author's field research) authorised hundreds of Israeli tour guides to work in Bethlehem in response to the growing number of tourists arrivals. For tourists, it seems much easier to contract or to work with Israeli tourism agents, guides, and buses, all of which can travel freely through checkpoints and from site to site, leaving Palestinian tourism operators to hope for whatever business remains. While Israel presents this move as an example of 'cooperation' and 'economic peace', Palestinians experience it as an assault on their livelihoods and encroachment into their territory, both physically and economically.

Apart from the economic consequences, the opening of Bethlehem to Israeli tour guides introduces a set of understandings and narratives about the city that are linked neither with the historic tourism run by the local Bethlehem tour agencies, nor the state-building narratives developed by the Palestinian ministries and schools. Israeli tour guides are trained separately, under a different government, through different universities and training programmes, and with a different constellation and Israeli representation of sites (Benvensitu 1949), through a Zionist strategy on which the space, the sphere, and symbols were reformulated so that Palestine fits into the Zionist narrative. In other words, a specific cultural heritage had to be constructed to harmonise with the religious narrative that tries to build legitimacy in order to justify the acquisition and control of the space with the aim of enhancing the Jewish consciousness and creating an international supportive movement (Ibrahim 2011). Israel has begun to make historical and 'cultural heritage' claims to tourist sites in the West Bank. A primary example is Rachel's Tomb in Bethlehem, which, as announced by Israeli Prime Minister Netanyahu in February 2010, would be included on a list of Israeli national heritage sites to be restored. While claimed as heritage for Israel, the site has been a part of the Palestinian city of Bethlehem since before the state of Israel was established, and thus has local significance to the community which may not be acknowledged when it is claimed as Israeli national heritage. Indeed, descriptions of the site on the Israeli Ministry of Tourism's website[1] do not mention the local Palestinian community of Bethlehem, who have been living with the tomb in their midst, and as a part of their daily realities, for centuries.

Commenting on advertisements such as a sales brochure for the ultra-Orthodox Jews West Bank settlements published in Brooklyn for member recruitment (see Shehadeh 2008: xiv), the Israeli Rafi Segal and Eyal Weizman (2003: 92) cleverly expose 'a cruel paradox':

> The very thing that renders the landscape "biblical" its traditional inhabitation and cultivation in terraces, olive orchards, and the existence of livestock, is produced by the Palestinians, whom the Jewish settlers came to replace. And so far the very people who cultivate the "green olive orchards" and render the landscape biblical are themselves excluded from the panorama. The Palestinians are there to produce the scenery and then disappear.

In addition, Elias Sanbar (2001: 87), a Palestinian historian and writer, articulates the strange exclusion of the Palestinians from the unfolding of Palestinian history, in particular in the Western world and thought, in his essay '*Out of Place, Out of Time*':

> The contemporary history of the Palestinians turns on a key date: 1948. That year, a country and its people disappeared from maps and dictionaries … The Palestinian people does not exist, said the new masters, and henceforth the Palestinians would be referred to by general, conveniently vague terms, as either "refugees" or in the case of a small minority that had managed to escape the generalised expulsion, "Israeli Arabs". A long absence was beginning.

The Argument

The preceding discussion notes that many Palestinians do not find sufficient expression in conventional pilgrim-based tourism and a potential shift from pilgrimage to 'atrocity' tourism is noticeable and starting to gain ground in Palestine (see Isaac 2009). Many tourists who visit Palestine and Israel in general and either Bethlehem, Ramallah or Nablus in particular book a trip – the so-called

---

1 http://www.goisrael.com/Tourism_Eng/Tourist%20Information/Attractions/Pages/default.aspx.

one-day tour – around the Segregation Wall and a visit to one of the refugee camps in these towns, provided by one of the incoming tour operators in Palestine. Whether this should be welcomed and encouraged by the various stakeholders involved, or conversely disapproved of and discouraged, raises wider issues and difficulties. A shift in whole or in part from pilgrimage to atrocity-based tourism is more than simple product changeover. It has a number of consequences, some of which are attractive and beneficial – in particular from the Palestinian perspective in their struggle against the occupying power by providing a critical look at the politics and history of Palestine – and others that are not.

Arguments in Favour

Despite the integral part that pilgrimage has played in the tourism industry in Palestine, most of the money earned in the Holy Land finds its way into the Israeli economy (Zoughbi-Janineh 2009). In addition, it is estimated that 92–4 per cent of every tourist dollar flows to Israel (The Portland Trust 2010). The value of pilgrimage in tourism should never be under estimated, however, it should not be allowed to dominate the market to the exclusion of other forms of tourism, which would bring benefits to a wider section of the community. As stated above many Palestinian stakeholders feel that their contemporary culture and the present political instability they are experiencing do not find reasonable expression in conventional pilgrim-based tourism. There are some concerns about the over dependence on pilgrimage raised by a number of Palestinian stakeholders (personal communication, Kokaly 2010), which could in the future impact on the region's development. Currently, Israel has a stranglehold on the international flow of tourists to Palestine, because Palestine has no control over its borders.

In an effort to ensure competitive advantage, The Bethlehem Tourism Master Plan produced by MOTA (2010), identified new forms of tourism market segments as potential opportunities to target in order to diversify their product portfolio, which is essential in the current political circumstances. Such product developments should be as a response to the growing demands of the consumers (MOTA 2010).

The aforementioned study by Bornhorst et al. (2010) reveals that the economic success variable most commonly mentioned by respondents in their study is visitor numbers. Many respondents highlighted overall visitor growth as a key measurement in determining the success of tourism. Economic success is an output measurement of destination success.

In spite of the various market segments and their behaviour within the pilgrimage group, a move from pilgrimage to 'atrocity' tourism results for a differentiated market. Simply, a wider range of products is sold to fewer customers possibly at a higher price. More revenues and thus more economic benefits are acquired from this different form of tourism for Palestinian local communities.

This type of tourism could also play a major role in introducing the tourists to the reality of the Palestinian–Israeli conflict a 'see it for yourself experience' and as such these touristic practices may endorse the Palestinian 'right of return', and highlight the alleged injustices committed by Israel. At the same time, Palestinians, through their will to stay on the land and to exist against all odds have strengthened their resilience and steadfastness (Isaac 2011). Tourists in this case can be drawn to the aspects of the horror and atrocities' characteristics such as the Segregation Wall, and the impacts of the Wall on Palestinian life through the destruction of the social and built environments.

In addition visits can be organised to Palestinian refugees' camps, where refugees can speak about their experiences and memories, and the uprooting and destruction of hundreds of Palestinian towns and villages between 1947 and 1949 and in the 1967 war. All these memories and places are examples of 'atrocity' tourism in Palestine, places associated with suffering and tragedies – namely heritage that hurts.

This raises the central question of to what extent can tourism be recruited to help and support the Palestinians in their struggle against the Israeli occupation?

Tourism has the potential to influence current international visitors in forwarding the message to their friends and relatives about the injustice committed by Israel (see Isaac and Hodge 2011). Further, an 'atrocity' tourism experience can be used as a political instrument in increasing the awareness of the plight of the Palestinian people, who live near the Wall, and are under Israeli occupation. At the same time, this form of tourism can provide the Palestinians with a hope to gain more political sympathy, and, importantly, empathy with their struggle by exposing tourists to the physical dimensions of this conflict, to reveal the 'facts on the ground', and a 'see it for yourself' experience.

Atrocity tourists may spend more time in destinations such as Palestine, in order to be able to comprehend the poignant blow and reflect on what is happening, in turn to be able to realise the 'real' issues of the conflict, (where communications and media to the world are seen to be partisan). This indeed, requires more time, to experience the reality of the Palestinians' everyday life that could lead to an increase in the 'length of stay' of visitors to Palestine.

Drawing attention to the alleged injustices perpetrated by Israel, 'atrocity' tourists can understand and judge this 'desperate' situation for themselves. The Western world remembers the Jewish holocaust, whereas the Palestinian '*Al Nakba*' has yet to be recognised and acknowledged. 'Atrocity' tourism in this sense can support this recognition through taking tourists to places associated with the suffering of the Palestinian people, or what can be termed as 'places of bother' (Isaac 2010b, Isaac and Platenkamp 2010), which raises some concerns of normative and existential questions. By entering this 'place of bother' a normative discussion will be stimulated, beyond the 'facts on the ground' and tourists can be challenged to reflect on their own judgment. Through these tours and activities, 'atrocity' tourists could dive into the cultural contexts in order to get information about what is happening in this region, and as a result, this raises important concerns such as, normative ones.

Figure 8.1 The Wall in front of a Palestinian house in Bethlehem
Source: Copyright © R. Isaac (2011).

Figure 8.1 shows one of the tours organised by a local tour operator in and around the Wall in Bethlehem. Here is the house of Claire Anastas in Bethlehem, hemmed in on three sides by the Wall. Her situation is dreadful and it is this which makes it dark tourism. Through such dark tourism tours, tourists and visitors are encouraged to imagine what it must be like to live in this house with its proximity to the Wall (as well as the other side) and thus to take these experiences home with them and tell others.

The first five star hotel Inter-Continental in Bethlehem is just 40 metres away from this gigantic wall.

Ashworth and Hartmann (2005) ask the simple question, why are tourists attracted to atrocity? As tourists are people, the question should be rephrased more generally to 'why are people attracted to atrocity?' Ashworth and Hartmann give three conceptual arguments (although, there are many more – see for example Rojek 1997, Seaton 1999, Tarlow 2005) in answering their question. First, the reason may be curiosity; to witness and experience that which is beyond the everyday, to engage with the extraordinary. The second argument is empathy, which relies upon the capacity of consumers of atrocities to identify with the individuals in the situation of atrocity being related. Therefore, atrocity tourism may play a role in providing empathy for the Palestinian cause.

The third is horror; the representation of horror and the emotions of fear and fascination that it evokes in consumers has always been a stable of various forms of literature, and more recently film and television (see Dann 2005).

Figure 8.2 The Wall at the entrance of Bethlehem
Source: Copyright © R. Isaac (2011).

Arguments Against

It appears that the positives outweigh the negatives in this scenario. This is definitely the case when 'atrocity' tourism is laden with so many expectations and is seen as a contribution to the Palestinian people in their struggle by furthering understanding of the real core of the conflict and thus potentially contributing to the resolution in the international community.

Some of the most important warnings about developing this form of tourism in Palestine stem from the experience of atrocity tourism which may have an impact upon individual tourists and consequently their home countries. For example, as Ashworth and Hartmann (2005: 12) state, 'increased contact with horror and suffering may make it more normal or acceptable, rather than shocking and unacceptable, if only as a defensive reaction of individuals when confronted by such appalling situations and conditions'. Tourists may be deterred rather than attracted by horror and tragedies, if they feel that they themselves could become victims of continuing terror, violence or troubled by the result of atrocity. There is also an argument that promoting attractions and destinations of atrocity may legitimise the atrocities and sufferings and those who committed them (Ashworth and Hartmann 2005).

From the moral perspective, atrocity tourism has negative connotations with the so-called 'exhibitionistic inclination' (Platenkamp 2007) in that the consumer wants to become aroused by seeing the miserable circumstances of others. This poses the question as to whether a country wants to be perceived and potentially promoted as a destination of misery, atrocity and tragedies, which some tourists may find titillating. Another question is to what extent local communities want to promote themselves as victims, selling the sites and commodifying the tragedies. As an African American visiting the sites of the slave trade on the Ghanaian coast demanded, 'Don't turn our memories into a tourist attraction' (Finley 2004: 111–113). Finley (2004: 13) in addition states, 'in the age of global tourism, memory itself becomes a commodity – a thing to be bought, sold, and traded'. These are all questions that require further thought and the answers have implications for management and marketing.

From the consumer's point view tourists want to have authentic experiences while they are on a holiday. This implies that they may also be confronted with unfamiliar experiences, outside of their comfort zone. As Urry and Larsen (2011: 1) suggest, part of the tourist experiences consists of gazing upon 'a set of different scenes, of landscapes or townscapes, which are out of ordinary. When tourists go away, they look at the environment with interest and curiosity'. Authentic experience in 'dark' tourism goes hand-in-hand with experiencing the true circumstances of a violent environment. This, as a result, pulls tourists out of their comfort zones. Tourists do not want to be taken out of their comfort zone. Nevertheless, tourists want to have the familiar and unfamiliar in the same time. The field of tension where this ambiguous experience located is exactly this comfort zone. They want to feel safe and unsafe in the same time. This is the fairground or dangerous sport situation, where the thrill comes from a danger that is constrained (Isaac and Ashworth 2012).

Atrocity tourism can negatively impact on the image of a country. South Africa for example, is still associated with apartheid. Another issue is that in any tourism destination there are many stakeholders with different interests and motivations for involvement in the tourism sector. Diverse stakeholders have different interests as to whether to encourage or discourage this form of tourism.

In addition another issue is that the motivations for visiting sites of atrocities and death, their motives and experiences are still under-researched. Despite studies such as that by Biran et al. (2011) we still need to answer the question of why people are drawn to such attractions.

How is it Possible to Change from Pilgrimage to 'Atrocity'?

Market Change

The short and more sensible answer to this market change approach would be to understand changes in the market to attract this segment. The number of tourists is increasing in many destinations and attractions where there is violence. There has long been tourism to destinations of current conflict. For example Belfast witnessed an increase in tourism in the early 1990s (*Time Magazine* 1993), and Richter (1980) notes a similar situation during the 1970s in the Philippines. In addition tourism is used as a political tool in Tibet (Schwartz 1991), and Pitts (1996) refers to the conflict or war tourists in Mexico, Zimbabwe and Burma. Indeed, there are many more, as Smith (1998: 205) suggests, sites or destinations associated with war, for example, probably constitute 'the largest single category of tourist attractions in the world'.

It could be concluded that there is a wide range of motivations to visit sites of atrocities and death. In spite of the variety of angles taken on atrocity tourism in the literature (e.g. Miles 2002, Sharpley 2005, Stone 2006, Stone and Sharpley 2008), the main enquiry about who the tourists are, who searches for this type of attraction and why they are attracted to them remains unanswered.

Potential Scenarios

There are a number of core issues within the preceding discussion that can now be brought together. The introduction or underpinning of 'sites of atrocities and horror' within the tourism product confronts the question of the relationship between this and the dominant existing forms of tourism. There is a spectrum of opportunities reduced here to two concise scenarios: 1. the supplementary scenario and 2. the parallel development scenario.

Supplementary Scenario

In this scenario, atrocity tourism can and is seen as a supplement to the existing dominant pilgrimage tourism. It is introduced to enhance the pilgrimage tourism experience by bringing tourists' attention to the suffering of the Palestinian people under the Israeli occupation. As a supplement 'atrocity' tourism can be offered as day or half-day excursions to tourists and visitors in Palestine. This has the potential to increase the length of stay of visitors. The main benefit of this scenario is that it requires no extra investment, because the product, which includes occupation, refugee camps, and the Segregation Wall is already in existence. It is this form of tourism which is starting to gain ground in Palestine managed by a Palestinian tour operator which promotes so-called 'political tours' focusing on atrocities and the suffering of the Palestinian people, as well as providing a critical examination of the history and politics of the Palestinian–Israeli conflict.

This scenario raises a central question, which is whether such initiatives directed at the existing markets, which have expressed only a secondary interest in 'atrocity' tourism, should be promoted, extended and enhanced by the various Palestinian stakeholders?

Parallel Development Scenario

A more ambitious approach would be to establish atrocity tourism as a primary motive for a visit and as the dominant activity in Palestine, catering for a separate market segment alongside the leading market segment of pilgrimage based tourism. This scenario raises two options. First, a new set of products served by new facilities and providing new experiences would need to be developed and promoted as a complete holiday package, alongside, but rather different from, those currently on offer and marketed to quite different customers. Indeed, the facilities and products need to deal with the interpretation and management of the sites. Although, such holiday packages should also link with other Palestinian heritage tourism products, for example, Palestinian festivals, and other community-based tourism attractions connected to the Palestinian people. In addition there should be tours that enable participants to be educated about the on-going Palestinian–Israeli conflict, to meet with various Palestinian people, Christian as well as Muslim communities, human rights organisations and the Palestinian summer school, which provides students and participants with the opportunity to learn Arabic at Palestinian universities. Secondly, the development of any facilities and enhancement of the sites and attractions would need to be revised once a final peace agreement has been made with Israel. For example, there would be no Wall (although, the site of its existence would remain). This is short-term thinking for the development and strengthening of this atrocity tourism. In reality, it is unlikely that Israel will reach a final peace agreement with the Palestinians which includes demolishing the Wall, ending the occupation, the recognition of the '*Al Nakba*' of 1948 and 1967, allowing the free movement of the Palestinians in and within Palestine, and withdrawing from Palestine according to the United Nations Resolutions within the 'Green Line' borders of 1967 with its capital East Jerusalem. However, for the longer-term, this part of history – the occupation and associated violence – and heritage needs to be maintained, protected and enhanced for future Palestinian generations. A new set of museums (e.g. occupation museum) and attractions need to be developed and marketed as part of the Palestinian heritage. The interpretations and management of these sites need to aim at reconciliation and for the motto 'never again'. Nonetheless, this scenario raises one more question: can two different products be sold to different market segments in the same small territory of Palestine at the same time? The experiences from many tourist destinations in the Mediterranean such as Spain, Italy and Turkey (Ashworth and Tunbridge 2005), suggest that they can if the market segments can be separately targeted and the tourists separately managed at a destination. Whether such complicated marketing and destination management organisation (DMO) skills exist in Palestine, however, is uncertain. Although, there are examples of such training such as that which took place at Bethlehem University, the EU-funded TEMPUS project from 2004–2007 (see Isaac 2008).

Conclusion

This chapter uses the case of Palestine to examine the processes and instruments in the potential shift in and the possibility of expanding from pilgrimage to 'other types' of tourism, in particular so-called 'atrocities' or thanatourism. This chapter also explores the answers to the basic question of why there is a shift; the process and thus consequences of such changes, and the chapter sheds light on how 'dark' tourism practices in Palestine could help to legitimise the Palestinian 'right of return', and eventually the acknowledgement of '*Al Nakba*' in 1948 and 1967.

Considering these two scenarios, one can respond with the answer 'let's have a bit of each', with obvious advantages being 'cherry-picked' and taking into account that there will be no real and just peace with Israel in the short-term. As discussed atrocity tourism is already gaining ground in Palestine with the support of NGOs, social and human rights organisations, tourism organisations as well as small tour operators who are promoting this type of niche tourism as a segment of the special interest market. However, it is not expected that this would form the mainstream of tourism in Palestine.

This atrocity tourism indeed could play a major role in uncovering the reality of the Palestinians' suffering and abuse by the Israeli occupation, in all its facets. Walking near the Segregation Wall, understanding the impacts of the Wall on natural resources, landscapes and on Palestinians' economic and social lives, listening to the stories of uprooting and destruction of olive trees and houses as a result of the Wall, are more tangible than seeing a photograph or reading a newspaper. Groups of people and visitors are led around the different cities and villages in Palestine, to be exposed to 'the reality' of the situation and take these experiences home with them and tell others.

To conclude, the tourism context of Palestine is not a case of the aestheticised/ fetishised violence in the present, but it is tourism of an apparently clearly 'dark' variety that stands separately from its pilgrimage counterparts, that tourists head to Palestine, not only *despite* violence, but *because* of it. They want to experience and witness the 'real' daily life of the Palestinians. However, this type of experience is only possible to a certain extent. The degree to which this is possible is dependent on the tension of the limits of the comfort zone of the tourists. The more tourists are challenged to come out of their comfort zone, the more they feel threatened by the violent aspect of Israeli occupation. Therefore, tour operators and tourism organisations in Palestine should be prepared to include this tension, between the tourist comfort zone and the threatening violence of Israeli occupation in their products and offers. An important difference with the discussion about dark and heritage sites, like Auschwitz (Thurnell-Read 2009) of young travellers' experiences of Holocaust tourism, and the former sites of the slave trade on the Ghanaian coast (Finley 2004) is the situation. In Ghana and Auschwitz, these sites and places are constructed because they are related to heritage and memory. While in Palestine, the situation is 'real', and genuine. It is an on-going conflict and situation of violence, with which visitors and individuals would seek to actively engage.

References

Affouneh, S. 2010. 'The Wall is a snake: The impact of the Wall on Palestinian children's education: Facts and photos', a paper presented at the Sumud and the Wall Conference in Bethlehem, Palestine 30 April–1 May 2010.

Andoni, G. 1993. *Non-Violence Tax Resistance in Beit Sahour*, Beitsahour: Palestinian Centre for Rapprochement between People.

Ashworth, G.J. and Hartman, R. 2005. *Horror and Human Tragedy Revisited: The Management of Sites of Atrocities for Tourism*, New York: Cognizant Communication Corporation.

Ashworth, G. and Tunbridge, J. 2005. 'Moving from blue to grey tourism: Reinventing Malta', *Tourism Recreation Research*, 30(1), 45–54.

Avnery, U. 2011. 'Sad and happy' [Online 15 January], available at: http://www.ramallahquakers.org/pdfs/r3septresources-- happy%20and%20sad%20 day%20by%20uri%20avnery%20sept%2017.pdf [accessed 15 January].

Barghouti, M. 2000. *I saw Ramallah*, New York: Anchor Books.

Benvensitu, M. 1949. *Sacred Landscape: The Buried History of the Holy Land since 1948*, Middle Eastern Studies Association, California: University of California Press.

Biran, A., Poria, Y. and Oren, G. 2011. 'Sought experiences at (dark) heritage sites', *Annals of Tourism Research*, 38(3), 820–41.

Bornhosrt, T., Ritchie, R.J.B. and Sheehan, L. 2010. 'Determinants of tourism success for DMOs and destinations: An empirical examination of stakeholders' perspective', *Tourism Management*, 31, 572–89.

B'Tselem 2007. 'Statistics on checkpoints and roadblocks' [online 11 November], available at: www.btselem.org/english/Freedom_of_Movement/Statistics.asp [accessed 11 November].

Buhalis, D. 2000. 'Marketing the competitive destination of the future', *Tourism Management*, 21(1), 97–116.

Butler, R. 1980. 'The concept of a tourist area cycle of evolution: Implications for management of resources', *Canadian Geographer*, 24, 5–12.

Christaller, W. 1963. 'Some consideration of tourism location in Europe: The peripheral regions–underdeveloped countries–recreation areas', *Regional Science Association Papers*, XII, Lund Congress.

Cooper, C. and Jackson, S. 1989. 'The destination area life cycle: The Isle of Man case study', *Annals of Tourism Research*, 16, 377–98.

Dann, G. 2005. 'Children of the dark', in Ashworth, G. and Hartmann, R. (eds) *Horror and Human Tragedy Revisited: The Management of Sites Atrocities for Tourism*, New York: Cognizant Communication Corporation.

Donnelly, M.P. and Vaske, J.J. 1997. 'Factors influencing membership in tourism promotion authority', *Journal of Travel Research*, 35(4), 50–55.

Dwyer, L., Forsyth, P. and Prasade, R. 2000. 'The price competitiveness of travel and tourism: A comparison of 19 destinations', *Tourism Management*, 21(1), 9–22.

Faulkner, B., Oppermann, M. and Fredline, E. 1999. 'Destination competitiveness: An exploratory examination of South Australia's core attractions', *Journal of Vacation Marketing*, 5(2), 125–39.

Finley, C. 2004. 'Authenticating dungeons, whitewashing castles: The former sites of the slave trade on the Ghanaian coast', in Medina Lasansky, D. and McLaren, B. (eds) *Architecture and Tourism*, Oxford: Berg.

Go, F.M. and Govers, R. 2000. 'Integrated quality management for tourist destinations: A European perspective on achieving competitiveness', *Tourism Management*, 21(1), 79–88.

Gormsen, E. 1981. 'The spatio-temporal development of international tourism: Attempt at a centr–periphery model', in *La Consommation D'Espace Par le Tourisme et sa Preservation*, Aix-en-Provence: CHET, pp. 150–79.

Hall, C.M. 2004. *Tourism and Politics: Policy, Power and Place*, New York: Wiley.

Hall, C.M. and O'Sullivan, V. 1996. 'Tourism, political instability and violence', in Pizam, A. and Mansfeld, Y. (eds) *Tourism, Crime and International Security Issues*, New York: Wiley.

Halper, J. 2008. *An Israeli in Palestine: Resisting Dispossession, Redeeming Israel*, London: Pluto Press.

Harker, C. 2009. 'Student im/mobility in Birzeit, Palestine', *Mobilities*, 4(1), 11–35.

Ibrahim, N. 2011. 'The politics of heritage in Palestine: A conflict of two narratives' [online 7 May], available at: http://www.thisweekinpalestine.com/details.php?id=3358anded=192andedid=192 [accessed 1 May].

Isaac, R.K. 2008. 'Master of Arts in Tourism and Pilgrimage', *Tourism, Hospitality, Planning and Development*, 5(1), 73–6.

Isaac, R.K. 2009. 'Alternative tourism: Can the Segregation Wall in Bethlehem be a tourist attraction?' *Tourism and Hospitality Planning and Development*, 6(3), 247–54.

Isaac, R.K. 2010a. 'Alternative tourism: New forms of tourism in Bethlehem for the Palestinian tourism industry', *Current Issues in Tourism*, 13(1), 21–36.

Isaac, R.K. 2010b. 'Moving from pilgrimage to responsible tourism: The case of Palestine', *Current Issues in Tourism*, 13(6), 579–90.

Isaac, R.K. 2011. 'Steadfastness and the Wall conference in Bethlehem, Palestine', *Tourism Geographies*, 13(1), 152–7.

Isaac, R.K. and Ashworth, G.J. 2012. 'Moving from pilgrimage to "dark" tourism: Leveraging tourism in Palestine', *Tourism Culture and Communication*, 11, 149–64.

Isaac, R.K and Hodge, D. 2011. 'An exploratory study: Justice tourism in controversial areas. The case of Palestine', *Tourism Planning and Development*, 8(1), 101–8.

Isaac, R.K. and Platenkamp, V. 2010. 'Volunteer tourism in Palestine: A normative perspective', in Moufakkir, O. and Kelly, I. (eds) *Tourism Progress and Peace*, Wallingford: CAB International.

Judd, D.R. 1995. 'Promoting tourism in US cities', *Tourism Management*, 16(3), 175–87.

Keane, M.J. 1997. 'Quality and pricing in tourism destinations', *Annals of Tourism Research*, 21(1), 117–30.

Kozak, M. 2002. 'Destination benchmarking', *Annals of Tourism Research*, 29(2), 497–519.

Mangion, M.L., Durbarry, R. and Sinclair, M. 2005. 'Tourism competitiveness: Price and quality', *Tourism Economics*, 11(1), 45–68.

Miles, W. 2002. 'Auschwitz: Museum interpretation and atrocity tourism', *Annals of Tourism Research*, 29, 1175–8.

Miossec, J. 1977. 'Un Modéle de L 'Espace Touristique', *Le E'espace Gégraphique*, 6, 41–8.

MOTA 2010. *Master Plan for Developing Tourism in Bethlehem*, Bethlehem: MOTA.

Murphy, P., Pritchard, M. and Smith, B. 2000. 'The destination product and its impact on traveller perceptions', *Tourism Management*, 21(1), 43–52.

Neumayer, E. 2004. 'The impact of political violence on tourism: Dynamic economic estimation in a cross-national panel', *Jounal of Conflict Resolution*, 48(2), 259–81.

Nieuwhof, A. 2011. 'Everyone can help to Welcome Palestine in 2012' [online 22 December], available at: http://electronicintifada.net/content/interview-everyone-can-help-welcome-palestine-2012/10706 [accessed 22 December].

OCHA 2007. 'Closure update – Occupied Palestinian territories', *United Nations Office for the Coordination of Humanitarian Affairs* [online 1 December], available at: http://www.ochaopt.org/documents/ClosureUpdateOctiber2007.pdf [accessed 1 December].

OCHA 2010a. 'Occupied Palestinian territories movement access', *United Nations Office for the Coordination of Humanitarian Affairs* [online 20 March], available at: http://www.ochaopt.org/documents/ocha_opt_movement_access_2010_06_16_english.pdf [accessed 20 March].

OCHA 2010b. 'Occupied Palestinian territories route projection', *United Nations Office for the Coordination of Humanitarian Affairs* [online 2 April], available at: http://www.ochaopt.org/documents/ocha_opt_route_projection_july_2010.pdf [accessed 2 April].

Otto, J.E. and Ritchie, J.R.B. 1996. 'The service experience in tourism', *Tourism Management*, 17(3), 165–74.

Pappé, I. 2006. *The Ethnic Cleansing of Palestine*, Oxford: Oneworld.

Pearce, D.G. 1997. 'Competitive destination analysis in Southeast Asia', *Journal of Travel Research*, 35(4), 16–24.

Pitts, W.J. 1996. 'Uprising in Chiapas, Mexico: Zapata lives, tourism falters', in Pizam, A. and Mansfeld, Y. (eds) *Tourism, Crime and International Security Issues*, New York: Wiley.

Pizam, A., Tarlow, P. and Bloom, J. 1997. 'Making tourists feel safe: Whose responsibility is it?' *Jounal of Travel Research*, 36(1), 23–8.

Platenkamp, V. 2007. 'Contexts in tourism and leisure studies. A cross-cultural contribution to the production of knowledge', PhD dissertation, Wageningen University.

Richter, L.K. 1980. 'The political uses of tourism: A Philippine case study', *The Journal of Developing Area*, 14(2), 237–357.

Richter, L.K. and Waugh, J.R. 1986. 'Terrorism and tourism as a logical companions', *Tourism Management*, 7(4), 230–38.

Ritchie, J.R.B. and Crouch, G.I. 2000. 'The competitive destination: A sustainability perspective', *Tourism Management*, 21(1), 53–65.

Ritchie, J.R.B. and Crouch, G.I. 2003. *The Competitive Destination: A Sustainable Tourism Perspective*, Oxon, UK: CABI Publishing.

Roehl, W.S. 1995. 'The June 4, 1989, Tiananmen Square incident and Chinese tourism', in Lew, A.A. and Yu, L. (eds) *Tourism in China: Geographic, Political and Economic Perspectives*, Boulder, CO: West View Press.

Rojek, C. 1997. 'Indexing, dragging and the social construction of tourist sights', in Rojek, C. and Urry, J. (eds) *Touring Cultures: Transformations of Travel and Theory*, London: Routledge.

Sanbar, E. 2001. 'Out of place, out of time', *Mediterranean Historical Review*, 16(1), 87–94.

Schwartz, R. 1991. 'Travellers under fire: Tourists in the Tibetan uprising', *Annals of Tourism Research*, 18(4), 588–604.

Seaton, A.V. 1999. 'War and thanatourism: Waterloo 1815–1914', *Annals of Tourism Research*, 26, 130–58.

Segal, R. and Weizman, E. 2003. 'The mountain. Principles of building in heights', in Segal, R. and Weizman, E. (eds) *A Civilian Occupation. The Politics of Israeli Architecture*, Tel Aviv: Babel.

Sharpley, R. 2005. 'Travels to the edge of atrocityness: Towards a typology of atrocity tourism', in Ryan, C., Page, S. and Aitken, M. (eds) *Taking Tourism to the Limits: Issues, Concepts and Management Perspectives*, Oxford: Elsevier.

Shehadeh, R. 2008. *Palestinians Walks*, London: Profile Books.

Smith, V.L. 1998. 'War and tourism: An American ethnography', *Annals of Tourism Research*, 25, 202–27.

Sönmez, S.F. 1998. 'Tourism, terrorism and political instability', *Annals of Tourism Research*, 25(2), 416–56.

Stone, P. 2006. 'An atrocity tourism spectrum: Towards a typology of death and macabre related tourist sites, attractions and exhibitions', *Tourism: An Interdisciplinary International Journal*, 52, 145–60.

Stone, P. and Sharpley, R. 2008. 'Consuming atrocity tourism: A thanatological perspective', *Annals of Tourism Research*, 35(2), 574–95.

Taraki, L. and Giacaman, R. 2006. 'Modernity aborted and reborn: Way of being urban in Palestine', in Taraki, L. (ed.) *Living Palestine: Family Survival,*

Resistance and Mobility Under Occupation, New York: Syracuse University Press, pp. 1–50.

Tarlow, P.G. 2005. 'Dark tourism: The appealing dark side of tourism and more', in *Niche Tourism: Contemporary Issues, Trends and Cases*, Oxford: Elsevier.

The Portland Trust 2010. 'Palestinian economic bulletin', 5 October 2010.

Thurnel-Read, T. 2009. 'Engaging Auschwitz: An analysis of young traveller's experience of Holocaust tourism', *Journal of Tourism Consumption and Practice*, 1(1), 26–52.

Time Magazine 1993. 'Holidays in hell', August, 142(8), 50.

Urry, J. and Larsen, J. 2011. *The Tourist Gaze: Leisure and Travel in Contemporary Societies*, 3rd edition, London: Sage Publications.

Zoughbi-Janineh, C. 2009. 'The development of rural tourism in the hidden parts of Palestine: A case study from the Bethlehem district', in Isaac et al. (eds) *Voices in Tourism Development: Creating Spaces for Tacit Knowledge and Innovation*, Breda: NHTV expertise series 8.

Chapter 9

Violence, Tourism, Crime and the Subjective: Opening New Lines of Research

Sônia Regina da Cal Seixas, João Luiz de Moraes Hoeffel,
David Botterill, Paula V Carnevale Vianna, Michelle Renk

Introduction

In this chapter we explore some new territory, literally for the UK-based member of our authoring team who visited Brazil to conduct fieldwork in 2012, and conceptually, as we attempt a dialogue across several disciplines – environmental sociology, tourism studies, criminology and the sociology of violence and mental health. The complexity of disciplinary influences, international experiences, and different academic and national identities of the authoring team mirrors the complexity of investigating violence, tourism, crime and the subjective in our fieldwork locale – the beach town of Caraguatatuba, located on the coast of the State of São Paulo, Brazil. The research process that has led to this chapter has been complex and occasionally chaotic just like the turbulent condition of everyday life in Caraguatatuba. We, therefore, present our chapter as a work in progress with very tentative findings on opening up new lines of research within the general subject of this book.

We begin the chapter with a description of the context of our case study in two sections. First, we capture the rapid economic and social change experienced in the town since the 1970s and second, we offer some specific observations on the concomitant fast growth of tourism since the mid-1980s. The reductionist separation of tourism development from the general trajectory of social change is a tactic we return to later in our analysis and we acknowledge here that it is fraught with paradox as in getting a sharper focus on the specifics of tourism and violence we then have to rebuild its relationship to more generic processes of change. Next, we provide a range of social indicators that demonstrate the social vulnerability of Caraguatatuba over the past four decades. Vulnerability is the state of being susceptible to damage caused by exposure to pressures associated with environmental and social changes, and is related to an incapacity to adapt. It results in individual and social suffering (Adger and Kelly 2001). We provide indicators of mortality, crime and health to demonstrate the increasing vulnerability of the residents and visitors to the town.

Finally, we offer an exploratory analysis of violence and tourism. Two major strands of thinking are presented. The first draws upon the often under-reported ontological fact of tourism's close relationship with normative, moral and legal transgression (Uriely et al. 2011). Under this research strand, we consider explicit indicators of violence – physical assault and homicide – and argue that in promoting a transgressive possibility then tourism is complicit in creating a criminogenic environment for the alcohol and substance abuse that is closely associated with property crime, violent assault and homicide. The second research line sketches our formative thinking on tourism and social suffering. We explore the paradox that in Caraguatatuba tourism is both *subject to* and is *contributing to* an escalating atmosphere of violence created by rapid, turbulent and chaotic social and environmental change. As a result, tourists, second home owners, migrant workers and residents are all subject to varying degrees of social suffering.

Research Context

The northern coastal stretch of the state of São Paulo is made-up of four municipalities (Caraguatatuba, Ilhabela, São Sebastião and Ubatuba) and covers an area of 1,947.7 km^2. In 2010 it had a population of 281,779, 98.6 per cent of whom live in urban settings. At this time Caraguatatuba (the largest of the four municipalities) had 100,840 inhabitants, 95.9 per cent living in urban areas. Ilhabela, São Sebastião, and Ubatuba still have 84 per cent of their original vegetation (Atlantic Forest); while in Caraguatatuba this figure is 74 per cent (SOS Mata Atlântica and INPE 2009). Caraguatatuba is located 186 km from the city of São Paulo and its 29 km of Atlantic sea coast encompass 17 stretches of beach, some of them being among the most beautiful along the state's Atlantic Coast. It is therefore located in a very important leisure and tourist region.

In the 1950s, a highway was built to extend from the Paraiba Valley, between Rio de Janeiro and São Paulo, to the Northern Coast. The result was that the region became one of the most popular tourist areas in the state, allowing for economic recovery as traditional agriculture and fishing activities declined. Demographic growth, boosted by ever-growing tourism, real-estate speculation, and lack of planning, has prompted significant environmental changes which have strongly affected the quality of life of local residents in the four municipalities (Seixas et al. 2011). Population growth on the north coast shows an increase from 48,000 in 1970 to 282,000 in 2010, a fivefold increase over 40 years. The city of Caraguatatuba shows even stronger population growth from 15,000 in 1970 to 100,840 in 2012, a twelvefold increase. Between 2000 and 2010, population growth in Caraguatatuba reached 2.62 per cent per year, significantly above the annual rate for the state (1.35 per cent) and Brazil (1.55 per cent) for the same period (IBGE 2012). The north coast communities are directly affected by the megalopolis of São Paulo, in 2010 with an estimated 20 million people, and to a lesser extent the 12 million residents of Rio de Janeiro. Both cities are within 3–4 hours' drive times from points along the north coast.

These drivers of social change have led to significant impacts on both socio-environmental vulnerability and exposure of the local population to environmental risks and hazards, which are likely to increase with the impact of major projects involving the extraction of oil and natural gas, such as the Mexilhão Project (Petrobras), the projected Caraguatatuba–São Sebastião Highway, regional landfills, and a planned prison facility.

Tourism in Caraguatatuba

The semi-tropical environment of forest and beaches along the north coast of São Paulo State provides a high quality leisure resource protected by legislation in the form of the State Park of the Serra do Mar. The town of Paraty, a UNESCO World Heritage Site recognised for its seventeenth-century town centre, and the resorts of Ubatuba and Ilhabela are the most well-known and popular tourism destinations. Paraty attracts significant numbers of international tourists. Ubatuba developed as a resort for wealthy Paulistas (residents of the city of São Paulo) in the 1960s and promotes itself as a forerunner of beach resorts in Brazil offering high quality resort infrastructure and high-end condominium and hotel accommodation. Ilhabela is a popular and expensive holiday home island. Day visitor numbers to the island are controlled by its off-shore location and limited ferry services. Caraguatatuba is a much more recent tourism destination on the north coast. It has a long beach frontage and accommodates large volumes of day visitors particularly in the holiday season and on festival weekends. The most striking aspect of its very recent tourism development has been the dramatic increase in condominium buildings since 1996 that has greatly expanded the holiday accommodation in the city.

Tourism development on the north coast, but particularly in Caraguatatuba, is driven by the demographic forces and concomitant social transformations that surround it. A function of this influence is the rapid growth of high-rise condominium buildings in Caraguatatuba. These developments are almost entirely as a result of the general growth in the Brazilian economy and the increased disposable income amongst a wider range of social classes and an appetite for leisure spending among residents of the inland cities of the state of São Paulo, including the megalopolis of São Paulo itself. In response, speculative real estate developers and the construction industry sought to provide lower cost condominium holiday homes on the north coast. This was facilitated, in part, by permissive planning laws that enabled an intensity of site development not found elsewhere on the north coast that reduced unit development costs. In Caraguatatuba this resulted in the construction of approximately 7,000 high density holiday units over the period 1996–2005 in prime tourist locations in the city (Weissberg et al. 2011).

Each unit has a maximum capacity of eight persons and thus the investment in holiday homes produced a maximum additional capacity of 56,000 bed nights in a city of approximately 100,000 residents, over a nine-year period. Low construction costs and entry level pricing of holiday homes left little or no margin for infrastructure investment, consequently, the surrounding street pavements and lighting are inadequate. There has been little or no investment in water supply and waste water treatment, and, as a result, the sea water is often unfit for bathing and pollution has had an adverse effect on the local fishing industry (Seixas et al. 2012a). Planning regulation tightened in 2006/07 and this halted development dramatically as speculators lost interest (Weissberg et al. 2011). The hiatus in development was short lived, however, and observations made in the city in 2012 confirm the ongoing construction of several new holiday home complexes.

The changes to the physical infrastructure of the city are not the only legacy of these developments. The developers sequestered prime sites in the city for condominium use and the social spaces of the beaches have subsequently become 'de facto' privatised for the exclusive use of the new second home owners. Occupation of the condominiums is highly seasonal and for large periods of the year and during the weekdays in the shoulder season they lay vacant. At peak holiday times the neighbourhoods are lively, interesting parts of the tourism offering of the city but over many months they are akin to a new urban wasteland occupying prime city tourist resources. Those residents who do occupy the units on a longer term basis, often comprising 'at risk' groups of the elderly or problematic young adults sent to live away from the city homes of the family, are isolated from the city's social services and the network of community aid.

Indicators of Vulnerability in Caraguatatuba

The rapid changes in demography and economy have produced a myriad of new social problems. For example, Caraguatatuba was rated the most violent municipality in the State of São Paulo in 2008 and the prevalence of depression and AIDS is also high for state parameters. In this section of our chapter we report a range of indicators that capture the vulnerability of the town and its populations.

Our investigation interrogates a range of official data sources. Police statistics are used to calculate death rates from external causes (accidents, homicides and suicides), and notification of cases and of deaths from AIDS is taken from data produced by state health agencies. Data on AIDS is included because for some time this epidemic has been considered the materialisation, in the health area, of the degree of violence in a given region (McKenzie et al. 2012, Minayo 2006, Reichenheim et al. 2011). In our study, information referring to the notification of cases of AIDS, and mortality from AIDS, was gathered per 100,000 inhabitants.

Secondary databases were also used, such as the type available and systematised in publications such as *Mapas de Violência* (Maps of Violence) (Waiselfisz 1998, 2011a, 2011b). Since 1998, Waiselfisz has coordinated projects for compiling data on violence in Brazil and the results are available on the Internet in table and map formats by state (Waiselfisz 1998, 2011a, 2011b). All this data was derived from the Information System on Mortality (*Sistema de Informações Sobre Mortality – SIM*), which centralises information on deaths across Brazil.

The database of the Seade Foundation, specifically the item entitled *Justiça e Segurança* (Justice and Security) provided analysis of police reports of different types of crime registered in the municipality of Caraguatatuba. Based on the absolute data available on this database rates per 100,000 inhabitants were calculated, enabling a comparative evaluation of the town of Caraguatatuba and state-wide averages. Using a similar methodology, historical series on deaths from external causes for the municipality and, comparatively for the entire State of São Paulo, were constructed and analysed. This information is useful as an important indicator of the relationship between violence and health (Souza 1993). Rates per 100,000 inhabitants were calculated using the Vital Statistics Database of the Seade Foundation. To supplement the information, interviews were held with professionals in the area of mental health, with the purpose of drawing up a profile of the diagnoses of depression and their interrelationship with the broad raft of social changes that have been occurring in the municipality.

According to data from 'Map of Violence 2012' (Waiselfisz 2011b, 2012), Caraguatatuba was in 91st place among the 5,560 municipalities in Brazil, between 2006 and 2008, in terms of the number of homicides in municipalities with populations of 10,000 or over. It was in 44th place during the same period in the number of homicides of youth in municipalities of 10,000 or more young inhabitants. It should be noted that the neighbouring municipality of São Sebastião was in 73rd place in the number of deaths of young people from traffic accidents in municipalities with 10,000 or more young inhabitants, in the period from 2006 to 2008. The remaining coastal municipalities of the State failed to show such high rates of violence.

The deaths considered in the study are those classified in the *International Classification of Diseases* (ICD–10, 10th Revision), in the broad group of 'External Causes of Death' (chapter XX), categories X85 to Y09 (homicides). This group is defined as intentional assault against third parties, using any means to cause damage, injury or death of the victim. In Table 9.1 (below) we show a series from 2003 to 2007 for the 16 coastal municipalities of the State of São Paulo.

In 2010, 49,932 deaths from aggression were reported in Brazil, corresponding to 26.2 deaths from homicide per 100,000 inhabitants. This rate was not calculated for 2,677 of the 5,569 municipalities in the country (48.07 per cent), the average population per municipality being 5,230 (Waiselfisz 2012). This lack of information was due either to the absence of deaths in such areas or to a lack of statistical significance of the rate shown. On the Map of Violence for 2012 (Waiselfisz 2012), Caraguatatuba was listed as the 162nd most violent municipality in the country. The municipality also ranked in second place in the state, with 147 deaths, at a rate of 50.1 deaths per 100,000 inhabitants. During the same period São Sebastião recorded a total of 53 deaths, corresponding to 26.2 per 100,000 inhabitants (Waiselfisz 2012).

In order to better understand the information shown on the Map of Violence, the data on police occurrences and different types of crime that are committed and recorded in the municipality of Caraguatatuba were studied. Table 9.2 was constructed on the basis of the secondary data gathered from the Seade Foundation Database, specifically in the item entitled 'Justice and Security'. Table 9.3 was

Table 9.1 Death figures and respective homicide rate,[1] municipalities of São Paulo shore, 2003–2007

National Ranking	State Ranking	Municipality	Pop. (1000)	No. of Homicides					Rate Homicide
				2003	2004	2005	2006	2007	
Northern Coast									
273	3	Caraguatatuba	101.1	74	51	55	78	40	39.6
1232	72	Ilhabela*	27.0	6	4	6	7	2	18.5
721	29	São Sebastião	78.6	50	40	35	38	20	25.5
806	32	Ubatuba	83.4	28	21	26	35	20	24.0
Lower 'Santista'									
998	50	Bertioga*	45.8	15	15	9	13	7	21.1
943	45	Cubatão	122.9	85	50	39	21	27	22.0
1250	76	Guarujá	311.3	149	78	52	103	57	18.3
775	31	Itanhaém	94.0	37	23	23	27	23	24.5
1235	73	Mongaguá*	48.8	22	9	11	10	6	18.5
1680	119	Peruíbe	67.3	38	22	10	19	10	14.8
960	47	Praia Grande	253.2	122	66	48	61	55	21.7
1988	152	Santos	418.4	98	95	59	80	53	12.7
1941	148	São Vicente	333.3	103	76	49	63	43	12.9
Southern Coast									
2605	235	Cananéia*	14.5	1	3	2	0	2	9.2
1521	104	Iguape*	29.0	5	4	9	4	1	16.1
1090	58	Ilha Comprida*	10.1	0	0	1	3	2	19.9

Notes: [1] Rates per 100,000 inhabitants. * Aggregate homicide rate (years 2005–07). For the remaining municipalities rates refer to 2007.
Source: Created from Waiselfisz 2011a.

drawn up on the basis of the rates per 100,000 inhabitants for the State of São Paulo, in order to evaluate the position of the municipality as compared with the state-wide average. The data referring to Caraguatatuba stands out very negatively.

Regarding deaths from traffic accidents, Figure 9.1 indicates a trend toward stabilisation between 1980 and 1996 in the State of São Paulo, followed by a fall during the period from 1996 to 2000, and then a new trend toward stabilisation from then on. Although Caraguatatuba follows this general trend, it consistently shows higher rates than the state as a whole. In regard to this trend in accidents, it should be noted that Brazilian transit laws became more severe with the National Motor Vehicle Code, effective as of 1997. Since this time the country is no longer world champion in traffic deaths, although figures are still high. In respect of

Table 9.2 Police report rates[1] according to type of crime, Caraguatatuba, SP, Brazil, 1997–2007

Year/ Category	1997	1998	1999	2000	2001	2002	2003	2004	2005	2006	2007
Police Reports	8179	8348	9367	10005	10241	10576	10828	9920	8980	7585	7894
Crimes Against the Person	1977	2045	2294	2546	2442	2547	2597	2558	2229	2194	2382
Homicide 1st and 2nd Degree	56	47	73	71	62	77	91	51	68	86	45
Robberies	339	351	480	456	562	536	695	662	709	449	394
Thefts	1039	995	913	916	1216	1451	1851	1853	1798	1550	1602
Drug Abuse – Traffic	66	63	56	44	43	39	59	56	54	87	161
Drug Abuse – Use	167	88	78	114	126	126	83	75	26	21	40

Note: [1] Rates per 100,000 inhabitants.
Source: Created from *Justiça e Segurança*, Fundação SEADE, available at www.seade.gov.sp.

Table 9.3 Police report rates according to type of crime,[1] State of São Paulo, 1997–2007

Year/ Category	1997	1998	1999	2000	2001	2002	2003	2004	2005	2006	2007
Police Reports	5344	5966	6700	6564	6792	6756	6705	6696	6675	6544	6617
Crimes Against the Person	1289	1346	1422	1412	1403	1443	1506	1542	1589	1530	1543
Homicide 1st and 2nd Degree	49	48	51	48	47	45	41	35	30	27	24
Robberies	435	531	603	583	585	587	640	594	565	533	523
Thefts	688	775	804	794	853	871	992	1002	970	1001	952
Drug Abuse – Traffic	21	23	25	24	25	30	34	35	38	43	54
Drug Abuse – Use	35	37	43	47	55	54	55	52	50	52	56

Note: [1] Rates per 100,000 inhabitants.
Source: Created from *Justiça e Segurança*, Fundação SEADE, available at www.seade.gov.sp.

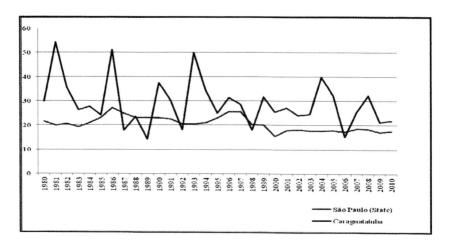

Figure 9.1 Traffic accidents mortality rates (per 100,000 inhabitants), State of São Paulo and municipality of Caraguatatuba, 1980–2010

traffic accident mortality, Caraguatatuba has another particular characteristic: its very flat topography has encouraged the use of bicycles but the improvements in the road leading to the town and the heavy influx of automobiles and heavy lorries has proved to be an added and constant risk to the local cycling population.

Comparative suicide rates are a less reliable comparator due to the small number of cases in Caraguatatuba. As shown below, this leads to fluctuation in time series data. Even so, the municipality's suicide rate is above the state average (Figure 9.2).

The homicide rate in the State of São Paulo rose steadily until 1999, followed by a considerable fall, and then stabilisation as of 2008 (Figures 9.3 and 9.6). The fall in the State's homicide rates was not uniform. According to Waiselfisz (2012), violence has recently migrated from the most populous and metropolitan municipalities in Brazil to the medium-sized municipalities. The Map of Violence recognises that the most vulnerable municipalities are the 'new centers of growth [outside Greater São Paulo]'. In the early 1990s such towns and cities, including Caraguatatuba, began attracting investment and migratory flows without the corresponding public policies and services to address the population. Although homicide rates in Caraguatatuba were high in the 1980s, they increased rapidly as of the mid-1990s and rose to a peak in 2001. Since then they have accompanied the downward trend in the State, but levels are still four times those of the State as a whole.

The municipality of Caraguatatuba shows high rates of both notification of, and death from, AIDS in comparison with the other municipalities along the Northern Coast and in the State of São Paulo in general. The neighbouring port city of São Sebastião also shows high levels for this indicator. It should be noted that, in

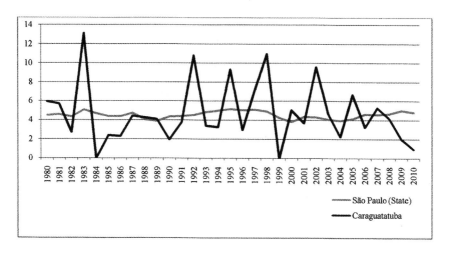

**Figure 9.2 Suicide mortality rates (per 100,000 inhabitants), State of
São Paulo and municipality of Caraguatatuba, 1980–2010**

evaluating the death rate, different from the other graphs presented, Caraguatatuba
has not been following the falling trend seen in the State. Table 9.4 shows, at three
important moments, the number of cases of AIDS notified in the four municipalities
of the Northern Coast and the totals for the Northern Coast and the entire State.
Although data from the 1990s was not considered totally reliable we chose to use
it in order to provide at least some information on this point in time.

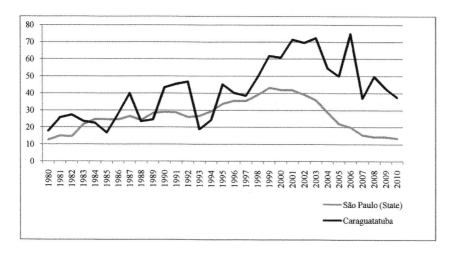

**Figure 9.3 Homicide mortality rates (per 100,000 inhabitants), State of
São Paulo and municipality of Caraguatatuba, 1980–2010**

Table 9.4 Number of AIDS notifications, State of São Paulo, Caraguatatuba, Ilhabela, São Sebastião and Ubatuba, 1990, 2000 and 2010

Region/Year	1990	2000	2010
Caraguatatuba	1	38	26
Ilhabela	0	1	0
São Sebastião	7	29	14
Ubatuba	0	22	2
Litoral Norte	8	90	42
São Paulo State	4116	10294	6360

Source: Created from DATASUS 2012; IBGE 2012 and Fundação SEADE 2012.

Death rates from AIDS in Caraguatatuba (Figure 9.4) show a pattern similar to that for the State in general until 1996, the year when the federal law of general access to retroviral therapy went into effect.

Since then the rates in the State of São Paulo have fallen consistently. The municipality of Caraguatatuba showed oscillating figures (1.15 to 17.97 deaths per 100,000 inhabitants), with a sharp rise as of 2003 (figures 9.4 and 9.5). This may be an accurate reflection of reality, or it may merely be the result of more accurate reporting of cause of death on certificates. Even so, this source of data is considered inadequate, since more than 10 per cent of all deaths in the municipality

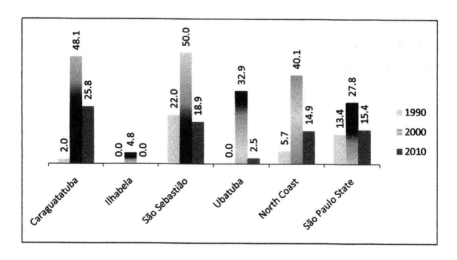

Figure 9.4 Rate of AIDS notification (per 100,000 inhabitants), São Paulo State, Caraguatatuba, Ilhabela, São Sebastião and Ubatuba, 1990, 2000 and 2010

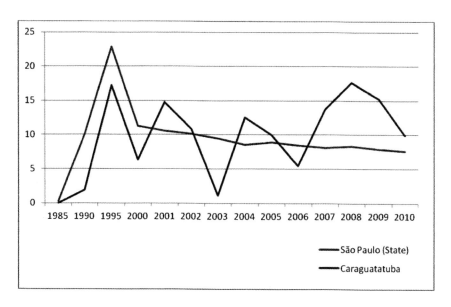

Figure 9.5 AIDS mortality rate (per 100,000 inhabitants), São Paulo State and municipality of Caraguatatuba, 1985–2010

indicate no defined cause. In an interview with the person responsible for the AIDS programme in the municipality, delayed diagnosis was indicated as one of the main challenges for lowering the death rate.

Although this study does not allow for statistical inferences, a correlation can be seen between the rates of police occurrences (especially drug trafficking, which has increased since 2003), deaths from assault and battery, and deaths from AIDS, consistently higher than those for the State, overall (see Figure 9.6 below).

Barcellos et al. (2001) in an evaluation of the spatial progression of AIDS in Brazil, especially near the country's borders, showed that the main directions of the spread of the epidemic could be detected by monitoring three groups of highways in the country, namely: 1. the stretches of highway that connect the central-western and northern regions; 2. the coastal areas of the southeast and south; and 3. the highway connections between the states of São Paulo, Mato Grosso and Mato Grosso do Sul. In all three cases, higher incidence of AIDS corresponds statistically to more complex networks of illegal drug traffic. In some locations, besides these connections, there has been an increase in the movement of people and merchandise, and this increases the possibility of contact between local populations and infected individuals coming from other places. Therefore, the populations in coastal tourist towns are also likely to be at higher than average risk of contracting AIDS, and the rapid and intense growth of Caraguatatuba could become a further factor of its vulnerability.

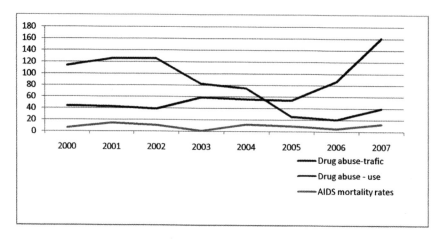

**Figure 9.6 Rates of drug abuse (traffic), drug abuse (use) and AIDS
mortality (per 100,000 inhabitants), municipality of
Caraguatatuba, 2000–2007**

Social Suffering, Violence and Tourism

The social pathology of Caraguatatuba, as partially represented in the range
indicators of vulnerability in Figure 9.6, might better be understood if located
within the discussions about social suffering. Kleinman et al. (1997) argue that
social suffering is a result of 'what political, economic and institutional power
does to people and, reciprocally, from [*sic*] how these forms of power themselves
influence responses to social problems' (p. ix). In order to demonstrate the
efficacy of social suffering to account for the consequences of the rapid social
and environmental changes effecting Caraguatatuba in the past 40 years, we focus
our discussion on the current state of community mental health before we attempt
to lay bare the particular forms of political, economic and institutional power
contained in tourism's conflation with social suffering.

We propose that depression offers a conduit to understanding how violence
and tourism are interconnected through the intervention of the drug economy.
This is because depression is a response of the subjective to the powers inherent
in tourism that potentially destabilise relatively stable categories of human
experience, including trauma, violence, pain, illness and death. We observed the
destabilisation as an ever-present edgy feel in the resort and, as we have argued
elsewhere, the transgressive possibility that attends tourism feeds ontological
disorder (Botterill et al. 2013). First, we report interviews with health professionals
in the field that point towards the influence of the drug economy on community
mental health. Second, we will suggest mechanisms that merge tourism with the
lawless and violent world of the drug economy. By these retroductive moves we
argue that tourism is complicit in violence, both symbolic and actual.

Psychoanalysis holds that the concept of depression, although derived from psychiatry, cannot be considered a clinical entity. We have adopted as our reference here the position set down by Rowe (2009: 1), who, at the beginning of her book *Depression, the Way Out of Your Prison* by writing 'Depression is not an illness or a mental disorder but a defense against pain and fear'. This assertion reinforces what we see in psychoanalysis, where, in general, depression is considered a 'position of the subject' (Dias 2004: 9). This implies that there are two currents to be considered. On the one hand, there is a need to define the notion of subject and the laws of the functioning of the unconscious. On the other, depressive episodes can be seen in different clinical states of hysterical, obsessional and phobic neuroses (Dias 2004). The depressed subject is essentially a defeated, silent and downhearted subject, one who falls before the fall (Dias 2003: 83).

Semi-structured interviews were held with four participants (one doctor – a psychiatrist who has recently taken on the role of a forensic psychiatrist – now based at a hospital; and three nursing technicians who work in the Municipal Health Department). The doctor was asked about her understanding of depression on the basis of her work with patients at the health centre and the presence of depression among them. She was also asked to talk about the socio-cultural aspects of the municipality and region, especially concerning levels of violence. The topics for discussion in the interviews with the health technicians were focused on the way health services are organised, the global environmental changes that the municipality has faced in recent decades, and the most recent data on violence.

The psychiatrist (who was interviewed for this present study) explained how she had become concerned with the high number of cases of depression, and could see that these numbers were well above the international expectations of the WHO. The psychiatrist, together with a nursing technician, analysed the records of patients at the health centre in terms of mental health, and they were able to identify some of the particularities of the municipality. One specific question stood out for the psychiatrist: why were there so many mental health cases in Caraguatatuba, especially of psychosis? The data showed that, in 2006, 20 per cent of the total population of the municipality (including both adults and children) had sought municipal mental health services at least once in their lives. This percentage is considered absurdly high for a municipal outpatient mental health clinic.

One fact noted by the psychiatrist was that not all of these patients were residents of the municipality, suggesting that at least some of her patients were likely to be second home owners. Municipal records of property occupation and ownership are not reliable indicators of actual residence as there are property tax implications and payment avoidance is a well-known problem for municipalities on the coast. Studied case by case, she counted 8,000 open patient files who frequented the clinic on a regular basis and were medicated. The psychiatrist also noted that 62 per cent of the patients treated were diagnosed with depression. In addition, nearly all the patients declared some direct involvement with abusive consumption of alcohol and/or illegal drugs. It is important to emphasise that such involvement refers not only to individual substance abuse and dependence.

Many persons are classified as co-dependents, defined as immediate family members of dependents who go to a clinic for medication because they find no other way to cope with the problems of drug and alcohol dependency amongst family members and are themselves diagnosed with depression. Although the raw data might be masking aspects of reality, they are nonetheless alarming. Even if one recognises that there are different methods for systematising the data, one cannot deny the unusual character of the fact that 62 per cent of the population who frequent the public mental health services in Caraguatatuba are diagnosed with depression.

The Drug Economy and Tourism

In the following discussion we continue to evidence the localised relationships between depression, the drug economy and violent crime on the north coast before making the arguably more difficult retroductive move to associate tourism within the transgressive and pathological domains of our case study area. Given the drug-related context of the violence in the state it would seem reasonable to deduce that the particularly high incidents of homicide in Caraguatatuba are also drug-related. Interview respondents confirmed the pivotal influence of the drug economy on the rates of crime and violence in the city.

For example, the forensic psychiatrist respondent working in the city was quite clear about the circumstances surrounding the deaths of many of the victims of violence, 'The violence is directly connected with alcohol and drugs'. Extant research on drug addiction in our case study area is difficult to locate. The only published study we could find was carried out in psychiatric hospitals in Greater São Paulo with cocaine users. The authors concluded that 'Drug use is a serious public health problem in Greater São Paulo and this is shown by the great amount of hospital admissions due to drug addiction. Crack users have lower socioeconomic status and more often engage in violence and crimes' (Ferreira Filho et al. 2003: 752). The forensic psychiatrist respondent in our study confirmed this assessment for Caraguatatuba too, but was also quick to point out that crack is the bi-product of cocaine, is therefore the drug of lower socio-economic groups and is often targeted by policy makers because the images of the poor, consuming drugs, is 'ugly'. In contrast, she pointed to the popular image of the middle class cocaine user who is 'shown on (soap opera) TV programs as sensible … the person next to us … a TV star'. She insisted, therefore, that in her experience drug use was not a class issue and that the demonisation of lower class drug consumption simply deflected from the pervasive, across classes, problem of drug use.

The market for drugs in Caraguatatuba is built around the in-migration of new residents to the city, both migrant workers and second home owners. One respondent painted a vivid picture of how the demand and supply in Caraguatatuba for alcohol, drugs and the bodies of the sex industry are driven, in part, by the in-migration of a labour force from rural areas of Brazil such as Acre. The manpower is needed to serve construction projects, including those associated with tourism –

condominium and retail developments. Thus, the market for holiday homes and the demands of other new enterprises conjointly fuel the transgressive possibility in the communities of the north coast.

A health respondent recounted how she had encountered many lone male workers in her practice. Typically they are separated from their families by thousands of miles and suddenly find themselves earning previously unimagined levels of income. From a monthly salary of Reais (R$) 6,000, R$1,000 is sent home leaving the young men with a monthly disposable income of R$5,000 (approximately US$2,500). The workers live in hostels, often located in unplanned developments with no community infrastructure. Work patterns are very demanding. There is little for them to do in the short amount of spare time they have except to drink, perhaps experiment with drugs and accept the invitations of prostitutes. The extent of the problem was detailed by our respondent who reported that there are around 8,000 cases of young people facing alcohol and/or drug addiction who are currently receiving treatment. In her work as a clinical psychiatrist the respondent has treated both those that consume – the workers who have psychotic breakdowns, the tourist who buys a 'bad' fix, and those that supply – the drug dealers, or most likely the families of drug dealers, and the prostitutes who themselves turn to alcohol and drug abuse as a survival strategy. In her testimony she recounted several such cases including one of a prostitute who found a sufficient source of income from the migrant workers to buy a house and a car in just two years but was deeply depressed and threatening suicide.

Alongside the potential consumers of the migrant workforce, the tourist market for drugs begins, as in many tourist areas around the world, with the consumption of alcohol on the beaches and in the beach side cafes. These tourism spaces close to the condominiums are exploited by drug suppliers, in some cases using children as young as 10 or 11 as vendors to offer a range of drug products. Soon the tourists are drawn to the city by the attraction of the easy availability of drugs. But the supply chain for drugs is not limited to identifiable tourist spaces. Respondents in our study spoke of the involvement in drug supply of many of the businesses that service the needs of the tourist, 'I treat the wife of one drug dealer here and he gave me his business card! They are bold and they live among us as popcorn street vendor, butcher, night club owner and teacher. They hold respected roles in our society ... drugs are easy money'.

It was also pointed out to us that the new holiday homes are sometimes used by 'casual' drug dealers from the nearby cities who use them as cheap weekend accommodation and a base from which to off-load their supplies perhaps unbeknown, or ignored, by the property owners who may even have a family connection to the dealer. The overall extent of drug dealing in Caraguatatuba is confirmed by the data in tables 9.2 and 9.3 above. These report that rates of drug dealing arrests in Caraguatatuba are three times the state average. Notwithstanding the possibility of a more effective policing regime in the city as an explanation of these differences in offending rates, it is unlikely that a more vigilant policing regime could account for such high comparative levels of offending in the city.

Thus, we begin to paint a picture of the messy inter-relations between tourism and the transgressive and pathological conditions in our case study area. But what of the violent homicides associated with the supply chain of the drug economy on the north coast? It is surely not possible that tourists occupying holiday homes are in any way associated with acts of violence that occur in parts of the city where tourists do not go and between gangs who would certainly not self-identify as tourists. On the surface, the empirical evidence would not support a connection, but let us explore this question in a little more depth.

The retroductive move, legitimised under critical realist ontology, is vital at this point in our analysis. Botterill et al. (2013) have shown how surface indicators of violence in a tourist city are only a start point for exploring the depth of social reality that provides the conditions necessary for its existence. They identify several 'mechanisms' that make violence possible despite the otherwise exemplary efforts of many stakeholders in the city to protect public safety. In their article, evidence drawn from several studies of violence in the city points to a mechanism of 'unresolved tension' within the public safety community. A further retroductive move identifies two deeper mechanisms. In respect of alcohol-related violence, Botterill et al. (ibid.) identify the mechanism 'acquiescence of transgression' and, in respect of sexual violence, a mechanism 'collusion of denial', both operating across the security and public safety community in their case study city in Australia. Our purpose in referring to this article is not to suggest that the same mechanisms are at work in the Caraguatatuba case study as our evidence is insufficient to draw such parallels. Instead we use it to legitimise the form of deep analysis used in this case study and we would encourage interested readers of this chapter to look at this earlier work, and Platenkamp and Botterill (2013), for a fuller account of critical realist ontology.

In the Caraguatatuba case study, we identify an additional mechanism, 'immunisation', which acts to protect the veil of virtuous innocence associated with tourism. Recent media coverage of the violent clashes between drug gangs and the police in São Paulo demonstrates the power of this mechanism in respect of tourism's 'immunisation' from drug gang violence. The managing director of Brazil Funding, a private company that advises European investors on putting their money into Brazil, responded to reportage of the recent violence on the BBC news website as follows, 'We are seeing a big wave of crime in Sao Paulo, which is not good for its image or tourism. But Sao Paulo is a huge, sprawling city, we are talking 19 million people, and the violence is taking place in the very poor parts of the city on its outskirts. Most people are completely unaffected' (BBC 2012a). And Julia Carneiro, the BBC's Rio de Janeiro correspondent comments,

> The conflict has brought great fear to the poorer part of the population and to policemen and their families, but has not affected the richer neighbourhoods – Brazil's inequality is reflected also when it comes to security. If this situation doesn't change and crime does not spread to the central areas, it shouldn't be a matter of concern for tourists (BBC 2012b).

What such statements overlook are the deeper connections between poverty and the potential amounts of money to be made by drug dealing that fuels the drug economy on the one hand, and, on the other, the transgressive act of purchasing drugs. As a respondent in our study of Caraguatatuba commented 'when a person starts the search for drugs they become indicted in the violent, lawless world of the drug dealer'. Thus all consumers of drugs, including experimenting tourists or bored migrant worker, become indicted in the violent homicide associated with the drug economy simply by the act of seeking to purchase drugs. Tourists may not be the victim or the murderer but they are complicit in the crime, and tourism's veil of virtuous innocence begins to shred. Meanwhile, the ontological powers of the 'immunisation' mechanism continue to deflect and protect tourism from closer scrutiny.

Conclusion

We have argued that the rapid social and environmental change experienced in our case study location has produced, and continues to reproduce, social suffering. Violence, its actual physical manifestation in crimes and in its symbolic form (Bourdieu and Wacquant 1992), has a profound impact on the subjective of both residents and visitors alike. We have sought to show how tourists and tourism are not immune from social suffering. Tourists and tourism therefore contribute to, and are reactive of, enduring structures of political and economic power and are complicit in the social pathology of Caraguatatuba.

Acknowledgements

We thank Sao Paulo State Foundation for Research Support (FAPESP, Brazil) for financial support for the research that led to this chapter (FAPESP, n. 2010/20811–5 and 2011/51714–8), and CNPq for the fellowship granted to the first author.

References

Adger, W.N. and Kelly, P.M. 2001. 'Social vulnerability and resilience', in W.N. Adger, P.M. Kelly and N.H. Ninh (eds) *Living with Environmental Change: Social Vulnerability, Adaptation and Resilience in Vietnam*, London: Routledge, 19–34.
Barcellos, C., Peiter, P., Rojas, L.I. and Matida, A. 2001. *A geografia da AIDS nas fronteiras do Brasil. Trabalho realizado para o 'Diagnóstico Estratégico da Situação da AIDS e das DST nas Fronteiras do Brasil'* [online], Convênio Ministério da Saúde/CN DST/SIDA; Population Council e USAID, 2001,

available at: http://www.igeo.ufrj.br/fronteiras/pesquisa/fronteira/p02pub03. htm [accessed 15 July 2012].

BBC 2012a. 'Sao Paulo sees big jump in murders' [online], available at: http://www. bbc.co.uk/news/world-latin-america-20441716 [accessed 28 November 2012].

BBC 2012b. 'Brazil's World Cup work overshadowed by police murders', [online], available at: http://www.bbc.co.uk/news/business-20427230 [accessed 26 November 2012].

Botterill, D., Seixas, S.C. and Hoefel, J-L. 2013. 'Tourism and transgression: Resort development, crime and the drug economy', *Tourism Planning and Development*,11(1), 27–41.

Botterill, D., Pointing, S., Clough, A., Hayes-Jonkers, C., Jones, T. and Rodriguez, C. 2013. 'Violence, backpackers, security and critical realism', *Annals of Tourism Research*, http://dx.doi.org/10.1016/j.annals.2013.01.007.

Bourdieu, P. and Wacquant, L. 1992. *An Invitation to Reflexive Sociology*, Chicago: The University of Chicago Press.

Dias, M.M. 2003. *Aposição do sujeito na depressão: uma abordagem psicanalista, Caderno do Seminário: Neuroses e Depressão Lições I à IV*, Campinas: Instituto de Psiquiatria de Campinas.

Dias, M.M. 2004. *Caderno do Seminário: Neuroses e Depressão Lições VI à XII*, Campinas: Instituto de Psiquiatria de Campinas.

Ferreira Filho, O.F., Turchi, M.D., Laranjeira, R. and Castelo, A. 2003. 'Epidemiological profile of cocaine users on treatment in psychiatrics hospitals, Brazil', *Rev Saude Publica*, 37(6), 751–9.

IBGE 2012. *Censo 2010*, [online], available at: http://www.ibge.gov.br/home/ estatistica/populacao/censo2010/default.shtm [accessed 9 July 2012].

Kleinman, A., Das, V. and Lock, M. (eds) 1997. *Social Suffering*, Berkeley: University of California Press.

McKenzie, K., Fingerhut, L., Walker, S., Harrison, A., and Harrison, J.E. 2012. 'Classifying external causes of injury: History, current approaches, and future directions', *Epidemiologic Reviews*, 34(1), 4–16.

Minayo, M.C.S. 2006. 'A inclusão da violência na agenda da saúde: trajetória histórica', *Ciência e Saúde Coletiva*, 11, 1259–67.

Platenkamp, V. and Botterill, D. 2013. 'Critical realism, rationality and tourism knowledge', *Annals of Tourism Research*, 41, 110–29.

Reichenheim, M.E., Souza, E.R., Moraes, C.L., Jorge, M.H.P.M., Passos da Silva, C.M.F. and Minayo, M.C.S. 2011. 'Health in Brazil 5. Violence and injuries in Brazil: The effect, progress made, and challenges ahead', *Lancet*, 377, 1962–75.

Rowe, D. 2009. *Depression: The Way out of Your Prison*, London: Routledge.

Seixas, S.R.C., Hoeffel, J.L.M., Renk, M., Vieira, S.A., Freire de Mello, L. and Vianna, P.V.C. 2011. 'Mudanças ambientais globais, vulnerabilidade e risco: impactos na subjetividade em Caraguatatuba, litoral norte Paulista', *Revista VITAS Visões Transdisciplinares sobre Ambiente e Sociedade*, 1, 1–28.

Seixas, S.R.C., Renk, M., Hoeffel, J.L.M., Conceição, A.L. and Asmus, G.F. 2012a. 'Global environmental changes and impacts on fishing activities in the northern coast of São Paulo, Brazil', in W.G. Holt (ed.) *Urban Areas and Global Climate Change*, Bingley, UK: Emerald Group Publishing, 299–317.

SOS Mata Atlântica, Instituto de Pesquisas Espaciais 2009. *Atlas dos Remanescentes Florestais da Mata Atlântica: Período 2005–2008*, São Paulo: Relatório Parcial.

Souza, E.R. 1993. 'Violência velada e revelada: estudo epidemiológico da mortalidade por causas externas em Duque de Caxias, Rio de Janeiro', *Cadernos de Saúde P*ública, 9(1), 48–64.

Uriely, N., Ram, Y., and Malach-Pines, A. 2011. 'Psychoanalytic sociology of deviant tourist behaviour', *Annals of Tourism Research*, 38(3), 1061–9.

Waiselfisz, J.J. 1998. *Mapa da violência: os jovens do Brasil. Juventude, violência e cidadania. Unesco Brasil* [online], available at: www.mapadaviolencia.org.br [accessed 18 July 2012].

Waiselfisz, J.J. 2011a. *Mapa da violência: os jovens do Brasil* [online], available at: www.mapadaviolencia.org.br [accessed 5 July 2012].

Waiselfisz, J.J. 2011b. *Mapa da violência: os novos padrões da violência homicida no Brasil* [online], available at: www.mapadaviolencia.org.br [accessed 7 July 2012].

Waiselfisz, J.J. 2012. *Mapa da violência 2012: os novos padrões da violência homicida no Brasil* [online], available at: www.mapadaviolencia.org.br [accessed 15 March 2012].

Weissberg, D., Guimarães, A.C.M. and Neto, P.R.M. 2011. 'The discipline of the market by a master plan: The case of building summer condominiums in Caraguatatuba', *Revista Univap*, 17(2), 24–31.

Chapter 10

New Approaches in the Research on Terrorist Attacks Affecting Tourism Demand

Wolfgang Aschauer

Introduction

Since 11 September 2001, and numerous other terrorist attacks in different parts of the world, alongside epidemics, natural disasters, risks and crises, their impacts have gained considerably more importance in tourism research. Terrorist attacks represent a specific form of tourism crises, because usually the destinations are hit unprepared. Symbolic images of fright and destruction are rooted in the minds of potential travellers (Freyer 2004), and the loss in demand may strongly affect the tourism industries (Mansfeld 1999) and the local population (UNDP 2003).

With the example of terrorist attacks, negative effects can arise from an economic perspective (effects on the tourism supply sector), a socio-cultural perspective (effects on the population, changes in intercultural relations) and a political perspective (political instability as a result of terror), and can cause critical conditions for affected destinations. Until today, most of the contributions from tourism studies are restricted to economic effects. They primarily refer towards the measurement of loss in demand by terrorist attacks (Aly and Strazicich 2001, Pizam and Smith 2000, Pizam and Fleischer 2002, Frey, Luechinger and Stutzer 2005, Goodrich 2002) as well as towards preventive actions and coping strategies generally known as risk and crisis management (Blake and Sinclair 2003, Israeli and Reichel 2002, Stafford, Yu and Armoo 2002). An interdisciplinary consideration of this phenomenon should, however, connect approaches from sociology, psychology, economics and the politics of tourism.

The following model (Figure 10.1) provides a systematic overview of possible research approaches to the multifaceted impacts of terror on tourism.[1]

By adopting a social science-based perspective, effects on tourism demand, as well as cultural processes of change as a consequence of terrorist attacks, can be

---

1 The illustrated model functioned as the basis for a research project that analysed the impacts of terrorist attacks on tourist demand (secondary analysis of spatial-temporal effects of terror by using existing tourism statistics), on the supply sector and crisis management in selected destinations (guided interviews with hotel managers) and on attitudes and behaviour of tourists (quantitative interviews). Three affected regions (Bali – Indonesia, Sinai – Egypt and Madrid/Catalonia – Spain) were examined and compared (Aschauer 2008).

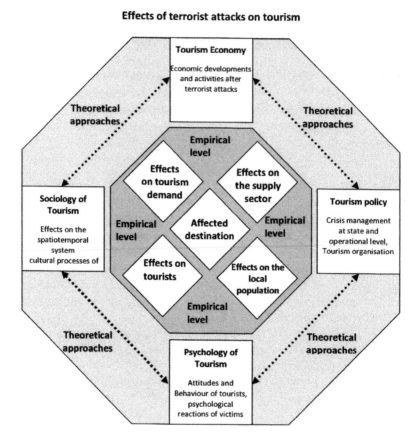

Figure 10.1 A model of scientific approaches regarding effects of terrorist attacks on tourism

analysed. An economic perspective may emphasise effects on the supply sector as well as aspects of crisis management at the public and private level.[2] By contrast the discipline of psychology has had a less central role in the study of tourism in crises destinations. However, it can contribute effectively towards our understanding of the experiences and behaviours of travellers and the affected populations. Until now, existing studies are mostly restricted to reactions of victims and relatives after terrorist attacks (Stotland 2002, Marshall et al. 2007).

---

2   The arrows between the disciplines in Figure 10.1 hint towards a necessary cross linking of the results. Statistical data of tourism demand is central for a destination to forecast further economic development. National crisis management influences the local population and travellers being confronted with new security measures.

Fieldwork including potential travellers in the source markets and on location is desirable. Such approaches could be further developed with research on potential travellers in the tourist generating markets and those on holiday at the sites of terrorist incidents. If we consider empirical research on terrorism affecting tourism demand, most of the studies are based on estimations of aggregated effects of terrorism events on the industry by using time-series models (Enders and Sandler 1991, Aly and Strazicich 2001). However, quantitative data that is only related to the flow of tourists allows only speculative assumptions with respect to the causes of spatio-temporal fluctuations in tourism. Further potentially influential elements including psychological (tourist mentality), economic-societal (crisis management, media) and political-cultural factors (travel alerts, cultural distance from locals) are hardly examined in existing research. Thus, alternative explanations drawn from individual preferences of tourists are included in the study for this chapter. Based on former empirical results (tourists visiting the terrorism-affected regions of Bali and the Sinai Peninsula (Aschauer 2008)), a follow-up survey of the local population in Salzburg (seen as future potential tourists) was conducted. Potential tourists in major tourist generating countries (like Austria) may have a more negative destination image of Bali and of the Sinai region (due to influences of critical media reports) in comparison with tourists on location.

Additionally, the research tries to integrate several explanations as to why destinations threatened by terrorism are perceived as insecure and unattractive by potential travellers. The aim of the empirical approach in this chapter is therefore twofold: first, the destination images of travellers on location and of the local population of Salzburg are compared to demonstrate differences in experiences of informed travellers (on location) with stereotypes of uninformed and inexperienced potential tourists (in their daily routine with or without any experience with the destinations or plans to visit them). Secondly, the study tries to find psychological explanations as to why specific groups of travellers are susceptible to a higher fear of terrorist attacks which manifest themselves in an unpopular destination image (with regard to destination quality, attitudes towards the locals, perceptions of security and terrorism fear).

The Effects of Terrorist Attacks on Tourism Demand

Tourists in general show a clear preference for tranquillity and peaceful social environments (Neumayer 2004, Reisenger and Mavondo 2005). Therefore destinations threatened by terrorism have a considerable handicap to maintain achieved growth rates in tourism demand. The impact of terrorism on tourism demand is a widely researched area but studies generally prove a significant negative impact of terrorism on tourist demand (Enders and Sandler 1991). Comprehensive explanations of the complex tourist mentality, as well as alternative approaches, alongside the analysis of tourism statistics are virtually non-existent.

Summarising the studies relying on tourism statistics six main results concerning the relationships between terrorism and tourism demand can be reported.

In a comprehensive study Neumayer (2004) demonstrated that politically motivated violence has a stronger effect on tourism demand than criminality. In comparison to several indicators measuring political violence in destinations, homicide rates do not exert a significant influence on tourism demand.

Terrorist attacks as a particularly dramatic form of political violence hit destinations completely unprepared and are described as 'over-night crises' (Kuschel and Schröder 2002). Pizam and Smith (2000) found that the higher the severity of an attack the more extensive is media coverage, which in turn has greater impacts on tourism demand. Nevertheless, the second main result shows that terrorist attacks exert rather a short-term effect, rather than a long-term effect, on destinations hit by terrorism (Aly and Strazicich 2001).

The tourism industry seems to be surprisingly resilient and even after attacks with a high number of victims former growth rates can be normally re-achieved within one year. Considering the two destinations selected for this study tourism flows after the terrorist attacks in Egypt and in Bali confirm the findings of Aly and Strazicich (2001). Despite numerous terrorist attacks (e.g. Luxor 1998, Taba 2004, Sharm el Sheik 2005 and Dahab 2006) the number of tourist arrivals in Egypt almost doubled between 2000 (5.5 million arrivals) and 2007 (11.1 million arrivals) (see Hussien 2009). Also in Bali, which suffered from two terrorist attacks in October 2002 and October 2005, tourism is again flourishing. The effects of the terrorist attacks on Bali were for both incidents limited to one year. In 2003, there was a clear decrease in international tourist arrivals (23 per cent), which in part can also be attributed to the Iraqi war and the SARS epidemics in May 2003. Tourism recovered very quickly in 2004 (together with a high growth rate of 47 per cent) (Aschauer 2005). Also after the second attack, tourism dropped considerably following the attack, which was represented in a decrease of 5 per cent in the year 2005 and 9 per cent in the year 2006; but again, the period of 2007–2009 saw a tremendous rebound of tourism in Bali, accompanied with growth rates of above 30 per cent (2007), 18 per cent (2008) and 13 per cent in 2009. Therefore the results of Pizam's study (1999) that permanent attacks are able to damage tourism in the long run until the terrorism threat is under control again are confirmed.

The Bali attacks can also be used as an example for the third main result which highlights that the frequency of terrorist attacks can be a stronger predictor of tourism losses than the severity of attacks. This was also the case with regard to Israel (Pizam and Fleischer 2002); while Krakover (2001) demonstrated that both the severity and the frequency of the terror acts are negatively correlated with tourism demand. The situation in Bali indicates that the second attack leads to a deeper violation of the destination image. Although the severity of the terrorist attack was considerably lower, the loss in tourism demand was similar and equally long-lasting in comparison to the first bombings.

Vester (2001) emphasises the importance of differentiating between terrorist attacks that violate society and public order (e.g. 9/11, Madrid 2004, London

2005) and terrorist attacks directly aimed at tourists in holiday destinations (e.g. Bali and Sinai). The fourth main result claims stronger effects of attacks, where tourists are the main target. Attacks against the public order can also affect tourism, but statistical data (for instance for Madrid 2004) confirm rather low effects on tourism. In the first three months after the terrorist attack (April to June 2004) in Madrid, the rate of German tourists was 10 per cent lower compared to the year before, but during the summer season tourism numbers returned to their normal performance (Aschauer 2008). Travellers seem to be aware that nowadays several Western European countries have to live with the terrorist threat and that subsequent attacks in the Western world cannot easily be foreseen. If tourists are hit by terrorism they clearly recognise their role as explicit targets and react more emotionally with fear and insecurity.

The fifth result concentrates more on the spatial effects of terrorist attacks. Sönmez (1998) distinguishes between substitution effects and generalisation effects. The assumption that tourists are rational consumers also strengthens the thesis that terrorist attacks in one destination result in substitution with a destination perceived as safe (e.g. Gu and Martin 1992).

Concerning Egypt and the Middle East, Mansfeld (1996) identifies shifts from states perceived as politically unstable (e.g. Egypt, Israel, Jordan) to states perceived as rather secure (e.g. Turkey). Severe attacks, which can be seen as a breach of the peace (e.g. 9/11) or where tourists are the main target (e.g. Bali 2002) can lead to a generalisation effect, which means that tourists presume entire regions to be at risk. The events of 11 September for instance led to a global shock for the tourism industry. Destinations dependent on the US market, as well as destinations which were linked to the conflict were particularly hard hit. There was, for instance, a heavy drop in tourism demand in the whole middle-east region (−30 per cent between September and December 2001) because Arabic states were across-the-board perceived as sympathisers of Al-Qaeda and Islamist terror groups (UNWTO 2002).

Nevertheless Sönmez (1998) argues for the need to take other factors into consideration, for instance intensive marketing efforts, currency exchange rates as well as the habits of different local and international markets. This leads us to the last main result that the effects of terrorist attacks are culturally different. Glaeßer (2005) argues that national involvement is of crucial importance. If nationals from major source markets are victims of the attack this will result in higher media coverage within the specific countries. This, in turn, fuels fears in the affected generating market. The geographical closeness of the affected destinations can have a positive and a negative influence. If terrorist attacks happen in nearby countries, potential tourists will be better informed and can more easily assess the risks of travelling for themselves. Many destinations, being confronted with terrorism, pay attention to local markets in their efforts to compensate for losses in long-haul travelling (see UNWTO 2004). On the other hand, a high popularity of the destination corresponds with comprehensive media reports, which can lead to severe damage of the destination image. Due to their higher geographical knowledge local markets are also able to switch from affected destinations to other nearby tourist places.

The geographical and cultural distance of destinations is one crucial marker of different cultural effects but there are general cultural differences in risk perceptions as well. Pizam et al. (2004) demonstrate that travellers from Ireland, the United States and from Israel can be characterised by a higher risk propensity. This is compared to value studies (Hofstede 1980 and Schwartz 1994) which confirm that for example Japanese society can be characterised by a higher uncertainty avoidance, which leads to a higher sensitivity with regard to terrorist attacks.

A New Empirical Approach in the Research of Terrorism Affecting Tourism Demand

In general, instead of statistically analysing tourism flows this chapter adopts a new strategy in the analysis of the effects of terrorism on tourism demand. The main idea is to focus on individual preferences of tourists. Here the concept of the destination image held by travellers should be emphasised, being a crucial factor in tourism choice and marketing (e.g. Jenkins 1999, Baloglu and Mangaloglu 2001).

However, as Sönmez et al. highlight: 'the impact of terrorism on destination image has been virtually ignored in literature' (Sönmez et al. 1999: 13). One step in this direction is the study of Araña and León (2008), who used individual tourist data and a decision-making approach to get an insight of tourists' perceptions of traumatic events. Two split surveys (pre- and post-September 2001) were conducted following the method of discrete choice experiments to study the preferences of tourists for specific destinations. They found that primarily Middle East countries (e.g. Turkey and Tunisia) reduced their image values as a consequence of 9/11. However, the study results are limited to Germany and focus on a terrorist attack not directly related to tourism. Yechiam et al. (2005) mention that three dimensions, namely cultural aspects, personal experiences and the costs of avoiding the risk, are crucial to explaining different reactions of tourists concerning the impact of terrorist attacks.

The empirical approach, adopted in this chapter, derives possible influence factors from a comprehensive research project on the effects of terrorism on tourism, where three countries – Bali, Egypt and Spain – were examined and compared.

In a qualitative study hotel managers were interviewed about the causes of losses in tourism demand and a survey was conducted with more than 900 tourists on location to measure attitudinal and behavioural characteristics of travellers in destinations affected or threatened by terrorist attacks (Aschauer 2008, 2010).[3] The study results served as the starting point of a follow-up study with potential

---

3   Due to the fact that, during fieldwork, the second terrorist attack in Bali occurred, it was for the first time possible to analyse immediate reactions of travellers to a terrorist attack (Aschauer 2005, 2010).

travellers in their home countries. The population of Salzburg was surveyed to compare the destination image and risk perceptions of potential tourists in their daily routine with travellers on location.[4]

On the other hand it is of particular interest to look at different levels of tourists' mentality as important predictors of a positive or negative evaluation of threatened or affected destinations.

Research Questions, Study Design and Hypothesis

Based on the existing literature, the main factors influencing destination image and risk perception (concerning terrorist attacks), which were operationalised in this study are summarised in Table 10.1. In summary, two main research questions serve as a theoretical starting point for the empirical analyses:

1. How do potential tourists, at home, perceive the place image of destinations threatened by terrorism (Bali and Sinai) in comparison to tourists on location?
2. Which factors of tourists' mentality contribute significantly to the explanation of a negative place image as well as an increased fear of terrorist attacks?

Concerning the first research question, it is hypothesised that informed and experienced travellers on location will have a better image of the destination compared to uninformed and inexperienced potential tourists at home (*Hypothesis 1*).

The second research question tries to find explanations for a negative image of the terrorism-threatened destinations and a high fear of terrorism. The statistical method of hierarchical OLS-regressions including all proposed levels of variables serves as a fruitful approach to clarify the influences of several psychological constructs integrated in this study.[5]

At Level 1 (on the very left side of Table 10.1), the independent factors of the study are listed, on the one hand socio-demographic parameters of the sample (gender, age, marital status, children and qualifications) as well as sensation

---

4 Of course the comparison has its limits because in Bali and in the Sinai region travellers from different nations were interviewed (e.g. mainly Australian and German tourists in Bali and mainly Italian, British and German tourists in the Sinai region). But the population of this Austrian city can be seen as a sample of potential travellers in their quotidian world whose destination image is mainly built on media reporting and there is in general only little specific knowledge of the destination. It is particularly interesting how terrorism in famous tourist destinations affects not only travellers on location but also potential tourists in Western source markets.

5 With this technique, the relevance of explanatory factors is justified because with several steps, more predictors of different levels are included (see Urban and Mayerl 2011).

Table 10.1 Operationalisation of the main constructs and indicators in the survey

Socio-demographic parameters/personal characteristics	Level of travel parameters	Tourist mentality in regard to travelling under terrorism risk	Dependent level (destination image, risk perception terrorism)
1. Socio-demographic variables • Gender (male, female) • Age (metric scale) • Marital status (single, in relationship) • Children (no, yes) • Qualification (below vs. above qualification for university entrance) **2. Sensation seeking (personality)** *(BSSS → Short scale Sensation seeking, reduced from 8 to 7 items due to a higher reliability; Cronbach α = 0.84)*	**1. Roles of tourists** *(International Tourist Roles Scale, 16 items reduced to 6 items, single factor solution Cronbach α = 0.72)* **2. Information seeking** • Touristic information seeking (two items, Likert-Scale, Cronbach α = 0.77) • Country-specific information seeking (two items, Likert-Scale, Cronbach α = 0.62) **3. Destination-specific factors** • Former stay in destination (no, yes) • Attraction of destination (4 items Bali, 6 items Sinai, Likert-Scale, Cronbach α = 0.90 (Bali), 0.70 (Sinai)) **4. Travel parameters** • Travel intensity (number of holiday trips per year, metric scale) • Long-haul travel experience (number of intercontinental trips) • Travelling with underage children (no, yes) • Preference for package tours (no, yes) • Preference for individual travelling (no, yes)	• Following media reporting about terrorist attacks (5 Items, Likert-Scale, Cronbach α = 0.81) • Knowledge about attacks in Bali, Sinai (index, three questions on attacks in Bali, Sinai, 0 = false answers, 1 = at least one right answer) • Experiences with terrorism-affected or threatened destinations (index, four questions, 0 = no experience, 4 = very experienced) • Importance of security during travelling (3 Items, Likert-Scale, Cronbach α = 0.90)	**1. Destination image** • Attitudes to destinations Bali, Sinai (cognitive component) (7 items, Likert-Scale, index negative–positive judgement, low consistency) • Perception of the locals (cultural component) (8 items, Likert-Scale, index negative–positive judgement, Cronbach α = 0.8) • Judgement of security (4 items, Likert-Scale, Cronbach α = 0.66) **2. Risk perception** • Risk perception → 1 Item, Likert-Scale, fear of terrorist attacks in the destination 1 = would not occupy my mind to 5 = would strongly occupy my mind

seeking as a stable and independent personal construct. The indicator for sensation seeking was constructed using seven items of the eight item-BSSS scale (Hoyle et al. 2002), due to a higher internal consistency of the shorter scale (Cronbach $\alpha = 0.84$). Pizam et al. (2004) combined the risk propensity of young adults with numerous travel characteristics and tourism specific behaviours. It transpired that sensation seekers prefer adventurous and sportive activities as well as entertainment offers.

Thus it is hypothesised that socio-demographic variables exert only a little influence on the destination image of the two threatened regions Bali and Sinai but sensation seeking is a crucial factor regarding terrorism fear (*Hypothesis 2*).

Travel parameters and holiday needs are located at the next (independent) level. The standardised scale of Jiang et al. (2000) for holiday preferences was reduced to six items and leads to a single factor solution. Therefore potential tourists in the city of Salzburg can be differentiated in relation to their open-mindedness towards the destination which results in a high motivation for strangeness and a preference of individual travel styles and intercultural contacts. Again it is assumed that this dimension leads significantly to a better destination image and to a lower risk perception (*Hypothesis 3*). Information seeking does not have an influence on qualitative destination image but a high effect on the perception of locals, security perceptions and terrorism fear. While touristic information seeking increases security concerns, country-specific information seeking decreases the fear of terrorism (*Hypothesis 4*).

Destination specific factors positively influence the destination image as well as the risk perceptions. If tourists are attracted by Asian and Oriental destinations they value both destinations higher and demonstrate fewer security concerns (*Hypothesis 5*).

On the third level, the crucial factors measuring the tourist mentality in relation to the terrorism threat can be found. It is hypothesised that these factors are statistically the most relevant factors explaining the fear of terrorism (*Hypothesis 6*).

Finally knowledge about terrorism (following media reporting, knowledge of attacks in Bali and Sinai) as well as experiences with terrorism (operationalised through former visits in terrorism-threatened destinations or knowledge of narratives from affected destinations) leads to a better destination image as well as to a lower risk perception (*Hypothesis 7*). Contrary to those factors a higher value of security leads to a higher fear of terrorism (*Hypothesis 8*).

Study Procedures

Between April and June 2007, 125 inhabitants of the city of Salzburg took part in the survey. One part of the sample was interviewed about the destination image of Bali (n = 62) and the other half of the sample about the destination image of the Sinai region (n = 63). The other indicators were used for all participants, namely socio-demographic and travel parameters, the sensation seeking scale and the measurement of tourism mentality in relation to the terrorist threat in tourist destinations. The sample has to be seen as a convenience sample, the answers were gained from respondents in the city who had time to answer the survey. Due to the broad distribution of sampling points throughout different urban districts the sample can be considered to be largely coherent with the geographical structure of the inhabitants of Salzburg.

Concerning age and education the sample cannot be seen as representative because of a higher proportion of younger people (median age: 31, mode: 23 years) and a higher proportion of highly educated individuals. 28.2 per cent have a qualification for university entrance (compared to 12.2 per cent of the Salzburg population) and 17.7 per cent of the participants have already achieved a higher degree (compared to 12.4 per cent found in official statistics) (see Statistik Austria, http://www.statistik.at/blickgem/gemDetail.do?gemnr=50101). There is also a slightly higher proportion of women in the sample (56.8 per cent, compared to 52.45 per cent in the city of Salzburg).[6]

Due to the selection criteria of the local inhabitants of Salzburg, the participants of the study had only a little experience of the two destinations. More than one quarter have already been either to Bali or to Egypt and more than 70 per cent of the sample have already travelled to a destination outside of Europe. Most of the participants (42.7 per cent) prefer package tours while one third of the sample normally favours an independent travel style. The travel characteristics indicate a sample of rather experienced travellers, which may not represent perfectly the Austrian population.

Empirical Results

The first research question of the study deals with the destination image of potential tourists in their daily routine in comparison with tourists on location. In general one survey question refers to attitudes about which larger touristic regions are highly threatened by terrorism. The results of Figure 10.2 demonstrate that (Northern) African destinations as well as tourist areas in the Middle East are highly associated with terrorism. Destinations in Asia, Northern and Southern America are generally perceived as rather secure, while in Australia and Europe no terrorism risk is assumed.

After these general estimations of the terrorist threat in major world regions the place images of two destinations already confronted with terrorism, namely the Sinai region and Bali were examined and compared with the views of tourists on location. The first hypothesis assumes that travellers on location have a better

---

6   So results referring to the whole sample should be treated with caution because they do not really reflect the Salzburg population. By contrast, results based on influential factors on destination image and terrorism fear can be seen as valid, because the group sizes (of different ages and education groups) are high enough to analyse socio-demographic and travel-related differences between the participants.

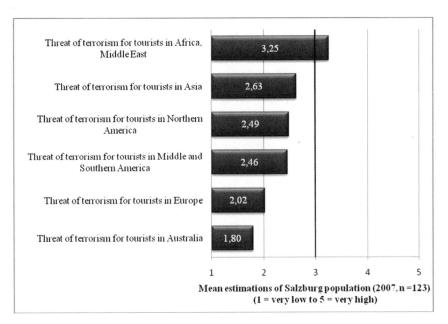

Figure 10.2 Perceptions of the terrorism threat in different world regions (opinions of Salzburg sample)

image of the destinations in all aspects compared to potential tourists at home. Table 10.2 (below) presents all the mean differences in the indicators which were presented to the respondents as semantic differential (−3 reflects the left pole and +3 reflects the right pole). Analysing all different aspects (cognitive judgement, local population and security) the hypothesis is only partly confirmed for Bali. Compared to tourists on location potential Austrian tourists place more emphasis on the attractiveness of beaches and there are no significant differences regarding climatic conditions and pollution. Additionally, tourists on location judge locals more importunate, while the Salzburg population estimates them as more reserved. Regarding the risk of terrorism attacks and political stability, no significant differences were found. However, most of the indicators demonstrate that tourists on location give the destination generally a higher value (e.g. good value for money, lots worth seeing, high quality of infrastructure, friendliness and openness of locals, safety and criminality).

Table 10.3 (below) demonstrates the differences between the two samples (international tourists on location versus the Salzburg population) for the Sinai region. The results using mainly the same indicators as in Bali lead to similar conclusions. Generally, tourists in the Sinai region value the destination higher than potential Austrian tourists (e.g. value for money, climatic conditions, quality of infrastructure, openness of locals) but, again, not in all aspects. Regarding security, a big difference between the two samples can be found. The Salzburg population

Table 10.2 Differences of the destination image between travellers in Bali and potential tourists in Austria (Bali)

Destination Image components	Destination Image Variables	Travellers on location (Bali, 2005) vs. Salzburg population (at home, 2007)	n	mean	Sig.
	poor value for money – good value for money	on location	215	2.30	.00
		at home	47	1.11	
	unpleasant climatic conditions – pleasant climatic conditions	on location	217	1.89	.09
		at home	54	1.48	
	unattractive beaches – attractive beaches	on location	216	0.87	.02
		at home	55	1.51	
Cognitive Judgement	little worth seeing – lots worth seeing	on location	216	1.94	.03
		at home	55	1.44	
	low quality of infrastructure – high quality of infrastructure	on location	215	1.13	.00
		at home	48	0.35	
	polluted environment – clean environment	on location	212	-0.66	.13
		at home	46	-0.20	
	dull scenery – impressive scenery	on location	215	2.08	.04
		at home	53	1.57	

			N	Mean	p
Judgement of local population	unfriendly – friendly	on location	217	2.38	.01
		at home	53	1.91	
	uncommunicative with tourists – open with tourists	on location	215	1.97	.00
		at home	52	1.04	
	importunate – reserved	on location	212	-0.43	.00
		at home	50	0.46	
	hectic – patient	on location	214	1.32	.95
		at home	53	1.30	
Judgement of security	unsafe – safe	on location	216	1.54	.00
		at home	57	-0.04	
	high criminality – low criminality	on location	206	1.00	.01
		at home	55	0.31	
	politically unstable – politically stable	on location	187	-0.04	.17
		at home	48	-0.38	
	danger of terrorist attacks – no danger of terrorist attacks	on location	208	-0.05	.46
		at home	58	-0.22	

Table 10.3 Differences of the destination image between travellers in Bali and potential tourists in Austria (Sinai)

Destination Image components	Destination Image Variables	Travellers on location (Sinai, 2005) vs. Salzburg population (at home, 2007)	n	mean	sig
	poor value for money – good value for money	on location	266	1.61	.01
		at home	54	0.98	
	unpleasant climatic conditions – pleasant climatic conditions	on location	271	1.94	.00
		at home	62	0.66	
	unattractive beaches – attractive beaches	on location	271	1.25	.29
		at home	58	1.50	
Cognitive Judgement	little worth seeing – lots worth seeing	on location	266	1.64	.14
		at home	61	1.98	
	low quality of infrastructure – high quality of infrastructure	on location	271	1.00	.00
		at home	59	0.25	
	polluted environment – clean environment	on location	266	0.60	.00
		at home	56	-0.45	
	dull scenery – impressive scenery	on location	271	0.97	.00
		at home	60	-0.10	

Category	Item	Condition	N	Mean	p
Judgement of local population	unfriendly – friendly	on location	272	1.64	.14
		at home	56	1.32	
	uncommunicative with tourists – open with tourists	on location	266	1.17	.00
		at home	51	0.35	
	importunate – reserved	on location	260	-0.68	.64
		at home	58	-0.79	
	hectic – patient	on location	265	0.94	.16
		at home	52	0.58	
Judgement of security	unsafe – safe	on location	275	1.05	.00
		at home	61	-0.26	
	high criminality – low criminality	on location	247	0.73	.00
		at home	58	-0.71	
	politically unstable – politically stable	on location	242	0.09	.01
		at home	57	-0.49	
	danger of terrorist attacks – no danger of terrorist attacks	on location	251	-0.21	.00
		at home	62	-1.02	

sees the Sinai Peninsula as highly insecure in comparison to tourists at the location. In all aspects, high mean differences are found between the two samples, especially in indicators dealing with safety, criminality and the terrorism threat.

The second research aim of the survey was to identify characteristics of tourists which may explain negative destination images as well as an increased fear of terrorist attacks. Besides the three main analysed levels of destination image (negative versus positive attitudes, negative versus positive perceptions of locals and judgement of security), which were built as index variables (see Table 10.4 for further information) a fourth dependent variable measuring the potential fear of terrorism in the two destinations (on a five-point scale) was added. The three levels (socio-demographic and personal factors, travel parameters and tourists' mentality with regard to the terrorism threat) were treated as independent factors and four hierarchical OLS- regressions were run to identify the relevant predictors and the total effect size of the different levels explaining the dependent variables.

Regarding the first level, it was hypothesised that socio-demographic indicators exert only a small influence on the dependent variables, while the risk propensity (sensation seeking) is assumed to be a crucial predictor regarding terrorism fear. In total, this hypothesis can be confirmed, but sensation seeking has to be seen as a rather weak predictor (beta = -0.22).

Socio-demographic indicators have indeed no influence on terrorism fear but they exert a clear effect on perceptions of destination image. Women demonstrate more positive attitudes towards the destinations and express lower security concerns compared to men. Older residents in Salzburg express more positive attitudes towards the local population in the destinations compared to younger people.

Concerning the second level (travel parameters) the third hypothesis has to be rejected. It was assumed that holiday preferences representing open-mindedness (search for strangeness, individuality and intercultural contacts) lead to a better destination image and to lower terrorism fears. This factor has a negative significant influence on the judgement of the destination (contrary to the expectations). Also the fourth hypothesis, referring to the information seeking behaviour cannot be confirmed. Information seeking has a significant influence on terrorism fear but both factors (touristic information seeking and country-specific information seeking lead to a higher fear of terrorist attacks). Additionally, country-specific information seeking has a positive influence on the qualitative judgement of the destination.

Destination specific factors (e.g. attractiveness of destination) have no significant influence (neither on destination image nor on terrorism fear) but a former stay in the region leads to a more positive judgement of the holiday destination. Long-haul travel experience leads to a rather negative judgement of the locals in the destinations.

On the third level, the factors representing tourism mentality in relation to the terrorism risk were analysed. Hypothesis 6, assuming that these factors are statistically the most relevant factors explaining terrorism fear cannot be confirmed

Table 10.4 Hierarchical regression analysis – effects of socio-demographic characteristics. Travel parameters and tourist mentality on destination image and terrorism fear

Model 1: Socio-demographic characteristics	Beta	Model 2: Socio-demographic characteristics and travel parameters	Beta	Model 3: Socio-demographic characteristics, travel parameters, tourist mentality	Beta	r² (%)	Dependent variables
Gender (females)	.33 (.76)**	Gender (females)	.35 (.81)**			12.7	*Negative vs. positive attitudes towards destination*
Age	.35 (.03)**	Age	.26 (.02)*				
		Country-specific information seeking	.30 (.43)**			21.2	
		Already stayed there	.30 (.78)**				
		Open-mindedness	-.34 (-.49)*				
				Gender (females)	.33 (.74)**		
				Country-specific information seeking	.28 (.39)*		
				Already stayed there	.30 (.76)*	19.2	
				Open-mindedness	-.35 (-.50)*		
Age	.34 (.02)*					4.1	*Negative vs. positive perception of locals*
		Age	.31 (.02)+			4.6	
		Long-haul travel experience	-.31 (-.04)*				
				Long-haul travel experience	-.38 (-.05)**	6.8	
Gender (females)	.22 (.50)+					2.6	*Judgement of security*
		No influence				-	
				Gender (females)	.24 (.56)+	-	
Sensation Seeking	-.22 (-.27)+					4.7	*Fear of terrorist attacks in destination*
		Touristic information seeking	.19 (.23)+				
		Country-specific information seeking	.20 (.30)+			4.8	
				Importance of Security	.44 (.47)***	16.8	

Notes: Hierarchical OLS-Regressions; Missing: pairwise; + = p <0.10; * = p<0.05; ** = p < 0.01; corrected r² and standardised regression coefficients (beta) as well as unstandardised coefficients (in brackets).

because only one factor (the importance of security on travelling) turned out to be significant (confirmation of Hypothesis 8).

Finally other factors (e.g. knowledge of attacks in Bali and Sinai) as well as experiences with terrorism (operationalised through former visits in terrorism-threatened destinations or knowledge of narratives from affected destinations) failed to exert a significant influence on destination image as well as on terrorism fear. Therefore Hypothesis 7, supposing that these factors are mostly relevant, cannot be confirmed.

Conclusion

In this chapter a new approach to the analysis of terrorist attacks affecting tourism demand was adopted. Instead of a secondary analysis of international tourist arrivals after terrorist attacks, a case study of the local population of Salzburg which can be seen as a sample of potential western travellers in their quotidian world was conducted and the results were compared with a former study of tourists on location. A standardised questionnaire measured the destination image of two terrorism affected regions (Bali and Sinai) and focused on psychological characteristics of individual travellers to shed light on tourist mentality in times where security concerns during travelling are of crucial importance. The follow-up study after a comprehensive research on tourists in affected destinations enables a comparison of the destination image of experienced travellers (on location) with destination-inexperienced potential tourists in a typical Western European source market (the population of Salzburg).

It has to be stated that the comparison has its limits because in Bali and in the Sinai region travellers from different nations were interviewed (mainly Australian and German tourists in Bali and mainly Italian, British and German tourists in the Sinai region). These results are compared with selected inhabitants from the city of Salzburg (convenience sample) reflecting potential Western travellers in their quotidian world. After terrorist attacks it is of particular importance for the affected regions to attract exactly those potential markets to re-achieve normal growth rates in tourism. The first hypothesis regarding the comparison of the destination image assumes that potential tourists in their daily routine give more negative judgements on the destinations, and express especially security concerns. This hypothesis can only partly be confirmed because in Bali single indicators are even more positively judged by the Salzburg population and no significant differences regarding security concerns appear. Nevertheless the attitudes towards the Sinai regions reflect unpopular views, especially with regard to the terrorism threat, safety and criminality. In addition, Bali is given a higher value in comparison to the Sinai region. This is also a confirmation of the study of Araña and León (2008) who found out that primarily Middle East countries (in their study Turkey and Tunisia) reduced their image values as a consequence of 9/11. It seems that particularly the destination image of Arab regions is harmed in the long-term and that tourists are more sensitive to terrorism or political insecurities in these places.

The second aim of the study was to find out how indicators of tourist mentality influence the destination image as well as the fear of future terrorist attacks. Four variables functioned as dependent constructs, namely the qualitative judgement of the destination, the view of the local populations, security issues and the fear of terrorist attacks. In general, the effects of these variables are considerably lower than expected and several hypotheses had to be rejected.

Sensation seeking was presumed to be an important predictor of understandings of destination image and terrorism fear but only one significant influence on terrorism fear could be found. Contrary to the assumption (Hypothesis 3) holiday preferences (operationalised in the dimension open-mindedness) have no significant influence on destination image and on terrorism fear. Thus the famous tourist typologies (e.g. Plog 2001) are perhaps not as relevant with regard to the fear of terrorism. It could not be confirmed that open-minded travellers perceive unfamiliar destinations as more secure compared to the psychocentric tourists' views. Open-mindedness leads even to a higher critical view of classical mass-tourism destinations like Bali and the Sinai Peninsula because allocentrics seem to favour clearly alternative tourist destinations. Additionally long-haul travel experiences lead to negative judgements of locals. This result may reflect a more realistic judgement of a population by experienced travellers compared to stereotypical views of destination peoples by inexperienced locals in Austria.

Interestingly, information seeking leads to a higher fear of terrorist-attacks. Tourists, being highly informed of the destination thus recognise the terrorist threat but maybe this does not lead to avoidance of the destination. This assumption is strengthened because highly informed tourists judge the destinations more positively than tourists who are not well informed before travelling. These results are a clear sign that informed tourists (about destinations in general as well as about terrorism) can be seen as rational consumers, while uniformed tourists express emotional reactions. They are susceptible to the message of fear from terrorists and decide to avoid terrorism-affected destinations.

Tourist mentality with regard to terrorist attacks was presumed as a strong predictor of terrorism fear and destination image but only one factor, namely the importance of security during travelling exerts a strong influence on terrorism fear. Here an interaction has to be assumed because both variables – importance of security and fear of terrorism – influence each other. Finally other factors (e.g. knowledge of attacks in Bali and Sinai) as well as experiences with terrorism (operationalised through former visits in terrorism-threatened destinations or knowledge of narratives from affected destinations) failed to exert a significant influence on destination image as well as on terrorism fear.

Although the study has its limits (lacking comparability and representativeness) it can be seen as a starting point to follow new approaches in the research of tourism demand. This approach, favouring destination image and tourist mentality is able to offer new explanations as to why terrorism affected destinations suffer only short-term on the one hand or long-term on the other. In general, larger samples are needed to strengthen the preliminary results of this study, because the lack of significant findings can also be traced back to the rather small sample size (n = 125) and to small group sizes. Representative cross-national studies in the source markets, using a multiplicity of indicators may be able to clarify tourists´ preferences and security concerns and to illuminate which tourist types particularly avoid crises destinations.

References

Aly, H.Y. and Strazicich, M.C. 2001. 'Terrorism and tourism. Is the impact permanent or transitory?' [online], available at: http://fama2.us.es:8080/turismo/turismonet1/economia%20del%20turismo/economia%20del%20turismo/terrorism%20and%20tourism.pdf [accessed 1 February 2012].

Araña, J.E. and León, C.J. 2008. 'The impact of terrorism on tourism demand: A stated preference approach', *Annals of Tourism Research*, 35(2), 299–315.

Aschauer, W. 2005. 'Psychologische Effekte als direkte Folge von Terroranschlägen. Touristen vor und nach den Bali-Attentaten 2005', *Irics-Beiträge*, Trans 16, available at: http://www.inst.at/trans/16Nr/12_1/aschauer16.htm [accessed 9 February 2012].

Aschauer, W. 2008. *Tourismus im Schatten des Terrors. Eine vergleichende Analyse der Auswirkungen von Terroranschlägen (Bali, Sinai, Spanien)*, München: Profil.

Aschauer, W. 2010. 'Perceptions of tourists at risky destinations. A model of psychological influence factors', *Tourism Review*, 65(2), 4–20.

Baloglu, S. and Mangaloglu, M. 2001. Tourism destination images of Turkey, Egypt, Greece and Italy as perceived by US-based tour operators and travel agents', *Tourism Management*, 22, 1–9.

Blake, A. and Sinclair, M.T. 2003. 'Tourism crisis management. US response to September 11', *Annals of Tourism Research*, 30(4), 813–32.

Enders, W. and Sandler, T. 1991. 'Causality between transnational terrorism and tourism: The case of Spain', *Terrorism*, 14, 49–58.

Frey, B.S., Luechinger, S. and Stutzer, A. 2005. 'Calculating tragedy: Assessing the costs of terrorism', *CESifo Working Paper*, 1341, 1–31.

Freyer, W. 2004. 'Von "Schutz und Sicherheit" zu "Risiko und Krisen" in der Tourismusforschung', in W. Freyer and S. Groß (eds) *Sicherheit in Tourismus und Verkehr*, Dresden: Fit, 1–13.

Glaeßer, D. 2005. *Handbuch Krisenmanagement im Tourismus. Erfolgreiches Entscheiden in schwierigen Situationen*, Berlin: Erich Schmidt.

Goodrich, J.N. 2002. 'September 11, 2001 attack on America: A record of the immediate impacts and reactions in the USA travel and tourism industry', *Tourism Management*, 23, 573–80.

Gu, Z. and Martin T.L. 1992. 'Terrorism, seasonality and international air tourist arrivals in central Florida: An empirical analysis', *Journal of Travel and Tourism Marketing*, 1, 3–15.

Hofstede, G. 1980. *Culture's Consequences: International Differences in Work-related Values*, Beverly Hills: Sage Publications.

Hoyle, R.H. et al. 2002. 'Reliability and validity of a brief measure of sensation seeking', *Personality and Individual Differences*, 32, 401–14.

Hussien, R. 2009. 'The horizon of developing the Egyptian marketing tourism in EU', *Annals of Faculty of Economics*, 4(1), 836–9, available at: http://steconomice.uoradea.ro/anale/volume/2009/v4-management-and-marketing/169.pdf [accessed 9 February 2012].

Israeli, A.A. and Reichel, A. 2002. 'Hospitality crisis management practices: The Israeli case', *Hospitality Management*, 22, 353–72.

Jenkins, O.H. 1999. 'Understanding and measuring tourist destination images', *International Journal of Tourism Research*, 1, 1–15.

Jiang, J., Havitz, M.E. and O'Brien, R.M. 2000. 'Validating the international tourist role scale', *Annals of Tourism Research*, 27(4), 964–81.

Krakover, S. 2001. 'Estimating the effects of atrocious events on the flow of tourists to Israel', in G. Ashworth and R. Hartmann (eds) *Tourism, War and the Commemoration of Atrocity*, New York: Cognizant Communication Corp.

Kuschel, R. and Schröder, A. 2002. *Tourismus und Terrorismus. Interaktionen, Auswirkungen und Handlungsstrategien*, Dresden: Fit.

Mansfeld, Y. 1996. 'Wars, tourism and the "Middle East" factor', in A. Pizam and Y. Mansfeld (eds) *Tourism, Crime and International Security Issues*, Chichester: Wiley, 265–78.

Mansfeld, Y. 1999. 'Cycles of war, terror and peace: Determinants and management of crisis and recovery of the Israeli tourism industry', *Journal of Travel Research*, 38, 30–36.

Marshall, R.D. et al. 2007. 'The psychology of ongoing threat: Relative risk appraisal, the September 11th attacks and terrorism-related fears', *American Psychologist*, 62(4), 304–16.

Neumayer, E. 2004. 'The impact of violence on tourism: Dynamic econometric estimation in a cross-national panel', *Journal of Conflict Resolution*, 48(2), 259–81.

Pizam, A. 1999. 'A comprehensive approach to classifying acts of crime and violence at tourism destinations', *Journal of Travel Research*, 38, 5–12.

Pizam, A. and Smith, G. 2000. 'Tourism and terrorism. A quantitative analysis of major terrorist acts and their impact on tourism destination', *Tourism Economics*, 6(2), 123–38.

Pizam, A. and Fleischer, A. 2002. 'Severity vs. frequency of acts of terrorism: Which has a larger impact on tourism demand', *Journal of Travel Research*, 40, 337–9.

Pizam, A. et al. 2004. 'The relationsship between risk-taking, sensation seeking and the tourist behaviour of young adults: A cross-cultural study', *Journal of Travel Research*, 42, 251–60.

Plog, S.C. 2001. 'Why destination areas rise and fall in popularity', *Cornell Hospitality Quarterly*, 42(3), 13–24.

Reisinger, Y. and Mayondo, F. 2005. 'Travel anxiety and intentions to travel internationally: Implications of travel risk perception', *Journal of Travel Research*, 43, 212–25.

Schwartz, S. H. 1994. 'Beyond individualism/collectivism. New cultural dimensions of values', in, U. Kim et al. (eds) *Individualism and Collectivism. Theory, Method and Applications*, London, New Delhi: SAGE Publications, 85–122.

Sönmez, S. 1998. 'Tourism, terrorism and political instability', *Annals of Tourism Research*, 25(2), 416–56.

Sönmez, S., Apostolopoulos, Y. and Tarlow, P. 1999. 'Tourism in crises: Managing the effects of terrorism', *Journal of Travel Research*, 38(1), 13–18.

Stafford, G., Yu, L. and Armoo, A.K. 2002. 'Crisis management and recovery. How Washington, D.C. hotels responded to terrorism', *Cornell Hotel and Restaurant Administration Quarterly*, 27–40.

Statistik Austria. 'Ein Blick auf die Gemeinde', available at: http://www.statistik.at/blickgem/gemDetail.do?gemnr=50101 [accessed 21 June 2012].

Stotland, N.L. 2002. 'The psychology of terror: Primary care representations', *Primary Care Update for OB/GYNS*, 9(3), 90–93.

United Nations Development Program (UNDP) 2003. *Bali Beyond the Tragedy: Impact and Challenges for Tourism-Led Development in Indonesia*, Denpasar: Consultative Group Indonesia, UNDP and the World Bank.

UNWTO (ed.) 2002. 'The impact of the September 11 attacks on tourism. The light at the end of the tunnel', special report, Madrid.

UNWTO (ed.) 2004. 'Crisis guidelines for the tourism industry', available at: http://www.unwto.org/mkt/committees/recovery/crisis_en.pdf [accessed 9 February 2012].

Urban, D. and Mayerl, J. 2011. *Regressionsanalyse: Theorie, Technik und Anwendung*, 3rd edition, Wiesbaden: VS Verlag.

Vester, H.G. 2001. 'Terror und Tourismus', *Aus Politik und Zeitgeschichte. Beiträge zur Wochenzeitung: "Das Parlament"*, 47, 3–5.

Yechiam, E., Barron, G. and Erev, I. 2005. 'The role of personal experience in contributing to different patterns of response to rareterrorist attacks', *Journal of Conflict Resolution*, 49(3), 430–39.

Chapter 11

'What Makes Violence in Backpacker Tourism Possible?' A Critical Realist Study of Tourism and the Governance of Security

David Botterill, Shane Pointing, Charmaine Hayes-Jonkers,
Trevor Jones, Cristina Rodriguez, Alan Clough

Introduction

On 25 September 2011, 20 Brazilian backpackers were assaulted by five men in a hostel in Rio de Janeiro, stealing money, a computer and cameras. The hostel is near a military area, yet the backpackers complained about the lack of security (Loureiro 2011). Welsh student Katherine Horton was raped and killed by two fishermen on the island of Koh Samui, Thailand, in the evening of New Year's Day in 2006 (BBC News 2007). In 2010, Ian Horton, her father, was cleared of a charge of rape. His defence attorney told the court that Horton had suffered 'difficulties' in coming to terms with the murder and rape of his daughter (BBC News 2010). On 2 October 2011, a female, Estonian backpacker, 27, was followed from an inner city night club before being threatened with a knife, then sexually assaulted, on the foreshore at the northern end of the Cairns esplanade, the fourth female backpacker victim of a sexual assault in Cairns in just over two weeks (Bester 2011).

News media reporting of violent incidents involving backpackers provokes intense emotional audience reaction. News media coverage is, however, limited to audiences that 'connect' with the story line and it is unlikely that news reports of these incidents have any impact beyond specific geographic boundaries and linguistic communities. News media reporting of the worldwide extent of incidents such as these are clearly unreliable indicators of the total numbers of violent backpacker experiences. The absence of any systematic statistics on the extent of violence in backpacking should not deter investigation, however, as the events that are described above happened and will continue to happen. The resultant loss of lives, the devastating consequences for the survivors, and the impact upon the victims' families following incidents such as these are a sufficient justification to warrant attention within tourism studies. Our intention in presenting these examples is simply to use them as an entry point for a chapter that seeks to take up the challenge set by Botterill and Jones (2010) to get beneath the relationship between tourism and crime.

Realism, Tourism and Security

In this chapter we adopt a realist position and pose the question, 'What makes violence in backpacker tourism possible?' Our realist position is informed by two central tenets of what has become Critical Realism. Bhaskar (1978) first introduced the notion of a layered social ontology in his *A Realist Theory of Science*. Table 11.1 displays social ontology in three layers as domains of science: the Empirical, the Actual and the 'Deep' and their entities, or expressions, of the domains. The second tenet proposes that not only is the ontology of the social world layered but that it is also transformational. Bhaskar (1989) developed his Transformational Model of Social Action, and Archer (1995) has elaborated and extended Bhaskar's account in her *Morphogenetic Approach*. Fleetwood (2007) summarised the specific identity of this position as follows:

> While traditionally most commentators recognize that society consists of agents and structures (and institutions) the debate centers upon the way they interact. Agents do not create or produce institutions/social structures *abinitio*, rather they *re*create, *re*produce, and/or *transform* a set of pre-existing institutions/ social structures. Society continues to exist only because agents reproduce and/ or transform those institutions/social structures that they encounter in their social actions. Every action performed requires the pre-existence of some institutions/ social structures which agents draw upon in order to initiate that action, and in doing so reproduce and/or transform them (Fleetwood 2007: 259).

Table 11.1 Layered ontology

Domain	Entity
Empirical	Experiences and perceptions
Actual	Events and actions
'Deep'	Social structures, institutions, rules, mechanisms, resources, norms, conventions, values, powers, relations

We begin our realist analysis of events such as those described above by presenting the relevant sensitising conceptual frames of the literature of tourism studies and criminology. These are positioned in Table 11.1 as representations of the accumulated accounts of the empirical and actual found within the literature of the two academies. This takes the form of a selective review of two literatures on backpacker motivation and behaviour from tourism studies, and the governance of security from within criminology. Each of these conceptual frames is then translated into the specific context of this chapter – the city of Cairns in the Far Northern Region of Queensland. Contemporary, illustrative local evidence (both empirical and actual) of the backpacker phenomenon and a multi-agency approach to the governance of security is provided. Realist analysis adopts the process of retroduction, sometimes also called abduction (Sayer 1992), in order to propose potential explanatory accounts of observable events. Retroduction entails the idea of going back from, underneath, or behind observed patterns or regularities to discover what produces them. It is a rejection of positivism's pattern model of explanation. That is, that explanation can be achieved by establishing regularities, or constant conjunctions.

For critical realists, establishing such regularities is only the beginning of the process. What is then required is to locate the structures or mechanisms of the 'deep' that have produced the regularity through creative activity involving disciplined scientific imagination and the use of analogies and metaphors. As an initial round of retroduction, our explorations of conceptual frames and local practices suggest a deepening of our initial research question into a tentative set of explanatory mechanisms. Retroduction one takes the form of interactions with the relatively enduring motivations, values and practices of backpacking, the hidden sensitivities of tourism stakeholders to the projection of negative destination images, and the turn to plural policing, crime prevention and community safety initiatives as a central plank of government policy response to crime. Our initial assumption is that there are un-reconciled tensions between these mechanisms. Empirical data from an ongoing three year research project (Hayes-Jonkers, Pointing and Clough 2011a, Pointing, Hayes-Jonkers and Clough 2012) aiming to reduce the incidence of alcohol-related assault in the night time economy (NTE) of the Cairns central business district (CBD) are presented in the form of three elements extracted from the full data set.

The first element demonstrates the approach to the governance of security within our case study city. We present the initial outcomes of a project which mapped the crime prevention and public safety stakeholder network addressing alcohol-related violence in Cairns. The second element recounts the ongoing responses of multiple agencies to a particular incident, the violent assault of a German female backpacker that occurred as she made her way back to her accommodation in the early hours of 7 September 2010. The third element explores the issue of 'Mad Monday' – a commercial product offered by a backpacker hostel located in Cairns. In a discussion we return to 'tensions' of retroduction one in order to develop a realist, practically adequate, answer to our initial research question, 'What makes violence in backpacker tourism possible?' This is achieved by considering the nuanced ways in which the preliminary identified mechanisms intersect, reproduce and constrain the pre-existing structures of the Cairns model of the governance of security, and to offer two further retroductions exploring what possible other mechanisms sit beneath the first. We oscillate between abstract mechanisms and further examples of the empirical and the actual to show how their powers – sometimes exercised and observed – facilitate and constrain violence in backpacker experiences. We conclude by summarising our realist explanations for the possibility of violence in backpacker experience and consider the implications of our research for backpacker safety in other contexts.

Backpacker Motivation and Behaviour in the Tourism Studies Literature

Our intention here is to identify the relatively enduring strands of thought on backpacker motivation and behaviour across nearly 40 years of scholarship. We identify three phases, first, an antecedent period culminating in the 'naming' of the backpacker phenomenon by Pearce (1990). Second, the subsequent 15-year exploration, and reporting, of studies of backpacker experiences up to, and contributing to, the edited collection of Richards and Wilson (2004a). Thirdly, studies that subsequently sought to elaborate on contemporary trends in backpacking and to place these within broader questions confronting the social sciences. Typically, but not exhaustively, these later studies have addressed issues such as identity formation, social cohesion and social exclusion, economic and social development and debates surrounding the concept of mobility. Prior to the labelling of backpacking within the tourism literature, several antecedent studies begin to sketch out the territory of backpacker motivation; for a longer account see the summary in Pearce and Loker-Murphy (1995).

Towner's (1985) observations on the motivations of the upper class young men of the seventeenth- and eighteenth centuries who sought the hidden, strange and exotic offerings of the Grand Tour in order to become cultured, rounded and educated proscribe the early origins of the practice, and provide a virtuous gloss to more earthy explorations and pleasures. Adler's (1985) writing about late nineteenth-century 'tramping' introduced the motivations of adventure, sightseeing and the opportunity to find casual work. Eric Cohen's 'drifter' (Cohen 1973), inspired by his meeting, in the central Andes town of Ayacucho, with a young German student of chemistry who had spent seven months traversing the continent from the Atlantic coast of Brazil (Cohen 2004), set the desire for an intensity of experience and the expression of alienation through escape as markers of more 'modern' motivations. Vogt's (1976) wanderers pencilled in the turn to the markers of social recognition, prestige, and inner satisfactions of travel, and the achievement of autonomy, independence and freedom of action gained through 'wandering'. Riley's (1988) study of long-term budget tourists added the draw of socialisation with fellow tourists and local residents through a deliberate strategy of avoiding the mainstream tourism destinations.

These influences were captured by Pearce (1990) who listed the following traits in his seminal article on backpacking: environmental and cultural experiences, meeting people, cheap living, social activities, escaping pressing life choices, occasional work to extend travel time, and an emerging sub-culture focus on health and outdoor activities. Pearce and his colleagues subsequently conducted a number of studies in Australia that further reinforced the concept and positioned Australia at the forefront of backpacker destinations. Other scholars embarked on studies in different backpacking destinations, often using the ethnographer's tool kit. For our arguments, we draw attention to three particular developments in understanding backpacker motivation and behaviour from this second period: an emphasis on personal change through self-discovery rather than radical counter-culture transformation of society (Binder 2004), the relational identity of backpackers as ensconced in symbolic values rather than absolute traits (Sorenson 2003, Welk 2004), and the institutionalisation of backpacking as represented by the creation of backpacker enclaves (Cohen 2004, Richards and Wilson 2004b).

As a consequence of these observed shifts, the backpacker experience somewhat closed in on itself. Backpacker enclaves (central nodes through which backpackers pass and urban enclaves) became the 'stuff' of backpacking, 'places of fleeting, spontaneous, but friendly and pleasant (and frequently intimate) encounters between individuals belonging to a shared but loosely defined subculture ... serve as meeting places and provide for the hedonistic desires of backpackers for food, drink, drugs, rest and "having a good time"' (Cohen 2004: 47). Exploration and experimentation, as reported in these studies, is more likely expressed as over-stepping normative boundaries of behaviour and entering the subjective 'other' (Binder 2004). Tales of adventure and experiences of cultural diversity become the content of backpacker storytelling, designed to reinforce a shared commitment to an otherwise unspoken code of honour amongst fellow backpackers, that nods to the virtuous tradition of earlier times. Such conversations occur while having a good time or just hanging out in enclaves that offer safety and security, reinforcing the preference to inward-looking socialisation within the backpacker subculture rather than encounters with a cultural 'other' (Richards and Wilson 2004b).

From 2005 on the literature has reflected a growing diversity of backpacking *types* within an overall *form* of tourism (Uriely 2009). Prominent here is a broadening of age categories of backpacker to include the career break and mid-life crisis inspired sojourn and the grey-nomad backpacker, that created a diversity of product offering, as exemplified by the flashpacker (Jarvis and Peel 2010). At the same time, a growing literature on the negative impact of the excesses of the backpacker enclave has developed, recording not just the antagonisms between the backpackers and their nemesis – the tourist – but also between resident communities and the backpacking community itself (Wilson Richards and MacDonnell 2008). The isolation of the drifter, the arduousness of the tramper, the quest for novelty of the wanderer and long term budget tourist seem but faint echoes in the more recent backpacker experience literature (Hannam and Diekmann 2010). The adventurous and packaged 'experiences' are now, in the main, the same adventurous experiences as those of the tourist and consequently are subject to commercialisation and protective risk management regimes (Welk 2010).

Yet the motivations of early seekers of these experiences seem to be exactly those that create the enduring cravings of subsequent generations of the backpacking community, at least for Pearce and Foster's (2007: 1294–5), 'high involvement socialites' and 'externally-driven thrill seekers'. So how, where and when do the enduring motivations of the backpacker find expression? Stepping out of the cocooning enclaves in search of 'edgy' spaces, groups of backpackers feeling emboldened by their shared sense of virtuous identity, continue to seek an adrenalin rush and to demonstrate mastery of their world and, thus, accumulate the bragging rights. One such new 'edgy' space, we suggest, at least in developed economies, is the by now ubiquitous city space of the NTE. It is in these new urban spaces, under the cover of night and in beckoning stylised night clubs, that backpackers earn their badges of exploration and adventure rather than during the daytime activities of packaged adventure tourism products. The data in this chapter suggests that in contemporary backpacking form, these enduring motivations interact to reinforce the vulnerability of, at least young backpackers to violent experiences in the NTE. The institutionalising of the infrastructure and the 'turning in' of the experience that might appear to protect the backpacker community has, perhaps, inadvertently increased its vulnerability. As a police liaison officer with the Far Northern Region of the Queensland Police Service noted in an interview about her work, including the safety talks she gives regularly to new arrivals of young adult tourists to Cairns, 'it's as if they lose their common sense'.

The Cairns Backpacker Context

In Australia, a large, self-identified backpacker industry has emerged due to the promotion of adventure and environment activities for backpackers and the existence of government actions and private sector incentives for those seeking to develop more facilities for this market. Cairns is considered a backpacker tourism enclave in Australia, uniquely located between two major and contrasting World Heritage sites: the Great Barrier Reef Marine Park and the Wet Tropics Rainforest in Far Northern Queensland. Consequently, Cairns has become both a main point of entry for backpackers into Australia and an important destination on the backpacker route in Australia (Prideaux Falco-Mammoneand Thompson 2006). Tourism Queensland estimate that around 160,000 annual backpacker tourists visit the Tropical North Queensland region, which equates to 28 per cent of the estimated total of 583,000 backpacker tourists to Australia in 2011. Eighty per cent are in the 15 to 29-year-old age range and the top five reported activities include the beach (swimming, diving, surfing) 91 per cent, eating out 91 per cent, sightseeing 89 per cent, shopping for pleasure 80 per cent, and pubs/clubs and discos 80 per cent (Tourism Queensland 2011).

The marketing strap line for Cairns, 'Don't leave Queensland without getting a little crazy in Cairns' (Backpacking Queensland 2011), chosen by the backpacking and independent travel industry body for the State – Backpacking Queensland – emphasises the importance of the NTE of Cairns to the Queensland backpacker experience. Oral evidence collected in 2010 as part of an ongoing study from the backpacker community in Sydney confirmed the reputation of two specific NTE venues in Cairns that significantly contribute to its identity as a 'party city'. One backpacker hostel in Cairns has developed a specific 'product' to capture this aspect of Cairns' reputation (TripAdvisor 2011). Part of the hostel offering is 'Mad Monday', described on the hostel website as 'the ultimate night of insanity, madness, and political incorrectness, as we tear up the Cairns nightclubs with the infamous Mad Monday Party and Bar Crawl'

(Asylum Cairns 2011). Andrews (2009) has documented organised forms of similar activities in Magaluf, Spain.

We acknowledge, of course, that backpacking in Cairns is not all about partying but the CBD and the NTE do seem to us to offer backpackers something of a last frontier of adventure, excitement and coincidentally the possibility of criminogenic behaviour and violent backpacker experiences. The commercialisation of the edgy space of the NTE, with its emphasis on alcohol-induced insanity and mayhem, has itself provoked a substantial and significant response from the local community. The development of policy and practice at the local level is demonstrated in the proceeding discussion through an account of the Cairns' model of community safety. Local multi-agency partnerships are a result of a much broader shift in government response to crime and it is to the generic criminology literature that captures the rise of the governance of security that we now turn.

Criminological Literature on the 'Governance of Security'

Criminological treatments of policing have traditionally focused upon the specialist state bureaucracy – 'the police' – tasked with law enforcement, crime investigation, public reassurance and peace-keeping (Reiner 2000). Recent work, however, has highlighted the 'pluralisation' of policing, rendering visible a range of 'policing' activities and agencies beyond the police (Crawford Lister Blackburn and Burnett 2005, Jones and Newburn 2006). Policing – in terms of peacekeeping, law enforcement and regulation – is now undertaken by a range of public, commercial and voluntary agencies as well as the public police (Johnston 1992, 2000, Jones and Newburn 1998). Indeed, it is argued that governance more generally is increasingly organised and funded under the auspices of a range of state and non-state actors. Wood and Shearing (2007) have argued that these developments in the policing and security landscape are so significant that an entirely new theoretical paradigm is needed to make sense of them. On this view, the complexities of governance require an explanation using a framework of 'nodal governance' because governance at all levels of social organisation is typically complex, and the various governance systems throughout social space interact with even greater complexity. Nodal governance is an elaboration of contemporary network theory that explains how a variety of actors operating within social systems interact along networks to govern the systems they inhabit (Burris Drahosand Shearing 2005).

Under nodal governance, collective outcomes are pursued within a network of 'nodes' some of which are state institutions, but the majority of which are made up of commercial or community actors. Wood and Shearing define nodes as 'sites of knowledge, capacity and resources that function as governance auspices or providers' (2007: 27). For these writers, then, the term 'policing' is too 'state-centric' and contributes to an unhelpful scholarly 'myopia' about policing beyond the police (Shearing 2006). The term 'security governance' is suggested as capturing more effectively the fundamental changes that have occurred in recent decades (Johnston and Shearing 2003). Although these conceptual arguments have been contested robustly by leading authors in the field (Reiner 2010), there is now wide agreement that – empirically at least – regulation, order maintenance, and law enforcement activities are increasingly 'pluralised' in contemporary societies. It is possible to identify a number of elements to this pluralisation. Perhaps the most important has been the expansion of the commercial security sector in many nations (Johnston 1992, Jones and Newburn 1998).

Various factors have contributed to the expansion of 'policing for profit', including spiralling demands on public providers, the active privatisation of policing functions, and a range of broader structural changes in contemporary industrial societies that exacerbate concerns about risk and insecurity (Jones and Newburn 2006). A key factor is the significant growth in the urban spaces which form the 'natural habitat' of private security rather than the public police, such as commercially-owned shopping malls, entertainment complexes and retail parks. Policing has also seen a diversification of provision *within* the state sector. Examples include the emergence of local authority patrol forces and municipal police forces (Loader 2000), and the creation of new auxiliary ranks within public police organisations. These relatively new forms of 'policing' have supplemented longer-established law enforcement and regulatory agencies operating largely within the public sector including functionally/spatially specialised police forces (such as transport police), and specialist investigatory/regulatory bodies attached to national and local government (such as environmental health officers). In addition, some authors have highlighted the development of informal policing forms such as voluntary citizen patrols or even vigilantism (Johnston 1996).

The diversification of security organisation and provision reflects more fundamental changes in the nature of contemporary security governance. There has been a shift in the mentalities, technologies and practices of security governance towards proactive and risk-oriented approaches. The terminology of 'security' (as opposed to 'policing') entails future-orientation and a preventive logic. Commodification of security provision has encouraged a forward-looking preventive mentality that grates against more reactive criminal justice approaches based on the retrospective punishment of past wrongs (Zedner 2007). Shaped by the instrumental objective of loss reduction, risk oriented forms of thinking have a close fit with market sensibilities, but do not sit comfortably with these more traditional punitive approaches (Johnston and Shearing 2003). This has resulted in a proliferation of different kinds of security provision, which are more hidden and consensual than traditional forms. For example, they place more emphasis on surveillance (often using new technologies such as closed circuit television (CCTV)), and deploy a range of other interventions to modify behaviour.

Security is increasingly embedded, designed into the physical structure of premises, so that the layout of the built environment reduces the possibility of non-compliance (Newman 1972, Coleman 1985). Such 'adaptive' forward looking, instrumental approaches to crime control have emerged alongside (rather than replaced completely) traditional reactive and expressive criminal justice responses (Garland 2001). An important part of the adaptive responses is the active 'responsibilisation' of a wide range of actors in the arena of crime control. Growing emphasis on multi-agency partnerships in crime prevention, and the promotion of community safety via a coordinated network of state, commercial and community actors has been a noted development in a number of countries (Hughes 2007). Indeed, these shifts have particular relevance for the governance of security in 'tourist spaces' (Hughes 2010, Jones 2010), and it is to a particular example of such tourist space that we now turn.

Element 1: The Cairns Model of Community Safety in the NTE

Cairns city achieved *International Safe Communities* accreditation in 2008 through a partnership comprising community, local government and service delivery agencies (Cairns Regional Council 2011). Population growth and demographic changes have been forecast, and a formal infrastructure and social planning framework has been established by the Cairns Regional Council and the Queensland Government. An integrated suite of crime prevention and community safety initiatives has been identified as a sub-goal of the planning framework (Cairns Regional Council 2011). The existing structure of the community safety stakeholder network (Hayes-Jonkers et al. 2011b), and strategic and operational practices by public and private security have been documented in Cairns (Hayes-Jonkers et al. 2011a) and will be described in detail below.

A programme of research studying alcohol-related violence in the Cairns' late-night entertainment precinct has identified the geographical boundaries of the precinct (Figure 11.1, below) and a network of actors addressing this sort of violence (Figure 11.2, below). The Cairns late-night entertainment precinct is an area of approximately 0.8 square kilometres comprising a retail, restaurant and late-night entertainment precinct and adjacent seafront esplanade. The area is used intensively by backpackers, and at night, use of the precinct turns to providing nightclub and other alcohol-related entertainment. Twenty-six premises licensed to sell liquor after midnight are located in this precinct, with a total capacity of approximately 18,000 patrons. The precinct comprises open spaces where patrons congregate, two taxi ranks, a public transport hub, a casino and a conference centre. There are several perceived night-time, violence 'hot spots'. Streets to the north and northwest leading out of the late-night entertainment precinct serve as pedestrian egress to the main backpacker accommodation facilities (Figure 11.1).

In the Cairns NTE, there is substantial functional overlap between public policing and private security operations to assess risk and implement interventions to ameliorate it (Figure 11.2) (Hayes-Jonkers et al. 2011a). The level of formal interaction and co-operation between public and private security, as well as businesses, regulatory bodies, local government and others is highly reciprocal and may almost be said to be approaching mutual dependence. This co-operation

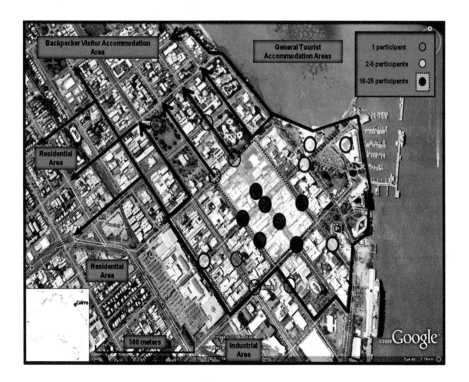

**Figure 11.1 The late-night entertainment precinct with identified hotspots
and pedestrian egress routes**

encompasses strategic[1] and operational[2] levels, and has been functioning for
nearly two decades. This model includes formal agreements through Memoranda
of Understanding (MOU), incorporating data and information sharing and
coordinated, proactive interventions, as well as capacity building through strategic
partnerships. For example, a recently-formalised 'liquor accord', based on a MOU
between the Cairns City Licensees Safety Association, the Queensland Police
Service and Cairns' Regional Council has consolidated and extended established
roles and responsibilities, as well as communication networks involving licensed
premises in the inner city (Hayes-Jonkers et al. 2011a).

A number of shared communication and operational procedures have been
established, including a continuously monitored CCTV system with real-time
communication to the scene, and a 'secure' taxi rank patrolled by a security

---

1   The strategic level includes high level decision making by those in authority. For
example: high-ranking police officers and private security managers.

2   The operational level includes those people who work at the 'front line' or 'on the
ground'. For example: crowd controllers or licensed venue owners.

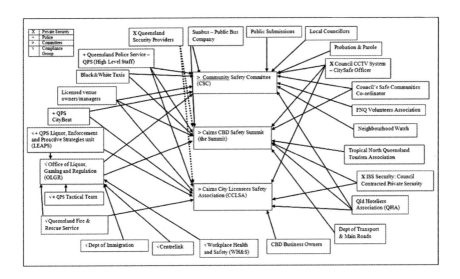

**Figure 11.2 The community-based crime prevention framework in
         Cairns city**

marshal during peak periods. These above mentioned operational procedures operate within regulations set down by the Queensland Government. Under the Liquor Act 1992, licensed venue owners/managers are also required to carry out a Risk-Assessment Management Plan, which includes factors such as: Responsible Service of Alcohol (RSA), transport services, security lighting, dealing with unduly intoxicated and disorderly patrons on the premises, dealing with minors on the premises, training of staff, designated outdoor smoking areas and the number of patrons on premises. Security providers are also required by legislation to uphold a code of conduct, which is written by the security firm, but must be approved by the regulatory body. The operation of security personnel in licensed venues in Cairns includes: stringent identification checks at the door; the use of electronic identification scanners in a minority of venues, recently commenced awareness training of the effects of drugs and alcohol on patrons, and a poorly defined, informal 'Duty of Care' requirement.

Interview respondents stated this 'Duty of Care' may mean that venue security officers are responsible for monitoring the safety of patrons outside of the venue within 50 metres of the front of the premises, and responsibility for monitoring the area around the venue after closing to ensure that patrons leave the area safely and anti-social behaviour and violence does not occur near the venue after closing time. In December 2010, the Queensland Government made changes to the Penalties and Sentencing Act 1992, the Bail Act 1980 and the Liquor Act 1992 to enable police, magistrates and liquor accords to ban problem patrons from venues and city centres. The Cairns City Model of Practice for Security

Providers is purposefully based on the principles of strategic and operational risk management (Hayes-Jonkers et al. 2011a). Private security management attend strategic planning committees to assist in the development and implementation of interventions to reduce alcohol-related, anti-social behaviour and violence issues in the NTE and to pre-empt pertinent issues. These strategic planning meetings incorporate a risk management approach to identify and specify existing and potential risks to patrons and property, nomination of risk tolerance levels, and actions to reduce or remove risk (Hayes-Jonkers et al. 2011a).

Written agreements between stakeholders provide governance on the extent of cooperation, collaborative intervention strategies and data and information sharing, and operational issues such as allowing street security to enter venues to assist venue security and providing formal permission for venue security to assist street security, as well as clearly outlining roles, responsibilities, duty of care and process protocols to be followed by the agreeing agencies. Each agent in the Cairns late-night entertainment precinct has a focus on assault prevention but approaches the problem from their own particular perspective: it is everybody's business but no-one's core business. The focus of the police is law enforcement; the focus of licensed premises owners is safe and economically viable businesses; the focus of private security is to facilitate this business through patron safety; and the focus of liquor licensing is enforcement and compliance. The risk assessment and removal approach of the Cairns Community Crime Prevention Model tacitly acknowledges the physical and psychosocial existence of backpacker enclaves. The risks inherent in these enclaves are acknowledged, calculated and accepted by the community crime prevention structure.

In addition, these partnerships facilitate coordinated operations between the police and private security in Cairns city (Hayes-Jonkers et al. 2011a). These practices exemplify the move from post-crime focus to pre-crime focus and the move from generic to plural policing. The community-based crime prevention approach to alcohol-related violence in Cairns has been constructed specifically around the issue of alcohol-related violence in the inner city of Cairns, and has been found to be exemplary in its co-operation, collaboration and information sharing through combined stakeholder focusing of effort (Hayes-Jonkers et al. 2011a). These structures exist within an Australian community crime prevention model (Attorney General's Department 2008). This model is endorsed by the policy framework of local, state and national governments, with associated resourcing allocated. This model aims to 'develop and support collaborative and coordinated partnerships and approaches to community safety and crime prevention with key government and non-government stakeholders' (Queensland police 2010). Community safety is defined as 'the right of all individuals living, working or visiting Cairns to go about their daily pursuits without fear or risk of harm or injury; and it is the shared responsibility of Government agencies and all other people in the community to ensure this is possible' (Cairns Regional Council 2011).

Element 2: Response of the Community Safety Network to a Violent Incident

The Cairns Post newspaper announced in front-page headlines on Tuesday 7 September 2010 that the Cairns High School had been closed because of a serious assault on a young female German backpacker at 1.30 a.m. that morning. The following day, the police had already identified the licensed venue where the woman had her last drink for the night, interviewed staff and security from that venue and viewed CCTV footage from the venue as well as from the open-space urban CCTV. Police released live footage of the female backpacker leaving the inner city on foot then called upon the public to report any information. The following day a description of the offender was circulated by the police and on Sunday 12 September 2010, five days after the assault, a 15-year-old male was arrested for the crime. However, the ripple effect through the community safety network was longer lasting than the five-day police investigation. Committee meetings were called almost immediately to identify how this attack on an overseas tourist could have happened within such a heavily policed area. A member of parliament, city councillors, police, council officers, security personnel, managers of taxi and bus companies, licensees, hoteliers and more congregated to analyse the attack and propose why it occurred and identify the 'hole' in the inner city plural policing.

The following issues were identified as contributing to this identified 'hole' in community safety in the inner city: the area is outside of the CCTV system and there is poor lighting in the area; backpackers are walking back to their accommodation close to the inner city; females are walking home alone late at night to their accommodation; international backpackers are seemingly unaware of possible safety issues in the city and backpackers are not utilising public transport due to cost. After many months of discussion, the community safety network decided a free bus should be made available to backpackers to alleviate the issue of them walking back to accommodation. It was determined that this was the most immediate solution available. However, issues of lighting etc. would be considered for the long-term future in order to ensure the general area is made safer. A steering committee was established and support was gathered from community agencies. Negotiations commenced to implement the 'Get Home Safe Bus' (GHSB) proposal. At the date of writing, 13 December 2011, 15 months after the attack, the proposal is still in discussion. Governance and funding issues are yet to be resolved.

Discussion

Retroduction applied to uncover dysfunction in the Cairns Model of Public Safety
The Cairns Model of Public Safety has yet to be the subject of a systematic evaluation. The observations made in this chapter relate only to the research question we pose in respect to violence in one community of its constituency – backpackers. A significant strand of pre-crime strategy is to adopt high profile public

awareness campaigns to counter crime. These have been deployed extensively in the Cairns model to address issues such as domestic violence, property crime and drug consumption. Almost exclusively the target audience of the campaigns has been Cairns residents. In an ongoing study of policing tourists in the Far North Region, some beat police officers indicate that in both domestic violence and in property crime, tourists and tourism properties can account for at least half of the reported incidents. Where tourists have been considered in the Cairns model then it is usually only in the context of the potential *resident on tourist* crime and only for some types of crimes but not others. For example, as we discuss below in respect of sexual assault, the response of the public safety committee is obscured by pre-occupations over economic interests. Furthermore, the need for awareness campaigns about tourists offending, (tourist to tourist offending and tourist on resident offending) has yet to be fully considered in the Cairns model, despite the considerable tourist population in the city. Thus, while the model is generally exemplary in many of its features it appears dysfunctional in respect of its handling of tourism and crime and this retroduction posits an explanatory account for this.

The deliberations surrounding the GHSB proposal, detailed in Element 2, begin to expose the ways in which interventions to reduce crime involve a complex interplay of individual and institution, agency and structure, and power play (Pawson and Tilley 1997). Tensions between actors in the public safety network arose throughout the discussion of the GHSB proposal but particularly when the normative practices of the pre-crime community – the strategy of awareness raising among vulnerable communities, for example – comes into conflict with the interests of tourism stakeholders in the Cairns public safety model. Within the tourism stakeholders we note a passive ambivalence, if not unspoken reluctance, to embrace interventions such as the GHSB. We assign these actions to, on the one hand, the protection of the economic interests of the transportation sector and, on the other, the more generally held belief that the destination image would be damaged by the inferred risks to backpacker safety in the city associated with the adoption of the GHSB. When asked how the GHSB might be marketed to his backpacker clients, one backpacker owner answered 'as an additional service to our guests', alongside, presumably, free internet use and the airport courtesy bus!

A further factor limiting tourism stakeholders' enthusiasm for the GHSB, we suggest, is the satisfaction of backpacker expectations. As we discussed earlier, backpacker motivations are expressed through the Cairns NTE. The licensees of the NTE are ever mindful of the experiences sought by their customers. As an owner of a night club commented, 'We're here in the "show" business ... the business of providing the perception of risk with the reality of safety'. Consequently, the backpackers themselves, through the expression of their motivations, collude to limit the effectiveness of the public safety model. The possibility of normative transgressions and potentially criminogenic behaviours are, therefore, protected. We now make the move to retroduction and ask what mechanism holds the dysfunction in place.

Our suggestion is that a mechanism – denial – exists in both the backpacking community and tourism stakeholders in respect of violence and that this mechanism sits beneath the initial retroductions we make. The surface tensions between the motivations of backpackers, the fear of negative destination imagery and models of public safety are, we suggest, dysfunctional in the Cairns model and, furthermore, are held in place by a deep collusion of denial. The imperative of the pre-crime policy community to raise awareness of crime, or to launch a service such as the night time bus in response to a violent crime, dampens yet further the muted enthusiasm of the tourism stakeholders to pre-crime interventions precisely because such strategy heightens the possibility of damaging destination imagery and loss of livelihood. Here, the mechanism of denial transforms from its previously identified expression as tacit collusion between backpackers and tourism stakeholders, to actions that shape the institutions of the Cairns model. The gaze of the governance of security community is very firmly fixed on the resident population, while the tourism stakeholders engaged in public safety do little to redirect it, even in the face of violent crime. This is a strong example of what realists call the morphogenisis (Archer 1995) of social structure.

The transformational principle, then, centres upon the institutions/social structures that are the *ever-present condition, and the continually reproduced and/or transformed outcome, of human agency*. Agents, acting purposefully or consciously, unconsciously draw upon, and thereby reproduce, modify, and/or transform the institutions/social structures that facilitate their actions in daily life. (Fleetwood 2007: 259).

Retroduction applied to violence in nature and in society, and the demarcation of civility
The identification of denial as an explanatory mechanism sets us on a new line of analysis. Following the realist intention to persistently apply retroduction, we must now reformulate our question to ask 'what makes the denial of violence in backpacker tourism possible?'. We do this by considering violence in the context of the tourism proposition in the Far North Region. In sharp contrast to the denial that restricts the use of pre-crime messages in the social world to avert violence, one set of pre-crime/community safety messages that are constantly reinforced and even exonerated by tourism stakeholders in the region are those associated with the violent capacity of nature in the Far North Region of Queensland. Tourists to the Far Northern Region are surrounded by media messages, conversations and in-place signage about the dangers of crocodiles, marine stingers, snakes, and even Cassowaries,[3] both before and during their visit. A fear of the violent potential lurking within the wilderness of the tropical rainforest, or of the creatures beneath the glimmering surface of coastal waters and estuarine creeks, is encouraged and contributes to the distinctiveness of the tourism destination.

---

3   A large flightless bird capable of wounding or killing humans, although documented deaths are rare.

In situ conversations with local inhabitants and accounts in the local press reinforce the formal warnings in a plethora of new phrases; being 'croc-aware' or 'stinger-savvy' is the way to stay safe on holiday. Tourist attractions exploit the sinister potential of violent nature; tourist experiences are delivered to emphasise proximity to the untamed. A voyeuristic exposure to the violence of nature is considered a commercial winner. Tourism stakeholders' open celebration of violence in nature thus contrasts sharply with their actions in relation to violence in human behaviour. There is a deeper ontological mechanism operating here that comfortably locates violence in nature and simultaneously diverts attention away from considering it in humanity. Our earlier assumption that it is in the NTE that the backpacker is now most likely to encounter the 'wild', presents this mechanism as somewhat ironic. The mechanism in question rests on a clear demarcation between the animal and human species. That demarcation is represented by the claim that the human species is different because it has evidenced a process of civilisation. Furthermore, differentiations such as this are made possible, we suggest, by adopting Elias's (1978) notion of figurations which is explained in the next section.

Retroduction applied to contrasting figurations, violence and the veil of Western civility
We suggest that beneath the paradoxical acceptance of violence in nature but its denial in humanity lays the demarcation claim of civility. Following Elias (1978) we see the mechanism of civility existing as a figuration, 'the connections between power, behavior, emotions and knowledge in (to a greater or lesser extent) long-term perspective' (Norbert Elias Foundation 2011). In our study, many figurations are at work. International tourists to Cairns travel to a foreign destination but they remain immersed in particular figurations of civility bounded by national histories, cultural identities, norms and behaviours – British, Canadian, Japanese, Korean, Chinese, for example. In the Far North Region, local figurations prevail in the form of a dominant Western, white Australian figuration and a subordinate, contrasting, figuration of the indigenous Aboriginal and Torres Strait Islanders. These two local figurations are conditioned by markedly different and relatively recent histories of violence, subordination and domination. Each figuration orders what is civil and uncivil behaviour, how gender, sexual and racial relations should be conducted, what constitutes violence and, as if casting a veil over these interactions, we see, as a further expression of the dominant local figuration, the local model of the governance of security described in Element 1.

Element 3: The Issue of 'Mad Monday'

We cannot, here, provide deep explorations of these figurations. This would require a trans-national study of considerable magnitude. Instead, we return to the domains of experience and the actual in Table 11.1 and present findings of a related study into Element 3, the 'Mad Monday' issue in order to demonstrate the powers figurations as a mechanism. The public and private spaces and of the NTE are not just peopled by a backpacking community held together by an honour or code that includes consensual and casual sex and excessive consumption of alcohol (Wilson and Richards 2008). These are shared spaces, occupied by other social groups whose behaviour is conditioned by sometimes quite different and contrasting figurations of civility. Mingling with the backpackers are groups of other international tourists, Asian youth tourists on extended working or language holidays in the region, for example. On certain days of the week, local youths, both men and women, cruise the streets and bars intent on making the most of the visiting flesh, while in the shadows, the homeless, predominantly of Aboriginal and Torres Strait Islander origins, congregate to socialise, smoke, drink and sleep. Many individuals in such groups have a habit of excessive consumption of alcohol; some have histories of mental illness. Observations from fieldwork on two Monday evenings in the Cairns NTE and from a 14-day monitoring exercise in the CCTV surveillance control room are presented below in a vignette to demonstrate the multi-use of spaces in the CBD and to indicate the workings of the mechanism 'figurations of civility'.

It's Monday evening. We stroll past the Asylum hostel. Around 50 participants in Mad Monday and identifiable by their $10 "inmate" T-shirts (already liberally splattered with felt tip pen slogans – homophobic, sexual and racist) wobble their noisy way along Grafton Street towards the city. We walk slowly and they catch us up. A police car appears and an officer jumps out demanding to know where the "spliff"[4] is? A rather one-sided exchange ends with a stern warning. We are all passing a public park. On its benches sit solitary males of, likely, Aboriginal and Torres Strait Islander identity. In floodlights at the centre of the park a white vehicle, doors open, painted with a message "Taking care of youth up to the age of 21". A microwave oven sits on a shelf in the van. Neither "inmates" nor park dwellers seem to notice one another.

Charlie, a girl in her 20s wearing a maroon Mad Monday organisers T-shirt discovers we know her home town; joyful, rather slurred, celebrations. We ask what's going on, she tells us, "and the best bit is, it's all videoed and played at breakfast the next morning". We follow the inmates to their first bar where many consume copious amounts of 2 for 1 "chasers", chant slogans, scribble on T-shirts, and play a "pile up" game on the dance floor. At 10 p.m., end of the 2 for 1, the group drifts to the next bar; heterosexual couples make slow progress down the street, tarrying in intimate clinches. Thirty minutes later we wander into the bar, smiled at by the bouncers. The group is dancing to loud hip-hop and joining in with familiar lyrics. Charlie greets us as if we are long lost relatives. She tells us that the bar owner is involved in organising Mad Monday. We ask

---

4   A handmade cannabis cigarette.

what happens next, "up to the Woolshed for drinking games and taking clothes off". The atmosphere is of a private party and feeling more exposed as voyeurs in this bar, we decide to get ahead of the "inmates" and make our way to the next venue.

In the street we recognise a few stray "inmates", already falling off the pace, and approach the door of the next venue, "You can go in free tonight lads, but just to the downstairs bar". We enter, it's very quiet, we go home. Elsewhere in the city congregations of homeless, some already heavily intoxicated, socialise. The staff of the CCTV control room monitor the street spaces. They record unpredictable behaviours of both backpackers and homeless. Conversations in the homeless groups are getting louder and behaviours are interpreted in the control room as more threatening. A group of tourists stroll by, they are hassled for a cigarette. An altercation is taking place within the group. Street security is alerted, the police advised. They move in, and move on the alleged perpetrators. Those perceived to be "drunk" are picked up by the Diversionary[5] van and taken to a hostel to sleep-off the effects of the alcohol. The "inmates" are rolling up to the next bar, they are loud and boisterous. Tourists stroll by, an "inmate" shouts obscenities and "moons" the tourists. Security calls the police, there is an exchange, no action is taken. The "inmates" are ushered to the temporarily "private" upstairs bar of the Woolshed.

The veil of the Western figuration of civility displays a double standard and nods towards a racist tendency. One set of tolerances towards drunk and disorderly behaviour for the backpackers, another for the homeless.

Re-visiting Element 2: Response of the Community Safety Network to a Violent Incident

As we noted in our first paragraph, allegations of serious sexual assault signal particularly painful clashes of figurations. During fieldwork interviews within the community safety network they provoked strong emotions. One respondent, the only police volunteer of a particular Asian national identity (a male), recounted the following incident during a face-to-face interview with the lead author.

The police volunteer received a phone call from 'a friend'. A young woman (of the same national identity as the volunteer) was distraught and inconsolable; the friend was very worried for the young woman's safety and asked for help. The volunteer agreed to meet the young woman. She could not stop crying. At a second meeting she alleged that she had been raped by a local male youth whom she had met on a night out in the central business district. The victim eventually agreed to go to the police station with the volunteer. Her emotional state compounded

---

5   The name given to this social service which is used to divert persons to sober-up shelters rather than being taken into police custody.

the difficulties she faced in communicating in English. The interviews with the police were transacted through the volunteer, who acted as a translator. Following normal police protocols, a physical examination was arranged. The girl could not cope with the invasion of her privacy, became very distressed and refused the examination. She also insisted that she would not reveal her identity to the police. No investigation could, therefore, be conducted and the young woman returned home earlier than expected.

Under these conditions, the veil of the governance of security becomes tattered and torn as it attempts to shroud multiple, complex figurations of civility: racialised, sexualised and gendered. The violent incidents described in our chapter shred the veil. The ordering of power, emotion, behaviour and knowledge implicit within figurations of civility displays disarming fragility. The mechanisms of the ontological 'deep' that we identify through our retroductions, combined with the transformational power of their interactions with future events are, we propose, the necessary but not sufficient conditions by which violence in backpacking is made possible.

Conclusion

This chapter commenced with the presentation of elements selected from a rigorous, substantial and published study into alcohol-related violence in the city of Cairns. We have worked from these entities of experience and events through retroduction to identify mechanisms in the 'deep' (as a reminder see Table 11.1). Our explorations of the 'deep' have revealed mechanisms that we have labelled 'collusion of denial', 'demarcation of civility' and 'figurations'. The transformational powers of these emergent mechanisms have been re-considered by returning to the elements of our case study. Thus, we have striven to produce an account of realist scholarship that reasserts, 'the possibility of an explanatory social science that would aspire to the standards of empirical and theoretical rigor of the natural sciences, while fully acknowledging the indispensably communicate-interpretive dimensions of social life' (Benton 2009: 211).

Our study is set in a particular location and we acknowledge, therefore, that for some researchers there would be limited validity of our findings for other backpacker destinations. However, we would argue that the transcendent moves between the domains of science provided by the depth ontology of Critical Realism opens the possibility of explanations beyond the specific context. Furthermore, the Critical Realist acceptance of epistemological relativism invites explanatory accounts based on qualitative data. Firstly, many other Western societies are popular destinations for backpackers and they have concomitantly engaged with the turn to the governance of security in response to crime. We would therefore expect the presence of 'tensions' in many destinations. Secondly, a collusion of denial between the tourism stakeholders and the backpackers will also be operating. Thirdly, we would further suggest that the stronger the dependence of the economy on tourism in the destination region, the wider the spread of collusion becomes and it is likely to extend beyond the actors with a direct stake in tourism. Fourthly, the demarcation of civility in the human species will also be present although the contrast to violence in nature may be less marked than it is in the Far Northern Region. While we would concede that the figurations of civility in any tourist destination are shaped by the pattern and volumes of tourists and the social structures of the host society, we would assert that, at the very least, the mechanisms identified in this study provide a theoretical starting point for further elaboration and testing in Western societies.

Backpacker destinations in non-Western society present more of a challenge to our findings. Figurations of civility in the new backpacker destinations in Latin America, Africa and Asia will vary greatly from those we observe in the Far North Region of Australia and domestic figurations of civility will respond to crimes of violence in these places in markedly different ways. Public policy responses to crime and measures of accountability applied to regimes of policing are likely to take quite different forms; more authoritarian perhaps, and thus less likely to employ the governance of a security model. Scholars researching these backpacker destinations might, therefore, borrow from Symbolic Interactionism (Botterill and Platenkamp 2012) and adopt our findings as a set of sensitising concepts rather than as an explanatory template.

References

Adler, J. 1985. 'Youth on the road: Reflections on the history of tramping', *Annals of Tourism Research*, 12(3), 7–29.

Andrews, H. 2009. '"Tits out for the boys and no back chat": Gendered space on holiday', *Space and Culture*, 12(2), 166–82.

Archer, M. 1995. *Realist Social Theory: The Morphogenetic Approach*, Cambridge: Cambridge University Press.

Asylum Cairns 2011. Home page, available at: www.users.on.net/~asylumcairns/cairns_hostel.html [accessed 4 November 2011].

Attorney General's Department 2008. *Australian Government Crime Prevention Initiatives*, available at: http://www.crimeprevention.gov.au/ [accessed 6 November 2011].

Backpacking Queensland 2011. *Cairns and Tropical North*, available at: www.backpackingqueensland.com/cairns-and-tropical-north/ [accessed 4 November 2011].

BBC News 2007. 'Thai murder victim's final hours', *BBC*, available at: http://news.bbc.co.uk/2/hi/uk_news/wales/6276023.stm [accessed 4 November 2011].

BBC News 2010. 'Thai death father Ian Horton cleared of rape in Cardiff', *BBC*, available at: http://news.bbc.co.uk/2/hi/uk_news/wales/south_east/8651687.stm [accessed 4 November 2011].

Benton, T. 2009. 'Conclusion: Philosophy, materialism and nature – comments and reflections', in S. Moog and R. Stones (eds) *Nature, Social Relations and Human Needs: Essays in Honour of Ted Benton*, Basingstoke: Palgrave Macmillan, 208–43.

Bester, C. 2011. 'Taskforce zeros in on sex attackers', *Cairns Post*, available at: http://www.cairns.com.au/news/ [accessed 4 October 2011].

Bhaskar, R. 1978. *A Realist Theory of Science*, Hassocks: Harvester Press.

Bhaskar, R. 1989. *The Possibility of Naturalism*, Hassocks: Harvester Press.

Binder, J. 2004. 'The whole point of backpacking: Anthropological perspectives on the characteristics of backpacking', in G. Richards and J. Wilson (eds) *The Global Nomad: Backpacker Travel in Theory and Practice*, Clevedon: Channel View Publication, 92–108.

Botterill, D. and Jones, T. 2010. *Tourism and Crime: Key Themes*, Oxford: Goodfellow.

Botterill, D. and Platenkamp, V. 2012. *Key Concepts in Tourism Research*, London: Sage.

Cairns Regional Council 2011. *Safe Communities Program*, available at: http://www.cairns.qld.gov.au/community-information/community-services/safe-communities-program [accessed 8 November 2011].

Cohen, E. 1973. 'Nomads from affluence: Notes on the phenomenon of drifter-tourism', *International Journal of Comparative Sociology*, 14, 89–103.

Cohen, E. 2004. 'Backpacking: Diversity and change', in G. Richards and J. Wilson (eds) *The Global Nomad: Backpacker Travel in Theory and Practice*, Clevedon: Channel View Publications, 43–59.

Coleman, A. 1985. *Utopia on Trial: Vision and Reality in Planned Housing*, London: Hilary Shipman.

Crawford, A., Lister, S., Blackburn, S. and Burnett, J. 2005. *Plural Policing: The Mixed Economy of Visible Patrols in England and Wales*, Bristol: Policy Press.

Elias, N. 1978. *The Civilizing Process: The History of Manners*, [translation from German by Edmund Jephcott of *Über den Prozeß der Zivilisation. Soziogenetische und psychogenetischeUntersuchungen*, vol. 1], Oxford: Blackwell.

Fleetwood, S. 2007. 'Austrian economics and the analysis of labour markets', *Review of Austrian Economics*, 20, 247–67.

Garland, D. 2001. *The Culture of Control: Crime and Social Order in Contemporary Society*, Oxford: Oxford University Press.

Hannam, K. and Diekmann, A. 2010. 'From backpacking to flashpacking: Developments in backpacker tourism research', in K. Hannam and A. Diekmann (eds) *Beyond Backpacker Tourism: Mobilities and Experiences*, Clevedon: Channel View Publications, 1–7.

Hayes-Jonkers, C.S., Pointing, S. and Clough, A.R. 2011a. 'Comparison of strategic and operational good practice for private security personnel in the night-time economy and the Cairns City Model', *Security Journal*, available at: http://www.palgrave-journals.com/sj/journal/vaop/ncurrent/abs/sj201124a. html [accessed 3 October 2011].

Hayes-Jonkers, C.S., Pointing, E.S. and Clough, A. 2011b. 'A Comparison of strategic and operational good practice for private security personnel in the night-time economy and the Cairns City Model. 5th Annual Critical Criminology Conference, The Cairns Institute, Cairns, 7–8 July 2011.

Hughes, G. 2007. *The Politics of Crime and Community*, Basingstoke: Palgrave.

Hughes, G. 2010. 'The preventative turn in crime control and its relationship with tourism', in D. Botterill and T. Jones (eds) *Tourism and Crime: Key Themes*, Oxford: Goodfellow Publishers, 69–88.

Jarvis, J. and Peel, V. 2010. 'Flashpacking in Fiji: Reframing the global nomad in a developing destination', in K. Hannam and A. Diekmann (eds) *Beyond Backpacker Tourism: Mobilities and Experiences*, Clevedon: Channel View Publications, 21–39.

Johnston, F. 1992. *The Rebirth of Private Policing*, London: Routledge.

Johnston, F. 2000. *Policing Britain: Risk, Security and Governance*, London: Longman.

Johnston, L. 1996. 'What is vigilantism?' *British Journal of Criminology*, 36(2), 220–36.

Johnston, L. and Shearing, C. 2003. *Governing Security: Explorations in Policing and Justice*, London: Routledge.

Jones, T. 2010. 'Governing security in tourist spaces', in D. Botterill and T. Jones (eds) *Tourism and Crime: Key Themes*, Oxford: Goodfellow Publishers, 167–86.

Jones, T. and Newburn, T. 1998. *Private Security and Public Policing*, Oxford: Clarendon Press.

Jones, T. and Newburn, T. (eds) 2006. *Plural Policing: A Comparative Perspective*, London: Routledge.

Loader, I. 2000. 'Plural policing and democratic governance', *Social and Legal Studies*, 9(3), 323–45.

Loureiro, C. 2011. 'Grupoarmadoasaltaalberguezonasul do rio', Globo.com, available at: http://g1.globo.com/rio-de-janeiro/noticia/2011/09/grupo-armado-assalta-albergue-na-zona-sul-do-rio.html accessed 5 November 2011].

Newman, O. 1972. *Defensible Space: Crime Prevention through Urban Design*, New York: Macmillan.

Norbert Elias Foundation 2011. 'Figurational studies: Some concepts, principles and major research areas. Norbert Elias Foundation, available at: http://www. norberteliasfoundation.nl/network/concepts.php [accessed 5 November 2011].

Pawson, R. and Tilley, N. 1997. *Realistic Evaluation*, London: Sage Publications.

Pearce, P.L. 1990. 'The backpacker phenomenon: Preliminary answers to basic questions', unpublished doctoral dissertation, James Cook University, Australia.

Pearce, P.L. and Loker-Murphy, L. 1995. 'Young budget tourists: Backpackers in Australia', *Annals of Tourism Research*, 22(4), 819–43.

Pearce, P.L. and Foster, F. 2007. 'A "University of Travel": Backpacker learning', *Tourism Management*, 28(5), 1285–98.

Pointing, S., Hayes-Jonkers, C. and Clough, A. 2012. 'The role of an open-space CCTV system in limiting alcohol-related assault injuries in a late-night entertainment precinct in a tropical Queensland city, Australia', *Injury Prevention*, 18, 58–61.

Prideaux, B., Falco-Mammone, F. and Thompson, M. 2006. 'Backpacking in the tropics: A review of the backpacker market in Cairns and their travel patterns within Australia', unpublished research report (Vol. 1), James Cook University: Australia.

Queensland Police 2010. *Crime Prevention*, available at: http://www.police.qld.gov.au/programmes/cscp/ [accessed 8 November 2011].

Reiner, R. 2000. *The Politics of the Police*, 3rd Edition, Oxford: Oxford University Press.

Reiner, R. 2010. 'Citizenship, crime, criminalization: Marshalling a social democratic perspective', *New Criminal Law Review*, 13(2), 241–61.

Richards, G. and Wilson, J. 2004a. 'Drifting towards the global nomad', in G. Richards and J. Wilson (eds) *The Global Nomad: Backpacker Travel in Theory and Practice*, Clevedon: Channel View Publications, 3–13.

Richards, G. and Wilson, J. 2004b. 'The global nomad: Motivations and behaviour of independent tourists worldwide', in G. Richards and J. Wilson (eds) *The Global Nomad: Backpacker Travel in Theory and Practice*, Clevedon: Channel View Publications, 14–39.

Riley, P.J. 1988. 'Road culture of international long-term budget tourists', *Annals of Tourism Research*, 15(3), 313–28.

Sayer, A. 1992. *Method in Social Science: A Realist Approach*, New York: Routledge.

Shearing, C. 2006. Reflections on the refusal to acknowledge private governments', in J. Wood and B. Dupont (eds) *Democracy, Society and the Governance of Security*, Cambridge: Cambridge University Press, 11–32.

Sorensen, A. 2003. 'Backpacker ethnography', *Annals of Tourism Research*, 30(4), 847–67.

Tourism Queensland 2011. *International Backpacker Market Snapshot*, available at: http://www.tq.com.au/tqcorp_06/fms/tq_corporate/special_interests/backpacking/International%20Backpackers%20Market%20Snapshot%20-%20Year%20ended%20June%202011.pdf [accessed 4 November 2011].

Towner, J. 1985. 'The Grand Tour: A key phase in the history of tourism', *Annals of Tourism Research*, 12(3), 297–333.

TripAdvisor 2011. *Asylum Cairns Backpacker Hostel*, available at: http://www.tripadvisor.com.au/Hotel_Review-g255069-d285634-Reviews-Asylum_Cairns_Backpacker_Hostel-Cairns_Cairns_District_Queensland.html [accessed 2 November 2011].

Uriely, N. 2009. 'Deconstructing tourist typologies: The case of backpacking', *International Journal of Culture, Tourism and Hospitality Research*, 3(4), 306–12.

Vogt, J.W. 1976. 'Wandering: Youth and travel behaviour', *Annals of Tourism Research*, 4(1), 26–41.

Welk, P. 2004. 'The beaten track: Anti-tourism as an element of backpacker identity construction', in G. Richards and J. Wilson (eds) *The Global Nomad: Backpacker Travel in Theory and Practice*, Clevedon: Channel View Publications, 77–91.

Welk, P. 2010. 'Town of 1770, Australia', in K. Hannam and A. Diekmann (eds) *Beyond Backpacker Tourism: Mobilities and Experiences*, Clevedon: Channel View Publications, 169–86.

Wilson, J., Richards, G. and MacDonnell, I. 2008. 'Intra-community tensions in backpacker enclaves: Sydney's Bondi beach', in K. Hannam and I. Ateljevic (eds) *Backpacker Tourism: Concepts and Profiles*, Clevedon: Channel View Publications, 199–214.

Wilson, J. and Richards, G. 2008. 'Suspending reality: An exploration of enclaves and the backpacker experience', *Current Issues in Tourism*, 11(2), 187–202.

Wood, J. and Shearing, C. 2007. *Imagining Security*, Portland: Willan Publishing.

Zedner, L. 2007. 'Pre-crime and post-criminology?' *Theoretical Criminology*, 11(2), 262–81.

Chapter 12

Quest for Life: From Pilgrimage to Medical Tourism to Transplant Trafficking[1]

Nancy Scheper-Hughes

For the purpose of this chapter I want to situate my research and writings on the traffic and trade of humans for their organs—what journalists benignly call "transplant tourism"—into the larger category of medical migrations. While *Homo sapiens* is above all a global colonizing and travelling species, in recent decades, increasing numbers of people have crossed the globe and slipped under national borders (often illegally) for biomedical, experimental, or alternative medical, surgical, or cosmetic interventions and/or bodily transformations. They travel for health, beauty, and what John Janzen long ago described as the quest for therapy. The elderly and well insured are searching for cures to the maladies that accompany aging, chronic, non-contagious illnesses and afflictions, from obesity and diabetes to congestive heart disease to dental care and depression. Women travel in search of cures of infertility for reproductive technologies through IVF or renting surrogate wombs. Men travel in search of cures for sexual dysfunction. Others travel in search for cures for addictions and psychiatric illnesses, including the many South American elite who enjoy the benefits of Cuba's medicalized revolution in private spas specializing in drug addiction cures in a country that claims it never experienced a drug addiction epidemic. Meanwhile, Chinese heroin users travel across China to special addiction recovery centers that follow to the letter an American imported 12 step program that is seemingly "out of step" with post-Maoist political, medical, and moral realities (Hyde 2011).

Americans travel across the Canadian border to purchase expensive drugs—Lipitor, Viagra, Xanex, Zoloft—more cheaply. Those suffering ailments that have no known cure travel far and wide to participate in clinical trials, experimental genetic medicine or stem cell transplants not yet (or likely ever to be) approved in their own countries. While most medical migrants are biomedically savvy, well-read and self-informed, other medical travelers have lost their lives in the pursuit of false or non-existent cures, like New Age pilgrims to the high desert of Sedona, Arizona who perished in a Native American sweat lodge managed by a huckster-hippie guru. Or Coretta Scott King, suffering from ovarian cancer, who died in the clinic of a private hospital in Baja owned by a counterfeit US doctor

---

1 This chapter is adapted from a Festschrift held in honor of Professor Benedicte Ingstad at the University of Oslo, Norway, May 14, 2011.

wanted by the FBI. But among those Americans and Europeans to flock to central Brazil for psychic surgeries at the hands of a notorious charlatan, João Teixeira de Faria, known as João de Deus ("John of God"), many return miraculously healed, including one of my own recent Brazilian doctoral students who, diagnosed with incurable cancer, and having nothing to lose, put herself in the hands of João de Deus, a man she described as a despicable fraud. So much for the long-standing thesis that magical cures are based in faith.

The term medical migrations conjures up an image of affluent Westerners taking advantage of the health care resources of poor nations. But today many medical migrants are poor and medically disenfranchised persons desperately seeking drugs, therapies and surgeries that they cannot get at home. Some are undocumented persons traveling without tourist visas, including, Mexicans who enter the US surreptitiously in search of, not employment, but American health care at public hospitals and emergency rooms, fueling a strong popular backlash in conservative communities in the Southwest and to the angry, protectionist rhetoric—no health care to illegals that led to Arizona's harsh anti-immigration Act.

Jessica Santillan, a pretty teenager and the daughter of an undocumented domestic worker lay dying in 2003 at Duke University Hospital following a botched heart–lung transplant finagled by the interventions of a wealthy North Carolina construction worker. The organs, designated for another patient, were transplanted in Jessica whose blood type was incompatible. The girl's suffering and death touched the hearts of many Americans while unleashing the anger of other Americans who saw Jessica's death as a kind of brutal poetic justice. The immigrant child had no right to the organs of an American (Wailoo 2006). There are no easy ways to capture all the divergent experiences of medical travelers that contribute to their medical migrations. Some are haves and others are decidedly have-nots in the global and medical order of things—the autonomous, self-managed, independent medical tourist on the one hand, and the exploited kidney sellers that Lawrence Cohen and I have written about.[2]

Contemporary medical migrations can be linked to earlier healing pilgrimages—those depicted in Chaucer's *Canterbury Tales* or the medieval North African Muslims who sought treatment from Bori priests in what is now Nigeria and the medieval Mediterraneans who traveled to bathe in the healing waters of Pamu-kkule, in what is now Turkey—or to the early nineteenth-century therapeutic travels that were tied to climate, topology, and medical ecology—from the brisk, cold healing airs of the mountains, the dry airs of the desert, or the healing airs of mineral springs. Three themes emerge: *mobility*—the conditions that shape who can and who cannot participate in medical migrations; *localities*—the destinations of medical migrants, contextualizing these within the larger political economy of sickness and health care; *bodies and biologies*—the specificities of the bodies,

---

2 See our essays in Scheper-Hughes and Wacquant 2004, *Commodifying Bodies* (Sage); in Ong and Collier (eds) 2007, *Global Assemblages* (Blackwell); and Roberts and Scheper-Hughes (eds) 2011, *Medical Migrations*, special issue of *Body & Society* (Sage).

corporalities and subjectivities involved in medical migrations. They are as diverse as the pleasure journeys of medical tourists in search of plastic surgeries in luxurious spas in Costa Rica (Ackerman 2010) and the forced migrations of kidney sellers and of medical refugees seeking better health care, and even research subjects recruited to participate in medical research and clinical trials as proxy bodies/subjects for those in the developed world who refuse to have anything to do with biomedical researchers (Whitmarsh 2011).

The extraordinary mobility that has accompanied the processes we call neoliberal globalization provide possibilities as well as constraints, often side by side. They show how borders produce and are themselves produced through various kinds of medical migrations. The experience of travel is a constitutive experience of the subject in the late modern world. But of course mobility is always contingent. The ability to move, to be mobile, is a defining feature of individual life in today's world for only certain populations and subjects. Crossing borders and reshaping bodies, via participation in biomedical technologies are characteristics of the global cosmopolitan. Many others are unable to participate in border hopping and medical transformation. The opportunity for bodily transformation, for health and life is shaped by the most basic and yet complex of human efforts—the ability to move.

Transplant Travels

Global capitalism and the spread of advanced medical and biotechnologies have incited new tastes, desires and demands for the skin, bone, blood, organs, tissue and reproductive and genetic material of others. Fresh kidneys are the new "blood diamonds" in the global organs trade. This new commodity is both an organ of opportunity *and* the organ of last resort for buyers and sellers, making the trade appear like a "win-win" solution to an intractable problem of kidney supplies.

The plot thickens considerably with the appearance of highly organized and extensive criminal networks of organs brokers and human traffickers who operate transnationally to link desperate and affluent or well insured transplant patients—mostly desperate kidney and a smaller number of liver patients—with equally desperate organ sellers and with the essential third party—enterprising surgeons—all of them—buyers, sellers, surgeons—often willing to travel great distances, to and in search of "parts unknown," evokes a timeless moral and ethical "gray zone"[3]—as described by Primo Levi with respect to behavior in the death camps at Auschwitz—that is, the lengths to which an individual should go in the interests of saving, prolonging or even simply enhancing one's life at the expense

---

3   This is a reference to Primo Levi's description, in his book *The Drowned and the Saved*, of the extent to which inmates of the concentration camps would collaborate with the enemy in order to survive.

of diminishing another person's life or sacrificing cherished cultural and political values (such as social solidarity, justice, or equity).

I have described the criminal aspects of the traffic in humans for their disposable organs and tissues. I have publicized the scars left not only on the ruined bodies of disillusioned sellers but on the geo-political landscapes where the illicit transplant trade has taken root. In an effort to get the attention of medical professionals, human rights organizations, regulatory agencies and government officials I have used forceful language. I have described organs buying and brokering as "neo-cannibalism," as biolust, body theft, and even as bioterrorism. I have called surgeons involved in brokered living donor transplants as "outlaws," "vultures," part of an international "organs mafia" and their local recruiters as "kidney-hunters." I described the buyers—the transplant tourists and travelers as the ethically impaired, giving no more thought to helping themselves to kidneys purchased from depressed, displaced, disgraced and debt-ridden slum and shantytown dwellers than if they were living collections of "spare" organs, detachable, and disposable "supplements," to be used like so many energizer batteries or swallowed like multi-vitamins.

Nonetheless, the first challenge for the anthropologist-ethnographer is to define the situation adequately. What are we dealing with, anthropologically speaking? How should we name the beast? *Medical Migrations? Transplant Tourism? Commerce in Organs? Trafficking in Organs? Trafficking in Humans (for organs)? Organized Crime? Medical Human Rights Abuses? Crimes Against Humanity?* What journalists benignly call "transplant tourism" involves more than consenting individuals engaged in intimate bodily exchanges and backdoor transplants that are privately arranged. Each illicit transplant involves an extensive and highly organized criminal network of well-placed intermediaries with access to leading transplant surgeons, excellent public and private hospitals, laboratories, offshore bank accounts, police protection and often the tacit approval of and blessing of government officials.

Transplant trafficking is a dangerous game and the high risk players in the global "transplant mafia," who think they are invincible and above the law, can suddenly find themselves shoved up against a wall and handcuffs slapped on their wrists. Surgeons have been pulled out of operating rooms, and transplant tourist patients carried out of illicit private transplant units in stretchers and taken to nearby public hospitals. In Istanbul, Dr Sonmez and his Israeli partner of many years, Dr Zaki Shapira were arrested during a shootout in Sonmez's private hospital in Yesil Behar as police and angry relatives of a Turkish kidney donor who had broken into the hospital to rescue the donor—exchanged fire.

In Durban, South Africa, the final trigger in a slow moving police sting of a private NETCARE clinic at St. Augustine's Hospital was the madcap escape down a back stairwell of the clinic of the designated living donor for an Israeli transplant tourist. The donor, in this instance also an Israeli—most of the donors were trafficked Brazilians, Romanians and new Russian immigrants to Israel—changed his mind, and cell phoned his wife to meet him at the international airport. The local Durban broker for the Israeli network, Sushan Meir, called the police to say that a man was escaping the country with $20,000 that he had stolen from Meir. Today the Netcare organs trafficking case has gone to trial, after many delays, and six of the 12 parties that have been indicted, including the Netcare Medical Corporation, have pleaded guilty through plea bargains. At the time of this writing (May 2011) four surgeons and two transplant coordinators have refused a plea bargain agreement and are awaiting trial. I am to serve as the opening witness. The surgeons have been charged with fraud, deceit, organized crime, money laundering, trafficking in minors (five of the 109 illegals paid for transplant providers were technically minors in their teens). The final charge is assault with a deadly weapon and inflicting grave harm to the bodies of living donors and recipients alike, given the criminal organization of the dual surgeries.

What motivates an intelligent person of high professional standing to enter an illicit human trafficking scheme that pits stranded kidney patients in one country against the appalling "bio-availability" of desperate peasants from demolished agricultural villages in Eastern Europe, displaced stevedores from the watery barrios of Manila, and hungry men from the decaying slums of a Brazilian port city? What kind of moral worlds do kidney hunters and organs traffickers and their clients inhabit? How do they justify their actions? These intimate exchanges of life-giving body parts concern more than medical necessity or medical self-defense and individual life-saving. In this particular case, the Durban Netcare illustration, they entail complicated histories—for the Brazilian kidney sellers a history of plantation slavery followed by contemporary patron–client debt bondage, for the Moldovan and Romanian kidney sellers, a history of the end of the Soviet Union and the collapse and impoverishment of the Soviet's client agrarian states human.

For the South African transplant surgeons the history concerned the end of apartheid and a new democratic state that could no longer afford financing public transplants (for what was only the minority white population that needed them). The new state had to save its resources for acute illness and infectious diseases and for primary care for children, pregnant women and workers. Transplant was privatized and the surgeons had few patients who could pay. The Netcare clinics and their doctors easily fell prey to the Israeli broker, Ilan Perry, who promised their clinics an exclusive deal, one that came with, in the end several hundred guaranteed transplant patients and their "invisible" organs providers.

For the Israeli transplant patients and their Israeli brokers and handler there is another history that, I argue, plays a role—a strong survivalist ethos born of the Holocaust. In the case of Gaddy Tauber, the Brazilian-based Israeli agent of Ilan Perry for his extensive organs trafficking scheme, far more was at stake in arranging these complicated and illicit transnational operations than large sums of money. Greed, yes, but also revenge, restitution and even reparation for his childhood in a Romanian transit-detention camp at the end of WWII. Redemption, resurrection, and reparations on the one hand, organ stealing, blood libels, and seething resentment on the other make the global traffic in humans for organs a unique, unstable and particularly dangerous proposition, a political tragedy in the making of truly epic and Shakespearean dimensions.

In previously published articles and book chapters I have described the criminal aspects of the global traffic in humans for their transplantable organs and tissues. I have publicized the scars left not only on the ruined bodies of disillusioned sellers but on the geopolitical landscapes where the illicit transplant trade has taken root. In an effort to get the attention of medical professionals, journalists, human rights organizations, regulatory agencies and government officials I have used forceful, even scandalous, language at times. I described organs brokering as "neo-cannibalism," as "bioterrorism," as body theft, and, as human trafficking. I have referred to the surgeons involved in transplant tour schemes as renegades, "outlaws," and "vultures," the international brokers as an "organs mafia," and their local accessories and accomplices as "kidney-hunters."

Kidney buyers fared no better in my descriptions. They were described as the ethically impaired giving no more thought to dipping into the bodies of economically demolished Moldovans and Brazilian slum dwellers than if they had been actual, rather than pseudo-cadavers. As for the kidney sellers, I presented reams of data from my decade of travel (yes, the anthropologist, too, is part of these new medical migrations) to the sites of kidney brokering and selling in several countries showing the "victims" to be medically, economically, socially, and existentially reduced by their "entrapment" in the global organs trade.

I was not wrong in so doing. Transplant tourism, a term I invented in 1999 to facilitate intimate interviews and participant observations of/with the parties involved in the organs trade, is a euphemism for transplant trafficking, a global multi-million dollar criminal industry involved in the transfer of fresh kidneys (and half-livers) from poor and desperate "sellers" to the seriously, if not mortally, ill and relatively affluent and mobile transplant patients. Those involved at the top of transplant tour schemes are not nice people. I have met, interviewed, photographed and videotaped dozens of the high level transplant brokers (who like to style themselves as "international transplant coordinators") both inside and outside of jail and prisons. Some kidney brokers are corrupt businessmen who rival Bernard Madoff in their socio-pathological indifference to the wellbeing of those—patients and surgeons as well as kidney sellers—who got caught up in the scheme. The pre-screening and blood and tissue matching promised to patients who "signed on" to the scheme was often non-existent, as the tragic case of Moshe Tati's poisoned kidney illustrates.

Among the cohort of consumer-hungry and malnourished Afro-Brazilian men trafficked 4,500 miles from the slums Recife to a large private hospital in Durban, were several men who had to be returned to Brazil as damaged goods because they were found on examination to have only one operant kidney or were themselves mortally ill with previously undiagnosed diseases.

South African Medical Safaris

The Cape of Good Hope figured in the Dutch colonial imagination as a *"lui-lekker* land," a place of natural beauty, ease, and plenty, where even "the savages" seemed hardly to labor to feed and decorate bodies described by the first European visitors as healthy, supple, and full-bodied. When Jan Van Riebeeck, the head merchant for the Dutch East India Company, and his men arrived and established the first European settlement in the Cape in the mid-seventeenth century, they had no intention of exploring the vast interior of the peninsula. Van Riebeeck wished to contain the first European settlement to the cultivation of a network of coastal gardens to serve as a supply station for ships en route between Europe and the East (Coetzee 1988, Scheper-Hughes 2006). In the late nineteenth century, South African health authorities tried to make their country a destination for early modern medical travelers. Health authorities promoted the nation as a salubrious location for ailing Europeans, touting the healthiness of its climate. For a time South Africa attracted ailing British colonial employees stationed in India who needed to recover from tropical afflictions, in a temperate climate thought to be more suited for their Northern constitutions.

After a after a lapse of 200 years South Africa has once again re-emerged as a destination for medical travelers, but this time for advanced medical technologies like plastic surgery and for illicit organ transplants. "Scalpel safaris" and "transplant tours" have nothing to do with the temperate and healthy climate of colonial South Africa. Rather, they are the legacy of apartheid: the surplus population of highly trained surgical specialists no longer supported by the public health sector. In the New South Africa, the provision of basic health care has become a right for all citizens, but the state no longer pays for more expensive medical interventions, including organ transplantation which moved into the private sector. This created a demand for well-insured or relatively wealthy paying patients that led to the aggressive importing of kidney patients via international organs brokers and human traffickers that infiltrated the largest private medical corporation in South Africa, Netcare, whose surgeons are now in prosecution, their trial about to begin in June, in which I am to serve as the opening witness.

Lax regulation of private medicine produced an environment conducive to illicit transplants that enriched private clinics while public health services for the majority of South Africans lag. There is no trickle down from transplant tourism to the public health sector in most developing nations. Thus, transplant tourism is a kind of category fallacy, an invention of the news media and the global tourism industry. The organization of international transplant tours in Turkey, USA, Kosovo, and South Africa by and for the Diasporic Jewish community raises important questions about the nature of "flexible citizenship" built around the quest for health, longevity, and for improved quality of life. The ability of Israelis to travel to Durban, South Africa for illegal transplants (with kidneys trafficked from Brazil and Romania) in private Netcare clinics employing the third generational heirs of Christiaan Barnard—British, Afrikaner and Indian South African-trained transplant surgeons, and reimbursed by Israel's national health care "sick funds" underscores the differences between legitimate *medical tourism* and criminal forms of *transplant trafficking*, based on the transfer of energy, vitality and solid organs from one population to another and more economically advantaged population.

All medical tourism programs are rooted in a highly commercialized and commodified medicine and health care. Medical tourism does not conceive of health care as a *right or an entitlement of citizens* (as recognized in many constitutions, such as those of Brazil and South Africa) but rather as a commodity that can be bought and sold through global medical markets. Medical tourism is based on a neoliberal paradigm of commercialized medicine and individual "choice" that imply the ability of those who can do so to travel often great distances to purchase elsewhere what they cannot buy or otherwise procure at home. Thus, medical tourism and medical commerce go hand in hand. All forms of medical tourism leads to international competition among hospitals and health care corporations to establish themselves as international medical institutions and centers of excellence, and all based on the ability to pay.

In an effort to avoid semantic confusion I employ the term "transplant traffic," one that is synonymous with international "drug traffic" and international sex traffic, all of which rely on organized crime, brokers, and vulnerable people who are used as "mules." However, even medical tourism is not free of criticism; there are ethical concerns, especially when the resources (medical doctors, nurses, and medical facilities) devoted to providing medical care to patients from outside of a country undermine the country's ability to provide the same services for its own population.

The Rise of Transplant Trafficking

WANTED: Kidney Donor—healthy, white, male 25–40, non-smoker, blood group O positive. *Donor Suitably Rewarded. Must be willing to travel.* Reply—Box 202, Jerusalem (*Makor Rishon*, Israeli newspaper).

FOR SALE: *Eu, Manuel da Silva, 38 anos, trabalhador rural, pai de tres meninos doentes, disposto a vender em qualque lugar, qualquer orgao do qual tenha dois e cuja remocao nao cause minha morte imediata* (*Diario de Pernambuco*, newspaper in Recife, Brazil).

[I, Manuel da Silva, 38 years old, rural worker, father of three sick children, am prepared to sell anywhere (in the world) any organ of which I have two and the immediate removal of which will not cause my immediate demise.]

As kidney transplant surgery spread rapidly to all corners of the world, new demands and new scarcities for "fresh" kidneys emerged. The right to buy and sell kidneys from poor nations and to outsource and reimburse dialysis patients to enterprising transplant units elsewhere in the world emerged as a global solution to local organs scarcities. In Japan, Egypt, the Gulf States, and Israel—where cultural reservations about tampering with the dead body and a palpable level of discomfort with brain death makes harvesting organs from deceased donors difficult, the only solution is to get the kidneys from loving relatives or from paid strangers living elsewhere. That "elsewhere" turned out to be wherever poor people in debt, in distress—the disgraced, the dispossessed and the displaced—could be convinced to part with a "surplus" organ.

Organized "transplant tours" began in the late 1970s when wealthy Arab patients from the Gulf states began to go abroad for transplant surgeries they could not get at home. They went to India to purchase kidneys in the Bombay Organs Bazaar until they came home infected with hepatitis and later with HIV. Then, they went to private hospitals in the Philippines staffed by American-trained surgeons who "guaranteed" healthy kidneys from carefully screened sellers. Those requiring hearts, livers and other less divisible organs, went to China, where organs were in plentiful supply on the dates that multiple executions were held. In China and the Philippines Saudis and Kuwaitis met up with Japanese and a smaller number of transplant tourists from Canada, Europe and the United States. Israeli kidney patients observed the medical exodus of Arab-Israeli and Palestinian transplant tourists to Baghdad where they were transplanted in one of Saddam's military hospitals at bargain basement prices ($10,000 including a fresh living donor's kidney) while they remained tethered to dialysis machines. Israelis demanded equal access to safe and affordable commercial transplants abroad with paid living donors.

When criticized for turning to Palestinian day laborers to supply Israeli patients with purchased kidneys, outlaw surgeons joined forces with organs brokers knowledgeable about Israel's national medical insurance program. All Israeli citizens have access to government subsidized and regulated medical insurance that reimbursed Israeli patients for medical treatments abroad that they could not get at home. In the mid-1990s several hundred Israelis were transplanted in Turkey with kidneys procured from poor Turks and from rural Moldovans and Romanians lured by the promise of a cash windfall in exchange for a little discomfort and an invisible spare kidney.

Following the deaths of several Israeli transplant patients following transplant tours, quality control was improved and access to "five star" hospitals and to the most highly qualified surgical staff worldwide, from Singapore to New York City and Cape Town to Durban were available to those who could pay between $120,000–$200,000. The kidney providers were procured by knife-wielding thugs in dozens of agricultural villages in rural Moldova, Ukraine, and Romania where the rural economies had collapsed following the break-up of the Soviet Union. If the trafficked kidney sellers got cold feet on the eve of their kidney-removal operations they were sometimes threatened that they had better get up on the operating table if they ever wanted to see their home and loved ones again. If not, their body might be found "floating somewhere in the Bosporus Strait."

If Moldovan kidney sellers speak bitterly of having being coerced, deceived, cheated, and assaulted by their Ukrainian, Russian, Turkish and Brooklyn, New York brokers and handlers, a fresh, young Brazilian kidney sellers cohort spoke positively about their transplant brokers and traffickers who were seen (quite literally) as godfathers, both tough and loving. In the slums of Jardin São Paulo, Areias, and Barro, tucked in-between the elite high rise apartments of the swanky beachfront neighborhood Boa Viagem and the Guarrarapes International Airport, kidney selling was promoted by organs traffickers as a way of escaping from the *favela*, stepping on a jet plane and returning home with a fistful of American greenbacks.

More than 100 working-class guys from Recife, none of them ever in trouble with the law, signed up to sell a kidney through a local network headed by a retired military police officer, who was well known in the neighborhood, Capitão Ivan Bonifácio da Silva. Captain Ivan moved comfortably in the sketchy neighborhoods near Boa Viagem, especially in local bars, like the rundown "The Egyptian," where working class guys would hang out after a humiliating day of selling bottles of water or Coca-Colas on the beach, lugging crates of manioc in the open air market, or tinkering with broken cars, bicycles, or washing machines in their outdoor workshops. Life is hard in Recife's hardscrabble slums which are dominated by strongmen. Captain Ivan had the *jeito* (manner) of a local boss, having grown up poor himself and knowing how to talk to common people without putting on airs. Ivan's military police background and his connections to local death squads and hired guns "from below" and his connections to "higher ups" in the Brazilian justice and prison system, lent the captain a mantle of respectability and total immunity from prosecution, or so he thought. Ivan thought he was "untouchable" and he boasted that recruiting kidney sellers from the poor was easy because he was feared and he was "respected a lot" in the slums of Recife because he had "killed a lot of them—the bad ones." So, recruiting the "*meninos*," the boys of Recife, was easy. All he had to do was to drop hints at the local bars where he hung out in 2001 that quick cash was to be had by the courageous. All you had to do was go through a minor operation in a place called Durban. "Where is Durban?" the guys asked each other. "England," one said, "Belgium" said another. When they learned that Durban was in Africa a few got a little nervous. "Isn't that a jungle?—Will they have good hospitals there?" Captain Ivan assured them that he had been there, with his wife, and the hospital was even more beautiful than the Royal Portuguese Hospital in Recife. Saint Augustine's Hospital was a hospital fit for movie stars! "OK—sign me up!" said Paulo, and then Pedro, and Gervasio, and Geremias and Alberty and João fell into line, one by one.

Captain Ivan had not cooked up this plan on his own. He himself was recruited by a local expatriate Israeli, also a retired military man, a captain like himself, Gadalya (Gaddy) Tauber.

After retiring from the military in Israel, Tuber began traveling the world, selling his skills in police and security training. He met Captain Ivan in 1997 at a SWAT training class in Miami. They got along well, and da Silva invited Tuber to

Brazil where they set up a consulting firm specializing in police and prison security training. They also tried to break into the legal weapons trade—selling arms to the military and police in Pernambuco—and were awarded an $8.5 million contract by the former governor of Pernambuco, Miguel Arrais, but the deal collapsed. Meanwhile, Tauber fell in love with Brazil and with Terezinha Medeiros, an attractive and sophisticated lawyer in her fifties. When the arms deal fell through, Gaddy had no way of making a living in Brazil and was forced to return to Israel. There, in 1999, he was approached by Ilan Perry, a businessman with a background in medical insurance who was involved in setting up a global transplant scheme. Perry offered Tauber a way to return to Recife as a local agent for his "company." All that Captain Tauber had to do was to find someone in Recife who could recruit people willing to travel abroad and sell a kidney to Israeli transplant patients. "I refused outright," Gaddy said. "I had no idea that such things were possible, and I found it all distasteful."

But three years later, in 2002, Tauber was approached by the wife of an old friend of his, Eva Ramon. Her description of the pressing need of Israeli transplant patients stranded on dialysis machines caused Tauber to change his mind and this time he returned to Brazil on a mission. Once again he teamed up with Captain Ivan da Silva, and in no time at all a new criminal network had formed: a pyramid structure with Ilan Perry at the top, and everyone got a cut. Gaddy, who was in charge of financial operations in Recife, made $10,000 on each successful transplant. Captain da Silva, who recruited donors though local "kidney hunters," received $5,000 for every kidney procured. Silvio Bourdoux, a military police doctor and colonel who handled medical screening and blood matching, at an upscale clinic in Recife was paid $500 for every donor that was prescreened. Gaddy Tauber was the crime boss, the Brazilian "rep" for Ilan Perry. Captain Ivan's wife was also involved; she traveled with the donors to South Africa where they were taken to a safe house to await their operation. A parallel structure existed in Johannesburg with parallel brokers operating in tandem in Israel. But that is another story. Tauber received the money needed to organize the trips directly from Perry and deposited it under the name of his Brazilian girlfriend, Terezinha, who served as the "accountant" for the scheme. Together, Gaddy and his team rounded up more than 50 donors to send to South Africa where 38 of them were actually relieved of a "spare" kidney. The *meninos* (or "boys" as the kidney sellers were called) were easy prey. As soon as the first two or three returned safely from Durban and began flashing wads of hundred dollar bills, the word was out, and the kidney hunters did not have to do anything but take down names—more than a hundred of them. The boys had spent their entire lives in Recife's rundown, working-class neighborhoods, in concrete slab houses whose roof tiles shook every few minutes as jet planes roared overhead. They wanted to travel, too, to see the world and to come back, their pockets bulging. It was a buyers' market, and the price for a "fresh" kidney fell almost immediately from $10,000 for the first few sellers to $6,000 and then down to $3,000 by the time a Brazilian sting (Operation Scalpel) interrupted the gang. Even so, there was no lack of enthusiasm among the unemployed and indebted some of whom tried to bribe their way to the head of the kidney express waiting line. Among the kidney sellers of Recife was the affable and handsome Afro-Brazilian Alberty Alfonso da Silva who eagerly left his job as a night watchman and his mud hut where he slept on a piece of cardboard for a flight to Durban South Africa (his first time in a plane) for the price of a kidney and a bonus of $6,000. The caper did not change his life very much. He used his kidney loot to pay some child support he owed to a former girlfriend, and then he paid off part of a used car debt. In the end, he lost the car because he could not meet his monthly payments. He sold the car for a jalopy, and the jalopy for a bicycle and the bike, finally, for a good pair of Nike running shoes for $100. Obviously, Alberty's focus was on mobility.

Have Kidney, Will Travel—João's African Safari

Recife, September 2003

Rogerio Bezerra da Silva, a 31-year-old car mechanic, was living with his wife and two kids in a two-room shack behind his parent's slightly larger shack in the sticky hot, working-class 'hood of Jardim São Paulo, tucked between Recife's Aeroporto Internacional dos Guararapes and a commuter train station just behind the elegant beach-front community of Boa Viagem in Recife. Rogerio and his buddies, stripped down to their shorts, unemployed and always strapped for cash, would pass the time playing dominoes and placing bets on numbers at tables set up outside a local bar "The Egyptian." Between bottles of Antarctica beer and the occasional shot of cachaça (a strong sugar cane brandy) the "boys" of Jardim São Paulo (hereafter Jardim) hatched schemes that would take them away to a big city somewhere else in the world—not São Paulo, *anywhere but* São Paulo!—where they could make some real money. Every five minutes or so a lumbering jet would take off from the international airport almost clipping the roofs of their little concrete slab homes, as if to mock their immobility, their economic and social paralysis. "This place is *porra*—a shit hole" one would say, while another would wave his fist at the offending plane rumbling overhead and interrupting their conversation and shaking them out of their dreams.

The "boys" of Jardim as they were called by their brokers, Gaddy Tauber and Captain Ivan, were an easy prey. All the traffickers needed was some bait, and that was easily provided. The international transplant ring was now a more sophisticate and well-organized operation. In the early years when it functioned in Turkey and in Eastern Europe the kidney recruits had been lied to and tricked into traveling abroad by local thugs and bullies only to learn on their arrival that their job was to provide a kidney to a stranger. It was a dangerous strategy that often ended up badly for everyone. Now, the scheme operated more smoothly, as a pyramid scheme. The international coordinators at the top of the scheme made millions of dollars, tucked away in off shore bank accounts in Cyprus and Italy as well as in

Israel where the scheme originated, those in the middle, the national coordinators, like Gaddy and Captain Ivan in Brazil, and Rod Kimberly and Sushan Meir in South Africa made tens of thousands of dollars, their kidney hunters trawling poor neighborhoods for kidney sellers made thousands, and the little fish at the bottom of the feeding chain were the sellers, paid as little as $3,000. The first sellers recruited—Gerson, João and Mercondes—were treated well ("like kings," they said) in South Africa, housed in tourist hotels and in elegant private homes rather than in the dingy, locked safe houses that would soon enough crop up for the following groups of sellers. The first kidney sellers from Recife were paid "extravagantly" for their kidneys: $10,000.

In Durban the first sellers were taken on holiday tours, not as elegant, perhaps, as the entertainment arranged for the foreign transplant patients and their families, but still something to talk about when they returned home. There would be photos of Zulu dancers, giraffe, wildebeest and ostriches taken at a small private wild game farm not far from Durban. As soon as the first three kidney sellers—João, Gerson, and Mercondes—returned to Recife from South Africa they were recruited into the scheme as bounty hunters working on small commissions—finders' fees, as it were. They were told to search among intimates for others willing to travel and cash in on the kidney express windfall. From trafficked to traffickers in just one month. As soon as the sellers-turned-kidney hunters began flashing wads of $100 bills—more money than these guys would ever see in their entire lives—the word was out and the brokers did not have to do anything but agree to take down the names and contact numbers of willing sellers, more than 100 asked to be inscribed. The *meninos* of Jardim wanted to travel, to see the world, and to come back, with their pockets bulging, so that they could take their families shopping in Recife's famous galleria, "Shopping Center" almost walking distance from their homes.

The local kidney hunters in Recife could afford to be choosey, and they chose the way the poor of Brazil always have, selecting their family members, in-laws, close friends and neighbors first, and eliminating those they did not know personally and "could not trust." It was a buyer's market and the price for a "fresh" kidney fell almost immediately to $6,000 and then—just as Brazilian police were closing in on them—to $3,000. Even so, there was no lack of enthusiasm among the boys of Jardim who began to imagine that their ship had finally come in.

Throughout the 18 months that the Brazil to South Africa (or Recife-to-Durban) kidney express was in full steam, the carpenters, bricklayers, night watchmen, street salesmen, market venders, bicycle messengers, water carriers, fishermen and curbside car mechanics met among their friends in local bars, in little *praças*, and in car repair garages and in outdoor woodworking shops to hear the experiences of those who had gone first and to pass around photos of the "transplant tours"—Pedro in the plane en route to Durban; Gervasio in his well-appointed hospital room at St. Augustine's hospital; Alberty in his floppy hospital togs hugging his favorite Zulu nurse; and best of all, João Calvalcanti on safari: "Imagine!—Me among the giraffes and zebra of South Africa!"

Those on the "waiting list" as kidney sellers for the Durban express tried to push their own case forward, to jump the list, so that they could be next in line. Some tried to bribe the new intermediaries and kidney hunters stuffing some of their hard earned cash into the hands or pocket of a broker. "Don't forget me," said Rogerio, as he slipped several crumpled bills into João's shirt pocket. Rogerio's neighbor Paulo had tipped off both Rogerio and his brother Ricardo about the kidney selling deal. Paulo, an unemployed railroad worker, was recruited by João Cavalcanti and Paulo recruited Rogerio and Ricardo. Kidney recruiting in Jardim reads like a page of Biblical "be-gots." You had to be inside the network, and nominated by a "knowing" person to be accepted by the dealers and get one's foot inside the door.

Finally, Rogerio made the final cut with his brother. Their blood was drawn for screening at a local laboratory in Derby, Recife and they were "clean—no trace of drugs or communicable disease." Even better both men were blood type O (common among the people of Northeast Brazil) making them universal blood (and kidney) donors. Tissue cross-matching was left up to the discretion of the South African transplant team. Rogerio told his wife and children that he had found well-paying work in South Africa, and that he would be painting a highway billboard sign that would take a few weeks. He would return home in time for them to go on a shopping spree before Christmas. It would be the first real Christmas celebration, filled with toys and Christmas stockings, that he and his family had ever had.

Rogerio was warned by Captain Ivan, who treated the boys like a kind but stern father: "Be careful with your money. $6,000 may seem like a fortune but it can disappear if you waste it on booze, drugs, and loose women." He frightened the young men with stories of an unchecked AIDS epidemic in South Africa. No "screwing" around, he drummed into them, to little avail it turned out. The second warning from Captain Ivan was that there was to be "no going back on the decision" once the international air tickets were purchased. "No one makes a fool of me," Captain Ivan, a self-described former leader of a death squad in the poor marginal neighborhoods of Recife. "They trusted me a lot," Ivan said, "because I killed them a lot, but only the bad ones," he chuckled from his prison cell. Nobody was forced to go to Durban, but once the wheels started to turn, there was no going back either. "Right! You understand, don't you?" And the eager kidney sellers nodded their heads. They were "cool."

St. Augustine's Hospital, November 2003

Before he knew it, Rogerio awoke in St. Augustine's hospital with a painful wound that began at his last rib and wound itself across his flank. It hurt like hell, he said, but the South African nurses were so kind, so attentive, and so unlike any nurses he has ever encountered in Brazil. When Rogerio cried out the only word he learned in English while in English-speaking Durban—"PAIN!"—the nurses in crisp white uniforms would come and give him another injection. As soon as he was able to get out of bed Rogerio wanted to check in with his recipient, a middle-aged Israeli man named Agiana Robel. Rogerio had felt so sorry for him when they met, just once, before they were wheeled into their operating rooms. Agiana was so weak, so anemic, and so pale that his thin skin was almost translucent. The man could only smile faintly at Rogerio, but Agiana's wife cried on meeting the Brazilian stranger who was willing to rescue her husband and the father of their four children.

Agiana had suffered a lot to get this far. His first kidney seller, Shlomo Zohar, a young Israeli man in deep financial trouble who (Rogerio learned later) was paid $20,000, more than twice what he was promised, for his bona fide Israeli kidney, had a change of heart just as he was being prepped for surgery. Shlomo, the recalcitrant kidney seller, called his wife on his cell phone and told her to meet him at the international airport. Then he ducked out of the hospital by a back stairwell to meet his wife at the airport. In the meantime, the local broker, Meir Sushan, was alerted by his client's surgeon that the kidney provider had escaped! Sushan notified the airport police in Johannesburg international airport that a thief was about to make off for Israel with $18,000 that did not belong it him. There was something strange said about a missing kidney.

With Agiana Robel, "trussed" and ready for his transplant, the frantic transplant organizers quickly came up with a substitute, Rogerio Bezzeira, who was ready and waiting in the secured Durban "safe house" (a dingy two bedroom apartment with no view of the ocean) that was such a disappointment to the latest crop of kidney selling transplant tourists. "We were expecting to stay at a Holi-day Inn" Rogerio said, bringing to mind the absurdist Brazilian comedy of the 1970s, about a travelling circus caravan named Holi-day. Rogerio and his brother along with another willing kidney seller (Wesley da Silva) hoped to use their kidney cash to open a car and bicycle repair shop. Rogerio fondly recalled the lovely Mozambican Portuguese-speaking woman and interpreter for the boys, Dalila, who had even prepared a barbeque at her home. Guilt-stricken she took the young men aside and asked them if they had cold feet and perhaps wanted to opt out of the scheme. If so, she promised to arrange it for them. This beautiful "rich" woman, living in a suburban ranch style house that looked like a Hollywood film set, had no idea what the kidney deal meant for the hungry Brazilians. For them it was not a burden; it was the opportunity of a lifetime. There was no way any of them would be crazy enough to even consider changing their mind.

But as Rogerio was puzzling about this, Dalila appeared in his hospital room, her pretty face pinched with anxiety. "Get up! You've got to get out of here as quickly as you can," she told him. "The police are after us!" Rogerio could hardly move he was in so much pain. One of the nurses gave Rogerio another shot and rubbed some calming ointment under his bandaged wound. They made him get up and use the toilet and even as he was relieving himself, to his horror, Dalila stepped inside and began stuffing crisp new dollar bills into his hands. "Take this and hide it," she said. But Rogerio, still groggy from his injection did not know where to hide it. "Quick, put it under your bandages," Dalila suggested, but doing that hurt dreadfully. "Aye! Aye!," he groaned.

It did not take the Durban police very long to find Rogerio and his buddies hiding out at the safe house, to arrest them, and to relieve them of their kidney-cash. The foiled escape and the arrest of Shlomo Zohar was exactly what South African Police Captain, Louis Helberg, of the commercial crime branch had been waiting for. They had been tipped off in March 2003 about the transatlantic trafficking scheme and they had staked out St. Augustine's Hospital, observing all the comings and goings at the private Netcare Transplant unit there. On December 3, 2003 the police made their move and 11 people were arrested in Durban while in Recife almost simultaneously nine members of the organs trafficking ring were arrested. A photo of Rogerio and his brother, heads in their hands, appeared on the front pages of *The New York Times*.

Rogerio hardly knew what felt worse, his oozing excoriated kidney wound or the end of his fantasy of self-improvement. Not only would he be returning home, an arrested and released felon, but empty-handed. The dream of opening his own auto repair garage where he could greet his customers in fresh overalls with his name and that of his brother emblazoned across his back had evaporated. He would have to return to his fate as an ordinary curbside car repair man. And he would not be able to go on the little African safari he had planned with the help of Rod Kimberly, the English-speaking organs broker who was also arrested and who had pleaded guilty. Unlike João, Rogerio would not be returning home flashing his color photos of wild animals—giraffe and rhinos—to his children and his neighbors. He would be lucky if he could buy a few postcards of elephants at the Durban airport as he was deported home, hurting, humiliated and empty-handed.

Back in Recife, Rogerio met up with João, Gerson, Mercondes, Geremias, Alberty and others who had taken part in the transplant tours before him. They were called to the police station in Recife to give depositions to Police Chief Karla Gomes, then in court before Judge Amanda and again had to appear before Senator Raymond Pimentel ("the pretty one" as he was called by the sellers) for a congressional investigation of the organs trafficking scheme in Recife. There, in the congressional auditorium the boys of Jardim saw and heard a very different Captain Ivan. He was no longer the swaggering, boastful, boisterous authoritarian, wheeler and dealer, but reduced to a quivering mass of recrimination and paranoid accusations. Captain Ivan maintained his innocence throughout the hearings. He blamed Gaddy Tauber for everything, and he had a particular venom toward the kidney seller English translator for the group, Geremias, whose English was more refined than the captain's.

Gaddy Tauber remained cool, silent, and composed during the court hearings and he refused to be separated from, or treated any differently than, the working-class boys of Jardim. Though offered a private prison cell commensurate with his education and military rank, a constitutional right maintained even in the new democratic, post-military state, Tauber insisted on sharing the cell with the boys he had led astray, or (as he saw it) helped to bootstrap out of their grinding poverty. The Brazilian guys were impressed with Gaddy's show of jailhouse solidarity.

The boys from Jardim defended themselves before Judge Amanda as best they could. In his deposition Geremias asked the judge a rhetorical question that stunned many observers in the courtroom: "What father seeing a bullet headed straight for his children's heads wouldn't throw his own body in front of the gun to defend them?" When the judge countered that Geremias's three children were not facing a *death* threat, Geremias responded: "No, your honor, but they were facing something even worse, a *life* threat." Geremias explained before the court that he had lost his job as an English teacher and he was suddenly facing homelessness with his wife, Vera, and their children. "To save my family," he argued, "I would have sold not only a kidney, but an eye, part of my liver, or even my heart, and I would have died a happy man." Geremias also defended his traffickers saying that Captain Tauber, an Israeli stranger, was the only person to help him out when every Brazilian official from every social service agency had turned him down in his time of dire need. "Where were the social workers and the psychologists to help me and my family?" He addressed Judge Amanda: "Gaddy may have been, as you say, a crook who was taking advantage of the desperation of the poor, but, even so, we all gained something from it."

On a return visit in 2006 the boys from Brazil were a little more critical about their situation. Although the kidney sellers do not regret their caper they are paying a big price for what they did. Things have not turned out so well for them. Many lost their jobs and never recovered them. Their faces appeared in newspapers and on TV and everyone knows them as the "*mutilados*"—the mutilated ones. Even their wives and children suffer from the stigma.

Geremias was frightened to learn that he had a kidney stone in his kidney of last resort. Alberty had lost weight and his energy—he was sleeping all the time—and wondered if maybe, when the surgeons put him under anesthesia, they had not done more to him, maybe even removing part of his liver. He had become very nervous. João Cavalcanti's wife left him, taking his children with her. She could not stand the shame of what her husband had done and the fact that he had lied to her.

Some of the fellows meet up from time to time at a bar or at João's woodworking shop to reminisce about their "transplant holiday" until it derailed. Alberty had a few regrets. He never heard back from Luanne, the woman from New York City (as black as himself and married to a skinny, disabled Jewish man). Both seemed very sick, and Alberty did not begrudge saving Luanne's life with his best, most active kidney. But he imagined that Luanne was a wealthy woman, indeed, and that she could have helped Alberty out a little bit more. He hoped that she could find him a job as a bell hop or a porter in a big hotel in New York City. Back sleeping on a piece of wet cardboard, Alberty also wishes that he could have stayed a few extra days in that luxury hospital with a semi-private room, clean sheets, a color TV set and all the food he could want, even if the hospital food was awful and he missed his beans and rice and especially his *fejoada*, black bean stew, on Saturdays.

Despite everything, the boys from Brazil like to reminisce about the city of Durban which they describe as a dream-like city, super modern; a city of white people in black Africa. They are embarrassed today when they recall how they thought that Africa was a wild and savage place and joke that they were the only "wild animals" exported to Africa from the urban jungles of northeast Brazil. They tell their children stories about Durban, about how all the people were beautiful, all the nurses were kind, all the streets were clean, and all the beaches lined with boardwalks and amusement parks, and how all the shopping malls were filled with wonderful things that could not be seen anywhere in Brazil. The coffee, too, was something to admire, said Alberty da Silva. "It was like ambrosia," he mused. "What did they call it?" And then the words slid off Alberty's tongue— "cappuccino!" Alberty savored his first cappuccino in the little café built inside the airy atrium of St. Augustine's Hospital. Sitting there and drinking his cappuccino, Alberty said, made him feel for all the world, like a real tourist on holiday, even though his surgical wound hurt him so much.

Scars—Visible and Invisible

Although the Brazilian "*meninos*" recruited by Gaddy Tauber and his transplant trafficking gang defended themselves saying that although they had been "fooled," deceived, and exploited, they refused to accept that they had been "*trafficked*." One of the Recife kidney sellers interrupted my testimony before the Brazilian Congressional Hearings in 2003:

> No way! No matter what that woman had to say, it was me, my choice. Eu, Pedro da Silva, I trafficked myself! Nobody put a knife to my throat, nobody forced me to get on that plane. I did it to get out of my stinking slum and to see the world and to buy some necessities for my children. I had an opportunity and I took it.

In 2006 several of the kidney sellers of Recife, including Geremias, Cicero, Pedro, Paulo, Alberty, João, Gerson, Hernani, who had gotten caught up in Captain Gaddy Tauber's organ trafficking scheme met to figure out how they could get reparations for their missing kidneys and subsequently messed up lives. They were trying to organize an NGO, an Association of Disillusioned (or Disenchanted) Organ Donors—*Associacao de Doadores Disilusionados* (or *Disencantados*). The name was still in debate. At their first meeting, the disenchanted sellers aired their complaints: loss of work, loss of income, of strength, and most of all, a loss of social standing. They reported chronic pain, weakness, anxiety, depression, family discord, and personal rejection, as well as medical problems, all attributed (by them) to their missing kidneys. "None of us were told how hard it would go for us," Cicero said. Paulo agreed: "The pain was so bad that for three days in the hospital I was praying to be the next one to die." Geremias noted that they were treated OK until the doctors got what they wanted and then they were thrown out like *lixo*, garbage, and put back on a plane, with their cash stuffed under their bandages, and warned by Roddy [the

Durban broker] not to show they were in pain because the customs/immigration people might be suspicious.

Alberty da Silva lost his job and took an inferior job as a night watchman that gave him lots of time to think, and to worry. "My health has gone down," he told me. "What if those surgeons in Durban took more than just a kidney?" A common fear among kidney sellers the world over. He badgered me so much that we went to a local hospital and waited in lines all day so that Alberty could have an X-ray to determine if the "rest of him" was still intact. He was relieved for a few days until we returned to the X-ray clinic for the results and found after several more hours of waiting that his medical file had gone missing. Alberty then explained that his real concern was whether the missing kidney had or could affect his sexual potency, a common fear among male kidney sellers who equate the missing kidney with their reproductive organs.

I finally got out to the distant rural suburb of Janga in July 2006 to visit Geremias's new home and to meet his family. While the house was not nearly so fine as the mansion imagined by the fellows he had left behind in the slums near Boa Viagem airport and was just a concrete slab with four barn like rooms with unfinished cement floors and a muddy back yard, Geremias was still proud of it and he smiled broadly as ushered me inside the gate and quieted the skinny puppy yapping at my heels. Geremias pulled himself up to his full 5'4" height as he motioned for me to sit down on a hard kitchen chair: "*Bem Vindo!*" he said. "Welcome inside my kidney."

"What about your scar, Geremias?" I asked, as I knew that his wife Vera found his body less attractive because of it. "I have the solution," he said. "I'm going to have a tattoo artist weave a large Amazonian snake all around it so that this, he said pointing to one end, will be the head, and this, will be the tail. It will be an expensive tattoo, in multi-color, but it will be worth it, *nao* eh?" Rogerio had set the pattern by covering his ugly saber like scar with a dragon tattoo.

Kidney and transplant trafficking casts light on the dark underbelly of neo-liberal globalization, on the rapacious demands it creates and the predatory claims it makes on the bodies of the "biodisposables" of the world but also the dreams it engenders about the possibilities for a better life and a mobile existence. For the kidney buyers their scars are carried lightly and signify a release from the corporal entombment of dialysis machines. For the itinerant Brazilian kidney sellers their scars carry embodied memories of suffering and exploitation, to be sure, but also of a momentary release from the slums and the first chance they had to travel and see the world, and to return with a wad of dough in one's pocket, and an empty, itching empty pocket where their missing kidney used to sleep.

To a great many people, connected to the trade, organs trafficking is not like the traffic in guns, drugs and "illicit" sex) a "rotten trade" or a trade in "bads." Instead, kidney selling is seen as a "sweet" trade, a trade in "goods" that promise hope and deliverance. And that is the ultimate dilemma. Over the past decade, kidney selling and human trafficking for organs have lost the ability to shock. Although initially protested through the circulation of urban legends of kidnapping and body theft, organ selling soon became an acceptable, if a somewhat sorry quick fix for chronic problems in living. Today, organ selling has become a "body tax" on the world's poor, who have always been treated as supernumerary and disposable. The governments of Iran, Israel, Saudi Arabia, Singapore, Philippines, and the US either have instituted or are trying to institute regulated systems that would allow cash payments to living kidney donors or (alternatively) special subsidies or entitlements including medical insurance, immigration papers, working papers, or best of all, citizenship and a passport. The film *Dirty Pretty Things* got it quite right in this regard.

The criminal networks of brokers and human traffickers operating transplant tours that linked desperately ill and insured transplant patients with desperately poor and medically uninsured kidney and half-liver sellers and with enterprising surgeons, all shared one characteristic and motive—all of them willing to travel great distances in the pursuit of some kind of freedom and mobility—either freedom from the constraints of dialysis or a chance to see the world, even if that meant through the barred windows of a safe house and a hospital ward in Turkey or South Africa. If anthropologists once made the observations that kinship was not about blood, and that marriage was not about love, then we can perhaps conclude that trafficking in persons to sell a sale kidney abroad is not about "gifting," unless perhaps, despite the inherent exploitation involved, it is, for some, a gift of travel.

Acknowledgements

This chapter reflects on two generative themes that reflect Benedicte's life as an anthropologist-ethnographer and that of her family, especially her father, Helga the Navigator![4] The first theme is global travel and migrations. The second theme reflects Benedicte's research and writings on the experience of disability and illness in global perspective,[5] across time and space, history, geography, and culture but especially the creativity and resilience of the disabled despite the many obstacles—metaphorical, physical and material—they are forced to overcome. In my forthcoming book—*A World Cut in Two—The Global Traffic in Humans for Organs* (University of California Press, forthcoming)—I include an anecdote about Benedicte that I hope she will not mind. It appears in the middle of a chapter on body love in a section about the veneration of Catholic relics, in which I recall my first generation Czech mother's enormous store of beribboned relics of splinters of the bones of various saints, miniscule bits of Saint Teresa of Avila's Carmelite veil, a dot of blood from a stigmatic Italian monk and so on. In the rag-tag immigrant neighborhood of Williamsburg, Brooklyn in the early

4   Ingstad, B., Fugelli, P. 2009. *Helse på norsk. God helse slik folk ser det*, Gyldendal; Ingstad, B. 2009. *Eventyret. En biografi om Helge Ingstad*, Oslo: Gyldendal.
5   Ingstad, B., Whyte, S.R. 2007. *Disability in Local and Global Worlds*, University of California Press.

1950s, Catholic school children exchanged relics like bubble gum cards—"*I'll take two of your Padre Pio's for one of my Saint Bernadette Soubirous.*" I write: "The family relics bring to mind my first visit to Oslo where my wonderful anthropologist—host, Benedicte Instad, brought me to see many memorable sites and museums where I could feast my eyes on incredible Viking Ships, actually see up close the paintings of Edvard Munch, and finally St Olaf's Church where the patron saint's arm bone is displayed in a reliquary." Then, a recent convert to Catholicism, Benedicte like Cardinal Newman and like my German Lutheran father who became a Catholic after, he said, the Vatican Council helped inch the medieval Catholic Church toward the age of reason, Benedicte is a "conditional" Catholic. One of her conditions was her avoidance of the unseemly display of Norway's patron saint's arm bone, his ulna, in a silver reliquary for popular consumption and private devotion and veneration. Benedicte drew the line when it came to venerating the bodily remains of saints even when they were national heroes. This chapter also draws on my article, "Tati's Holiday and João's Kidney Safari," *Body & Society*, June 2011.

References

Ackerman, S.L. 2010. "Plastic paradise: Transforming bodies and selves in Costa Rica's cosmetic surgery tourism industry," *Medical Anthropology: Cross-Cultural Studies in Health and Illness*, 29(4), 403–23.

Scheper-Hughes, N. 2011. "Tati's Holiday and João's Kidney Safari," *Body & Society*, June 2011.

Wailoo, K. 2006. "A death retold: Jesica Santillan, the bungled transplant, and paradoxes of medical citizenship," *Studies in Social Medicine*, University of North Carolina Press.

Chapter 13

Afterword:
The Experience of 'Matter Out of Place'

Catherine Palmer

Introduction

In the Introduction to this volume Andrews states that the relationship between tourism and violence is a neglected area within studies of tourism, tourists and local communities. Whilst a key aim of the volume has been to address this gap the specific focus and the arguments presented in each chapter go beyond the usual case study examples of the impact and implications of violence on consumer behaviour, risk perception or travel flows; aspects that have tended to drive the tourism-violence agenda (Alvarez and Campo 2014, Boakye 2012, Taylor 2006, Neumayer 2004, Ryan 1993). Although the influence of crime and terrorist attacks is represented here they are employed to support broader discussions ranging from the ontological roots of violence (Botterill et al. Chapter 11) to the relationship between tourism and social suffering (Seixas Chapter 9). Overall, each chapter contributes towards a wider agenda that sees tourism as a lens through which to examine the role and function of violence in society. As Andrews notes '[t]he study of tourism has a duty to think through violence to examine not only tourism but also the nature and place of violence in society at large'.

My purpose here is not to present a summary overview of each chapter as to do so would merely repeat what Andrews provides in her Introduction. Furthermore, each contributor clearly sets out the relevance and significance of the focus adopted for understanding the role of violence within tourism. My intention is rather to offer some general thoughts on what a focus on violence in and through tourism may reveal about the human condition. In doing so I will draw from the chapters to illustrate my arguments. I also intend to suggest areas for further research in support of a wider research agenda (of which violence is a key component) focusing on tourism and conflict.

All of the chapters in this volume demonstrate that violence is a manifestation of conflict although it needs to be acknowledged that not all conflict involves or leads to violence. Evidence of conflict can be highly visible for example terrorism, war, feud and protest marches but it can also be invisible, lying low, hidden away until an act of violence erupts into the open shattering the taken-for-grantedness of everyday life. Suicide is one example of invisible conflict in the sense that the inner turmoil, struggle or conflict that underpins what the World Health Organisation defines as self-directed violence is not always visible to the family and friends of the individual concerned. The physical effects of violence in tourism can be invisible in the sense discussed by Lozanski (Chapter 3) where tourists associate violence with images of otherness, or where linguistic violence is constitutive of place image as illustrated by Platt (Chapter 5). However, for the most part, within tourism violence is the shadow that lurks outside the hotel compound, clings to the back of the tour bus or catches the traveller unawares (see Botterill et al. Chapter 11, Seixas et al. Chapter 9, Meskell 2005).

Although violence may be part of the experience of being human, as the contributions to this volume demonstrate it does not therefore follow that violence is intrinsic to human behaviour. It is not merely a label or a category of behaviour to be deciphered, investigated and corrected as this ignores the complex conditioning influence of social structure and cultural specificity. It also ignores the experience of violence at the level of the individual as revealed through studies of long-term conflict in countries and regions as diverse as India, Northern Ireland and the Middle East (Kelly 2008, Chatterji and Mehta 2007, Das 2007, Thornton et al. 2004, Bowman 1989). In terms of tourism, the chapters by Isaac and Selwyn (this volume) provide insightful expositions of the long-term consequences for tourists and local communities of living with violence as a manifestation of conflict.

Tourists are also exposed to the ubiquity of the conflict-violence-tourism meleé not just through media reports of atrocities but also through the travel advice on many, but not all, official government websites. Such advice not only constructs approaches to and understandings of the other it also offers a moral compass against which 'we' can locate ourselves relative to other people and places. 'Our' moral compass is employed to justify how we think about, behave towards and react to violent events that rupture the taken-for-grantedness of daily life. Butler's (2006) critical dissection of the political aftermath of September 11 illustrates this point when she argues that paranoia is sustained by a fantasy of omnipotence where our moral values are seen as better than your moral values. This fantasy provided a framework by which the Bush administration justified and legitimised its response to the terrorist attacks 'a frame for understanding violence emerges in tandem with the experience, and … the frame works to both preclude certain kinds of questions, certain kinds of historical inquiries, and to function as a moral justification for retaliation' (Butler 2006: 4).

Although violence is a terrible and unwelcome experience for many individuals and communities it is not a universal urge as the contributors to two edited collections focusing on the meanings of violence illustrate (see Stanko 2003, Aijmer and Abbink 2000). Here, violence is a contingent and context driven act or practice shaped by the social and cultural context in which it takes place. As Aijmer (2000: 19) notes the social context offers a way 'of reading violence as it occurs in the world'. Such a perspective is useful because the activity of tourism is a social context and the case studies included here provide particular readings of violence as encountered through the context and experience of tourism and travel.

Tourism as Social Context

The chapters in this volume illustrate that the touristification of brutality, the link between tourism and violence is not a recent phenomenon, despite the emergence of *Dark Tourism* as a focus for scholarly activity. Indeed, Andrews provides a rather chilling example of this link in her Introduction through a discussion of the special excursion trains provided to enable people to watch the appalling treatment of black Americans in the southern United States of America during the nineteenth- and twentieth centuries. Voyeurism associated with death, brutality and violence is a significant part of tourism as the previously mentioned *Dark Tourism* phenomenon illustrates and this is reflected in media stories highlighting the commercialisation of the macabre.

The British broadsheet newspaper *The Guardian* illustrates the growing demand for attractions and disturbing experiences by reporting on the opening up to the public of the home of Dorothea Puente, a notorious 1980s serial killer in the United States. The tour includes showing visitors the place in the garden where the victim's bodies were buried (Coldwell 2013). Such a tour is in line with a plethora of similar experiences ranging from Jack the Ripper walking tours in London to the Cù Chi tunnel experience in Vietnam. Tours like these illustrate a point made by Roberts (Chapter 2) in his discussion of the non-places of tourism that violence permeates the spaces and places of tourism as a form of latent energy to which tourists are attracted.

The attraction of horror, fear, pain, suffering and death as vicarious experience is questioned by Isaac's discussion (this volume) of atrocity tours to the Segregation Wall in Bethlehem, part of which involves visiting the house of Claire Anastas, a local Palestinian woman whose house is surrounded by the Wall. Tourists are encouraged to imagine what it must be like to live in the house, to empathise with the individual's plight and in so doing make a wider connection to the plight of the Palestinian people in general. Through encounters with the materiality of violence – the house, the Wall – tourists come face to face with the daily consequences of living with violence. Violence is literally and symbolically brought *home* to them. Atrocity tours provide tourists with an alternative experience of space and time one where tourism turns from a moment of pleasure into what Roberts (this volume) refers to as a moment of violence.

In coming face to face with violence in this way tourists are encountering the other through the face of pain where face not only refers to the actual face of the individual it also refers to the collective social face of groups, communities, nations, states and so forth. My argument here draws from Levinas's (1991) philosophy of face where to encounter another's face is to encounter more than a physical human face it is to encounter an expression that speaks of otherness; an otherness imprinted with the practical and emotional resonances of history, politics, culture and gender. Selwyn (Chapter 7) offers two challenging examples of the face of otherness through a focus on Bosnia-Herzogovina and the West Bank both of which present us with particular 'faces'. For example, *Birthright* tours to Israel offered to young Jewish Americans illustrate how tourism is used to construct and communicate a face of pain, the pain of a people and of a landscape torn apart by violent conflict.

The *Birthright* tour in Israel and the one-day tour to the Palestinian house of Claire Anastas demonstrates how violence and conflict are employed through the medium of tourism to construct and maintain a relationship between individuals, states and the stateless. These relationships are constructed in relation to the social and political systems of thought within which such tours are organised. Tourism facilitates 'relations between strangers' (see Machlis and Burk 1983) both through and against violence. In some cases this is done as a way of encouraging empathy and solidarity with the lives of those being visited. Arguably, by bringing tourists face-to-face with the other tourism becomes a vehicle for demanding 'we' take social and ethical responsibility for the plight of the other in the sense intended by Levinas when he argued 'the face presents itself, and demands justice' (1991: 294).

Matter out of Place

So what does the seemingly endless fascination with violence, death and conflict reveal about being human? If violence has meaning then what are we are meant to understand by the ways in which it is packaged for tourists as part of the pleasure periphery? There are no easy answers to these questions as the issues inherent in the conflict-violence-tourism meleé are complex and challenging. Nevertheless one possible response relates to how we engage with the social world as a way of locating the self in relation to other ways of thinking and being. Conflict and violence are part of the fabric of social relations that serve to connect or disconnect one individual or group to another. This is not meant to imply that violence as a manifestation of conflict is a positive thing, but rather to acknowledge that pain and suffering are as much a part of the social world as goodness and light. As we orientate ourselves we locate ourselves in relation to a complex matrix of relationships with other people, places and beliefs (Strathern et al. 1990). Conflict and violence present us with moments of rupture that breakdown and through the relationships and structures underpinning the social order to such an extent that they resemble what Douglas (2002) has referred to as 'matter out of place'.

Douglas's (2002: 43) examination of dirt as matter out of place is highly instructive here because '[i]t implies two conditions: a set of ordered relations and a contravention of that order'. Violence does not merely contravene the order of things it interrupts and dislocates the lifeworld from its structural moorings. It is an aberrant anomaly that shows up in stark relief that social relations as a way of ordering the world are neither stable nor harmonious. To quote again from Douglas (2002: 48) '[a]ny given system of classification must give rise to anomalies, and any given culture must confront events which seem to defy its assumptions. It cannot ignore the anomalies which its schema produces'. As an anomaly, as matter out of place violence is a polluting behaviour and just as Douglas (2002) argues in relation to dirt by examining how different societies understand, use and experience violence we can learn something about the prevailing social order governing the behaviour of the group. This is so irrespective of whether the social order is formed by an indigenous or an industrialised system of thought.

The chapters in this volume show quite clearly that the physical, symbolic and linguistic manifestations of violence within tourism reveal the systems of thought governing those who perpetrate the violence and those affected by it. For example, Scheper-Hughes (Chapter 12) argues that violence linked to the illegal trafficking of human organs referred to as 'transplant tourism' is part of a wider 'trade' category of medical travellers seeking cures, cosmetic interventions or bodily transformations unavailable to them in the places where they live. The ability or otherwise of individuals to seek out treatments that all too often are illegal and/ or unethical in their own countries tells us something of the dominant structures and process governing the contemporary world. For Scheper-Hughes neo-liberal globalisation has provided complex networks of mobility that have facilitated the trafficking of organs and other dubious medical practices. The ability to move, to be mobile is part of a global system that privileges the rights of the individual over those of the majority who all too often are disenfranchised and dispossessed. The trafficking of violence packaged as a form of tourism where the organ or procedure is part of the package 'holiday' is the consequence of a system of ordering based on the principle of freedom; freedom of markets, freedom as individual choice (albeit highly contingent), and freedom experienced as the temporary or permanent removal of pain.

Hertzog (Chapter 6) provides a further illustration of violence as a reflection on systems of ordering and of thought in her discussion of war violence as interpreted and presented through battlefield tourism generally, and specifically in relation to the French battlefields of World War I. Here, the development of battlefields as tourist attractions involved the physical display of war violence as the trenches and tunnels were preserved and opened up to visitors and the creation of symbolic landscapes where the planting of trees represented the missing soldiers. In this example, the physical and the symbolic representations of violence are constant reminders of a time when the social order was thrown aside, ruptured and dislocated. Such representations support Douglas's argument that any given culture must confront events, which seem to defy its assumptions. Battlefield tourism provides opportunities for confronting and reflecting upon a significant breakdown in global social relations and a questioning of the assumptions by which these relations had been maintained prior to the breakdown.

Some forms of tourism are, therefore, a way of confronting and reflecting upon conflict and violence through a vicarious encounter with the remnants of violence. When tourists avoid destinations associated with violence, as Aschauer describes in Chapter 10 they are making a conscious decision to do so even if that decision is not always an informed one. Of course, such decisions are based upon an understandable and reasonable desire to avoid potentially dangerous or risky situations. But avoidance is also a way of maintaining the social order through a deliberate non-engagement with the world of the other. However, tourists as victims of crime or terrorist attacks often have little opportunity to avoid such experiences or indeed they may have no choice in doing so because of the situation in which they find themselves. So, whether as unwelcome experience, through conscious avoidance or as purposeful engagement violence in the context of tourism is a catalyst for contemplation of the basis upon which the social order is and should be maintained.

The Purification Ritual

I have argued above that violence is a polluting behaviour that like dirt defiles the assumptions upon which a particular social reality is constructed and controlled. When associated with tourism the social reality affected is that which 'governs' the role and status of tourism within the value system of the tourist and the destination community. As several of the contributors to this volume have stated tourism is for many, although not all people, a time for relaxation a time away from the rules, duties and obligations of daily life. The cultural value of tourism, its significance for many individuals is evidenced by the extensive literature base that links tourism to activities and concepts such as pilgrimage, the sacred, ritual and myth (Badone and Roseman 2004, Selwyn 1996, Graburn 1983).

So, just as '[r]eflection on dirt involves reflection on the relation of order to disorder, being to non-being, form to formlessness, life to death' (Douglas 2002: 7) reflection on violence encountered and experienced through tourism involves reflection on the systems of order that tourists and the societies from which they emanate hold as fundamental to being, to social structure and ultimately to the maintenance of life. By rupturing the systems of thought wherein tourism is a highly valued activity violence exposes the cosmological significance of tourism within those societies where it is encouraged and valued, as Inglis (2000: 4) argues tourism gathers 'to itself a little cluster of special values ... to be on vacation is to become conscious of these values and to cherish them in a way often excluded from everyday life'.

An interesting issue here is again highlighted by Douglas's argument that cultures define themselves in relation to their rituals of purity such that the purification practices designed to eliminate dirt as pollution are enacted as a way of re-ordering the environment, of making social reality conform to the ideas and categories of thought that maintain the established social order. Tourism is a means by which purification can be achieved it is a purifying ritual providing moments of freedom from the obligations that constrain many people's lives. Violence pollutes the cosmological values that enable tourism to function as a purifying ritual capable of maintaining the social order. Values that for many societies owe their existence to the social and economic transformations resulting from the industrial revolution (Inglis 2000); transformations such as the legalisation of leisure time through paid holidays, systems of transport and accommodation provision, the delivery of pleasure and entertainment experiences.

Inglis argues that through such transformations the social meanings of a vacation gradually accumulated and wove themselves into the ideals and values associated with contemporary tourism 'for a value to *be* a value, it concentrates, in action and symbol, something of the best of life. Vacations mean what they mean because we look to them to bring out that best, in life and in us' (2000: 6). Vacations are not intended to be polluted by violence, they are meant to be as Cohen and Taylor (1992) have argued escape attempts from the routine realities of everyday life. Yet as Andrews argues in Chapter 4 destinations such as the Balearics may not be an escape for women as the marketing and merchandising of particular activities and attractions all too frequently portray women as sexually available and as subordinate to men. The language of subordination employed by tourism is according to Andrews a form of symbolic violence reasserting a social order of unequal gender relations.

Such an argument illustrates Butler's (2004) position that the category of gender is a symbolic form of violence because it forces bodies (and thus individuals) into preordained categories, preordained through systems of social reproduction where conformity to a gender 'norm' is both expected, regulated and reinforced. The concept of symbolic violence emerges from Bourdieu's (1991) examination of language as symbolic power, which Platt (Chapter 5) astutely highlights plays a significant role in creating the myths and stereotypes that position certain places as particular types of tourist destination. So although the purpose of tourism is to purify the mind and body of the tourist there lurks within it the potential for danger, as what is impure cannot always be eradicated since 'all social systems are built on contradiction' (Douglas 2002: 173). The contradiction of tourism is that it may bring both pleasure and pain.

Conclusion

As noted earlier the aim of this book is to provide a space for exploring the role and function of violence in society through the lens of tourism. The case studies presented by each contributor, together with this afterword, illustrate that violence as matter out of place pollutes the social order by rupturing the value system that tourist-generating societies hold as being fundamental to the maintenance of life. In this sense its 'purpose' is to act as a threshold between that which is acceptable and that which is not, that which we value and that which we decry. Violence through tourism brings the individual into contact with him or herself both the violent self and the non-violent self and in doing so asks that a judgment be made about how to relate to and live alongside other ways of thinking and being.

So where do we go from here? I offered one response in my introduction by stating my intention to offer suggestions for further research as part of a wider agenda focusing on tourism and conflict. As already stated despite the fact that not all conflict involves or leads to violence, violence is a manifestation of conflict and in order to think through violence whether as part of tourism or as part of the lifeworld the wider context within and from which it emanates needs to be taken into account. This of course is fraught with difficulties because of the complex, frequently long-standing and seemingly intractable political, social and economic factors inherent in many conflict situations whether these are interpersonal, local, regional or global. However, doing something is better than doing nothing and given the global reach of tourism this activity provides an opportunity to bring disparate and often unconnected people into contact with each other. We need to be mindful here that tourism is a generic category and as such not all types of tourism are capable of shining a light on conflict and violence in society. Likewise, not all tourists are the same, some are open to difference and dialogue as part of the holiday experience whilst others are not seeing the whole point of a holiday as being to get away from the challenges of daily life. A tourism and conflict research agenda needs to acknowledge and unpick such contextual characteristics as part of an overarching approach.

It is not possible to suggest an all-encompassing research agenda here, assuming there is such a thing in the first place. What I can offer are potential lines of enquiry that others may wish to add to in the future. For example, it would be useful to know more about the ways in which the language of violence operates in and through tourism, whether this is symbolic, spoken, visual or virtual. How might this help us to better understand tourism's role in both supporting and challenging conflict and violence? There are numerous case studies of conflict in relation to tourism all of which make a significant contribution to understanding conflict. These studies range from ones focusing on a particular conflict (Stein 2008) to studies of a specific type of conflict (Butler and Suntikul 2013), or as is the case with this volume studies of a particular outcome of conflict. However, more research is needed that leads into practical suggestions to raise awareness and support the individuals and communities who live with conflict whilst also providing the tourist destination. What are tour companies that may describe their product as alternative or ethical or NGOs already doing in this respect? To what extent can tours such as that described by Isaac (this volume) stimulate post trip connections with the individual or group visited? What might be the benefits of any such connections?

Although there are numerous studies that focus on the significance and role of tourism in developing and marketing destinations in the aftermath of conflict – or at least when there is a sustained movement towards peace – for example Novelli et al. (2012), Alluri (2009), Anson (1999) not enough has been done on destinations experiencing long term sustained conflict.

A final research suggestion is anthropological in its borrowing from Mary Douglas as it seeks to explore conflict through tourism as a form of secular defilement indicative of particular patterns of belief and social ordering. As Douglas (2002: 35) argues 'we shall not expect to understand other people's ideas of contagion, sacred or secular, until we have understood our own'. I argue that we cannot hope to understand, confront and challenge conflict generally or through tourism until we can recognise how our own patterns of belief contribute to the way the world *is* and how it could and should be. The anthropology of tourism and conflict is a possible way forward.

References

Aijmer, G. and Abbink, J. (eds) 2000. *Meanings of Violence: A Cross-Cultural Perspective*, Oxford: Berg.

Aijmer, G. 2000. 'Introduction: The idiom of violence in imagery and discourse', in G. Aijmer and J. Abbink (eds) *Meanings of Violence: A Cross-Cultural Perspective*, Oxford: Berg, 1–21.

Alluri, Rina M. 2009. 'The role of tourism in post-conflict peacebuilding in Rwanda', Swiss peace Working Paper 2, Bern: Swisspeace, available at: http://www.isn. ethz.ch/Digital-Library/Publications/Detail/?ots591=0c54e3b3-1e9c-be1e-2c24-a6a8c7060233&lng=en&id=111583 [accessed 5 December 2013].

Alvarez, Maria D. and Campo, S. 2014. 'The influence of political conflicts on country image: A study of Israel's image', *Tourism Management*, 40, 70–78.

Anson, C. 1999. 'Planning for peace: The role of tourism in the aftermath of violence', *Journal of Travel Research*, 38, 57–61.

Badone, E. and Roseman, S. (eds) 2004. *Intersecting Journeys: The Anthropology of Pilgrimage and Tourism*, Urbana: University of Illinois.

Boakye, K.A. 2012. 'Tourists' views on safety and vulnerability. A study of some selected towns in Ghana', *Tourism Management*, 33(2), 327–33.

Bowman, G. 1989. 'Fucking tourists sexual relations and tourism in Jerusalem's Old City', *Critique of Anthropology*, 9(2), 77–93.

Butler, J. 2004. *Undoing Gender*, New York: Routledge.

Butler, J. 2006. *Precarious Life. The Powers of Mourning and Violence*, London: Verso.

Butler, R. and Suntikul, W. (eds) 2013. *Tourism and War*, Abingdon: Routledge.

Chatterji, R. and Mehta, D. 2007. *Living with Violence. An Anthropology of Events and Everyday Life*, Abingdon: Routledge.

Cohen, S. and Taylor, L. 1992. *Escape Attempts: The Theory and Practice of Resistance in Everyday Life*, 2nd ed., Abingdon: Routledge.

Coldwell, W. 2013. 'Dark tourism: Why murder sites and disaster zones are proving popular', *The Guardian*, [online, 31 October], available at: http.// theguardian.com/travel/2013/oct/31/dark-tourism-murder-sites-disaster-zones [accessed 5 December 2013].

Das, V. 2007. *Life and Words: Violence and the Descent into the Ordinary*, Berkeley: University of California Press.

Douglas, M. [1966] 2002. *Purity and Danger*, London: Routledge.

Graburn, N.H.H. 1983. 'The anthropology of tourism', *Annals of Tourism Research*, 10(1), 9–33.

Inglis, F. 2000. *The Delicious History of the Holiday*, Abingdon: Routledge.

Kelly, T. 2008. 'The attractions of accountancy: Living an ordinary life during the second Palestinian intifada', *Ethnography*, 9(3), 351–76.

Levinas, E. 1991. *Totality and Infinity: Essay on Exteriority*, A. Lingis (trans.), Dordrecht, NL: Kluwer Academic Publishers.

Machlis, G.E. and Burch, W.R. 1983. 'Relations between strangers: Cycles of structure and meaning in tourist systems', *The Sociological Review*, 31(4), 666–92.

Meskell, L. 2005. 'Sites of violence: Terrorism, tourism and heritage in the archaeological present', in L. Meskell and P. Pels (eds) *Embedding Ethics: Shifting Boundaries of the Anthropological Profession*, Oxford: Berg, 123–46.

Neumayer, E. 2004. 'The impact of political violence on tourism: Dynamic cross-national estimation', *Journal of Conflict Resolution*, 48(2), 259–81.

Novell, M., Morgan, N. and Nibigira, C. 2012. 'Tourism in a post-conflict situation of fragility', *Annals of Tourism Research*, 39(3), 1446–69.

Ryan, C. 1993. 'Crime, violence, terrorism and tourism: An accidental or intrinsic relationship?' *Tourism Management*, 14(3),173–83.

Selwyn, T. (ed.) 1996. *The Tourist Image: Myths and Myth Making in Tourism*, Chichester: John Wiley & Sons Ltd.

Stanko, E. (ed.) 2002. *The Meanings of Violence*, Abingdon: Routledge.

Stein, R. 2008. *Itineraries in Conflict. Israelis, Palestinians and the Political Lives of Tourism*, London: Duke University Press.

Strathern, M., Peel, J., Toren, C., Spencer, J. and Ingold, T. 1990. *The Concept of Society is Theoretically Obsolete*, Manchester: GDAT.

Taylor, P. 2006. 'Getting them to forgive and forget: Cognitive based marketing responses to terrorist acts', *International Journal of Tourism Research*, 8(3), 171–83.

Thornton, C., Kelters, S., Feeney, B. and McKittrick, D. 2004. *Lost Lives*, 2nd ed., Edinburgh: Mainstream Publishing.

Index